Lecture Notes in Computer Science 11294

Commenced Publication in 1973
Founding and Former Series Editors:
Gerhard Goos, Juris Hartmanis, and Jan van Leeuwen

More information about this series at http://www.springer.com/series/7408

Ruzica Piskac · Philipp Rümmer (Eds.)

Verified Software

Theories, Tools, and Experiments

10th International Conference, VSTTE 2018
Oxford, UK, July 18–19, 2018
Revised Selected Papers

 Springer

Editors
Ruzica Piskac
Yale University
New Haven, CT, USA

Philipp Rümmer (iD)
Uppsala University
Uppsala, Sweden

ISSN 0302-9743   ISSN 1611-3349 (electronic)
Lecture Notes in Computer Science
ISBN 978-3-030-03591-4   ISBN 978-3-030-03592-1 (eBook)
https://doi.org/10.1007/978-3-030-03592-1

Library of Congress Control Number: 2018960421

LNCS Sublibrary: SL2 – Programming and Software Engineering

This Springer imprint is published by the registered company Springer Nature Switzerland AG
The registered company address is: Gewerbestrasse 11, 6330 Cham, Switzerland

Preface

This volume contains the proceedings of the 10th International Working Conference on Verified Software: Theories, Tools, and Experiments (VSTTE 2018), held during July 18–19, 2018, as part of the Federated Logic Conference (FLoC) in Oxford, UK, and affiliated with the 30th International Conference on Computer-Aided Verification (CAV).

The goal of the VSTTE conference series is to advance the state of the art in the science and technology of software verification, through the interaction of theory development, tool evolution, and experimental validation. We solicited contributions describing significant advances in the production of verified software, i.e., software that has been proven to meet its functional specifications. Submissions of theoretical, practical, and experimental contributions were equally encouraged, including those that focus on specific problems or problem domains. We were especially interested in submissions describing large-scale verification efforts that involve collaboration, theory unification, tool integration, and formalized domain knowledge. We also welcomed papers describing novel experiments and case studies evaluating verification techniques and technologies. The topics of interest included education, requirements modeling, specification languages, specification/verification/certification case studies, formal calculi, software design methods, automatic code generation, refinement methodologies, compositional analysis, verification tools (e.g., static analysis, dynamic analysis, model checking, theorem proving, satisfiability), tool integration, benchmarks, challenges, and integrated verification environments.

The inaugural VSTTE conference was held at ETH Zurich in October 2005, and the following editions took place in Toronto (2008 and 2016), Edinburgh (2010), Philadelphia (2012), Atherton (2013), Vienna (2014), San Francisco (2015), and Heidelberg (2017).

This year there were 24 submissions. Each submission was reviewed by at least three Program Committee members. The committee decided to accept 19 papers for presentation at the conference. The program also included three invited talks, given by Cesare Tinelli (University of Iowa, USA), Stuart Matthews (Altran UK), and Rayna Dimitrova (University of Leicester, UK).

We would like to thank the invited speakers and the authors for their excellent contributions to the program this year, the Program Committee and external reviewers for diligently reviewing the submissions, and the organizers of FLoC and CAV 2018 for their help in organizing this event. We also thank Natarajan Shankar for his tireless stewardship of the VSTTE conference series over the years.

The VSTTE 2018 conference and the present volume were prepared with the help of EasyChair.

August 2018

Ruzica Piskac
Philipp Rümmer

Organization

Program Committee

June Andronick	CSIRO—Data61 and UNSW, Australia
Martin Brain	University of Oxford, UK
Michael Butler	University of Southampton, UK
Supratik Chakraborty	IIT Bombay, India
Roderick Chapman	Protean Code Limited, UK
Cristina David	University of Cambridge, UK
Dino Distefano	Facebook and Queen Mary University of London, UK
Mike Dodds	University of York, UK
Patrice Godefroid	Microsoft Research, USA
Arie Gurfinkel	University of Waterloo, Canada
Liana Hadarean	Synopsys, USA
Bart Jacobs	KU Leuven, Belgium
Swen Jacobs	CISPA and Saarland University, Germany
Cezary Kaliszyk	University of Innsbruck, Austria
Andy King	University of Kent, UK
Tim King	Google, USA
Vladimir Klebanov	SAP, Germany
Akash Lal	Microsoft Research, India
Nuno Lopes	Microsoft Research, UK
Alexander Malkis	Technical University of Munich, Germany
Yannick Moy	AdaCore, France
Gennaro Parlato	University of Southampton, UK
Andrei Paskevich	Université Paris-Sud, LRI, France
Ruzica Piskac	Yale University, USA
Markus Rabe	University of California, Berkeley, USA
Philipp Rümmer	Uppsala University, Sweden
Peter Schrammel	University of Sussex, UK
Natarajan Shankar	SRI International, USA
Tachio Terauchi	Waseda University, Japan
Mattias Ulbrich	Karlsruhe Institute of Technology, Germany
Philipp Wendler	LMU Munich, Germany
Thomas Wies	New York University, USA
Greta Yorsh	Queen Mary University of London, UK
Aleksandar Zeljić	Uppsala University, Sweden
Damien Zufferey	MPI-SWS, Germany

Additional Reviewers

Amani, Sidney
Ekici, Burak
Kirsten, Michael
Lewis, Corey

Margheri, Andrea
Paul, Lucas
Wang, Qingxiang
Winkler, Sarah

Abstracts of Invited Talks

Contract-based Compositional Verification of Infinite-State Reactive Systems

Cesare Tinelli

Department of Computer Science, The University of Iowa, USA
cesare-tinelli@uiowa.edu

Abstract. Model-based software development is a leading methodology for the construction of safety- and mission-critical embedded systems. Formal models of such systems can be validated, via formal verification or testing, against system-level requirements and modified as needed before the actual system is built. In many cases, source code can be even produced automatically from the model once the system designer is satisfied with it. As embedded systems become increasingly large and sophisticated, the size and complexity of models grows correspondingly, making the verification of top-level requirements harder, especially in the case of infinite-state systems. We argue that, as with conventional software, contracts are an effective mechanism to establish boundaries between components in a system model, and can be used to aid the verification of system-level properties by using compositional reasoning techniques. Component-level contracts also enable formal analyses that provide more accurate feedback to identify sources of errors or the parts of a system that contribute to the satisfaction of a given requirement. This talk discusses our experience in designing an assume-guarantee-based contract language on top of the Lustre modeling language and leveraging it to extend the Kind 2 model checker with contract-based compositional reasoning techniques.

Verified Software: Theories, Tools, ...
and Engineering

Stuart Matthews

Altran Technologies, SA
stuart.matthews@altran.com

Abstract. Continual innovation of software verification theories and tools is essential in order to meet the challenges of ever-more complex software-intensive systems. But achieving impact ultimately requires an understanding of the engineering context in which the tools will be deployed. Based on our tried-and-trusted methods of high-integrity software development at Altran, I will identify key features of the industrial landscape in which software verification tools have to operate, and some of the pitfalls that can stop them being adopted, including regulation, qualification, scalability, cost justification, and the overall tool ecosystem. Within this context I will present Altran's own on-going research and development activities in verified software technologies. The talk will conclude by drawing some key lessons that can be applied to avoid the traps and pitfalls that tools encounter on their journey to succesful deployment.

Synthesis of Surveillance Strategies for Mobile Sensors

Rayna Dimitrova

Department of Informatics, University of Leicester, UK
rd307@leicester.ac.uk

Abstract. The increasing application of formal methods to the design of autonomous systems often requires extending the existing specification and modeling formalisms, and addressing new challenges for formal verification and synthesis. In this talk, I will focus on the application of reactive synthesis to the problem of automatically deriving strategies for autonomous mobile sensors conducting surveillance, that is, maintaining knowledge of the location of a moving, possibly adversarial target. By extending linear temporal logic with atomic surveillance predicates, complex temporal surveillance objectives can be formally specified in a way that allows for seamless combination with other task specifications. I will discuss two key challenges for applying state-of-the-art methods for reactive synthesis to temporal surveillance specifications. First, naively keeping track of the knowledge of the surveillance agent leads to a state-space explosion. Second, while sensor networks with a large number of dynamic sensors can achieve better coverage, synthesizing coordinated surveillance strategies is challenging computationally. I will outline how abstraction, refinement, and compositional synthesis techniques can be used to address these challenges.

The talk is based on joint work with Suda Bharadwaj and Ufuk Topcu.

Contents

A Tree-Based Approach to Data Flow Proofs

Jochen Hoenicke, Alexander Nutz$^{(\boxtimes)}$, and Andreas Podelski

University of Freiburg, Freiburg im Breisgau, Germany
{hoenicke,nutz,podelski}@cs.uni-freiburg.de

Abstract. In this paper, we investigate the theoretical foundation for the cost/precision trade-off of data flow graphs for verification. We show that one can use the theory of tree automata in order to characterize the loss of precision inherent in the abstraction of a program by a data flow graph. We also show that one can transfer a result of Oh et al. and characterize the power of the proof system of data flow proofs (through a restriction on the assertion language in Floyd-Hoare proofs).

1 Introduction

Data flow proofs are safe inductive annotations of the data flow graph of a program. In this paper we explore the potential and the limitations of data flow proofs for program verification on a theoretical level.

Farzan and Kincaid recently showed that data flow proofs can be used effectively for software verification [5]. Oh et al. showed that a static program analysis can often be computed significantly faster on the data flow graph than on the control flow graph [13,14].

Compared to proofs that annotate the control flow graph (Floyd proofs[1]), data flow proofs have the advantage of being *sparse* [13,14]. *Temporal sparseness* means the data flow graph abstracts away from the linear ordering of statements in the control flow graph and only retains a partial order. *Spatial sparseness* eliminates the need to "carry over" information about a variable from where it is assigned to where it is used over many locations where that information is irrelevant. Additionally, in verification data flow proofs exhibit *projective sparseness*. Data flow graphs are often not connected, thus one may discard all components that are not connected to the property.

The other side of the medal is that data flow proofs are limited in proving power because the data flow graph loses some information that is present in the control flow graph.

We formalize the notion of a "data flow" and use tree languages to denote sets of data flows. We observe that the tree language induced by taking all the

---

[1] Note the subtle difference between Floyd-style proofs [8] and Hoare-style proofs [10]: The former are annotations of the control flow graph while the latter are annotations of the program's source code.

© Springer Nature Switzerland AG 2018
R. Piskac and P. Rümmer (Eds.): VSTTE 2018, LNCS 11294, pp. 1–16, 2018.
https://doi.org/10.1007/978-3-030-03592-1_1

traces of the control flow graph and converting them to data flow trees is non-regular even for very simple examples. However, we show that the path-closure of this non-regular language is always regular, and that it is indeed equal to the language of data flow trees obtained from simply unwinding the data flow graph. We gain the insight that the loss of proving power of data flow proofs compared to Floyd proofs is a consequence of this overapproximation.

Based on these tree languages, we can extend existing language based refinement schemes using tree interpolation to obtain a CEGAR-style algorithm that computes a data flow proof from a data flow graph of a program with some property.

We also characterize the proving power of data flow proofs semantically by comparing them to Floyd proofs. We arrive at the result that the proving power of data flow proofs precisely equals that of Floyd proofs that are based on the Cartesian abstraction of the given program.

Our contributions are the following:

- We introduce data flow trees as a means to formally compare the data flow denotations of the control flow graph and the data flow graph.
- We show that the step from the data flow trees of the control flow graph to the data flow trees of the data flow graph corresponds precisely to the step from some tree language to its path-closure.
- We characterize the proving power of data flow proofs (a consequence of the loss of precision through the path-closure) by showing that it equals the proving power of Floyd proofs over the Cartesian abstraction of a program.
- We show how to construct a set of constrained Horn clauses from a data flow graph whose models correspond to data flow proofs for the underlying program.

2   Example

We present an example program that illustrates a particular trait of the abstraction introduced by the data flow graph. Note that the example is not chosen to show efficiency of data flow proofs; for example it does not exploit the fact that the data flow graph is inherently parallel because the program is sequential.

The example depicted in Fig. 1 illustrates the abstraction of the program introduced by the data flow graph. In the top-left corner the program P is depicted as a control flow graph. P initializes its variables x and y to 0. Then it runs a loop an arbitrary number of times and increments both variables in each iteration. Finally it checks a property that at the end of the loop the sum of x and y is non-negative. This is expressed by an assume statement that guards the error location ℓ_{err}. Thus, the error location is reachable if and only if the property can be violated. In the bottom-left corner the set Traces(P) of error traces of P is given as a regular expression. This is the language of the control flow graph P if it is interpreted as a finite automaton with the accepting state ℓ_{err} where the alphabet consists of the statements. The program P is correct

P:

P#:

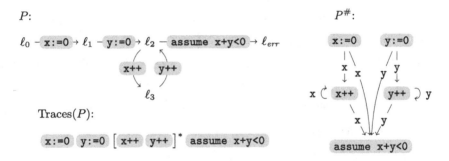

Traces(P):

Fig. 1. Program P as a control flow graph, the traces of P as a regular expression, and the data flow graph of P, called $P^{\#}$.

DFT(Traces(P)):   DFT(P#):

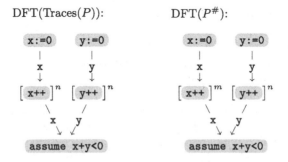

Fig. 2. The set of data flow trees where each element is the data flow graph of a trace in Traces(P) (left-hand side, with $n \in \mathbb{N}$), and the set of data flow trees induced by $P^{\#}$ (right-hand side, with $m, n \in \mathbb{N}$).

if all of its traces are infeasible, i.e., cannot be executed because of a blocking assume statement.

The right part of Fig. 1 depicts the data flow graph $P^{\#}$ of P. For each statement of the control flow graph P there is a corresponding node in the data flow graph $P^{\#}$. The edges are labelled by variables. An edge (s_1, x, s_2) in the data flow graph is added if the statement s_1 defines the value of a variable x, s_2 uses the variable x, and there is a path $s_1 \ldots s_2$ in the control flow graph, such that x is not defined by another statement between s_1 and s_2.

It is possible to convert each trace into a data flow graph by interpreting it as a control flow graph that only executes this single trace. This data flow graph is acyclic. Thus it forms a DAG. By copying nodes with multiple outgoing edges a data flow tree for each trace is induced. For the traces of P the set of corresponding data flow trees is sketched on the left-hand side of Fig. 2. The square brackets with superscript n denote that x++ (resp. y++) can be taken n times respectively, i.e., the tree has height $n + 2$ and each inner node is an x++ (resp. y++) node. All edges are labelled with x (resp. y). Since the number of occurrences of x++ and y++ in any trace of P is the same, the two branches must have the same height.

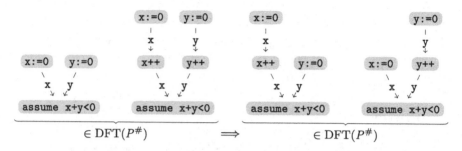

Fig. 3. The set DFT($P^\#$) is path-closed. This means that if the two data flow trees on the left are contained, so are the two data flow trees on the right.

The data flow graph $P^\#$ also induces a set of data flow trees. These can be seen as the trees accepted by a tree automaton similar to $P^\#$. These are given on the right-hand side of Fig. 2. The data flow graph cannot ensure that the statements x++ and y++ are taken the same number of times. Thus, we use m and n to denote that the number of repetitions of these statements may differ in each branch.

In fact, the set DFT(Traces(P)) is not a regular tree language, since a finite tree automaton cannot ensure that the two branches are of the same height. On the other hand, DFT($P^\#$) is a regular tree language recognized by a deterministic root-frontier (also called top-down) tree automaton. The language class accepted by root-frontier tree automata are the *path-closed* languages. In Fig. 3 we illustrate the consequences of path-closure to the tree language DFT(Traces(P)). Given this intuition, we can observe that DFT($P^\#$) equals the path closure of DFT(Traces(P)) in this example. We will show in Sect. 4 that this is the case for all programs.

However, even though the abstraction introduced by $P^\#$ is very coarse, we can still prove P correct on it. This is because the property also holds for all the data flow trees obtained from $P^\#$. It does not depend on x++ and y++ to be executed the same number of times. One might wonder if there is an easy syntactic way to see if there is a data flow proof. However, this is not the case as the following example shows. If one changes the error guard to assume x-y<0, the program is still correct (the error state in the control flow graph is not reachable) but it is unprovable using the data flow graph. This is because the property does not hold for the trees in DFT($P^\#$) where $m \neq n$.

As we will see in Sect. 5, being provable in the data flow graph abstraction coincides precisely with the fact that P has a *Cartesian* Floyd proof, i.e., it suffices to only reason about each variable independently. In this example, the Cartesian assertion $x \geq 0 \wedge y \geq 0$ is a safe inductive loop invariant for P.

3 Preliminaries

In this section we fix our notation for trees and tree languages and present the notion of path-closure and afterwards we fix our notation for programs and Floyd proofs.

3.1 Path-Closed Tree Languages

Trees. We use standard notation for trees, following Comon et al. [2]. A ranked alphabet (A, r) consists of an alphabet A for the node labels and a rank function $r\colon A \to \mathbb{N}$ that determine the number of children for each node. An *index set* I is some finite set. Let Pos_t be a prefix-closed set of positions $Pos_t \subseteq I^*$. Then we define a *tree* t as a mapping from positions to alphabet symbols, i.e., $t\colon Pos_t \to A$, such that the rank of the alphabet symbol at each position equals the number of children at that position.

Intuitively, a position identifies a node in the tree by identifying the path from the root to that node through a sequence of directions. The empty word ϵ denotes the root position. The child of position p at the index i is denoted by $\mathrm{child}_t(i, p) \stackrel{def}{=} pi$. Similarly, we use $\mathrm{parent}_t(pi) = p$ to denote the parent position of pi.

For $a \in A$ with rank $r(a) = n$ and trees $t_1, \dots, t_n$ we denote by $a(t_1, \dots, t_n)$ the tree with root a and children $t_1, \dots, t_n$. Given two trees t_1, t_2, and a position $p \in Pos_{t_1}$, we define the *tree substitution* $t_1[p \leftarrow t_2]$ as the tree that is obtained by substituting the subtree at p in t_1 by the tree t_2.

Path-Closed Tree Languages. The following definition of path-closedness follows the one made by Martens et al. [11]. A tree language $\mathcal{L}$ is *path-closed* if for every $t \in \mathcal{L}$ and for every position $p \in Pos_t$ it is the case that if $t[p \leftarrow a(t_1, \dots, t_n)] \in \mathcal{L}$ and $t[p \leftarrow a(s_1, \dots, s_n)] \in \mathcal{L}$, then $t[p \leftarrow a(t_1, \dots, s_i, \dots, t_n)] \in \mathcal{L}$ for each $i \in \{1, \dots, n\}$. This is illustrated in Fig. 4. The path-closed languages are precisely the ones recognizable by deterministic top-down (root-to-leaf) tree automata.

Note the precondition that the tree t is equal in the two trees can be weakened to the precondition that the nodes on the path from the root to the parent of the tree that we exchange are labelled with identical symbols.

The path-closure of a tree language $\mathcal{L}$ is the smallest path-closed superset of $\mathcal{L}$, i.e.,

$$\mathrm{path\text{-}closure}(\mathcal{L}) \stackrel{def}{=} \bigcap \{\mathcal{L}' \mid \mathcal{L}' \supseteq \mathcal{L} \land \mathcal{L}' \text{ is path-closed}\}$$

A path-closed tree language $\mathcal{L}$ is uniquely defined by the set of its tree paths, i.e., the set of all paths (with directions) from any leaf in any tree to the root.

$$\begin{aligned}
\mathrm{tree\text{-}paths}(\mathcal{L}) \stackrel{def}{=} \{(p_1, a_1) \dots (p_n, a_n) \mid {} & \exists t \in \mathcal{L}.p_1 \text{ is a leaf of } t \land p_n = \epsilon \\
& \land \forall i < n.p_{i+1} = \mathrm{parent}(p_i) \\
& \land \forall i \leq n.t(p_i) = a_i\}
\end{aligned}$$

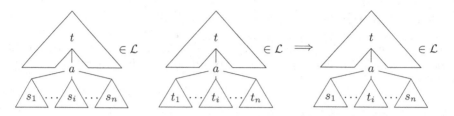

Fig. 4. Illustration of path-closure, taken from [11]: If the left and the middle tree are in the tree language $\mathcal{L}$, then, for $\mathcal{L}$ to be path-closed, the right tree must also be contained.

3.2   Programs, Specifications, Floyd Proofs

We fix a set of *program variables Var*. We use names like $x, y, x_1, \ldots$ for program variables. We use first-order logical formulas over the program variables. We use names like $\varphi, \psi, \varphi_1, \ldots$ for logical formulas. By $\top$ (resp. $\bot$) we denote the formula that is always true (resp. false). Given a formula φ, we denote the set of program variables occurring in φ as $\mathrm{vars}(\varphi)$. For representing state changes we use formulas over *Var* and *Var'* $\overset{def}{=} \{x' \mid x \in Var\}$, where x' captures the value of the program variable after the state change.

We denote program statements by $\sigma, \sigma_1, \cdots \in \Sigma$. *Assignment statements* are of the form $\boxed{\texttt{x := e}}$ where x is a program variable and e is an expression over the program variables. *Assume statements* are of the form $\boxed{\texttt{assume } \varphi}$ where φ is a logical formula over the program variables.

We use statement formulas over primed and unprimed program variables to describe the semantics of a statement. The function $\mathrm{sf} \colon \Sigma \to Formulas$ assigns a statement formula to a statement as follows.

$$\mathrm{sf}(\boxed{\texttt{x := e}}) \overset{def}{=} x' = e \wedge \bigwedge_{y \in Var \setminus \{x\}} y' = y$$

$$\mathrm{sf}(\boxed{\texttt{assume } \varphi}) \overset{def}{=} \varphi \wedge \bigwedge_{y \in Var} y' = y$$

Program with Specification P. We define programs by their control flow graph. A program $P = (\Sigma, Loc, \ell_0, \ell_{err}, \delta)$ consists of

- a finite set of statements Σ,
- a finite set of program locations Loc,
- an initial location $\ell_0 \in Loc$,
- an error location $\ell_{err} \in Loc$,
- and a transition relation $\delta \subseteq Loc \times \Sigma \times Loc$.

A program is correct if every sequence of statements leading from the initial location to the error location is infeasible.

For simplicity, we assume that each statement $\sigma \in \Sigma$ occurs only once in the program. Thus we can define a source and a target function for a statement as

$$\text{src}(\sigma) \overset{def}{=} \ell \quad \text{tgt}(\sigma) \overset{def}{=} \ell' \quad \text{where } (\ell, \sigma, \ell') \in \delta$$

P can be viewed as a finite automaton over the alphabet Σ. Then the language of the automaton P is the set of all sequences of statements that start in ℓ_0 and end in ℓ_{err} and that respect the control flow. We call this set the *traces* of P and denote it by $\text{Traces}(P)$. We make the following assumptions on the form of P that do not restrict expressivity but avoid some corner cases. This will allow for a simpler presentation later in the paper.

- There is only one statement in P that leads to the error location ℓ_{err}; we call this statement the *error guard* σ_{err}.
- The program starts with an assume statement that initializes every variable to a nondeterministic value. If there are no variables, the program starts with `assume true`. By convention, these initialization statements do not read any variables.
- There is no location that is not visited by any trace.

Program Paths. We define a *program path* of P as a sequence of statements where the target location of a statement is always identical with the source location of the statement that directly follows. Intuitively, the paths of P are all the connected segments of all the traces of P. Formally:

$$\text{Paths}(P) \overset{def}{=} \{\sigma_1 \sigma_2 \dots \sigma_n \in \Sigma^* \mid \forall i \in \{1, \dots, n-1\}. \text{tgt}(\sigma_i) = \text{src}(\sigma_{i+1})\}$$

Assertions, Hoare Triples. An *assertion* is a logical formula over the program variables *Var* and describes an *abstract program state*, i.e., a set of valuations of the program variables.

We use the standard notation of *Hoare triples*. The Hoare triple $\{\varphi\} \sigma \{\psi\}$ holds if the formula $\varphi \wedge \text{sf}(\sigma) \rightarrow \psi'$ is valid.

Floyd Proof. A Floyd proof for program P is a mapping ι of locations in *Loc* to assertions, i.e., $\iota \colon Loc \rightarrow Formulas$, such that $\iota(\ell_0) = \top$, and $\iota(\ell_{err}) = \bot$, and for every control flow edge $(\ell, \sigma, \ell') \in \delta$ the following Hoare triple holds.

$$\{\iota(\ell)\} \quad \sigma \quad \{\iota(\ell')\}$$

We say a program is *correct* if there exists a Floyd proof for it. We say that a trace τ is *infeasible* if there exists a Floyd proof for the straight-line program that corresponds to τ.

4   Data Flow in Data Flow Graph vs. Data Flow in Program Traces

In this section we formally introduce the data flow graph, its denotation as a data flow tree language, and the data flow tree language induced by the traces of a program. Then we compare the two languages.

The Functions use *and* def. The ingredients for constructing a data flow graph are the control flow graph together with the functions use and def.

The function use: $\Sigma \to 2^{Var}$ assigns every statement σ a set of variables that are read by σ. The function def: $\Sigma \to 2^{Var}$ assigns every statement σ a set of variables that are written by σ.

For this section we rely on the reader's intuition for what it means that a statement reads or writes a variable. For our result concerning tree languages it is irrelevant how use and def are chosen. We will give well-formedness constraints for use and def in Sect. 5.

Data Flow Graph. Following [12] we define the *reaching definitions* of a location $\ell \in Loc$ wrt. a variable $x \in Var$ as all the statements that define x and that are the beginning of a control flow path to ℓ where x is not overwritten.

$$\mathrm{RD}_P(x, \ell) \overset{def}{=} \{\sigma_0 \in \Sigma \mid \sigma_0 \sigma_1 \ldots \sigma_n \in \mathrm{Paths}(P)$$
$$\wedge \mathrm{tgt}(\sigma_n) = \ell$$
$$\wedge x \in \mathrm{def}(\sigma_0)$$
$$\wedge \forall i \in \{1, \ldots, n\}.x \notin \mathrm{def}(\sigma_i)\}$$

A data flow edge connects two statements and is decorated with a program variable. The data flow edge (σ, x, σ') exists in P if σ is a reaching definition for x at $\mathrm{src}(\sigma')$, and σ' reads x. The *data flow graph* $P^{\#}$ of a program P is the set of all the data flow edges that exist in P. Formally:

$$P^{\#} \overset{def}{=} \{(\sigma, x, \sigma') \in \Sigma \times Var \times \Sigma \mid \sigma \in \mathrm{RD}_P(x, \mathrm{src}(\sigma')) \wedge x \in \mathrm{use}(\sigma')\}$$

For a trace τ we define $DFG(\tau)$ as the data flow graph of the straight-line program that corresponds to τ.

Data Flow Trees. We define *data flow trees* as a special kind of trees.

Definition 1 (Dataflow tree). *Let Σ be a set of statements and Var be the set of variables used in Σ. Let* use *and* def *be two functions mapping statements to sets of variables. Then we define a* data flow tree t *as a tree where*

- *the ranked alphabet is (Σ, rank), where* rank *is the function that assigns a statement the cardinality of its use-set, i.e.,*

$$\mathrm{rank}(\sigma) \overset{def}{=} |\mathrm{use}(\sigma)|,$$

- *the index set is the set of program variables, i.e.,*

$$Pos_t \subseteq Var^*,$$

- *for every position p and every variable x that is used by statement $t(p)$ there exists a position p' in Pos_t that is the child of p at index x and whose statement $t(p')$ defines x, i.e.,*

$$\forall p \in Pos_t, x \in \mathrm{use}(t(p)).\exists p' \in Pos_t.p' = \mathrm{child}_t(x, p) \wedge x \in \mathrm{def}(t(p')).$$

We call a data flow tree that has a data flow proof *infeasible*.

The infeasibility of a data flow tree implies the infeasibility of all of its linearizations $\{\tau \mid \text{DFT}(\text{DFG}(\tau))\}$. However, the other direction does not hold in general: A data flow tree may be feasible even though all of its linearizations are infeasible. It follows from Theorem 2 that this is not the case if we restrict ourselves to Cartesian assertions.

4.1 Data Flow Trees from the Data Flow Graph

We define the set data flow trees that is denoted by the data flow graph $P^{\#}$.

Definition 2 (Data flow trees of $P^{\#}$). *The denotation of $P^{\#}$, $\text{DFT}(P^{\#})$, is the set of data flow trees such that every edge in every tree corresponds to an edge in $P^{\#}$:*

$$\text{DFT}(P^{\#}) = \{t \mid t \text{ is a data flow tree}$$
$$\wedge \forall (p, \text{child}_t(x, p)) \in Pos_t^2.(t(\text{child}_t(x, p)), x, t(p)) \in P^{\#}$$
$$\wedge t(\epsilon) = \sigma_{err}\}$$

Given the data flow graph $P^{\#}$, it is easy to construct a (deterministic, root-to-frontier) tree automaton that accepts precisely the language $\text{DFT}(P^{\#})$.

4.2 Data Flow Trees from the Control Flow Graph

For intuition, the data flow tree belonging to a trace τ of P is obtained in two steps. First we build the data flow graph of τ, $\text{DFG}(\tau)$, which has the shape of a directed acyclic graph (DAG). Second we convert this acyclic graph to a tree by duplicating nodes going backwards from the last statement of τ, which is the error statement σ_{err}. So σ_{err} will be the root of the tree.

Note that in case of a loop-free data flow graph, the DFT-operator yields a singleton set. We will sometimes abuse notation, and use the singleton set to refer to its element.

Definition 3 (Data flow trees of P). *The data flows of a program P are given as the data flows tree of all traces of P:*

$$\text{DFT}(\text{Traces}(P)) \overset{def}{=} \{\text{DFT}(\text{DFG}(\tau)) \mid \tau \in \text{Traces}(P)\}$$

We observe that that the tree language denoted by $P^{\#}$ is an overapproximation of the tree language obtained from the traces of P.

Proposition 1. $\text{DFT}(P^{\#})$ *is a superset of* $\text{DFT}(\text{Traces}(P))$, *i.e.,*

$$\text{DFT}(P^{\#}) \supseteq \text{DFT}(\text{Traces}(P)).$$

4.3 $\text{DFT}(P^\#) = \text{path-closure}(\text{DFT}(\text{Traces}(P)))$

We collect some facts about the relationship between $\text{DFT}(\text{Traces}(P))$ and $\text{DFT}(P^\#)$ that we already know:

- $\text{DFT}(\text{Traces}(P))$ is in general neither regular nor path-closed.
- $\text{DFT}(P^\#) \supseteq \text{DFT}(\text{Traces}(P))$.
- $\text{DFT}(P^\#)$ is regular and path-closed.

The following theorem will show that $\text{DFT}(P^\#)$ is precisely the path-closure of $\text{DFT}(\text{Traces}(P))$.

Theorem 1. *The data flow tree language denoted by $P^\#$, is equal to the path-closure of the data flow tree language derived from P, i.e.,*

$$\text{DFT}(P^\#) = \text{path-closure}(\text{DFT}(\text{Traces}(P))).$$

Proof. "$\supseteq$": We know that $\text{DFT}(P^\#) \supseteq \text{DFT}(\text{Traces}(P))$ holds by Proposition 1. $\text{DFT}(P^\#)$ is clearly path-closed because the construction of the trees may use any combination of edges for the variables in the use-set of a given statement. The proof goal follows immediately from those two facts.

"$\subseteq$": We show that $\text{tree-paths}(\text{DFT}(P^\#)) \subseteq \text{tree-paths}(\text{DFT}(\text{Traces}(P)))$. Choose $tp = (p_1, \sigma_1) \dots (p_n, \sigma_n) \in \text{tree-paths}(\text{DFT}(P^\#))$. By definition, $P^\#$ contains the data flow edge $(\sigma_i, x, \sigma_{i+1})$ for every two adjacent elements of the tree path (p_i, σ_i) and (p_{i+1}, σ_{i+1}) with $1 \leq i \leq n-1$. Therefore, there must be a path in P that connects the two statements, i.e., $\sigma_i \sigma' \dots \sigma_{i+1} \in \text{Paths}(P)$ where x is not defined in between. When we concatenate the paths in P that we obtained from all pairs (σ_i, σ_{i+1}) on the tree path tp, we get an trace of our program, $\tau \in \text{Traces}(P)$. By construction, $\text{DFT}(\text{DFG}(\tau)) = t$ is a tree that contains tp. Thus, $tp \in \text{tree-paths}(\text{DFT}(\text{Traces}(P)))$. □

It is not true in general that the path-closure of a non-regular tree language is regular. Intuitively, one important reason for $\text{DFT}(\text{Traces}(P))$ having this property is that it is constructed from $\text{Traces}(P)$, a regular word language.

Corollary 1. *The tree language* $\text{path-closure}(\text{DFT}(\text{Traces}(P)))$ *is regular (even though $\text{DFT}(\text{Traces}(P))$ is in general not regular).*

5   Data Flow Proofs and Cartesian Floyd Proofs

In this section we give one more characterization of the power of data flow proofs. We define data flow proofs and Cartesian Floyd proofs. We start by giving an overview of the relevant sections of the paper by Oh et al. [13] and point out critical aspects like the functions use and def. Using on this technical apparatus, we prove the equivalence between data flow proofs and Cartesian Floyd proofs. Afterwards we give a set of Horn constraints that can be used to compute a data flow proof from a data flow graph if one exists.

Oh et al.'s Sparse Analysis. Oh et al.'s approach takes as input an off-the-shelf static analysis (consisting of an abstract domain and an abstract post operator) and a program. The output is a sparse analysis of the given program, i.e., an abstract post operator that effectively operates on the data flow graph of the program and yields the same analysis result as the original abstract post operator. A sparse analysis result can be seen as an inductive annotation of the data flow graph. Thus it can be seen as a data flow proof (introduced formally in the next paragraph), except that it does not have to be safe, i.e., it does not need to prove the error location unreachable.

One major obstacle that sparse analysis (and verification) faces is to obtain a suitable data flow graph. If the data flow graph has too few edges, the analysis may loose precision compared to the original one. (A verification procedure loses completeness in that case.) If the data flow graph has too many edges, the analysis may not run faster than the original one. Note that the existence of a data flow dependency is a semantic property both of the abstract domain and the program. For example the statement `x := x*2` has no effect in the sign-domain (assuming mathematical integers), and thus can be left out of the data flow graph.

Oh et al. define *precise* use and def functions dependent on the result of the original analysis (Definitions 3.12 and 3.10 respectively). They are precise in the sense they yield the smallest data flow graph that retains the original analysis result. Oh et al. also give a condition for safe overapproximations of these functions such that the sparse analysis does not loose precision (Definition 3.21, Theorem 3.23). In practice, they propose to run a preanalysis on an inexpensive abstract domain to obtain overapproximated use and def functions, and then run the sparse main analysis using those.

Data Flow Proof. We define a data flow proof as an inductive annotation of the data flow graph.

The nodes in $P^{\#}$ are statements. The set of incoming edges in $P^{\#}$ of statement σ where variable x is flowing in $P^{\#}$ is

$$in_{P^{\#}}(\sigma, x) \overset{def}{=} \{(\sigma', x, \sigma) \mid \exists \sigma'.(\sigma', x, \sigma) \in P^{\#}\}.$$

The sets of outgoing edges of statement σ in $P^{\#}$ are

$$out_{P^{\#}}(\sigma) \overset{def}{=} \{(\sigma, x, \sigma') \mid \exists \sigma' \exists x.(\sigma, x, \sigma') \in P^{\#}\}$$

A *data flow proof* κ for program P is a mapping from the edges of the data flow graph $P^{\#}$ to the set of formulas, i.e., $\kappa \colon P^{\#} \to Formulas$, such that

- for all statements $\sigma \in \Sigma$ with $use(\sigma) = \{x_1, ..., x_n\}$, and for all tuples of incoming edges $(e_{x_1}, ..., e_{x_n}) \in in_{P^{\#}}(\sigma, x_1) \times \cdots \times in_{P^{\#}}(\sigma, x_n)$ and for all outgoing data flow edges of σ, $e_{out} \in out_{P^{\#}}(\sigma)$

$$\{ \bigwedge_{1 \le i \le n} \kappa(e_{x_i}) \} \quad \sigma \quad \{\kappa(e_{out})\}, \qquad \text{if } \sigma \neq \sigma_{err}$$

$$\text{and} \quad \{ \bigwedge_{1 \le i \le n} \kappa(e_{x_i}) \} \quad \sigma_{err} \quad \{\bot\}, \qquad \text{if } \sigma = \sigma_{err}$$

– and for every data flow edge (σ, x, σ'), the formula $\kappa((\sigma, x, \sigma'))$ contains no variable other than x, i.e.,

$$\forall (\sigma, x, \sigma') \in P^{\#}. \, \text{vars}(\kappa((\sigma, x, \sigma'))) \subseteq \{x\}.$$

This definition follows Kincaid and Farzan [5] except that it also ensures the unreachability of the error location. The first condition ensures that for each statement every combination of assertions at its incoming data flow edges guarantees the assertion at all of its outgoing edges. The second condition states that each data flow edge $e = (\sigma, x, \sigma')$, $\kappa(e)$ contains only the variable x. Note that for a statement with an empty use-set the conjunction is empty, i.e., the Hoare triple should hold for the pre-condition $\top$.

Cartesian Floyd Proofs. Intuitively, Cartesian Floyd proofs allow only assertions that do not relate the values of different variables. We call an assertion φ a *Cartesian assertion* if it is $\top$, $\bot$, or a conjunction where each conjunct only refers to one program variable $x \in Var$, i.e.,

$$\varphi = \varphi_1 \wedge ... \wedge \varphi_n \text{ where } \text{vars}(\varphi_i) = \{x_i\}.$$

Let D_i denote the domain of the program variables x_i for each variable $x_i \in Var$. Then, $D_1 \times \cdots \times D_n$ is the domain of the program state (assuming a linear ordering of the variable set Var). Also, each φ_i defines a subset $M_i \subseteq D_i$ and the the Cartesian assertion $\varphi = \varphi_1 \wedge ... \wedge \varphi_n$ describes a set of states that is the Cartesian product $M_1 \times ... \times M_n$.

Definition 4 (Cartesian Floyd Proof). *A Floyd proof is called* Cartesian *if all of its assertions are Cartesian.*

Note that in principle every program with a Floyd proof can be made into a program with a Cartesian Floyd proof by replacing all variables by a single variable that holds the whole program state. This technique is usually called *packing* (or variable packing). However packing influences the shape of the data flow graph; packing all variables together yields a data flow graph that is isomorphic to the control flow graph. For further descriptions of packing see [3,13].

Oh et al. do not discuss Cartesian abstraction explicitly. However they distinguish non-relational and relational abstract domains and use variable packing for the relational domains. This amounts to our notion of Cartesian abstraction.

Safe use *and* def. Oh et al.'s define precise and overapproximated use and def functions. We adapt this to our notation and define safe use and def functions, which correspond to the overapproximated functions. This will allow us to relate

Data flow proofs to Cartesian Floyd proofs in Theorem 2. We implicitly allow overapproximations as one may use use and def function that are not minimal but safe.

We define the following *projection function* π, which, given a variable x and an assertion φ, extracts from φ only the constraint it puts on x.

$$\pi(x, \varphi) \stackrel{def}{=} \exists x_1, \dots, x_n.\varphi \quad \text{where } \{x_1, \dots, x_n\} = \text{Var} \setminus \{x\}$$

Definition 5 (Safe use and def). *Let σ be a statement, let φ and ψ be Cartesian assertions.*

- *We call def safe under the following condition:*
  If variable x is not contained in $\text{def}(\sigma)$, then the Hoare triple $\{\varphi\}\,\sigma\,\{\psi\}$ must hold if and only if ψ projected to x is a weakening of φ projected to x. Formally:

$$x \notin \text{def}(\sigma) \implies (\{\varphi\}\,\sigma\,\{\psi\} \iff \pi(x, \varphi) \models \pi(x, \psi))$$

- *We call use safe if, given $\{\varphi\}\,\sigma\,\{\psi\}$ holds, the weakened precondition, that only uses the projection to variables in $\text{use}(\sigma)$, is strong enough such that the parts of the postcondition that constrain variables in $\text{def}(\sigma)$ can still be concluded. Formally:*

$$\{ \bigwedge_{x \in \text{Var}} \pi(x, \varphi)\} \quad \sigma \quad \{ \bigwedge_{x \in \text{Var}} \pi(x, \psi)\}$$
$$\implies \quad \{ \bigwedge_{x \in \text{use}(\sigma)} \pi(x, \varphi)\} \quad \sigma \quad \{ \bigwedge_{x \in \text{def}(\sigma)} \pi(x, \psi)\}$$

Concrete Syntactic use and def. In Table 1 we give concrete definitions for use and def that are safe for any program in our programming language. The definition shows that there is an easily computable instance of use and def. However, there is much room for optimization here, in general and with respect to given program. More complicated programming languages (for example with pointers) may introduce the need for more involved definitions.

The main difficulty here is to correctly deal with assume statements. We introduce a fresh auxiliary variable $a \notin \text{Var}$. The data flow edges labelled with a allow data flow proofs to express that an assume statement blocks execution of another statement even though their variables are disjoint. Because a does not occur in any statement, no value constraint will be put on a, but data flow edges labelled by a may be annotated with $\bot$ expressing unreachability of the following statements.

Proposition 2. use *and* def, *as defined in Table 1, are safe* use- *and* def-*functions for any program.*

Table 1. Concrete use- and def-functions

σ	use(σ)	def(σ)
`x := e`	vars$(e) \cup \{a\}$	$\{x\}$
`assume` φ	$Var \cup \{a\}$	$Var \cup \{a\}$

Equivalence of Data Flow Proofs and Cartesian Floyd Proofs. We state the equivalence between data flow proofs and Cartesian Floyd proofs.

Theorem 2 (Data flow proof vs. Cartesian Floyd proof). *There exists a data flow proof for P if and only if there exists a Cartesian Floyd proof for P.*

Proof. A Cartesian proof can be seen as a non-sparse program analysis result for some abstract domain. A data flow proof can be seen as the result of a sparse program analysis for some abstract domain. Oh et al. show how one can be constructed from the other (Theorem 3.23, Appendix A, Appendix B in [13]).

This theorem allows us to justify the following proof rule:

> If P has a data flow proof then P is correct.

From Theorem 2 it immediately follows that the proof rule is sound, complete with respect to Cartesian Floyd proofs, and that the power of Cartesian Floyd proofs is the best we can achieve with data flow proofs.

Data Flow Proofs via Horn Constraint Solving. We can use standard tools for Horn constraint solving [1] in order to compute a data flow proof. Given a data flow graph $P^\#$, we construct a set of Horn clauses whose solution is a data flow proof for P.

For each node σ of $P^\#$ and every variable $x \in \mathrm{use}(\sigma)$ we introduce a predicate $I_{\sigma,x}(x)$. For every edge $(\sigma, x, \sigma') \in P^\#$, with $\mathrm{use}(\sigma) = \{x_1, \dots, x_n\}$, we add the following Horn constraint.

$$\forall x_1, \dots, x_n, x. I_{\sigma,x_1}(x_1) \wedge \dots \wedge I_{\sigma,x_n}(x_n) \wedge \mathrm{sf}(\sigma) \rightarrow I_{\sigma',x}(x')$$

For the error guard σ_{err}, with $\mathrm{use}(\sigma_{err}) = \{x_1, \dots, x_n\}$, we add the following Horn constraint.

$$\forall x_1, \dots, x_n, x. I_{\sigma_{err},x_1}(x_1) \wedge \dots \wedge I_{\sigma_{err},x_n}(x_n) \wedge \mathrm{sf}(\sigma_{err}) \rightarrow \bot$$

This set of Horn constraints corresponds to a slight reformulation of the constraints describing a data flow proof. The predicates $I_{\sigma,x}$ can be converted to a data flow proof and back as follows.

$$\kappa((\sigma, x, \sigma')) \stackrel{def}{=} I_{\sigma',x} \qquad I_{\sigma,x} \stackrel{def}{=} \bigvee_{e \in in_{P^\#}(\sigma,x)} \kappa(e)$$

If the Horn clause solver produces a counterexample (i.e., a derivation of $\perp$), then we can only conclude the absence of a Cartesian proof (not the incorrectness of the program). The counterexample produced by the Horn clause solver corresponds to a data flow tree. We now need to check whether there exists a linearization of the data flow tree that is a control flow trace. This check can be done using techniques from [7].

The general setting of Horn constraints allows us to go beyond the setting of data flow graphs; we leave this to future work.

6 Related Work

Farzan and Kincaid renewed the interest in data flow graphs in the context of verification. They propose to iteratively compute an annotation on the data flow graph, convert it to an annotation of the control flow graph, and use a possible counterexample for safety of the control flow graph to refine the data flow graph [5,6]. In this paper we assume that the data flow graph is fixed.

Farzan et al. [7] also introduced inductive data flow graphs, which achieve compact representations of many interleaving traces through a parallel representation. They use Craig interpolants to detect when interleaved statements don't influence each other. The branching of inductive data flow graphs is computed from interpolants where as in this paper it is fixed (given through the functions use and def).

Oh et al. [13,14] showed that any abstract interpretation-style program analysis can be done on the data flow graph instead of the control flow graph. We transfer their result into the setting of verification. While the step from analysis to verification is generally a trivial one, we account for several subtle differences between their setting and our setting of verification. The non-fixed assertion language has consequences for the computation of the data flow graph. The demand for a *safe* inductive annotation also means we have to formulate a set of constraints instead of an abstract post operator. Our setting furthermore allows us to leverage a third dimension of sparseness (next to so-called temporal and spatial sparseness mentioned by Oh et al.); in particular we only consider program parts that have a data flow to the error guard.

Denaro et al. [4] investigated the potential of data flow analysis for software testing. They show experimentally that the set of data flows of the executions of a program is significantly different from the data flows denoted by the data flow graph.

The notion of viewing a control flow graph as the denotation of a set of traces as in trace refinement schemes [9] has inspired the view on the data flow graph as a denotation of a set of data flow trees.

7 Future Work

Much of the effectiveness of sparse program analysis depends on the computation of a good data flow graph, and the same is to be expected for program verification through data flow proofs. One question is if the counterexamples to the existence of a data flow proof that a verification procedure yields can be exploited effectively to refine the functions use and def, through variable packing or through other techniques.

The path-closedness of the data flow graph, together with the nonregularity of DFT(Traces(P)) points to a potential for refinement that leads to languages that are no longer path-closed. More generally one perspective opened by our work is a new notion of data flow proofs that considers finer sets of data flow trees than the data flow graph.

References

1. Bjørner, N., Gurfinkel, A., McMillan, K., Rybalchenko, A.: Horn clause solvers for program verification. In: Beklemishev, L.D., Blass, A., Dershowitz, N., Finkbeiner, B., Schulte, W. (eds.) Fields of Logic and Computation II. LNCS, vol. 9300, pp. 24–51. Springer, Cham (2015). https://doi.org/10.1007/978-3-319-23534-9_2
2. Comon, H., et al.: Tree automata techniques and applications (2007)
3. Cousot, P., Cousot, R., Feret, J., Mauborgne, L., Miné, A., Rival, X.: Why does astrée scale up? Formal Methods Syst. Des. **35**(3), 229–264 (2009)
4. Denaro, G., Pezzè, M., Vivanti, M.: On the right objectives of data flow testing. In: ICST, pp. 71–80. IEEE Computer Society (2014)
5. Farzan, A., Kincaid, Z.: Verification of parameterized concurrent programs by modular reasoning about data and control. In: POPL, pp. 297–308. ACM (2012)
6. Farzan, A., Kincaid, Z.: DUET: static analysis for unbounded parallelism. In: Sharygina, N., Veith, H. (eds.) CAV 2013. LNCS, vol. 8044, pp. 191–196. Springer, Heidelberg (2013). https://doi.org/10.1007/978-3-642-39799-8_12
7. Farzan, A., Kincaid, Z., Podelski, A.: Inductive data flow graphs. In: POPL, pp. 129–142. ACM (2013)
8. Floyd, R.W.: Assigning meanings to programs. Math. Aspects Comput. Sci. **19**, 19–32 (1967)
9. Heizmann, M., Hoenicke, J., Podelski, A.: Refinement of trace abstraction. In: Palsberg, J., Su, Z. (eds.) SAS 2009. LNCS, vol. 5673, pp. 69–85. Springer, Heidelberg (2009). https://doi.org/10.1007/978-3-642-03237-0_7
10. Hoare, C.A.R.: An axiomatic basis for computer programming. Commun. ACM **12**(10), 576–580 (1969)
11. Martens, W., Neven, F., Schwentick, T.: Deterministic top-down tree automata: past, present, and future. In: Logic and Automata, volume 2 of Texts in Logic and Games, pp. 505–530. Amsterdam University Press (2008)
12. Nielson, F., Nielson, H.R., Hankin, C.: Principles of Program Analysis. Springer, Heidelberg (1999). https://doi.org/10.1007/978-3-662-03811-6
13. Oh, H., et al.: Global sparse analysis framework. ACM Trans. Program. Lang. Syst. (TOPLAS) **36**, 8:1–8:44 (2014)
14. Oh, H., Heo, K., Lee, W., Lee, W., Yi, K.: Design and implementation of sparse global analyses for C-like languages. In: PLDI, pp. 229–238. ACM (2012)

Executable Counterexamples in Software Model Checking

Jeffrey Gennari[1], Arie Gurfinkel[2(✉)], Temesghen Kahsai[3], Jorge A. Navas[4], and Edward J. Schwartz[1]

[1] Carnegie Mellon University, Pittsburgh, USA
[2] University of Waterloo, Waterloo, Canada
`arie.gurfinkel@uwaterloo.ca`
[3] University of Iowa, Iowa City, USA
[4] SRI International, Menlo Park, USA

Abstract. Counterexamples—execution traces of the system that illustrate how an error state can be reached from the initial state—are essential for understanding verification failures. They are one of the most salient features of Model Checkers, which distinguish them from Abstract Interpretation and other Static Analysis techniques by providing a user with information on how to debug their system and/or the specification. While in Hardware and Protocol verification, the counterexamples can be replayed in the system, in Software Model Checking (SMC) counterexamples take the form of a textual or semi-structured report. This is problematic since it complicates the debugging process by preventing developers from using existing processes and tools such as debuggers, fault localization, and fault minimization.

In this paper, we argue that for SMC the most useful form of a counterexample is an *executable mock environment* that can be linked with the code under analysis (CUA) to produce an executable that exhibits the fault witnessed by the counterexample. A mock environment is different from a unit test since it can interface with the CUA at the function level, potentially allowing it to bypass complex logic that interprets program inputs. This makes mock environments easier to construct than unit tests. In this paper, we describe the automatic environment generation process that we have developed in the SeaHorn verification framework. We identify key challenges for generating mock environments from SMC counterexamples of complex memory manipulating programs that use many external libraries and function calls. We validate our prototype on the verification benchmarks from Linux Device Drivers in SV-COMP. Finally, we discuss open challenges and suggests avenues for future work.

This material is based upon work supported by the Office of Naval Research under contract no. N68335-17-C-0558 and by the Defense Advanced Research Projects Agency (DARPA) and Space and Naval Warfare Systems Center, Pacific (SSC Pacific) under contract no. N66001-18-C-4011. Any opinions, findings and conclusions or recommendations expressed in this material are those of the author(s) and do not necessarily reflect the views of the Office of Naval Research, DARPA, or SSC Pacific. We acknowledge the support of the Natural Sciences and Engineering Research Council of Canada (NSERC), RGPAS-2017-507912.

© Springer Nature Switzerland AG 2018
R. Piskac and P. Rümmer (Eds.): VSTTE 2018, LNCS 11294, pp. 17–37, 2018.
https://doi.org/10.1007/978-3-030-03592-1_2

1   Introduction

Software testing is the most widely used technique for assuring quality of a software system. Automated testing tools, such as fuzzers, generate a *test input* (or a test-case), which are concrete values for program inputs that are fed to the Code Under Analysis (CUA). If the execution raises an exception, crashes, or produces unexpected output, then that test-case triggers a bug. Developers are familiar with such test-cases and can use them to help understand the nature of the bug and develop a fix.

Although testing can be very effective at finding bugs, it cannot uncover all bugs because exhaustively enumerating all program inputs is not possible. A complementary approach to testing is Software Model Checking (SMC)[1]. SMC has several advantages over testing. First, it can (symbolically) explore all program executions, and as a result, it can prove the *absence* of bugs in addition to finding them. Unlike some forms of testing (e.g., mutational fuzzing), SMC is completely automated and does not require user-provided test-cases or inputs.

One of the most important features of SMC (and Model Checking in general) is its ability to produce a counterexample when the property of interest is violated. A counterexample is a trace through the system that shows how the system reaches an error state from the initial state. The current state-of-the-art is for SMC tools to generate counterexamples as a machine readable document describing a set of assignments of variables to their corresponding values, or traces through an abstract transition system. For example, the SLAM verification project uses a special text format and a special visualizer for its counterexamples, and the Linux Driver Verification project uses an XML-based format indicating the line numbers and function calls that were executed. Most recently, the Software Verification Competition (SV-COMP) has adopted an XML-based format for its counterexamples.

These counterexample formats are often enhanced by a variety of visualizers to illustrate the relationship between a counterexample and a program. Most commonly, a visualizer simulates a debug session, by showing a counterexample as an execution over the program text. A recent study [25] has argued that a textual report from an analysis tool does not fit well into the usual development cycle, and that this is one of the leading reasons why developers do not adopt static program analysis tools.

In this paper, we argue that the most useful representation of a counterexample that a SMC can output for the developer is an *executable mock environment*. An executable mock environment E is a code module that implements the external environment used by the CUA C such that linking C and E together produces an executable that triggers the buggy execution witnessed by the counterexample. In other words, a mock environment lifts the counterexample into an executable code.

---

[1] Some authors make the distinction between static and dynamic SMC. The former analyzes statically all possible program executions while the latter is an adaptation for testing. Unless otherwise stated, we always refer to static SMC.

As an example, we show in Fig. 1 a simplified C snippet from the Linux Driver Verification Project (LDV) [26] and a conceptual C implementation of a mock environment. LDV programs are Linux kernel modules annotated with assertions that check for proper API usage (e.g., every lock is eventually unlocked and no lock is taken twice in a row). The C snippet shown on the left of Fig. 1 allocates external memory by calling ldv_ptr, a special LDV function that represents a memory interaction between the device driver and the kernel. To represent an error during this interaction, ldv_ptr can return a pointer value greater than a predefined absolute address[2]. The mock environment on the right of Fig. 1 triggers the error function (__VERIFIER_error) by returning an invalid pointer (2013) from ldv_ptr and yielding 457 when __VERIFIER_nondet_int is called.

```
1  extern int __VERIFIER_nondet_int(void);      1  void* ldv_ptr(void) {
2  extern int __VERIFIER_error(void);           2    static int ctr = 0;
3  extern void* ldv_ptr(void);                  3    switch (ctr++) {
4                                               4      case 0: return 2013;
5  int main(int argc, char* argv[]) {           5      default: abort();
6    void *p = ldv_ptr();                       6    }
7                                               7  }
8    if (p > (long) 2012) {                     8
9      if (__VERIFIER_nondet_int() > 456) {     9  int __VERIFIER_nondet_int(void) {
10       ...                                    10   static int ctr = 0;
11       __VERIFIER_error();                    11   switch (ctr++) {
12     }                                        12     case 0: return 457;
13   }                                          13     default: abort();
14   return 0;                                  14   }
15 }                                            15 }
```

Fig. 1. C snippet (left) and an example of a mock environment implementation (right)

Mock environments are natural to software developers. They are analogous to traditional test doubles, such as mock objects[3], which are often used to simulate complex behaviors or external services in testing. Mock objects tend to be limited in their implementation; they must be manually configured, and perhaps involve recompilation or specific program design strategies to achieve desired behaviors. Furthermore, the mocks themselves become additional dependencies that must be maintained with test-cases. Conversely, mock environments are automatically generated from counterexamples and capture all the conditions necessary to replay error traces through the CUA. Developers need not worry about configuration or environmental dependencies; they can simply run the executable counterexample using their traditional tools such as a debugger.

The main challenge in generating mocks is to synthesize an environment that is sufficient to trigger a bug in the CUA while being a realistic enough representation of the real environment to be of interest to the developer. In principle,

---

[2] The constant 2012 is added by the LDV team as part of kernel modeling.

[3] http://www.mockobjects.com/2009/09/brief-history-of-mock-objects.html.

mock generation can be reduced to symbolic execution, which would guarantee that the mock is consistent with the operational semantics of the program. Unfortunately, in practice, state-of-the-art symbolic execution engines do not scale to this task. Existing symbolic execution engines are good at exploring many shallow executions, or opportunistically finding bugs at an end of a long concrete execution. None are good at finding a targeted non-trivial execution that satisfies some constraints found by an SMC [6].

In summary, we make the following contributions: (1) formally define a concrete semantics for executable counterexamples, (2) describe a general framework for building executable counterexamples, (3) describe an instance of the framework as implemented in SEAHORN [22], a state of the art software analysis tool, and (4) present a preliminary experimental evaluation of our framework implementation in SEAHORN by benchmarking it on the Linux Driver Verification set of benchmarks from SV-COMP.

2   Concrete Semantics for Executable Counterexamples

In this section, we formally define what we mean by a *counterexample* and a *mock environment*. To do so, we first define a simple imperative language that has an explicit error state and a corresponding concrete semantics. We then show how this language can be extended to represent *external* functions and memory allocations.

2.1   A Simple Imperative Language

To simplify the presentation, we first define a simple language restricted to integers and pointers and without function calls. The syntax is described in Fig. 2. The set of program variables is $\mathcal{V} = \mathcal{V}_\mathcal{P} \cup \mathcal{V}_\mathcal{I}$, where $\mathcal{V}_\mathcal{P}$ and $\mathcal{V}_\mathcal{I}$ are the set of pointer and integer variables, respectively. We assume that the integer and pointer variables are disjoint, $\mathcal{V}_\mathcal{P} \cap \mathcal{V}_\mathcal{I} = \emptyset$. Integer and pointer variables are denoted with symbols $v_i \in \mathcal{V}_\mathcal{I}$ and $v_p \in \mathcal{V}_\mathcal{P}$, respectively. The symbol $v \in \mathcal{V}$ denotes a variable of either integer or pointer type. Boolean and arithmetic expressions are described by $b \in \mathsf{BExp}$ and $a \in \mathsf{AExp}$, respectively. We assume they are equipped with the standard boolean (op_b) and arithmetic (op_a) operators. Similarly, we define pointer expressions $p \in \mathsf{PExp}$, which are equipped with pointer equality and inequality operators (op_p).

We assume a classical structural operational semantics with a standard memory model for C programs. A pointer is a pair $\langle Loc, Offset \rangle$, where Loc is a unique identifier of a memory object of size $Sz(Loc)$ and $Offset$ is the byte offset in Loc, where $0 \le Offset < Sz(Loc)$. The number of possible memory objects is infinite. The special constant null is denoted by the pointer $(0, 0)$. We assume a function $Sz : Loc \mapsto \mathbb{N}$ that maps each memory object to its size.

$$
\begin{aligned}
&a ::= n \mid v_i \mid a_1 \ op_a \ a_n \\
&p ::= \mathsf{null} \mid v_p + a \\
&b ::= \mathbf{true} \mid \mathbf{false} \mid \mathbf{not} \ b \mid b_1 \ op_b \ b_2 \mid a_1 \ op_r \ a_2 \mid p_1 \ op_p \ p_2 \\
&S ::= \mathbf{skip} \mid \mathbf{error} \mid S_1; S_2 \mid \mathbf{if} \ b \ \mathbf{then} \ S_1 \ \mathbf{else} \ S_2 \mid \mathbf{while} \ b \ \mathbf{do} \ S \ \mathbf{end} \\
&\qquad v_p := \mathbf{alloc} \ (sz) \mid v_i := \mathbf{load} \ (p) \mid v_p := \mathbf{load} \ (v_p') \\
&\qquad \mathbf{store} \ (v_p, v_p') \mid \mathbf{store} \ (v_i, v_p') \mid v_i := a \mid v_p := p
\end{aligned}
$$

Fig. 2. A simple imperative language

$\langle \_, e_i, e_p, h, \omega \rangle \Rightarrow \langle e_i, e_p, h, \omega \rangle$	if $\omega = \mathrm{true}$
$\langle \mathbf{error}, e_i, e_p, h, \omega \rangle \Rightarrow \langle e_i', e_p, h, \mathrm{true} \rangle$	
$\langle v_p := \mathbf{alloc}(sz), e_i, e_p, h, \omega \rangle \Rightarrow$ $\langle e_i, e_p[v_p \mapsto c], h[c \equiv \langle Loc, 0 \rangle \mapsto \epsilon], \omega \rangle$	if $\omega = \mathrm{false}$ and $Loc \notin \mathsf{Dom}(h)$ and $Sz[Loc \mapsto sz]$
$\langle \mathbf{store}(v_p, v_p'), e_i, e_p, h, \omega \rangle \Rightarrow \langle e_i, e_p, h[e_p(v_p') \mapsto h(e_p(v_p))], \omega \rangle$	if $\omega = \mathrm{false}$
$\langle \mathbf{store}(v_i, v_p'), e_i, e_p, h, \omega \rangle \Rightarrow \langle e_i, e_p, h[e_p(v_p') \mapsto e_i(v_i)], \omega \rangle$	if $\omega = \mathrm{false}$
$\langle v_p := \mathbf{load}(v_p'), e_i, e_p, h, \omega \rangle \Rightarrow \langle e_i, e_p[v_p \mapsto h(v_p')], h, \omega \rangle$	if $\omega = \mathrm{false}$
$\langle v_i := \mathbf{load}(v_p), e_i, e_p, h, \omega \rangle \Rightarrow \langle e_i[v_i \mapsto h(v_p)], e_p, h, \omega \rangle$	if $\omega = \mathrm{false}$
$\langle v_p := p, e_i, e_p, h, \omega \rangle \Rightarrow \langle e_i, e_p[v_p \mapsto \mathcal{P}[\![p]\!](e_i, e_p)], h, \omega \rangle$	if $\omega = \mathrm{false}$
$\langle v_i := a, e_i, e_p, h, \omega \rangle \Rightarrow \langle e_i[v_i \mapsto \mathcal{A}[\![a]\!](e_i)], e_p, h, \omega \rangle$	if $\omega = \mathrm{false}$
$\langle \mathbf{skip}, e_i, e_p, h, \omega \rangle \Rightarrow \langle e_i, e_p, h, \omega \rangle$	
$\dfrac{\langle S_1, e_i, e_p, h, \omega \rangle \Rightarrow \langle e_i', e_p', h', \omega' \rangle}{\langle S_1; S_2, e_i, e_p, h, \omega \rangle \Rightarrow \langle S_2, e_i', e_p', h', \omega' \rangle}$	
$\dfrac{\langle S_1, e_i, e_p, h, \omega \rangle \Rightarrow \langle S_1', e_i', e_p', h', \omega' \rangle}{\langle S_1; S_2, e_i, e_p, h, \omega \rangle \Rightarrow \langle S_1'; S_2, e_i', e_p', h', \omega' \rangle}$	
$\langle \mathbf{if} \ b \ \mathbf{then} \ S_1 \ \mathbf{else} \ S_2, e_i, e_p, h, \omega \rangle \Rightarrow \langle S_1, e_i, e_p, h, \omega \rangle$	if $\mathcal{B}[\![b]\!](e_i, e_p) = \mathrm{true}$
$\langle \mathbf{if} \ b \ \mathbf{then} \ S_1 \ \mathbf{else} \ S_2, e_i, e_p, h, \omega \rangle \Rightarrow \langle S_2, e_i, e_p, h, \omega \rangle$	if $\mathcal{B}[\![b]\!](e_i, e_p) = \mathrm{false}$
$\langle \mathbf{while} \ b \ \mathbf{do} \ S \ \mathbf{end}, e_i, e_p, h, \omega \rangle \Rightarrow$ $\langle S; \mathbf{while} \ b \ \mathbf{do} \ S \ \mathbf{end}, e_i, e_p, h, \omega \rangle$	if $\mathcal{B}[\![b]\!](e_i, e_p) = \mathrm{true}$
$\langle \mathbf{while} \ b \ \mathbf{do} \ S \ \mathbf{end}, e_i, e_p, h, \omega \rangle \Rightarrow \langle e_i, e_p, h, \omega \rangle$	if $\mathcal{B}[\![b]\!](e_i, e_p) = \mathrm{false}$

Fig. 3. Operational semantics for language described in Fig. 2

To define a program state, we need environments that map both program variables and pointers to values, and a store that represents memory contents:

$$
e_i \in Env_{\mathcal{I}} = \mathcal{V}_{\mathcal{I}} \mapsto \mathbb{Z} \qquad e_p \in Env_{\mathcal{P}} = \mathcal{V}_{\mathcal{P}} \mapsto \langle Loc, \mathrm{Offset} \rangle
$$

$$
h \in \mathrm{Store} = \langle Loc, \mathrm{Offset} \rangle \mapsto \langle Loc, \mathrm{Offset} \rangle \ \cup \ \mathbb{Z} \ \cup \ \epsilon
$$

An integer environment $e_i \in Env_{\mathcal{I}}$ maps integer variables to integer values. A pointer environment $e_p \in Env_{\mathcal{P}}$ maps pointer variables to pointers. A store $h \in$ Store is a mapping from pointers to either pointers or integer values. The symbol

ϵ denotes that the pointer points to uninitialized memory. We use functions $\mathcal{P}, \mathcal{B}$, and $\mathcal{A}$ to express the semantics of pointer, boolean and arithmetic expressions:

$$\mathcal{P} : \text{PExp} \rightarrow (Env_{\mathcal{I}} \times Env_{\mathcal{P}}) \rightarrow \langle Loc, \text{Offset} \rangle$$
$$\mathcal{B} : \text{BExp} \rightarrow (Env_{\mathcal{I}} \times Env_{\mathcal{P}}) \rightarrow \mathbb{B}$$
$$\mathcal{A} : \text{AExp} \rightarrow Env_{\mathcal{I}} \rightarrow \mathbb{Z}$$

The semantics of boolean and arithmetic expressions is standard and the details are omitted for brevity. However, we describe here the semantics for pointers:

$$\mathcal{P}[\![p]\!](e_i, e_p) = \begin{cases} (0,0) & \text{if } p \equiv \text{ null or } (0,0) = e_p(p) \\ (Loc, o + \mathcal{A}[\![a]\!]e_i) & \text{if } p \equiv v_p + a \text{ and } (Loc, o) = e_p(v_p) \end{cases}$$

The structural operational semantics for our language is given in Fig. 3. A configuration $\langle S, e_i, e_p, h, \omega \rangle$ consists of a statement S, an integer environment e_i, a pointer environment e_p, a store h and a flag ω that indicates whether **error** has been executed. Given two configurations c_1 and c_2, the notation $c_1 \Rightarrow c_2$ means that c_2 is reachable from c_1 in one execution step according to the semantics. $\Rightarrow^*$ is the transitive closure of the $\Rightarrow$ relation. Our semantics tracks whether **error** is reached and sets ω to true if that is the case. The statement p:=**alloc**(sz) allocates a fresh memory object of size sz and returns a pointer to it. The statement $v_p := p$ performs pointer arithmetic but does not read from memory. The statements $v_p := \textbf{load}(v_p')$, $v_i := \textbf{load}(v_p)$, $\textbf{store}(v_i, v_p')$, and $\textbf{store}(v_p, v_p')$ read and write memory. We assume that memory operations abort execution when the pointer operand cannot be resolved to a legal offset of an allocated memory object. For simplicity, we do not keep track of such runtime error states in our semantics. The rest is standard so we omit the details.

2.2 Extending with External Functions and Memory

One key feature of SMC is that the environment of the CUA does not need to fully defined. For example, external functions, which are called by the CUA but whose implementations are not in the CUA, and memory regions allocated by external functions are both permitted by SMC. This is vital, for instance, when model checking of Linux device drivers, as the whole system is not available. However, partially defined programs cannot be represented by the operational semantics presented so far. To represent external functions and memory regions, we first extend our syntax with a new statement:

$$v := \textbf{extern\_alloc}(v_1, \ldots, v_n)$$

where the variables $v, v_1, \ldots, v_n$ can be either integers or pointers. Note that with some syntactic sugar this statement is enough to model both external function calls with parameters $v_1, \ldots, v_n$ and externally allocated memory.

We then extend our definition of a configuration as follows. In addition to $\langle S, e_i, e_p, h, \omega \rangle$, we need a global counter $\lambda \in \mathbb{N}$ used for a time-stamp. The counter is needed to distinguish external memory allocations across loop iterations. We also define two external environments e_i^{ext}, e_p^{ext} for integers and pointers whose values and memory are allocated externally, respectively:

$$e_i^{ext} \in ExternalEnv_\mathcal{I} = \mathbb{N} \times \overline{\mathcal{V_P}} \times Env_\mathcal{I} \times Env_\mathcal{P} \times Store \mapsto \mathbb{Z}$$
$$e_p^{ext} \in ExternalEnv_\mathcal{P} = \mathbb{N} \times \overline{\mathcal{V_P}} \times Env_\mathcal{I} \times Env_\mathcal{P} \times Store \mapsto (\mathrm{Loc}, \mathrm{Offset})$$

The environment e_i^{ext} (e_p^{ext}) is a mapping from a tuple consisting of: a timestamp, a vector of program variables representing the arguments to the function, and the standard environments (i.e., integer and pointer environments and the store). We are now ready to define the semantics of our new statement:

$$\langle v := \textbf{extern\_alloc}(v_1, \ldots, v_n), e_i, e_p, h, \omega, \lambda, e_i^{ext}, e_p^{ext} \rangle =$$

$$\begin{cases} \langle e_i[v \mapsto n], e_p, h, \omega, \lambda + 1, e_i^{ext}, e_p^{ext} \rangle \text{ if } v \in \mathcal{V_I} \text{ and} \\ \qquad\qquad\qquad\qquad\qquad\quad n = e_i^{ext}(\lambda, v_1, \ldots, v_n, e_i, e_p, h) \\ \langle e_i, e_p[v \mapsto c], h[c \equiv \langle Loc, O \rangle \mapsto \epsilon], \\ \quad \omega, \lambda + 1, e_i^{ext}, e_p^{ext} \rangle \qquad\quad \text{if } v \in \mathcal{V_P} \text{ and} \\ \qquad\qquad\qquad\qquad\qquad\quad \langle Loc, O \rangle = e_p^{ext}(\lambda, v_1, \ldots, v_n, e_i, e_p, h) \end{cases}$$

2.3   Counterexamples and Mock Environments

We can now formally define both *counterexamples* and *mock environments*:

Definition 1 (Counterexample and Mock Environment). *Given a program S_{entry}, a counterexample is defined as*

$$\langle S_{entry}, \emptyset, \emptyset, \emptyset, false, 0, e_i^{ext}, e_p^{ext} \rangle \Rightarrow^* \langle e_i, e_p, h, true, \lambda, e_i^{ext}, e_p^{ext} \rangle.$$

and a mock environment $\mathcal{E}$ *is defined as the pair of external environments,* $\langle e_i^{ext}, e_p^{ext} \rangle$.

The rest of this paper describes how to synthesize the external environments e_i^{ext} and e_p^{ext} from a SMC counterexample and how to combine it with the CUA in order to exercise the error location.

3   A Framework for Constructing Executable Counterexamples

In this section, we present our framework for generating mocks from counterexamples produced by a Software Model-Checker (SMC), and the process of generating an executable that links the code under analysis (CUA) (which may be partially defined) with the mock to form a fully defined executable. The framework is illustrated in Fig. 4. Rectangular boxes denote the main components, and the labeled arrows between these components denote the inputs and outputs of these components.

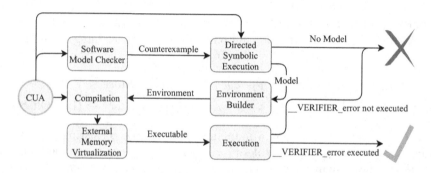

Fig. 4. Executable Counterexample Generation

The main components of the framework are: (a) a Software Model Checker, (b) Directed Symbolic Execution, (c) a Mock Environment Builder, and (d) an External Memory Virtualization. The input to the framework is the Code Under Analysis (CUA), which contains an embedded safety property. An output, if possible, is a fully-defined executable that takes no inputs and references no external functions, and that violates the safety property when it is executed. We summarize each component and corresponding assumptions in the rest of this section. An instance of this framework using the Software Model Checker SEAHORN is presented in Sect. 4.

Software Model Checker. In the first step, an SMC is used to identify a potential buggy behavior of the CUA. We assume that the SMC finds a counterexample, since otherwise nothing needs to be generated. We make minimal assumptions about SMC. First, we assume that the safety property is already combined with the CUA. This, for example, can be done via a common convention of reducing safety verification to checking reachability of a designated error function, such as the __VERIFIER_error function used by SV-COMP. Second, we assume that the SMC can produce a trace indicating the loops executed by the counterexample and their corresponding number of iterations. However, we do *not* require the SMC to produce a detailed trace. This is necessary to allow the SMC to use simplification and optimization techniques during verification, some of which might make it difficult to extract a detailed trace after the analysis. Third, we do not require the SMC to be sound with respect to the C operational semantics. This is a necessary assumption because most current SMC techniques sacrifice soundness for scalability. Common soundness issues are related to undefined behavior, bit-precise semantics of integer operations, or memory modeling. Although we do not make any assumption about the SMC's soundness, we hope that the SMC is sound with respect to *some* useful subset of the language's operational semantics.

Directed Symbolic Execution (DirSE). In this step, a counterexample produced by SMC is analyzed by Directed Symbolic Execution. The main purpose of DirSE is to reproduce the counterexample found by the SMC and produce a more precise counterexample with respect to the concrete semantics. First, DirSE produces a Control Flow Graph (CFG) of the program which is sliced with respect to the counterexample trace. A key observation is that the sliced CFG is acyclic since each loop is unrolled using the information from the trace. Recall that the SMC must produce counterexamples given as traces indicating the number of times loops are executed. However, since we do not require the SMC to produce a detailed trace, the sliced CFG can still contain a large number of paths. Next, DirSE tries to prove that __VERIFIER_error is still reachable. This search process can be quite challenging because of the need for bit-precise semantics of integer operations, potential undefined behavior, and the presence of external memory allocation and functions which are not defined in the CUA. A successful output of DirSE is a counterexample generated by a SMT solver using bit-level precision. If a counterexample cannot be obtained because DirSE determines that no buggy execution exists in the sliced CFG, the SMC's counterexample is deemed unsound and the counterexample generation process is aborted.

Mock Environment Builder (MB). This component takes the detailed trace produced by DirSE and produces a mock environment in the form of object code. Essentially, it "internalizes" all external functions by creating mocks for them. Thus, the main task for the mock builder is to produce all values and memory addresses for all the memory that is allocated outside of the CUA. This is quite challenging. While the addresses for return values can be extracted from the counterexample, the mock builder is not aware whether an external call is allocating memory or what happens to a pointer that is passed as a parameter.

External Memory Virtualization (EMV). The last component of the framework takes the executable binary produced by linking the CUA and the mock together, and ensures that, when executed, it violates the safety property. The main challenge is to ensure that all memory addresses generated by the MB are *valid* so that each memory access can be resolved to a legal offset of an allocated memory object, while at the same time the complete execution triggers a property violation. In our framework, the MB does not allocate memory and therefore, it cannot map the (abstract) memory addresses generated by DirSE to valid (i.e., allocated) memory. This is the main task of the EMV which translates between the two types of addresses. The EMV provides a virtual external memory to the executable, ensuring that no memory access ever triggers a program failure during the execution. More precisely, the EMV traps each memory access of the program, and, whenever the access appears to reference an unallocated memory region, it either redirects the access to a special memory region, or, simulates a valid memory access by providing a default value back to the program. Having multiple choices in how to map unallocated memory regions to valid ones is the reason why MB is decoupled from EMV.

Finally, we believe that our framework is general enough so that almost any verification tool can be plugged in. However, this does not mean that all tools can clearly benefit from all our components or the framework itself. For instance, Bounded Model Checking (BMC) can usually produce bit-precise counterexamples, and as a result would not benefit from DirSE. Some Test Case Generation (TCG) tools (see Sect. 6) model the concrete semantics of the program and allocate memory on-the-fly. Thus, they might not benefit from our framework at all. The main advantage of our framework is, however, that it separates the problem of model-checking a program from the generation of an executable counterexample. This is vital for scalability since it allows the SMC to perform abstractions which would be difficult, if not impossible, to apply on BMC and TCG tools.

4   Executable Counterexample Generation in SeaHorn

In this section, we present an instance of our framework using SEAHORN [22], a publicly available Software Model Checker. We organize the section following the same structure as Sect. 3 describing the implementation details of each of the four main components of the framework: Software Model Checker, Directed Symbolic Execution, Mock Environment Builder, and External Memory Virtualization.

The SEAHORN *Software Model Checker.* SEAHORN is a SMC for C/C++ programs based on the LLVM framework. It uses clang to compile programs to the LLVM intermediate representation, applies many of the LLVM optimizations to pre-process the code before analysis, and then uses a custom analysis engine based on Abstract Interpretation and Constrained Horn Clauses for verification. SEAHORN is sound with respect to its specialized semantics of C. In particular, it assumes that all integers are of arbitrary precision (i.e., unbounded or mathematical), and assumes a C-like memory model [23]. Furthermore, because SEAHORN relies on multiple LLVM components, which aggressively optimize undefined computations, the presence of undefined behavior (e.g., signed integer overflow, out-of-bound array access, and reads from uninitialized memory) in a program may significantly affect its interpretation.

Directed Symbolic Execution in SEAHORN. A high-level description for DirSE implemented in SEAHORN is shown in Fig. 5. The input to DirSE is a counterexample CEX produced by SEAHORN. The counterexample CEX only indicates which loop heads must be executed and for how many iterations, and represents many potential execution paths. From CEX, DIRSE first constructs a sliced acyclic CFG that contains all executions witnessed by CEX (line 1). Symbolic execution over the CFG is reduced to a Bounded Model Checking (BMC) problem. The verification condition of the CFG is encoded into a SMT formula ϕ, and the satisfiability of ϕ is checked by an SMT solver. The BMC is specialized for handling dynamically allocated memory. We use points-to analysis [23] to partition the memory used by the CFG into disjoint regions, represented by a points-to graph G_{Mem}. Next, all behaviors of the CFG are encoded into verification conditions ϕ using bit-precise semantics of all of the LLVM instructions (line 2). In the formula ϕ, we represent each memory region in G_{Mem} by an array, and each memory access is mapped to an array select or store operation respectively, by associating a pointer to its corresponding memory region. Finally, extra constraints ϕ_{alloc} are generated to map regions to memory addresses (line 3) which

DIRSE(CFG, CEX)
1   Build a sliced acyclic CFG based on the CEX
2   Let ϕ be the verification conditions of CFG
3   Let ϕ_{alloc} be the encoding of memory allocation constraints
4   **if** $\phi \wedge \phi_{alloc}$ is UNSAT (or timeout) **then**
5   **print** "no concrete CEX found"
6   **return** $\emptyset$
7   **else**
8   **return** model M of $\phi \wedge \phi_{alloc}$

Fig. 5. DirSE in SEAHORN implemented as a BMC problem

are consistent with the C memory model. These constraints ensure, for instance, that allocated pointers are not NULL, that they are disjoint, and that no two allocated segments intersect. More precise modeling of memory allocation is possible (e.g., all memory addresses are 4-byte or 8-byte aligned) but at the expense of increasing the solving time. Finally, an SMT solver checks for satisfiability of $\phi \wedge \phi_{alloc}$. If the solver returns UNSAT (or times out) the process is aborted. Otherwise, the model corresponding to the concrete counterexample is returned. The model is extended to contain meta-data information so that each variable in the model can be mapped back to its corresponding LLVM variable.

Mock Environment Builder in SEAHORN. A description of the MB is shown in Fig. 6. The MB produces an LLVM bitcode file that provides definitions for all of the external functions in the CUA. The MB proceeds in two phases. In the first phase (lines 2–6), the MB walks the concrete counterexample produced by DIRSE and collects all external calls of the form $v := f(\overline{v})$. It then uses the model M from DIRSE to find and record the return value v of the call-site. This represents the only possible side-effect since we assume external functions do not modify global state or any of their arguments. In the second phase (lines 7–9), the MB emits LLVM bitcode (function EMITCODE) defining each external function. For each external function f, it constructs a body B_f that tracks the number of times it is called and returns an appropriate value based on the order of the call. That is, in the first call to f, B_f returns the first value that f returned in the counterexample, in the second call it returns the second value, etc.

As an example, Fig. 7 shows the mocks (in LLVM bitcode) that MB generated for the Linux Driver Verification (LDV) program introduced earlier in Fig. 1. Lines 6–14 and 16–24 provide definitions for the two external functions in that code: __VERIFIER_nondet_int and ldv_ptr, respectively. Lines 1–4 define the global variables used by the two functions. Since the code of the two functions follows exactly the same structure, we focus on the definition of ldv_ptr. The function is assigned its own global counter, lambda_2, to track the number of

```
MockEnvironmentBuilder(CEX, MODEL)
  1    let m be a map String × (τ₁ × ... × τₖ → τᵣₑₜ) → Vec(int)
  2    foreach s ∈ CEX
  3        if s is external callsite v := f(v̄) then
  4            key = (nameof(f), typeof(f))
  5            m[key] := add(m[key], MODEL(v))
  6    endfor
  7    foreach ((f, T), VALS) ∈ m
  8        EmitCode(f, T, VALS)
  9    endfor

EmitCode(F, τ₁ × ... × τₖ → τᵣₑₜ, VALS)
 10    add global counter for λ_F initially to 0
 11    add function declaration for F with type τ₁ × ... × τₖ → τᵣₑₜ
 12    add function body:
 13        if (λ_F == 0) then VALS[0]
 14        else if (λ_F == 1) then VALS[1]
 15        ...
 16        else VALS[len(VALS) − 1]
 17        λ_F := λ_F + 1
```

Fig. 6. High-level description of the Mock Environment Builder in SeaHorn

```
 1   @lambda_1 = private global i32 0
 2   @lambda_2 = private global i32 0
 3   @int_vals = private constant [1 x i32] [i32 457]
 4   @ptr_vals = private constant [1 x i8*] [i8* inttoptr (i32 2013 to i8*)] ;
 5
 6   define i32 @__VERIFIER_nondet_int() {
 7   entry:
 8     %0 = load i32, i32* @lambda_1
 9     %1 = add i32 %0, 1
10     store i32 %1, i32* @lambda_1
11     %2 = i32* getelementptr inbounds ([1 x i32], [1 x i32]* @int_vals, i32 0, i32 0)
12     %3 = call i32 @__seahorn_get_value_i32(i32 %0, i32* %2, i32 1)
13     ret i32 %3
14   }
15
16   define i8* @ldv_ptr() {
17   entry:
18     %0 = load i32, i32* @lambda_2
19     %1 = add i32 %0, 1
20     store i32 %1, i32* @lambda_2
21     %2 = i8* bitcast ([1 x i8*]* @ptr_vals to i8*)
22     %3 = call i8* @__seahorn_get_value_ptr(i32 %0, i8* %2, i32 1)
23     ret i8* %3
24   }
25
26   declare i32 @__seahorn_get_value_i32(i32, i32*, i32)
27   declare i8* @__seahorn_get_value_ptr(i32, i8*, i32)
```

Fig. 7. Example of mock environment in LLVM bitcode corresponding to the C program in Fig. 1

calls. Lines 18–20 increment the counter each time the function is called. The function is also assigned a global array ptr_vals containing the values that will be returned by each call to ldv_ptr; these values are extracted from the concrete counterexample. (This array is called VALS in EMITCODE in Fig. 6). Finally, a call to our run-time library function __seahorn_get_value_ptr is used to retrieve an appropriate value from ptr_vals using the current value of lambda_2. We postpone the definitions of the two external functions, __seahorn_get_value_i32 and __seahorn_get_value_ptr, until we describe our next component.

External Memory Virtualization in SEAHORN. The EMV instruments the CUA with memory load and store hooks that control access to memory. This is achieved by replacing each load or store instruction in the CUA with a function call to the special functions __seahorn_mem_load and __seahorn_mem_store, respectively. Note that it is sufficient to instrument only instructions whose corresponding memory object might alias with an external object. The goal of these hooks is to map external "virtual" memory to real memory. This is vital because if a pointer that is externally allocated (e.g., p at line 6 on the left of Fig. 1) does not refer to a real memory address, the executable counterexample will probably crash when the pointer is dereferenced.

We have implemented EMV as an LLVM pass that replaces every load and store instructions with calls to the corresponding functions in our run-time library. A simplified version of the source code of these functions is shown in Fig. 8. We also present the implementation of the functions __seahorn_get_value_i32 and __seahorn_get_value_ptr discussed earlier. These functions check for a given value in a given global array and return it to the caller. The case of __seahorn_get_value_ptr is a bit more involved. Whenever a pointer to an external memory object is returned, we need to guess the size of the corresponding allocated object. Unfortunately, it is not possible in general. Instead, we guess the size based on the type. We assume that all addresses within the guessed regions are externally allocated.

The definition of __seahorn_mem_load and __seahorn_mem_store are shown on the right of Fig. 8. These functions decide whether a pointer being dereferenced is allocated by the CUA or not (is_valid_address). For this, we use the map absptrmap. If the dereferenced pointer is within the bounds of any of the memory objects externally allocated then the address is considered *invalid*, otherwise it is considered to be allocated by the CUA, and, therefore, *valid*. If the pointer is valid then both __seahorn_mem_load and __seahorn_mem_store implement the original semantics of load and store. Otherwise, a load returns a pointer pointing to a region with all its contents written by zeroes and store is ignored. Note that although simple, this solution is sufficient for many of our benchmarks.

```
1    const int MEM_REGION_SIZE_GUESS = 4196;
2    const int TYPE_GUESS = sizeof(int);
3    std::map<intptr_t, intptr_t, std::greater<intptr_t>>
4    absptrmap;
5
6    void __VERIFIER_error() {
7      printf("[sea] __VERIFIER_error was executed\n");
8      exit(1);
9    }
10
11   int32_t __seahorn_get_value_i32(int ctr, intptr_t *g_arr, int g_arr_sz) {
12     if (ctr >= g_arr_sz)
13       return 0;
14     else
15       return g_arr[ctr];
16   }
17
18   intptr_t __seahorn_get_value_ptr(int ctr, intptr_t *g_arr, int g_arr_sz) {
19     if (ctr >= g_arr_sz) return 0;
20     intptr_t absptr = g_arr[ctr];
21     size_t sz = MEM_REGION_SIZE_GUESS * TYPE_GUESS;
22     absptrmap[absptr] = absptr + sz;
23     return absptr;
24   }
25
26   bool is_external_address (void *addr) {
27     intptr_t ip = intptr_t (addr);
28     auto it = absptrmap.lower_bound (ip+1);
29     if (it == absptrmap.end()) return false;
30     intptr_t lb = it->first;
31     intptr_t ub = it->second;
32     return (ip >= lb && ip < ub);
33   }
34
35   bool is_valid_address (void *addr) {
36     return !is_external_address (addr);
37   }
38
39   void __seahorn_mem_load (void *dst, void *src, size_t sz) {
40     if (is_valid_address (src)) {
41       memcpy (dst, src, sz);
42     } else {
43       // ignore read from an illegal memory address
44       bzero(dst, sz);
45     }
46   }
47
48   void __seahorn_mem_store (void *src, void *dst, size_t sz) {
49     if (is_valid_address (dst)) {
50       memcpy (dst, src, sz);
51     } else { // ignore write to illegal memory address
52     }
53   }
```

Fig. 8. External Virtualization implemented in SEAHORN

5   Experimental Evaluation

In this section, we report on the evaluation of our framework as implemented in SEAHORN. Our goal is to show that the generation of executable counterexamples is feasible on a set of non-trivial benchmarks. In the future, it would be interesting to evaluate the effectiveness of executable counterexamples compared to other outputs from an SMC, such as textual reports. All experiments were done on a 16 core, 3.5 GHz Intel Xeon CPU and 64 GB of RAM. Each component of our framework was restricted to 5 min CPU and 4 GB memory limits.

For the evaluation, we took all benchmarks in the Systems, DeviceDrivers, and ReachSafety categories of SV-COMP 2018. These categories are representative of real code. In total, this yielded 356 unsafe benchmarks. From those, our SMC solved 144, failed in 18, and ran out of resources in 194. DirSE successfully concretized 141 counterexamples (out of 144). The three failures are due to an abstraction mismatch between SMC and DirSE: SMC is not bit-precise but DirSE is bit-precise. MB and EMV were successful on all 141 concretized counterexamples. Finally, we ran all the binaries witnessing a counterexample. We observed three outcomes: (a) the executable found the dedicated error function __VERIFIER_error in 24 cases, (b) the executable terminated but it did not execute __VERIFIER_error in 44 cases, and (c) the executable ran out of resources in 73 cases.

Table 1. Experimental results for validated counterexamples in SEAHORN

Program	SMC		DirSE		MB+EMV	Exec
	T(s)	#CP	T(s)	#BB	T(s)	T(s)
module_get_put-drivers-net-wan-farsync	8.72	3	12.66	11	0.7	0.0
32_7_linux-32_1-drivers-staging-keucr-keucr	2.38	3	0.88	11	2.17	0.0
32_7_single_drivers-usb-image-microtek	0.76	3	0.02	6	0.78	0.0
linux-3.12-rc1-144_2a-drivers-net-wireless-mwifiex-mwifiex_usb	23.39	3	13.82	15	0.74	0.0
32_7_cilled_linux-32_1-drivers-usb-image-microtek	0.64	3	0.01	6	0.79	0.0
32_7_cilled_linux-32_1-drivers-media-dvb-dvb-usb-dvb-usb-dib0700	2.19	3	0.48	11	2.76	0.0
32_7_cilled_linux-32_1-drivers-isdn-capi-kernelcapi	0.92	3	6.37	11	1.51	0.0
32_7_cilled_linux-32_1-drivers-media-video-mem2mem_testdev	5.28	3	3.5	16	0.8	0.0
32_7_cilled_linux-32_1-drivers-usb-storage-usb-storage	30.59	3	124.27	11	1.68	0.0
32_7_single_drivers-staging-media-dt3155v4l-dt3155v4l	2.63	3	5.47	12	0.93	0.0
43_1a_cilled_linux-43_1a-drivers-misc-sgi-xp-xpc	105.8	5	2.64	31	2.0	0.0
m0_drivers-usb-gadget-g_printer-ko-106_1a-2b9ec6c-1	8.35	2	0.41	16	0.65	0.0
linux-3.12-rc1.tar.xz-144_2a-drivers-staging-media-go7007-go7007-loader	0.82	5	0.24	35	0.44	0.0
205_9a_linux-3.16-rc1.tar.xz-205_9a-drivers-net-ppp-ppp_synctty	44.32	6	3.46	61	0.71	0.0
205_9a_linux-3.16-rc1.tar.xz-205_9a-drivers-net-wan-hdlc_ppp	195.22	5	57.41	52	0.66	0.0
43_2a_linux-3.16-rc1.tar.xz-43_2a-drivers-usb-host-max3421-hcd	2.3	4	5.28	36	0.82	0.0
linux-stable-9ec4f65-1-110_1a-drivers-rtc-rtc-tegra	0.78	6	0.2	35	0.52	0.0
linux-stable-39a1d13-1-101_1a-drivers-block-virtio_blk	1.71	5	7.04	37	0.52	0.0
linux-stable-42f9f8d-1-111_1a-sound-oss-opl3	6.03	4	14.08	22	0.61	0.0
linux-stable-2b9ec6c-1-106_1a-drivers-usb-gadget-g_printer	51.12	4	28.46	37	0.67	0.0
linux-stable-39a1d13-1-101_1a-drivers-block-virtio_blk	1.63	6	0.84	33	0.66	0.0
linux-stable-2b9ec6c-1-106_1a-drivers-usb-gadget-g_printer	43.1	4	17.29	26	0.69	0.0
linux-stable-d47b389-1-32_7a-drivers-media-video-cx88-cx88-blackbird	39.48	4	27.18	96	0.75	0.0
linux-4.2-rc1.tar.xz-08_1a-drivers-md-md-cluster	5.84	5	12.0	23	0.68	0.0

The detailed results for the successful 24 cases are shown in Table 1. The table reports on the time in seconds taken by the SMC, DirSE, MB, and counterexample execution, respectively. We also show the number of CFG cut-points (#CP) of the counterexample returned by SMC and the number of basic blocks (#BB) that DirSE considered based on the counterexample. Note that sometimes DirSE takes significantly longer than SMC. This is expected because DirSE uses more complex semantics. Mock construction and execution take a negligible amount of time.

Analysis of Results and Current Limitations. Results show that constructing executable counterexamples is possible using current Software Model Checking techniques. The main challenge is improving techniques for extracting the memory model assumed by the SMC. Manually inspecting the failing cases shows that the pointers extracted from external allocation sites are often dereferenced further. Our current strategy traps such dereferences and replaces them with some default values. While this is sometimes sufficient, it does not always work. We have tried replacing such addresses by symbolic memory and using a symbolic execution engine, but this did not scale.

One manual solution we found is to replace external dereferences by external functions calls. For example, dereferencing an external field foo->f is replaced by a call to an external function get_foo_f(foo) that returns the value of the field. Such external calls are trapped by the mock to produce the required value. Selectively applying this manual technique, we converted several failing cases to successful executable counterexamples. For example, Fig. 9 shows the changes for usb_urb-drivers-input-misc-keyspan_remote.ko_false-unreach-call.cil.out.i.pp.i. Three get functions are added to wrap around memory references (the original code is in comments). These functions allow the MB to inject the right values to guide the program toward the counterexample. While currently this is a manual process, we believe it can be significantly automated in the future.

```
1   extern __u8 get_bEndpointAddress(struct usb_endpoint_descriptor const *e) ;
2   extern __u8 get_bmAttributes(struct usb_endpoint_descriptor const *e);
3   extern struct device* get_dev(struct usb_interface *iface);
4
5   __inline static int usb_endpoint_dir_in(struct usb_endpoint_descriptor const *ed) {
6     /* return (((int const )ed->bEndpointAddress & 128) == 128); */
7     return (((int const) get_bEndpointAddress(ed) & 128) == 128);
8   }
9   __inline static int usb_endpoint_xfer_int(struct usb_endpoint_descriptor const *ed) {
10    /* return (((int const )ed->bmAttributes & 3) == 3);  */
11    return (((int const )get_bmAttributes(ed) & 3) == 3);
12  }
13  __inline static void *usb_get_intfdata(struct usb_interface *intf ) {
14    void *tmp___7 ;
15    /* struct device const* dev = (struct device const *)(& intf->dev); */
16    struct device const* dev = get_dev(intf);
17    tmp___7 = dev_get_drvdata(dev);
18    return (tmp___7);
19  }
20
21  int main(void) {
22    /* struct usb_interface *var_group1; */
23    struct usb_interface *var_group1 = ldv_undefined_pointer();
24    ...
25  }
```

Fig. 9. Example of manual modifications to generate executable counterexample

6   Related Work

Generating executable tests from Software Model Checking counterexamples is not a new idea. One of the earliest approaches was proposed by Beyer et al. [3]. However, they do not consider programs that manipulate memory or use external functions.

Executable Counterexamples from SMC. Rocha et al. [29] propose EZProofC, a tool to extract information about program variables from counterexamples produced by ESBMC [12] and generate executable programs that reproduce the error. First, EZProofC extracts the name, value, and line number for each variable assignment in the counterexample. Second, the code is instrumented so that the original assignment statements are replaced with assignments of the corresponding values in the counterexample. This approach is closely related to ours, but there are some important differences. First, EZProofC assumes that it is easy to match assignments in ESBMC counterexamples to the original source code. This assumption does not hold if verification is combined with aggressive optimization or transformations. In our experience, such optimizations are essential for scalability. In contrast, we make no such assumptions. More importantly, EZProofC does not deal with dereferences of pointers allocated by external functions. We found this to be prevalent in benchmarks, difficult to address, and is a primary focus of our work.

Muller and Ruskiewicz [28] produce .NET executable from a Spec# program and a symbolic counterexample. Counterexamples may include complex types including classes, object creation, and initialization of their fields. There are again some key differences. First, they target Spec#, a language without direct pointer manipulation, while we target C. As a result, our memory models differ significantly since Spec# is type-safe while C is not. Second, their executables simulate the verification semantics as defined by the verifier rather than the concrete semantics as defined by the language. Instead, our executables simulate the concrete semantics of C programs. As a result, their executables cannot guarantee the existence of an error even when an error is exercised since it might be ruled out by the concrete semantics. In contrast, in our approach an error is always consistent with the concrete semantics when the executable triggers it. A downside to our approach, however, is that our approach might fail to generate a successful executable counterexample when the verification semantics differ significantly from the concrete semantics. Third, their executables do not contain the original CUA but instead an abstraction of it where loops are modeled with loop invariants and methods with contracts.

Csallner and Smaragdakis [14] propose CnC (Check 'n' crash), a tool that uses counterexamples identified by ESC/Java [15], to create concrete test-cases (set of program inputs) that exercise the identified violation. Test-cases are then fed to the testing tool JCrasher [13]. When ESC/Java identifies a violation, CnC turns the counterexample into a set of constraints, which are solved to yield a program that exercises the violation. CnC is able to produce programs that contain numeric, reference, and array values. As in our framework, the executables produced by CnC simulate the concrete semantics of the underlying language (Java for CnC). Apart from using different memory models, the main distinction is that CnC aims at generating test-cases, while we focus on generating mocks that synthesize the external environment of the program. Test-cases are, in general, harder to produce because of the difficulty of ensuring that library calls produce the outputs needed to exercise the error. Instead, we try to generate the coarsest mocks for those library calls that can still exercise the error. Therefore, we believe our methodology can scale better for larger applications.

Recently, Beyer et al. [4] proposed an approach similar to Rocha et al. [29]. Given a counterexample in the SV-COMP [2] *witness automaton* format, original source is instrumented by assigning values from the counterexample. The approach is supported by CPAChecker [5] and Ultimate Automizer [24]. Similar to Rocha et al. [29], they do not deal with externally allocated pointers.

Test Case Generation. Dynamic Model Checking (DMC) adapts Model Checking to perform testing. One of the earliest DMC tools is VeriSoft [16] which has been very successful at finding bugs in concurrent software. The tool provides a simulator that can replay the counterexample but it does not generate executables. Test-case generation tools such as Java PathFinder [32], DART [18], EXE [8], CUTE [30], Klee [7], SAGE [19], and PEX [31] generate test-cases that can produce high coverage and/or trigger shallow bugs based on dynamic symbolic execution (DSE). The Yogi project [1,20,21] combines SMC with testing to improve scalability of the verification process. They compute both over- and under-approximations of the program semantics so that they can both prove absence of bugs and finding errors in a scalable way. Yogi tools have been integrated in the Microsoft's Static Driver Verifier. Christakis and Godefroid [9] combine SAGE [19] and MicroX [17] to prove memory safety of the ANI Windows Image Parser. SAGE starts from a random test case and performs DSE while computing procedure summaries. MicroX computes sets of inputs and outputs for ANI functions without any provided information while allocating memory on-the-fly for each uninitialized memory address. They model precisely the concrete semantics of the program: "symbolic execution of an individual path has *perfect precision*: path constraint generation and solving is then *sound* and *complete*".

These tools model the concrete semantics of the program and allocate memory on-the-fly while we deliberately allow the SMC to use abstract semantics or even be unsound. By doing so, the verification process can scale. The challenge for us is to synthesize an environment that can exercise the error in the presence of uninitialized memory, while for these tools, the process of lifting an error execution to a test case is relatively simpler.

Guided Symbolic Execution. Hicks et al. [27] propose two heuristics to guide symbolic execution (SE) to reach a particular location. The first uses a distance metric to guide SE while the second uses the callgraph to run SE in a forward manner while climbing up through the call chain. Christakis et al. [11] introduce a program instrumentation to express which parts of the program have been verified by a static analysis tool, and under which assumptions. They use PEX [31] to exercise only those unverified parts. The same authors [10] instrument the code of a static analysis tool to check for all known unsound cases and provide a detailed evaluation about it. In all these cases, symbolic execution is guided in an intelligent manner to reach certain locations of interest. However, none of these techniques focus on dealing with memory.

7   Conclusion

We presented a new framework to generate mock environments for the Code Under Analysis (CUA). A mock environment can be seen as actual binary code that implements the external functions that are referenced by the CUA so that the CUA execution mirrors the counterexample identified by the Model Checker. We believe that having executable counterexamples is essential for software engineers to adopt Model Checking technology since they would be able to use their existing toolchain. Moreover, we described formally the concrete semantics of executable counterexample based on a simple extension to the standard operational semantics for C programs. This significantly differs from the textual-based counterexample representation used by SV-COMP tools. Finally, we have implemented an instance of the framework in SEAHORN, and tested it on benchmarks from SV-COMP 2018. Although the initial results are promising, more work remains to be done, especially to handle counterexamples with more complicated memory structures.

Acknowledgments. Authors would like to thank Natarajan Shankar for his invaluable comments to improve the quality of this paper.

References

1. Beckman, N.E., Nori, A.V., Rajamani, S.K., Simmons, R.J.: Proofs from tests. In: Proceedings of the ACM/SIGSOFT International Symposium on Software Testing and Analysis, ISSTA 2008, Seattle, WA, USA, 20–24 July 2008, pp. 3–14 (2008)
2. Beyer, D.: Software verification with validation of results. In: Legay, A., Margaria, T. (eds.) TACAS 2017. LNCS, vol. 10206, pp. 331–349. Springer, Heidelberg (2017). https://doi.org/10.1007/978-3-662-54580-5_20
3. Beyer, D., Chlipala, A., Henzinger, T.A., Jhala, R., Majumdar, R.: Generating tests from counterexamples. In: 26th International Conference on Software Engineering (ICSE 2004), Edinburgh, UK, 23–28 May 2004, pp. 326–335 (2004)
4. Beyer, D., Dangl, M., Lemberger, T., Tautschnig, M.: Tests from witnesses. In: Dubois, C., Wolff, B. (eds.) TAP 2018. LNCS, vol. 10889, pp. 3–23. Springer, Cham (2018). https://doi.org/10.1007/978-3-319-92994-1_1
5. Beyer, D., Keremoglu, M.E.: CPACHECKER: a tool for configurable software verification. In: Gopalakrishnan, G., Qadeer, S. (eds.) CAV 2011. LNCS, vol. 6806, pp. 184–190. Springer, Heidelberg (2011). https://doi.org/10.1007/978-3-642-22110-1_16
6. Beyer, D., Lemberger, T.: Software verification: testing vs. model checking. In: Strichman, O., Tzoref-Brill, R. (eds.) Hardware and Software: Verification and Testing. LNCS, vol. 10629, pp. 99–114. Springer, Cham (2017). https://doi.org/10.1007/978-3-319-70389-3_7
7. Cadar, C., Dunbar, D., Engler, D.R.: KLEE: unassisted and automatic generation of high-coverage tests for complex systems programs. In: 8th USENIX Symposium on Operating Systems Design and Implementation, OSDI 2008, San Diego, California, USA, 8–10 December 2008, pp. 209–224 (2008)

8. Cadar, C., Ganesh, V., Pawlowski, P.M., Dill, D.L., Engler, D.R.: EXE: automatically generating inputs of death. ACM Trans. Inf. Syst. Secur. **12**(2), 10:1–10:38 (2008)
9. Christakis, M., Godefroid, P.: Proving memory safety of the ani windows image parser using compositional exhaustive testing. In: D'Souza, D., Lal, A., Larsen, K.G. (eds.) VMCAI 2015. LNCS, vol. 8931, pp. 373–392. Springer, Heidelberg (2015). https://doi.org/10.1007/978-3-662-46081-8_21
10. Christakis, M., Müller, P., Wüstholz, V.: An experimental evaluation of deliberate unsoundness in a static program analyzer. In: D'Souza, D., Lal, A., Larsen, K.G. (eds.) VMCAI 2015. LNCS, vol. 8931, pp. 336–354. Springer, Heidelberg (2015). https://doi.org/10.1007/978-3-662-46081-8_19
11. Christakis, M., Müller, P., Wüstholz, V.: Guiding dynamic symbolic execution toward unverified program executions. In: Proceedings of the 38th International Conference on Software Engineering, ICSE 2016, Austin, TX, USA, 14–22 May 2016, pp. 144–155 (2016)
12. Cordeiro, L.C., Fischer, B., Marques-Silva, J.: SMT-based bounded model checking for embedded ANSI-C software. IEEE Trans. Softw. Eng. **38**(4), 957–974 (2012)
13. Csallner, C., Smaragdakis, Y.: JCrasher: an automatic robustness tester for Java. Softw. Pract. Exper. **34**(11), 1025–1050 (2004)
14. Csallner, C., Smaragdakis, Y.: Check 'n' crash. In: Proceedings of the 27th International Conference on Software Engineering - ICSE 2005, p. 422. ACM Press, New York (2005)
15. Flanagan, C., Leino, K.R.M., Lillibridge, M., Nelson, G., Saxe, J.B., Stata, R.: Extended static checking for Java. In: Proceedings of the 2002 ACM SIGPLAN Conference on Programming Language Design and Implementation (PLDI), Berlin, Germany, 17–19 June 2002, pp. 234–245 (2002)
16. Godefroid, P.: VeriSoft: a tool for the automatic analysis of concurrent reactive software. In: Grumberg, O. (ed.) CAV 1997. LNCS, vol. 1254, pp. 476–479. Springer, Heidelberg (1997). https://doi.org/10.1007/3-540-63166-6_52
17. Godefroid, P.: Micro execution. In: 36th International Conference on Software Engineering, ICSE 2014, Hyderabad, India, 31 May–07 June 2014, pp. 539–549 (2014)
18. Godefroid, P., Klarlund, N., Sen, K.: DART directed automated random testing. In: Proceedings of the ACM SIGPLAN 2005 Conference on Programming Language Design and Implementation, Chicago, IL, USA, 12–15 June 2005, pp. 213–223 (2005)
19. Godefroid, P., Levin, M.Y., Molnar, D.A.: Automated whitebox fuzz testing. In: Proceedings of the Network and Distributed System Security Symposium, NDSS 2008, San Diego, California, USA, 10th February-13th February 2008 (2008)
20. Godefroid, P., Nori, A.V., Rajamani, S.K., Tetali, S.: Compositional may-must program analysis: unleashing the power of alternation. In: Proceedings of the 37th ACM SIGPLAN-SIGACT Symposium on Principles of Programming Languages, POPL 2010, Madrid, Spain, 17–23 January 2010, pp. 43–56 (2010)
21. Gulavani, B.S., Henzinger, T.A., Kannan, Y., Nori, A.V., Rajamani, S.K.: SYNERGY: a new algorithm for property checking. In: Proceedings of the 14th ACM SIGSOFT International Symposium on Foundations of Software Engineering, FSE 2006, Portland, Oregon, USA, 5–11 November 2006, pp. 117–127 (2006)
22. Gurfinkel, A., Kahsai, T., Komuravelli, A., Navas, J.A.: The SeaHorn verification framework. In: Kroening, D., Păsăreanu, C.S. (eds.) CAV 2015. LNCS, vol. 9206, pp. 343–361. Springer, Cham (2015). https://doi.org/10.1007/978-3-319-21690-4_20

23. Gurfinkel, A., Navas, J.A.: A context-sensitive memory model for verification of C/C++ programs. In: Ranzato, F. (ed.) SAS 2017. LNCS, vol. 10422, pp. 148–168. Springer, Cham (2017). https://doi.org/10.1007/978-3-319-66706-5_8

24. Heizmann, M., et al.: Ultimate automizer with SMTInterpol. In: Piterman, N., Smolka, S.A. (eds.) TACAS 2013. LNCS, vol. 7795, pp. 641–643. Springer, Heidelberg (2013). https://doi.org/10.1007/978-3-642-36742-7_53

25. Johnson, B., Song, Y., Murphy-Hill, E., Bowdidge, R.: Why don't software developers use static analysis tools to find bugs? In: Proceedings of the 2013 International Conference on Software Engineering, ICSE 2013, pp. 672–681 (2013)

26. LDV: Linux Driver Verification. http://linuxtesting.org/ldv

27. Ma, K.-K., Yit Phang, K., Foster, J.S., Hicks, M.: Directed symbolic execution. In: Yahav, E. (ed.) SAS 2011. LNCS, vol. 6887, pp. 95–111. Springer, Heidelberg (2011). https://doi.org/10.1007/978-3-642-23702-7_11

28. Müller, P., Ruskiewicz, J.N.: Using debuggers to understand failed verification attempts. In: Butler, M., Schulte, W. (eds.) FM 2011. LNCS, vol. 6664, pp. 73–87. Springer, Heidelberg (2011). https://doi.org/10.1007/978-3-642-21437-0_8

29. Rocha, H., Barreto, R., Cordeiro, L., Neto, A.D.: Understanding programming bugs in ANSI-C software using bounded model checking counter-examples. In: Derrick, J., Gnesi, S., Latella, D., Treharne, H. (eds.) IFM 2012. LNCS, vol. 7321, pp. 128–142. Springer, Heidelberg (2012). https://doi.org/10.1007/978-3-642-30729-4_10

30. Sen, K., Agha, G.: CUTE and jCUTE: concolic unit testing and explicit path model-checking tools. In: Ball, T., Jones, R.B. (eds.) CAV 2006. LNCS, vol. 4144, pp. 419–423. Springer, Heidelberg (2006). https://doi.org/10.1007/11817963_38

31. Tillmann, N., de Halleux, J.: Pex–white box test generation for.NET. In: Beckert, B., Hähnle, R. (eds.) TAP 2008. LNCS, vol. 4966, pp. 134–153. Springer, Heidelberg (2008). https://doi.org/10.1007/978-3-540-79124-9_10

32. Visser, W., Pasareanu, C.S., Khurshid, S.: Test input generation with java pathfinder. In: Proceedings of the ACM/SIGSOFT International Symposium on Software Testing and Analysis, ISSTA 2004, Boston, Massachusetts, USA, 11–14 July 2004, pp. 97–107 (2004)

Extending VIAP to Handle Array Programs

Pritom Rajkhowa$^{(\boxtimes)}$ and Fangzhen Lin

Department of Computer Science,
The Hong Kong University of Science and Technology,
Clear Water Bay, Kowloon, Hong Kong
{prajkhowa,flin}@cse.ust.hk

Abstract. In this paper, we extend our previously described fully automated program verification system called VIAP primarily for verifying the safety properties of programs with integer assignments to programs with arrays. VIAP is based on a recent translation of programs to first-order logic proposed by Lin [1] and directly calls the SMT solver Z3. It relies more on reasoning with recurrences instead of loop invariants. In this paper, we extend it to programs with arrays. Our extension is not restricted to single dimensional arrays but general and works for multidimensional and nested arrays as well. In the most recent *SV-COMP* 2018 competition, VIAP with array extension came in second in the ReachSafety-Arrays sub-category, behind *VeriAbs*.

Keywords: Automatic program verification · Array · Structure
Multi-dimensional · Nested · First-order logic
Mathematical induction · Recurrences · SMT · Arithmetic

1 Introduction

Arrays are widely used data structures in imperative languages. Automatic verification of programs with arrays is considered to be a difficult the task as it requires effective reasoning about loops and nested loops in case of multidimensional arrays. We have earlier reported a system called VIAP [2] that can prove non-trivial properties about programs with loops without using loop invariants. In this paper, we extend VIAP to arrays. In particular, we show how our system can handle multidimensional arrays. While there have been a few systems that can prove some non-trivial properties about one-dimensional arrays automatically, we are not aware of any that can do so for multidimensional arrays. Systems like Dafny [3],VeriFast [4] and Why [5] can indeed prove non-trivial properties about programs with multidimensional arrays, but they require user-provided loop invariant(s). Program verification is in general an undecidable problem, so there cannot be a fully automated system that works in all cases. Still, it is worthwhile to see how much one can do with fully automatic systems, hence the interest competitions like SV-COMP for fully automated systems.

ⓒ Springer Nature Switzerland AG 2018
R. Piskac and P. Rümmer (Eds.): VSTTE 2018, LNCS 11294, pp. 38–49, 2018.
https://doi.org/10.1007/978-3-030-03592-1_3

In the following, we first describe how our system works. We then discuss some related work and finally make some concluding remarks.

2 Translation

Our translator consider programs in the following language:

```
E ::= array(E,...,E) |
      operator(E,...,E)
B ::= E = E |
      boolean-op(B,...,B)
P ::= array(E,...,E) = E |
      if B then P else P |
      P; P |
      while B do P
```

where the tokens E, B, P stand for integer expressions, Boolean expressions, and programs respectively. The token `array` stands for program variables, and the tokens `operator` and `boolean-op` stand for built-in integer functions and Boolean functions, respectively. Notice that for `array`, if its arity is 0, then it stands for an integer program variable. Otherwise, it is an array variable. Notice also that while the notation `array[i][j]` is commonly used in programming languages to refer to an array element, we use the notation `array(i,j)` here which is more common mathematics and logic.

Our system actually accepts C-like programs which are converted to these programs by a preprocessor. In particular, goto-statements are removed using the algorithm proposed in [6].

Given a program P, and a language X, our system generates a set of first-order axioms denoted by Π_P^X that captures the changes of P on X. Here by a language we mean a set of functions and predicate symbols, and for Π_P^X to be correct, X needs to include all program variables in P as well as any functions and predicates that can be changed by P.

The set Π_P^X of axioms are generated inductively on the structure of P. The algorithm is described in details in [1] and an implementation is [2]. This paper extends it to handle arrays. The inductive cases are given in table provided in the supplementary information depicted in[1]. There are two primitive cases, one for integer assignment and one for array element assignment. Before we describe them, we first describe our representation of arrays.

We consider arrays as first-order objects that can be parameters of functions, predicates, and can be quantified over. In first-order logic, this means that we have sorts for arrays, and one sort for each dimension. In the following, we denote by int the integer sort, and $array_k$ the k-dimensional array sort, where $k \geq 1$.

To denote the value of an array at some indices, for each $k \geq 1$, we introduce a special function named $dkarray$ of the arity:

$$dkarray : array_k \times int^k \rightarrow int,$$

---

[1] https://goo.gl/2ZBGUr.

as we consider only integer valued arrays. Thus $d1array(a, i)$ denotes the value of a one-dimensional array a at index i, i.e. $a[i]$ under a conventional notation, and $d2array(b, i, j)$ stands for $b[i][j]$ for two-dimensional array b. We can also introduce a function to denote the size of an array. However, we do not consider it here as the programs that we deal with in this paper does not involve operations about array sizes and we assume that all array references are legal.

Recall that we generate a set of axioms for a program P under a language X. The generated set of axioms captures the changes of P on X, so X needs to include all functions and predicates that can be changed by P. Therefore if a program makes changes to, say a two-dimensional array, then X must include $d2array$.

When we translate a program to first-order axioms, we need to convert expressions in the program to terms in first-order logic. This is straightforward, given how we have decided to represent arrays. For example, if E is $a(1, 2)+b(1)$, where a is a two-dimensional array and b a one-dimensional array, then $\hat{E}$, the first-order term that corresponds to E, is $d2array(a, 1, 2) + d1array(b, 1)$.

We are now ready to describe how we generate axioms for assignments, First, for integer variable assignments:

Definition 21. If P is V = E, and $V \in X$, then Π_P^X is the set of the following axioms:

$$\forall x.X1(x) = X(x), \text{ for each } X \in X \text{ that is different from } V,$$
$$V1 = \hat{E}$$

where for each $X \in X$, we introduce a new symbol $X1$ with the same arity standing for the value of X after the assignment, and $\hat{E}$ is the translation of the expression E into its corresponding term in logic as described above.

For example, if P_1 is

```
I = a(1,2)+b(1)
```

and X is $\{I, a, b, d1array, d2array\}$ (a and b are for the two array variables in the assignment, respectively), then $\Pi_{P_1}^X$ is the set of following axioms:

$$I1 = d2array(a, 1, 2) + d1array(b, 1),$$
$$a1 = a,$$
$$b1 = b,$$
$$\forall x, i.d1array1(x, i) = d1array(x, i),$$
$$\forall x, i, j.d2array1(x, i, j) = d2array(x, i, j).$$

Again we remark that we assume all array accesses are legal. Otherwise, we would need axioms like the following to catch array errors:

$$\neg in\text{-}bound(1, b) \rightarrow arrayError,$$
$$\neg in\text{-}bound((1, 2), a) \rightarrow arrayError,$$

where $in\text{-}bound(i, array)$ means that the index i is within the bound of $array$, and can be defined using array sizes.

Definition 22. If P is V(e1,e2,...,ek) = E, then Π_P^X is the set of the following axioms:

$\forall x. X1(x) = X(x)$, for each $X \in \boldsymbol{X}$ which is different from $dkarray$,

$dkarray1(x, i_1, ..., i_k)$
$$= ite(x = V \wedge i_i = \hat{e}_1 \wedge \cdots \wedge i_k = \hat{e}_k, \hat{E}, dkarray(x, i_1, ..., i_k)),$$

where $ite(c, e, e')$ is the conditional expression: if c then e else e'.

For example, if P_2 is b(1)=a(1,2)+b(1), and $\boldsymbol{X}$ is $\{I, a, b, d1array, d2array\}$, then $\Pi_{P_2}^X$ is the set of following axioms:

$I1 = I$,

$a1 = a$,

$b1 = b$,

$\forall x, i. d1array1(x, i) =$
$\qquad ite(x = b \wedge i = 1, d2array(a, 1, 2) + d1array(b, 1), d1array(x, i))$,

$\forall x, i, j. d2array1(x, i, j) = d2array(x, i, j)$.

Notice that $b1 = b$ means that while the value of b at index 1 has changed, the array itself as an *object* has not changed. If we have array assignments like a=b for array variables a and b, they will generate axioms like $a1 = b$.

We now give two simple examples of how the inductive cases work described in the tables[2] provided as supplementary material mentioned previously. See [1] for more details.

Consider P_3 which is the sequence of first P_1 then P_2:

```
I = a(1,2)+b(1);
b(1)=a(1,2)+b(1)
```

The axiom set $\Pi_{P_3}^X$ is generated from $\Pi_{P_1}^X$ and $\Pi_{P_2}^X$ by introducing some new symbols to connect the output of P_1 with the input of P_2:

$I2 = d2array(a, 1, 2) + d1array(b, 1)$,

$a2 = a$,

$b2 = b$,

$\forall x, i. d1array2(x, i) = d1array(x, i)$,

$\forall x, i, j. d2array2(x, i, j) = d2array(x, i, j)$,

$I1 = I2$,

$a1 = a2$,

$b1 = b2$,

$\forall x, i. d1array1(x, i)$
$\qquad = ite(x = b2 \wedge i = 1, d2array2(a2, 1, 2) + d1array2(b2, 1), d1array2(x, i))$,

$\forall x, i, j. d2array1(x, i, j) = d2array2(x, i, j)$,

---

[2] https://goo.gl/2ZBGUr.

where $I2, a2, b2, d1array2, d2array2$ are new symbols to connect P_1's output with P_2's input. If we do not care about the intermediate values, these temporary symbols can often be eliminated. For this program, eliminating them yields the following set of axioms:

$$I1 = d2array(a, 1, 2) + d1array(b, 1),$$
$$a1 = a,$$
$$b1 = b,$$
$$\forall x, i.d1array1(x, i) =$$
$$ite(x = b \wedge i = 1, d2array(a, 1, 2) + d1array(b, 1), d1array(x, i)),$$
$$\forall x, i, j.d2array1(x, i, j) = d2array(x, i, j).$$

The most important feature of the approach in [1] is in the translation of loops to a set of first-order axioms. The main idea is to introduce an explicit counter for loop iterations and an explicit natural number constant to denote the number of iterations the loop executes before exiting. It is best to illustrate by a simple example. Consider the following program P_4:

```
while I < M {
    I = I+1;
}
```

Let $\boldsymbol{X} = \{I, M\}$. To compute $\Pi_{P_4}^X$, we need to generate first the axioms for the body of the loop, which in this case is straightforward:

$$I1 = I + 1,$$
$$M1 = M$$

Once the axioms for the body of the loop are computed, they are turned into inductive definitions by adding a new counter argument to all functions and predicates that may be changed by the program. For our simple example, we get

$$\forall n.I(n + 1) = I(n) + 1, \tag{1}$$
$$\forall n.M(n + 1) = M(n), \tag{2}$$

where the quantification is over all natural numbers. We then add the initial case, and introduce a new natural number constant N to denote the terminating index:

$$I(0) = I \wedge M(0) = M,$$
$$I1 = I(N) \wedge M1 = M(N),$$
$$\neg(I(N) < M(N)),$$
$$\forall n.n < N \rightarrow I(n) < M(n).$$

One advantage of making counters explicit and quantifiable is that we can then either compute closed-form solutions to recurrences like (1) or reason about them using mathematical induction. This is unlike proof strategies like k-induction where the counters are hard-wired into the variables. Again, for more details about this approach, see [1] which has discussions about related work as well as proofs of the correctness under operational semantics.

3   VIAP

We have implemented the translation to make it work with programs with a C-like the syntax used SymPy to simplify algebraic expressions and compute the closed-form solutions to simple recurrences, and finally verified assertions using Z3. The resulting system, called VIAP, is fully automated. We reported in an earlier paper [2] how it works on integer assignments. We have now extended it to handle arrays. We have described how the translation is extended to handle array element assignments in the previous section. In this section, we describe some implementation details.

We have already mentioned that temporary variables introduced during the translation process can often be eliminated, and that SymPy can be used to simplify algebraic expressions and compute closed-form solutions to simple recurrences. All of these have already been implemented for basic integer assignments and described in our earlier paper [2], therefore we do not repeat them here. For arrays, an important module that we added is for instantiation.

Our main objective is translating a program to first-order logic axioms with arithmetic. This translation provides the relationship between the input and output values of the program variables. The relationship between the input and output values of the program variables is independent of what one may want to prove about the program. SMT solver tools like Z3 is just an off shelf tool, so we never considered using the built-in array function there.

3.1   Instantiation

Instantiation is one of the most important phases of the pre-processing of axioms before the resulting set of formulas is passed on an SMT-solver according to some proof strategies. The objective is to help an SMT solver like Z3 to reason with quantifiers. Whenever an array element assignment occurs inside a loop, our system will generate an axiom like the following:

$$\forall x_1, x_2...x_{k+1}, n.dkarray_i(x_1, x_2...x_{k+1}, n+1) =$$
$$ite(x_1 = A \land x_2 = E_2 \land ... \land x_{k+1} = E_{h+1}, E,$$
$$dkarray_i(x_1, x_2...x_{k+1}, n)) \tag{3}$$

where

- A is a k-dimensional array.
- $dkarray_i$ is a temporary function introduced by translator.
- x_1 is an array name variable introduced by translator, and is universally quantified over arrays of k dimension.

- $x_2,....,x_{k+1}$ are natural number variables representing array indices, and are universally quantified over natural numbers.
- n is the loop counter variable universally quantified over natural numbers.
- $E, E_2, ..., E_{k+1}$ are expressions.

For an axiom like (3), our system performs two types of instantiations:

- **Instantiating Arrays**: this substitutes each occurrence of variable x_1 in the axiom (3) by the array constant A, and generates the following axiom:

$$\forall x_1, x_2...x_{k+1}.dkarray_i(A, x_2...x_{k+1}, n+1)$$
$$= ite(x_2 = E_2 \wedge ... \wedge x_{k+1} = E_{h+1}, E, dkarray_i(A, x_2...x_{k+1}, n)) \quad (4)$$

- **Instantiating Array Indices**: This substitutes each occurrence of variable x_i, $2 \leq i \leq k$, in the axiom (4) by E_i, and generates the following axiom:

$$\forall n.dkarray_i(A, E_2...E_{k+1}, n+1) = E \quad (5)$$

Example 1. This example shows the effect of instantiation on a complete example. Consider the following Battery Controller program from the SV-COMP benchmark [7,8]:

```
1.      int COUNT , MIN ,i=1 ;
2.      int volArray[COUNT];
3.      if( COUNT %4 != 0) return ;
4.      while(i <= COUNT /4) {
5.          if (5 >= MIN ){ volArray [i*4-4]=5; }
6.              else { volArray [i*4-4]=0; }
7.          if (7 >= MIN ){ volArray [i*4-3]=7; }
8.              else { volArray [i*4-3]=0; }
9.        if (3 >= MIN ){ volArray [i*4-2]=3; }
10.             else { volArray [i*4-2]=0; }
11.         if (1 >= MIN ){ volArray [i*4-1]=1; }
12.             else  { volArray [i*4-1]=0; }
13.         assert ( volArray[i]>=MIN ||volArray[i]==0);
14.         i=i+1; }
```

Our system generates the following set of axioms after the recurrences from the loop are solved by SymPy:

1. $COUNT1 = COUNT$
2. $j1 = j$
3. $volArray1 = volArray$
4. $MIN1 = MIN$
5. $i1 = ite(((COUNT\%4) == 0), (N_1 + 1), 1)$
6.

$$\forall x_1, x_2.d1array1(x_1, x_2)$$
$$= ite((COUNT\%4) == 0, d1array_{13}(x_1, x_2, N_1), d1array(x_1, x_2))$$

7.

$$\forall x_1, x_2, n_1.d1array_{13}(x_1, x_2, (n_1 + 1)) = ite(1 \geq MIN,$$
$$ite(x_1 = volArray \wedge x_2 = (n_1 + 1) * 4 - 1, 1, d1array_{13}(volArray, x_2, n_1)),$$
$$ite(x_1 = volArray \wedge x_2 = (n_1 + 1) * 4 - 1, 0,$$
$$\quad ite(3 \geq MIN,$$
$$\quad\quad ite(x_1 = volArray \wedge x_2 = (n_1 + 1) * 4 - 2, 1, d1array_{13}(volArray, x_2, n_1))$$
$$\quad\quad ite(x_1 = volArray \wedge x_2 = (n_1 + 1) * 4 - 2, 0,$$
$$\quad\quad\quad ite(7 \geq MIN,$$
$$\quad\quad\quad\quad ite(x_1 = volArray \wedge x_2 = (n_1 + 1) * 4 - 3, 1, d1array_{13}(volArray, x_2, n_1)),$$
$$\quad\quad\quad\quad ite(x_1 = volArray \wedge x_2 = (n_1 + 1) * 4 - 3, 0,$$
$$\quad\quad\quad\quad\quad ite(5 \geq MIN,$$
$$\quad\quad\quad\quad\quad\quad ite(x_1 = volArray \wedge x_2 = (n_1 + 1) * 4 - 4, 1,$$
$$\quad\quad\quad\quad\quad\quad\quad d1array_{13}(volArray, x_2, n_1)),$$
$$\quad\quad\quad\quad\quad\quad ite(x_1 = volArray \wedge x_2 = (n_1 + 1) * 4 - 4, 0,$$
$$\quad\quad\quad\quad\quad\quad\quad d1array_{13}(volArray, x_2, n_1)))))))))$$

8. $\forall x_1, x_2.d1array_{13}(x_1, x_2, 0) = d1array(x_1, x_2)$
9. $(N_1 + 1) > (COUNT/4)$
10. $\forall n_1.(n_1 < N_1) \rightarrow (n_1 + 1) \leq (COUNT/4)$

where $(COUNT\%4) == 0$ is copied directly from the conditional `COUNT%4 !=0` in the program and is converted to $(COUNT\%4) = 0$ in Z3.

The instantiation module will then generate the following new axioms from the one in 7:

1. $\forall n_1.0 \leq n_1 < COUNT \rightarrow$
   $d1array_{13}(volArray, (n_1 + 1) * 4 - 1, n_1 + 1) = ite(1 \geq MIN, 1, 0)$
2. $\forall n_1.0 \leq n_1 < COUNT \rightarrow$
   $d1array_{13}(volArray, (n_1 + 1) * 4 - 2), n_1 + 1) = ite(3 \geq MIN, 1, 0)$
3. $\forall n_1.0 \leq n_1 < COUNT \rightarrow$
   $d1array_{13}(volArray, (n_1 + 1) * 4 - 3, n_1 + 1) = ite(7 \geq MIN, 1, 0)$
4. $\forall n_1.0 \leq n_1 < COUNT \rightarrow$
   $d1array_{13}(volArray, (n_1 + 1) * 4 - 4, n_1 + 1) = ite(5 \geq MIN, 1, 0)$

For the the following assertion to prove:

$$d1array_{13}(volArray, n_1 + 0, N_1) \geq 2 \vee d1array_{13}(volArray, n_1 + 0, N_1) = 0$$

VIAP successfully proved the assertion irrespective of the value of `COUNT`. On the other hand, tools like CBMC [5] and SMACK+Corral [9] which prove this assertion for arrays with small values of `COUNT=100` fail when the COUNT value is non-deterministic or bigger(`COUNT=10000`) and this has been also reported by [8]. Other tools like UAutomizer [10], Seahorn [11], ESBMC [12], Ceagle [13], Booster [14], and Vaphor [15] fail to prove the assertion even for a small value of `COUNT`. To our knowledge, Vaphor [15] and VeriAbs [16] are the only other systems that can prove this assertion regardless of the value of `COUNT`.

3.2 Proof Strategies

Currently, VIAP tries to prove the given assertion by first trying it directly with Z3. If this direct proof fails, it tries a simple induction scheme which works as follows: if N is a natural number constant in the assertion $\beta(N)$, it is replaced by a new natural number variable n and proves the universal assertion $\forall n \beta(n)$ using an induction on n. There is much room for improvement here, especially in the heuristics for doing the induction. This is an active future work for us.

3.3 Multi-dimensional Arrays

Finally, we show an example of a program with multi-dimensional arrays. In fact, with our approach, nothing special needs to be done here. Consider the following program for doing matrix addition:

```
1.     int i,j,A[P][Q],B[P][Q],C[P][Q];
2.     i=0;j=0;
3.     while(i < P){
4.         j=0;
5.         while(j < Q){
6.             C[j][i] = A[i][j]+B[i][j];
7.             assert(C[i][j] == A[i][j]+B[i][j])
8.             j=j+1;}
9.         i=i+1;}
```

For this program, our system generates the following set of axioms:

1. $P1 = P$
2. $Q1 = Q$
3. $A1 = A$
4. $B1 = B$
5. $C1 = C$
6. $i1 = (N_2 + 0)$
7. $j1 = j_5(N_2)$
8. $\forall x_1, x_2, x_3.d2array1(x_1, x_2, x_3) = d2array5(x_1, x_2, x_3, N_2)$
9.

$$\forall x_1, x_2, x_3, n_1, n_2.d2array2(x_1, x_2, x_3, (n_1 + 1), n2)$$
$$= ite(x_1 = C \wedge x_2 = n1 \wedge x_3 = n_2,$$
$$d2array2(A, n_1 + 0, n_2 + 0, n_1, n_2) + d2array2(B, n_1 + 0, n_2 + 0, n_1, n_2),$$
$$d2array2(x1, x2, x3, n1, n2))$$

10. $\forall x_1, x_2, x_3, n_2.d2array2(x_1, x_2, x_3, 0, n_2) = d2array5(x_1, x_2, x_3, n_2)$
11. $\forall n_2.(N_1(n_2) \geq Q)$
12. $\forall n_1, n_2.(n_1 < N_1(n_2)) \rightarrow (n_1 < Q)$
13. $\forall n_2.j_5((n_2 + 1)) = (N_1(n_2) + 0)$
14. $\forall x_1, x_2, x_3, n_2.d2array5(x_1, x_2, x_3, (n_2 + 1)) = d2array2(x_1, x_2, x_3, N_1(n_2), n_2)$

15. $j_5(0) = 0$
16. $\forall x_1, x_2, x_3.d2array_5(x_1, x_2, x_3, 0) = d2array(x_1, x_2, x_3)$
17. $(N_2 \geq P)$
18. $\forall n_2.(n_2 < N_2 \rightarrow (n_2 < P))$

and the following assertion to prove:

$$\forall n_1, n_2.d2array_5(C, (n_1 + 0), (n_2 + 0), N_2)$$
$$= d2array_5(A, (n_1 + 0), (n_2 + 0), N_2) + d2array_5(A, (n_1 + 0), (n_2 + 0), N_2).$$

VIAP proved it in 30 s using the direct proof strategy. In comparison, given that the program has multi-dimensional arrays and nested loops, state-of-art systems like SMACK+Corral [9], UAutomizer [10], Seahorn [11], ESBMC [12], Ceagle [13], Booster [14], VeriAbs [16] and Vaphor [15] failed to prove it.

Verifiability: VIAP is implemented in python. The source code, benchmarks and the full experiments are available in [17].

4 Related Work

Tools like Dafny [3], VeriFast [4] and Why [5] can prove the correctness of a program with multi-dimensional array only if provided with suitable invariants, however, VIAP is a fully automatic prover. The Vaphor tool [15], is a Horn clause base approach which uses the Z3 [18] solver in the back-end, and cannot handle array program with non-sequential indices, unlike VIAP. Seahorn [11] is another horn clause based verification framework. Seahorn can only prove 3 out of 88 programs from the Array-Example directory of SV-COMP benchmarks. There is a sizable body of work that considers the verification of C programs including programs with an array such as SMACK+Corral [9], UAutomizer [10], ESBMC [12], Ceagle [13]. The major limitation of UAutomizer is that it can only handle most of the programs with array when the property is not quantified. Ceagle [13] and SMACK+Corral [9] got first and second position in the ReachSafety-Arrays sub-category of ReachSafety category. SMACK+Corral is not very effective when it comes to dealing with multi-dimensional programs. Similarly, the Booster [14] verification tool failed when interpolants for universally quantified array properties (like programs with multidimensional array) became hard to compute.

5 Concluding Remarks and Future Work

In this paper, we describe an approach to prove the correctness of imperative programs with arrays in a system we implemented in an earlier work, called VIAP. VIAP is continuously evolving. In the future, we will work on incorporating proofs of the following in VIAP - (1) programs with more advanced data structures like linked lists, binary trees. (2) program termination (3) and object-oriented programs in languages like Java.

Acknowledgment. We would like to thank Jianmin Ji, Peisen YAO, Anand Inasu Chittilappilly and Prashant Saikia for useful discussions. We are grateful to the developers of Z3 and SymPy for making their systems available for open use. All errors remain ours. This work was supported in part by the HKUST grant IEG16EG01.

References

1. Lin, F.: A formalization of programs in first-order logic with a discrete linear order. Artif. Intell. **235**, 1–25 (2016)
2. Rajkhowa, P., Lin, F.: VIAP - automated system for verifying integer assignment programs with loops. In: 19th International Symposium on Symbolic and Numeric Algorithms for Scientific Computing, SYNASC 2017, 21–24 September, Timisoara, Romania (2017)
3. Leino, K.R.M.: Dafny: an automatic program verifier for functional correctness. In: Clarke, E.M., Voronkov, A. (eds.) LPAR 2010. LNCS (LNAI), vol. 6355, pp. 348–370. Springer, Heidelberg (2010). https://doi.org/10.1007/978-3-642-17511-4_20
4. Jacobs, B., Smans, J., Philippaerts, P., Vogels, F., Penninckx, W., Piessens, F.: VeriFast: a powerful, sound, predictable, fast verifier for C and Java. In: Bobaru, M., Havelund, K., Holzmann, G.J., Joshi, R. (eds.) NFM 2011. LNCS, vol. 6617, pp. 41–55. Springer, Heidelberg (2011). https://doi.org/10.1007/978-3-642-20398-5_4
5. Filliâtre, J.-C., Paskevich, A.: Why3 — where programs meet provers. In: Felleisen, M., Gardner, P. (eds.) ESOP 2013. LNCS, vol. 7792, pp. 125–128. Springer, Heidelberg (2013). https://doi.org/10.1007/978-3-642-37036-6_8
6. Erosa, A.M., Hendren, L.J.: Taming control flow: a structured approach to eliminating goto statements. In: Bal, H.E. (ed.) Proceedings of the IEEE Computer Society ICCLs, Toulouse, France, pp. 229–240 (1994)
7. Program Committee/Jury: SV-COMP: Benchmark Verification Tasks (2018)
8. Chakraborty, S., Gupta, A., Unadkat, D.: Verifying array manipulating programs by tiling. In: Ranzato, F. (ed.) SAS 2017. LNCS, vol. 10422, pp. 428–449. Springer, Cham (2017). https://doi.org/10.1007/978-3-319-66706-5_21
9. Carter, M., He, S., Whitaker, J., Rakamaric, Z., Emmi, M.: Smack software verification toolchain. In: 2016 IEEE/ACM 38th International Conference on Software Engineering Companion (ICSE-C), pp. 589–592, May 2016
10. Heizmann, M., et al.: Ultimate automizer with SMTInterpol. In: Piterman, N., Smolka, S.A. (eds.) TACAS 2013. LNCS, vol. 7795, pp. 641–643. Springer, Heidelberg (2013). https://doi.org/10.1007/978-3-642-36742-7_53
11. Gurfinkel, A., Kahsai, T., Komuravelli, A., Navas, J.A.: The SeaHorn verification framework. In: Kroening, D., Păsăreanu, C.S. (eds.) CAV 2015. LNCS, vol. 9206, pp. 343–361. Springer, Cham (2015). https://doi.org/10.1007/978-3-319-21690-4_20
12. Cordeiro, L., Morse, J., Nicole, D., Fischer, B.: Context-bounded model checking with ESBMC 1.17. In: Flanagan, C., König, B. (eds.) TACAS 2012. LNCS, vol. 7214, pp. 534–537. Springer, Heidelberg (2012). https://doi.org/10.1007/978-3-642-28756-5_42
13. Wang, D., Zhang, C., Chen, G., Gu, M., Sun, J.: C code verification based on the extended labeled transition system model. In: Proceedings of the MoDELS 2016 Demo and Poster Sessions co-located with ACM/IEEE 19th International Conference on Model Driven Engineering Languages and Systems (MoDELS 2016), 2–7 October 2016, Saint-Malo, France, pp. 48–55 (2016)

14. Alberti, F., Ghilardi, S., Sharygina, N.: Booster: an acceleration-based verification framework for array programs. In: Cassez, F., Raskin, J.-F. (eds.) ATVA 2014. LNCS, vol. 8837, pp. 18–23. Springer, Cham (2014). https://doi.org/10.1007/978-3-319-11936-6_2

15. Monniaux, D., Gonnord, L.: Cell morphing: from array programs to array-free horn clauses. In: Rival, X. (ed.) SAS 2016. LNCS, vol. 9837, pp. 361–382. Springer, Heidelberg (2016). https://doi.org/10.1007/978-3-662-53413-7_18

16. Chimdyalwar, B., Darke, P., Chauhan, A., Shah, P., Kumar, S., Venkatesh, R.: VeriAbs: verification by abstraction (competition contribution). In: Legay, A., Margaria, T. (eds.) TACAS 2017. LNCS, vol. 10206, pp. 404–408. Springer, Heidelberg (2017). https://doi.org/10.1007/978-3-662-54580-5_32

17. Rajkhowa, P., Lin, F.: VIAP tool and experiments (2018). https://github.com/VerifierIntegerAssignment/VIAP_ARRAY

18. de Moura, L., Bjørner, N.: Z3: an efficient SMT solver. In: Ramakrishnan, C.R., Rehof, J. (eds.) TACAS 2008. LNCS, vol. 4963, pp. 337–340. Springer, Heidelberg (2008). https://doi.org/10.1007/978-3-540-78800-3_24

Lattice-Based Refinement in Bounded Model Checking

Karine Even-Mendoza[1(✉)], Sepideh Asadi[2], Antti E. J. Hyvärinen[2],
Hana Chockler[1], and Natasha Sharygina[2]

[1] King's College London, London, UK
{karine.even_mendoza,hana.chockler}@kcl.ac.uk
[2] Università della Svizzera italiana, Lugano, Switzerland
{antti.hyvaerinen,sepideh.asadi,natasha.sharygina}@usi.ch

Abstract. In this paper we present an algorithm for bounded model-checking with SMT solvers of programs with library functions—either standard or user-defined. Typically, if the program correctness depends on the output of a library function, the model-checking process either treats this function as an uninterpreted function, or is required to use a theory under which the function in question is fully defined. The former approach leads to numerous spurious counter-examples, whereas the later faces the danger of the state-explosion problem, where the resulting formula is too large to be solved by means of modern SMT solvers.

We extend the approach of user-defined summaries and propose to represent the set of existing summaries for a given library function as a *lattice* of subsets of summaries, with the meet and join operations defined as intersection and union, respectively. The refinement process is then triggered by the lattice traversal, where in each node the SMT solver uses the subset of SMT summaries stored in this node to search for a satisfying assignment. The direction of the traversal is determined by the results of the concretisation of an abstract counterexample obtained at the current node. Our experimental results demonstrate that this approach allows to solve a number of instances that were previously unsolvable by the existing bounded model-checkers.

1 Introduction

Bounded model checking (BMC) amounts to verifying correctness of a given program within the given bound on the maximal number of loop iterations and recursion depth [10]. It has been shown very effective in finding errors in programs, as many errors manifest themselves in short executions. As the programs usually induce a very large state space even at bounded depth, there is a need for scalable tools to make the verification process efficient. The satisfiability modulo theories (SMT) [22] reasoning framework is currently one of the most successful approaches to verifying software in a scalable way. The approach is based on modeling the software and its specifications in propositional logic, while

© Springer Nature Switzerland AG 2018
R. Piskac and P. Rümmer (Eds.): VSTTE 2018, LNCS 11294, pp. 50–68, 2018.
https://doi.org/10.1007/978-3-030-03592-1_4

expressing domain-specific knowledge with first-order theories connected to the logic through equalities. Successful verification of software relies on finding a model that is expressive enough to capture software behavior relevant to correctness, while sufficiently high-level to prevent reasoning from becoming prohibitively expensive—the process known as *theory refinement* [28]. Since in general more precise theories are more expensive computationally, finding such a balance is a non-trivial task. Moreover, often there is no need to refine the theory for the whole program. As the modern approach to software development encourages modular development and re-use of components, programs increasingly use library functions, defined elsewhere. If the correctness of the program depends on the implementation of the library (or user-defined) functions, there is a need for a modular approach that allows us to refine only the relevant functions. Yet, currently, the theory refinement is not performed on the granularity level of a single function, hence BMC of even simple programs can result in a state explosion, especially if the library function is called inside a loop.

In this paper, we introduce an approach to efficient SMT-based bounded model checking with lattices of summaries for library functions, either taken from known properties of the functions or user-defined. Roughly speaking, the lattice is a *subset lattice*, where each element represents a subset of Boolean expressions (that we call *facts*) that hold for some subset of inputs to the function; the *join* and *meet* operators are defined as union and intersection, respectively (see Sect. 2 for the formal definition). The counter-example-guided abstraction refinement (CEGAR) [14,16] that we describe in this paper is lattice-based, is triggered by a traversal of the lattice, and the CEGAR loop is repeated until one of the following outcomes occurs: (i) we prove correctness of the bounded program (that is, absence of concrete counterexamples), (ii) we find a concrete counterexample, or (iii) the current theory together with the equalities in the lattice is determined insufficient for reaching a conclusion.

The following motivational example illustrates the use of lattices with LRA (quantifier-free linear real arithmetic) theory.

Example 1. The code example in Fig. 1 describes the *greatest common divisor* (GCD) algorithm. We assume that both inputs are positive integers. The program is safe with respect to the assertion $g \leq x$. However, with the LRA theory, an SMT solver cannot prove correctness of the program, as GCD is not expressible in LRA. The standard approach is to have $gcd(x, y)$ assume any real value; thus, attempting to verify this program with an SMT solver and the LRA theory results in an infinite number of spurious counterexamples.

In the example, we augment the solver with a set of *facts* about the *modulo* function, arranged in a meet semilattice. These facts are taken from an existing set of lemmas and theorems of the Coq proof assistant [3] for $a\%n$:

$$f_1 \equiv z\_mod\_mult \equiv$$

$$\equiv a \ mod \ n = 0 \text{ with the assumption } a == x * n \text{ for some positive integer } x;$$

$$f_2 \equiv z\_mod\_pos\_bound \wedge z\_mod\_unique \equiv$$

```
1 int gcd(int x, int y) {
2    int tmp;
3      while(y != 0) {
4        tmp = x%y;
5          x=y;
6          y=tmp; }
7      return x;
8 }
```

```
1 int main(void) {
2      int x=45;
3      int y=18;
4      int g = gcd(x,y);
5
6      assert(g <= x);
7 }
```

Fig. 1. The GCD program using *modulo* function

$$\equiv (0 \le a \bmod n < n) \wedge (0 \le r < n \implies a = n * q + r \implies r = a \bmod n)$$

for some positive integers r and q, with the assumption $(n > 0) \wedge (a \ne x * n)$;

$$f_3 \equiv z\_mod\_remainder \wedge z\_mod\_unique\_full \equiv$$

$$\equiv (n \ne 0 \implies (0 \le a \bmod n < n \vee n < a \bmod n \le 0)) \wedge ((0 \le r < n \vee n < r \le 0)$$

$$\implies a = b * q + r \implies r = a \bmod n) \text{ with the assumption } \mathbf{true}.$$

The assumptions are different from the original guards in [3], as these are re-written during the build of the meet semilattice. The original subset lattice consists of all subsets of the set $\{f_1, f_2, f_3\}$. It is analysed and reduced as described in Sect. 3 to remove contradicting facts and equivalent elements. In this example, the set $\{f_3\}$ generalises $\{f_1\} \sqcup \{f_2\}$. Figure 2 shows the original subset lattice on the left, and the resulting meet semilattice of facts on the right.

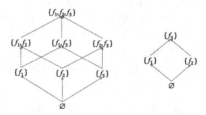

Fig. 2. Original subset lattice of facts and reduced meet semilattice for the *modulo* function in LRA

In the lattice traversal, we start from the bottom element $\emptyset$ and traverse the meet semilattice until we either prove that the program is safe or find a real counterexample (or show that a further theory refinement is needed). In this example, we traverse the lattice until the element $\{f_3\}$, which is sufficient to prove that the program is safe. Specifically, the fact f_1 is used to prove loop termination, and the fact f_2 is used to prove the assert.

Our algorithms are implemented in the bounded model checker HiFROG [5] supporting a subset of the C language and using the SMT solver OpenSMT

[29]. We demonstrate the lattice construction on several examples of lattices for the *modulo* function. The facts for the lattice construction are obtained from the built-in theorems and statements in the Coq proof assistant [3].

Our preliminary experimental results show that lattice-traversal-based CEGAR can avoid the state-explosion problem and successfully solve programs that are not solvable using the standard CEGAR approach. The lattices are constructed using data from an independent source, and we show that even with a relatively small lattice we can verify benchmarks which either are impossible to verify in less precise theories or are too expensive to verify with the precise definition. Our set of benchmarks is a mix of our own crafted benchmarks and benchmarks from the software verification competition SV-COMP 2017 [4].

The full paper, HiFrog tool, and lattices and programs used in our experiments, are available at http://verify.inf.usi.ch/content/lattice-refinement.

Related Work. Lattices are useful in understanding the relationships between abstractions, and have been widely applied in particular in Craig interpolation [20]. For instance [33] presents a semantic and solver-independent framework for systematically exploring interpolant lattices using the notion of interpolation abstraction. A lattice-based system for interpolation in propositional structures is presented in [23], further extended in [6,32] to consider size optimisation techniques in the context of function summaries, and to partial variable assignments in [30]. Similar lattice-based reasoning has also been extended to interpolation in different SMT theories, including the equality logic with uninterpreted functions [8], and linear real arithmetic [7]. The approach presented in this work is different from these in that we do not rely on interpolation, and work in tight integration with model checking.

In addition to interpolation, also computationally inexpensive theories can be used to over-approximate complex problem. This approach has been used in solving equations on non-linear real arithmetic and transcendental functions based on linear real arithmetic and equality logic with uninterpreted functions [12,13,31]; as well as on scaling up bit-vector solving [5,27,28]. Parts of our work can be seen as a generalisation of such approaches as we support inclusion of lemmas from more descriptive logics to increase the expressiveness of computationally lighter logics.

Abstract interpretation [18] uses posets and lattices to model a sound approximation of the semantics of code. Partial completeness and completeness in abstract interpretation [17,19,25,26] refers to the no loss of precision during the approximation of the semantics of code. Giacobazzi et al. [25,26] present the notation of backward and forward completeness in abstract interpretation and show the connection between iteratively computing the backward (forward)-complete shell to the general CEGAR framework [16]; however the completeness of their algorithm depends on the properties of the abstraction while our algorithm has no such requirements.

Interesting work on combining theorem provers with SMT solvers include the SMTCOQ system [24]. Our work uses facts from the Coq library, but differs from SMTCOQ in that we import the facts directly to the SMT solver instead of giving the SMT solver to Coq.

2 Preliminaries

Lattices and Subset Lattices. For a given set X, the family of all subsets of X, partially ordered by the inclusion operator, forms a *subset lattice* $L(X)$. The $\sqcap$ and $\sqcup$ operators are defined on $L(X)$ as *intersection* and *union*, respectively. The top element $\top$ is the whole set X, and the bottom element $\bot$ is the empty set $\emptyset$. The height of the subset lattice $L(X)$ is $|X| + 1$, and all maximal chains have exactly $|X| + 1$ elements. We note that $L(X)$ is a De-Morgan lattice [11], as meet and join distribute over each other. In this paper, we consider only lattices where X is a finite set.

A *meet-semilattice* is a partially ordered set that has a $\sqcap$ for any subset of its elements (but not necessarily $\sqcup$).

Bounded Model Checking. Let P be a loop-free program represented as a transition system, and a *safety property* t, that is, a logical formula over the variables of P. We are interested in determining whether all reachable states of P satisfy t. Given a program P and a safety property t, the task of a model checker is to find a counter-example, that is, an execution of P that does not satisfy t, or to prove the absence of counter-examples on P. In the bounded symbolic model checking approach followed in the paper the model checker encodes P into a logical formula, conjoins it with the negation of t, and checks the satisfiability of the encoding using an SMT solver. If the encoding is unsatisfiable, the program is safe, and we say that t holds in P. Otherwise, the satisfying assignment the SMT solver found is used to build a counter-example.

Function Summaries. In HIFROG, function summaries are Craig interpolants [20]. The summaries are extracted from an unsatisfiable SMT formula of a successful verification, are over-approximations of the actual behavior of the functions, and are available for other HIFROG runs. We use the definition of function summaries [35] and SMT summaries [5] as in our previous works; examples of function summaries are available at http://verify.inf.usi.ch/hifrog/tool-usage.

HIFROG and User-Defined Summaries. The tool HIFROG [5] consists of two main components: an *SMT encoder* and an *interpolating SMT solver OpenSMT2* [29], and uses *function summaries* [34]. It is possible to provide to HIFROG a library of *user-defined summaries*, which are treated in the same way as function summaries by the SMT solver. We note that the whole set of summaries is uploaded to the SMT solver at once, which can lead to time-outs due to the formula being too large. In contrast, our approach by using lattices only uploads the subset of summaries that are necessary for solving the current instance of the library function. In the encoding of the experimental sections and examples we will use the quantifier-free SMT theories for equality logic with uninterpreted functions (EUF), linear real arithmetic (LRA), and fixed-width bit vectors. Note that fixed-width bit vectors are essentially propositional logic.

3   Construction of the Lattice of Facts

In this section we formally define the semilattice of facts for a given library function and describe an algorithm for constructing it; the inner function calls in the algorithm are explained at the end of Sect. 3.2. We note that while the size of the semilattice can be exponential in the number of the facts, the construction of the semilattice is done as a *preprocessing step* once, and the results are used for verification of all programs with this function.

3.1   Definitions

A fact for a library function g with its assumption is added to the set of facts F_g as $(assume(X) \land fact(g))$ expression, where X is a constraint on the domain of the input to g under which $fact(g)$ holds. For example, for the *modulo* function, we can have a fact $assume((a \geq 0) \land (n > 0)) \land a\%n \geq 0$. For every fact $(assume(X) \land fact(g))$, we add a fact $assume(\neg X) \land \textbf{true}$ to F_g. As we discuss later, this is done in order to ensure that the lattice covers the whole domain of input variables for the function g.

Given a set of facts F_g for a library function g, the subset lattice $L(F_g)$ is constructed as defined in Sect. 2. The height of $L(F_g)$ is $|F_g|+1$ by construction, and the width is bounded by the following lemma on the width of a subset lattice.

Lemma 1. *For a set S of size s, let $L(S)$ be the subset lattice of S. Then, the width of $L(S)$ is bounded by $\binom{s}{\lfloor \frac{s}{2} \rfloor}$.*

Proof. The bound follows from Sperner's theorem [9] that states that the width of the inclusion order on a power set is $\binom{s}{\lfloor \frac{s}{2} \rfloor}$. $\square$

Not all elements in $L(F_g)$ represent non-contradictory subsets of facts. For example, a fact $f_1 = assume((a > 0) \land (n > 0)) \land a\%n \geq 0$ and a fact $f_2 = assume(a = 0) \land a\%n = 0$ are incompatible, as the conjunction of their assumptions does not hold for any inputs. In addition, some elements are equivalent to other elements, as the facts are subsumed by other facts. We remove the contradictory elements from the lattice, and for a set of equivalent elements we leave only one element. We denote the resulting set by $L^{min}(F_g) \subseteq L(F_g)$, and the number of facts in an element E, as $\#E$ ($E \in L(F_g)$).

It is easy to see that $L^{min}(F_g)$ is a *meet semilattice*, since if two elements are in $L^{min}(F_g)$, they are non-contradictory, and hence their intersection (or an element equivalent to the intersection) is also in $L^{min}(F_g)$. In general, we do not expect the $\top$ element, representing the whole set F_g, to be in $L^{min}(F_g)$. Rather, there is a set of *maximal* elements of $L^{min}(F_g)$, each of which represents a maximal non-contradictory subset of facts of F_g; we denote the set of *maximal* elements of $L^{min}(F_g)$ as $maxL^{min}(F_g)$.

In the next subsection we describe the algorithm for constructing $L^{min}(F_g)$.

3.2   Algorithm

The construction of a meet semilattice of facts for a library function g given a set of conjunctions of facts and their constraints expressed as assume statements, is described in Algorithm 1. The algorithm consists of five main components:

Construct a subset lattice from the input. For every statement and its assumption, we construct a fact f_g (line 1); given the set F_g of all facts, we construct a subset lattice $L(F_g)$ as defined in Sect. 3.1 (line 2).

Consistency check. For every element in the subset lattice we analyse the subset of facts corresponding to this element (lines 3–10); if the subset contains no contradictions (lines 6–7), we add the node to the meet semilattice (line 8).

Equivalence check. Remove equivalent elements from the meet semilattice (lines 11–20).

Cleanup. After the execution of the checks and removal of elements above, it is possible that in the resulting structure, an element has a single predecessor (lines 21–25). In this case, we unify the element with its predecessor (line 23). This process is repeated iteratively until all elements have more than one predecessor, except for the direct successors of the $\perp$ element.

Overlapping Assumes. Strengthen an assumption to avoid overlapping between elements (line 26).

The result of the algorithm is the meet semilattice $L^{min}(F_g)$, as defined in Sect. 3.1. Clearly, the exact $L^{min}(F_g)$ depends on the input set of statements, as well as on the theory. We note, however, that $L^{min}(F_g)$ can be used by the SMT solver with a different theory than the one in which it was constructed, as long as an encoding of the facts in SMT-LIB2 format with this logic exists. For example, the reduced meet semilattice in Fig. 2 can be used in EUF, even when its construction is done via propositional logic, since the encoding of f_1, f_2, and f_3 exists in EUF. Algorithm 1 invokes the following procedures:

- $\#E$: the number of facts in an element E (defined in Sect. 3.1);
- `buildSubsetLattice`: construct a *subset lattice* $L(F_g)$ given a finite set F_g of facts;
- `minimise`: given an element $E \in L(F_g)$, remove any fact $f_g \in E$ such as that $\exists E' \subset E.(\bigwedge_{f'_g \in E' - \{f_g\}} f'_g) \implies f_g$, starting from the smallest to the largest E' (i.e., remove a fact f_g if other facts in E imply f_g; that way, we minimise the size of the E);
- `checkSAT`(F): determine the satisfiablity of a formula F;
- `swap`(E_1, E_2): swap the current subset of facts in E_1 with E_2, while (roughly speaking) each element keeps its own edges;
- `immediateLower`(E): get all immediate predecessors of the element E;
- `immediateUpper`(E): get all immediate successors of the element E;

Algorithm 1. Construction of $L^{min}(F_g)$

Input : $facts = \{(X_1, Y_1), \ldots, (X_n, Y_n)\}$: set of pairs of assumptions and facts.

Output: $L^{min}(F_g)$

1 $F_g \leftarrow \bigcup_{(X,Y) \in facts} \{assume(X) \wedge Y, assume(\neg X) \wedge \mathbf{true}\}$

2 $L(F_g) \leftarrow \mathtt{buildSubsetLattice}(F_g)$

3 **foreach** *element* $E \in L(F_g)$ **do**

4 $\quad$ $\mathtt{minimise}(E)$ //remove facts that are generalised by other facts in E

5 $\quad$ $Query \leftarrow \bigwedge_{f_g \in E} f_g$

6 $\quad$ $\langle result, \_ \rangle \leftarrow \mathtt{checkSAT}(Query)$

7 $\quad$ **if** *result is* **SAT then**

8 $\quad\quad$ | Add E to $L^{min}(F_g)$

9 $\quad$ **end**

10 **end**

11 **foreach** *two elements* $E_{lower}, E_{upper} \in L^{min}(F_g)$ *such that* E_{lower} *is lower than* E_{upper} **do**

12 $\quad$ $Query \leftarrow \neg(\bigwedge_{f_g \in E_{lower}} f_g \iff \bigwedge_{f_g \in E_{upper}} f_g)$

13 $\quad$ $\langle result, \_ \rangle \leftarrow \mathtt{checkSAT}(Query)$

14 $\quad$ **if** *result is* **UNSAT then**

15 $\quad\quad$ **if** $\#E_{lower} < \#E_{upper}$ **then**

16 $\quad\quad\quad$ | $\mathtt{swap}(E_{upper}, E_{lower})$

17 $\quad\quad$ **end**

18 $\quad\quad$ Remove E_{lower} from $L^{min}(F_g)$

19 $\quad$ **end**

20 **end**

21 **foreach** *element* $E \in L^{min}(F_g)$ **do**

22 $\quad$ **if** $(\#immediateUpper(E)$ is $1) \wedge (\#immediateLower(immediateUpper(E))$ is $1)$ **then**

23 $\quad\quad$ | Remove E from $L^{min}(F_g)$

24 $\quad$ **end**

25 **end**

26 $L^{min}(F_g) \leftarrow \mathtt{fixOverlapsAssume}(L^{min}(F_g))$

27 **return** $L^{min}(F_g)$

- $\mathtt{fixOverlapsAssume}(L^{min}(F_g))$: for each meet element $E \in L^{min}(F_g)$, change the assumptions of E's immediate successors to fix any overlapping assumptions. $assume(X)$ of an immediate successor with a trivial fact is updated by intersecting with negations of all (original) assumes of the rest of the immediate successors of E, when removing any successor with (altered) $assume(X)$ equals to $false$. $assume(X)$ of an immediate successor with facts in F_g is strengthen by intersecting with the negation of an $assume(X)$ of overlapping elements with facts in F_g.

In Fig. 2, for example, the $assume(X)$ statement of f_2 originally was $(n > 0)$ thus the $assumes$ of f_1 and f_2 overlap over many values, e.g., when $a = n$; in the example in Fig. 2 we fix the $assume$ of f_2 to avoid such overlapping.

4   Lattice-Based Bounded Model Checking

In this section we describe the Lattice-Based Counterexample-Guided Abstraction Refinement algorithm for verifying programs with respect to a safety property. We present a formal notation for the data structure we use in the refinement algorithm and show that the refinement algorithm can prove safety of a program with respect to a given bound.

4.1   Definitions

For a program P and a safety property t such as that $P \cup \{t\}$ has functions which are missing the full definition in the current level of abstraction, we denote the set of all such functions in $P \cup \{t\}$ as G, thus $G = \{g_1, \ldots, g_m\}$. Each function $g \in G$ has a meet semilattice $L^{min}(F_g)$. The set of all meet semilattices of functions in G is $\mathcal{L}_G^{min} = \{L^{min}(F_{g_1}), \ldots, L^{min}(F_{g_m})\}$.

For each statement $s \in P \cup \{t\}$ with $g \in G$ function, we create an instance of $L^{min}(F_g)$. The set $\mathcal{L}_{G,K}^{min}$ is a set of all instances of all meet semilattices in $\mathcal{L}_G^{min}$. A meet semilattice instance $L_i^{min}(F_g) \in \mathcal{L}_{G,K}^{min}$ is the i-th instance of function g in $P \cup \{t\}$ where $1 \leq i \leq k_g$, and $k_g \in K$ is the number of instance of g in $P \cup \{t\}$. For simplicity of the description of the refinement, we assume each s has at most one function $g \in G$; if there is more than one g, one can write an equivalent code that guarantees this property. Note that Algorithms 3, 4 and 2 change instances of meet semilattices and not the meet semilattice itself; since each statement with a function g requires a different set of facts and thus must traverse the meet semilattice independently with its instance.

During Algorithm 3, we mark elements $E \in L_i^{min}(F_g)$ as **Safe** and add any such E to the cut of $L_i^{min}(F_g)$. A cut of $L_i^{min}(F_g)$ is a set of all elements with an in-edge in the cut-set of the graph representation of $L_i^{min}(F_g)$. For example, possible cuts in the reduced meet semilattice in Fig. 2 can be: $\{\{f_1\}, \{f_2\}\}$ or $\{\{f_3\}\}$.

Definition 1. Let $X_{L_i^{min}(F_g)} \subset L_i^{min}(F_g)$ be a subset of elements. We say $X_{L_i^{min}(F_g)}$ is a cut of $L_i^{min}(F_g)$ if all chains from $\emptyset$ to element(s) $E_{max} \in max L_i^{min}(F_g)$ contain at least one element in $X_{L_i^{min}(F_g)}$.

where E_{max} is a *maximal* element; maximal elements of a meet semilattice and a set of maximal elements are described in Sect. 3.1.

We use the elements in the cut of $L_i^{min}(F_g)$ in the proof of Theorem 1; we show Algorithm 2 returns **Safe** when a program with a given bound and a property is **Safe**, because the union of all assumptions of elements in $X_{L_i^{min}(F_g)}$ captures the whole domain of the inputs of g,

Lemma 2. *Given a cut $X_{L_i^{min}(F_g)}$ of function $g : \mathbb{D}_{in} \to \mathbb{D}_{out}$ the union of all assumptions (assume statements) of all facts in the cut is $\mathbb{D}_{in}$.*

Proof. We prove by induction that for a subset lattice $L(F_g)$: for any element $E \in L(F_g)$ its *assume* refers to the same domain as the union of *assumes* of all successors of E element.

(base) the union of *assume*s of all successors of $\emptyset$ element is $\mathbb{D}_{in}$: from line 1 in Algorithm 1 we know that the union of *assume*s of all successors of $\emptyset$ element is $\mathbb{D}_{in}$ by construction of F_g, and $\emptyset$ element has no assumption and thus captures all the input domain.

(step) for each element $E \in L(F_g)$, the union of *assume*s of all successors of E is equivalent to the *assume* of E. Since $L(F_g)$ is a subset lattice, then all immediate upper elements of an element $E \in L(F_g)$ contain exactly one additional fact from F_g. From line 1 in Algorithm 1, we know that any fact $(assume(X) \wedge Y)$ has the opposite fact $(\neg assume(X) \wedge \mathbf{true})$, thus union of any such pair of facts in F_g leaves the original *assume* of E the same; since each of the successor of E must contain either an original fact or its complementary fact, we get that the *assume* of the union of the successors of E stays the same as required.

Since all chains start from $\emptyset$ which refers to the whole domain $\mathbb{D}_{in}$, and since the *assume* of an element is a union of *assume*s of its immediate successors as proved by induction above, then if there is a cut where the union of all *assume*s of all facts in the cut is not $\mathbb{D}_{in}$ then there is a chain from $\emptyset$ to maximal element without an element in the cut, which contradict the definition of a cut. When extract $L^{min}(F_g)$, we only fix overlapping *assume*s thus the union of *assume*s stays the same in a cut and therefore refers to the whole domain as before. $\square$

Note that, the rest of the changes of elements in $L^{min}(F_g)$ do not affect the union of *assume*s; consistency check removes elements with no contribution to the input domain (as these equivalent to false), equivalence check affects only the number of possible cuts, and cleanup removes elements with the same *assume* with a weaker fact in compare to their single immediate successor.

4.2   Algorithm

Algorithm 2 takes the symbolically encoded program P with a safety property t and constructs an over-approximating formula $\hat{\varphi}$ of the problem in a given initial logic (line 1). Algorithm 2 refines $\hat{\varphi}$ by adding and removing facts from meet semilattices $L^{min}(F_g) \in \mathcal{L}_G^{min}$ according to the traversal on an instance of the meet semilattice per refined expression (main loop, lines 3–21); the algorithm terminates once it has proved the current $\hat{\varphi}$ is **Safe** (lines 8–10), after extracting a real counterexample (lines 14–16), or after using all facts in meet semilattices of $\mathcal{L}_G^{min}$ while still receiving spurious counterexamples (lines 17–19 or 23). The refinement in Algorithm 2 is finite and returns **Unsafe** if t does not hold in P. Algorithm 2 returns **Safe** if and only if the facts in $\mathcal{L}_G^{min}$ can refine functions in $\hat{\varphi}$ and t holds in P.

A counterexample in the last known precision is returned when t does not hold in P and the facts in $\mathcal{L}_G^{min}$ can refine the over-approximate functions in $\hat{\varphi}$. Algorithm 2 checks if CE is a spurious counterexample similarly to the counterexample check in [28] and returns either true with a real counterexample when all queries are **SAT**, or false otherwise. The solver produces an interpretation for the variables or a partial interpretation of uninterpreted functions and uninterpreted predicates in the case of EUF, for statements $s \in P \cup \{t\}$ in the current precision. The counterexample validation determines whether the conjunction of s and CE with an interpretation or partial interpretation is **UNSAT** in a more precise theory; an **UNSAT** result in any of the queries indicates that the counterexample is indeed spurious. A more precise theory can be the theory of bit-vectors as in [28] or the theory the meet semilattice was built with; if no available description of the function g with the current query exist in any preciser theory, we assume CE is spurious.

The data structures used in Algorithm 2 are described in Sect. 4.1. Note that Algorithm 2 allocates a new instance of a meet semilattice $L_i^{min}(F_g) \in \mathcal{L}_{G,K}^{min}$ for each i-th instance of function g in $P \cup \{t\}$, thus the main loop in lines 3–21 refers only to these instances of meet semilattices, where i, k_g, g, K, G are defined in Sect. 4.1.

Algorithm 2. Lattice-Based Counterexample-Guided Refinement

Input : $P = \{s_1 := (x_1 = t_1), \ldots, s_n := (x_n = t_n)\}$: a program, t: safety property, $\mathcal{L}_G^{min} = \{L^{min}(F_{g_1}), \ldots, L^{min}(F_{g_m})\}$: a set of meet semilattices.

Output: $\langle \mathbf{Safe}, \bot \rangle$ or $\langle \mathbf{Unsafe}, CE \rangle$ or $\langle \mathbf{Unsafe}, \bot \rangle$

1 $\hat{\varphi} \leftarrow \bigwedge_{s \in P \cup \{t\}} \texttt{convert}(s)$

2 $\mathcal{L}_{G,K}^{min} \leftarrow \bigcup_{s \in P \cup \{t\}, g \in G, i \in \{1, \ldots, k_g(\in K)\}} (L_i^{min}(F_g) \leftarrow \texttt{initialiseLI}(s, L^{min}(F_g)))$

3 **while** $\exists L_i^{min}(F_g) \in \mathcal{L}_{G,K}^{min} : element(L_i^{min}(F_g))$ *has upper element* **do**

4 $\quad$ $\chi \leftarrow \bigwedge_{L_i^{min}(F_g)' \in \mathcal{L}_{G,K}^{min}} \texttt{currentFacts}(L_i^{min}(F_g)')$

5 $\quad$ $Query \leftarrow \hat{\varphi} \wedge \chi$

6 $\quad$ $\langle result, CE \rangle \leftarrow \texttt{checkSAT}(Query)$

7 $\quad$ **if** *result is* **UNSAT then**

8 $\quad\quad$ **if** $(\forall L_i^{min}(F_g)'' \in \mathcal{L}_{G,K}^{min} : isSafe(L_i^{min}(F_g)'')) \vee (\chi$ *is* **true**$)$ **then**

9 $\quad\quad\quad$ **return** $\langle \mathbf{Safe}, \bot \rangle$ //Safe - Quit

10 $\quad\quad$ **end**

11 $\quad\quad$ $\mathcal{L}_{G,K}^{min} \leftarrow \texttt{updateCutAndWalk}(\mathcal{L}_{G,K}^{min})$ //element is safe, continue traversal

12 $\quad$ **end**

13 $\quad$ **else**

14 $\quad\quad$ **if** $checkRealCE(Query, CE)$ **then**

15 $\quad\quad\quad$ **return** $\langle \mathbf{Unsafe}, CE \rangle$ //Real Counterexample - Quit

16 $\quad\quad$ **end**

17 $\quad\quad$ **if** $!refine(Query, CE, P, t, \mathcal{L}_{G,K}^{min})$ **then**

18 $\quad\quad\quad$ **return** $\langle \mathbf{Unsafe}, \bot \rangle$ //Cannot Refine - Quit

19 $\quad\quad$ **end**

20 $\quad$ **end**

21 **end**

22 // End Of Main Loop

23 **return** $\langle \mathbf{Unsafe}, \bot \rangle$ //Cannot refine - Quit

---

Sub-Algorithm 3 is a high-level description of `updateCutAndWalk` sub-procedure. For the current instance of a meet semilattice $L_i^{min}(F_g)$ where E is the current element, `updateCutAndWalk` marks E as safe, adds E to the cut of $L_i^{min}(F_g)$, and traverses on an instance of a meet semilattice via `walkRight` either on $L_i^{min}(F_g)$ (if not yet safe) or (else) on any instance with no cut yet. Note that the sub-procedure `walkRight` changes the same instance of a meet semilattice until Algorithm 2 is in either lines 9, 15, 18, or 22, or Algorithm 3 is in lines 3–5.

Algorithm 3. `updateCutAndWalk` - Mark element as safe and traverse the semilattice

---

Input : $\mathcal{L}_{G,K}^{min}$: a set of meet semilattice instances.
Output: $\mathcal{L}_{G,K}^{min}$ after traversal

1   $L_i^{min}(F_g) \leftarrow$ last changed meet semilattice instance in $\mathcal{L}_{G,K}^{min}$

2   Mark current element in $L_i^{min}(F_g)$ as **Safe**

3   **if** $isSafe(L_i^{min}(F_g))$ **then**

4     $\forall L_i^{min}(F_g)' \in \mathcal{L}_{G,K}^{min} . \neg isSafe(L_i^{min}(F_g))' \implies \text{reset}(L_i^{min}(F_g)')$

5   Set $L_i^{min}(F_g)$ to be an item from the set
     $\{L_i^{min}(F_g)'' | L_i^{min}(F_g)''' \in \mathcal{L}_{G,K}^{min} \land \neg isSafe(L_i^{min}(F_g))'''\}$

6   **end**

7   `walkRight`$(L_i^{min}(F_g))$

8   **return** $\mathcal{L}_{G,K}^{min}$ // Returns back to the main loop in Alg. 2 line 11

A high-level description of the sub-procedure `refine` is given in Algorithm 4, and describes the refinement of a single CE via instances of a meet semilattice. The main loop (lines 1–13) searches $L_i^{min}(F_g)$ which refines CE, the inner loop (lines 3–9) adds facts from elements in $L_i^{min}(F_g)$ until CE is refined or a maximal element is reached; in the latter case we drop the changes in $L_i^{min}(F_g)$ (lines 10–12) and try a different $L_{i'}^{min}(F_{g'})$. The refinement successes if the query (line 5) detects CE is a spurious counterexample without using a more precise theory (lines 4–8) but using new added facts (line 10, previous loop). The refinement fails if for all $L_i^{min}(F_g) \in \mathcal{L}_{G,K}^{min}$, no element could refine the current CE (lines 17–19). The refinement order is determined by the way Algorithm 4 goes over statements $s \in P \cup \{t\}$ (line 1), which is done according to sets of basic heuristics defined in [28].

We describe the rest of the function calls in general; let s be a statement $s \in P \cup \{t\}$, F be a logical formula, CE a counterexample, x a meet semilattice of a statement s with a function g, and x' an instance of a meet semilattice x. Algorithms 2, 3, and 4 invoke the following procedures:

- `convert`(s): create a symbolic formula in the initial logic;
- `checkSAT`(F): determine the satisfiablity of a formula F;
- `checkRealCE`(F, CE): is true if CE is a valid counterexample of formula F;
- `element`(x'): retrieve the current element in x' or $\top$ for x' with a full cut;

Algorithm 4. refine with a Single Counterexample

Input : *Query* and *CE* formulas, and $P =$
$\{s_1 := (x_1 = t_1), \ldots, s_n := (x_n = t_n)\}$: a program, t: safety property,
$\mathcal{L}_{G,K}^{min}$: a set of meet semilattice instances.
Output: *true* or *false*

```
1  for s ∈ P ∪ {t} with L_i^min(F_g) ∈ L_{G,K}^min do
2  │   n ← element(L_i^min(F_g)) //To reset later to original location
3  │   while element(L_i^min(F_g)) has upper element do
4  │   │   χ' ← currentFacts(L_i^min(F_g))
5  │   │   ⟨result, _⟩ ← checkSAT(Query ∧ CE ∧ χ')
6  │   │   if result is UNSAT then
7  │   │   │   break // Refined the current CE
8  │   │   end
9  │   │   if result is SAT then
10 │   │   │   walkUpper(L_i^min(F_g))
11 │   │   end
12 │   end
13 │   if element(L_i^min(F_g)) ∈ maxL_i^min(F_g) ∧ result is SAT then
14 │   │   reset(L_i^min(F_g), n)
15 │   end
16 end
17 if all L_i^min(F_g) ∈ L_{G,K}^min reset location in line 11 then
18 │   return false // Returns and terminates the main loop in Alg. 2 lines 17-18
19 end
20 return true // Returns back to the main loop in Alg. 2 line 17
```

- currentFacts(x'): retrieves the formula of facts in x' which is either a union of all elements in the cut, an intersection of the facts in the current element, or *true* if the current element is the $\emptyset$;
- walkRight(x'): simulate a traversal of x' as described below;
- walkUpper(x'): simulate a traversal of x' from the current element to elements with stronger subset of facts;
- initialiseLI(s, x): create an instance of a meet semilattice x' for s and operation(s), if a meet semilattice exists in L_G^{min} for operation(s);
- operation(s): retrieve the operation or function call name in s;
- isSafe(x'): indicate if x' refines g in s with **Safe** result as described above, an **Unsafe** result of the refinement is taken care in the loop itself and does not need a sub-procedure;
- reset(x'): set the current element of simulation of the lattice traversal to be $\bot$ and initialise the inner state of the search on the meet semilattice instance.

Note that, the function updateCutAndWalk is Algorithm 3, and the function refine is Algorithm 4, both are been called in the main loop of Algorithm 2, lines 11 and 17 respectively.

Traversal of a Meet Semilattice. For function g such as that g is over-approximated in the initial theory and g has a meet semilattice $L^{min}(F_g) \in \mathcal{L}_G^{min}$, the algorithm creates an instance of a meet semilattice $L_i^{min}(F_g)$ to simulate the traversal of the meet semilattice in a DFS style per instance of g. Several instances of a meet semilattice of g are required for example when g is part of a loop.

A traversal on an instance of a meet semilattice $L_i^{min}(F_g)$ starts with $\emptyset$ element, adding no facts to the query $\hat{\varphi}$. During execution, if $\hat{\varphi}$ is **SAT** in the current precision, then the next element on the traversal is one of the immediate successors of the current element, as long as no real counterexample is obtained, in which case the algorithm terminates and returns **Unsafe** with the counterexample. After reaching an element in $maxL_i^{min}(F_g)$ during the traversal indicates that the facts in the elements of $L_i^{min}(F_g)$ cannot refine the $i-th$ instance of g with respect to the spurious counterexample, which can also terminate the refinement in Algorithm 2 and returns **Unsafe**.

Once the query $\hat{\varphi}$ with facts of $E \in L_i^{min}(F_g)$ is **UNSAT**, the traversal skips the successors of E, marks E as safe, adds E to $X_{L_i^{min}(F_g)}$, and continues with one of the siblings of E according to the DFS order from left to right; if there are no remaining siblings of E, the traversal of $L_i^{min}(F_g)$ terminates, and outputs the cut $X_{L_i^{min}(F_g)}$; there is no use of a current element of the meet semilattice $L_i^{min}(F_g)$ once the traversal terminates and only the facts in its cut are used.

For a program with several instances of meet semilattices, once Algorithm 2 finds a cut $X_{L_i^{min}(F_g)}$, the cut is added to χ' as a union of all elements in the cut with their facts. This allows using the facts in the cut for searching cuts on the rest of the instances of meet semilattices.

The following theorem shows that if Algorithm 2 outputs a positive result (that is, the program is safe with respect to the given bound), then there are no counterexamples up to the given depth in the program.

Theorem 1. *Given a program P, a safety property t, a set of functions $(g \in)$ G, and a set of instances of meet semilattices $\mathcal{L}_{G,K}^{min}$ for the functions in G, if there exists a cut $X_{L_i^{min}(F_g)}$ in the meet semilattice of facts $L_i^{min}(F_g)$ for each instance $i \in k_g$ of the function g such that the result of solving the program with each element in $X_{L_i^{min}(F_g)}$ is **UNSAT**, then the program is safe with respect to the given bound and the property.*

Proof (Sketch). Algorithm 2 returns **Safe** in line 8 when all $L_i^{min}(F_g)$ are safe with respect to their cuts $X_{L_i^{min}(F_g)}$. The last query (Algorithm 2, line 6) just before satisfying the condition in line 8 is a conjunction of union of elements of cuts $X_{L_i^{min}(F_g)}$ of each of the instances of the meet semilattice. By Lemma 2, the union of *assume* statements of elements in the cut is the input domain $\mathbb{D}_{in}$ of g, for all instances $i \in k_g$ of all $g \in G$. Therefore, if no satisfying assignment has been found in the cut, there is no satisfying assignment in $\mathbb{D}_{in}$ of g, for all instances of g in the unwound program P. Therefore, the result is **UNSAT**, and the program is safe with respect to the given bound.   □

The cut we use, is a disjunction (i.e., union of elements in a cut) of a conjunction of facts (i.e., intersection of all facts in an element in a cut); when using more than a single cut in *Query*, the expression is a conjunction of the expression of a cut above. The full proof of Theorem 1 is shown in the full version of the paper http://verify.inf.usi.ch/content/lattice-refinement using a formal definition of the expression of a cut.

5   Implementation and Evaluation

This section describes the prototype implementation and the evaluation of the lattice-based counterexample-guided refinement framework.

The algorithm is implemented on the SMT-based function summarisation bounded model checker HIFROG[5] and uses the SMT solver OPENSMT[29]. The experiments run on a Ubuntu 16.04 Linux system with two Intel Xeon E5620 CPUs clocked at 2.40 GHz. The timeout for all experiments is at 500 s and the memory limit is 3 GB.

The scripts for the build of a meet semilattice, the meet semilattice for modulo operation, the complete experimental results, and the source code, are available at [1,2]. The script contains greedy optimisations of Algorithm 1 to avoid, if possible, exponential number of SAT-solver calls; lines 3–10: starting the loop from the smallest subsets of facts, once a small subset of facts of an element is contradictory, all its upper elements are pruned; lines 11–19: considers only pairs of (roughly speaking) connected elements.

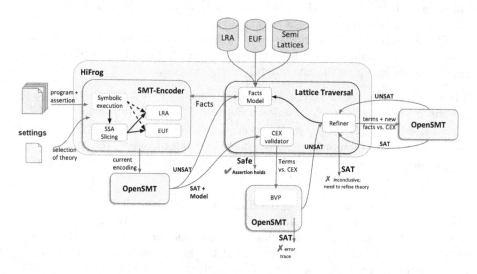

Fig. 3. The SMT-based model checking framework implementing a lattice-based counterexample-guided refinement approach used in the experiments

The overview of interaction between HIFROG, the refiner in HIFROG and the SMT solver OPENSMT is shown in Fig. 3. In the current prototype we add facts of the meet semilattice as SMT summaries, while checking before using a summary that its *assume* formula holds for better performance. The definition of the cut stays the same and contains only facts from F_g. The spurious counterexample check is done via the CEX validator using bit-vector logic (see [28]); any function that has no precise encoding is then added as a candidate to refine as HiFrog cannot validate a counterexample in the context of this function.

The lattice traversal component contains 3 sub-components: (1) *facts model* which contains the pure model (the meet semilattice) we load to HiFrog and instances of a meet semilattice per expression we refine, (2) the *CEX valida- tor* that validates the counterexample and reports real counterexamples in case found, and (3) the *refiner* which does the refinement, adds facts to and removes facts from the encoding, interacts with the CEX validator and terminates the refinement for each of the three possible cases. The OpenSMT instances use either EUF or LRA for modeling and bit-vectors for CEX validation.

Extraction of Facts. The preprocessing step of our framework is extracting a set of facts F_g for a function g. The facts can be imported from another program or a library. In the experimental results, we import facts from the Coq proof assistant [3], where $g := mod$ is modulo function. We use a subset of lemmas, theorems and definitions of modulo from [3] as is, as the data is simple to use, well known, and reliable. We translate the facts into the SMT-LIB2 format manually (see [1] for the results of translation).

Validation. The validation test is as follow; given a function g, a set of facts F_g, a statement s such that a fact $f_s \in F_g$ is sufficient to verify s, assure that $s \wedge f_s$ is **UNSAT** via a model checker. A complementary validation test is the sanity check which verifies that the facts are not contradictory. We describe in details the validation tests for modulo operator in the full version of the paper http:// verify.inf.usi.ch/content/lattice-refinement; thus the function g is *mod* and the set of facts is $F_g := F_{mod}$.

Experimental Results. We use a meet semilattice for refinement of modulo func- tion with a set of 20 facts which are a small arbitrary subset of modulo operation properties; the width and height of the modulo meet semilattice are 21 and 18 respectively; the raw data is taken from the Coq proof assistant [3] (see [1] for a meet semilattice sketch). The **UNSAT** proof of queries during the refinement are done using either OpenSMT [29] or Z3 [21], using a none-incremental mode of the solvers, due to known problems in the OpenSMT implementation; we expect better experimental results in terms of time and memory consumption once improving the implementation.

Our benchmarks consist of 74 C programs using the modulo operator at least few times; in 19 benchmarks the modulo operator is in a loop. The benchmarks set is a mix of 19 SV-COMP 2017 benchmarks [4] (8 **Unsafe** and 11 **Safe** bench- marks), our own 24 benchmarks including some hard arithmetic operations with modulo and multiplication, and 31 crafted benchmarks with modulo operator

Table 1. Verification results of lattice refinement against CBMC [15], theory refinement [28], and EUF and LRA without lattice refinement. #-number of instances, FP SAT-false positive SAT result, TO-time out of 500 s, MO-Out of Memory of 3GB

Approach	# instances solved		# instances unsolved	
	SAT	UNSAT	FP SAT	TO,MO
LRA Lattice Ref.	**23**	32	9	**10,0**
EUF Lattice Ref.	**23**	8	33	**10,0**
Theory Ref.	22	18	20	11,3
CBMC 5.7	**23**	**34**	1	6,10
PURE LRA	**23**	7	34	**10,0**
PURE EUF	**23**	6	35	**10,0**

(20 **Unsafe** and 35 **Safe** benchmarks). Table 1 provides the summary of the experimental results.

We compared our implementation of lattice-based refinement approach in HiFrog against: pure LRA encoding and pure EUF encoding in HiFrog, theory-refinement mode of HiFrog, and CBMC version 5.7 (the winner of the software model checking competition falsification track in 2017). CBMC version 5.7 `--refine` option performs as the standard CBMC version, and thus is not included in Table 1.

Even with a prototype implementation of meet semilattices of facts, HiFrog fares quite well in comparison to established tools. In particular, it has better resource consumption than CBMC and theory-refinement mode of HiFrog, while also having much better results proving safety of programs than HiFrog without lattices; and moreover HiFrog with meet semilattices of facts has the same performance as HiFrog with a lightweight theory only, and yet is able to prove safety of more benchmarks than before. The lattice base refinement approach can still fail to prove safety when other operations are abstracted from the SMT encoding (e.g., SHL, SHR, pointer arithmetic) or, in LRA when the code contains non-linear expressions. Another reason is related to the modeling itself: a small sample of 20 facts can be insufficient to prove safety, as well the combination of several meet semilattices might require smarter heuristics. None of the approaches in the comparison reports **Unsafe** benchmarks as **Safe**. The full table of results and the set of benchmarks are available at [1].

Acknowledgments. We thank Grigory Fedyukovich for helpful discussions.

References

1. http://verify.inf.usi.ch/content/lattice-refinement
2. https://scm.ti-edu.ch/projects/hifrog/
3. The coq proof assistant. https://coq.inria.fr/

4. Competition on software verification (SV-COMP) (2017). https://sv-comp.sosy-lab.org/2017/

5. Alt, L., et al.: HiFrog: SMT-based function summarization for software verification. In: Legay, A., Margaria, T. (eds.) TACAS 2017. LNCS, vol. 10206, pp. 207–213. Springer, Heidelberg (2017). https://doi.org/10.1007/978-3-662-54580-5_12

6. Alt, L., Fedyukovich, G., Hyvärinen, A.E.J., Sharygina, N.: A proof-sensitive approach for small propositional interpolants. In: Gurfinkel, A., Seshia, S.A. (eds.) VSTTE 2015. LNCS, vol. 9593, pp. 1–18. Springer, Cham (2016). https://doi.org/10.1007/978-3-319-29613-5_1

7. Alt, L., Hyvärinen, A.E.J., Sharygina, N.: LRA interpolants from no man's land. Hardware and Software: Verification and Testing. LNCS, vol. 10629, pp. 195–210. Springer, Cham (2017). https://doi.org/10.1007/978-3-319-70389-3_13

8. Alt, L., Hyvärinen, A.E.J., Asadi, S., Sharygina, N.: Duality-based interpolation for quantifier-free equalities and uninterpreted functions. In: Stewart, D., Weissenbacher, G. (eds.) Proceedings of FMCAD 2017, pp. 39–46. IEEE (2017)

9. Anderson, I.: Combinatorics of Finite Sets. Clarendon Press, Oxford (1987)

10. Biere, A., Cimatti, A., Clarke, E., Zhu, Y.: Symbolic model checking without BDDs. In: Cleaveland, W.R. (ed.) TACAS 1999. LNCS, vol. 1579, pp. 193–207. Springer, Heidelberg (1999). https://doi.org/10.1007/3-540-49059-0_14

11. Birkhoff, G.: Lattice Theory, 3rd edn. AMS, Providence (1967)

12. Cimatti, A., Griggio, A., Irfan, A., Roveri, M., Sebastiani, R.: Invariant checking of NRA transition systems via incremental reduction to LRA with EUF. In: Legay, A., Margaria, T. (eds.) TACAS 2017. LNCS, vol. 10205, pp. 58–75. Springer, Heidelberg (2017). https://doi.org/10.1007/978-3-662-54577-5_4

13. Cimatti, A., Griggio, A., Irfan, A., Roveri, M., Sebastiani, R.: Satisfiability modulo transcendental functions via incremental linearization. In: de Moura, L. (ed.) CADE 2017. LNCS (LNAI), vol. 10395, pp. 95–113. Springer, Cham (2017). https://doi.org/10.1007/978-3-319-63046-5_7

14. Clarke, E., Grumberg, O., Jha, S., Lu, Y., Veith, H.: Counterexample-guided abstraction refinement. In: Emerson, E.A., Sistla, A.P. (eds.) CAV 2000. LNCS, vol. 1855, pp. 154–169. Springer, Heidelberg (2000). https://doi.org/10.1007/10722167_15

15. Clarke, E., Kroening, D., Lerda, F.: A tool for checking ANSI-C programs. In: Jensen, K., Podelski, A. (eds.) TACAS 2004. LNCS, vol. 2988, pp. 168–176. Springer, Heidelberg (2004). https://doi.org/10.1007/978-3-540-24730-2_15

16. Clarke, E.M., Grumberg, O., Jha, S., Lu, Y., Veith, H.: Counterexample-guided abstraction refinement for symbolic model checking. J. ACM **50**(5), 752–794 (2003)

17. Cousot, P.: Partial completeness of abstract fixpoint checking. In: Choueiry, B.Y., Walsh, T. (eds.) SARA 2000. LNCS (LNAI), vol. 1864, pp. 1–25. Springer, Heidelberg (2000). https://doi.org/10.1007/3-540-44914-0_1

18. Cousot, P., Cousot, R.: Abstract interpretation: a unified lattice model for static analysis of programs by construction or approximation of fixpoints. In: Proceedings of the 4th ACM SIGACT-SIGPLAN Symposium on Principles of Programming Languages, POPL 1977, pp. 238–252. ACM, New York (1977)

19. Cousot, P., Cousot, R.: Systematic design of program analysis frameworks. In: Proceedings of the 6th ACM SIGACT-SIGPLAN Symposium on Principles of Programming Languages, POPL 1979, pp. 269–282. ACM, New York (1979)

20. Craig, W.: Three uses of the Herbrand-Gentzen theorem in relating model theory and proof theory. J. Symbolic Logic **22**, 269–285 (1957)

21. de Moura, L., Bjørner, N.: Z3: an efficient SMT solver. In: Ramakrishnan, C.R., Rehof, J. (eds.) TACAS 2008. LNCS, vol. 4963, pp. 337–340. Springer, Heidelberg (2008). https://doi.org/10.1007/978-3-540-78800-3_24

22. Detlefs, D., Nelson, G., Saxe, J.B.: Simplify: a theorem prover for program checking. J. ACM **52**(3), 365–473 (2005)

23. D'Silva, V., Kroening, D., Purandare, M., Weissenbacher, G.: Interpolant strength. In: Barthe, G., Hermenegildo, M. (eds.) VMCAI 2010. LNCS, vol. 5944, pp. 129–145. Springer, Heidelberg (2010). https://doi.org/10.1007/978-3-642-11319-2_12

24. Ekici, B., Mebsout, A., Tinelli, C., Keller, C., Katz, G., Reynolds, A., Barrett, C.: SMTCoq: a plug-in for integrating SMT solvers into Coq. In: Majumdar, R., Kunčak, V. (eds.) CAV 2017. LNCS, vol. 10427, pp. 126–133. Springer, Cham (2017). https://doi.org/10.1007/978-3-319-63390-9_7

25. Giacobazzi, R., Quintarelli, E.: Incompleteness, counterexamples, and refinements in abstract model-checking. In: Cousot, P. (ed.) SAS 2001. LNCS, vol. 2126, pp. 356–373. Springer, Heidelberg (2001). https://doi.org/10.1007/3-540-47764-0_20

26. Giacobazzi, R., Ranzato, F., Scozzari, F.: Making abstract interpretations complete. J. ACM **47**(2), 361–416 (2000)

27. Ho, Y.S., Chauhan, P., Roy, P., Mishchenko, A., Brayton, R.: Efficient uninterpreted function abstraction and refinement for word-level model checking. In: FMCAD, pp. 65–72. ACM (2016)

28. Hyvärinen, A.E.J., Asadi, S., Even-Mendoza, K., Fedyukovich, G., Chockler, H., Sharygina, N.: Theory refinement for program verification. In: Gaspers, S., Walsh, T. (eds.) SAT 2017. LNCS, vol. 10491, pp. 347–363. Springer, Cham (2017). https://doi.org/10.1007/978-3-319-66263-3_22

29. Hyvärinen, A.E.J., Marescotti, M., Alt, L., Sharygina, N.: OpenSMT2: an SMT solver for multi-core and cloud computing. In: Creignou, N., Le Berre, D. (eds.) SAT 2016. LNCS, vol. 9710, pp. 547–553. Springer, Cham (2016). https://doi.org/10.1007/978-3-319-40970-2_35

30. Jančík, P., Alt, L., Fedyukovich, G., Hyvärinen, A.E.J., Kofroň, J., Sharygina, N.: PVAIR: partial variable assignment InterpolatoR. In: Stevens, P., Wasowski, A. (eds.) FASE 2016. LNCS, vol. 9633, pp. 419–434. Springer, Heidelberg (2016). https://doi.org/10.1007/978-3-662-49665-7_25

31. Kutsuna, T., Ishii, Y., Yamamoto, A.: Abstraction and refinement of mathematical functions toward smt-based test-case generation. Int. J. Softw. Tools Technol. Transfer **18**(1), 109–120 (2016)

32. Rollini, S.F., Alt, L., Fedyukovich, G., Hyvärinen, A.E.J., Sharygina, N.: PeRIPLO: a framework for producing effective interpolants in SAT-based software verification. In: McMillan, K., Middeldorp, A., Voronkov, A. (eds.) LPAR 2013. LNCS, vol. 8312, pp. 683–693. Springer, Heidelberg (2013). https://doi.org/10.1007/978-3-642-45221-5_45

33. Rummer, P., Subotic, P.: Exploring interpolants. In: Formal Methods in Computer-Aided Design (FMCAD), pp. 69–76. IEEE (2013)

34. Sery, O., Fedyukovich, G., Sharygina, N.: FunFrog: bounded model checking with interpolation-based function summarization. In: Chakraborty, S., Mukund, M. (eds.) ATVA 2012. LNCS, pp. 203–207. Springer, Heidelberg (2012). https://doi.org/10.1007/978-3-642-33386-6_17

35. Sery, O., Fedyukovich, G., Sharygina, N.: Interpolation-based function summaries in bounded model checking. In: Eder, K., Lourenço, J., Shehory, O. (eds.) HVC 2011. LNCS, vol. 7261, pp. 160–175. Springer, Heidelberg (2012). https://doi.org/10.1007/978-3-642-34188-5_15

Verified Certificate Checking
for Counting Votes

Milad K. Ghale[1(✉)], Dirk Pattinson[1], Ramana Kumar[2], and Michael Norrish[3]

[1] Australian National University, Canberra, Australia
{milad.ketabghale,dirk.pattinson}@anu.edu.au
[2] Data61, CSIRO and UNSW, Kensington, Australia
ramana.kumar@cl.cam.ac.uk
[3] Data61, CSIRO, and ANU, Canberra, Australia
michael.norrish@data61.csiro.au

Abstract. We introduce a new framework for verifying electronic vote counting results that are based on the Single Transferable Vote scheme (STV). Our approach frames electronic vote counting as certified computation where each execution of the counting algorithm is accompanied by a certificate that witnesses the correctness of the output. These certificates are then checked for correctness independently of how they are produced. We advocate verification of the verifier rather than the software used to produce the result. We use the theorem prover HOL4 to formalise the STV vote counting scheme, and obtain a fully verified certificate checker. By connecting HOL4 to the verified CakeML compiler, we then extract an executable that is guaranteed to behave correctly with respect to the formal specification of the protocol down to machine level. We demonstrate that our verifier can check certificates of real-size elections efficiently. Our encoding is modular, so repeating the same process for another different STV scheme would require a minimal amount of additional work.

1 Introduction

The main contribution of this paper is a new framework for verifiably correct vote counting. Electronic voting is becoming more and more prevalent worldwide. But almost scandalously, the current state of affairs leaves much to be desired, given that the public vote is a cornerstone of modern democracy. Indeed electronic techniques as they are used now may be seen as a step back from traditional paper based elections.

For example, the vote counting software that is used in Australia's most populous state, New South Wales, was found to contain errors that had an impact in at least one seat that was wrongly filled with high probability. This was reported in specialist publications [5] as well as the national press [3].

When counting ballots by hand, the counting is monitored by scrutineers, usually members of the general public or stakeholders such as party representatives. In contrast, computer software that is used to count ballots merely produces a final result. Moreover, in many cases, the source code of these programs

© Springer Nature Switzerland AG 2018
R. Piskac and P. Rümmer (Eds.): VSTTE 2018, LNCS 11294, pp. 69–87, 2018.
https://doi.org/10.1007/978-3-030-03592-1_5

is commercial in confidence, and there is no evidence of the correctness of the count that could be seen as analogous to scrutineers in traditional, paper-based vote counting.

It is universally recognised that transparent and verifiable vote counting is a key constituent to establish trustworthiness, and subsequently trust, in the final outcome. The computer-based methods currently in use fail to meet both expectations.

In the literature on electronic voting, the notion of *universal verifiability* of vote counting (any voter can check that the announced result is correct on the basis of the published ballots [14]) has long been recognised as being central, both for guaranteeing correctness, and building trust, in electronic elections. This notion has three subproperties; verifiability of casting votes as intended by voters, recording votes as intended, and counting votes as recorded [8]. The aim of this paper is only to address the last property, namely *verifiability of the tallying process*.

The approach presented here combines the concept of certifying algorithms [17] with formal specification and theorem proving to address this challenge. In a nutshell, a *certifying algorithm* is an algorithm that produces, with every execution, an easily-verifiable certificate of the correctness of the computed result. This certificate can then be scrutinised by a verifier, independently of the tools, hardware or software that were used to create the certificate.

Our focus in this paper is on the *certificate verifier*. We briefly discuss a concise formal specification of *single transferable vote* (STV), a complex, preferential voting system used e.g. in Ireland, Malta, New Zealand and Australia for multi-seat constituencies. From this specification, we develop a notion of *certificate* so that correct certificates guarantee correctness of election results. The main body of our work concerns the *verifier* (certificate checker), and we present a synthesis of the verifier that is itself fully verified down to the machine-code level.

This proceeds in four steps.[1] First, we formalise the vote counting protocol as a sequence of steps inside the HOL theorem prover where every step corresponds to an action taken by a counting officer in a paper-based setting. There are two kinds of stages that we call *judgements* in analogy to typing assertions in type theory. Final judgements just declare the set of winners. NonFinal judgements represent the current state of the count as a tuple, corresponding to a snapshot of the stage of the count in a paper-based setting. The formalisation of the voting protocol then takes the form of *rules* that specify how to advance from one judgement to the next, thereby progressing the count. The applicability of particular rules are described by side conditions that are in turn formalised by HOL predicates. A correct certificate is then simply a sequence of judgements where each judgement is justified through its predecessor by means of a correct rule application. The task of the verifier is then simply to process a list of judge-

---

[1] Source code of the formalisation can be found at https://github.com/MiladKetabGhale/Checker.

ments and ascertain that this is indeed the case. In particular, our specification of rules is purely descriptive.

Second, in tandem with the logical specification of each rule, we define a boolean-valued function that checks whether or not the rule has been applied correctly. This then directly gives rise to the verifier that, at every step, just checks whether any of the rules is applicable, using the corresponding boolean-valued function.

Third, we establish correspondence between the logical definitions and their computational counterparts. This boils down to formally establishing that the logical specification holds if and only if the boolean-valued function returns true, which in turn implies the correctness of the certificate verifier. This allows us to conclude that a valid certificate indeed implies that the election protocol has been carried out in accordance to the specification.

In the fourth, and last step, we synthesise an implementation of the verifier and produce a proof of this implementation's correctness. This is achieved by using proof-producing synthesis [18] of CakeML code from the HOL definitions, then using the verified CakeML compiler [22] to produce the machine code. To perform computation on an actual certificate, we define the formal syntax for certificates, and a parser in HOL, that we combine with the I/O mechanisms of CakeML to obtain the verifier. The result is an executable verifier that provably validates a certificate if and only if the certificate witnesses a correct execution of the vote counting protocol.

In summary, our slogan is "verify the verifier". Rather than verifying the *program* that performs an election count, we demand that a program produces a certificate that we can then independently verify. This has several advantages. For one, it is much less labour intensive to verify the verifier, compared with verifying the counting program. Second, having verifiable certificates at hand establishes the count-as-recorded property [8]. Third, we achieve correctness over a minimal trust base through the use of CakeML.

In the remainder of the paper, we describe our framework in detail and demonstrate that it can handle real-world size elections by evaluating it on historical data of elections conducted in Australia.

2   The Protocol and Its HOL Formalisation

Single Transferable Vote is a preferential voting scheme that is used in multi-seat constituencies. Voters rank (possibly a subset of) candidates by assigning numerical preferences to candidates where no two candidates may be given the same preference. This allows us to represent ballots as duplicate free lists of candidates where the list order reflects the preference order.

Each election defines a *quota*, i.e. a minimal set of votes that a candidate must receive in order to be elected. The count starts by counting all voters' *first preferences*, and candidates who reach the quota are elected, but in general there will still be seats to fill. This is effected by two mechanisms:

1. Transfer of surplus votes. Votes for elected candidates in excess of the quota are distributed to (and counted in favour of) the next preference listed on the ballot.
2. Elimination of candidates. The candidate with the *least* number of first preferences is eliminated from the election, and their votes are then distributed to the next listed preference on the ballot.

We give a precise definition of STV below. The main idea of distributing surplus votes is to account for *additional* candidates favoured by a voter if their first preference is already elected, whereas elimination honours voters' follow-on preferences if their first preference *cannot* be elected. Of course, the key question is precisely which ballots should be considered surplus and distributed to the next preferences, as follow-on preferences will generally differ. This is the purpose of a third mechanism:

3. Fractional Transfer. *All* surplus votes are transfered to the next preference, but at a *reduced* weight that is proportional to the size of the surplus.

For example, if a candidate exceeds the quota by 20%, all first preference votes for that candidate are re-assigned a weight of 0.2 and injected back into the count, and regarded as first-preference votes for the subsequently listed candidate. In other words, the number of first preference votes for a candidate is the sum of the *weights* of ballots where that candidate is listed as first preference. The initial weight of all ballots is 1.

There are various versions of STV. They mainly differ in how and when ballots are transferred and candidates are elected, the calculation of the transfer value, and the various tie breaking methods used to determine which candidate is to be excluded, and the quota being used. Here, we deal with a generic version of STV that incorporates all three mechanisms outlined above, and is very similar to the method used to elect members of the Australian Senate, and incidentally also to the scheme used elect the representatives of the student union at the Australian National University. Throughout, we do not assume a particular definition of the quota, but take this as a parameter. Design decisions in the precise formulation of the scheme are resolved as follows:

Step-by-step surplus transfer. Surplus votes of elected candidates that have exceeded the quota are transferred in order of number of first preferences received. That is, surplus votes of the candidate with the largest number of first preferences are transferred first.

Electing after each transfer. After each transfer of surpluses, candidates that reach the quota after surplus votes are being elected immediately.

The description of the formal protocol that we are analysing uses the following terminology. A *continuing candidate* is a candidate that has neither been elected nor eliminated. The *first preference* of a ballot is the most preferred continuing candidate, and the *transfer value* of a ballot is the fractional weight of a ballot. We keep track of the following data throughout:

- the set of *uncounted ballots*
- a *tally* for each candidate, the sum of the transfer values of all ballots counted in the candidate's favour
- a *pile* for each candidate that contains all ballots counted in favour of the respective candidate
- an queue of candidates that await surplus transfer

Initially, the queue for surplus transfer, as well as the piles associated to the individual candidates are empty, all ballots are uncounted, and all candidates are continuing. From this initial state, the protocol proceeds as follows:

1. determine the set of *formal* ballots, i.e. those ballots that represent a total order of preferences over a subset of candidates, each of which receives an initial transfer value of 1.
2. determine the number of first preference votes (the tally) for each continuing candidate. In doing this, record which vote is counted for which candidate by adding the ballot paper to the respective pile.
3. if there are unfilled seats, all candidates that have reached the quota are elected, and are added to the transfer queue in order of their tally.
4. if all the vacancies have been filled, counting terminates and the result is announced.
5. if the number of unfilled vacancies equals or exceeds the number of continuing candidates, all continuing candidates are elected and the result is announced.
6. if there are still vacancies, all ballots are counted, and the transfer queue is not empty, remove the first candidate from the transfer queue and transfer their votes (the votes on their pile) to the next preference by declaring these votes to be uncounted and the transfer value given by

$$\text{new value} = \frac{\text{number of votes of elected candidate} - \text{quota}}{\text{number of votes of elected candidate}} \qquad (1)$$

Subsequent transfer values are computed as the product of the current value with previous transfer value.

7. if there are still vacancies, all ballots are counted, and all surplus votes are transferred, choose the candidate with the least amount of first preference votes and exclude that candidate from the set of continuing candidates. All votes counted in favour of the eliminated candidate are transferred to the next preference (with unchanged transfer value).

The purpose of setting aside the ballots counted for particular candidates in the second step is precisely for the purpose of possibly transferring these ballots later, in case the candidate is either elected or eliminated.

2.1   An Example Certificate

As argued in the introduction, in the framework of certified computation, each step of the protocol is evidenced. Each of the steps outlined above is formalised as a rule that progresses the count. Rules have side conditions (e.g. candidates having reached the quota, or all ballots being counted) and rule application changes the data that we track throughout the count (e.g. updating the tally, or removing a candidate from the set of continuing candidates). We given an example certificate in Fig. 1. Here, we have a small election with three candidates A, B and C, and an initial set of ballots containing $b_1 = ([A, C], 1)$, $b_2 = ([A, B, C], 1)$, $b_3 = ([A, C, B], 1)$, $b_4 = ([B, A], 1)$, $b_5 = ([C, B, A], 1)$. Each ballot is a pair, where the first component is a preference-ordered list of candidates, and the second is the transfer value (initially set to 1). The certificate consists of a *header* that specifies the quota as a fraction (computed according to the Droop quota [10]), the number of seats to be filled, and the list of candidates being voted on. The fourth line is the election result, and the remainder of the certificate consists of the intermediate steps that lead to this outcome.

The certificate records every step of the count, where a step corresponds to a rule application, and the rules themselves are modelled on valid actions that of counting officers to progress the count. The inspection of a certificate therefore corresponds to witnessing all the individual steps that take place in a hypothetical counting station.

Intermediate stages of the count record six pieces of information, separated by semicolons: the ballots the are still to be counted, the tallies of all candidates, the ballots counted in favour of each candidate, the transfer queue, and finally the sets of continuing and elected candidates. We briefly illustrate the protocol using the certificate in Fig. 1 as an example, going though the protocol step-by-step.

count. First preferences for each candidates are computed, and ballots counted in favour of particular candidates are placed onto that candidate's pile. Here, A is the first preference on b_1, b_2, and b_3 (leading to a tally of 3), and B receives b_4, and C receives b_5. Tallies are updated so that tally of A becomes 3, and B and C each reach 1.

elect. Candidate A exceeds the quota, and is elected. The transfer value of all ballots counted in A's favour changes to $1/9$ according to formula (1). The updated pile of A reflects this change in transfer values, and now contains $([A, C],$

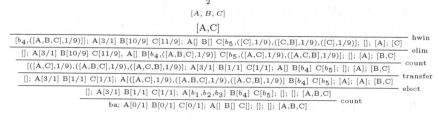

Fig. 1. Example certificate

$1/9$), ($[A, B, C]$, $1/9$), and ($[A, C, B]$, $1/9$). The data associated with B and C doesn't change.

transfer. As there are vacancies and no one else has reached or exceeded the quota, the surplus of A is dealt with. The list of uncounted ballots is updated to contain the votes for A (with transfer values updated in the previous step).

count. As there are uncounted ballots (again), tallies are updated. As A is no longer a continuing candidate, the votes are counted in favour of the highest-ranked continuing candidate. That is, C receives two new votes (each of value $1/9$) which are ($[A, C]$, $1/9$) and ($[A, C, B]$, $1/9$). Candidate B receives one vote, which is ($[A, B, C]$, $1/9$).

elim. No continuing candidate has reached the quota, one vacancy is still unfilled, and all ballots are (again) counted. Hence the candidate with the lowest tally is eliminated (in this case, B) and their votes (with unchanged transfer values) are again injected into the count.

hwin. The only continuing candidate, that is C, is elected and as we have filled all the vacancies, a final stage has been obtained.

To validate certificates of this form, we first parse the textual representation into actual data structures, and then check the certificates for correctness on the basis of a HOL formalisation that we now describe.

2.2   The HOL Formalisation

Elections are *parameterised* by the data in the header (candidates, quota and number of vacancies) that remain constant throughout the count. We use the term *judgement* for the data-structure representation of the various stages of the count. They come in two flavours: final judgements announce the winners, and non-final judgements are intermediate stages of the execution of the protocol.

Definition 1 (Judgements). *We formalise judgements as a datatype with two constructors. The first constructor,* Final w *represents a final stage of the computation, where w is the final list consisting of all of the declared elected candidates. The second constructor,* NonFinal (ba, t, p, bl, e, h) *is an intermediate stage of the computation, where ba is the list of uncounted ballots at this point, t is the tally list recording the number of votes of each candidate has received up to this point, p is the pile list of votes assigned to each candidate, bl is the list of elected whose surplus have not yet been transferred, e is the list of elected candidates by this point, and h is the list of continuing (hopeful) candidates up to this stage.*

> judgement $=$
>   NonFinal (*ballots* $\times$ *tallies* $\times$ *piles* $\times$ *cand list* $\times$ *cand list* $\times$ *cand list*)
> | Final (*cand list*)

We use lists (instead of sets, or multisets) mainly for convenience of formalisation in HOL, but this is not used in an essential way either in the definition, or in the formalisation, of the counting rules that we give later. By choosing to formalise the tally and pile as lists rather than functions operating on the list of candidates, judgements become an instance of the equality type class which we use later on in specification and reasoning about counting rules. Additionally, this formulation reduces the gap between an actual certificate and its abstract syntactic representation which we refer to as a *formal certificate*.

As a (formal) certificate consists of a sequence of judgements, each of which represents a state of the count, we need to verify the correctness of the transitions between successive judgements. Each rule consists of three main components:

– a specification of how premiss and conclusion relate
– side conditions that specifies when a rule is applicable
– a number of implicit assertions that guarantee the integrity of the data.

For example, we expect a valid certificate to have no duplication in the list of elected or continuing candidates, and every candidate must have only one tally and one pile at every non-final judgement.

Crucially, the specification of the counting rules is purely *descriptive*. To effectively check certificates, we augment each (specification of a) rule with an actual decision procedure that, given two judgements, returns either true or false, depending on whether the rule is applicable or not. The decision procedure and the formal specification are connected by (formal) proofs of soundess and completeness, as shown in the figure below.

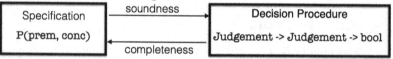

Here, *soundness* refers to the fact that the decision procedure only stipulates that a rule has been correctly applied if the application is in accordance with the specification and *completeness* says that this will happen whenever the rule is applicable. The decision procedures are actual functions in HOL that we then translate and extract using CakeML to guarantee machine-level correctness, and both soundness and completeness are established formally in HOL. We illustrate this in detail with the elimination rule.

Integrity Constraints. The integrity constraints for the elimination rule are identical to those of other rules. For example, the name of each candidate appears only once in the initial list of competing candidates. Also, at every stage of the count, every candidate has exactly one tally and one pile (of votes counted in their favour). Therefore, if a judgement in a certificate maliciously allocates no tally, or more than one tally for a single candidate, this error is detected and the certificate is rejected as invalid. We express the fact that tallies need to be recorded for every candidate as follows:

$$\text{Valid\_PileTally } t \; l \iff \forall c.\, \text{mem } c \; l \iff \text{mem } c \; (\text{map fst } t)$$

The above predicate is paired with computational twins, and soundness and completeness connect both. Here, given lists t and l, the function

Valid_PileTally_dec1 decides if every first element of each pair in t is a member of l.

>   Valid_PileTally_dec1 $[]$ l $\Longleftrightarrow$ true
>   Valid_PileTally_dec1 $(h::t)$ l $\Longleftrightarrow$ mem (fst h) l $\wedge$ Valid_PileTally_dec1 t l

Additionally, the function Valid_PileTally_dec2 determines if each element of l appears as the first component of a pair in t.

>   Valid_PileTally_dec2 t $[]$ $\Longleftrightarrow$ true
>   Valid_PileTally_dec2 t $(l_0::ls)$ $\Longleftrightarrow$
>   if mem l_0 (map fst t) then Valid_PileTally_dec2 t ls
>   else false

We prove that the formal specification Valid_PileTally corresponds with the functions Valid_PileTally_dec1 and Valid_PileTally_dec2. Therefore we ensure that tallies and piles are distinctively allocated to candidates.

> $\vdash$ Valid_PileTally t l $\Longleftrightarrow$ Valid_PileTally_dec1 t l $\wedge$ Valid_PileTally_dec2 t l

Side Conditions. Item 7 of the protocol on Page 5 specifies when and how a candidate shall be eliminated from the election. It stipulates that

a. there are still seats to fill
b. there are no votes to count at this stage and there are no pending transfers
c. the candidate c has the least tally
d. eliminate the candidate c
e. votes of the eliminated candidate c are transferred according to the next preference with the same transfer value.

To illustrate how clauses of the protocol are formalised explicitly, we explain the way that we have specified item (d) inside HOL. We introduce the predicate equal_except which formally asserts when two lists are equal except for one exact element.

>   equal_except c l nl $\Longleftrightarrow$
> $\exists l_1 \; l_2. \; l = l_1 + l_2 \wedge nl = l_1 + [c] + l_2 \wedge \neg$mem c l_1 $\wedge$ $\neg$mem c l_2

The computational twin of this definition decides whether two list match with the exception of one element. This is the function equal_except_dec.

>   equal_except_dec c $[]$ $= []$
>   equal_except_dec c $(h::t)$ $=$ if $c = h$ then t else $h::$equal_except_dec c t

We formally establish that this function implements the specification given by the equal_except predicate.

> $\vdash$ mem c h $\wedge$ distinct h $\Rightarrow$ equal_except c (equal_except_dec c h) h

Moreover, modulo extensional equality, the function equal_except_dec is unique.

$$\vdash \text{mem } c \; h_2 \wedge \text{equal\_except } c \; h_1 \; h_2 \Rightarrow h_1 = \text{equal\_except\_dec } c \; h_2$$

Having defined the implicit integrity constraints, and the explicit side conditions in the definition of *elimination*, we can present the formalisation of this rule in HOL as a predicate.

The ELIM_CAND rule specifies what it means to legitimately eliminate a given candidate c. It relates three data items: a candidate, a triple composed of three fixed parameters which are the quota, vacancies, and the initial list of candidates, and two judgements j_1 and j_2 (the premiss and the conclusion of the rule).

ELIM_CAND $c \; (qu,st,l) \; j_1 \; j_2 \iff$
$\exists t \; p \; e \; h \; nh \; nba \; np.$
    $j_1 = \text{NonFinal } ([],t,p,[],e,h) \wedge \text{Valid\_Init\_CandList } l \wedge$
    $(\forall c'. \text{mem } c' \; (h +\!\!+ e) \Rightarrow \text{mem } c' \; l) \wedge \text{distinct } (h +\!\!+ e) \wedge \text{Valid\_PileTally } p \; l \wedge$
    $\text{Valid\_PileTally } np \; l \wedge \text{length } (e +\!\!+ h) > st \wedge \text{length } e < st \wedge$
    $\text{distinct } (\text{map fst } t) \wedge \text{Valid\_PileTally } t \; l \wedge$
    $(\forall c'. \text{mem } c' \; h \Rightarrow \exists x. \text{mem } (c',x) \; t \wedge x < qu) \wedge \text{mem } c \; h \wedge$
    $(\forall d. \text{mem } d \; h \Rightarrow \exists x \; y. \text{mem } (c,x) \; t \wedge \text{mem } (d,y) \; t \wedge x \leq y) \wedge \text{equal\_except } c \; nh \; h \wedge$
    $nba = \text{get\_cand\_pile } c \; p \wedge \text{mem } (c,[]) \; np \wedge$
    $(\forall d'.$
        $d' \neq c \Rightarrow$
            $\forall l. (\text{mem } (d',l) \; p \Rightarrow \text{mem } (d',l) \; np) \wedge (\text{mem } (d',l) \; np \Rightarrow \text{mem } (d',l) \; p)) \wedge$
    $j_2 = \text{NonFinal } (nba,t,np,[],e,nh)$

The first and the fourth component of j_1 which correspond to the list of uncounted ballots and the backlog are both empty. This realises the condition (a) stated above. It is also required that h the list of continuing candidates in the premise j_1, and nh the updated list of continuing candidates in j_2 satisfy the predicate equal_except so that condition (d) is met. Each of the conjuncts in the definition of ELIM_CAND encapsulates part of the item 7 in the protocol.

Similar to the case of equal_except, for each of the conjuncts, we define a computational counterpart and prove the equivalence of the conjunct with its computational realisation. Conjunction of these computational definitions is ELIM_CAND_dec, which is the computational equivalent of the predicate ELIM_CAND.

ELIM_CAND_dec $c \; (qu,st,l) \; (\text{NonFinal } (ba,t,p,bl,e,h)) \; (\text{NonFinal } (ba',t',p',bl',e',h')) \iff$
  $\text{null } ba \wedge \text{null } bl \wedge \text{null } bl' \wedge t = t' \wedge e = e' \wedge \text{length } (e +\!\!+ h) > st \wedge \text{length } e < st \wedge$
  $\neg\text{null } l \wedge \text{distinct } l \wedge \text{list\_MEM\_dec } (h +\!\!+ e) \; l \wedge \text{distinct } (h +\!\!+ e) \wedge$
  $\text{Valid\_PileTally\_dec1 } p \; l \wedge \text{Valid\_PileTally\_dec2 } p \; l \wedge \text{Valid\_PileTally\_dec1 } p' \; l \wedge$
  $\text{Valid\_PileTally\_dec2 } p' \; l \wedge \text{distinct } (\text{map fst } t) \wedge \text{Valid\_PileTally\_dec1 } t \; l \wedge$
  $\text{Valid\_PileTally\_dec2 } t \; l \wedge \text{mem } c \; h \wedge \text{less\_than\_quota } qu \; t \; h \wedge$
  $h' = \text{equal\_except\_dec } c \; h \wedge \text{bigger\_than\_cand } c \; t \; h \wedge ba' = \text{get\_cand\_pile } c \; p \wedge$
  $\text{mem } (c,[]) \; p' \wedge \text{subpile1 } c \; p \; p' \wedge \text{subpile2 } c \; p' \; p$
ELIM_CAND_dec $c \; v_0 \; (\text{Final } v_1) \; v_2 \iff \text{false}$
ELIM_CAND_dec $c \; v_3 \; (\text{NonFinal } v_{11}) \; (\text{Final } v_5) \iff \text{false}$

By drawing upon the correspondence established between conjuncts of the elimination specification and computational counterpart, we prove that ⊢ELIM_-CAND_dec = ELIM_CAND. The same procedure is followed to achieve formal specification, computational definitions, and their correspondence for the rest of counting rules.

2.3   The Certificate Verifier

Clearly, one way to verify the result of a computation is to simply re-compute (possibly using a verified program) [2]. While this makes perfect sense for a *deterministic* program, voting protocols generally employ tie-breaking techniques that lead to non-determinism. In the case of STV, for example, this applies when two candidates are tied for exclusion. In this situation it is permissible to eliminate *either* of the candidates. From the perspective of certified computation, this is a non-issue, as the certificate simply records which choice has been made (and why this choice is permissible). Compared to simply re-computing, the verification of a certificate provides another significant advantage: in case of diverging results, we gain information on precisely what step of the (incorrect) computation is to blame for the wrong result. Computationally, the additional advantage is simplicity and speed: the verification of the verifier is considerably simpler than that of a fully-fledged implementation, and certificate checking is also generally faster than re-computing.

The verification of certificates comprises two steps. First we need to validate whether the first judgement of the certificate is a valid initial state of the count. A valid initial judgement is one where candidate's tally is zero, their piles are empty, and both the transfer queue and the list of elected candidates are both empty as well.

initial_judgement $l\ j$ $\Longleftrightarrow$
$\exists\ ba\ t\ p\ bl\ e\ h.$
$\quad j = \mathsf{NonFinal}\ (ba,t,p,bl,e,h) \wedge (\forall\ c.\ \mathsf{mem}\ c\ (\mathsf{map}\ \mathsf{snd}\ t) \Rightarrow c = 0) \wedge$
$\quad (\forall\ c.\ \mathsf{mem}\ c\ (\mathsf{map}\ \mathsf{snd}\ p) \Rightarrow c = [\,]) \wedge bl = [\,] \wedge e = [\,] \wedge h = l$

Second, we check whether transitions from one judgement to the next is according to one of the rules that define the count.

Valid_Step_Spec *params* $j_0\ j_1$ $\Longleftrightarrow$
HWIN *params* $j_0\ j_1$ $\vee$ EWIN *params* $j_0\ j_1$ $\vee$ COUNT *params* $j_0\ j_1$ $\vee$
TRANSFER *params* $j_0\ j_1$ $\vee$ ELECT *params* $j_0\ j_1$ $\vee$
$\exists\ c.\ \mathsf{mem}\ c\ (\mathsf{snd}\ (\mathsf{snd}\ params)) \wedge$ ELIM_CAND c *params* $j_0\ j_1$

We can therefore check whether a transition from one judgement to the next is correct by simply considering the disjunction of all rules.

Valid_intermediate_judgements *params* J $\Longleftrightarrow$
$J \neq [\,] \wedge (\exists\ w.\ \mathsf{last}\ J = \mathsf{Final}\ w) \wedge$
$\forall\ J_0\ J_1\ j_0\ j_1.\ J = J_0 \mathbin{+\!\!+} [j_0;\ j_1] \mathbin{+\!\!+} J_1 \Rightarrow$ Valid_Step_Spec *params* $j_0\ j_1$

Putting the specification of a valid initial judgement with valid sequence of judgements together, we obtain the specification for a valid certificate:

Valid_Certificate $params$ $[\,]$ $\Longleftrightarrow$ false
Valid_Certificate $params$ ($first\_judgement::rest\_judgements$) $\Longleftrightarrow$
 initial_judgement (snd (snd $params$)) $first\_judgement$ $\wedge$
 Valid_intermediate_judgements $params$ ($first\_judgement::rest\_judgements$)

For checking a formal certificate we therefore first verify that certificate starts at a permissible initial stage. We then iteratively check that transitions have happened correctly, and that the terminating state is a final one where winners are declared. The above specification of a valid vertificate, corresponds to the following computational formal certificate checker.

Check_Parsed_Certificate $params$ $[\,]$ $\Longleftrightarrow$ false
Check_Parsed_Certificate $params$ ($first\_judgement::rest\_judgements$) $\Longleftrightarrow$
 Initial_Judgement_dec (snd (snd $params$)) $first\_judgement$ $\wedge$
 valid_judgements_dec $params$ ($first\_judgement::rest\_judgements$)

The correctness of this definition rests on the equivalences we have already established between the specifications and their computational counterparts, namely, Initial_Judgement_dec and initial_judgement, and valid_judgements_dec and valid_judgements. Consequently a formal certificate is validated if and only if it is valid according to the HOL specification of Valid_Certificate.

Check_Parsed_Certificate $params$ J $\Longleftrightarrow$ Valid_Certificate $params$ J

Since the HOL specification realises the protocol, a formal certificate is validated if and only if it meets the protocol's expectation.

3   Translation into CakeML and Code Extraction

The verified certificate-checking function, Check_Parsed_Certificate, described above, is a good starting point for a verifier, but still has two shortcomings: it is a function in logic rather than an executable program, and as a consequence, its inputs must be provided as elements of the respective data types, whereas certificates are purely textual. We now demonstrate how to address these shortcomings and obtain a verified executable for checking certificates. Our final theorem about the verifier executable is presented at the end of this section.

Parsing. The input to the verifier is a textual certificate file, in a format similar to Fig. 1. We specify this file format indirectly, by defining an executable specification of a certificate parser.

```
Check_Certificate lines ⟺
  case lines of
    quota_line::seats_line::candidates_line::winners_line::jlines ⇒
      case
        (parse_quota quota_line,parse_seats seats_line,
         parse_candidates candidates_line,parse_candidates winners_line,
         mapm parse_judgement jlines)
      of
        (Some quota,Some seats,Some candidates,Some winners,Some judgements) ⇒
          Check_Parsed_Certificate (quota,seats,candidates)
          (rev (Final winners::judgements))
      | _ ⇒ false
  | _ ⇒ false
```

Specifically, we define functions that take a string representing a line in the file and return either None or Some x, where x is the parsed information from the line. Given these parsing functions—parse_quota, parse_seats, etc.—we write the verifier as a function, above, that parses lines from the file then calls Check_Parsed_Certificate to do the verification.

Translation into CakeML and I/O Wrapper. Using prior work on proof-producing synthesis [18] we can automatically synthesise an implementation of the function Check_Certificate in the programming language CakeML. The synthesis tool for CakeML produces a theorem relating the semantics of the synthesised program back to the logical function. However, the result is a *pure* function that expects the lines of a file as input. To actually open the file and read lines from it, we write the impure wrapper check_count (making use of the CakeML Basis Library) around the pure function, and verify the wrapper using Characteristic Formulae for CakeML, as described by Guéneau et al. [13]. The result is a complete CakeML program whose I/O semantics is verified, witnessed by the theorem check_count_compiled below, to implement Check_Certificate on lines from standard input.

To elaborate further on the above step, the impure wrapper check_count calls two impure functions parse_line and loop. The former, calls I/O functions to read one line at a time from the concrete certificate given as lines on the standard input and parse it. It comprises two phases; one for the header of the certificate file consisting of the quota, seats number, and initial list of candidates, and the other is for parsing judgement lines. If the parsing fails due to malformedness of a line, the parser messages the appropriate error on the standard output with the line number included. However, if it succeeds, the parsed line is fed to the loop function to check if the transition from two consecutive parsed judgement lines is a valid step. The parsing and checking of judgement lines continues until either all steps are verified as correct, or an incorrect step is encountered. The following theorem asserts that the loop function returns the correct output None if and only if the initial line of judgements in the certificate file is indeed valid and all steps taken to move from one judgement line to its successor are correct.

loop $params$ i (Final w) j_0 js = None $\Longleftrightarrow$
    EVERY (IS_SOME ∘ parse_judgement) js ∧
    Check_Parsed_Certificate $params$ (rev (Final w::j_0::map (the ∘ parse_judgement) js))

Compilation in Logic. Finally, we would like an executable verifier in machine code (rather than CakeML code). To produce this, we use the verifed CakeML compiler [22], which can be executed within the theorem prover itself. This is a time-consuming process: compilation within logic can be a thousand times slower (e.g., half an hour) than running the compiler outside the logic (a second or two). But the payoff is a final theorem which only mentions the final generated machine-code implementation: all dependence on the CakeML language and implementation is discharged by proof.

Final Theorem. The final theorem, which we explain further below, is about the generated machine code, represented by the constant check_count_compiled.

⊢ wfCL cl ∧ wfFS fs ∧
    x64_installed check_count_compiled (basis_ffi cl fs) mc ms ⇒
    ∃io_events fs'.
        machine_sem mc (basis_ffi cl fs) ms ⊆
        extend_with_resource_limit { Terminate Success io_events } ∧
        extract_fs fs io_events = Some fs' ∧
        (stdout fs' "Certificate OK\n" $\Longleftrightarrow$
            Check_Certificate (lines_of (get_stdin fs)))

We assume (x64_installed) that this code is loaded into memory in an x86-64 machine represented by mc and ms, and that the command line (cl) and file system (fs) are well-formed. The conclusion of the theorem concerns the semantics (machine_sem) of executing the machine: it will terminate successfully (or fail if there is not enough memory) with a trace of I/O events (io_events) such that if we replay those events on the initial file system, we obtain a resulting file system fs' for which the string "Certificate OK\n" is printed on standard output if and only if Check_Certificate succeeds on the lines of standard input.

4   Experimental Results

We have tested our approach against some of the past Australian Legislative Assembly elections in the Australian Capital Territory for years 2008 and 2012 (Fig. 2).[2] The certificates were produced by the Haskell program extracted from our previous formalisation of the same protocol in Coq [11].

We also evaluated the verifier on certificates obtained through randomly generated ballots. We vary two parameters: the number of ballots and the size of each ballot. Figure 3 shows the results on certificates where the number of candidates is fixed at 20, vacancies are 5, and the length of each ballot is 12. Also we

---

[2] Tests were conducted on one core of an Intel Core i7-7500U CPU 2.70 GHz × 4 Ubuntu 16.4 LTS.

electoral	ballots	vacancies	candidates	time (sec)	certificate size (MB)	year
Brindabella	63334	5	19	86	54.4	2008
Ginninderra	60049	5	27	118	83.0	2008
Molonglo	88266	7	40	329	211.2	2008
Brindabella	63562	5	20	75	74.5	2012
Ginninderra	66076	5	28	191	90.1	2012
Molonglo	91534	7	27	286	158.7	2012

Fig. 2. ACT Legislative Assembly 2008 and 2012

keep the number of ballots, vacancies, and length of each ballot fixed at 100000, 1, and 10 respectively, in order to see the effect of increase in the length of each ballot (Fig. 4). We have also implemented the protocol in an unverified certifying Haskell program.[3] The unverified program was then tested on ballots of the same ACT Legislative Assembly elections. We have then verified the certificates produced by this program for each of the districts. The result shows that the certificates of the districts for the year 2012 are valid. Also the certificate of Molonglo electorate 2008 is verified as correct. However, the two electorates of Brindabella and Ginninderra 2008, despite declaring the final winners correctly, were *invalid* as an error occurs in an intermediate transition on line 6 in both certificates.

ballots	certificate size	time (sec)
400000	523.6	4224
200000	253.3	938
100000	131.1	461

ballot length	certificate size	time (sec)
6	60.2	140
12	124.0	298
18	180.5	325

Fig. 3. Varying number of ballots

Fig. 4. Varying length of each ballot

Based on the aforementioned error message, we only need to inspect a very small part of the certificate. Upon closer inspection, we uncovered a subtle error in the implementation of the elimination rule. On the other hand, the same program successfully (and correctly) computes election results for other districts, substantiating the subtlety of the error. We argue that precisely because of such delicacies in the STV protocol and hence their implementation, we advocate that vote counting be carried out in a certified way, with a minimal trust base such as demonstrated in this paper.

5   Discussion

Universal verifiability is a security requirement introduced for measuring verifiability of an election result by any member of the public [8]. The literature

---

[3] Source code can be found in the Github repository given in the second page.

on election protocol design agrees on the textual formulation of the concept, despite the fact that they vary in the technical implementation of the property [8]. Moreover, it is accepted that satisfaction of the property rests on verifying three subproperties, namely cast-as-intended, recorded-as-intended, and count-as-recorded [8], and also demonstration of the eligibility verifiability as an explicitly or implicitly stated prerequisite [16].

Our framework only aims at addressing verification of the count-as-recorded subproperty. We do not attempt to introduce an election protocol for answering expectations of the universal verifiability. Therefore, verification of other two subproperties and the eligibility criterion falls outside the focus of the current work. However, our tool can be perfectly employed by any election protocol which accommodates STV scheme and uses Mixnets [4] for anonymising and decrypting ballots. For example, some protocols require authorities to produce a witness for tallying, and then verify it is a proof of correctness for the announced tallying result [6]. Such systems can adapt certification and the checker for (a) offering an independently checkable witness of tallying, and (b) verifying the certificate in a provably correct way. Finally, the certificates which the checker operates on include the exact ballots published by election authorities after the tallying is complete, and are therefore publicly available. Hence, the certificate would not compromise privacy concerns such as vote buying or voter coercion any more than the existing practice of ballot publication.

The framework employs CakeML to achieve an end-to-end verification of certificates. Therefore we prove that executable checker is verified to behave according to its specification in HOL, which operates in a different environment. To obtain this level of verification, we rely on the verified proof-synthesis tool of CakeML, the mechanism for producing deeply embedded equivalent assertions of HOL functions into CakeML environment, the Characteristic Formulae of CakeML to assert that the pure (deeply embedded functions) behave consistently with the impure I/O calls, and the verified compiler that generates executables that provably respect all of the above proofs.

Furthermore, the separation of the program from proofs offered in the combined CakeML and HOL environment makes our formalisation easier to understand. In particular, we believe that external scrutineers should be able to examine the specification of the framework to understand what it does, rather than having to also get to grips with CakeML proofs and computational components. HOL4's rich rewriting tactics and libraries also allow us to express the protocol and discharge related proofs with a minimum amount of lines of encoding.

We have demonstrated the practical feasibility of our approach by means of case studies. For example, the certificates of the Molonglo district, the biggest Legislative Assembly electorate in Australia, are checked in just five minutes.

Our framework is modular in two different ways. On the one hand, the formalisation realises the counting scheme as a set of standalone logical rules. On the other hand, each of the rules comprises independent assertions. Since every STV election consists of counting, elimination, transfer, electing and declaration of winners, we only need to change some of these rules locally to capture different variants. For example, the STV version used in the Senate elections of Australia requires transfer of excess votes of an elected candidate before any other rule can apply. This difference can be formalised in our system simply by modifying a single component of the TRANSFER rule. So for establishing verification results, we simply have to discharge a few correspondences in HOL. Furthermore, the steps of translation into CakeML and the process of extracting a verified executable remains mostly unaffected.

6   Related Work

Given that our main concern is with the count-as-recorded property, we provide an overview of existing work from the perspective of their tally verification methods. We also compare with related work that combines theorem proving and certified computation.

The existing certificate-producing implementations of vote counting mainly formalise a voting protocol inside the Coq theorem prover and then prove some desired properties about the formalised specification, and then extract the development into Haskell [11,20,23] or OCaml [21] programs. Since the semantics of the target and source of the extraction method differ, and there is no proof that the translation occurs in a semantic-preserving way, verification of the specification does not provably extend to the extracted program. Moreover, these work are either not accompanied by a checker [11], or their checker is an unverified Haskell/OCaml program [20,21,23]. One therefore has to trust both the extraction mechanism and the compiler used to produce the executable.

In the context of certified computation, Alkassar et al. [1] combine certified computation and theorem proving with methods of code verification to establish a framework for validation of certifying algorithms in the C programming language. With the help of the VCC tool [9], pre- and postconditions are generated that are syntactically generalized in the Isabelle theorem prover and then discharged. The user has to trust the VCC tool, and there is duplication of effort in that one has to generalise the conditions imposed by the VCC and then implement them manually in Isabelle to prove. To ameliorate this disadvantage, Noschinski et al. [19] replace the intermediate step where VCC is invoked by the AutoCorres [12] verifier which provably correctly translates (part of) the C language into Isabelle in a semantics-preserving manner. Nonetheless one has to trust that the machine code behaviour corresponds to its top-level C encoding.

Some election protocols [8,15] do require a witness for the tallying result, which should then be verified for correctness. Other work (e.g., [7]) implements algorithms in programming environments such as Python. However the algorithm, the correctness proof of the algorithm, and the implementation occur in different unverified environments. Finally, Cortier et al. [6] present simple formally stated pre- and post-conditions for elections that allow voting for one candidate. This is done inside the dependently-typed programming language $F^\star$. The $F^\star$ environment is implemented by a compiler that translates into RDCIL, a dialect of .NET bytecode. The verification also depends on the external SMT solver Z3. The size of these tools' implementations makes for a very large trusted code base.

7   Conclusion

Correct, publicly verifiable, transparent election count is a key constituent of establishing trustworthiness in the final outcome. The tool developed here has clarity in encoding, precision in formulation, and modularity in implementation so that it can be taken as a framework for verifying STV election results down to machine level.

References

1. Alkassar, E., Böhme, S., Mehlhorn, K., Rizkallah, C.: A framework for the verification of certifying computations. J. Autom. Reason. **52**(3), 241–273 (2014)
2. Blum, M., Kannan, S.: Designing programs that check their work. In: Proceedings of the 21st Annual ACM Symposium on Theory of Computing, 14–17 May 1989, Seattle, Washington, USA, pp. 86–97 (1989)
3. Brooks, L., Griffits, A.: NSW council elections: computer 'guesstimate' might have ignored your vote. ABC News, September 2017. http://www.abc.net.au/news/2017-09-14/computer-algorithms-may-sway-local-council-elections/8944186
4. Chaum, D.: Untraceable electronic mail return addresses and digital pseudonyms. In: Gritzalis, D.A. (ed.) Secure Electronic Voting, pp. 211–219. Springer, Boston (2003). https://doi.org/10.1007/978-1-4615-0239-5_14
5. Conway, A., Blom, M., Naish, L., Teague, V.: An analysis of New South Wales electronic vote counting. In: Proceedings of the ACSW 2017, pp. 24:1–24:5 (2017)
6. Cortier, V., Eigner, F., Kremer, S., Maffei, M., Wiedling, C.: Type-based verification of electronic voting protocols. In: Focardi, R., Myers, A. (eds.) POST 2015. LNCS, vol. 9036, pp. 303–323. Springer, Heidelberg (2015). https://doi.org/10.1007/978-3-662-46666-7_16
7. Cortier, V., Galindo, D., Glondu, S., Izabachène, M.: Election verifiability for Helios under weaker trust assumptions. In: Kutyłowski, M., Vaidya, J. (eds.) ESORICS 2014. LNCS, vol. 8713, pp. 327–344. Springer, Cham (2014). https://doi.org/10.1007/978-3-319-11212-1_19
8. Cortier, V., Galindo, D., Küsters, R., Müller, J., Truderung, T.: Verifiability notions for e-voting protocols. IACR Cryptology ePrint Archive 2016, 287 (2016)
9. Dahlweid, M., Moskal, M., Santen, T., Tobies, S., Schulte, W.: VCC: contract-based modular verification of concurrent C. In: 31st International Conference on Software Engineering, ICSE 2009, Vancouver, Canada, 16–24 May 2009, Companion Volume, pp. 429–430 (2009)
10. Droop, H.R.: On methods of electing representatives. J. Stat. Soc. Lond. **44**(2), 141–202 (1881). http://www.jstor.org/stable/2339223
11. Ghale, M.K., Goré, R., Pattinson, D.: A formally verified single transferable voting scheme with fractional values. In: Krimmer, R., Volkamer, M., Braun Binder, N., Kersting, N., Pereira, O., Schürmann, C. (eds.) E-Vote-ID 2017. LNCS, vol. 10615, pp. 163–182. Springer, Cham (2017). https://doi.org/10.1007/978-3-319-68687-5_10

12. Greenaway, D., Andronick, J., Klein, G.: Bridging the gap: automatic verified abstraction of C. In: Beringer, L., Felty, A. (eds.) ITP 2012. LNCS, vol. 7406, pp. 99–115. Springer, Heidelberg (2012). https://doi.org/10.1007/978-3-642-32347-8_8

13. Guéneau, A., Myreen, M.O., Kumar, R., Norrish, M.: Verified characteristic formulae for CakeML. In: Yang, H. (ed.) ESOP 2017. LNCS, vol. 10201, pp. 584–610. Springer, Heidelberg (2017). https://doi.org/10.1007/978-3-662-54434-1_22

14. Kremer, S., Ryan, M., Smyth, B.: Election verifiability in electronic voting protocols. In: Gritzalis, D., Preneel, B., Theoharidou, M. (eds.) ESORICS 2010. LNCS, vol. 6345, pp. 389–404. Springer, Heidelberg (2010). https://doi.org/10.1007/978-3-642-15497-3_24

15. Küsters, R., Truderung, T., Vogt, A.: Accountability: definition and relationship to verifiability. In: Proceedings of the 17th ACM Conference on Computer and Communications Security, CCS 2010, Chicago, Illinois, USA, 4–8 October 2010, pp. 526–535 (2010)

16. Küsters, R., Truderung, T., Vogt, A.: Verifiability, privacy, and coercion-resistance: new insights from a case study. In: 32nd IEEE Symposium on Security and Privacy, S&P 2011, 22–25 May 2011, Berkeley, California, USA, pp. 538–553 (2011)

17. McConnell, R.M., Mehlhorn, K., Näher, S., Schweitzer, P.: Certifying algorithms. Comput. Sci. Rev. 5(2), 119–161 (2011)

18. Myreen, M.O., Owens, S.: Proof-producing translation of higher-order logic into pure and stateful ML. J. Funct. Program. 24(2–3), 284–315 (2014)

19. Noschinski, L., Rizkallah, C., Mehlhorn, K.: Verification of certifying computations through autocorres and simpl. In: Badger, J.M., Rozier, K.Y. (eds.) NFM 2014. LNCS, vol. 8430, pp. 46–61. Springer, Cham (2014). https://doi.org/10.1007/978-3-319-06200-6_4

20. Pattinson, D., Schürmann, C.: Vote counting as mathematical proof. In: Pfahringer, B., Renz, J. (eds.) AI 2015. LNCS (LNAI), vol. 9457, pp. 464–475. Springer, Cham (2015). https://doi.org/10.1007/978-3-319-26350-2_41

21. Pattinson, D., Tiwari, M.: Schulze voting as evidence carrying computation. In: Ayala-Rincón, M., Muñoz, C.A. (eds.) ITP 2017. LNCS, vol. 10499, pp. 410–426. Springer, Cham (2017). https://doi.org/10.1007/978-3-319-66107-0_26

22. Tan, Y.K., Myreen, M.O., Kumar, R., Fox, A.C.J., Owens, S., Norrish, M.: A new verified compiler backend for CakeML. In: Garrigue, J., Keller, G., Sumii, E. (eds.) Proceedings of the 21st ACM SIGPLAN International Conference on Functional Programming, ICFP 2016, Nara, Japan, 18–22 September 2016, pp. 60–73. ACM (2016). http://doi.acm.org/10.1145/2951913.2951924

23. Verity, F., Pattinson, D.: Formally verified invariants of vote counting schemes. In: Proceedings of the Australasian Computer Science Week Multiconference, ACSW 2017, Geelong, Australia, 31 January–3 February 2017, pp. 31:1–31:10 (2017). http://doi.acm.org/10.1145/3014812.3014845

Program Verification in the Presence of I/O
Semantics, Verified Library Routines, and Verified Applications

Hugo Férée[1]($\boxtimes$), Johannes Åman Pohjola[2,3]($\boxtimes$), Ramana Kumar[3,5P],
Scott Owens[1], Magnus O. Myreen[2], and Son Ho[4]

[1] School of Computing, Univerity of Kent, Canterbury, UK
H.Feree@kent.ac.uk
[2] CSE Department, Chalmers University of Technology, Gothenburg, Sweden
[3] Data61, CSIRO/UNSW, Sydney, Australia
johannes.amanpohjola@data61.csiro.au
[4] École Polytechnique, Paris, France
[5] DeepMind, London, UK

Abstract. Software verification tools that build machine-checked proofs of functional correctness usually focus on the algorithmic content of the code. Their proofs are not grounded in a formal semantic model of the environment that the program runs in, or the program's interaction with that environment. As a result, several layers of translation and wrapper code must be trusted. In contrast, the CakeML project focuses on end-to-end verification to replace this trusted code with verified code in a cost-effective manner.

In this paper, we present infrastructure for developing and verifying impure functional programs with I/O and imperative file handling. Specifically, we extend CakeML with a low-level model of file I/O, and verify a high-level file I/O library in terms of the model. We use this library to develop and verify several Unix-style command-line utilities: cat, sort, grep, diff and patch. The workflow we present is built around the HOL4 theorem prover, and therefore all our results have machine-checked proofs.

1 Introduction

Program verification using interactive theorem provers is at its most pleasant when one reasons about shallow embeddings of the program's core algorithms in the theorem prover's native logic. For a simple example, consider this shallow embedding in the HOL4 theorem prover[1] of a program that given two lists returns the longest:

$$\text{longest } l \; l' = \text{if length } l \geq \text{length } l' \text{ then } l \text{ else } l'$$

---

[1] https://hol-theorem-prover.org/.

© Springer Nature Switzerland AG 2018
R. Piskac and P. Rümmer (Eds.): VSTTE 2018, LNCS 11294, pp. 88–111, 2018.
https://doi.org/10.1007/978-3-030-03592-1_6

Reasoning about such a shallow embedding is a breeze. The definition above is an equation in the HOL4 logic, so in a proof we can always replace the left-hand side with the right-hand side. The numbers and lists it uses are those of the HOL4 library, so all pre-existing theorems and proof procedures for them are directly applicable to our development. There is no need for the indirection and tedium of explicitly invoking the semantic rules of some calculus, program logic or programming language semantics.

This approach, while convenient, leaves two gaps in the verification story:

1. Any properties we prove are about a mathematical function in the HOL4 logic, and do not apply to the real program that runs outside of the logic, other than by a questionable informal analogy between functions in logic and procedures in a programming language.
2. Software must interact with its environment in order to be useful, but our toy verification example above is a pure functional program, i.e., it is unable to interact with its environment.

An overarching goal of the CakeML project[2] [20] is to create a verification framework that plugs both of these gaps, so as to maintain a small trusted computing base (TCB) without sacrificing the convenience of working with shallow embeddings. Our focus in this paper is how to plug the second gap. In particular, we are concerned with verifying impure functional programs in CakeML that interact with their environment in ways typically required by console applications: programs that receive input via command-line arguments and stdin, read from and write to the file system, and produce output via stdout and stderr.

The other components of this overarching story have largely been established in previous work. Our proof-producing translation [26] allows us to generate executable code from shallow embeddings for the pure parts of our code, so that shallow verifications done at the algorithm level in HOL4 can be automatically transferred to CakeML programs that implement the algorithm. Our program logic [13] based on characteristic formulae (CF) [7] supports the verification of the impure parts of CakeML programs. Finally, our verified compiler [33] allows us to transport whatever properties we verified using translation and CF to properties about concrete machine code for several mainstream architectures (x86-64, ARMv6, ARMv8, RISC-V, MIPS).

Our specific contributions in this paper are:

- We enrich CakeML with a low-level programmer's model of file I/O, which goes far beyond our previous toy read-only file I/O model [13]. The new model of read and write operations covers the non-determinism that is inherent in the fact that e.g. writing n bytes to a stream may sometimes fail to write all n bytes, or indeed any bytes at all.
- On top of this file I/O model, we write a verified TextIO library in CakeML that abstracts away from the low-level details. Instead it exposes an interface of familiar high-level functions for file handling, such as inputLine. These

---

[2] https://cakeml.org/.

functions do not expose the aforementioned non-determinism to the user, e.g. `inputLine` is verified to always return the first line of the stream, provided the file system satisfies a natural liveness property.
- We present a case study of a verified implementation of the `diff` and `patch` command-line utilities.

The case study serves two main purposes. First, it shows that our approach can be used to verify interesting programs. Second, it illustrates how our specific contributions fit into the bigger picture of our verification story. The bulk of the verification effort is cast in terms of a shallow embedding of the core algorithms, such as the auxiliary function `longest` above. Yet our file system model and `TextIO` library, together with our proof-producing translation, CF program logic, and verified compilation, allow us to transfer our theorems about the core algorithm to theorems about the environmental interactions of the machine code that implements the algorithm.

The end-result is a theorem with a remarkably small TCB: the HOL4 theorem proving system[3]; a simple Standard ML program that writes the compiled bytes of machine code into a file; the linker that produces the executable; the loading and I/O facilities provided by the operating system as wrapped by the `read`, `write`, `open` and `close` functions of the C standard library; our model of making I/O system calls over our foreign function interface (FFI); and our machine code semantics. Together, these constitute the whole formalisation gap. Notably, we do not need to trust any code extraction procedure standing between the verified model of each application and its code-level implementation, nor do we need to trust the compiler and runtime system that bridge between source code and machine code.

All of our code and proofs are contained in CakeML's 2.1 release, available at https://code.cakeml.org/. The example programs are in the `examples` directory, and the file system model and library is in the `basis` directory. The `examples` directory also contains verified implementations of `cat`, `grep`, and `sort` that we have developed using the techniques and tools presented in this paper. For lack of space we will not discuss these other examples further.

The CF-verified functions of the `TextIO` library, which is the topic of this paper, have been used as opaque building blocks in a recent paper [15] on synthesis of impure CakeML code.

2   Overview

In this section, we present an overview of how we achieved our results: we first give background on how CakeML handles interaction with the outside world; then explain how we instantiate the mechanism to a model of file I/O; and how we build a verified `TextIO` library on top; and finally present a verification case study that uses the new `TextIO` library.

---

[3] https://hol-theorem-prover.org/.

CakeML supports interaction with the environment via a foreign function interface (FFI) based on byte arrays that is very open-ended: the precise implementation of the FFI is an external—and thus potentially unverified—program that must be linked with the output of the CakeML compiler.

At the source code level, CakeML programs may contain FFI calls, written #(p) s ba, where p is the FFI port name, s is an (immutable) string argument, and ba is a (mutable) byte array argument. The FFI call may read the contents of s and ba, affect the state of the external environment, and relay information back to the caller by writing to ba. After compilation this becomes a subroutine call to, e.g., the label ffiwrite if the port name happens to be write. This subroutine must be present in the FFI implementation we link with.

The semantics of the CakeML language is parameterised on an *FFI oracle* that describes the effect of FFI calls on the outside environment. For each port name used by the program under consideration, the FFI oracle provides an *oracle function* of type:

$$\text{byte list} \rightarrow \text{byte list} \rightarrow {}'state \rightarrow (\text{byte list} \times {}'state) \text{ option}$$

The semantics of the aforementioned FFI call #(p) s ba is then given by $p\_oracle\ st\ s\ ba$, where st is the current state of the external environment. If $p\_oracle\ st\ s\ ba = \text{Some }(st', ba')$, the result is that the state of the environment is updated to st' and the contents of ba' are written to ba. If the oracle returns None, the FFI call fails.

The design described above allows us to enrich CakeML with our file system model by instantiating, rather than modifying, its semantics: our file system model is simply an FFI oracle. Specifically, the ${}'state$ type variable above is instantiated to a concrete type that models the file system. It describes which files are present and their contents, the set of file descriptors currently in use, and a *non-determinism oracle* for modelling the possibility that reading and writing may process fewer characters than expected. We define oracle functions for standard file system operations—write, read, open_in, open_out, and close—that describe their expected behaviour in terms of state updates to the file system model. (Sect. 3.2)

For each of the file system operations described above, we supply an implementation of the corresponding FFI call. These are simple C functions that are responsible for unmarshalling the byte array it receives from CakeML into the format that, e.g., the write standard library function expects. For the purposes of our verification story, we trust that the behaviour of these C functions is correctly modelled by the oracle functions described above. Hence we have strived to keep their implementations simple enough so that it is reasonable to assess their correctness by inspection. (Sect. 3.1)

We implement and verify a TextIO library for CakeML and integrate it into CakeML's basis library. The library is written entirely in the CakeML language and verified with respect to our file system model using the CF program logic. We handle low-level details such as non-deterministic write failures and marshalling of parameters to byte arrays in a way that does not expose them to the user during programming and verification. For example, the `TextIO.inputLine` function takes a file descriptor as argument, and returns the first unread line in the file as a string provided one exists and `NONE` otherwise. Its CF specification is kept at the same level of abstraction as the preceding sentence. (Sect. 4)

As a case study, we develop a verified implementation of the `diff` command-line tool. The core algorithm, i.e., computing a longest common subsequence of two sequences and presenting their deviations from this subsequence in the `diff` format, is developed and verified as a shallow embedding in HOL4. We verify the correctness of this algorithm against a specification taken directly from the POSIX standard description of `diff`. Thanks to the `TextIO` library described above, and the CakeML translator and CF program logic described in previous work, with minimal effort we can lift our theorems about a pure, shallowly embedded HOL function on sequences, to theorems about the I/O behaviour of a command-line tool. The main theorem says that the output produced on `stdout` is the same as the diff computed by the shallow embedding, when given as arguments two sequences corresponding to the contents of the files whose names are given as command-line arguments, and that appropriate error or usage messages are printed to `stderr` when called for. Thanks to the CakeML compiler correctness theorem, we can further transfer this result to a theorem about the I/O behaviour of the resulting binary. (Sect. 5)

3   File System Interaction

The Foreign Function Interface allows us to call foreign—and thus potentially unverified—functions within CakeML programs. Each such function needs to be modelled by a function in HOL (the *FFI oracle*), and to establish trust, they should be carefully scrutinised for semantic equivalence. This is why we should define as few of them as possible, and their code must be kept simple.

We have implemented in C a small set of foreign functions for command-line arguments and file system operations, enough to write the examples which will be described in Sect. 5 and Appendix A. In this section we present the file system FFI, and describe how we model the file system itself.

3.1   File System Model

We want to be able to treat input and output operations in a uniform manner on both conventional files, which are identified by a filename, and streams, especially the standard streams `stdin`, `stdout` and `stderr`. The datatype *inode* models a file system object as being either a file with an associated path, or a stream with an associated name.

```
Datatype inode = UStream mlstring | File mlstring
```

We model the state of the file system using the following record datatype:

```
IO_fs = <|
  inode_tbl : (inode, char list) alist;
  files : (mlstring, mlstring) alist;
  infds : (num, inode × num) alist;
  numchars : num llist
|>
```

The first two fields are association lists which describe the file system's contents: `files` maps each filename with its `inode` identifier (meant to be an argument of the File constructor); and `inode_tbl` associates each existing `inode` with its contents. Then, `infds` maps each file descriptor (encoded as a natural number) to an `inode` and an offset. The latter list could easily be extended to contain more detailed attributes, such as the mode on which a file has been opened (read-only, append mode, etc.). The last field is a non-determinism oracle modelled as a lazy list of natural numbers, whose purpose will be explained shortly.

Remark 1. This model could be made more detailed in many ways and is meant to grow over time. Its limitations can be understood as implicit assumptions on the correctness of CakeML programs using our file system FFI. For example, we assume that the program has exclusive access to the file system (i.e. no concurrent program writes to the same files as ours); file permissions are ignored (`inode_tbl` will need to be extended to take this into account); file contents are assumed to be finite (infinite contents could have been used to model pipes fed by another program running concurrently); streams are assumed to be distinct from regular files, although in practice standard streams also correspond to named files (e.g./dev/std* on Linux). There is also no representation of the directory structure of the file system: the `files` field can be seen as a unique directory listing all the existing files. This simple model is nonetheless sufficient to reason about interesting examples (detailed in Sect. 5) and to show the feasibility of more involved features.

Foreign function implementations form part of our trusted computing base, so we want them to be small, simple and easily inspectable. Thus, the C implementation for the write operation—and respectively for read, open and close—will be a simple wrapper around C's `write` function. We choose `write` because it is well specified (see POSIX standard [17, p. 2310]), and because it is the most low-level entry point available to us that does not commit us to the particulars of any one operating system.

The main issue with `write` is that it is not deterministic: given a number of characters to write, it may not write all of them—and possibly none—depending on various factors. Some factors are included in our model (e.g. whether the end of the file is reached) but others like signal interruptions are not. This is the non-determinism that we model with the numchars oracle. More precisely, numchars is a lazy list of integers whose head is popped on each read or write operation to bound the number of read/written characters.

$\vdash$ write fd n $chars$ $fs =$
  do
    (ino, off) $\leftarrow$ assoc fs.infds fd;
    $content$ $\leftarrow$ assoc fs.inode_tbl ino;
    assert $(n \leq$ length $chars)$;
    assert $(fs$.numchars $\neq \,[\![\,]\!])$;
    $strm$ $\leftarrow$ lhd fs.numchars;
    let k $=$ min n $strm$
    in
     Some
      $(k,$
       fsupdate fs fd 1 $(off + k)$
        (take off $content$ @ take k $chars$ @ drop $(off + k)$ $content))$
  od

Fig. 1. Write operation on files in HOL

We can now specify basic operations on the file system, namely open, close, read and write, in terms of our file system model. Here write is the most interesting one and the rest of the section will mostly focus on it. We give the definition of write in Fig. 1, which informally can be read: given a file descriptor, a number of characters to write, a list of characters to write, and a file system state, write looks up the inode and offset associated with the file descriptor, fetches its contents, asserts that there are enough characters to write and that the lazy list is not empty. Its head is then used to decide how many characters at most will be written. Then, the number of written characters is returned, and the file system is updated using fsupdate, which drops one element of the lazy list, shifts the offset and updates the contents of the file accordingly.

3.2 File System FFI

We will now take a closer look at the C-side FFI implementation and its HOL oracle, focusing again on the write operation. The C type of such a function is

```
void ffiwrite (unsigned char *c, long clen, unsigned char *a, long alen)
```

where clen and alen are the respective lengths of the arrays c of immutable arguments and a of mutable arguments/outputs. On the HOL side, this corresponds to an oracle function of type

$$\text{byte list} \rightarrow \text{byte list} \rightarrow \,'state \rightarrow (\text{byte list} \times \,'state) \text{ option}$$

where the argument of type $'state$ represents a resource on which the function has an effect—which in our case will be the file system state—and the inputs of type byte list encode respectively the immutable argument c and the state of the array a at the beginning of the call. The return type is an option type in order to handle malformed inputs, which returns the state of the array a after the call, and the new state of the resource.

In the case of the write function, this corresponds to the HOL specification shown in Fig. 2. It takes the file descriptor (encoded as eight bytes in c), the number of characters to write as well as an offset from a (both encoded on two bytes in the second array), and calls the write operation (defined in Fig. 1) on the file system with these parameters. As write may fail to write all the requested bytes, it may be necessary to call it several times successively on decreasing suffixes of the data, which is why we use an offset to avoid unnecessary copying. After this, the first byte of the array is updated with a return code (0 on success, 1 on failure) followed by the number of written bytes, encoded on two bytes.

$$
\begin{aligned}
&\vdash \mathsf{ffi\_write}\ c\ (a_0 :: a_1 :: a_2 :: a_3 :: a)\ \mathit{fs} = \\
&\quad \mathsf{do} \\
&\qquad \mathsf{assert}\ (\mathsf{length}\ c = 8); \\
&\qquad \mathit{fd}\ \leftarrow\ \mathsf{Some}\ (\mathsf{byte8\_to\_int}\ c); \\
&\qquad n\ \leftarrow\ \mathsf{Some}\ (\mathsf{byte2\_to\_int}\ [a_0;\ a_1]); \\
&\qquad \mathit{off}\ \leftarrow\ \mathsf{Some}\ (\mathsf{byte2\_to\_int}\ [a_2;\ a_3]); \\
&\qquad \mathsf{assert}\ (\mathsf{length}\ a \geq n + \mathit{off}); \\
&\qquad \mathsf{do} \\
&\qquad\quad (\mathit{nw},\mathit{fs'})\ \leftarrow\ \mathsf{write}\ \mathit{fd}\ n\ (\mathsf{implode}\ (\mathsf{drop}\ \mathit{off}\ a))\ \mathit{fs}; \\
&\qquad\quad \mathsf{Some}\ (0w :: \mathsf{int\_to\_byte2}\ \mathit{nw}\ @\ a_3 :: a,\mathit{fs'}) \\
&\qquad \mathsf{od} +\!\!+ \mathsf{Some}\ (1w :: a_1 :: a_2 :: a_3 :: a,\mathit{fs}) \\
&\quad \mathsf{od}
\end{aligned}
$$

Fig. 2. Oracle function for `write`. The $+\!\!+$ operator returns the first argument unless it is None, and the second argument otherwise.

Note that the arbitrary, and fixed size of the inputs and outputs allow to address 2^{64} file descriptors and read/write 2^{16} bytes at once, which has not been a restriction in practice so far.

Now let's see how this FFI call is implemented in C. The other file system FFI functions are handled similarly. Note that we trust this implementation to behave according to its specification, namely ffi_write.

```c
void ffiwrite (unsigned char *c, long clen, unsigned char *a, long alen){
    assert(clen = 8);
    int fd = byte8_to_int(c);
    int n = byte2_to_int(a);
    int off = byte2_to_int(&a[2]);
    assert(alen >= n + off + 4);
    int nw = write(fd, &a[4 + off], n);
    if(nw < 0){ a[0] = 1; }
    else{ a[0] = 0; int_to_byte2(nw,&a[1]); }
}
```

All it does is the corresponding system call, and marshalling its inputs and output between integers and fixed-sized sets of bytes using some easily-verifiable marshalling functions (bytes*_to_int and int_to_bytes*).

4   A Verified TextIO Library

In this section, we illustrate how we built a standard library of high-level input-output functions on top of the previously described foreign functions as well as their specification. For this, we first need to reason about the file system, i.e., express separation logic properties about it. We are then able to write and prove correctness properties about the file system operations in the CF program logic.

4.1   File System Properties

First, as we have seen in Sect. 3.2, when we make FFI calls from CakeML we use a mutable byte array for carrying input and output. The following property asserts that an array of length 2052 (i.e. 2048 plus 4 bytes to encode the two two-byte arguments) is allocated at the address iobuff_loc.

$$\vdash \mathsf{IOFS\_iobuff} = \mathsf{SEP\_EXISTS}\ v.\ \mathsf{W8ARRAY}\ \mathsf{iobuff\_loc}\ v * \&(\mathsf{length}\ v \geq 2052)$$

Then, any program involving write will almost surely require the following property on the file system's non-determinism oracle:

$$\vdash \mathsf{liveFS}\ \mathit{fs} \iff$$
$$\mathsf{linfinite}\ \mathit{fs}.\mathsf{numchars} \wedge$$
$$\mathsf{always}\ (\mathsf{eventually}\ (\lambda\, ll.\ \exists\, k.\ \mathsf{lhd}\ ll = \mathsf{Some}\ k \wedge k \neq 0))\ \mathit{fs}.\mathsf{numchars}$$

Indeed, according to Fig. 1, something can only be written if the head of *fs*.numchars is non-zero. To write at least one character, one thus has to try writing until it is actually done. This will succeed if the non-determinism oracle list contains a non-zero integer, and is characterised by the following temporal logic property:

$$\mathsf{eventually}\ (\lambda\, ll.\ \exists\, k.\ \mathsf{lhd}\ ll = \mathsf{Some}\ k \wedge k \neq 0)\ \mathit{fs}.\mathsf{numchars}$$

Then, to ensure that this property still holds after an arbitrary number of read or write operations, we need to ensure that it always holds and that the lazy list is infinite, hence the definition of liveFS. Another way to put it is that the file system will never block a write operation forever, which is not a strong assumption to make.

We wrap the previous property with other checks on the file system—namely that its open file descriptors can be encoded into eight bytes, and that they (as well as all valid filenames) are mapped to existing inodes—to state that the file system is well-formed.

$\vdash$ wfFS fs $\iff$
   ($\forall fd.$
     $fd \in$ fdom (alist_to_fmap fs.infds) $\Rightarrow$
     $fd \leq$ maxFD $\wedge$
     $\exists\, ino\ off.$
       assoc fs.infds $fd =$ Some $(ino, off)\ \wedge$
       $ino \in$ fdom (alist_to_fmap fs.inode_tbl)) $\wedge$
   ($\forall\, fname\ ino.$
     assoc fs.files $fname =$ Some $ino \Rightarrow$ File $ino \in$ fdom (alist_to_fmap fs.inode_tbl)) $\wedge$
   liveFS fs

Now here is the main property of file systems.

$$\vdash \text{IOFS } fs = \text{IOx fs\_ffi\_part } fs * \text{IOFS\_iobuff} * \&\text{wfFS } fs$$

It states that we have a buffer for file system FFI calls, and that the well-formed file system fs is actually the current file system.

More precisely, IOx fs_ffi_part fs means that there is a ghost state encoding a list of FFI calls whose successive compositions (like `ffi_write` from Fig. 2) produce the file system fs.

The latter property was heavily used when specifying various low-level I/O functions, but we need more convenient user-level properties. In particular, most programs using I/O will use the standard streams. Thus we need to ensure that they exist, are open on their respective file descriptors (i.e. 0, 1, and 2), and that standard output and error's offsets are at the end of the stream, all of which are ensured by the stdFS property.

The following property asserts that this is the case for the current file system and also abstracts away the value of fs.numchars.

$$\vdash \text{STDIO } fs = (\text{SEP\_EXISTS } ns.\ \text{IOFS } (fs \text{ with numchars} := ns)) * \&\text{stdFS } fs$$

Indeed, the value of this additional field is not relevant, and we only need to know that it makes the file system "live". It would otherwise be cumbersome to specify it, as we would need to know how many read and write calls have been made during the execution of the program, which itself depends on fs.numchars (the smaller its elements are, the higher the number of calls).

We also define convenient properties such as stdout fs out (and respectively for standard input and error), which states that the content of the standard output stream is out (and similarly for the other two streams), as well as the function add_stdout fs out which appends the string out at the end of the standard output of the file system fs to out. The specifications of `TextIO.output` and `TextIO.print` in Fig. 3 and of `diff` in Fig. 4 provide typical examples of their usage.

4.2   Library Implementation and Specifications

In the same way that a typical standard library is supposed to expose high-level functions to the user and hide their possibly intricate implementation, one of the main challenges of a verified standard library is to provide simple and reusable *specifications* for these functions so that users can build high-level verified programs on top of it. Once again, we take the `write` FFI call as a running example and build a user-level function `TextIO.output` which will be used in most of our examples in Sect. 5.

Now that we have an FFI call for `write`, we define (in CakeML's concrete syntax) a function `writei` which on file descriptor `fd` and integers `n` and `i`, encodes these inputs properly for the `write` FFI call, and keeps trying to write `n` bytes from the array `iobuff` from the offset `i` until it actually succeeds to write at least one byte.

As it is a quite low-level function, its specification won't be reproduced here, but the key point is that it requires the file system to be well-formed, and thus to verify the liveFS property. Its correctness, and especially termination, relies on the fact that, according to the latter property, the file system will always eventually write at least one byte. Its proof is mainly based on the following derived induction principle over lazy lists:

$$\vdash (\forall ll.\ P\ ll \lor \neg P\ ll \land Q\ (\text{the}\ (\mathsf{LTL}\ ll)) \Rightarrow Q\ ll) \Rightarrow$$
$$\forall ll.\ ll \neq [\![]\!] \Rightarrow \mathsf{always}\ (\mathsf{eventually}\ P)\ ll \Rightarrow Q\ ll$$

In words: in order to prove that Q holds for a non-empty lazy list such that P always eventually holds, it suffices to prove a) that whenever P holds of a lazy list, so does Q, and b) whenever P does not hold and Q holds of the list's tail, Q holds of the entire list. In the proof these get instantiated so that P is a predicate stating that the next write operation will write at least one byte, and Q is the CF Hoare triple for `writei`.

The `writei` function takes care of some part of the non-determinism induced by the `write` system call. We can then use it to define a function `write` which will actually write all the required bytes and whose outcome is thus fully deterministic. But this is yet another intermediate function whose specification has a fair number of hypotheses and whose Hoare triple is quite involved. We thus define SML-like user-level functions like `TextIO.output` and `TextIO.print` whose specifications involve the high-level property STDIO defined in Sect. 4.1. The latter are given in Fig. 3, in the form app p f_v *args* P (POSTv *uv*. Q) essentially meaning that whenever the separation logic precondition P is satisfied, the function named f, on arguments *args* (related to HOL values with relations like FD, STRING or UNIT) terminates on a value *uv* which satisfies the postcondition Q.

From a user's perspective, these theorems simply state that on a standard file system, the return type of these functions is `unit` and they produce a standard file system, modified as expected.

⊢ FD *fd fdv* ∧ get_file_content *fs fd* = Some (*content,pos*) ∧ STRING *s sv* ⇒
  app *p* TextIO_output_v [*fdv*; *sv*] (STDIO *fs*)
    (POSTv *uv*.
        &UNIT () *uv* *
        STDIO (fsupdate *fs fd* 0 (*pos* + strlen *s*) (insert_atl (explode *s*) *pos content*)))
⊢ STRING *s sv* ⇒
  app *p* TextIO_print_v [*sv*] (STDIO *fs*)
    (POSTv *uv*. &UNIT () *uv* * STDIO (add_stdout *fs s*))

Fig. 3. Specifications for `TextIO.output` and `TextIO.print`

5   Case Study: A Verified Diff

In this section, we present verified implementations of `diff` and `patch`, using the method described in preceding sections. For space reasons the presentation here will focus mostly on `diff`. The end product is a verified x86-64 binary, which is available for download[4]. We focus on implementing the default behaviour. Hence it falls somewhat short of being a drop-in replacement for, e.g., GNU `diff`: we do not support the abundance of command-line options that full implementations of the POSIX specification deliver.

At the heart of `diff` lies the notion of *longest common subsequence* (LCS). A list *s* is a *subsequence* of *t* if by removing elements from *t* we can obtain *s*. *s* is a *common subsequence* of *t* and *u* if it is a subsequence of both, and an LCS if no other subsequence of *t* and *u* is longer than it.

lcs *s t u* ⟺
common_subsequence *s t u* ∧
∀ *s'*. common_subsequence *s' t u* ⇒ length *s'* ≤ length *s*

`diff` first computes an LCS of the two input files' lines[5], and then presents any lines not present in the LCS as additions, deletions or changes as the case might require.

We implement and verify shallow embeddings for a sequence of progressively more realistic LCS algorithms: a naive algorithm that runs in exponential time with respect to the number of lines; a dynamic programming version that runs in quadratic time; and a further optimisation that achieves linear best-case performance[6].

On top of the latter LCS algorithm, we write a shallow embedding diff_alg *l l'* that given two lists of lines returns a list of lines corresponding to the verbatim output of `diff`. To give the flavour of the implementation, we show the main loop that diff_alg uses:

---

[4] https://cakeml.org/vstte18/x86_binaries.zip.

[5] The LCS is not always unique: both [*a, c*] and [*b, c*] are LCSes of [*a, b, c*] and [*b, a, c*].

[6] There are algorithms that do better than quadratic time for practically interesting special cases [3]; we leave their verification for future work.

```
diff_with_lcs [] l n l' n' =
  if l = [] ∧ l' = [] then [] else diff_single l n l' n'
diff_with_lcs (f::r) l n l' n' =
  let (ll,lr) = split ((=) f) l; (l'l,l'r) = split ((=) f) l'
  in
    if ll = [] ∧ l'l = [] then
      diff_with_lcs r (tl lr) (n + 1) (tl l'r) (n + 1)
    else
      diff_single ll n l'l n' @
      diff_with_lcs r (tl lr) (n + length ll + 1) (tl l'r)
        (n' + length l'l + 1)
```

The first argument to `diff_with_lcs` is the LCS of l and l', and the numerical arguments are line numbers. If the LCS is empty, all remaining lines in l and l' must be additions and deletions, respectively; the auxiliary function diff_single presents them accordingly. If the LCS is non-empty, partition l and l' around their first occurrences of the first line in the LCS. Anything to the left is presented as additions or deletions, and anything to the right is recursed over using the remainder of the LCS.

We take our specification of `diff` directly from its POSIX standard description [17, p. 2658]:

The diff utility shall compare the contents of *file1* and *file2* and write to standard output a list of changes necessary to convert *file1* into *file2*. This list should be minimal. No output shall be produced if the files are identical.

For each sentence in the above quote, we prove a corresponding theorem about our `diff` algorithm:

$$\vdash \text{patch\_alg (diff\_alg } l \ r) \ l = \text{Some } r$$
$$\vdash \text{lcs } l \ r \ r' \Rightarrow$$
$$\text{length (filter is\_patch\_line (diff\_alg } r \ r')) =$$
$$\text{length } r + \text{length } r' - 2 \times \text{length } l$$
$$\vdash \text{diff\_alg } l \ l = []$$

The convertibility we formalise as the property that `patch` cancels `diff`. The minimality theorem states that the number of change lines printed is precisely the number of lines that deviate from the files' LCS[7].

We apply our synthesis tool to diff_alg, and write a CakeML I/O wrapper around it:

```
fun diff' fname1 fname2 =
  case TextIO.inputLinesFrom fname1 of
      NONE => TextIO.print_err (notfound_string fname1)
    | SOME lines1 =>
```

---

[7] Note that this differs from the default behaviour of the GNU implementation of diff, which uses heuristics that do not compute the minimal list if doing so would be prohibitively expensive.

```
      case TextIO.inputLinesFrom fname2 of
          NONE => TextIO.print_err (notfound_string fname2)
        | SOME lines2 => TextIO.print_list (diff_alg lines1 lines2)
  fun diff u =
    case CommandLine.arguments () of
        (f1::f2::[]) => diff' f1 f2
      | _ => TextIO.print_err usage_string
```

We prove a CF specification shown in Fig. 4 stating that: if an unused file descriptor is available, and if there are two command-line arguments that are both valid filenames, the return value of diff_alg is printed to stdout; otherwise, an appropriate error message is printed to stderr. Note that we have a separating conjunction between the file system and command-line, despite the fact that both conjuncts describe the FFI state. This is sound since they are about two disjoint, non-interfering parts of the FFI state; for details we refer the reader to [13].

diff_sem cl fs =
   if length $cl = 3$ then
      if inFS_fname fs (EL 1 cl) then   ⊢ hasFreeFD fs ⇒
         if inFS_fname fs (EL 2 cl) then   app p diff_v [Conv None []]
            add_stdout fs (STDIO fs * CMDLN cl)
            (concat   (POSTv uv.
               (diff_alg (all_lines fs (EL 1 cl))   &UNIT () uv *
               (all_lines fs (EL 2 cl))))   STDIO (diff_sem cl fs) *
         else add_stderr fs (notfound_string (EL 2 cl))   CMDLN cl)
      else add_stderr fs (notfound_string (EL 1 cl))
   else add_stderr fs usage_string

Fig. 4. Semantics for diff (left) showing how it changes the file system state, and its specification (right) as a CF Hoare triple.

For an indication of where the effort went in this case study, we can compare the size of the source files dedicated to each part of the development. Definitions and proofs for LCS algorithms are 1098 lines of HOL script, and definitions and proofs for the diff and patch algorithms is 1270 lines. Translation of these algorithms to CakeML, and definition and verification of the CakeML I/O wrapper comprises 200 lines of proofs in total. Of these, 59 lines are tactic proofs for proving the CF specification from Fig. 4. These proofs are fairly routine and consist mostly of tactic invocations for unfolding the next step in the weakest precondition computation; in particular, none of it involves reasoning about file system internals. We conclude that our contributions in previous sections do indeed deliver on their promise: almost all our proof effort was cast in terms of shallow embeddings, yet our end product is a theorem about the I/O behaviour of the binary code that actually runs, and at no point did we have to sweat the small stuff with respect to the details of file system interaction.

6   Related Work

There are numerous impressive systems for verifying algorithms, including Why3 [11], Dafny [22], and F* [32] that focus on effective verification, but at the algorithmic level only. Here we focus on projects whose goal includes either generating code with a relatively small TCB, reasoning about file systems, or verification of Unix-style utilities.

Small-TCB Verification. One commonly used route to building verified systems is to use the unverified code extraction mechanisms that all modern interactive theorem provers have. The idea is that users verify properties of functions inside the theorem prover and then call routines that print the in-logic functions into source code for some mainstream functional programming language outside the theorem prover's logic. This is an effective way of working, as can be seen in CompCert [23] where the verified compile function is printed to OCaml before running. The printing step leaves a hole in the correctness argument: there is no theorem relating user-proved properties with how the extracted functions compile or run outside the logic. There has been work on verifying parts of the extraction mechanisms [12,24], but none of these close the hole completely. The CakeML toolchain is the first to provide a proof-producing code extraction mechanism that gives formal guarantees about the execution of the extracted code outside of the logic. In a slightly different way, ACL2 can efficiently execute code with no trusted printing step, since their logic is just pure, first-order Common Lisp. However, the Common Lisp compiler must then be trusted in a direct way, rather than only indirectly as part of the soundness of the proof assistant.

The above code extraction mechanisms treat functions in logic as if they were pure functional programs. This means that specifications can only make statements relating input values to output values; imperative features are not directly supported. The Imperative HOL [6] project addresses this issue by defining an extensible state monad in Isabelle/HOL and augmenting Isabelle/HOL's code extraction to map functions written in this monadic style to the corresponding imperative features of the external programming languages. This adds support for imperative features, but does not close the printing gap.

The above approaches expect users to write their algorithms in the normal style of writing functions in theorem provers. However, if users are happy to adapt to a style supported by a refinement framework, e.g., the Isabelle Refinement Framework [21] or Fiat [9], then significant imperative features can be introduced through proved or proof-producing refinements within the logic. The Isabelle Refinement Framework lets users derive fast imperative code by stepwise refinement from high-level abstract descriptions of algorithms. It targets Imperative HOL, which again relies on unverified code extraction. Fiat aims to be a mostly automatic refinement engine that derives efficient code from high-level specifications. The original version of Fiat required use of Coq's unverified code extraction. However, more recent versions seem to perform refinement all the way down to assembly code [8]. The most recent versions amount to proof-producing compilation inside the logic of Coq. Instead of proving that the compiler will always produce semantically compatible code, in the proof-producing setting, each run of the tools produces a certificate theorem explaining that this compilation produced a semantically compatible result.

The Verified Software Toolchain VST [4] shares many of the goals of our effort here, and provides some of the same end-to-end guarantees. VST builds a toolchain based on the CompCert compiler, in particular they place a C dialect, which they call Verifiable C, on top of CompCert C minor and provide a powerful separation logic-style program logic for this verification-friendly version of C. VST can deal with input and output and, of course, with highly imperative code. Much like CakeML, VST supports using an oracle for predicting the meaning of instructions that interact with the outside world [16], though to the best of our knowledge this feature has not been used to reason about file system interaction. VST can provide end-to-end theorems about executable code since verified programs can be compiled through CompCert, and CompCert's correctness theorem transfers properties proved at the Verifiable C level down to the executable. The major difference wrt. the CakeML toolchain is that in VST one is always proving properties of imperative C code. In contrast, with CakeML, the pure functional parts can be developed as conventional logic functions in a shallow embedding, i.e. no complicated separation logic gets in the way, while imperative features and I/O are supported by characteristic formulae. We offer similar end-to-end guarantees by composing seamlessly with the verified CakeML compiler.

The on-going CertiCoq project [2] aims to do for Coq what CakeML has done for HOL4. CertiCoq is constructing a verified compiler from a deeply embedded version of Gallina, the language of function definitions in the Coq logic, to the C minor intermediate language in CompCert and from there via CompCert to executable code. This would provide verified code extraction for Coq, that is similar to CakeML's partly proof-producing and partly verified code extraction. In their short abstract [2], the developers state that this will only produce pure functional programs. However, they aim for interoperability with C and thus might produce a framework where pure functions are produced from CertiCoq, and the imperative parts and I/O parts are verified in VST.

File Systems and Unix-Style Utilities. There is a rather substantial literature on file system modelling and verification [1,5,10,14,30], but comparatively little work on reasoning about user programs on top of file systems. An exception is Ntzik and Gardner [28], who define a program logic for reasoning about client programs of the POSIX file system. Their emphasis is on directory structure and pathname traversal, which we do not consider on our model, but apart from this, the two models are equivalent (our `files` field behaves as a single directory containing all file names). The programs they consider are written in a simple while language enriched with file system operations; this is sufficient for their aims since their aim is to study the correctness of file system algorithms in the abstract, not binary correctness of implementations as in the present paper. As a case study they consider the `rm -r` algorithm, in which they expose bugs in several known implementations.

Kosmatov et al. [34] mention a verification of the `Get_Line` function in Spark ADA [25].[8] The file system is modelled by ghost variables that represent the file contents and current position of the file under consideration. The `fgets` function from `libc` is annotated with a contract that describes its behaviour in terms of updates on the ghost variables, and is thus part of the TCB in the same way as the system calls that we model by the FFI oracle is part of our TCB. This effort uncovered several long-standing bugs in the implementation of `Get_Line`.

In terms of investigating `diff` from a formal methods point of view, Khanna et al. [19] study the three-way `diff` algorithm and attempt to determine what its specification is; the surprising conclusion is that it satisfies few, if any, of the properties one might expect it to. It does not attempt to verify two-way `diff`, which is the topic of the present paper; instead, it takes the properties of `diff` that we prove in Sect. 5 as given.

Recently, Jeannerod et al. [18] verified an interpreter for a shell-like language called CoLiS using Why3. The model of the underlying file system and the behaviour of external commands is kept abstract, since the paper's main focus is on the CoLiS language itself. Verification of shell scripts that invoke verified external commands such as our `diff` in, e.g., the setting of Jeannerod et al. extended with a file system model, would be an interesting direction for future work.

7 Conclusion

We have demonstrated that the CakeML approach can be used to develop imperative programs with I/O for which we have true end-to-end correctness theorems. The applications are verified down to the concrete machine code that runs on the CPU, subject to reasonable, and documented, assumptions about the underlying operating system. Verifying these applications demonstrates how it is possible to separate the high-level proof task, such as proofs about longest common subsequence algorithms, from the details of interacting with files and processing command-line arguments. In this way, the proof task naturally mimics the modular construction of the code.

Acknowledgements. The first and fourth authors were supported by EPSRC Grant EP/N028759/1, UK. The second and fifth authors were partly supported by the Swedish Research Council. We would also like to thank the anonymous reviewers for their constructive and insightful comments and corrections.

A   Appendix: Further Example Programs

For the benefit of readers, we describe our verified implementations of the `grep`, `sort`, and `cat` command-line utilities.

---

[8] The verification is described in more detail in a blog post by Yannick Moy: https://blog.adacore.com/formal-verification-of-legacy-code.

A.1   Cat

A verified `cat` implementation was presented in our previous work on CF [13]. The `cat` implementation presented here differs in two respects: first, it is verified with respect to a significantly more low-level file system model (see Sect. 3.1). Second, it has significantly improved performance, since it is implemented in terms of more low-level I/O primitives. Hence this example demonstrates that reasonably performant I/O verified with respect to a low-level I/O model is feasible in our setting. Here is the code:

```
fun pipe_2048 fd1 fd2 =
   let val nr = TextIO.read fd1 2048 in
      if nr = 0 then 0 else (TextIO.write fd2 nr 0; nr) end

fun do_onefile fd =
   if pipe_2048 fd TextIO.stdOut > 0 then do_onefile fd else ();

fun cat fnames =
   case fnames of
      [] => ()
   | f::fs => (let val fd = TextIO.openIn f in
                        do_onefile fd; TextIO.close fd; cat fs end)
```

The difference over the previous implementation is `pipe_2048`, which gains efficiency by requesting 2048 characters at a time from the input stream, rather than single characters as previously. We elide its straightforward CF specification, which essentially states that the output produced on `stdout` is the concatenation of the file contents of the filenames given as command line arguments. The `cat` implementation above does not handle exceptions thrown by `TextIO.openIn`; hence the specification assumes that all command line arguments are valid names of existing files.

A.2   Sort

The sort program reads all of the lines in from a list of files given on the command-line, puts the lines into an array, sorts them using Quicksort, and then prints out the contents of the array. The proof that the printed output contains all of the lines of the input files, and in sorted order, is tedious, but straightforward.

We do not use an existing Quicksort implementation, but write and verify one from scratch. Unlike the various list-based Quicksort algorithms found in HOL, Coq, and Isabelle, we want an efficient array-based implementation of pivoting. Hence we implement something more akin to Hoare's original algorithm. We sweep two pointers inward from the start and end of the array, swapping elements when they are on the wrong side of the pivot. We stop when the pointers pass each other. Note that we pass in a comparison function: our Quicksort is parametric in the type of array elements.

```
fun partition cmp a pivot lower upper =
let
  fun scan_lower lower =
  let val lower = lower + 1 in
    if cmp (Array.sub a lower) pivot
    then scan_lower lower
    else lower end

  fun scan_upper upper = ...

  fun part_loop lower upper =
  let
    val lower = scan_lower lower
    val upper = scan_upper upper in
    if lower < upper
    then let val v = Array.sub a lower in
        (Array.update a lower (Array.sub a upper);
        Array.update a upper v;
        part_loop lower upper)
      end
    else upper end in
  part_loop (lower - 1) (upper + 1) end;
```

Because this is intrinsically imperative code, we do not use the synthesis tool, but instead verify it with CF directly. The only tricky thing about the proof is working out the invariants for the various recursive functions, which are surprisingly subtle, for an algorithm so appealingly intuitive.

Our approach to verifying the algorithm is to assume a correspondence between the CakeML values in the array, and HOL values that have an appropriate ordering on them. The Quicksort algorithm needs that ordering to be a *strict weak order*. This is a less restrictive assumption than requiring it to be a linear order (strict or otherwise). Roughly speaking, this will allow us to assume that unrelated elements are equivalent, even when they are not equal. Hence, we can sort arrays that hold various kinds of key/value pairs, where there are duplicate keys which might have different values.

$$\begin{aligned}
\textsf{strict\_weak\_order}\ r \iff \\
\textsf{transitive}\ r \land (\forall x\ y.\ r\ x\ y \Rightarrow \neg r\ y\ x) \land \\
\textsf{transitive}\ (\lambda x\ y.\ \neg r\ x\ y \land \neg r\ y\ x)
\end{aligned}$$

Even though we are not using the synthesis tool, we do use its refinement invariant combinators to maintain the CakeML/HOL correspondence. This enforces a mild restriction that our comparison function must be pure, but greatly simplifies the proof by allowing us to reason about ordering and permutation naturally in HOL.

The following is our correctness theorem for partition. We assume that there is a strick weak order cmp that corresponds to the CakeML value passed in as the comparison. We also assume some arbitrary refinement invariant a on the elements of the array. The $\_ \to \_$ combinator lifts refinement invariants to functions.

$\vdash$ strict_weak_order $cmp \wedge (a \to a \to \text{Bool})\ cmp\ cmp\_v\ \wedge$
  pairwise $a\ elems_2\ elem\_vs_2 \wedge elem\_vs_2 \neq [\,] \wedge$
  $\text{INT}\ (\&\text{length}\ elem\_vs_1)\ lower\_v\ \wedge$
  $\text{INT}\ (\&(\text{length}\ elem\_vs_1 + \text{length}\ elem\_vs_2 - 1))\ upper\_v\ \wedge$
  $(pivot, pivot\_v) \in \text{set}\ (\text{front}\ (\text{zip}\ (elems_2, elem\_vs_2))) \Rightarrow$
  app ffi_p partition_v $[cmp\_v;\ arr\_v;\ pivot\_v;\ lower\_v;\ upper\_v]$
    (ARRAY arr_v ($elem\_vs_1$ @ $elem\_vs_2$ @ $elem\_vs_3$))
    (POSTv $p\_v.$
        SEP_EXISTS $part_1\ part_2.$
            ARRAY arr_v
              ($elem\_vs_1$ @ $part_1$ @ $part_2$ @ $elem\_vs_3$) $*$
              &partition_pred cmp (length $elem\_vs_1$) $p\_v\ pivot$
                $elems_2\ elem\_vs_2\ part_1\ part_2$)

We can read the above as follows, starting in the conclusion of the theorem. Partition takes 5 arguments cmp_v, arr_v, $pivot\_v$, $lower\_v$, and $upper\_v$, all of which are CakeML values. As a precondition, the array's contents can be split into 3 lists of CakeML values $elems\_vs_1$, $elems\_vs_2$, and $elems\_vs_3$.[9] Now looking at the assumptions, the length of $elem\_vs_1$ must be the integer value for the lower pointer. A similar relation must hold for the upper pointer, so that $elem\_vs_2$ is the list of elements in-between the pointers, inclusive. We also must assume that the pivot element is in segment to be partitioned (excluding the last element).

The postcondition states that the partition code will terminate, and that there exists two partitions. The array in the heap now contains the two partitions instead of $elem\_vs_2$. The partition_pred predicate (definition omitted), ensures that the two partitions are non-empty, permute $elem\_vs_2$, and that the elements of the first are not greater than the pivot, and the elements of the second are not less. These last two points use the shallowly embedded cmp and $elems_2$, rather than cmp_v and $elems\_vs_2$.

A.3   grep

grep <regex> <file> <file>... prints to stdout every line from the files that matches the regular expression <regex>. Unlike sort, diff and patch which need to see the full file contents before producing output, grep can process lines one at a time and produce output after each line. The main loop of grep reads a line, and prints it if it satisfies the predicate m:

```
fun print_matching_lines m prefix fd =
  case TextIO.inputLine fd of NONE => ()
  | SOME ln => (if m ln then (TextIO.print prefix; TextIO.print ln)
               else ();
               print_matching_lines m prefix fd)
```

---

[9] @ appends lists.

For each filename, we run the above loop if the file can be opened, and print an appropriate error message to `stderr` otherwise:

```
fun print_matching_lines_in_file m file =
  let val fd = TextIO.openIn file
  in (print_matching_lines m (String.concat[file,":"]) fd;
     TextIO.close fd)
  end handle TextIO.BadFileName =>
     TextIO.print_err (notfound_string file)
```

The latter function satisfies the following CF specification (eliding `stderr` output):

$$\vdash \mathsf{cf\_let}\ (\mathsf{Some}\ \text{``a''})\ (\mathsf{cf\_con}\ \mathsf{None}\ [\,])$$
$$(\mathsf{cf\_let}\ (\mathsf{Some}\ \text{``b''})$$
$$(\mathsf{cf\_app}\ p\ (\mathsf{Var}\ (\mathsf{Long}\ \text{``Commandline''}\ (\mathsf{Short}\ \text{``arguments''}))))$$
$$[\mathsf{Var}\ (\mathsf{Short}\ \text{``a''})])$$
$$(\mathsf{cf\_let}\ (\mathsf{Some}\ \text{``c''})$$
$$(\mathsf{cf\_app}\ p\ (\mathsf{Var}\ (\mathsf{Long}\ \text{``List''}\ (\mathsf{Short}\ \text{``hd''}))))\ [\mathsf{Var}\ (\mathsf{Short}\ \text{``b''})])$$
$$(\mathsf{cf\_let}\ (\mathsf{Some}\ \text{``d''})$$
$$(\mathsf{cf\_app}\ p\ (\mathsf{Var}\ (\mathsf{Long}\ \text{``IO''}\ (\mathsf{Short}\ \text{``inputLinesFrom''}))))$$
$$[\mathsf{Var}\ (\mathsf{Short}\ \text{``c''})])\dots)))\ st\ (\mathrm{CMDLN}\ cl * \mathrm{STDIO}\ fs)$$
$$(\mathrm{POSTv}\ uv.\dots)$$

The postcondition states that the output to `stdout` is precisely those lines in f that satisfy m, with f and a colon prepended to each line. The three assumptions mean, respectively: that f is a string without null characters, and fv is its corresponding deeply embedded CakeML value; that our view of the file system has a free file descriptor; and that m is a fully specified (i.e., lacking preconditions) function of type `char lang` and mv is the corresponding CakeML closure value.

The main function of `grep` is as follows:

```
fun grep u =
  case CommandLine.arguments () of
    [] => TextIO.print_err usage_string
  | [_] => TextIO.print_err usage_string
  | (regexp::files) =>
    case parse_regexp (String.explode regexp) of
      NONE => TextIO.print_err (parse_failure_string regexp)
    | SOME r =>
        List.app (fn file => print_matching_lines_in_file
                                (build_matcher r) file) files
```

`parse_regexp` and `build_matcher` are synthesised from a previous formalisation of regular expressions by Slind [31], based on Brzozowski derivatives [29].

The semantics of **grep** is given by the function **grep_sem**, which returns a tuple of output for **stdout** and **stderr**, respectively.

> grep_sem $(v_0::regexp::filenames)$ $fs =$
> if null $filenames$ then ("",explode usage_string)
> else
>   case parse_regexp $regexp$ of
>   None $\Rightarrow$ ("",explode (parse_failure_string (implode $regexp$)))
> | Some r $\Rightarrow$
>   let $l =$
>   map (grep_sem_file (regexp_lang r) fs)
>   (map implode $filenames$)
>   in (flat (map fst l),flat (map snd l))
> grep_sem _ $v_2 =$ ("",explode usage_string)

regexp_lang is a specification of build_matcher due to Slind, and grep_sem_-file is a semantics definition for print_matching_lines_in_file. The final CF specification states that the output to the std* streams are as in grep_sem, and has two premises: that there is an unused file descriptor, and that Brzozowski derivation terminates on the given regular expression [10].

References

1. Amani, S., et al.: Cogent: verifying high-assurance file system implementations. In: Conte, T., Zhou, Y. (eds.) Proceedings of the Twenty-First International Conference on Architectural Support for Programming Languages and Operating Systems, ASPLOS 2016, Atlanta, GA, USA, 2–6 April 2016, pp. 175–188. ACM (2016). https://doi.org/10.1145/2872362.2872404
2. Anand, A., et al.: CertiCoq: a verified compiler for Coq. In: Coq for Programming Languages (CoqPL) (2017)
3. Apostolico, A., Galil, Z. (eds.): Pattern Matching Algorithms. Oxford University Press, Oxford (1997)
4. Appel, A.W.: Verified software toolchain. In: Barthe, G. (ed.) ESOP 2011. LNCS, vol. 6602, pp. 1–17. Springer, Heidelberg (2011). https://doi.org/10.1007/978-3-642-19718-5_1
5. Arkoudas, K., Zee, K., Kuncak, V., Rinard, M.: Verifying a file system implementation. In: Davies, J., Schulte, W., Barnett, M. (eds.) ICFEM 2004. LNCS, vol. 3308, pp. 373–390. Springer, Heidelberg (2004). https://doi.org/10.1007/978-3-540-30482-1_32
6. Bulwahn, L., Krauss, A., Haftmann, F., Erkök, L., Matthews, J.: Imperative functional programming with Isabelle/HOL. In: Mohamed, O.A., Muñoz, C., Tahar, S. (eds.) TPHOLs 2008. LNCS, vol. 5170, pp. 134–149. Springer, Heidelberg (2008). https://doi.org/10.1007/978-3-540-71067-7_14

---

[10] Finding a termination proof for the kind of Brzozowski derivation we use is an open problem that is not addressed by Slind's work nor by the present paper. See, e.g., Nipkow and Traytel [27] for a discussion.

7. Charguéraud, A.: Characteristic formulae for the verification of imperative programs. In: Proceeding of the 16th ACM SIGPLAN International Conference on Functional Programming, ICFP 2011, pp. 418–430 (2011). https://doi.org/10.1145/2034773.2034828

8. Chlipala, A., et al.: The end of history? Using a proof assistant to replace language design with library design. In: Summit on Advances in Programming Languages (SNAPL). Schloss Dagstuhl - Leibniz-Zentrum fuer Informatik (2017). https://doi.org/10.4230/LIPIcs.SNAPL.2017.3

9. Delaware, B., Pit-Claudel, C., Gross, J., Chlipala, A.: Fiat: deductive synthesis of abstract data types in a proof assistant. In: Principles of Programming Languages (POPL), pp. 689–700. ACM (2015). https://doi.org/10.1145/2676726.2677006

10. Ernst, G., Schellhorn, G., Haneberg, D., Pfähler, J., Reif, W.: Verification of a virtual filesystem switch. In: Cohen, E., Rybalchenko, A. (eds.) VSTTE 2013. LNCS, vol. 8164, pp. 242–261. Springer, Heidelberg (2014). https://doi.org/10.1007/978-3-642-54108-7_13

11. Filliâtre, J.-C., Paskevich, A.: Why3—where programs meet provers. In: Felleisen, M., Gardner, P. (eds.) ESOP 2013. LNCS, vol. 7792, pp. 125–128. Springer, Heidelberg (2013). https://doi.org/10.1007/978-3-642-37036-6_8

12. Glondu, S.: Vers une certification de lextraction de Coq. Ph.D. thesis, Universit Paris Diderot (2012)

13. Guéneau, A., Myreen, M.O., Kumar, R., Norrish, M.: Verified characteristic formulae for CakeML. In: Yang, H. (ed.) ESOP 2017. LNCS, vol. 10201, pp. 584–610. Springer, Heidelberg (2017). https://doi.org/10.1007/978-3-662-54434-1_22

14. Heisel, M.: Specification of the Unix file system: a comparative case study. In: Alagar, V.S., Nivat, M. (eds.) AMAST 1995. LNCS, vol. 936, pp. 475–488. Springer, Heidelberg (1995). https://doi.org/10.1007/3-540-60043-4_72

15. Ho, S., Abrahamsson, O., Kumar, R., Myreen, M.O., Tan, Y.K., Norrish, M.: Proof-producing synthesis of CakeML with I/O and local state from monadic HOL functions. In: International Joint Conference on Automated Reasoning (IJCAR) (2018, to appear)

16. Hobor, A.: Oracle Semantics. Princeton University, Princeton (2008)

17. IEEE Computer Society, The Open Group: The open group base specifications issue 7. IEEE Std 1003.1, 2016 Edition (2016)

18. Jeannerod, N., Marché, C., Treinen, R.: A formally verified interpreter for a shell-like programming language. In: Paskevich, A., Wies, T. (eds.) VSTTE 2017. LNCS, vol. 10712, pp. 1–18. Springer, Cham (2017). https://doi.org/10.1007/978-3-319-72308-2_1

19. Khanna, S., Kunal, K., Pierce, B.C.: A formal investigation of Diff3. In: Arvind, V., Prasad, S. (eds.) FSTTCS 2007. LNCS, vol. 4855, pp. 485–496. Springer, Heidelberg (2007). https://doi.org/10.1007/978-3-540-77050-3_40

20. Kumar, R., Myreen, M.O., Norrish, M., Owens, S.: CakeML: a verified implementation of ML. In: POPL 2014: Proceedings of the 41st ACM SIGPLAN-SIGACT Symposium on Principles of Programming Languages, pp. 179–191. ACM Press, January 2014

21. Lammich, P.: Refinement to Imperative/HOL. In: Urban, C., Zhang, X. (eds.) ITP 2015. LNCS, vol. 9236, pp. 253–269. Springer, Cham (2015). https://doi.org/10.1007/978-3-319-22102-1_17

22. Leino, K.R.M.: Dafny: an automatic program verifier for functional correctness. In: Clarke, E.M., Voronkov, A. (eds.) LPAR 2010. LNCS (LNAI), vol. 6355, pp. 348–370. Springer, Heidelberg (2010). https://doi.org/10.1007/978-3-642-17511-4_20

23. Leroy, X.: A formally verified compiler back-end. J. Autom. Reason. **43**(4), 363–446 (2009)
24. Letouzey, P.: Extraction in Coq: an overview. In: Beckmann, A., Dimitracopoulos, C., Löwe, B. (eds.) CiE 2008. LNCS, vol. 5028, pp. 359–369. Springer, Heidelberg (2008). https://doi.org/10.1007/978-3-540-69407-6_39
25. McCormick, J.W.: Building High Integrity Applications with Spark ADA. Cambridge University Press, Cambridge (2015)
26. Myreen, M.O., Owens, S.: Proof-producing translation of higher-order logic into pure and stateful ML. J. Funct. Program. **24**(2–3), 284–315 (2014)
27. Nipkow, T., Traytel, D.: Unified decision procedures for regular expression equivalence. In: Klein, G., Gamboa, R. (eds.) ITP 2014. LNCS, vol. 8558, pp. 450–466. Springer, Cham (2014). https://doi.org/10.1007/978-3-319-08970-6_29
28. Ntzik, G., Gardner, P.: Reasoning about the POSIX file system: local update and global pathnames. In: Aldrich, J., Eugster, P. (eds.) Proceedings of the 2015 ACM SIGPLAN International Conference on Object-Oriented Programming, Systems, Languages, and Applications, OOPSLA 2015, part of SPLASH 2015, Pittsburgh, PA, USA, 25–30 October 2015, pp. 201–220. ACM (2015). https://doi.org/10.1145/2814270.2814306
29. Owens, S., Reppy, J.H., Turon, A.: Regular-expression derivatives re-examined. J. Funct. Program. **19**(2), 173–190 (2009). https://doi.org/10.1017/S0956796808007090
30. Ridge, T., Sheets, D., Tuerk, T., Giugliano, A., Madhavapeddy, A., Sewell, P.: SibyLFS: formal specification and oracle-based testing for POSIX and real-world file systems. In: Miller, E.L., Hand, S. (eds.) Proceedings of the 25th Symposium on Operating Systems Principles, SOSP 2015, Monterey, CA, USA, 4–7 October 2015, pp. 38–53. ACM (2015). https://doi.org/10.1145/2815400.2815411
31. Slind, K.L.: High performance regular expression processing for cross-domain systems with high assurance requirements. Presented at the Third Workshop on Formal Methods And Tools for Security (FMATS3) (2014)
32. Swamy, N., et al.: Dependent types and multi-monadic effects in F*. In: 43rd ACM SIGPLAN-SIGACT Symposium on Principles of Programming Languages (POPL), pp. 256–270. ACM, January 2016. https://www.fstar-lang.org/papers/mumon/
33. Tan, Y.K., Myreen, M.O., Kumar, R., Fox, A., Owens, S., Norrish, M.: A new verified compiler backend for CakeML. In: ICFP 2016: Proceedings of the 21th ACM SIGPLAN International Conference on Functional Programming, pp. 60–73. ACM Press, September 2016
34. Kosmatov, N., Marché, C., Moy, Y., Signoles, J.: Static versus dynamic verification in Why3, Frama-C and SPARK 2014. In: Margaria, T., Steffen, B. (eds.) ISoLA 2016. LNCS, vol. 9952, pp. 461–478. Springer, Cham (2016). https://doi.org/10.1007/978-3-319-47166-2_32

TWAM: A Certifying Abstract Machine for Logic Programs

Rose Bohrer$^{(\boxtimes)}$ⓘ and Karl Craryⓘ

Carnegie Mellon University, Pittsburgh, PA 15213, USA
crary@cs.cmu.edu

Abstract. Type-preserving (or typed) compilation uses typing derivations to certify correctness properties of compilation. We have designed
and implemented a typed compiler for an idealized logic programming
language we call T-Prolog. The crux of our approach is a new *certifying
abstract machine* which we call the Typed Warren Abstract Machine
(TWAM). The TWAM has a dependent type system strong enough
to show programs obey a semantics based on provability in first-order
logic (FOL). We present a soundness metatheorem which (going beyond
the guarantees provided by most typed compilers) constitutes a partial
behavior correctness guarantee: well-typed TWAM programs are sound
proof search procedures with respect to a FOL signature. We argue why
this guarantee is a natural choice for significant classes of logic programs.
This metatheorem justifies our design and implementation of a certifying
compiler from T-Prolog to TWAM.

1   Introduction

Compiler verification is important because compilers are essential and because
compiler bugs are easy to introduce, yet often difficult to catch. Most work on
compiler verification has been done in the setting of imperative or functional
programming; little has been done for logic programming. The most successful compilers [16,17] use an approach we will call *direct verification*, showing
that compilation of any valid program results in a refinement thereof. Multiple
approaches have been tried for logic programming, but none have resulted in a
executable verified compiler for logic programs.

Compiler verification is an equally interesting problem in the case of logic
programming. Logic programs are often easier to write correctly than programs
in other paradigms, because a logic program is very close to being its own specification. However, the correctness advantages of logic programming cannot be
fully realized without compiler verification. Beyond the intellectual interest in
compiler correctness, there is a practical concern for correctness of logic program
compilation: practical implementations can be large. For example, SWI-Prolog is
estimated at over 600,000 lines of code [36]. While our certifying compiler is much
smaller, it provides a natural first step toward production-scale verification.

© Springer Nature Switzerland AG 2018
R. Piskac and P. Rümmer (Eds.): VSTTE 2018, LNCS 11294, pp. 112–134, 2018.
https://doi.org/10.1007/978-3-030-03592-1_7

Certifying compilation [23] is an approach to verification wherein the compiler outputs a formal certificate (in our case, type annotations) that the compiled program satisfies some desired property. Certifying compilation, unlike direct verification, has the advantage that the certificates can be distributed with the compiled code and checked independently by third parties, which is useful, e.g., for ascertaining trust in code downloaded from the Web. Additional engineering advantages include the ability to write multiple independent checkers for improved confidence, to share a certificate language between multiple compilers for the same language, or even to share the certificate language between compilers for different languages so long as the target language and specification language are suitable for both (e.g. they have similar dynamic semantics but different static semantics). The flip side is that compiler bugs are not found until the compiler sees a program that elicits the bug. In the worst case, bugs might be found by the compiler's users, rather than its developers.

Traditionally, the other cost of certifying compilation [23] is that only type and memory safety are certified, not dynamic correctness. In contrast, we certify *search soundness*, which is a non-trivial dynamic correctness property. This leap has only been made recently in the context imperative and functional languages [6,14]. We provide their logic programming counterpart. The sense in which we do so is made precise in Theorem 1.

Theorem 1 (*Search Soundness*): Let P be a logic program and Q a query formula. If query ?- Q. succeeds on program P, then $P \vdash \sigma(Q)$ is derivable in first-order (minimal) logic for some substitution σ.

We choose not to certify completeness with respect to, e.g., Prolog's depth-first semantics. For important classes of programs (typecheckers, proofcheckers, expert systems), soundness is fundamental: Checkers should accept only valid programs and valid proofs, while expert systems should provide only justified advice. Otherwise, a user might run an unsafe program, believe an untrue statement, or take unreasonable actions. Theorem 1 says that all such guarantees which hold of the source transfer to the compiled code. While completeness is desirable, soundness is our priority because preventing undesired behavior is often more impactful than ensuring desired behavior.

Ignoring completeness is valuable because it allows us to use provability as the semantics of logic programs, abstracting over operational details like proof search order. This imprecision is sometimes a feature, e.g. when we wish to let the compiler reorder clauses for performance.

In Theorem 1, the logic programs are programs in our T-Prolog language. In order to keep the correspondence with first-order logic close, T-Prolog enforces the occurs check and removes cut and negation-as-failure[1]. T-Prolog also supports (simple) inductive data types. Since untyped Prolog is most familiar, our examples are untyped Prolog, or equivalently all terms have the same type `term`.

The heart of this work is the development of our compilation target, the Typed Warren Abstract Machine (TWAM), a dependently-typed *certifying*

---

[1] See Sect. 6 for how these features might be supported.

abstract machine for logic programs, inspired by the Warren Abstract Machine (WAM) [35]. TWAM diverges from WAM in several ways to simplify our formal development: (1) we use continuation-passing style (CPS) for success continuations instead of a stack and (2) we sometimes replace compound instructions (such as those for managing backtracking) with a smaller set of simpler, more orthogonal instructions. As formalized and proved in Sect. 3, soundness of the TWAM type system says that well-typed programs are sound proof search procedures for their first-order logic (FOL) signature. We have implemented a compiler from T-Prolog to TWAM and an interpreter for TWAM code, which we have tested on a small library of 468 lines. The result is a certifying compiler with a special-purpose proof checker as its trusted core: the TWAM typechecker.

Background: Dependent Types and Proof Terms. Our type system integrates first-order (minimal) logic (FOL) to specify the semantics of logic programs. We use the variable M to range over FOL terms, D to range over FOL proofs, a to range over (simple) types, and A to range over propositions. The type-theoretic analog of the quantifier $\forall x{:}a.\ \phi$ is the dependent function type $\Pi x{:}a.\tau$. When the name x is not referenced in τ, this is equivalent to the simple function type $a \Rightarrow \tau$. We borrow some notations from the logical framework LF [13], a type system corresponding to first-order minimal logic. Our proof language is minimalistic, consisting of constants, modus ponens, instantiation, abstraction, and variables. More information about proof terms for first-order logic is available in Sørensen [32, Chap. 8]. We refer to proof terms D as just "proofs" to avoid confusion with simply-typed FOL terms M. We use juxtaposition $D\ D$ to indicate modus ponens and $D\ M$ for universal quantifier instantiation. Abstraction $\lambda x.\ D$ can range over either proofs $x{:}A$ or term $x{:}a$. We write $\lambda x{:}\alpha.\ D$ wherever both abstraction over proofs and abstraction over individuals are permissible. Similarly, we write θ where both terms M and proofs D may appear.

$$\begin{array}{lll}
\text{FOL propositions } A & ::= c & \mid\ \forall x : a.\ A \mid A \Rightarrow A \mid A\ M \\
\text{FOL terms} & M ::= x & \mid\ c \mid M\ M \\
\text{FOL proofs} & D ::= x & \mid\ c \mid D\ \theta \mid \lambda x : \alpha.\ D
\end{array}$$

In Sect. 2 we will extract a constant c for each type, constructor, and clause of a program. This collection of constant declarations is called a *FOL signature*, written Σ. The compiler generates a FOL signature from an arbitrary T-Prolog program. This signature provides a precise formal specification of what it means for proof search to find a valid proof.

While we attempt to introduce key WAM concepts as we go, unfamiliar readers will benefit from reading Aït-Kaci [1]. A gentler version of this paper with extended proofs, definitions, and a simply-typed variant of WAM is available [4].

2   Certifying Compilation in Proof-Passing Style

We briefly demonstrate (Fig. 1) the T-Prolog source syntax and the extraction of a FOL signature Σ from a T-Prolog program. We consider addition on the Peano naturals as a running example, i.e., a predicate plus(N_1,N_2,N_3) that holds when $N_1 + N_2 = N_3$. We write 0 and 1+ for the Peano natural constructors. We also write, e.g., 1 as shorthand for $1+ 0$. A T-Prolog program consists of standard Prolog syntax plus optional type annotations. Throughout the paper, we write vectors in bold, e.g.; $\boldsymbol{a}$ below. Throughout, a ranges over simple (inductive) types while A is ranges over propositions in FOL. All terms in the untyped fragment of T-Prolog have a distinguished simple type, term.

- A type a in T-Prolog translates to a FOL type a.
- A term constructor $c\colon \boldsymbol{a} \to a$ translates to a FOL term constructor of the same type. For untyped c, the result and all arguments translate to term.
- A predicate $p\colon \boldsymbol{a} \to$ type translates to a FOL constant $P\colon \boldsymbol{a} \to \mathbb{B}$ where $\mathbb{B}$ is the type of booleans.
- A clause C of form G :- $\mathrm{SG}_1, \ldots, \mathrm{SG}_n$. translates to a FOL proof constructor $c\colon \forall_{\mathbf{FV}(C)}.\ \boldsymbol{SG} \to G$ where $\mathbf{FV}(C)$ is the set of free variables of clause C and $\boldsymbol{SG}$ consists of one argument for each subgoal. This is the universal closure of the Horn clause $\boldsymbol{SG} \to G$.
- The query ?- Q is translated to a distinguished predicate named $Query$ with one proof constructor $QueryI : \forall_{\mathbf{FV}(Q)}.\ Q \to Query^2$.

(no type declarations)	0: term
	$1+$: term $\Rightarrow$ term
	$Plus$: term $\Rightarrow$ term $\Rightarrow$ term $\Rightarrow \mathbb{B}$

```
plus(0,N,N).
plus(1+(N_1),N_2,1+(N_3))  :-
   plus(N_1,N_2,N_3).

?- plus(N_1, 0, 1+(0)).
```

$Plus$-Z: $(\forall N\colon \text{term}.\ Plus\ 0\ N\ N)$
$Plus$-S: $(\forall N_1\colon \text{term}.\ \forall N_2\colon \text{term}.\ \forall N_3\colon \text{term}.$
$\quad Plus\ N_1\ N_2\ N_3 \to$
$\qquad Plus\ (1+\ N_1)\ N_2\ (1+\ N_3))$
$QueryI$:$(\forall N_1\colon \text{term}.\ Plus\ N_1\ 0\ 1 \to Query)$

Fig. 1. Example T-Prolog program and FOL signature

The TWAM certification approach can be summed up in a slogan:

Typed Compilation + Programming As Proof Search = Proof-Passing Style

Typed compilation uses the type system of the target language to ensure that the program satisfies some property. Previous work [34] has used typed compilation to ensure intermediate languages are safe (do not segfault). One of our insights is that by combining this technique with the programming-as-proof-search paradigm that underlies logic programming, our compiler can certify a much stronger property: search soundness (Theorem 1).

A TWAM program must contain enough information that the TWAM type-checker can ensure that a proof of the query exists for each terminating runs of the program. We achieve this by statically ensuring that whenever *each* proof

---

[2] Note that $Query$ has no free variables. This simplifies the proof of Theorem 1 because it depends heavily on substitution reasoning.

search procedure p returns, the corresponding predicate P will have a proof in FOL. This amounts to (1) annotating each return point with the corresponding FOL proof and (2) reasoning statically about constraints on T-Prolog terms with dependent *singleton types* $\mathfrak{S}(M : a)$ containing exactly the values that represent some FOL term M of simple type a[3]. Singleton typing information is needed to typecheck almost any FOL proof term. For example, an application of *Plus-Z* only checks whether we statically know that the first argument is 0 and that the second and third arguments are equal, all of which are learned during unification.

This *proof-passing* style of programming is a defining feature of the TWAM type system. It is worth noting that these proofs never need to be inspected at runtime and thus can be (and in our implementation, are) *erased* before execution. In the following syntax, we annotate all erasable type annotations and subterms with square brackets. The Simply-Typed WAM [4] shows how TWAM works after erasure. Because proofs are only performed during type-checking, they have no (direct) runtime overhead, compared to runtime proof computations, which are expensive. At the same time, we do simplify WAM (e.g. with heap-allocated environments) in order to make developing a type system more feasible. For this reason, we do not expect our current implementation to be competitive with production compilers.

3   The Typed WAM (TWAM)

In this section, we develop the main theoretical contributions of the paper: the design and metatheory of the TWAM. We begin by introducing the syntax and operational semantics of TWAM by example. We then develop a type system for TWAM which realizes proof-passing style. We give an outline of the metatheory, culminating in a proof (Sect. 3.5) of Theorem 1.

3.1   Syntax

We begin by presenting the syntaxes for TWAM program texts, machine states (as used in the operational semantics), and typing constructs, which are given in Fig. 2. We call the formal representation of a TWAM program text a *code section* C. Each basic block in the program has its own identifier ℓ^C; the code section maps identifiers to *code values*, which we range over with variable v^C. Code values are always of the form $[\lambda x : \alpha.]\mathsf{code}[\Gamma](I)$ where I is a basic block (instruction sequence), $\lambda x : \alpha$ (possibly empty) specifies any FOL (term and/or proof) parameters of the basic block, and Γ is a *register file type* specifying the expected register types at the beginning of the basic block. Recall that the square brackets above indicate that λ-abstractions and type annotations are needed only for certification and that because they do not influence the operational semantics,

---

[3] Our running example is untyped ($a = \mathtt{term}$ throughout) because untyped Prolog is well-known, but we will still present the typing rules in their full generality.

basic block	$I ::= \mathtt{succeed}[D:Query] \mid \mathtt{jmp}\ op \mid \mathtt{mov}\ r_d, op; I$
	$\mid \mathtt{put\_str}\ c, r; I \mid \mathtt{unify\_var}\ r, [x:a.]\ I \mid \mathtt{unify\_val}\ r, [x:a].\ I$
	$\mid \mathtt{get\_val}\ r_1, r_2; I \mid \mathtt{get\_str}\ c, r; I \mid \mathtt{put\_var}\ r, [x:a.]\ I$
	$\mid \mathtt{close}\ r_d, r_e, (\ell^C\ [\boldsymbol{\theta}]); I \mid \mathtt{push\_bt}\ r_e, (\ell^C\ [\boldsymbol{\theta}]); I$
	$\mid \mathtt{put\_tuple}\ r_d, n; I \mid \mathtt{set\_val}\ r; I \mid \mathtt{proj}\ r_d, r_s, i; I$
operands	$op ::= \ell \mid r \mid op\ [\theta] \mid [\lambda x:\alpha.]\ op$

trails	$T :: \langle\rangle \mid (tf :: T)$
trail frames	$tf ::= (w_{\mathrm{code}}, w_{\mathrm{env}}, tr)$
traces	$tr ::= \langle\rangle \mid (x{:}a@\ell^H) :: tr$
code section, heap	$C ::= \{\ell_1^C \mapsto v_1^C, \ldots, \ell_n^C \mapsto v_n^C\} \quad H ::= \{\ell_1^H \mapsto v_1^H, \ldots, \ell_n^H \mapsto v_n^H\}$
heap values	$v^H ::= \mathbf{FREE}[x:a] \mid \mathbf{BOUND}\ \ell^H \mid c\langle \ell_1^H, \ldots, \ell_n^H\rangle$
	$\mid \mathtt{close}(w_{\mathrm{code}}, w_{\mathrm{env}}) \mid (\boldsymbol{w})$
code values	$v^C ::= [\lambda \boldsymbol{x}:\boldsymbol{\alpha}.]\mathtt{code}[\varGamma](I)$
word values	$w ::= \ell^C \mid \ell^H \mid w\ [M] \mid w\ [D] \mid [\lambda x:a.]\ w \mid [\lambda x:A.]\ w$
register files	$R ::= \{\mathtt{r0} \mapsto w_0, \ldots, \mathtt{rn} \mapsto w_n\}$
machines	$m ::= (\varDelta, T, C, H, R, I) \mid \mathtt{write}(\varDelta, T, C, H, R, I, c, \ell, \boldsymbol{\ell})$
	$\mid \mathtt{read}(\varDelta, T, C, H, R, I, \boldsymbol{\ell}) \mid \mathtt{twrite}(\varDelta, T, C, H, R, I, r, n, \boldsymbol{w})$

value types	$\tau ::= \mathfrak{S}(M:a) \mid \varPi\boldsymbol{x}:\boldsymbol{\alpha}.\neg\varGamma \mid \mathtt{x}[\tau]$
register file types	$\varGamma ::= \{\mathtt{r0}: \tau_0, \ldots, \mathtt{rn}: \tau_n\}$
heap, code types	$\varPsi ::= \{\ell_1^H: \tau_1, \ldots, \ell_n^H: \tau_n\} \quad \varXi ::= \{\ell_1^C: \tau_1, \ldots, \ell_n^C: \tau_n\}$
spine types	$J ::= \varGamma \mid \varPi x:a.\ J \quad J_t ::= \boldsymbol{a} \Rightarrow \{r_d: \tau\}$
signatures	$\varSigma ::= \cdot \mid \varSigma, c: \forall\boldsymbol{x}:\boldsymbol{a}.\ \boldsymbol{A} \to A \mid \varSigma, c: a_1 \Rightarrow \cdots \Rightarrow a_n \Rightarrow a$

Fig. 2. TWAM instructions, machine states, typing constructs

they can be type-erased before execution. Note that when the λ-abstractions are type erased, their matching (FOL) function applications will be as well. Brackets also appear in the syntax of machine states (e.g., $\mathbf{FREE}[x:a]$): these too are erased because they are used only in the metatheory and are not required at runtime. Recall also that $\varPi$ is a dependent function type, which is analogous to the quantifier $\forall x.\ \phi$.

3.2 Example: Code Section for Plus

We continue the running example: we present a code section which contains the implementation of the plus proof search procedure, consisting of two code values named plus-zero/3 and plus-succ/3. Like all TWAM code, it is written in continuation-passing style (CPS): code values never return, but rather return control to the caller by invoking a success continuation passed in to the callee through a register. The code section also includes an implementation of an example query, plus(N, 0, 1+(0)), consisting of a code value named query/0. When the query succeeds, it invokes the top-level success continuation, which is a code value named init-cont/0.

As is typical in continuation-passing-style, code values have no return type because they never return. The type of a code value is written $\varPi\boldsymbol{x}{:}\boldsymbol{\alpha}.\ \neg\varGamma$, where $\boldsymbol{x}{:}\boldsymbol{\alpha}$ records any FOL terms and proofs passed as static arguments, while $\varGamma$ records any heap values passed at runtime through the register file.

Example 1 (Implementing plus)

```
# Entry point to plus, implements
# case plus(0,N,N) and tries
# plus-succ/3 on failure
plus-zero/3  ↦  [λN₁N₂N₃ : term.]code[
  {A₁ : 𝔖(N₁), A₂ : 𝔖(N₂), A₃ : 𝔖(N₃),
   ret: ((Plus N₁ N₂ N₃) ⇒ ¬{})}](
  put_tuple X₁, 4;
    set_val A₁;
    set_val A₂;
    set_val A₃;
    set_val ret;
  push_bt X₁, (plus-succ/3 [N₁ N₂ N₃]);
  get_str A₁, 0;
  get_val A₂, A₃;
  jmp (ret [(Plus − Z N₂)]))
```

```
# plus(1+(N_1), N_2, 1+(N_3))
#     :- plus(N_1,N_2,N_3).
plus-succ/3  ↦  [λN₁N₂N₃ : term.]code[
  {env: x[𝔖(N₁), 𝔖(N₂), 𝔖(N₃),
   ((Plus N₁ N₂ N₃) ⇒ ¬{})]}](
  proj A₁, env, 1;
  proj A₂, env, 2;
  proj A₃, env, 3;
  proj ret, env, 4;
  get_str A₁, 1+;
  #Set arg 1 of rec. call to N_1-1
    unify_var A₁, [NN₁ : term.]
  get_str A₃, 1+;
  #Set arg 3 of rec. call to N_3-1
    unify_var A₃, [NN₃ : term.]
  #tail-call optimization: add
  #Plus-S constructor when called
  mov ret, [(λD: Plus NN₁ N₂ NN₃.]
    ret [(Plus-S NN₁ N₂ NN₃ D)]);
  jmp (plus-zero/3 [NN₁ N₂ NN₃]))
```

Example 2 (Calling plus)

```
init-cont/0  ↦
  [λN: term. λD: (Plus N 0 (1+ 0)).]
  code[{}](succeed[(QueryI N D):Query])
```

```
# plus(N, 0, 1+(0))
query/0  ↦  code[{}](
  put_var A₁, [N: term].
  put_tuple X₁, 0;
  close ret, X₁, (init-cont/0 [N]);
  put_str A₂, 0;
  put_str A₃, 1+;
    unify_val A₂, [_: term.]
  jmp (plus-zero/3 [N 0 (1+ 0)]))
```

The query entry point is query/0. The plus entry point is plus-zero/3, which is responsible for implementing the base case $A_1 = 0$. Its type annotation states that the argument terms N_1 through N_3 are passed in arguments A_1 through A_3. The success continuation (return address) is passed in through ret, but may only be invoked once *Plus* N_1 N_2 N_3 is proved.

The instructions themselves are similar to the standard WAM instructions. plus-zero/3 is implemented by attempting to unify A_1 with 0 and A_2 with A_3. If the plus-zero/3 case succeeds, we return to the location stored in ret, proving *Plus* N_1 N_2 N_3 in FOL with the *Plus-Z* rule. If the case fails, we backtrack to plus-succ/3 to try the *Plus-S* case. plus_succ/3 in turn makes a recursive call to plus-zero/3 to prove the subgoal $NN_1 + N_2 = NN_3$, where NN_1 and NN_3 are the predecessors of N_1 and N_3. The mov instruction implements proof-passing for tail-calls. Dynamically speaking, we should not need to define a new success continuation because we are making a tail call. However, while *Plus* NN_1 N_2 NN_3 implies *Plus* N_1 N_2 N_3, deriving the latter also requires applying *Plus-S* after proving the former. This mov instruction simply says to apply *Plus-S* (statically) before invoking ret. Because only the proof changes, the mov can be erased before executing the program.

Machines. As shown in Fig. 2, the state of a TWAM program is formalized as a tuple $m = (\Delta, T, C, H, R, I)$ (or a special machine read or write: see, e.g., Sect. 3.3). Here T is the *trail*, the data structure that implements backtracking. The trail consists of a list of *trail frames* (tf), each of which contains a failure continuation (location and environment) and a *trace* (tr), which lists any bound variables which would have to be made free to recover the state in which the failure continuation should be run. In WAM terminology, each frame implements one choice point. The *heap H* and *code section C* have types notated Ψ and Ξ, $R : \Gamma$ is the register file, and I represents the program counter as the list of instructions left in the current basic block. Typical register names are A_i for arguments, X_i for temporaries, ret for success continuations, and env for environments. Δ contains the free term variables of H; it is used primarily in Sect. 3.5. The *heap H* contains the T-Prolog terms. Heap value $\mathbf{FREE}[x : a]$ is a free variable x of type a and $c\langle \ell_1, \ldots, \ell_n \rangle$ is a *structure*, i.e., a *functor* (cf. constructor in FOL) c applied to arguments $\langle \ell_1, \ldots, \ell_n \rangle$. As in WAM, the heap is in disjoint-set style, i.e. all free variables are distinct and pointers $\mathbf{BOUND}$ ℓ can be introduced when unifying variables; $\mathbf{BOUND}$ ℓ and ℓ represent the same FOL term. TWAM heaps are acyclic, as ensured by an occurs check. The heap also contains success continuation closures $\mathrm{close}(w_{\mathrm{code}}, w_{\mathrm{env}})$ and n-ary tuples $(\boldsymbol{w})$ (used for closure environments), which do not correspond to T-Prolog terms.

3.3 Operational Semantics

We give the operational semantics by example. Due to space constraints, see the extended paper [4] for formal small-step semantics (judgements $m \longmapsto^* m'$ and m done). Those judgments which will appear in the metatheory are named in this section. We give an evaluation trace of the query ?- plus(N,0,1+(0)). For each line we describe any changes to the machine state, i.e. the heap, trail, register file, and instruction pointer. As with the WAM, the TWAM uses special execution modes *read* and *write* to destruct or construct sequences of arguments to a functor (we dub this sequence a *spine*). When the program enters read mode, we annotate that line with the list ℓs of arguments being read, and when the program enters write mode we annotate it with the constructor c being applied, the destination location ℓ and the argument locations ℓs. If we wish, we can view the final instruction of a write-mode spine as two evaluation steps (delimited by a semicolon), one of which constructs the last argument of the constructor and one of which combines the arguments into a structure. We write $H\{\{\ell^H \mapsto v^H\}\}$ for heap H extended with new location ℓ^H containing v^H, or $H\{\ell^H \mapsto v^H\}$ for updating an existing location. $R\{r \mapsto w\}$ is analogous. Updates $H\{\ell^H \mapsto v^H\}$ are only guaranteed to be acyclic when the occurs check passes (should the occurs check fail, we backtrack instead). Below, all occurs checks pass, and are omitted for brevity. Spines, backtracking, and no-ops are marked in monospace.

```
     query/0  ↦  code[{}](                        Outcome:
 1   put_var A₁, [N:term].                         H←H{{ℓ₁↦FREE[N:term]}}, R←R{A₁↦ℓ₁}
 2   put_tuple X₁, 0;                              H←H{{ℓ₂↦()}}, R←R{X₁↦ℓ₂};
 3   close ret, X₁, (init-cont/0 [N]);            H←H{{ℓ₃↦close(init-cont/0 [N], ℓ₂)}},
                                                   R←R{ret↦ℓ₃};
 4   put_str A₂, 0;                                H←H{{ℓ₄↦0}}, R←R{A₂↦ℓ₄}
 5   put_str A₃, 1+;                               H←H{{ℓ₅↦FREE[_: term]}},
                                                   R←R{A₃↦ℓ₅}, c = 1+; ℓ = ℓ₅, ℓs = ⟨⟩
 6     unify_val A₂, [_: term.]                    ℓs←⟨ℓ₄⟩; H←H{ℓ₅↦1+ ⟨ℓ₄⟩}
 7   jmp plus-zero/3[···]                          I←(C(plus-zero/3) [N 0 (1+ 0)])


     plus-zero/3: ([λN₁N₂N₃ : term.]
     code[{A₁ : 𝔖(N₁), A₂ : 𝔖(N₂), A₃ : 𝔖(N₃), ret : ((Plus N₁ N₂ N₃) ⇒ ¬{})}](
 8   put_tuple X₁, 4;                              ℓs = ⟨⟩, n = 4
 9     set_val A₁;                                 ℓs = ⟨ℓ₁⟩
10     set_val A₂;                                 ℓs = ⟨ℓ₁, ℓ₄⟩
11     set_val A₃;                                 ℓs = ⟨ℓ₁, ℓ₄, ℓ₅⟩
12     set_val ret;                                ℓs = ⟨ℓ₁, ℓ₄, ℓ₅, ℓ₃⟩;
                                                   H←H{{ℓ₆↦(ℓ₁, ℓ₄, ℓ₅, ℓ₃)}}, R←R{X₁↦ℓ₆}
13   push_bt X₁, (plus-succ/3[···]);              T←(plus-succ/3[N₁ N₂ N₃], ℓ₆, ⟨⟩) :: ⟨⟩
14   get_str A₁, 0;                                WRITE: H←H{ℓ₁↦0},
                                                   T←(plus-succ/3[N₁N₂N₃], ℓ₆, ⟨ℓ₁⟩) :: ⟨⟩
15   get_val A₂, A₃;                               BT:T←⟨⟩, I←plus-succ/3...,
                                                   H←H{ℓ₁↦FREE[N : term]}}

     plus-succ/3  ↦  [λN₁N₂N₃ : term.]
     code[{env: x[𝔖(N₁), 𝔖(N₂), 𝔖(N₃), (Plus N₁ N₂ N₃) ⇒ ¬{}]](
16   proj A₁, env 1;                               R←R{A₁↦ℓ₁}
17   proj A₂, env 2;                               R←R{A₂↦ℓ₄}
18   proj A₃, env 3;                               R←R{A₃↦ℓ₅}
19   proj ret, env, 4;                             R←R{ret↦ℓ₃}
20   get_str A₁, 1+;                               WRITE: c = 1+, ℓ = ℓ₁, ℓs = ⟨⟩}
21     unify_var A₁, [NN₁: term.]                  H←H{{ℓ₇↦FREE[NN₁ : term]}}
                                                   R←R{A₁↦ℓ₇}, ℓs = ⟨ℓ₇⟩;
                                                   H←H{ℓ₁↦1+ ⟨ℓ₇⟩}
22   get_str A₃, 1+;                               READ:ℓs = ⟨ℓ₄⟩
23     unify_var A₃, [NN₃: term.]                  R←R{A₃↦ℓ₄}
24   mov ret, [(λD : (Plus NN₁ N₂ NN₃).)ret[(Plus − S NN₁ N₂ NN₃ D)]);
                                                   NOP:R←R{{ret↦[(λD:(Plus NN₁ N₂ NN₃).)]
                                                   ℓ₃[(Plus − S NN₁ N₂ NN₃ D)])}}
25   jmp (plus-zero/3 [···]));                     I←C(plus-zero/3) [NN₁ N₂ NN₃]

     plus-zero/3  ↦  [λN₁N₂N₃ : term.]
     code[{A₁ : 𝔖(N₁), A₂ : 𝔖(N₂), A₃ : 𝔖(N₃), ret : ((Plus N₁ N₂ N₃) ⇒ ¬{})}](
26   put_tuple X₁, 4;                              ℓs = ⟨⟩, n = 4
27     set_val A₁;                                 ℓs = ⟨ℓ₇⟩
28     set_val A₂;                                 ℓs = ⟨ℓ₇, ℓ₄⟩
29     set_val A₃;                                 ℓs = ⟨ℓ₇, ℓ₄, ℓ₄⟩
30     set_val ret;                                ℓs = ⟨ℓ₇, ℓ₄, ℓ₄, λ...ℓ₃⟩;
                                                   H←H{{ℓ₈↦(ℓ₇, ℓ₄, ℓ₄, λ...ℓ₃)}}
                                                   R←R{X₁↦ℓ₈}
31   push_bt X₁, (plus-succ/3 [···]);             T←(plus-succ/3 [N₁ N₂ N₃], ℓ₈, ⟨⟩) :: ⟨⟩
32   get_str A₁, 0;                                READ: ℓs = ⟨⟩, ℓ = ℓ₇; H←H{ℓ₇↦0}
33   get_val A₂, A₃;                               NOP:R(A₂) = R(A₃)
34   jmp (ret(Plus − Z N₂));                       I←C(R(ret)) (Plus − Z N₂)
                                                   = C(init-cont/0) [0 N₂ N₃
                                                   (Plus − S 0 N₂ NN₃ (Plus − Z N₂))])

35   init-cont/0:[λN:term D:(Plus N 0 1).]code[{}](succeed[(QueryI N D):Query])
```

All top-level queries follow the same pattern of constructing arguments, setting a success continuation, then invoking a search procedure. Line 1 constructs a free variable. Line 2 creates an empty environment tuple which is used to create a success continuation on Line 3. This means that if proof search succeeds, we will return to init-cont/0, which immediately ends the program in success. Line 4 allocates the number 0 at ℓ_4. Lines 5–6 are a write spine that constructs $1+ 0$. Because A_2 already contains 0, we can eliminate a common subexpression, reusing it for $1+ 0$. This is an example of an optimization that is possible in the TWAM. Line 7 invokes the main *Plus* proof search.

Lines 8–12 pack the environment in a tuple. Line 13 creates a trail frame which executes plus-succ/3 if plus-zero/3 fails. Its trace is initially empty: from this point on, the trace will be updated any time we bind a free variable. Line 14 dynamically checks A_1, observes that it is free and thus enters write mode. On line 14, we also bind A_1 to 0 and add it to the trace. Note that this is the first time we add a variable to the trace because we only do so when trail contains at least one frame. The trace logic is formalized in a judgement update_trail. When the trail is empty, backtracking would fail anyway, so there is no need to track variable binding.

Line 15 tries and fails to unify (judgement unify) the contents of A_2 and A_3, so it backtracks to plus-succ/3 (judgement backtrack).

Backtracking consists of updating the instruction pointer, setting all trailed locations to free variables, and loading an environment. The plus-succ/3 case proceeds successfully: the first get_str enters write mode because A_1 is free, but the second enters read mode because A_3 is not free. On Line 26 we enter the 0 case of plus with arguments $A_1 = A_2 = A_3 = 0$. All instructions succeed, so we reach Line 34 which jumps to line 35 and reports success.

3.4   Statics

This section presents the TWAM type system. The main typing judgement $\Delta; \Gamma \vdash I_{\Sigma;\Xi}$ ok says that instruction sequence I is well-typed. We omit the signature Σ and code section type Ξ when they are not used. A code section is well-typed if every block is well-typed. The system contains a number of auxiliary judgments, which will be introduced as needed. Note that the judgement $\Delta; \Gamma \vdash I_{\Sigma;\Xi}$ ok is not parameterized by the query directly; instead, the query is stored as $\Sigma(Query)$. The typing rule for succeed then looks up the query in Σ to confirm that proof search proved the correct proposition. Below, the notation $\Psi\{\ell: \tau\}$ denotes the heap type Ψ with the type of ℓ replaced by τ whereas $\Psi\{\{\ell: \tau\}\}$ denotes Ψ extended with a fresh location ℓ of type τ.

Success. We wish to prove that a program only succeeds if a proof D of the *Query* exists in FOL. We require exactly that in the typing rule:

$$\frac{\Delta \vdash D \colon Query}{\Delta; \Gamma \vdash \mathsf{succeed}[D \colon Query]; I \text{ ok}} \text{ SUCCEED}$$

The succeed rule is simple, but deceptively so: the challenge of certifying compilation for TWAM is how to satisfy the premiss of this rule. The proof-passing approach says we satisfy this premiss by threading FOL proofs statically through every predicate: by the time we reach the succeed instruction, the proof of the query will have already been constructed.

Proof-Passing. The jmp instruction is used to invoke and return from basic blocks. When returning from a basic block, it (statically) passes a FOL proof to the success continuation. These FOL proofs are part of the jmp instruction's *operand* op:

$$\frac{\Delta; \Gamma \vdash op : \neg\Gamma' \quad \Delta \vdash \Gamma' \leq \Gamma}{\Delta; \Gamma \vdash \mathtt{jmp}\ op, I\ \mathsf{ok}} \ \mathrm{JMP}$$

Here $\Delta \vdash \Gamma' \leq \Gamma$ means that every register of Γ' appears in Γ with the same type.

The *operands* consist of locations, registers, FOL applications, and FOL abstractions:

operands op ::= $\ell \mid r \mid op\ [\theta] \mid [\lambda x : \alpha.]\ op$

Operand typechecking is written $\Delta; \Gamma \vdash op : \tau$ and employs standard rules for checking FOL terms. Brackets indicate that argument-passing and λ-abstraction are type-erased. The mov instruction is nearly standard. It supports arbitrary operands, which are used in our implementation to support tail-call optimization, as seen in Line 24 of the execution trace.

$$\frac{\Delta; \Gamma \vdash op : \tau \quad \Delta; \Gamma\{r_d : \tau\} \vdash I\ \mathsf{ok}}{\Delta; \Gamma \vdash \mathtt{mov}\ r_d, op; I\ \mathsf{ok}} \ \mathrm{Mov}$$

Continuation-Passing. Closures are created explicitly with the close instruction: close $r_d, r_e, \ell^C[\theta]$ constructs a closure in r_d which, when invoked, executes the instructions at ℓ^C using FOL arguments θ and environment r_e. The environment is an arbitrary value which is passed to $\ell^C\ [\theta]$ in the register env. The argument $(\ell^C\ [\theta])$ is an operand, syntactically restricted to be a location applied to arguments.

$$\frac{\Gamma(r_e) = \tau \quad \Delta; \Gamma\{r_d : \Pi x : \alpha.\ \neg\Gamma'\} \vdash I\ \mathsf{ok}}{\Delta; \Gamma \vdash (\ell^C\ [\theta]) : (\Pi x : \alpha.\ \neg\Gamma'\{\mathtt{env} : \tau\})}{\Delta; \Gamma \vdash \mathtt{close}\ r_d, r_e, (\ell^C\ [\theta]); I\ \mathsf{ok}} \ \mathrm{CLOSE}$$

Trail frames are similar, but they are stored in the trail instead of a register:

$$\frac{\Delta; \Gamma \vdash I\ \mathsf{ok} \quad \Gamma(r_e) = \tau \quad \Delta; \Gamma \vdash (\ell^C\ [\theta]) : \neg\{\mathtt{env} : \tau\}}{\Delta; \Gamma \vdash \mathtt{push\_bt}\ r_e, (\ell^C\ [\theta]); I\ \mathsf{ok}} \ \mathrm{BT}$$

Singleton Types. The PUTVAR rule introduces a FOL variable x of simple type a, corresponding to a T-Prolog unification variable. Statically, the FOL variable is added to Δ. Dynamically, the TWAM variable is stored in r, so statically we have $r : \mathfrak{S}(x : a)$, i.e., r contains a representation of variable x.

$$\frac{\Delta, x \colon a; \Gamma\{r \colon \mathfrak{S}(x \colon a)\} \vdash I \text{ ok}}{\Delta; \Gamma \vdash \mathtt{put\_var}\ r, [x \colon a.]\ I \text{ ok}} \text{ PUTVAR}$$

Singleton typing knowledge is then exploited in proof-checking FOL proofs.

Unification. However, $\mathtt{put\_var}$ alone does not provide nearly enough constraints to check most proofs. Almost every FOL proof needs to exploit equality constraints learned through unification. To this end, we introduce a *static* notion of unification $M_1 \sqcap M_2$, allowing us to integrate unification reasoning into our type system and thus into FOL proofs. We separate unification into a judgement $\Delta \vdash M_1 \sqcap M_2 = \sigma$ which computes a most-general unifier of M_1 and M_2 (or $\bot$ if no unifier exists) and capture-avoiding substitution $[\sigma]\Delta$. We also introduce notation $[\![\sigma]\!]\Delta$ standing for $[\sigma]\Delta$ with variable substituted by σ removed, since unification often removes free variables which might located arbitrarily within Δ. All unification in T-Prolog is first-order, for which algorithms are well-known [18,29]. One such algorithm is given in the extended paper [4].

The $\mathtt{get\_val}$ instruction unifies its arguments. If no unifier exists, $\mathtt{get\_val}$ vacuously typechecks: we know statically that unification will fail at runtime and, e.g., backtrack instead of executing I. This is one of the major subtleties of the TWAM type system: all unification performed in the type system is *hypothetical*. At type-checking time we cannot know what arguments a function will ultimately receive, so we treat all arguments as free variables. The trick (and key to the soundness proofs) is that this does not disturb the typical preservation of typing under substitution. For example, after substituting concrete arguments at runtime, the result will still typecheck even if unification fails, because failing unifications typecheck vacuously.

$$\frac{\begin{array}{c}\Delta \vdash M_1 \sqcap M_2 = \bot\\ \Gamma(r_1) = \mathfrak{S}(M_1 \colon a) \quad \Gamma(r_2) = \mathfrak{S}(M_2 \colon a)\end{array}}{\Delta; \Gamma \vdash \mathtt{get\_val}\ r_1, r_2; I \text{ ok}} \text{ GETVAL-}\bot$$

$$\frac{\begin{array}{c}\Gamma(r_1) = \mathfrak{S}(M_1 \colon a) \quad \Gamma(r_2) = \mathfrak{S}(M_2 \colon a)\\ \Delta \vdash M_1 \sqcap M_2 = \sigma \quad [\![\sigma]\!]\Delta; [\sigma]\Gamma \vdash [\sigma]I \text{ ok}\end{array}}{\Delta; \Gamma \vdash \mathtt{get\_val}\ r_1, r_2; I \text{ ok}} \text{ GETVAL}$$

Tuples and Simple Spines. Tuples are similar to structures, except that they cannot be unified, may contain closures, and do not have read spines. The $\mathtt{proj}$ instruction accesses arbitrary tuple elements i:

$$\frac{\Gamma(r_s) = \mathrm{x}[\tau]\Gamma\{r_d \colon \tau_i\} \vdash I \text{ ok} \quad (\text{where } 1 \leq i \leq |\tau|)}{\Delta; \Gamma \vdash \mathtt{proj}\ r_d, r_s, i; I \text{ ok}} \text{ PROJ}$$

New tuple creation is started by $\mathtt{put\_tuple}$. Elements are populated by a *tuple spine* containing $\mathtt{set\_val}$ instructions. We check the spine using an auxilliary typing judgement $\Delta; \Gamma \vdash_{\Sigma; \Xi} I{:}J_t$ where J_t is a *tuple spine* type with form

$\tau_2 \Rightarrow \{r_d{:}x[\tau_1\tau_2]\}$. A tuple spine type encodes both the expected types of all remaining arguments τ_2 and a postcondition: when the spine completes, register r_d will have type $x[\tau_1\tau_2]$. The typing rules check each $\texttt{set\_val}$ in sequence, then return to the standard typing mode $\Delta; \Gamma \vdash I$ ok when the spine completes.

$$\frac{\Delta; \Gamma \vdash I : (\tau \to \{r_d : x[\tau]\})(\text{where } n = |\tau|)}{\Delta; \Gamma \vdash \texttt{put\_tuple}\ r_d, n; I \text{ ok}} \text{ PUTTUPLE}$$

$$\frac{\Gamma(r) = \tau\Gamma \vdash I{:}J_t}{(\Delta; \Gamma \vdash \texttt{set\_val}\ r; I) : (\tau \to J_t)} \text{ TSPINE-SETVAL}$$

$$\frac{\Delta; \Gamma\{r_d : \tau\} \vdash I \text{ ok}}{\Delta; \Gamma \vdash I : \{r_d : \tau\}} \text{ TSPINE-END}$$

Dependent Spines. While the $\texttt{get\_val}$ instruction demonstrates the essence of unification, much unification in TWAM (as in WAM) happens in special-purpose *spines* that create or destruct sequences of functor arguments. Because spinal instructions are already subtle, the resulting typing rules are as well.

We introduce an auxiliary judgement $\Gamma \vdash I_{\Sigma;\Xi} : J$ and dependent *functor spine types J*. As above, they encode arguments and a postcondition, but here the postcondition is the unification of two terms, and the arguments are dependent.

The base case is $J \equiv (M_1 \sqcap M_2)$, meaning that FOL terms M_1 and M_2 will be unified if the spine succeeds. When J has form $\Pi x{:}a.\ J'$, the first instruction of I must be a spinal instruction that handles a functor argument of type a (recall that the same instructions are used for both read and write mode, as we often do not know statically which mode will be used). The type J' describes the type of the remaining instructions in the spine, and may mention x. The spinal instruction $\texttt{unify\_var}$ unifies the argument with a fresh variable, while $\texttt{unify\_val}$ unifies the argument with an existing variable.

$$\frac{\Gamma(r) = \mathfrak{S}(M : a) \quad \Delta; \Gamma \vdash [M/x]I : [M/x]J}{\Delta; \Gamma \vdash \texttt{unify\_val}\ r, [x{:}\,a.]I : (\Pi x{:}\ a.\ J)} \text{ UNIFYVAL}$$

$$\frac{\Delta, x{:}\ a; \Gamma\{r{:}\ \mathfrak{S}(x{:}\ a)\} \vdash I : J}{\Delta; \Gamma \vdash \texttt{unify\_var}\ r, [x{:}\,a.]I : (\Pi x{:}\ a.\ J)} \text{ UNIFYVAR}$$

The instruction $\texttt{get\_str}$ unifies its argument with a term $c\ M_1\ \cdots\ M_n$ by executing a spine as described above. The $\texttt{put\_str}$ instruction starts a spine that (always) constructs a new structure.

$$\frac{\Sigma(c) = \boldsymbol{a} \to a \quad \Gamma(r) = \mathfrak{S}(M : a)}{\Delta; \Gamma \vdash I : (\Pi\boldsymbol{x}{:}\ \boldsymbol{a}.(M \sqcap c\ \boldsymbol{x}))}{\Delta; \Gamma \vdash \texttt{get\_str}\ c, r; I \text{ ok}} \text{ GETSTR}$$

$$\frac{\Sigma(c) = \boldsymbol{a} \to a}{\Delta, x{:}\ a; \Gamma\{r{:}\ \mathfrak{S}(x{:}\ a)\} \vdash I : (\Pi\boldsymbol{x}{:}\ \boldsymbol{a}.(x \sqcap c\ \boldsymbol{x}))}{\Delta; \Gamma \vdash \texttt{put\_str}\ c, r; I \text{ ok}} \text{ PUTSTR}$$

This completes the typechecking of TWAM instructions.

Machine Invariants. Having completed instruction checking, we prepare for the metatheory by considering the invariants on validity of machine states, which are quite non-trivial. Consider first the invariant for non-spinal machines:

$$\frac{\Delta \vdash C{:}\Xi \quad \Delta; \Gamma \vdash I \text{ ok} \quad \Delta \vdash H{:}\Psi \quad \Delta; \Psi \vdash R : \Gamma \quad \Delta; C; H \vdash T \text{ ok}}{\cdot \vdash (\Delta, T, C, H, R, I) \text{ ok}} \ Mach$$

Recall that machines include a context Δ containing the free variables of the heap H. We can[4] identify variables of Δ with heap locations, trivially ensuring that each variable appears exactly once in the heap. Premisses $\Delta \vdash C{:}\Xi$ and $\Delta; \Gamma \vdash I$ ok and $\Gamma; \Psi \vdash R : \Gamma$ simply say the code section, current basic block, and register file typecheck.

Premiss $\Delta \vdash H{:}\Psi$ says that all heap values obey their types and that the heap is acyclic. The encoding of acyclic heaps is subtle: while both the heap H and its type Ψ are unordered, the typing derivation is ordered. The rule for non-empty heaps $H\{\{\ell^H \mapsto v^H\}\}$ says that the new value v may refer only to values that appear earlier in the ordering:

$$\frac{\Delta \vdash H : \Psi \Delta; \Psi \vdash v^H : \tau \ell^H \notin Dom(H)}{\Delta \vdash H\{\{\ell^H \mapsto v^H\}\} : \Psi\{\{\ell^H : \tau\}\}}$$

Thus, the derivation exhibits a topological ordering of the heap, proving that it is acyclic. Section 3.5 shows this invariant is maintained because we only bind variables when the occurs check passes. The code section has no ordering constraint, in order to support mutual recursion.

Heap values for T-Prolog terms have singleton types:

$$\frac{\Delta(x) = a}{\Delta; \Psi \vdash \textbf{FREE}[x : a] : \mathfrak{S}(x : a)} \frac{\Delta; \Psi \vdash \ell^H : \mathfrak{S}(M : a)}{\Delta; \Psi \vdash \textbf{BOUND} \ \ell^H : \mathfrak{S}(M : a)}$$

$$\frac{\Sigma(c) = \textbf{\textit{a}} \to a \Delta; \Psi \vdash \ell_i^H : \mathfrak{S}(M_i : a_i)(\text{ for all } i)}{\Delta; \Psi \vdash_{\Sigma;\Xi} c\langle \ell_1^H, \dots, \ell_n^H \rangle : \mathfrak{S}(c \ \textbf{\textit{M}} : a)}$$

Premiss $\Delta; C; H \vdash T$ ok says the trail is well-typed. The empty trail $\langle \rangle$ checks trivially. A non-empty trail is well-typed if the result of *unwinding* the trace tr (i.e. making the traced variables free again), is well-typed.

$$\frac{\begin{array}{c} \text{unwind}(\Delta, H, tr) = (\Delta', H') \quad \Delta; (C, H') \vdash T \text{ ok} \\ \Delta \vdash H' : \Psi' \quad \Psi' \vdash w_{env} : \tau \quad \Delta; \Psi' \vdash \ell^C \ \boldsymbol{\theta} : \neg \{\text{env} : \tau\} \end{array}}{\Delta; C; H \vdash (\ell^C \ [\boldsymbol{\theta}], w_{env}, tr) :: T \text{ ok}} \ \textsc{Trail-Cons}$$

This completes the invariants for non-spinal machines.

Each of the typing invariant rules for spinal machines has an additional premiss, either $\Delta; \Psi \vdash \ell$ reads $\Pi x : \boldsymbol{a}.(c \ \textbf{\textit{M}} \ \textbf{\textit{M}}' \sqcap c \ \textbf{\textit{M}} \ \boldsymbol{x})$ (for a read spine) or $\Delta; \Psi \vdash (\ell^H, \ell^H, c)$ writes $\Pi \boldsymbol{x} : \boldsymbol{a}_2. \ x' \sqcap c \ \textbf{\textit{M}} \ \boldsymbol{x}$ (for a write spine). These are

---

[4] While this approach is preferable for the proofs, it is quite unreadable, so we used readable names in our presentation of the example instead.

some of the most complex rules in the TWAM. Nonetheless, their purpose can be explained naturally at a high level. For a read spine, the types a expected by the spine type must agree with the types of remaining arguments ℓ. For a write spine, the types of all values written so far must agree with the functor arguments and the destination must agree with functor result. Naturally, the yet-unwritten arguments must also agree with the functor type, but that is already ensured by the typing judgement $\Delta; \Gamma \vdash I{:}J$.

$$\frac{\Delta; \Psi \vdash \ell \colon \mathfrak{S}(M' \colon a)}{\Delta; \Psi \vdash \ell \text{ reads } \Pi x \colon a.\ (c\ M\ M' \sqcap c\ M\ x)}$$

$$\frac{\Delta \vdash C \colon \Xi \quad \Delta \vdash H \colon \Psi \quad \Delta; \Gamma \vdash I \colon J}{\Delta; \Psi \vdash \ell \text{ reads } J \quad \Delta \vdash T \text{ ok} \quad \Delta; \Psi \vdash R \colon \Gamma}$$

$$\cdot \vdash_{\Sigma; \Xi} \text{read}(\Delta, T, C, H, R, I, \ell) \text{ ok}$$

$$\frac{\Psi(\ell^H) = \mathfrak{S}(x' \colon a) \quad \Sigma(c) = a_1 \to a_2 \to a \quad \Delta; \Psi \vdash \ell^H \colon \mathfrak{S}(M \colon a_1)}{\Delta; \Psi \vdash (\ell^H, \ell^H, c) \text{ writes } \Pi x \colon a_2.\ x' \sqcap c\ M\ x}$$

$$\frac{\Delta \vdash C \colon \Xi \quad \Delta \vdash H \colon \Psi \quad \Delta; \Gamma \vdash I \colon J}{\Delta; \Psi \vdash (\ell^H, \ell, c) \text{ writes } J \quad \Delta \vdash T \text{ ok} \quad \Delta; \Psi \vdash R \colon \Gamma}$$

$$\cdot \vdash_{\Sigma; \Xi} \text{write}(\Delta, T, C, H, R, I, c, \ell^H, \ell) \text{ ok}$$

The case for tuple spines is similar to the write case.

3.5 Metatheory

Proofs of metatheorems are in the extended paper [4]. Here, we state the major theorems and lemmas. As expected, TWAM satisfies progress and preservation:

Theorem (Progress). *If $\Delta \vdash m$ ok then either m done or m fails or $m \longmapsto m'$.*

Theorem (Preservation). *If $\Delta \vdash m$ ok and $m \longmapsto m'$ then $\cdot \vdash m'$ ok.*

Here m fails means that a query failed in the sense that all proof rules have been exhausted—it does not mean the program has become stuck. m done means a program has succeeded. Search Soundness (Theorem 1) is a corollary:

Theorem 1 (Search Soundness). *If $\cdot \vdash_{\Sigma; \Xi} m$ ok and $m \longmapsto^* m'$ and m' done then there exists a context of term variables Δ and substitution σ such that $\Delta \vdash \sigma(Q)$ in FOL where $\Sigma(QueryI) = \forall_{FV(Q)}(Q \to Query)$.*

Proof (Sketch). By progress and preservation, m' ok. By inversion on m done, have $\Delta \vdash Query$ for $\Delta = \mathbf{FV}(H)$ where H is the heap from m'. By inversion on $QueryI$, have some σ such that $\Delta \vdash \sigma(Q)$. $\qquad\square$

We overview major lemmas, including all those discussed so far:

- Static unification computes most-general unifiers.
- Language constructs obey their appropriate substitution lemmas, even in the presence of unification.
- Dynamic unification is sound with respect to static unification.

- When the occurs check passes, binding a variable does not introduce cycles.
- Updating the trail maintains trail invariants and backtracking maintains machine state invariants.

Our notion of correctness for static unification follows the standard correctness property for first-order unification: we compute the most general unifier, i.e., a substitution which unifies M_1 with M_2 and which is a prefix of all unifiers.

Lemma (Unify Correctness). *If $\Delta \vdash M : a$ and $\Delta \vdash M' : a$ and $\Delta \vdash M \sqcap M' = \sigma$, then:*

- $[\sigma]M = [\sigma]M'$
- *For all substitutions σ', if $[\sigma']M = [\sigma']M'$ then there exists some σ^* such that $\sigma' = \sigma^*, \sigma$ up to alpha-equivalence.*

While this lemma is standard, it is essential to substitution. While we have numerous substitution lemmas (e.g. for heaps), we mention the lemma for instruction sequences here because it is surprisingly subtle.

Lemma (I-Substitution). *If $\Delta_1, x{:}\alpha, \Delta_2; \Gamma \vdash I$ ok and $\Delta_1 \vdash \theta{:}\alpha$ then we can derive $\Delta_1, [\theta/x]\Delta_2; [\theta/x]\Gamma \vdash [\theta/x]I$ ok.*

The most challenging cases are those involving unification. Unification is not always preserved under substitution; in this case, $[\theta/x]I$ is vacuously well-typed as discussed in Sect. 3.4. In the case where unification is preserved, we exploit the fact that the derivation for I computed the *most general* unifier, which is thus a prefix of the unifier from $[\theta/x]I$. At a high level, this suffices to show all necessary constraints were preserved by substitution.

The progress and preservation cases for unification instructions need to know that dynamic unification unify is in harmony with static unification.

Lemma (Soundness of unify). *If $\Delta \vdash M_1 : a$ and $\Delta \vdash M_2 : a$ and $\Delta \vdash H : \Psi$ and $\Delta; C; H \vdash T$ ok and $\Delta; \Psi \vdash \ell_1 : \mathfrak{S}(M_1 : a)$ and $\Delta; \Psi \vdash \ell_2 : \mathfrak{S}(M_2 : a)$ then*

- *If $\Delta \vdash M_1 \sqcap M_2 = \bot$ then have unify$(\Delta, H, T, \ell_1, \ell_2) = \bot$*
- *If $\Delta \vdash M_1 \sqcap M_2 = \sigma$ then have unify$(\Delta, H, T, \ell_1, \ell_2) = (\Delta', H', T')$ where $\Delta' = [\sigma]\Delta$ and $[\sigma]\Delta \vdash H' : [\sigma]\Psi$ and $\Delta', (C, H') \vdash T'$ ok.*

The Heap Update lemma says that when the occurs check passes, the result of binding a free variable is well-typed (with the new binding reflected by a substitution into the heap type Ψ). Because the typing invariant implies acyclic heaps, this lemma means cycles are not introduced.

Lemma (Heap Update). *If $\Delta \vdash H : \Psi$ and $\Psi(\ell_1) = \mathfrak{S}(x : a)$ then*

(a) *If $\Psi(\ell_2) = \mathfrak{S}(M : a)$ and $\ell_1 \notin_H \ell_2$, (the occurs check passes) then $\Delta \vdash H\{\ell_1 \mapsto \boldsymbol{BOUND}\ \ell_2\} : [M/x]\Psi$.*

(b) *If for all i, $\Psi(\ell_i') = \mathfrak{S}(M_i : a_i)$ and $\ell_1 \notin_H \ell_i'$ and $\Sigma(c) = \boldsymbol{a} \to a$, then $\Delta \vdash H\{\ell_1 \mapsto c\langle \ell_1', \ldots, \ell_n' \rangle\} : [c\ \boldsymbol{M}]\Psi.$*

This lemma is more subtle than its statement suggests, and demonstrates the subtle relationship between heaps, heap types, and heap typing derivations. Recall that heaps and heap types are unordered: the typing derivation itself exhibits a topological ordering as a witness that there are no cycles. The proof of Heap Update is constructive and proceeds by induction on the derivation: an algorithm can be given which computes a new topological ordering for the resulting heap. Introducing free variables and binding free variables both preserve the validity of the trail:

Lemma (Trail Update). *If $\Delta; C; H \vdash T$ ok then*

(a) *If $H(\ell^H) = \mathbf{FREE}[x : a]$ then*
$$\Delta; H\{\ell^H \mapsto w\} \vdash \text{udate\_trail}(x : a@\ell^H, T) \text{ ok}.$$
(b) *If ℓ^H fresh and x fresh then $\Delta; H\{\{\ell^H \mapsto \mathbf{FREE}\}\}[x : a] \vdash T$ ok.*

Claim (a) says that if we bind a free variable x to a term and add x to the trail (notated $x : a@\ell^H$ to indicate a variable x of type a was located at ℓ^H), the resulting trail is well-typed. The trail update_trail$(x : a@\ell^H, T)$ is well-typed under the heap $H\{\ell^H \mapsto w\}$ iff unwinding it results in a well-typed heap. Thus proving (a) amounts to showing that unwinding update_trail$(x : a@\ell^H, T)$ gives us the original heap, which we already know to be well-typed.

Claim (b) is a weakening principle for trails, which comes directly from the weakening principle for heaps (a heap $H : \Psi$ is allowed to contain extra unreachable locations ℓ which do not appear in Ψ). This claim shows that the trail does not need to be modified when a fresh variable is allocated, only when it is bound to a term. It relies on the following subclaim, which holds by induction on the trace tr contained in tf.

Claim. unwind$((\Delta, x{:}a), H\{\{\ell^H \mapsto \mathbf{FREE}[x{:}a]\}\}, tr) = (\Delta, H'\{\{\ell^H \mapsto \mathbf{FREE}[x{:}a]\}\})$ for some heap H'.

Recall that the typing rule for trails simply says whatever heap results from unwinding must be well-typed. This simplifies the proofs significantly: showing that an update preserves validity consists simply of showing that it does not change the result of backtracking (modulo perhaps introducing unused values).

Soundness of the backtracking operation simply says the resulting machine is well-typed. The proof is direct from the premises of the trail typing invariant.

Lemma (Backtracking Totality). *For all trails T, if $\Delta \vdash C : \Xi$, $\Delta \vdash H : \Psi$, and $\Delta; C; H \vdash_{\Sigma;\Xi} T$ ok then either backtrack$(\Delta, C, H, T) = m'$ and $\cdot \vdash m'$ ok or backtrack$(\Delta, C, H, T) = \bot$.*

While the full proof contains several dozen other lemmas, those discussed above demonstrate the major insights into why the TWAM type system is sound and why it enables certification for TWAM programs.

4   Implementation

Implementing a compiler from T-Prolog to TWAM, a TWAM runtime, and a TWAM typechecker allows us not only to execute T-Prolog programs, but crucially to validate the TWAM design. For example, implementation increased our confidence that the static and dynamic semantics are exhaustive. Testing the compiler and checker provides informal evidence that they are sufficiently complete in practice. Testing the checker also tests its soundness, validating simultaneously that it is faithful to the dynamics and that Theorem 1 holds of the implementation.

The proof-of-concept implementation, which consists of 5,000 lines of Standard ML, is available from the first author upon request. The TWAM typechecker, which constitutes the trusted core, is about 400 lines. The large majority of the core is implemented by straightforward (manual) translation of the TWAM typing rules into ML code. This is a small fraction of the code (less than 10%) and compares favorably with the trusted cores of general-purpose proof checkers. Our test suite has 23 test files totaling 468 lines, the largest of which is a library for unary and decimal arithmetic. Other files stress-test edge cases of T-Prolog and TWAM execution.

The tests showed that the TWAM checker often catches compiler bugs in practice. Many of these bugs centered around placing a value into the wrong register or wrong position of a tuple. Singleton types are effective at catching these bugs because distinct terms always have different singleton types. Prior typed intermediate languages are less certain to catch these bugs because they permit distinct terms to have the same type.

Not only did our implementation greatly increase confidence in the theory, but we believe that it demonstrates TWAM's potential for catching real bugs.

5   Related Work

We are the first to build a full certifying (or verified, in general) compiler for a Prolog-like language. In contrast, full compilers for imperative (C [17]) and functional (ML [16]) languages have been verified directly in proof assistants. The latter project also yielded a compiler from higher-order logic [21] to ML.

Compiler verification for Prolog has been explored, but past attempts did not yield a full compiler. Paper proofs were written for both concrete [30] and abstract [3,5] compiler algorithms. Some (but not all) passes of Prolog compilers were verified in Isabelle [28] and KIV [31]. Prolog source semantics have also been formalized, e.g., in Coq [15]. Compiling all the way from Prolog to WAM with proof has been noted explicitly [31] as a challenge. Previous formalized proofs reported 6 person-month development times, the same time that it took to develop our theory, proofs, and implementation. While the comparison is not direct because many details of the projects differ, we find it promising.

Certifying compilation includes type-preserving compilation [34] and proof-carrying code (PCC) [23]. In type-preserving compilation, the certificates are type annotations, while in PCC they are proofs in logic. Type-preserving compilation is typically more concise while PCC is typically more flexible. Certifying compilation has recently been applied to the Calculus of Constructions [6] and LLVM passes [14]. A significant fragment of the proof checker for LLVM is verified in Coq for reliability. Applying this approach to TWAM is non-trivial, but possible in theory. Their experience supporting optimizations suggest we could do the same for TWAM, with proportional verification effort.

Translation validation [27] is a related approach, with post-hoc, black-box (but still automatic) construction of certificates. Its black-box nature means it might support multiple compilers, but is also often brittle.

The first-order logic we used can be embedded in the logical framework LF [13]; We have chosen FOL over LF for the simple reason that it is much better known. LF is also the foundation of the programming language Elf [25] and proof checker Twelf [26]. A comparison of our approach with Elf is fruitful: Elf instruments execution to produce LF proofs, whereas we instrument *compilation* to produce a proof that *obviates the need* for execution to produce proofs, which is amenable to higher performance. Singleton types, which are featured prominently in TWAM, are not new [38], but we are the first to support unification on singletons.

TWAM is also a descendant of typed assembly language (TAL) [7–9,19,20]. Dependent types and TAL have been combined in DTAL [37], but DTAL employs a lightweight, restrictive class of dependent types in order to, e.g., eliminate array bounds checks when compiling DML [38]. Our class of dependent types is more expressive. DTAL typechecking also requires complex non-syntactic constraint generation and solving. While TWAM's unification constraints are non-trivial, they are syntactic and thus more likely to scale.

Abstraction interpretation for Prolog [33] provides another view on our work. The abstraction interpretation literature distinguishes between *goal-dependent* analyses which must be performed again for every query and *goal-independent* ones which are reusable across queries. Our type system is compositional, so most of the work is reusable across queries. When a new query is provided, on the query itself (and success continuation) must be checked again. This is true in large part because procedure typechecking is static and need not know what arguments will be supplied at runtime.

6   Future Work

Our proof-of-concept implementation has shown that the certifying compilation approach is viable for logic programs. What remains is to exploit this potential by building a production-quality optimizing compiler for a widely-used language. Full Prolog is a natural target: a first step can be achieved easily by reintroducing cuts and negations as failure into the language but leaving them out of the certification spec. That is, it is straightforward to support compilation of cut and negation while only providing a formal correctness guarantee for the "pure" subgoals. It is less obvious how to certify full Prolog precisely. The deepest challenge is that provability semantics are insufficient to certify non-logical

Prolog features, so a more complex approach using operational semantics may be needed.

Logic languages other than Prolog may benefit from certifying compilation, especially certification of search soundness. Lambda-Prolog [22] and Elf [24, 25] can both be easily interpreted with a provability semantics and have both been used in theorem-proving [11, 26] where soundness of proof checking is essential. It is expected that these languages could be supported by using a stronger logic for specifications. Certifying compilation for Datalog might be especially fruitful given Datalog's commercial successes [2, 12] and given that it is a subset of Prolog, one which typically omits cut and negation. The main challenge there would not be extending the specification language, but replacing our WAM-like design with a relational algebra-based forward-chaining interpreter as is typically used for Datalog.

The challenge of runtime performance should also not be ignored. TWAM's proximity to WAM and purely compile-time approach show promise for runtime efficiency. However, the WAM supports a well-known set of optimizations that have a significant impact in practice [1] and many of which we did not implement. Some of the most important optimizations, such as careful register allocation and common subexpression elimination, are already possible in TWAM. Many of the other important optimizations, such as jump-tables, are implemented with custom instructions, which we believe could be added to TWAM with modest effort. In short, the future work is to use the lessons learned from a proof-of-concept implementation for a simplified language to build a production-quality implementation for a production-quality language.

Acknowledgements. We thank the many collaborators and friends who read earlier drafts of this work, including Jean Yang, Jan Hoffman, Stefan Muller, Chris Martens, Bill Duff, and Alex Podolsky. We thank all of our anonymous reviewers, especially for their infinite patience with the technical details of the paper. Special thanks to the VSTTE organizers for allowing us additional space. The first author was partially supported by the NDSEG Fellowship.

References

1. Aït-Kaci, H.: Warren's Abstract Machine: A Tutorial Reconstruction. MIT Press, Cambridge (1991)
2. Aref, M., et al.: Design and implementation of the LogicBlox system. In: Sellis, T.K., Davidson, S.B., Ives, Z.G. (eds.) Proceedings of the 2015 ACM SIGMOD International Conference on Management of Data, Melbourne, Victoria, Australia, 31 May - 4 June, 2015, pp. 1371–1382. ACM (2015). http://doi.acm.org/10.1145/2723372.2742796
3. Beierle, C., Börger, E.: Correctness proof for the WAM with types. In: Börger, E., Jäger, G., Kleine Büning, H., Richter, M.M. (eds.) CSL 1991. LNCS, vol. 626, pp. 15–34. Springer, Heidelberg (1992). https://doi.org/10.1007/BFb0023755
4. Bohrer, R., Crary, K.: TWAM: a certifying abstract machine for logic programs. CoRR abs/1801.00471 (2018). http://arxiv.org/abs/1801.00471

5. Börger, E., Rosenzweig, D.: The WAM–definition and compiler correctness. In: Logic Programming: Formal Methods and Practical Applications, pp. 20–90 (1995)
6. Bowman, W.J., Ahmed, A.: Typed closure conversion for the calculus of constructions. In: Foster and Grossman [10], pp. 797–811. https://doi.org/10.1145/3192366.3192372
7. Crary, K.: Toward a foundational typed assembly language. In: Aiken, A., Morrisett, G. (eds.) Conference Record of POPL 2003: The 30th SIGPLAN-SIGACT Symposium on Principles of Programming Languages, New Orleans, Louisisana, USA, 15–17 January 2003, pp. 198–212. ACM (2003). https://doi.org/10.1145/640128.604149
8. Crary, K., Sarkar, S.: Foundational certified code in the Twelf metalogical framework. ACM Trans. Comput. Log. 9(3), 16:1–16:26 (2008). https://doi.org/10.1145/1352582.1352584
9. Crary, K., Vanderwaart, J.: An expressive, scalable type theory for certified code. In: Wand, M., Jones, S.L.P. (eds.) Proceedings of the Seventh ACM SIGPLAN International Conference on Functional Programming (ICFP 2002), Pittsburgh, Pennsylvania, USA, 4–6 October 2002, pp. 191–205. ACM (2002). https://doi.org/10.1145/581478.581497
10. Foster, J.S., Grossman, D. (eds.): Proceedings of the 39th ACM SIGPLAN Conference on Programming Language Design and Implementation, PLDI 2018, Philadelphia, PA, USA, 18–22 June 2018. ACM (2018). https://doi.org/10.1145/3192366
11. Gacek, A.: System description: Abella - a system for reasoning about computations. CoRR 2008 (2008). http://arxiv.org/abs/0803.2305
12. Hajiyev, E., et al.: Keynote address: QL for source code analysis. In: Seventh IEEE International Working Conference on Source Code Analysis and Manipulation (SCAM 2007) (SCAM), pp. 3–16, October 2007. https://doi.org/10.1109/SCAM.2007.31
13. Harper, R., Honsell, F., Plotkin, G.D.: A framework for defining logics. J. ACM 40(1), 143–184 (1993). https://doi.org/10.1145/138027.138060
14. Kang, J., et al.: Crellvm: verified credible compilation for LLVM. In: Foster and Grossman [10], pp. 631–645. https://doi.org/10.1145/3192366.3192377
15. Kriener, J., King, A., Blazy, S.: Proofs you can believe in: proving equivalences between prolog semantics in Coq. In: Peña, R., Schrijvers, T. (eds.) 15th International Symposium on Principles and Practice of Declarative Programming, PPDP 2013, Madrid, Spain, 16–18 September 2013, pp. 37–48. ACM (2013). https://doi.org/10.1145/2505879.2505886
16. Kumar, R., Myreen, M.O., Norrish, M., Owens, S.: CakeML: a verified implementation of ML. In: POPL 2014, pp. 179–191 (2014). https://doi.org/10.1145/2535838.2535841
17. Leroy, X.: Formal certification of a compiler back-end or: programming a compiler with a proof assistant. In: Morrisett, J.G., Jones, S.L.P. (eds.) Proceedings of the 33rd ACM SIGPLAN-SIGACT Symposium on Principles of Programming Languages, POPL 2006, Charleston, South Carolina, USA, 11–13 January 2006, pp. 42–54. ACM (2006). https://doi.org/10.1145/1111037.1111042
18. Martelli, A., Montanari, U.: An efficient unification algorithm. ACM Trans. Program. Lang. Syst. 4(2), 258–282 (1982). https://doi.org/10.1145/357162.357169
19. Morrisett, J.G., Crary, K., Glew, N., Walker, D.: Stack-based typed assembly language. J. Funct. Program. 13(5), 957–959 (2003). https://doi.org/10.1017/S0956796802004446

20. Morrisett, J.G., Walker, D., Crary, K., Glew, N.: From system F to typed assembly language. ACM Trans. Program. Lang. Syst. **21**(3), 527–568 (1999). https://doi.org/10.1145/319301.319345

21. Myreen, M.O., Owens, S.: Proof-producing translation of higher-order logic into pure and stateful ML. J. Funct. Program. **24**(2–3), 284–315 (2014). https://doi.org/10.1017/S0956796813000282

22. Nadathur, G., Miller, D.: An overview of Lambda-PROLOG. In: Kowalski, R.A., Bowen, K.A. (eds.) Logic Programming, Proceedings of the Fifth International Conference and Symposium, Seattle, Washington, USA, 15–19 August 1988, vol. 2, pp. 810–827. MIT Press (1988)

23. Necula, G.C., Lee, P.: The design and implementation of a certifying compiler. In: Davidson, J.W., Cooper, K.D., Berman, A.M. (eds.) Proceedings of the ACM SIGPLAN '98 Conference on Programming Language Design and Implementation (PLDI), Montreal, Canada, 17–19 June 1998, pp. 333–344. ACM (1998). https://doi.org/10.1145/277650.277752

24. Pfenning, F.: Elf: A language for logic definition and verified metaprogramming. In: Proceedings of the Fourth Annual Symposium on Logic in Computer Science (LICS 1989), Pacific Grove, California, USA, 5–8 June 1989, pp. 313–322. IEEE Computer Society (1989). https://doi.org/10.1109/LICS.1989.39186

25. Pfenning, F.: Logic programming in the LF logical framework. In: Logical Frameworks, pp. 149–181. Cambridge University Press, New York (1991). http://dl.acm.org/citation.cfm?id=120477.120483

26. Pfenning, F., Schürmann, C.: System description: Twelf—a meta-logical framework for deductive systems. In: CADE 1999. LNCS (LNAI), vol. 1632, pp. 202–206. Springer, Heidelberg (1999). https://doi.org/10.1007/3-540-48660-7_14

27. Pnueli, A., Siegel, M., Singerman, E.: Translation validation. In: Steffen, B. (ed.) TACAS 1998. LNCS, vol. 1384, pp. 151–166. Springer, Heidelberg (1998). https://doi.org/10.1007/BFb0054170

28. Pusch, C.: Verification of compiler correctness for the WAM. In: Goos, G., Hartmanis, J., van Leeuwen, J., von Wright, J., Grundy, J., Harrison, J. (eds.) TPHOLs 1996. LNCS, vol. 1125, pp. 347–361. Springer, Heidelberg (1996). https://doi.org/10.1007/BFb0105415

29. Robinson, J.A.: A machine-oriented logic based on the resolution principle. J. ACM **12**(1), 23–41 (1965). https://doi.org/10.1145/321250.321253

30. Russinoff, D.M.: A verified prolog compiler for the warren abstract machine. J. Log. Program. **13**(4), 367–412 (1992). https://doi.org/10.1016/0743-1066(92)90054-7

31. Schellhorn, G., Ahrendt, W.: Reasoning about abstract state machines: the WAM case study. J. UCS **3**(4), 377–413 (1997). https://doi.org/10.3217/jucs-003-04-0377

32. Sørensen, M.H., Urzyczyn, P.: Lectures on the Curry-Howard Isomorphism, vol. 149. Elsevier, Amsterdam (2006)

33. Spoto, F., Levi, G.: Abstract interpretation of prolog programs. In: Haeberer, A.M. (ed.) AMAST 1999. LNCS, vol. 1548, pp. 455–470. Springer, Heidelberg (1998). https://doi.org/10.1007/3-540-49253-4_32

34. Tarditi, D., Morrisett, J.G., Cheng, P., Stone, C.A., Harper, R., Lee, P.: TIL: a type-directed optimizing compiler for ML. In: PLDI, pp. 181–192. ACM (1996)

35. Warren, D.H.: An Abstract Prolog Instruction Set, vol. 309. Artificial Intelligence Center, SRI International Menlo Park, California (1983)

36. Wielemaker, J.: SWI-Prolog OpenHub Project Page (2018). https://www.openhub.net/p/swi-prolog. Accessed 28 Apr 2018

37. Xi, H., Harper, R.: A dependently typed assembly language. In: Pierce, B.C. (ed.) Proceedings of the Sixth ACM SIGPLAN International Conference on Functional Programming (ICFP 2001), Florence, Italy, 3–5 September 2001, pp. 169–180. ACM (2001). https://doi.org/10.1145/507635.507657

38. Xi, H., Pfenning, F.: Dependent types in practical programming. In: Appel, A.W., Aiken, A. (eds.) POPL 1999, Proceedings of the 26th ACM SIGPLAN-SIGACT Symposium on Principles of Programming Languages, San Antonio, TX, USA, 20–22 January 1999, pp. 214–227. ACM (1999). https://doi.org/10.1145/292540.292560

A Java Bytecode Formalisation

Patryk Czarnik, Jacek Chrząszcz, and Aleksy Schubert[(⊠)]

Institute of Informatics, University of Warsaw, ul. S. Banacha 2, 02–097 Warsaw, Poland
{czarnik,chrzaszcz,alx}@mimuw.edu.pl

Abstract. This paper presents the first Coq formalisation of the full Java bytecode instruction set and its semantics. The set of instructions is organised in a hierarchy depending on how the instructions deal with the runtime structures of the Java Virtual Machine such as threads, stacks, heap etc. The hierarchical nature of Coq modules neatly reinforces this view and facilitates the understanding of the Java bytecode semantics. This approach makes it possible to both conduct verification of properties for programs and to prove metatheoretical results for the language. Based upon our formalisation experience, the deficiencies of the current informal bytecode language specification are discussed.

Keywords: Formalisation · Coq · Semantics · Java bytecode

1 Introduction

Although originally designed as a target compilation language for Java, the Java bytecode becomes more and more useful for other languages such as Scala or Kotlin. Consequently multi-language applications executed on the common ground of a Java Virtual Machine gain in popularity. One way to ensure security of such mixed applications is to develop tools and techniques which work directly at the bytecode level.

Conception of such tools requires thorough understanding of bytecode and its semantics. They are described in natural language in the specification document [21] which leaves certain margin to the language implementers. As a result, real implementations usually differ in their operation, which is the result of particular implementation decisions (e.g. they can use a different scheduler). A formal specification of semantics, on the other hand, can be faithful to the specification document and hence it can serve as a common platform for expressing properties of many implementations.

This effort creates also an opportunity to systematically review the natural language specification of the Java Virtual Machine Language (JVML) [21]. As a result, certain assumptions made in the specification become explicit and inconsistencies are pointed out and resolved. This can be beneficial for future

This work was partially supported by the Polish NCN grant no 2013/11/B/ST6/01381.

R. Piskac and P. Rümmer (Eds.): VSTTE 2018, LNCS 11294, pp. 135–154, 2018.
https://doi.org/10.1007/978-3-030-03592-1_8

releases of the natural language specification document: it can gain better structure, more precise phrasing, less ambiguities and better consistency. The last point is especially appealing since the large size of a real programming language leads to big semi-formal description and maintaining its consistency becomes a challenging task.

For many programming languages the effort of formalisation can be done for a small core sublanguage so that the rest of the language is reducible to it through a desugaring translation. In this way full formalisation consists of two parts, a translation to the core language and a formalisation of the core itself. This approach was taken for instance for SML [23] and JML [18,31]. This method is not adequate for Java bytecode since JVML is the ultimate form that is executed by real machines. To cope with this difficulty we defined an abstract set of instructions following the design in [6] and then formalised it in Coq [9]. These abstractions are hierarchical in the sense that the lower the level, the closer the abstractions are to the actual JVM mnemonics.

In our design of the hierarchy, we rigorously took the approach to examine the way instructions use the runtime structures of the Java Virtual Machine such as threads, heap, method stack, operand stack etc. Each instruction operates on some selected runtime structures, e.g. the integer arithmetic instructions manipulate only the local operand stack, object field access uses the operand stack and the heap etc. This way of abstracting the instructions has important advantages such as:

- Hierarchical approach makes it possible to express elements of functionality on higher levels in the hierarchy; as a result numerous parts of formalisation need not be repeated.
- The hierarchy singles out particular submodels for the language for which interesting and useful metalanguage properties can be proved (e.g. to consider single-threaded Java one has to take the part of the hierarchy that avoids threads).
- The structure of metatheoretical proofs resembles the hierarchic structure of the definition of semantics; therefore proofs become easier to follow.

To obtain a manageable and general formalisation, we used the following techniques. First, the semantics is formalised as a relation. In this way it can be non-deterministic in places where the original description leaves certain freedom to implementations. This would be impossible in case of a formalisation as a computable function, which would correspond to a single implementation. Second, the whole semantics is written in the small-step fashion. It is more appropriate since the specification expressed in the natural language is in most cases also formulated in the small-step fashion. Moreover, many metatheoretic properties (e.g. immutability, purity etc.) are easier to formulate in this style. Third, our development uses the hierarchical nature of the Coq module system [5,33] (see Fig. 1) to separate different aspects of the virtual machine and to reflect our hierarchy of instructions and their semantics. In this way, the formal semantics is naturally divided into consistent fragments and is therefore easier to understand.

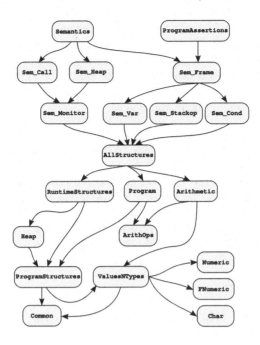

Fig. 1. Module dependencies in CoJaq.

The same hierarchical structure of modules can be used for proofs of metatheoretical properties of the JVML semantics: in this way, the structure of the proof follows the structure of the entity on which the proof is done and therefore it becomes clear and comprehensive.

In this paper we present a formalisation of the Java Virtual Machine language semantics for all 200 bytecode instructions. It is done within a Coq project, called CoJaq[1]. A long-term goal of this project is to create a platform to attain two objectives: to get the possibility to verify real programs and to prove metatheoretical properties of the bytecode language. The current paper presents a major step towards this goal.

The key achievements of the presented formalisation are:

- Full Java bytecode instruction set as fixed by The Java Virtual Machine Specification, Second Edition [21] together with a small-step operational semantics has been modelled in Coq. The formalisation groups the instructions according to their handling of the JVM runtime structures[2].
- A static semantic based upon types of values is developed. This static semantics is proved to be sound and complete with regard to the dynamic one.
- We proved a general theorem that locally operating programs for which Hoare-style logic rules apply at each step are partially correct.

---

[1] Available at http://cojaq.mimuw.edu.pl. Intermediate report appeared in [10].
[2] This does not include native method calls.

- The semantics is also a case study in mechanising of metatheory of programming languages in the spirit of POPLmark challenge [2]. This time the ability of proof assistants technology to formalise big languages is checked.
- The formalisation gives an opportunity to discuss design choices that were made during the creation of the bytecode language as well as to analyse the way the informal semantics is laid down.

In our formalisation we adopted a *post-linking view*: CoJaq only handles complete programs and hence is not able to deal with dynamic linking and class initialisation.

The paper is structured as follows. Section 2 presents the motivations for a hierarchical formalisation. The hierarchical definition of the JVML semantics is presented in Sect. 3. A proof that a simple type system for JVML is correct is presented in Sect. 4. The account of program verification in our semantics is presented in Sect. 5. This is followed in Sect. 6 by a discussion on the design of the Java bytecode language and its informal specifications. In Sect. 7 we report the related work and we conclude in Sect. 8.

2   The Need for Hierarchy of Instructions

Java bytecode consists of 200 mnemonics and their organisation in the natural language specification lacks almost any structure. A computerised formalisation performed in the same flat fashion would suffer from two main issues. First of all, a lot of code fragments would need to be repeated for many instructions. Almost every step in the semantics requires the same operations such as selection of a thread to execute and identification of the current instruction to execute. Secondly, with a flat definition consisting of so many cases it is difficult to conduct any kind of analytic work. Usually a metatheoretical proof requires a lot of proofs by induction over the subject language.

There are numerous situations where it is easy to recognise common patterns that make it possible to group instructions together. Here are some examples:

1. A set of instructions performing the same operation for different data types. This is the case of `iload`, `fload`, `aload`, and so on. Each instruction loads a local variable value and pushes it on the operand stack, but a single instruction is applicable only to a particular value types (`int`, `float`, and 'reference', respectively). A natural generalisation of this set of instruction is one *load* instruction parametrised with data type.
2. "Shorthand instructions" are defined for some most widely used argument values. For example, the meaning of `iload_0`, `iload_1`, `iload_2`, and `iload_3` is the same as `iload` with a suitable parameter. Taking also the conclusions of the previous point into account, the ultimate form of *load* is one instruction with two arguments: a variable index and a value type. This single instruction stands for 25 original JVML mnemonics.
3. Instructions related to arithmetic and comparison often behave in a similar way and differ only in the arithmetic operator. For example, `iadd`, `isub`,

imul, idiv, and imod all perform binary arithmetic operations on integers. They all pop two operands from the stack and push back one resulting value. It is convenient to group them in one metainstruction "binary arithmetic operation" parametrised with an actual operator. The semantics on structural level can now be defined in one place, and only the semantics of arithmetic operators needs to be defined separately simply as a function of type int $\times$ int $\rightarrow$ int. Unfortunately, division operators idiv and imod destroy such a clear image as they throw *ArithmeticException* in case of division by zero. Summing up, a binary arithmetic operation is parametrised with a type and an operator.

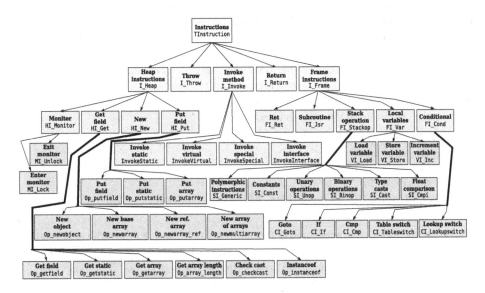

Fig. 2. Hierarchy of instruction abstractions

These examples of instruction groups, used e.g. in [27], and also hinted by JVM specification in Table 3.2 [21], are very efficient in reducing the number of instructions. They are very natural, still, they are rather ad hoc. Therefore, we decided to go one step further and complement the above structuring by finding an *inherent principle*, according to which the instructions can be combined into a comprehensive structure. This principle, which led us to the hierarchy in Fig. 2 is:

Instructions grouped together in one slot use the same runtime structures.

3   Hierarchical Definition of Semantics

The structural organisation of instructions is naturally reflected by the organisation of semantics. It can already be seen in a "big picture" view of Coq modules from our formalisation, Fig. 1, where the structure of modules implementing semantics to some extent reflects the hierarchy of instructions. The hierarchy is inspired by the tree-like structure of the JVM state. In this way the relations defining semantics of abstract instructions which are lower in the instruction hierarchy operate on a smaller fragment of the JVM state—exactly the one which is accessed by the real instructions represented by the abstract ones.

Let us present and explain the hierarchy of semantic relations on the example of if_icmpge 19 instruction, whose CoJaq representation is:

I_Frame (FI_Cond (CI_Cmp KInt CmpOp_ge offset19))

where *offset19* represents the target address *19*.

Let us assume that the virtual machine is in a state consisting of a single thread and a heap. The frame at the top of the call stack contains a local variable table, an operand stack, and a program counter (PC), pointing to the instruction of interest.

We start with presenting three relations *step*, *stepThread*, and *semInstr* from the Semantics module. These relations define the semantics on the top level of our instructions hierarchy, but they focus on different aspects of execution. The entry point is the relation *step* defined as:

Inductive *step (p: TProgram): TJVM → TJVM →* **Prop** :=
| *Step_thread:* **forall** ...,
  selectedThread jvm th →
  stepInThread p (th, h) (th', h') →
  oneThreadAndHeapChanged (th, h) (th', h') jvm jvm' →
    step p jvm jvm'.

The relation has three arguments *TProgram*, *TJVM* and *TJVM* (the result kind **Prop** indicates that this is a relation). It holds if for a given program *p* and a virtual machine state a transition to another state is possible. The only case of its definition says that *step* holds if and only if a thread *th* can be selected for execution, a step in this single thread is possible (*stepInThread*), and it results in a potential change of the thread internal state (*th* to *th'*) and the heap (*h* to *h'*). The auxiliary relation *oneThreadAndHeapChanged* applies these partial changes to the whole JVM state. This relation makes it possible for this semantics to work in memory models that offer sequential consistency only.

CoJaq supports mutithreading by means of non-deterministic choice. For a given input state, *step* may assign more than one output states, one for each possible choice of a thread. Similarly, in case when no thread can be chosen because of monitor state, i.e. when the program went to deadlock, the relation would not hold at all.

In the case of our example the only possibility for the relation to hold is that the relation *stepInThread* holds for the sole thread of the machine.

Inductive *stepThread (p: TProgram):*
  (TThread ∗ THeap) → (TThread ∗ THeap) → **Prop** :=
| *StepInThread_instruction_ok:* **forall** ...,
  th = threadMake thid null ((cm, fr) :: frs) →

> *getMethodBodyFromProgram p (cmQName cm) = Some code →*
> *getInstruction code (frameGetPC fr) = Some instr →*
> *semInstr p code instr (th, h) (Result (th', h')) →*
>   *stepInThread p (th, h) (th', h')*

The type of the relation illustrates the fact that a step within a thread may affect its internal state and the heap, but the state of the other threads is not even taken into account. The definition consists of five inductive cases handling normal and exceptional execution. The first case, given above, describes a step starting from a non-exceptional state and executing a single instruction. The first three premises select the current method code and the instruction to execute. Next, we refer to another relation *semInstr* to obtain the details of the single instruction execution. In this case we require that the instruction completes with a normal *Result*, i.e. without an exception. Finally, if the conditions are met, we prescribe that *stepInThread* holds for the given input state and the result state obtained from *semInstr*.

Another case concerns the situation when the instruction completes with an exception described in the specification, like *NullPointerException*.

> | *StepInThread_instruction_exn:* **forall** ...,
>   *th = threadMake thid null ((cm, fr) :: frs) →*
>   *getMethodBodyFromProgram p (cmQName cm) = Some code →*
>   *getInstruction code (frameGetPC fr) = Some instr →*
>   *semInstr p code instr (th, h) (Exception ecn) →*
>   *systemException ecn h h' eloc →*
>   *th' = threadMake thid eloc ((cm, fr') :: frs) →*
>   *stepInThread p (th, h) (th', h')*

Analogously to the style in which the natural language specification [21] describes standard exceptions, we specify only the class (*ecn*) of such exceptions in descriptions of particular instructions. Lower levels of the semantics hierarchy use a special type *TResultOrException*, being in fact a disjoint union of normal results and exception class names, to provide information about normal or exceptional instruction completion in an elegant way. Here, at the top level of the semantics, the exceptional case is handled so that a proper exception object is actually thrown.

The last three cases of the relation *stepThread* (skipped here) specify handling an exception that has been thrown earlier: either catching the exception, which results in a jump to an appropriate handler; passing uncaught exception to the outer method, which terminates the current one; or throwing another exception in case of an illegal monitor state.

Execution of a single instruction is formalised in the relation *semInstr* of Coq type

$$TProgram → TCode → TInstruction → (TThread*THeap)$$
$$→ TResultOrException (TThread*THeap) → \textbf{Prop}.$$

Its second and third arguments are the current method's code and the current instruction, already extracted form the program and the thread's state by *stepThread*. We can see here that the hierarchical design of the semantics helps to separate the concerns (threads, exceptions, actual instruction execution) and to avoid code duplications, as otherwise we would have to repeat the presented premises of *step* and *stepThread* cases in each case of *semInstr* or describe the allocation of exception objects in each place where an exception should be thrown. The relation is defined by 10 cases which correspond to 5 instructions at the top level of the hierarchy (*I_Frame*, *I_Heap*, and so on) multiplied by the fact that an instruction can complete normally or with an exception.

Coming back to our example, as the instruction is from the *I_Frame* category, two of the 10 cases are relevant here:

```
| SemInstr_frame: forall  ...,
    th = threadMake thid null ((cm, fr) :: frs) →
    th' = threadMake thid null ((cm, fr') :: frs) →
    M_Sem_Frame.semFrame code finstr fr (Result fr') →
      semInstr p code (I_Frame finstr) (th, h) (Result (th', h))
| SemInstr_frame_exn: forall  ...,
    th = threadMake thid null ((cm, fr) :: frs) →
    M_Sem_Frame.semFrame code finstr fr (Exception ecn) →
      semInstr p code (I_Frame finstr) (th, h) (Exception ecn)
```

Both cases decompose the input state of the thread to obtain the frame at the top of the call stack, refer to *semFrame* relation which gives the detailed semantics of this frame instruction. The first case applies the change in the frame state (*fr* to *fr'*) to the state of the whole thread. The heap and the rest of the call stack remain unchanged. The second case simply propagates the exception. Cases for instructions in other categories are similar but, as our principle governs, they affect different fragments of the state.

The *semFrame* relation, from the Sem_Frame module, specifies the semantics of frame instructions. Its type

$$TCode \rightarrow TFrameInstr \rightarrow TFrame \rightarrow TResultOrException\ TFrame \rightarrow \textbf{Prop}$$

shows us that instructions from this category operate on a single frame. Also the program as a whole is not required here, only the code of the current method. As before, the relation is determined by cases according to the particular frame instruction, i.e. *FI_Stackop*, *FI_Var*, *FI_Cond*, *FI_Jsr*, *FI_Ret*. Most instructions are handled in single cases, only *FI_Stackop* may raise exceptions and it requires an additional case to handle. For our example instruction *FI_Cond* only one case applies:

```
| SemFrame_cond: forall ...,
    M_Sem_Cond.semCond op vs vs' off_opt → stackTopValues vs vs' sk sk' →
    pc' = calculatePC off_opt code pc →
      semFrame code (FI_Cond op) (frameMake vars sk pc)
                               (Result (frameMake vars sk' pc'))
```

In this code fragment the parameter *op* denotes the special variant of *FI_Cond* instruction, which is *CI_Cmp KInt CmpOp_gt offset19*. For the case to hold, it is required that another specialised relation *semCond* holds for *op*. Together with the auxiliary relation *stackTopValues* it says that it permits the transformation of values at the top of the operand stack from *vs* to *vs'* and optionally generates a jump to *off_opt*. Lastly, the equation for *pc'* calculates the proper next instruction according to *off_opt* and the current position. The last line clearly explains that the instruction affects only two fields of a frame state: the operand stack *sk* and the PC, and it does not change local variables.

The precise semantics of the *FI_Cond* instruction does not interact with the whole frame, but only with the parts it really needs, i.e. the top values from the stack. The actual effect of the instruction on the values from the operand stack is implemented in the *semCond* relation (from the Sem_Cond module) of type *TCondInstr* → *list TValue* → *list TValue* → *option TOffset* → **Prop**, which, given the conditional instruction details (denoted as *op* in the previous paragraph), should be understood as a partial function from a list of values (popped from the operand stack) to the list of values (to be pushed back on the operand stack) and optional jump address. It is realised as an inductive relation with branches determined by the conditional instruction details *op*. Usually there is more than one branch per one type of conditional instruction, depending on whether the condition is met or not. Out of 9 cases that define the relation, two correspond to the instruction from our example:

| *SemCond_cmp_true:* **forall** ...,
  let *arithmetic* := *arithmeticForKind k* **in**
  M_ArithmeticTypes.arithCmpValues arithmetic cmpop arg1 arg2 true →
  semCond (CI_Cmp k cmpop off) [arg2;arg1] [] (Some off)
| *SemCond_cmp_false:* **forall** ...,
  let *arithmetic* := *arithmeticForKind k* **in**
  M_ArithmeticTypes.arithCmpValues arithmetic cmpop arg1 arg2 false →
  semCond (CI_Cmp k cmpop off) [arg2;arg1] [] None

The actual work is delegated to the Arithmetic module which does the comparison.[3] Since operations on different data types are structurally similar, different arithmetic modules are grouped together and selected according to the type ("kind") *k* by the function *arithmeticForKind*. In both cases two values are popped from the operand stack and no value is returned. Depending on the boolean result of the comparison a jump is triggered or not—in the latter case the program will simply go to the next instruction.

The hierarchical structure of semantics has a number of advantages. First of all, it prevents code duplication, as otherwise the *step* relation e.g. for all the *I_Frame* instructions would have almost identical premises corresponding to extracting the suitable fragment of the JVM state. Another advantage is the possibility to develop some proof techniques like VCGen, Hoare logic etc. only for fragments of the semantics, if the whole semantics is too complex to cover. The hierarchical structure of the semantics provides a natural delineation of fragments to do and to ignore. The approach to prove program properties (Sect. 5), together with the appropriate support in the ProgramAssertions module can serve as an example here, as it covers code fragments that use only instruc-

---

[3] The integer arithmetic was taken, in its major part, from Bicolano [27] by David Pichardie. The specification of floats was taken from the Coq contribution IEEE754 by Patrick Loiseleur.

tions from the *LFrame* category and operate within a single method. Finally, the hierarchical organisation of proofs corresponding to the design of the semantics helps to comprehend and manage them. The correctness of the static semantics described in the next part is an example of such proof.

4   Static Semantics

The correct operation of the semantics in the JVML strongly relies on the assumption that bytecode instructions have arguments of appropriate types. Therefore, the specification of each instruction is accompanied in JVM semantics [21] by a careful description of the types for its input and results. Revising the approach proposed in our earlier work [6], in CoJaq we decided to exclude explicit type conditions from the primary semantic rules. The type information can be, in fact, deduced from the form of the values manipulated by the instructions, but it is not given directly. Instead, we accompany definitions of the "dynamic" semantics with "static" semantics relations which operate at the level of types. In particular, the conditional instruction operation defined through

*semCond: TCondInstr → list TValue → list TValue → option TOffset → **Prop***

is accompanied by the relation

staticSemCond: TCondInstr → list TKind → list TKind → option TOffset →
Prop

which says that the operation in question given an operand stack with top elements of types enumerated in the first list returns a stack with the top elements replaced with values of types enumerated in the second list and optionally moves PC by the given offset. Note that both properties are relations so we can easily describe more than one allowed behaviour for a given input state. In this static semantics and other places where the term *kind* is used in the formalisation, we mean a simplified type information where all reference types (object types, array types etc.) are considered to be a single type *KRef* of references. This is the way type requirements are given in the majority of instruction specifications.

The consistency of the static and the dynamic view is proved through two properties which correspond to soundness and completeness properties of proof systems. First, we show that every possible step in the dynamic semantics has a counterpart in the static semantics. For *semCond* the fact is expressed by a property of the following form:

forall *op off_opt vs vs', semCond op vs vs' off_opt →*
   staticSemCond op (kindOfValues vs) (kindOfValues vs') off_opt.

Second, we demonstrate that every step in the static semantics is motivated by a corresponding step in the dynamic one:

forall *op off_opt ks ks', staticSemCond op ks ks' off_opt →*
   exists *vs vs', kindOfValues vs = ks ∧ kindOfValues vs' = ks'*
      ∧ semCond op vs vs' off_opt.

Full definitions and proofs are in the Sem_Cond module. Analogous properties and proofs are provided for other instructions from the I_Frame category (FI_Var, FI_Stackop etc.), and for I_Frame itself, which corresponds to 160 mnemonics. Beside potential applications for simplified analysis where actual values are not important, the proofs serve also as an assurance that the semantics has no anomalies. Moreover, this is an example of a large proof organised according to the hierarchy of instructions. In particular, the proof for I_Frame makes use of lemmas proved for FI_Cond, FI_Stackop, etc. Our experience shows us benefits of such a structural layout. Each of the lemmas defined for lower levels of the hierarchy is focused on a particular fragment of the state while at higher levels we can manage a whole branch at once. In this way we avoid a frequent obstacle in proof management for systems with sizeable number of constants where the proof context contains a big number of assumptions with a large size, which makes the process of proof development critically hard to get through. In our case, it proved especially useful as we gradually added new instructions during the development of CoJaq and the proof usually required changes only in one of the lemmas.

5   Program Verification

One of the design goals of the project was to build a formalisation applicable to real programs. Although the intended role of CoJaq itself is rather to be a base reference model for other tools, direct verification of a program in Coq is the most straightforward application and the first step to ensure that the formalisation is usable.

```
public static int m() {
    int i = 0;
    int n = 50;
    int r = 0;
    while (i < n) {
        r = i + r;
        i++;
        r = i + r;
    }
    return r;
}

        (a)
```

```
public static int m();

0:  iconst_0      // int i = 0;
1:  istore_0
2:  bipush 50     // int n = 50;
4:  istore_1
5:  iconst_0      // int r = 0;
6:  istore_2
7:  iload_0
8:  iload_1
9:  if_icmpge 26  // i >= n
12: iload_0
13: iload_2
14: iadd          //   i + r
15: istore_2      //   r = ...
16: iinc 0, 1     //   i++
19: iload_0
20: iload_2
21: iadd          //   i + r
22: istore_2      //   r = ...
23: goto 7        // end of loop
26: iload_2       // r is returned
27: ireturn
```

(b)

(c)

Fig. 3. An example of a method. (a) The Java source code of a method, (b) the corresponding bytecode, and (c) the control flow graph of the bytecode.

```
Definition code: TCode := codeFromList
  [(* 0*) I_Frame (FI_Stackop (SI_Const KInt (VInt (INum.zero))));
   (* 1*) I_Frame (FI_Var (VI_Store VIKInt var0));
   (* 2*) I_Frame (FI_Stackop (SI_Const KInt (VInt (INum.const n))));
   (* 3*) I_Frame (FI_Var (VI_Store VIKInt var1));
   (* 4*) I_Frame (FI_Stackop (SI_Const KInt (VInt (INum.zero))));
   (* 5*) I_Frame (FI_Var (VI_Store VIKInt var2));
   (* 6*) I_Frame (FI_Var (VI_Load VIKInt var0));
   (* 7*) I_Frame (FI_Var (VI_Load VIKInt var1));
   (* 8*) I_Frame (FI_Cond (CI_Cmp KInt ArithmeticOperators.CmpOp_ge
                            (offsetFromPosition 19%nat)));
   (* 9*) I_Frame (FI_Var (VI_Load VIKInt var0));
   (*10*) I_Frame (FI_Var (VI_Load VIKInt var2));
   (*11*) I_Frame (FI_Stackop (SI_Binop KInt ArithmeticOperators.BinOp_add));
   (*12*) I_Frame (FI_Var (VI_Store VIKInt var2));
   (*13*) I_Frame (FI_Var (VI_Inc var0 (INum.const 1)));
   (*14*) I_Frame (FI_Var (VI_Load VIKInt var0));
   (*15*) I_Frame (FI_Var (VI_Load VIKInt var2));
   (*16*) I_Frame (FI_Stackop (SI_Binop KInt ArithmeticOperators.BinOp_add));
   (*17*) I_Frame (FI_Var (VI_Store VIKInt var2));
   (*18*) I_Frame (FI_Cond (CI_Goto (offsetFromPosition 6%nat)));
   (*19*) I_Frame (FI_Var (VI_Load VIKInt var2));
   (*20*) I_Return (Some KInt)].
```

Fig. 4. Crucial fragments of the method code from Fig. 3 translated to our formalisation

A systematic process of JVML program verification can be performed as follows

1. We describe in Coq states between every two consecutive bytecode instructions.
2. Then for each instruction we prove that starting from a state satisfying the formula before an instruction if the semantic step of the instruction is taken then the resulting state satisfies the formula after the instruction. Special care must be taken for conditional jump instructions and the points of program where separate branches of the control flow join together.
3. When all transitions are described in this way, we can prove by induction that the program will always stay within the set of specified states, which is a form of partial correctness property.

Consider the program given in Fig. 3. It consists of initial assignments of constants to local variables and a loop that calculates the sum of first n odd numbers, which is equal to n^2. Its CoJaq counterpart is given in Fig. 4. First of all, note that labels in bytecode are positions in bytes, whereas in the Coq counterpart they are consecutive numbers. Second, the CoJaq code is parametrised by n, while in Java and JVML n is replaced by a concrete constant 50. The proof of program correctness is of course done for arbitrary (but small enough) n.

The proof process starts with proving a number of auxiliary lemmas about properties of *int32* numbers. After that we define properties describing the state before given instructions, e.g.:

```
Definition s8_prop frame :=
  pcToPosition (frameGetPC frame) = 8%nat
    ∧ exists i, exists r, stack_values frame [n; i] ∧ var_value frame var0 i
    ∧ var_value frame var1 n ∧ var_value frame var2 r ∧ r = i*i ∧ 0 <= i ∧ i <= n.
```

The above definition says (i) that the program counter of the current frame is at position 8, (ii) that the values on the operand stack correspond to the values of appropriate local variables, and (iii) that the abstract loop invariant is satisfied, i.e. $r=i*i$, where i is in the appropriate range.

Once the state properties are defined, we prove lemmas about their transitions, e.g.

```
Lemma trans_7_8: forall frame frame',
  s7_prop frame → SF.stepFrame code frame frame' → s8_prop frame'.
```

After proving transition lemmas, one can establish that reachable program states are described by the aforementioned state properties. Hence, one can show the partial correctness of the program, i.e., when it is started in the initial state and arrives after instruction 19 then the operand stack contains n^2:

```
Theorem partial_correctness: forall frameF,
  pcToPosition (frameGetPC frameF) = 20%nat →
    SF.stepsFrame code frame0 frameF → exists res,
      frameGetLocalStack frameF = [(VInt res)] ∧ Num.toZ res = (n * n).
```

The same proof methodology can be applied to different programs. In module ProgramAssertions we provide relevant infrastructure and a general theorem that code blocks for which our Hoare-like logic apply at each step are partially correct. This is available for instructions from the *LFrame* category.

6   Discussion on Bytecode Design

Efforts associated with the formalisation lead inevitably to reflections on the design of the natural language specification. We present here our main observations. We assume that some of them could be integrated easily into future releases of natural language specifications [15, 21], but some would require total rewrite of the documents, which we perceive as not only difficult, but also very risky since many people learned to read the documents in the current structure. Still, we find the remarks useful for the design of future low-level languages and their descriptions.

Missing Descriptions. Some of the issues concerning the design of JVM are nowhere described in the specification document [21]. The most prominent example here is the multithreading semantics, which is documented in the Java specification itself [15]. This would be acceptable if appropriate links were provided in the JVM description to the Java one, but many such links are missing. The reader is referred few times to [15, Chap. 17] as a general account for multithreading, but this is not reflected at the level of instruction description even though it is crucial for understanding the semantics of several instructions. In particular this concerns the *word tearing* feature allowed by the Java multithreading behaviour, but nowhere mentioned in the JVM specification.

To counterbalance the aforementioned poor description of some aspects, the operation of instructions in terms of monitors is described in a very detailed way in the JVM specification document. This shows again that the large size of the specification is inconsistent with regard to which facets of the description should be covered and which omitted.

Flat Structure of Specification. The specification of the instructions (Sect. 6.5 of [21]) is written in the spirit of traditional assembly languages documentation, where each instruction is described separately. This approach inevitably results in many duplications of text, which engineering practice instructs us to avoid. Beside literal duplications of large text fragments, which we mention below, we can observe that in many cases whole descriptions of instructions differ only in

- the type for which an instruction is defined, which is the case of e.g. `iaload`, `faload`, `laload`, `daload`, and `aaload` instructions;
- short snippets of text appearing only in selected cases, which is the case of e.g. `baload` instruction when compared to the above group.

Summarising all such cases, we found 17 schemes of instruction descriptions that serve to create as many as 61 actual descriptions. Even if having a complete description of an instruction in one place is clearly an advantage, the reader should be advised of a common pattern to which the specification of the given instruction adheres and, which is even more important, clearly warned about cinstruction.

Copy and Paste Caveats. By an analysis of the specification document we found several duplications of large fragments of text. For instance

- two paragraphs of text describing run-time exceptions related to the monitor state on method completion, which is repeated for all 6 `return` instructions and, in its major part, for `athrow` instruction,
- large fragments of text in descriptions of method invocation instructions. In our formal design we provide separate definitions for operations such as dynamic method lookup or passing arguments to a method, which helps us to avoid such duplications. In our opinion it would be reasonable to apply a similar approach in the text specification at least for those complex operations which require long descriptions.

In two cases the pasted text has been partially modified, leading to an error or confusion.

- Reference subtyping rules are repeated in descriptions of `aastore`, `checkcast`, and `instanceof` with small differences (e.g. "can be cast to TC by these run-time rules" vs "can be cast to TC by recursive application of these rules"). This may lead the reader to a confusion whether the differences are substantial, or whether there is a common ground and the different descriptions relate it from different perspectives, or it is just a result of a stylistic adjustments.
- Descriptions of `imul`, `lmul`, and `lsub` contain a note describing the case of arithmetic overflow. They incorrectly refer to sum instead of the appropriate operation—multiplication and subtraction, respectively.

Inconsistencies in the Instruction Set. The particular choice of instructions is in many places strange and results in numerous special cases that must be handled in an implementation and formalisation. These are natural sources of error in implementation of the bytecode and in many cases constitute obstacles to code reuse. Here are the most important deficiencies of the current design:

- Basically, the *load* and *store* instructions have different instances for different types. However, the address store instruction astore can be used both for reference types and for the returnAddress type, used by the subroutine mechanism. Surprisingly, the corresponding aload instruction is only allowed to load references.
- An asymmetry related to the above can also be found in case of jsr and ret. The former starts a subroutine by storing the return address on the operand stack while the latter fetches it directly from the local variables array. The address put on the stack by jsr is moved to a variable by the aforementioned astore instruction. Although it is acceptable that the address is kept in a variable, it would be more consistent to use the same schema, either a direct one or one with an intermediate stack step, to store the address and to retrieve it again.
- Integer division instructions idiv, ldiv, irem, and lrem throw ArithmeticException on division by zero. At the same time their floating point counterparts handle this situation locally. The latter choice is the result of the IEEE 754 specification, but these two diverging approaches could be unified.
- There is only one instruction that operates directly on local variables without the need to refer to the operand stack, namely iinc. This creates a single special case that requires separate handling in formalisation and implementation.
- The instructions checkcast and instanceof bring virtually the same primitive, but offer only a minimally different interface. This results in duplication of large parts in their descriptions and may be the source of errors.
- The specification provides cases for special handling of interface types (e.g. in the description of instanceof or checkcast). However, we could not find any way an object of an interface type could actually occur in the heap.

7   Related Work

A systematic reduction of a large set of JVML instructions to a small one by means of abstraction was given by Yelland [36]. He proposed a language μJVM with a modest set of instructions that transform program continuations. Next, a translation was provided for the actual bytecode instructions. In fact, one can view the work as a continuation style denotational semantics for the JVML written in Haskell, which makes it immediately modular and executable. One important advantage of the formalisation is that the Haskell type system corresponds there to type correctness verification. In our approach we formalise the language in small step fashion and the correctness proof for static checking in similar fashion is done separately. Moreover, μJVM works on a different level of abstraction—instructions in CoJaq correspond in a hierarchical way to instructions in the JVML, while in the case of μJVM a translation is required.

The semantics of Java and the JVML was given on paper in a notable book by Stark et al. [34]. A number of formal accounts of the JVML are available, which was summarised by Hartel and Moreau [17] and Freund and Mitchell [14]. We present here a brief overview of those realised in mechanised frameworks.

Formal Accounts of the Java Bytecode. There is a number of bytecode semantics done on paper. One of them is the already mentioned work of Stark et al. [34].

An early effort in this direction was done by Sata and Abadi [35]. They proposed a type based method of ensuring the correctness for the Java bytecode verification procedure with subroutines. The approach did not include objects and method calls. The work was further refined by Hagiya and Tozawa [16] so that separate variable access analysis was eliminated. Another variant of the Sata and Abadi work was given by O'Callahan [26] where continuations and polymorphic recursion were employed to extend the applicability of the original type system.

Bertelson [3] proposed a detailed dynamic semantics for over 60 instructions, although no formal properties of the system were shown.

Rose [32] proposed a framework of lightweight bytecode verification in the spirit of Leroy [20] (see below for a more extensive description), which is more general and based upon the principles of the proof-carrying code paradigm. She proved that checking of a lightweight certificate on device gives guarantees that are as strong as the ones provided by traditional bytecode verification procedure.

Freund and Mitchell [14] proposed a type system for a bytecode abstract language that consists of 22 instructions. As far as the works on paper are concerned, their effort covers probably the biggest number of important aspects of the language including classes, interfaces, constructors, methods, exceptions, and bytecode subroutines. They provided an operational semantics for the language and proved the soundness of their type system. At last they developed a program that conducts Java classes verification and uses the type system.

A notable review of the Java Virtual Machine specification [21] was presented by Coglio in [8], but the author focused on the bytecode verification algorithm.

Mechanised Formalisations of the JVML. Probably the earliest effort to mechanically formalise the JVML was done by Pusch [29]. She did it in Isabelle/HOL by direct representation of general instructions that group bytecode operations. The language covered low-level control flow, integer types, classes, methods, and arrays. She proved the correctness of the JVML verifier. The formalisation largely corresponds to an earlier formalisation on paper done by Qian [30], which was also formalised in Specware [7].

Bertot validated in Coq [4] the correctness of soundness proofs for the fragment of the JVML concerned with object initialisation. This work was based upon an early version of the work by Freund and Mitchell [13].

An important formalisation was proposed by Leroy [20]. This formalisation is focused on the JavaCard version of JVML and offers a Coq formal proof that the JVML verifier is correct and that a preverified type information can serve to guarantee type correctness after a type checking procedure is executed.

The group of Klein and Nipkow [19] proposed probably the most extensive work concentrated on the JVML verification. They provided a model of Java called Jinja and a formalisation of the JVM language model with 15 instructions that includes such aspects of the JVML as low-level control flow, integer numeric operations, classes, arrays, methods, exceptions, casts, and bytecode subroutines. They constructed a verified compiler of Jinja to their model of JVM as well as a JVML verifier. All the verification of the procedures was done in the proof assistant Isabelle/HOL. As a result they obtained a unified model for the source language, the virtual machine, and the compiler, which was later extended to cover Java Memory Model [22].

A considerable fragment (138 instructions) of JVML was formalised in an executable form in ACL2 [25]. The formalisation did not include exceptional behaviour nor floating point operations. Another big portion of the instruction set (over 70 instructions) was modelled by Pichardie [27] in Coq. The work was similar in spirit to the one of Bertelsen [3] and modelled directly the instructions. The semantics was done both in the small-step and big-step fashion and the two were proved equivalent. This was probably the most ambitious and largely successful attempt to make a formal account of the full bytecode instruction set. However, the drawback of this approach was such that the number of instructions made the formalisation unwieldy in the context of proving metatheorems for JVML e.g. that a JVML verification algorithm is correct.

Another attempt to formalise JVML was done by Atkey [1] in Coq. The most important feature of the attempt is that it uses the Coq program extraction to make possible extraction of OCaml programs that work as a JVM. In this way it is possible to efficiently validate the operational semantics encoded in Coq against real JVMs and test if the results obtained in the two environments agree.

Demange et al. [11] presented yet another formalisation of the JVML. The authors present a semantics of a chosen set of bytecode instructions in Coq and a translation of bytecode to a stackless representation to make a basis for formal analysis of bytecode compilation and its optimisation to native code in JIT or standard compilers. Moreover, a semantics in Coq is given for the target language. In this way they obtain two semantic accounts of the bytecode and they prove that they are equivalent.

Not only interactive theorem provers were used to formalise JVM. A formalisation in Maude rewriting system was proposed by Farzan et al. [12].

An interesting exercise in formal methods was proposed by Posegga and Vogt [28]. They showed how model checking can be applied to verify functional properties of a JVML program.

8   Conclusions

In working with complex systems, people usually are unable to think and act with complete system view in mind. They focus only on chosen aspects of program execution. In case of a machine that executes a program, this often agrees with the assumption that the state of certain runtime structures that govern the machine (in our case JVM) is irrelevant for the operation of the particular instruction while for others it is relevant. We took this view and hierarchised the JVML instructions based upon the way they operate on the runtime structures. In this way we obtained a decomposition of the whole set of 200 bytecode instructions [21] and formalised it in Coq. As a result we obtained a unique, hierarchical view of the Java virtual machine specification structure that is based on the runtime structure access patterns and that was hidden before. Based upon this formalisation, the natural language description can benefit from better organisation of the material and more precise phrasing. In addition, future descriptions of other low-level languages could benefit from these structuring ideas in a similar way, resulting in a more uniform presentation of mechanisms offered by the language.

References

1. Atkey, R.: CoqJVM: an executable specification of the Java virtual machine using dependent types. In: Miculan, M., Scagnetto, I., Honsell, F. (eds.) TYPES 2007. LNCS, vol. 4941, pp. 18–32. Springer, Heidelberg (2008). https://doi.org/10.1007/978-3-540-68103-8_2
2. Aydemir, B.E., et al.: Mechanized metatheory for the masses: the POPLMARK challenge. In: Hurd, J., Melham, T. (eds.) TPHOLs 2005. LNCS, vol. 3603, pp. 50–65. Springer, Heidelberg (2005). https://doi.org/10.1007/11541868_4
3. Bertelsen, P.: Dynamic semantics of Java bytecode. Future Gener. Comput. Syst. **16**(7), 841–850 (2000)
4. Bertot, Y.: Formalizing a JVML verifier for initialization in a theorem prover. In: Berry, G., Comon, H., Finkel, A. (eds.) CAV 2001. LNCS, vol. 2102, pp. 14–24. Springer, Heidelberg (2001). https://doi.org/10.1007/3-540-44585-4_3
5. Chrząszcz, J.: Modules in Coq are and will be correct. In: Berardi, S., Coppo, M., Damiani, F. (eds.) TYPES 2003. LNCS, vol. 3085, pp. 130–146. Springer, Heidelberg (2004). https://doi.org/10.1007/978-3-540-24849-1_9
6. Chrząszcz, J., Czarnik, P., Schubert, A.: A dozen instructions make Java bytecode. ENTCS **264**(4), 19–34 (2011)
7. Coglio, A., Goldberg, A., Qian, Z.: Toward a provably-correct implementation of the JVM bytecode verifier. In: Proceedings DARPA Information Survivability Conference and Exposition, 2000. DISCEX 2000, vol. 2, pp. 403–410. IEEE Computer Society (2000)
8. Coglio, A.: Improving the official specification of Java bytecode verification. Concurr. Comput.: Pract. Exp. **15**(2), 155–179 (2003). http://dblp.uni-trier.de/db/journals/concurrency/concurrency15.html#Coglio03
9. Coq development team: the Coq proof assistant reference manual V8.4. Technical Report 255, INRIA, France, March 2012. http://coq.inria.fr/distrib/V8.4/refman/

10. Czarnik, P., Chrząszcz, J., Schubert, A.: CoJaq: a hierarchical view on the Java bytecode formalised in Coq. In: Swacha, J. (ed.) Advances in Software Development, pp. 147–157. Polish Information Processing Society (2013)

11. Demange, D., Jensen, T., Pichardie, D.: A provably correct stackless intermediate representation for Java bytecode. In: Ueda, K. (ed.) APLAS 2010. LNCS, vol. 6461, pp. 97–113. Springer, Heidelberg (2010). https://doi.org/10.1007/978-3-642-17164-2_8

12. Farzan, A., Chen, F., Meseguer, J., Roşu, G.: Formal analysis of Java programs in JavaFAN. In: Alur, R., Peled, D.A. (eds.) CAV 2004. LNCS, vol. 3114, pp. 501–505. Springer, Heidelberg (2004). https://doi.org/10.1007/978-3-540-27813-9_46

13. Freund, S.N., Mitchell, J.C.: The type system for object initialization in the Java bytecode language. ACM Trans. Program. Lang. Syst. **21**(6), 1196–1250 (1999)

14. Freund, S.N., Mitchell, J.C.: A type system for the Java bytecode language and verifier. J. Autom. Reason. **30**(3–4), 271–321 (2003). https://doi.org/10.1023/A:1025011624925

15. Gosling, J., Joy, B., Steele, G., Bracha, G.: The Java Language Specification. The Java Series, 3rd edn. Addison Wesley, Boston (2005)

16. Hagiya, M., Tozawa, A.: On a new method for dataflow analysis of Java virtual machine subroutines. In: Levi, G. (ed.) SAS 1998. LNCS, vol. 1503, pp. 17–32. Springer, Heidelberg (1998). https://doi.org/10.1007/3-540-49727-7_2

17. Hartel, P.H., Moreau, L.: Formalizing the safety of Java, the Java virtual machine, and Java card. ACM Comput. Surv. **33**(4), 517–558 (2001)

18. Jacobs, B., Poll, E.: A logic for the Java modeling language JML. In: Hussmann, H. (ed.) FASE 2001. LNCS, vol. 2029, pp. 284–299. Springer, Heidelberg (2001). https://doi.org/10.1007/3-540-45314-8_21

19. Klein, G., Nipkow, T.: A machine-checked model for a Java-like language, virtual machine, and compiler. ACM Trans. Program. Lang. Syst. **28**(4), 619–695 (2006)

20. Leroy, X.: Bytecode verification on Java smart cards. Softw. Pract. Exper. **32**(4), 319–340 (2002)

21. Lindholm, T., Yellin, F.: The Java Virtual Machine Specification, 2nd edn. Addison-Wesley Professional, Boston (1999). Specification available at https://docs.oracle.com/javase/specs/jvms/se6/html/VMSpecTOC.doc.html

22. Lochbihler, A.: A Machine-Checked, Type-Safe Model of Java Concurrency : Language, Virtual Machine, Memory Model, and Verified Compiler. Ph.D. thesis, Karlsruher Institut für Technologie, Fakultät für Informatik, July 2012

23. Milner, R., Harper, R., MacQueen, D., Tofte, M.: The Definition of Standard ML - Revised. The MIT Press, Cambridge (1997)

24. MOBIUS Consortium: Deliverable 3.1: bytecode specification language and program logic (2006). http://mobius.inria.fr

25. Moore, J.S.: Proving theorems about Java and the JVM with ACL2. In: Broy, M., Pizka, M. (eds.) Models, Algebras and Logic of Engineering Software, pp. 227–290. IOS Press, Amsterdam (2003)

26. O'Callahan, R.: A simple, comprehensive type system for Java bytecode subroutines. In: Proceedings of POPL1999, pp. 70–78. ACM (1999)

27. Pichardie, D.: Bicolano - Byte Code Language in Coq (2006). http://mobius.inria.fr/bicolano. Summary appears in [24]

28. Posegga, J., Vogt, H.: Byte code verification for Java smart cards based on model checking. In: Quisquater, J.-J., Deswarte, Y., Meadows, C., Gollmann, D. (eds.) ESORICS 1998. LNCS, vol. 1485, pp. 175–190. Springer, Heidelberg (1998). https://doi.org/10.1007/BFb0055863

29. Pusch, C.: Proving the soundness of a Java bytecode verifier specification in Isabelle/HOL. In: Cleaveland, W.R. (ed.) TACAS 1999. LNCS, vol. 1579, pp. 89–103. Springer, Heidelberg (1999). https://doi.org/10.1007/3-540-49059-0_7

30. Qian, Z.: A formal specification of Java$\mathcal{M}$ virtual machine instructions for objects, methods and subroutines. In: Alves-Foss, J. (ed.) Formal Syntax and Semantics of Java. LNCS, vol. 1523, pp. 271–311. Springer, Heidelberg (1999). https://doi.org/10.1007/3-540-48737-9_8

31. Raghavan, A.D., Leavens, G.T.: Desugaring JML method specifications. Technical Report TR #00-03d, Iowa State University, March 2000

32. Rose, E.: Lightweight bytecode verification. J. Autom. Reason. **31**, 303–334 (2003)

33. Soubiran, E.: Développement modulaire de théories et gestion de l'espace de nom pour l'assistant de preuve Coq. Ph.D. thesis, Ecole Polytechnique (2010)

34. Stärk, R.F., Schmid, J., Börger, E.: Java and the Java Virtual Machine: Definition, Verification, Validation. Springer, Heidelberg (2001). https://doi.org/10.1007/978-3-642-59495-3

35. Stata, R., Abadi, M.: A type system for Java bytecode subroutines. ACM Trans. Program. Lang. Syst. **21**(1), 90–137 (1999)

36. Yelland, P.M.: A compositional account of the Java virtual machine. In: Proceedings of POPL1999, pp. 57–69. ACM (1999)

Formalising Executable Specifications
of Low-Level Systems

Paolo Torrini$^{(\boxtimes)}$, David Nowak, Narjes Jomaa, and Mohamed Sami Cherif

CRIStAL, CNRS & University of Lille, Lille, France
{p.torrini,d.nowak,n.jomaa}@univ-lille.fr, mohamedsami.cherif@yahoo.com

Abstract. Formal models of low-level applications rely often on the distinction between executable layer and underlying hardware abstraction. This is also the case for the model of Pip, a separation kernel formalised and verified in Coq using a shallow embedding. DEC is a deeply embedded imperative typed language with primitive recursion and specified in terms of small-step semantics, which we developed in Coq as a reified counterpart of the shallow embedding used for Pip. In this paper, we introduce DEC and its semantics, we present its interpreter based on the type soundness proof and extracted to Haskell, we introduce a Hoare logic to reason about DEC code, and we use this logic to verify properties of Pip as a case study, comparing the new proofs with those based on the shallow embedding. Notably DEC can import shallow specifications as external functions, thus allowing for reuse of the abstract hardware model (DEC can be found at https://github.com/2xs/dec.git [1]).

1 Introduction

Formal modelling and verification of OS kernels involve different aspects of theorem proving: realistic modelling of low-level systems, scalable verification of program behaviour with respect to abstract specifications, executable models, generation of efficient, certified low-level code. Models have often complex structures in terms of components and levels of abstraction [2–4]. A natural distinction arises between the mathematical modelling of low-level requirements, typically associated with an abstract model of the platform, and the executable model of the platform-independent application which we also call the service layer. Primarily, the abstract model needs to be extensible with respect to concrete models of specific architectures, whereas the executable model needs to be translated to an efficient implementation language. Working with a theorem prover such as Coq [5] or Isabelle [6], this is a difference that matters for the choice of the representation in the base language.

A deep embedding of an object language captures its abstract syntax in terms of abstract datatypes, therefore providing a reified representation that supports manipulation, notably translations, as well as operational specifications of behaviour, thus allowing for a naturally executable characterisation of control flow. However, reasoning about abstract datatypes involves a significant

© Springer Nature Switzerland AG 2018
R. Piskac and P. Rümmer (Eds.): VSTTE 2018, LNCS 11294, pp. 155–176, 2018.
https://doi.org/10.1007/978-3-030-03592-1_9

overhead in relation to the pervasive use of constructors and destructors. Moreover, conventional datatypes are not extensible. A shallow embedding consists of defining semantically the constructs of the object language in the base language, hence providing their characterisation in terms of denotational semantics, thus not only keeping the maths as simple as possible, but also allowing for extensibility in a non-problematic way. On the other hand, a shallow embedding does not provide any direct way to manipulate language constructs, and it makes it hard to separate object execution from evaluation in the base language.

Going back to our problem, we would generally like to associate the executable model with a deep embedding and the abstract platform model with a shallow one. Our approach consists in deeply embedding an object language that allows importing specifications written in the metalanguage as external function calls. We call the object language thus formalised a *deeply embedded language extension* (DLE). A DLE can be thought of as a domain specific extension of the base language, taking it closer to the target domain in the sense of syntax (i.e. with language constructs close to the instructions to be modelled) and of behavioural specification (i.e. with an operational semantics close to its model of execution).

2 Motivation

In this paper, we focus on the development of a specific DLE in connection with the formal development of the Pip protokernel [4,7–9]. Separation kernels [10] are systems designed to provably ensure noninterference properties with respect to distinct applications running on the same machine [2,3,11]. Usually a separation kernel is based on a formal model that is verified with respect to its security policy and translated to a low-level language for efficiency.

Pip is a separation kernel in which the kernel functionalities are reduced to a minimum needed to allow for efficient memory management and context switching (hence its characterisation as protokernel) [4]. It provides a service API allowing for partitions to be created, allocated memory and removed at runtime according to a hierarchical model. Partitions form a tree and each partition manages its own subpartitions. The security policy of Pip is based on three memory access properties: the parent partition can access the memory of its children (*vertical sharing*), sibling partitions cannot share memory with each other (*horizontal isolation*), and no partition can access kernel memory (*kernel isolation*). The Pip system is implemented in C and assembly, relying on a model written in Coq, the structure of which is shown in Fig. 1. The executable model, corresponding to the service API, is built on top of an abstract platform model that covers hardware abstraction layer (HAL) and hardware, the former in terms of the high-level specification of low-level, platform-specific C and assembly functions, the latter in terms of an abstract model of the physical memory and the MMU.

The service layer of Pip relies on a fragment of C that can be represented as a comparatively simple imperative language, one that is not difficult to capture

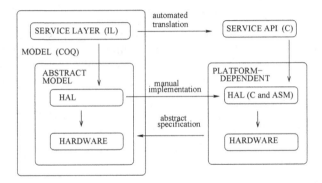

Fig. 1. The design of Pip: the system and its model

in functional terms. This fragment, which we call IL here, corresponds to a typed first-order sequential language with call-by-value, primitive recursion and mutable references. Crucially, we do not need to return pointers, to use call by reference, structures or arrays. Non-termination can always be ruled out relying on hardware parameters.

The executable model has been formalised in Coq on top of hardware abstraction using a shallow embedding of IL based on its monadic semantics, and the verification of the security properties, presented in [4], has been carried out directly on the MC code using an associated Hoare logic, without going through a higher-level model of the service layer. The service layer is about 1300 lines of what we specifically call *monadic code* (MC), semantically corresponding to IL, while the HAL is about 300 lines of monadic specification. The verification involves rather long proofs [9] (several tens of thousands of lines), of which over ten thousands for the abstract platform model.

Modelling Pip at the shallow level has made it possible to focus on system development from the start, independent of any work on language development. However, translation to a low-level language is mandatory for efficiency. The closeness of IL to a fragment of C made it possible to carry out automatically the translation of MC to C source code. Such translation, defined on Gallina abstract syntax, has been implemented in Haskell [12] and it returns efficient, yet unverified code. Unfortunately, verifying code obtained in this way seems rather hard, as it would involve comparing semantically two large languages such as C and Gallina.

We would like to obtain a certified translation at a comparatively lower cost, by focusing on a smaller source language, building a reified representation of our object language, and by targeting an existing formalisation of C such as CompCert C [13], defining a verified translator in Coq. For this reason, we have developed in Coq a DLE that we call DEC [1,14], as an object-level counterpart of IL. As a deep embedding, DEC can be the source of a translation function defined in Coq by pattern matching on the abstract syntax. Unlike MC, DEC has an interpreter based on its small-step operational semantics. This makes it possible to analyse the control flow in Coq, and it could help significantly in comparing formally the behaviour of a program with that of its translation to another language. Although in practice it is difficult to run the interpreter in Coq, it is possible to rely on the extraction mechanism to obtain an efficient program based specifically on the operational semantics of DEC rather than on generic Gallina evaluation.

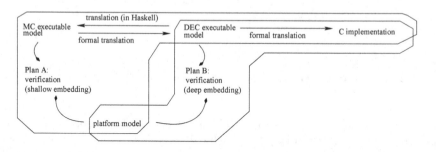

Fig. 2. Two verification plans: A and B

Given DEC, there are indeed two distinct possibilities for the verification of Pip, as shown in Fig. 2. Both plans involve translating the MC model to DEC. Plan A consists additionally in proving the semantic equivalence between the two models, relying for the rest on the verification of the security properties in the shallow embedding as presented in [4]. Plan B, on the other hand, consists in verifying properties directly on the DEC model. In this case, given the large size of the existing verification based on MC, one of the main priorities is to maximise its reuse in verifying DEC code. This can be achieved particularly for the abstract platform model, relying on the DLE character of DEC. In this paper we focus on the distinctive part of plan B, i.e. on DEC and on verification in the deep embedding, omitting the translation to C (which is ongoing work). Our contribution (beyond the semiformal characterisation of IL) consists in two aspects that are essential to our verification approach: the development of DEC as DLE (ca. 10,000 lines code), and the development of an appropriate Hoare logic for DEC (ca. 2,000 lines code), allowing for syntax-driven, compositional proofs and reuse of the abstract platform model. We applied our approach to a case study (ca. 2,000 lines code on top of a significant amount of reuse), proving auxiliary invariants of Pip functions in their translation to DEC.

In Sect. 3 we give a preliminary overview of IL, characterising it mathematically in terms of its operational semantics. In Sect. 4 we present the development of DEC, with its interpreter (Sect. 5) and the associated Hoare logic (Sect. 6). Section 7 presents the verification of Pip invariants based on DEC code, and compares it with their verification based on MC. In Sect. 8 we discuss related work, in Sect. 9 conclusions and further work.

3   Preliminaries

We start with a semiformal, mathematical specification of IL, the language we use to illustrate succinctly the operational semantics DEC is based on, and to connect it with MC through a mathematical specification of its denotational semantics. IL is parametric in the primitive types Typ (ranged over by by t), in the state type W, and in the actions Act, ranged over by a, associated with side effects and used to represent external functions. Values of primitive types are informally regarded as a set Val ranged over by v. Function types, ranged over by ft, are each defined by a tuple of primitive types for the parameters, and a primitive type for the return value. The syntax of IL is constituted of intrinsically well-typed expressions Exp and functions Fun (ranged over by e and f respectively). We rely on higher-order abstract syntax (HOAS), treating identifiers as formal variables and programs as closed terms, thus avoiding the need for environments. For brevity, we represent tuples as heterogeneous lists, which we treat as typed by type lists (denoted Typs), extending to them a standard list notation (including map). We use the Haskell convention for naming lists.

$$\mathsf{Exp}\ (t : \mathsf{Typ})\ :=\ \mathsf{val}\ t\ |\ \mathsf{cond}\ (\mathsf{Exp}\ \mathsf{Bool})\ (\mathsf{Exp}\ t)\ (\mathsf{Exp}\ t)$$
$$|\ \mathsf{binds}\ (t' : \mathsf{Typ})\ (\mathsf{Exp}\ t')\ (t' \to \mathsf{Exp}\ t)$$
$$|\ \mathsf{call}\ (ts : \mathsf{Typs})\ (\mathsf{Fun}\ t\ ts)\ (\mathsf{Exps}\ ts)\ |\ \mathsf{xcall}\ (ts : \mathsf{Typs})\ (\mathsf{Act}\ t\ ts)\ (\mathsf{Exps}\ ts)$$

$$\mathsf{Exps}\ (ts : \mathsf{Typs})\ :=\ \mathsf{map}\ \mathsf{Exp}\ ts$$

$$\mathsf{Fun}\ (t : \mathsf{Typ})\ (ts : \mathsf{Typs})\ :=\ \mathsf{fun}\ (ts \to \mathsf{Exp}\ t)\ ((ts \to \mathsf{Exp}\ t) \to ts \to \mathsf{Exp}\ t)\ \mathsf{Nat}$$

$$\mathsf{Act}\ (t : \mathsf{Typ})\ (ts : \mathsf{Typs})\ :=\ ts \to \mathsf{W} \to (\mathsf{W} * t)$$

We specify the small-step transition relation using configurations defined as pairs (s, X) where $s : \mathsf{W}$ is a state and X may be either an expression or a list of them. We make the presentation more concise by giving only the reduction rules and relying on evaluation contexts to specify call-by-value. Evaluation contexts allow us to compute the redex at each step. As usual [15], we write $[\_]$ to denote the hole in which to plug the redex in, and $C[e]$ to denote the splitting of an expression into context and redex.

$$\mathsf{Ctx}\ :=\ [\_]\ |\ \mathsf{binds}\ \_\ \mathsf{Ctx}\ (\mathsf{Exp}\ \_)\ |\ \mathsf{binds}\ \_\ \mathsf{Val}\ \mathsf{Ctx}\ |\ \mathsf{cond}\ \mathsf{Ctx}\ (\mathsf{Exp}\ \_)\ (\mathsf{Exp}\ \_)$$
$$|\ \mathsf{call}\ \_\ (\mathsf{Fun}\ \_\ \_)\ \mathsf{Ctxs}\ |\ \mathsf{xcall}\ \_\ (\mathsf{Act}\ \_\ \_)\ \mathsf{Ctxs}$$
$$\mathsf{Ctxs}\ :=\ \mathsf{Ctx}\ ::\ (\mathsf{Exps}\ \_)\ |\ \mathsf{Val}\ ::\ \mathsf{Ctxs}$$

$$\frac{\langle\ s\ \triangleright\ e\ \rangle \longrightarrow \langle\ s'\ \triangleright\ e'\ \rangle}{\langle\ s\ \triangleright\ C[e]\ \rangle \longrightarrow \langle\ s'\ \triangleright\ C[e']\ \rangle}$$

$$\langle\ s\ \triangleright\ \mathsf{binds}\ \_\ (\mathsf{val}\ v)\ e\ \rangle \longrightarrow \langle\ s\ \triangleright\ e\ v\ \rangle$$

$$\langle\ s\ \triangleright\ \mathsf{cond}\ (\mathsf{val}\ \mathsf{true})\ e_1\ e_2\ \rangle \longrightarrow \langle\ s\ \triangleright\ e_1\ \rangle$$

$$\langle\ s\ \triangleright\ \mathsf{cond}\ (\mathsf{val}\ \mathsf{false})\ e_1\ e_2\ \rangle \longrightarrow \langle\ s\ \triangleright\ e_2\ \rangle$$

$$\langle\ s\ \triangleright\ \mathsf{call}\ (\mathsf{fun}\ e_0\ e_1\ 0)\ (\mathsf{map}\ \mathsf{val}\ vs)\ \rangle \longrightarrow \langle\ s\ \triangleright\ e_0\ vs\ \rangle$$

$$\langle\ s\ \triangleright\ \text{call (fun } e_0\ e_1\ (S\ n))\ (\text{map val } vs)\ \rangle\ \longrightarrow\ \langle\ s\ \triangleright\ e_1\ (\text{fun } e_0\ e_1\ n)\ vs\ \rangle$$

$$\langle\ s\ \triangleright\ \text{xcall } ts\ a\ (\text{map val } vs)\ \rangle\ \longrightarrow\ \langle\ s'\ \triangleright\ \text{val } v\ \rangle\qquad\text{where}\quad a\ vs\ s\ =\ (s',v)$$

Notice that val simply lifts values to expressions, and the final value can be obtained by unlifting from an expression of form val v. The denotational semantics of IL can be defined along the lines of the monadic translation in [16], using a state monad with state W (see Appendix A). The result corresponds to the shallow embedding used in the formalisation of Pip [4].

4   The Deep Embedding

DEC [1] is a strongly normalising, functional imperative language with primitive recursion, implemented in Coq as an DLE based on IL, parametric in the type of the mutable state. The constructs of DEC are internally specified as functional ones. Nonetheless, Coq functions can be imported as external functions, and these can be stateful, although the totality requirement of the metalanguage ensures that they are terminating. In this sense, DEC is a functional language that can be extended with generic effects, as well as a deeply embedded functional interface which can be used to extend a stateful model. Unlike the HOAS-style presentation of IL, DEC relies on environments, on explicit typing relations, and on a semantic representation which uses propagation rules rather than evaluation contexts, following an approach closer to [17] and to the original presentation of structural operational semantics (SOS) [18], a choice made to allow for explicit manipulation of identifiers without the need to implement α-renaming. As a distinctive computational feature, DEC has typing relations with inductive principles which are strong enough to carry the weight of the type soundness proof, while minimising type annotation.

Relying on Coq modules, the definition of DEC is parametric in the type of the mutable state w and in the type of the identifiers Id, the latter required to have decidable equality. We model environments as homogeneous lists, and to this purpose, unlike in HOAS, we need to introduce a deep embedding of object types and values. Our object types (i.e. *deep* types) are lifted Gallina types (i.e. *shallow* ones). Their type could be treated as trivial hiding, i.e. $\Sigma(\lambda X{:}\texttt{Type},X)$, but we prefer to rely on a type class ValTyp:Type→Prop to ensure lifting is explicitly allowed, hence defining our type VTyp of value types as ΣValTyp, with associated lifting function vtyp: Type → VTyp. Deep values are defined by lifting shallow values, hiding their type, and their type Value is defined as ΣValueI, where

Inductive ValueI (T: Type) : Type := Cst (v: T).

and lifting is cst: ∀ T:Type, T → Value. Value environments and value typing contexts are then given types list(Id*Value) and list(Id*VTyp), respectively abbreviated as valEnv and valTC. The value typing relation ValueTyping:Value→VTyp→Type reduces to extracting and equating the shallow types of the two arguments, whereas the identifier typing relation IdTyping:valTC→Value→VTyp→Type relies on the application of the lookup function findE.

From the deep typing point of view, DEC is intended as a first-order language, therefore it would not be strictly necessary to allow for the body of program expressions to contain occurrences of function definitions, as opposed to function variables. However, allowing function definitions to be syntactical subexpressions leads to a stronger built-in induction principle. Partly for this reason, DEC is essentially designed as first-order fragment of a higher-order language. The deep type of function types

```
Inductive FTyp : Type := FT (prms_type: valTC) (ret_type: VTyp).
```

ensures the first-order restriction, requiring that parameters are deep datavalues. Function environments (funEnv) and function typing contexts (funTC) are defined as lists, in analogy to valEnv and valTC. The namespace distinction between value identifiers and function identifiers is enforced at the level of head normal forms, here called q-values and q-functions.

```
Inductive QValue : Type := Var (x: Id) | QV (v: Value).
```

The inductive type of expressions is mutually defined with functions, q-functions, and lifted expression lists that represent parameters.

```
Inductive Fun : Type := FC (fenv: funEnv) (tenv: valTC)
                           (e0 e1: Exp) (x: Id) (n: nat)
with QFun : Type := FVar (x: Id) | QF (f: Fun)
with Exp : Type := Val (v: Value) | Return (q: QValue)
         | IfThenElse (e1 e2 e3: Exp)
         | BindN (e1 e2: Exp) | BindS (x: Id) (e1 e2: Exp)
         | BindMS (fenv: funEnv) (venv: valEnv) (e: Exp)
         | Apply (qf: QFun) (args: Prms)
         | Modify {T1 T2: Type} {VT1: ValTyp T1} {VT2: ValTyp T2}
                  (XF: XFun T1 T2) (arg: QValue)
with Prms : Type := PS (es: list Exp).
```

The function constructor FC represents an *iterate*-style construct, where tenv gives the list of the formal parameters with their types, n is a natural number that represents fuel, e0 is the function body for n=0, e1 is the function body for n>0, x is the function identifier used in recursive calls, and fenv is the local function environment. Constructors Var and FVar lift identifiers to the corresponding head-normal forms. Similarly QV and QF lift normal forms. PS lifts expression lists to parameters. Concerning expressions, Val and Return are lifting constructors, IfThenElse represents conditional branching, BindN sequencing and BindS local binding of identifiers to expressions (i.e. let-style binding). BindMS allows for multiple binding of identifiers to normal forms, i.e. for local environments, and it is needed for internal processing in our environment-based representation. Apply represents application of recursive functions. Modify represents application of external one-argument functions, where the function type is T1→T2. Modify works as a constructor of generic effects, handled by the stateful functions associated with the corresponding record of type

```
Record XFun (T1 T2: Type) : Type := { x_mod : W→T1→W*T2 ;
         x_exec : W→T1→W := λw x, fst (x_mod w x) ;
         x_eval : W→T1→T2 := λw x, snd (x_mod w x) }.
```

For example, generic read and write actions can be defined as follows

```
Definition xf_read {T: Type} (f: W → T) : XFun unit T  := {|
    x_mod := fun x _ ⇒ (x, f x)  |}.
Definition xf_write {T: Type} (f: T → W) : XFun T unit := {|
    x_mod := fun _ x ⇒ (f x, tt)  |}.
```

Read and write instructions can then be defined, given UnitVT:ValTyp unit (here @ is used to make implicit arguments explicit).

```
Definition Read {T: Type} (VT: ValTyp T) (f: W → T) : Exp :=
    @Modify unit T UnitVT VT (xf_read f) (QV (cst unit tt)).
Definition Write {T: Type} (VT: ValTyp T) (f: T → W) (x: T) : Exp :=
    @Modify T unit VT UnitVT (xf_write f) (QV (cst T x)).
```

Notice that function definitions are meant to represent closed terms, as they may occur as subterms in expressions. For this reason, a function definition is defined as a closure with respect to its function identifiers, by including fenv as local function environment. This measure prevents variable capture and suffices to ensure we can type check recursive functions without annotating them with their return type.

The typing relations on expressions, functions, q-functions and parameters are defined by mutual induction, where MatchEnvs maps a binary relation over two lists.[1]

```
Inductive ExpTyping : funTC→valTC→funEnv→Exp→VTyp→Type := ...
  | Apply_Typing : ∀ (ftenv: funTC) (tenv fps: valTC) (fenv: funEnv)
                     (q: QFun) (ps: Prms) (pt: PTyp) (t: VTyp),
      pt = PT (map snd fps) → MatchEnvs FunTyping fenv ftenv →
      QFunTyping ftenv fenv q (FT fps t) →
      PrmsTyping ftenv tenv fenv ps pt →
      ExpTyping ftenv tenv fenv (Apply q ps) t
  | Modify_Typing : ∀ (ftenv: funTC) (tenv: valTC) (fenv: funEnv)
                       (T1 T2: Type) (VT1: ValTyp T1) (VT2: ValTyp T2)
                       (XF: XFun T1 T2) (q: QValue),
        QValueTyping tenv q (vtyp T1) →
        ExpTyping ftenv tenv fenv (@Modify T1 T2 VT1 VT2 XF q) (vtyp T2)
with QFunTyping : funTC→funEnv→QFun→FTyp→Type := ...
```

In the typing of function application, the type of the actual parameters is compared with that of the formal ones obtained from the q-function typing, which means either consulting the function typing context (ftenv) in case of an identifier, or else checking the function type. In the typing of external function calls the relevant types and the function definition are passed as a record.

Our function typing relation has a comparatively non-standard, algorithmic character.

---

[1] Details in 2xs/dec/src/langspec/LangSpec.v [14].

```
with FunTyping : Fun→FTyp→Type :=
 | Fun0_Typing: ∀ (ftenv: funTC) (tenv: valTC) (fenv: funEnv)
                  (e0 e1: Exp) (x: Id) (t: VTyp),
    MatchEnvs FunTyping fenv ftenv →
    ExpTyping ftenv tenv fenv e0 t →
    FunTyping (FC fenv tenv e0 e1 x 0) (FT tenv t)
 | FunS_Typing: ∀ (ftenv: funTC) (tenv: valTC) (fenv: funEnv)
                  (e0 e1: Exp) (x: Id) (n: nat) (t: VTyp),
    let ftenv' := (x, FT tenv t) :: ftenv in
    let fenv' := (x, FC fenv tenv e0 e1 x n) :: fenv in
    MatchEnvs FunTyping fenv ftenv → ExpTyping ftenv' tenv fenv' e1 t →
    FunTyping (FC fenv tenv e0 e1 x n) (FT tenv t) →
    FunTyping (FC fenv tenv e0 e1 x (S n)) (FT tenv t)
```

Given a function f := FC fenv tenv e0 e1 x n to type, while the types of the parameters are supplied by tenv, the return type needs to be inferred, either from e0 when n = 0, or else from e1. This involves also inferring the types of the local functions in fenv, not supplied by f. Hence the typing relation requires a function environment as argument, rather than just a function typing context, and given the function environment update in case of n > 0, type inference requires induction on the fuel.

We have developed our typing definitions in parallel with the proof of a type soundness theorem which in fact we carry out by mutual induction on the typing relations. However, the induction principle supplied automatically by Coq turned out to be weak, particularly given our use of lists to represent parameters and our typing of parameters

```
with PrmsTyping : funTC→valTC→funEnv→Prms→PTyp→Type :=
 | PS_Typing: ∀ (ftenv: funTC) (tenv: valTC) (fenv: funEnv)
                (es: list Exp) (ts: list VTyp),
      Forall2T (ExpTyping ftenv tenv fenv) es ts →
      PrmsTyping ftenv tenv fenv (PS es) (PT ts).
```

where Forall2T maps a relation on lists.

```
Inductive Forall2T {A B : Type} (R: A→B→Type): list A→list B→Type :=
 | Forall2_nilT : Forall2T R nil nil
 | Forall2_consT : ∀ x y l l',
       R x y → Forall2T R l l' → Forall2T R (x::l) (y::l').
```

We solved this problem by supplying customised and stronger mutual induction principles (called ExpTyping_str_rect for expressions and similarly for the other categories), obtained by instantiating a more general one, proved by means of the mutually recursive version of the fix tactic [5]. Reasoning by induction on the typing relations, we can prove that each well-typed object is uniquely typed. This is also the case for functions.

```
Lemma UniqueFunType (f: Fun) (ft1 ft2: FTyp)
       (k1: FunTyping f ft1) (k2: FunTyping f ft2) :  ft1 = ft2.
```

Although the typing of functions depends on their fuel, we can prove

```
         FunTyping (FC fenv tenv e0 e1 x (S n)) ft →
         FunTyping (FC fenv tenv e0 e1 x n) ft
```

and conversely

```
     sigT (fun ft0 ⇒ FunTyping (FC fenv tenv0 e0 e1 x (S n)) ft0) →
     FunTyping (FC fenv tenv0 e0 e1 x n) ft →
     FunTyping (FC fenv tenv0 e0 e1 x (S n)) ft.
```

The dynamic semantics of DEC, defined in terms of small-step rules, is comparatively standard and close to the IL presentation, though far less concise, as propagation rules are needed for each constructs. It relies on a notion of configuration parametrised by syntactic categories (i.e. expressions, parameters, q-values and q-functions).

```
Inductive AConf (T: Type) : Type := Conf (state: W) (qq: T).
```

The step rules for q-values and q-functions are just environment lookups.

```
Inductive QVStep : valEnv → AConf QValue → AConf QValue → Type
Inductive QFStep : funEnv → AConf QFun → AConf QFun → Type
```

The step rules for expressions and parameters (evaluated from left to right) are defined by mutual induction, using the principle supplied by Coq.

```
Inductive EStep: funEnv→valEnv→AConf Exp→AConf Exp→Type := ...
with  PrmsStep: funEnv→valEnv→AConf Prms→AConf Prms→Type := ...
```

The reduction rules for Apply and particularly the decreasing character of the recursive one (shown below), supplemented by the call-by-value propagation rules, ensures the termination of recursive functions in a way that corresponds to the *iterate*-style construct of IL. Here isValueList2T is used to check whether a list of expressions equals a list of lifted values, and mkVE:valTC→list Value→valEnv constructs a value environment from a typing context and a list of values of the same length.

```
| Apply_RS1 : ∀(fenv fenv': funEnv) (env: valEnv) (n: W) (e0 e1: Exp)
                   (es:list Exp) (vs:list Value) (x: Id) (i: nat) (pt:valTC),
  isValueList2T es vs → length pt = length vs → EStep fenv env
   (Conf Exp n (Apply (QF (FC fenv' pt e0 e1 x (S i))) (PS es)))
   (Conf Exp n (BindMS ((x,(FC fenv' pt e0 e1 x i))::fenv') (mkVE pt vs) e1))
```

Notice the use of BindMS to introduce a local environment, with the following step rules.

```
| BindMS_RS : ∀(fenv fenv': funEnv) (env env': valEnv) (n: W) (v: Value),
  EStep fenv env (Conf Exp n (BindMS fenv' env' (Val v))) (Conf Exp n (Val v))
| BindMS_PS : ∀(fenv fenvL:funEnv) (env envL:valEnv) (n n': W) (e e': Exp),
  EStep (fenvL++fenv) (envL++env) (Conf Exp n e) (Conf Exp n' e') →
  EStep fenv env (Conf Exp n (BindMS fenvL envL e))
                   (Conf Exp n' (BindMS fenvL envL e'))
```

The reduction rule of `Modify` enacts the monadic behaviour of the stateful action associated with `xf`, returning the value computed by `x_eval` and changing the state according to `x_exec`.

5   The SOS Interpreter

The small-step semantics can be used to compute well-typed programs in well-typed environments. First of all, we extend the definitions of transition steps to reflexive-transitive closures (represented by inductive types, e.g. `EClosure : funEnv → valEnv → AConf Exp → AConf Exp → Type`). Then, after using double induction on the step relation and its reflexive-transitive extension to prove a weakening lemma (for expressions as shown, and similarly for parameters)

```
Lemma weaken (fenv fenv':funEnv) (env env':valEnv) (n1 n2:W) (e1 e2:Exp):
EClosure fenv env (Conf Exp n1 e1) (Conf Exp n2 e2) →
EClosure (fenv ++ fenv') (env ++ env') (Conf Exp n1 e1) (Conf Exp n2 e2).
```

our strong mutual induction principle on typing suffices to prove a type soundness theorem, with the following formulation for expressions (and similarly for the other mutually defined categories).[2]

```
Lemma ExpEval (ftenv:funTC) (tenv:valTC) (fenv:funEnv) (e:Exp) (t:VTyp):
ExpTyping ftenv tenv fenv e t →
MatchEnvs FunTyping fenv ftenv → ∀ env: valEnv,
MatchEnvs ValueTyping env tenv → ∀ n: W,
Σ (λ v: Value, ValueTyping v t ⋆ Σ (λ n': W,
            EClosure fenv env (Conf Exp n e) (Conf Exp n' (Val v)))).
```

The use of Σ types ensures that the witnesses can be extracted from the proof. The proof can then be applied as a function, ensuring that a value of the expected type can always be obtained together with a final state for well-typed expressions in well-typed environments by a finite number of steps. Notice that usually induction on the typing relation only suffices to prove subject reduction, i.e.

```
Lemma ExpSubjectRed (ftenv:funTC) (tenv:valTC) (fenv:funEnv) (e:Exp) (t:VTyp):
    ExpTyping ftenv tenv fenv e t → MatchEnvs FunTyping fenv ftenv →
    ∀ (env: valEnv), MatchEnvs ValueTyping env tenv →
    ∀ (e': Exp) (n n': W), EStep fenv env (Conf Exp n e) (Conf Exp n' e') →
                    ExpTyping ftenv tenv fenv e' t.
```

whereas type soundness, in the case of a terminating language, involves a weak normalisation result typically provable by induction on the step relations. Our typing relations incorporate the inductive aspect on fuel, and therefore suffice

---

[2] Specification and proofs in `2xs/dec/src/DEC1` [1].

to prove normalisation. We prove determinism of evaluation, again by induction on typing.

```
Lemma ExpDeterm (ftenv:funTC) (tenv:valTC) (fenv:funEnv) (e:Exp) (t:VTyp):
  ExpTyping ftenv tenv fenv e t → FEnvTyping fenv ftenv →
  ∀ (env: valEnv), EnvTyping env tenv → ∀ (n n1 n2: W) (e1 e2: Exp),
  EStep fenv env (Conf Exp n e) ((Conf Exp n1 e1)) →
  EStep fenv env (Conf Exp n e) ((Conf Exp n2 e2)) → (n1 = n2) ∧ (e1 = e2).
```

Determinism together with weak normalisation give us strong normalisation, and indeed this makes it possible to ensure that our type soundness proof can be used as an SOS interpreter to evaluate DEC programs. We can run the interpreter on simple expressions, but Coq's evaluation mechanism (notoriously fragile [19]) currently does not carry us far enough, particularly in connection with our extensive use of dependent types.

Nonetheless, we can rely on the Coq extraction mechanism to obtain a certified and efficient implementation of the SOS interpreter. We used extraction to Haskell to generate code which we compiled and run with GHC. The presence of dependent types in our Coq code required some adjustments. In fact, when Coq types have no direct translation into Haskell, the extraction mechanism will use the Haskell type Any (which can be understood as the union of all possible types). This means that in order to print the result of running the interpreter, we need to supply explicitly the translated type using the Haskell function unsafeCoerce. As expected, the Haskell interpreter is recursively defined on a term that in Coq has the dependent type of the typing relation. In fact, the computational content of our carefully designed algorithm rests entirely on that relation, rather than on its arguments. Although such arguments have no computational role, they are still present in the extracted code, as they have computational types. But the lazy evaluation strategy of Haskell ensures that they are not evaluated, and thus they can be safely given the value undefined.

In the future we would like to tackle the aspect of evaluation in Coq too, in order to show the semantic adequacy of DEC with respect to MC. We have defined a translation of DEC to Gallina, relying on the strong induction principle on typing as we did for type soundness. Ideally we would like to show that for each DEC program, the proof term of this translation is equal to the term obtained from the SOS interpreter.

6   Hoare Logic

We defined a Hoare logic to verify well-typed DEC programs with respect to state properties expressed in Gallina. Our definitions of Hoare triples allow for the postcondition to depend on the value returned by the computation, following [20,21], and for the computation to depend on function and value environments. We provide the syntax {{ P }} fenv >> env >> e {{ Q }} to write triples for expressions, where the unary predicate P gives the precondition and the binary predicate Q the postcondition of running the SOS interpreter on a well-typed expression e in well-typed environments fenv for functions and env for values, corresponding to the following definition

```
Definition THoareTriple_Eval (P : W → Prop) (Q : Value → W → Prop)
         (fenv: funEnv) (env: valEnv) (e: Exp) : Prop :=
 ∀ (ftenv: funTC) (tenv: valTC) (t: VTyp)
   (k1: MatchEnvs FunTyping fenv ftenv) (k2: MatchEnvs ValueTyping env tenv)
   (k3: ExpTyping ftenv tenv fenv e t) (s s': W) (v: Value),
   EClosure fenv env (Conf Exp s e) (Conf Exp s' (Val v)) → P s → Q v s'.
```

where the transitive closure hypothesis states that the expression `e`, evaluated in state `s`, leads to value `v` in an updated state `s`. The syntax `{{ P }}` `fenv >> env >> ps` `{{ Q }}` and an analogous definition are used for Hoare triples for parameters. Notice that in contrast with the triples for MC [4] where well-typedness is shallow and implicit, here the typing information is deep and thus needs to be explicit. In principle, this explicitness could bring additional discriminating power, making it easier to distinguish between types that are meant to be different, with different actions associated to them, though modelled by the same shallow type. However, this comes to the cost of an overhead in the proofs. On the other hand, an untyped version of the triples could not rely on termination, and therefore would be rather weak in comparison with the shallow counterpart.

We supply a Hoare logic library based on our triples, notably including Hoare logic structural rules for each DEC construct, in order to allow for a verification style that is essentially syntax-driven. Most of these rules support bidirectional use, i.e. both by weakest precondition and strongest postcondition, and correspond to big-step rules. For example, the following is the main rule for `BindS`

```
{{P0}} fenv >> env >> e1 {{P1}} →
(∀ v: Value, {{P1 v}} fenv >> (x,v)::env >> e2 {{P2}}) →
{{P0}} fenv >> env >> BindS x e1 e2 {{P2}}
```

This rule allows a triple for the expression `BindS x e1 e2` to be broken down into sequential triples for `e1` and `e2` (the latter in an updated value environment). The main rule for the `Apply` constructor can be conveniently split into two distinct ones, in order to deal with the recursive update of the function environment, which does not take place with zero fuel

```
let f := FC fenv' tenv' e0 e1 x 0  in
  {{P0}} fenv >> env >> PS es {{P1}} →
  (∀ vs: list Value, {{P1 vs}} fenv' >> (mkVE tenv' vs) >> e0 {{P2}}) →
  {{{P0}} fenv >> env >> Apply (QF f) (PS es) {{P2}}
```

whereas it does otherwise (i.e. `fenv` is updated with the assignment of function `f0` to the identifier `x`)

```
let f0 :=  FC fenv' tenv' e0 e1 x n   in
let f1 :=  FC fenv' tenv' e0 e1 x (S n)  in
   {{P0}} fenv >> env >> PS es {{P1}} →
   (∀ vs, {{P1 vs}} (x, f0)::fenv' >> (mkVE tenv' vs) >> e1 {{P2}}) →
   {{P0}} fenv >> env >> Apply (QF f1) (PS es) {{P2}}
```

As another example, given an external function record xf: XFun t1 t2, the rule for Modify has more naturally the form of a weakest precondition (we show the case when the argument q is already a lifted value):

```
let q :=  QV (cst t1 v)  in let g :=  λs, xf.x_eval s v  in
let h :=  λs, xf.x_exec s v  in {{λ s. Q (g s) (h s)}}
         fenv >> env >> Modify xf q {{Q}}
```

The validity of these rules is proved by inverting the corresponding operational semantic rules, making use of the determinism of DEC.

7   Case Study: Verifying Properties of Pip

The model of Pip in the shallow embedding [4] is based on Gallina code which can be regarded as a monadic representation of IL. The LLI monad used in that representation is defined as an abstract datatype and it wraps together hardware state and undefined behaviours, analogously to applying a state transformer to an error monad [16, 22].

```
Definition LLI (A: Type) : Type := state → result (A * state).
Inductive result (A: Type) : Type :=
val: A → result A | undef: nat → state → result A.
```

The primitive types are Booleans and subsets of naturals. The HAL functions correspond to the actions in IL. The monadic operations ret and bind, which can be easily proved to satisfy the monadic laws

```
Definition ret : A → LLI A := fun a s ⇒ val (a, s).
Definition bind : LLI A → (A → LLI B) → LLI B := fun m f s ⇒
  match m s with | val (a, s') ⇒ f a s' | undef a s' ⇒ undef a s' end.
```

provide the semantics for sequencing, let binding and function application. Primitive recursion and conditional expressions are encoded in terms of the corresponding Gallina notions (see Appendix A for a semiformal definition of the corresponding denotational semantics).

The executable specification of Pip rests on a platform model which includes the representation of physical memory as association lists of physical addresses and values, and the specification of HAL primitives corresponding to architecture-dependent functions [4,9]. Stateful functions such as get and put are only used in the definition of the HAL primitives, thus ensuring that Pip services can access the state only through specific actions. A physical address is modelled as a page identifier (corresponding to a fixed-size chunk of memory) and an offset value called index.

```
Record page := {p :> nat; Hp: p < memorySize}.
Record index := {i :> nat;  Hi: i < pageSize}.
Definition paddr := page * index.
```

The `value` datatype sums up the types of values that can be found in the configuration pages.

```
Inductive value : Type:= | PE: Pentry → value | VE: Ventry → value
    | PP: page → value | VA: vaddr → value | I:  index  → value.
```

Here `Pentry` stands for physical entry, `Ventry` for virtual entry, and `vaddr` for virtual address. Physical entries (PTEs) associate a page with its accessibility information.

```
Record Pentry : Type:= {pa: page; present: bool; accessible: bool}.
```

The management of memory is based on a tree-like partition structure. The partition tree is a hierarchical graph in which each node contains a handle called partition descriptor (PD) together with the configuration of the partition, defined as a set of entities, the main one being the MMU configuration. This has the structure of a tree of fixed `levelNum` depth where physical addresses (including those pointing to possible children in the partition tree) are essentially leaves, whereas valid virtual addresses represent maximal branches. In fact, virtual addresses are modelled as lists of indices of length `levelNum+1`. Each of them is translated by the MMU either to the null address or to a physical one, by interpreting each index in the list as offset in the page table at the corresponding level in the MMU. Partitioning management also uses two auxiliary entities, which can be described as *shadows* of the MMU. The first shadow is used to find out which pages are assigned children, and it uses the type `Ventry`. The second shadow is used to associate each PD to the virtual address it has in the parent partition. The comparatively low-level representation of these structures in the Coq model is based on lists and relies on consistency invariants to ensure e.g. that a list represents a tree. The physical state in Pip is defined by the PD identifier of the currently active partition and the relevant part of the memory state (i.e. essentially, the configuration pages).

```
Record state: Type := {currentPartition: page; memory: list (paddr * value)}.
```

In the monadic model of Pip, this defines the state for the `LLI` monad [4,9].

In the deep embedding formalisation [1,23], we rely on a concrete module where `Id` is instantiated with strings, and `W` with `state`. The HAL primitives correspond to the actions which are executed as external function calls by means of `Modify`. Since the current definition of DEC does not include rules for error handling, we delegate undefined behaviour to each action, using `option` types. This involves some adjustments. For example, the original HAL primitive in [9] to read a physical address in a given page

```
Definition readPhysical (p: page) (i: index) : LLI page := bind get (λs,
```

```
match (lookup p i (memory s) page_beq index_beq) with
| Some (PP a) ⇒ ret a | Some _ ⇒ undefined 5 | None  ⇒ undefined 4 end).
```

gets translated to the following

```
Definition readPhysical' (p: page) (i: index) (s: state) : option page :=
  match (lookup p i (memory s) page_beq index_beq) with
    | Some (PP a) ⇒ Some a | _ ⇒ None end.
```

which can be lifted to DEC as external function.

```
Definition xf_read (p: page) : XFun (option index) (option page) :=
{| x_mod := fun (s: W) (x: option index) ⇒ (s, match x with
   | Some i ⇒ readPhysical' p i s | None ⇒ None end) |}.
Definition ReadPhysical (p:page) (x:Id) : Exp := Modify (xf_read p) (Var x).
```

The fact that the composition of state and error is essentially inverted by the translation is not problematic in our model: all the proofs on the hardware primitives turned out to be easy to adjust.

We translated to DEC three auxiliary functions which are defined in the MC model [9], called getFstShadow, writeVirtual and initVAddrTable. For each function, we proved the main invariant associated with it for its DEC translation, along the lines of the proofs in the shallow embedding, reusing the HAL model in the sense we have described above. The top-level proofs in the shallow embedding are comparatively small (about 50, 100 and 250 lines, respectively), but they are quite representative as they involve using several HAL primitives, sequencing and let-binding, reading from the state (getFstShadow), updating the state (writeVirtual), as well as a conditional and a recursive function (initVAddrTable). Following in the footsteps of the shallow proofs, the deep embedding results in comparable top-level proofs (about 100, 100 and 350 lines respectively), with an overhead due mainly to DEC type-checking, and to the lifting-unlifting of values on which properties may depend. In the case of getFstShadow, we have experimented with alternative definitions of HAL primitives, showing that the top-level proof does not change and therefore, in principle, that DEC could support refinement of abstract specifications. In the case of initVAddrTable, we also proved the invariant following a more thoroughly syntax-driven approach, in the spirit of our Hoare logic. This resulted in a significantly shorter top-level proof (about 170 lines, mainly instantiations of metavariables), though it involved proving additional HAL-level lemmas (about 300 lines) not supplied by the original model, yet general enough to be potentially reusable.

The function getFstShadow is used to return the physical page of the first shadow for a given partition, and it is implemented monadically using readPhysical as well as getSh1idx and Index.succ as HAL primitives.

```
Definition getFstShadow (p : page) : LLI page :=
  bind getSh1idx (λ x, bind (Index.succ x) (λ y, readPhysical p y)).
```

This function can be translated to DEC as follows

```
Definition GetFstShadow (p : page) : Exp :=
    BindS "x" GetSh1idx (BindS "y" (IndexSucc "x") (ReadPhysical p "y")).
```

where all the subexpressions are based on lifted primitives. The invariant that has been proved for the DEC code [1,23] is the following

```
Lemma GetFstShadowBind (p: page) (P: W → Prop) (fenv: funEnv) (env: valEnv):
{{λ s, P s ∧ PartitionDescriptorEntry s ∧ p ∈ (GetPartitions mltplxr s) }}
    fenv >> env >> (GetFstShadow p)
{{λ sh1 s, P s ∧ NextEntryIsPP p sh1idx sh1 s }}.
```

closely matching the shallow version in [9]. Here again `GetPartitions` and `NextEntryIsPP` are lifted HAL primitives. `GetPartitions` returns the list of all sub-partitions of a given partition, `NextEntryIsPP` returns a Boolean depending on whether the successor of the given index in the given configuration page points to the given physical page, whereas `PartitionDescriptorEntry` defines a specific property of the partition descriptor. The typing information that is explicit in the shallow embedding needs to be extracted from the deep type, and this makes for most of the overhead in the deep proof.

The function `writeVirtual` writes a virtual address to the physical memory and it is used to update configuration pages in the second shadow. It is a HAL primitive, and therefore can be adjusted and lifted to DEC as an external function. The associated invariant ensures that the given value is actually written to the given location, while the properties which do not depend on the updated part of the state are preserved. This example illustrates reuse quite well. Although the invariant requires a comparatively long proof in the shallow embedding, this proof can be replicated almost exactly in the deep embedding, using the same (of many) HAL lemmas.

The recursive function `initVAddrTable` is used to initialise the virtual addresses in the second shadow. Its translation has a comparatively complex DEC structure, involving a conditional and the use of `tableSize` as fuel.

```
Definition InitVAddrTableAux (f i: Id) (p:page) : Exp :=
BindN (WriteVirtual p i defaultVAddr)
        (IfThenElse (LtLtb i maxIndex) (BindS "y" (BindS "idx" (IndexSucc i)
            (ExtractIndex "idx")) (Apply (FVar f) (PS [VLift (Var "y")])))
                (Val (cst unit tt))).
```

```
Definition InitVAddrTable (p:page) (i:index) : Exp :=
Apply (QF (FC emptyE [("x",vtyp index)] (Val (cst unit tt))
            (InitVAddrTableAux "initVAddrTable" "x" p)
            "initVAddrTable" tableSize)) (PS[Val (cst index i)]).
```

The associated invariant ensures that after execution each entry of the given configuration table contains the default value `defaultVAddr`, regardless of the current index (`cidx`).

```
Lemma InitVaddrTableInv (p: page) (cidx: index)
    (fenv: funEnv) (env: valEnv) : {{λ  s, (λ idx : index , idx < cidx →
        (ReadVirtual table idx (memory s) = Some defaultVAddr)) }}
    fenv >> env >> InitVAddrTable p cidx
```

`{{λ _ s idx, ReadVirtual p idx (memory s) = Some defaultVAddr}}`.

The DEC structure of `InitVAddrTableAux` makes it convenient to adopt a syntax-driven approach based on the application of Hoare logic rules (as opposed to unfolding the definition of Hoare triple), in order to facilitate automation and maximise reuse. Indeed, it has been easy to write a tactic in Ltac (the scripting language of Coq) to semi-automate the application of such rules. In comparison, pattern-matching on terms in MC might be trickier. On the other hand, the impact of this basic form of automation is restricted by the need to instantiate metavariables with comparatively complex terms for properties. Moreover, the proof uses induction on `tableSize` (in analogy to the shallow one).

8 Related Work

Differences and complementarity between shallow and deep embedding have been widely discussed in functional programming, in relationship with the development of embedded domain specific languages (EDSLs) [24–27]. Combinations of shallow and deep embedding have been proposed e.g. in [25] to deal at once with the expression problem (related to extending a deeply embedded language) and the interpretation problem (related to extending the semantic interpretation of a shallow embedding). Their approach consists in extending a deeply embedded core language with a shallowly embedded front-end, thus the opposite of what we do with a DLE. In fact, they share our intent of separating the interpretation of the EDSL from that of the metalanguage. However, they want the high-level qualities of a shallow embedding (e.g. usability and extensibility of the syntax) for the top level part of the EDSL, whereas we need those qualities in the abstract model underneath (where in facts proofs tend to be, mathematically speaking, higher-level ones).

In applications of theorem proving, the difference between shallow and deep embedding has often been associated with a tradeoff between ease in dealing with mathematically higher-level proofs and language manipulation [28]. For example, Cogent [29] is a domain-specific language that has been used to verify file systems in the context of the seL4 project [3]. Targeting Isabelle, Cogent compiles both to a shallow embedding, used in higher-level verification, and to a deep one, used in verifying C source code (an approach that bears some analogy with our plan A mentioned in Sect. 2).

In the Coq community, refinement from abstract models based on shallow embedding to deeply embedded lower-level ones has been discussed in the context of higher-level formal development [30] as well as in hardware design [31,32]. CertikOS [2,33] provides a method to formally develop low-level applications in Coq, targeting an extension of CompCert Clight and assembly code [13], allowing for composition and refinement of modular specifications which can be imported as external functions into the deeply embedded CompCert frontend. In comparison, our notion of DLE has a radically lighter-weight, domain specific character, relying on a separation of concerns between verification of the executable model (discussed in this paper) and translation to the implementation language.

Moreover, unlike our basic Hoare logic, CertikOS provides advanced support for modular reasoning through contextual refinement [33].

9 Conclusions and Further Work

We have presented the core development of DEC as a DLE, with an interpreter based on its small-step operational semantics. The translation of DEC to C is ongoing work, and so is the proof that its denotational translation to the monadic code agrees with its operational semantics. As a preliminary experiment in using DEC as modelling language, we formalised functions of Pip in DEC and we proved model invariants associated with them. The DLE approach has proved fruitful in two main respects: it has enabled us to match neatly the modelling distinction between platform abstraction and service layer with a linguistic one between external and internal functions, hence defining a formal interface between the two; it has supported modular reuse of abstract platform components and associated proofs along that interface, within a framework that allows for direct manipulation of the executable code.

The notion of DLE is essentially oriented toward the design of intermediate, executable models. In the case of DEC, the DLE has been designed to ensure well-typedness and termination. This choice has been made to match the original model in the shallow embedding, rather than the ultimate C target. More generally, the idea we presented is to build domain specific modelling languages that support program development by refining stateful specifications into imperative code, while preserving in Coq the separation of concerns between layered modelling in a language with a comparatively simple model of execution, and translation to a richer implementation language.

Acknowledgments. We wish to thank all the other members of the Pip Development Team, especially Gilles Grimaud and Samuel Hym, Vlad Rusu and the anonymous reviewers for feedback and discussion. This work has been funded by the European Celtic-Plus Project ODSI C2014/2-12.

A Appendix: Denotational Semantics

We can define a denotational semantics of IL relying on a monadic translation similar to the one in [16] based on a state monad M with fixed state type W. The semantics is defined by a translation of IL to the monadic metalanguage (4–7), for types (Θ_t), expressions (Θ_e), expression lists (Θ_{es}) and functions (Θ_f), using the auxiliary definitions here also included (1–3).

$$
\begin{aligned}
\text{condM} : \; & M \text{ Bool} \rightarrow M \ t_1 \rightarrow M \ t_1 \rightarrow M \ t_1 \; := \\
& \lambda x_0 \ x_1 \ x_2. \text{ bind } x_0 \\
& (\lambda v_0. \text{ bind } x_1 \ (\lambda v_1. \text{ bind } x_2 \ (\lambda v_2. \text{ if\_then\_else } v_0 \ v_1 \ v_2)))
\end{aligned}
\tag{1}
$$

$$\begin{aligned}
\mathsf{mapM} : \; &(\forall t.\; \mathsf{Exp}\; t \to M\; t) \to \mathsf{Exps}\; ts \to M\; ts \; := \\
&\lambda f\; es.\; \mathsf{match}\; es\; \mathsf{with}\; [] \;\Rightarrow\; [] \\
&\qquad\qquad | \; e :: es' \Rightarrow \mathsf{bind}\; (f\; e)\; (\lambda x.\; (\mathsf{bind}\; (\mathsf{mapM}\; f\; es') \\
&\qquad\qquad\qquad\qquad\qquad (\lambda xs.\; \mathsf{ret}\; (x :: xs))))
\end{aligned} \tag{2}$$

$$\begin{aligned}
\mathsf{iterateM}\; &(ts : \mathsf{Typs})\; (t : \mathsf{Typ})\; (e_0 : \; ts \to M\; t) \\
&(e_1 : \; (ts \to M\; t) \to (ts \to M\; t)) \\
&(n : \mathsf{Nat})\; (xs : \; ts) : M\; t \; := \mathsf{match}\; n\; \mathsf{with} \\
&\; 0 \;\Rightarrow\; e_0\; xs \quad | \; S\; n' \Rightarrow\; e_1\; (\mathsf{iterateM}\; ts\; t\; e_0\; e_1\; n')\; xs
\end{aligned} \tag{3}$$

$$\begin{aligned}
\Theta_t\; (\mathsf{Exp}\; t) \quad &:= \; M\; t \\
\Theta_t\; (\mathsf{Exps}\; ts) &:= \; M\; ts \\
\Theta_t\; (\mathsf{Fun}\; t\; ts) &:= \; ts \to M\; t \\
\Theta_t\; (\mathsf{Act}\; t\; ts) &:= \; ts \to M\; t
\end{aligned} \tag{4}$$

$$\begin{aligned}
\Theta_e \; &: \; \forall t.\; \mathsf{Exp}\; t \to M\; t \\
\Theta_e\; (\mathsf{val}\; x) \qquad\qquad\quad &= \; \mathsf{ret}\; x \\
\Theta_e\; (\mathsf{binds}\; e_1\; (\lambda x : t.\; e_2)) &= \; \mathsf{bind}\; (\Theta_e\; e_1)\; (\lambda x : t.\; \Theta_e\; e_2) \\
\Theta_e\; (\mathsf{cond}\; e_1\; e_2\; e_3) \quad &= \; \mathsf{condM}\; (\Theta_e\; e_1)\; (\Theta_e\; e_2)\; (\Theta_e\; e_3) \\
\Theta_e\; (\mathsf{call}\; fc\; es) \qquad &= \; \mathsf{bind}\; (\Theta_{es}\; es)\; (\Theta_f\; fc) \\
\Theta_e\; (\mathsf{xcall}\; a\; es) \qquad &= \; \mathsf{bind}\; (\Theta_{es}\; es)\; a
\end{aligned} \tag{5}$$

$$\begin{aligned}
\Theta_{es} \; &: \; \mathsf{Exps}\; ts \to M\; ts \\
\Theta_{es}\; es &= \; \mathsf{mapM}\; \Theta_e\; es
\end{aligned} \tag{6}$$

$$\begin{aligned}
\Theta_f : \; &\mathsf{Fun}\; t\; ts \to ts \to M\; t \\
\Theta_f\; &(\mathsf{fun}\; (\lambda\; x : \; ts.\; e_0)\; (\lambda\; (r : \; ts \to \mathsf{Exp}\; t)\; (x : \; ts).\; e_1)\; n) \; = \\
&\mathsf{iterateM}\; ts\; t\; (\lambda\; x : \; ts.\; \Theta_e\; e_0) \\
&\qquad (\lambda\; (r : \; ts \to M\; t)\; (x : \; ts).\; \Theta_e\; e_1))\; n
\end{aligned} \tag{7}$$

References

1. Torrini, P., Nowak, D., Cherif, M.S., Jomaa, N.: The repository of DEC (2018). https://github.com/2xs/dec.git
2. Gu, R., et al.: CertiKOS: an extensible architecture for building certified concurrent OS kernels. In: OSDI, pp. 653–669 (2016)
3. Klein, G., et al.: seL4: formal verification of an OS kernel. In: Proceedings of the ACM SIGOPS 22nd Symposium on Operating Systems Principles, pp. 207–220 (2009)

4. Jomaa, N., Torrini, P., Nowak, D., Grimaud, G., Hym, S.: Proof-oriented design of a separation kernel with minimal trusted computing base. In: Proceedings of AVOCS 2018, 16 p. (2018). http://www.cristal.univ-lille.fr/~nowakd/pipdesign.pdf

5. Bertot, Y., Casteran, P.: Interactive Theorem Proving and Program Development. Coq'Art: The Calculus of Inductive Constructions. Springer, Heidelberg (2004). https://doi.org/10.1007/978-3-662-07964-5

6. Nipkow, T., Wenzel, M., Paulson, L.C.: Isabelle/HOL: A Proof Assistant for Higher-Order Logic. Springer, Heidelberg (2002). https://doi.org/10.1007/3-540-45949-9

7. Bergougnoux, Q., Grimaud, G., Iguchi-Cartigny, J.: Porting the Pip proto-kernel's model to multi-core environments. In: IEEE-DASC 2018, 8 p. (2018)

8. Yaker, M., et al.: Ensuring IoT security with an architecture based on a separation kernel. In: FiCloud 2018, 8 p. (2018)

9. Bergougnoux, Q., et al.: The repository of Pip (2018). http://pip.univ-lille1.fr

10. Zhao, Y., Sanan, D., Zhang, F., Liu, Y.: High-assurance separation kernels: a survey on formal methods. arXiv preprint arXiv:1701.01535 (2017)

11. Dam, M., Guanciale, R., Khakpour, N., Nemati, H., Schwarz, O.: Formal verification of information flow security for a simple ARM-based separation kernel. In: Proceedings of the 2013 ACM SIGSAC Conference on Computer & Communications Security, CCS 2013, pp. 223–234. ACM (2013)

12. Hym, S., Oudjail, V.: The repository of Digger (2017). https://github.com/2xs/digger

13. Blazy, S., Leroy, X.: Mechanized semantics for the Clight subset of the C language. J. Autom. Reason. **43**, 263–288 (2009)

14. Torrini, P., Nowak, D.: DEC 1.0 specification (2018). https://github.com/2xs/dec.git

15. Felleisen, M., Hieb, R.: The revised report on the syntactic theories of sequential control and state. Theor. Comput. Sci. **103**(2), 235–271 (1992)

16. Moggi, E.: Notions of computation and monads. Inf. Comput. **93**, 55–92 (1991)

17. Churchill, M., Mosses, P.D., Sculthorpe, N., Torrini, P.: Reusable components of semantic specifications. In: Chiba, S., Tanter, É., Ernst, E., Hirschfeld, R. (eds.) Transactions on Aspect-Oriented Software Development XII. LNCS, vol. 8989, pp. 132–179. Springer, Heidelberg (2015). https://doi.org/10.1007/978-3-662-46734-3_4

18. Plotkin, G.D.: A structural approach to operational semantics. J. Log. Algebr. Program. **60–61**, 17–139 (2004)

19. Leroy, X.: Using Coq's evaluation mechanisms in anger (2015). http://gallium.inria.fr/blog/coq-eval/

20. Cock, D., Klein, G., Sewell, T.: Secure microkernels, state monads and scalable refinement. In: Mohamed, O.A., Muñoz, C., Tahar, S. (eds.) TPHOLs 2008. LNCS, vol. 5170, pp. 167–182. Springer, Heidelberg (2008). https://doi.org/10.1007/978-3-540-71067-7_16

21. Swierstra, W.: A Hoare logic for the state monad. In: Berghofer, S., Nipkow, T., Urban, C., Wenzel, M. (eds.) TPHOLs 2009. LNCS, vol. 5674, pp. 440–451. Springer, Heidelberg (2009). https://doi.org/10.1007/978-3-642-03359-9_30

22. Wadler, P.: Comprehending monads. Math. Struct. Comput. Sci. **2**, 461–493 (1992)

23. Cherif, M.S.: Project report - modelling and verifying the Pip protokernel in a deep embedding of C (2017). https://github.com/2xs/dec.git

24. Gibbons, J., Wu, N.: Folding domain-specific languages: deep and shallow embeddings (functional pearl). In: Proceedings of the ACM SIGPLAN International Conference on Functional Programming, ICFP, vol. 49 (2014)
25. Svenningsson, J., Axelsson, E.: Combining deep and shallow embedding of domain-specific languages. Comput. Lang. Syst. Struct. **44**, 143–165 (2015)
26. Jovanovic, V., Shaikhha, A., Stucki, S., Nikolaev, V., Koch, C., Odersky, M.: Yinyang: concealing the deep embedding of DSLs. In: Proceedings of the 2014 International Conference on Generative Programming: Concepts and Experiences. GPCE 2014, pp. 73–82. ACM (2014)
27. Carette, J., Kiselyov, O., Shan, C.: Finally tagless, partially evaluated: tagless staged interpreters for simpler typed languages. J. Funct. Program. **19**, 509–543 (2009)
28. Wildmoser, M., Nipkow, T.: Certifying machine code safety: shallow versus deep embedding. In: Slind, K., Bunker, A., Gopalakrishnan, G. (eds.) TPHOLs 2004. LNCS, vol. 3223, pp. 305–320. Springer, Heidelberg (2004). https://doi.org/10.1007/978-3-540-30142-4_22
29. O'Connor, L., et al.: Refinement through restraint: bringing down the cost of verification. In: Proceedings of the 21st ACM SIGPLAN International Conference on Functional Programming, ICFP 2016, pp. 89–102. ACM (2016)
30. Delaware, B., Pit-Claudel, C., Gross, J., Chlipala, A.: Fiat: deductive synthesis of abstract data types in a proof assistant. In: Proceedings of the 42nd Annual ACM SIGPLAN-SIGACT Symposium on Principles of Programming Languages, POPL 2015, pp. 689–700 (2015)
31. Chlipala, A.: The Bedrock structured programming system: combining generative metaprogramming and Hoare logic in an extensible program verifier. In: Morrisett, G., Uustalu, T. (eds.) ACM SIGPLAN International Conference on Functional Programming, ICFP 2013, Boston, MA, USA, 25–27 September 2013, pp. 391–402. ACM (2013). https://doi.org/10.1145/2500365.2500592
32. Vijayaraghavan, M., Chlipala, A., Arvind, Dave, N.: Modular deductive verification of multiprocessor hardware designs. In: Kroening, D., Păsăreanu, C. (eds.) CAV 2015. LNCS, vol. 9207, pp. 109–127. Springer, Heidelberg (2015). https://doi.org/10.1007/978-3-319-21668-3_7
33. Gu, R., et al.: Deep specifications and certified abstraction layers. In: Proceedings of the 42nd Annual ACM SIGPLAN-SIGACT Symposium on Principles of Programming Languages, POPL 2015, pp. 595–608. ACM (2015)

A Formalization of the ABNF Notation and a Verified Parser of ABNF Grammars

Alessandro Coglio[(✉)]

Kestrel Institute, Palo Alto, CA, USA
coglio@kestrel.edu
http://www.kestrel.edu/~coglio

Abstract. Augmented Backus-Naur Form (ABNF) is a standardized formal grammar notation used in several Internet syntax specifications. This paper describes (i) a formalization of the syntax and semantics of the ABNF notation and (ii) a verified parser that turns ABNF grammar text into a formal representation usable in declarative specifications of correct parsing of ABNF-specified languages. This work has been developed in the ACL2 theorem prover.

Keywords: ABNF · Parsing · Verification

1 Problem, Contribution, and Outlook

Augmented Backus-Naur Form (ABNF) is a standardized formal grammar notation [9,18] used in several Internet syntax specifications, e.g. HTTP [11], URI [6], and JSON [8]. Since inadequate parsing may enable security exploits such as HTTP request smuggling [19], formally verified parsers of ABNF-specified languages are of interest. It is important to ensure that the formal specifications against which the parsers are verified are faithful to the ABNF grammars.

The work described in this paper contributes to this goal by providing:

1. A formalization of the syntax and semantics of the ABNF notation.
2. A verified parser that turns ABNF grammar text (e.g. the grammar of HTTP) into a formal representation usable in declarative specifications of correct parsing (e.g. correct HTTP parsing).

This work has been developed in the ACL2 theorem prover [14]. The development is available [24, books/kestrel/abnf], is thoroughly documented [25, abnf], and includes examples of use of the parser on several Internet grammars such as HTTP, URI, and JSON. It also includes a collection of operations to compose ABNF grammars and to check properties of them, but this paper does not describe these operations. Some of the excerpts of the development shown in this paper are slightly simplified for brevity.

Future work includes the development of verified parsers for ABNF-specified languages such as JSON and HTTP, and of a generator of verified parsers from ABNF grammars.

© Springer Nature Switzerland AG 2018
R. Piskac and P. Rümmer (Eds.): VSTTE 2018, LNCS 11294, pp. 177–195, 2018.
https://doi.org/10.1007/978-3-030-03592-1_10

2   Background

2.1   ABNF

ABNF adds conveniences and makes slight modifications to Backus-Naur Form (BNF) [3], without going beyond context-free grammars.

Instead of BNF's angle-bracket notation for nonterminals, ABNF uses case-insensitive names consisting of letters, digits, and dashes, e.g. `HTTP-message` and `IPv6address`. ABNF includes an angle-bracket notation for prose descriptions, e.g. `<host, see [RFC3986], Section 3.2.2>`, usable as last resort in the definiens of a nonterminal.

While BNF allows arbitrary terminals, ABNF uses only natural numbers as terminals, and denotes them via: (i) binary, decimal, or hexadecimal sequences, e.g. `%b1.11.1010`, `%d1.3.10`, and `%x.1.3.a` all denote the string '1 3 10'; (ii) binary, decimal, or hexadecimal ranges, e.g. `%x30-39` denotes any string 'n' with $48 \leq n \leq 57$ (an ASCII digit); (iii) case-sensitive ASCII strings, e.g. `%s"Ab"` denotes the string '65 98'; and (iv) case-insensitive ASCII strings, e.g. `%i"ab"`, or just `"ab"`, denotes any string among '65 66', '65 98', '97 66', and '97 98'. ABNF terminals in suitable sets represent ASCII or Unicode characters.

ABNF allows repetition prefixes $n*m$, where n and m are natural numbers in decimal notation; if absent, n defaults to 0, and m defaults to infinity. For example, `1*4HEXDIG` denotes one to four `HEXDIG`s, `*3DIGIT` denotes up to three `DIGIT`s, and `1*OCTET` denotes one or more `OCTET`s. A single n prefix abbreviates $n*n$, e.g. `3DIGIT` denotes three `DIGIT`s.

Instead of BNF's |, ABNF uses / to separate alternatives. Repetition prefixes have precedence over juxtapositions, which have precedence over /. Round brackets group things and override the aforementioned precedence rules, e.g. `*(WSP / CRLF WSP)` denotes strings obtained by repeating, zero or more times, either (i) a `WSP` or (ii) a `CRLF` followed by a `WSP`. Square brackets also group things but make them optional, e.g. `[":" port]` is equivalent to `0*1(":" port)`.

Instead of BNF's ::=, ABNF uses = to define nonterminals, and =/ to incrementally add alternatives to previously defined nonterminals. For example, the rule `BIT = "0" / "1"` is equivalent to `BIT = "0"` followed by `BIT =/ "1"`.

The syntax of ABNF itself is formally specified in ABNF [9, Sect. 4], after the syntax and semantics of ABNF are informally specified in natural language [9, Sects. 1–3]. The syntax rules of ABNF prescribe the ASCII codes allowed for white space (spaces and horizontal tabs), line endings (carriage returns followed by line feeds), and comments (semicolons to line endings).

2.2   ACL2

ACL2 is a general-purpose interactive theorem prover based on an untyped first-order logic of total functions that is an extension of a purely functional subset of Common Lisp [15]. Predicates are functions and formulas are terms; they are false when their value is `nil`, and true when their value is `t` or anything non-`nil`.

```
(defun fact (n)                      (defchoose below (b) (n)
  (if (zp n) 1 (* n (fact (- n 1))))) (and (natp b) (< b (fact n)))))

(defthm above                        (defun-sk between (n)
  (implies (natp n) (>= (fact n) n))) (exists (m)
                                         (and (natp m) (< (below n) m) (< m (fact n))))))
```

Fig. 1. Some simple examples of ACL2 functions and theorems

The ACL2 syntax is consistent with Lisp. A function application is a parenthesized list consisting of the function's name followed by the arguments, e.g. $x + 2 \times f(y)$ is written (+ x (* 2 (f y))). Names of constants start and end with *, e.g. *limit*. Comments extend from semicolons to line endings (like ABNF, incidentally).

The user interacts with ACL2 by submitting a sequence of theorems, function definitions, etc. ACL2 attempts to prove theorems automatically, via algorithms similar to NQTHM [7], most notably simplification and induction. The user guides these proof attempts mainly by (i) proving lemmas for use by specific proof algorithms (e.g. rewrite rules for the simplifier) and (ii) supplying theorem-specific 'hints' (e.g. to case-split on certain conditions).

The factorial function can be defined like **fact** in Fig. 1, where **zp** tests if **n** is 0 or not a natural number. Thus **fact** treats arguments that are not natural numbers as 0. ACL2 functions often handle arguments of the wrong type by explicitly or implicitly coercing them to the right type—since the logic is untyped, in ACL2 a 'type' is just any subset of the universe of values.

To preserve logical consistency, recursive function definitions must be proved to terminate via a measure of the arguments that decreases in each recursive call according to a well-founded relation. For **fact**, ACL2 automatically finds a measure and proves that it decreases according to a standard well-founded relation, but sometimes the user has to supply a measure.

A theorem saying that **fact** is above its argument can be introduced like **above** in Fig. 1, where **natp** tests if **n** is a natural number. ACL2 proves this theorem automatically (if a standard arithmetic library [24, books/arithmetic] is loaded), finding and using an appropriate induction rule—the one derived from the recursive definition of **fact**, in this case.

Besides the discouraged ability to introduce arbitrary axioms, ACL2 provides logical-consistency-preserving mechanisms to axiomatize new functions, such as indefinite description functions. A function constrained to be strictly below **fact** can be introduced like **below** in Fig. 1, where **b** is the variable bound by the indefinite description. This introduces the logically conservative axiom that, for every **n**, (below n) is a natural number less than (fact n), if any exists—otherwise, (below n) is unconstrained.

ACL2's Lisp-like macro mechanism provides the ability to extend the language with new constructs defined in terms of existing constructs. For instance, despite the lack of built-in quantification in the logic, functions with top-level quantifiers can be introduced. The existence of a value strictly between **fact** and below can be expressed by a predicate like between in Fig. 1, where defun-sk is a macro defined in terms of defchoose and defun, following a well-known construction [2].

3   ABNF Formalization

3.1   Abstract Syntax

The formalization starts by defining an abstract syntax of ABNF, based on the ABNF rules that define the concrete syntax of ABNF.[1] To ease validation by inspection, this abstract syntax closely follows the structure of the concrete syntax (as exemplified below) and abstracts away only essentially lexical details (e.g. white space, comments, and defaults of repetition prefixes). ACL2's FTY macro library for introducing structured recursive types [23] is used to define the abstract syntactic entities of ABNF—11 types in total.

```
rulelist = 1*( rule / (*c-wsp c-nl) )
rule = rulename defined-as elements c-nl
defined-as = *c-wsp ("=" / "=/") *c-wsp
elements = alternation *c-wsp
alternation = concatenation *(*c-wsp "/" *c-wsp concatenation)
concatenation = repetition *(1*c-wsp repetition)
repetition = [repeat] element
element = rulename / group / option / char-val / num-val / prose-val
group = "(" *c-wsp alternation *c-wsp ")"
option = "[" *c-wsp alternation *c-wsp "]"
num-val = "%" (bin-val / dec-val / hex-val)
bin-val = "b" 1*BIT [ 1*("." 1*BIT) / ("-" 1*BIT) ]
dec-val = "d" 1*DIGIT [ 1*("." 1*DIGIT) / ("-" 1*DIGIT) ]
hex-val = "x" 1*HEXDIG [ 1*("." 1*HEXDIG) / ("-" 1*HEXDIG) ]
c-wsp = WSP / (c-nl WSP)
c-nl = comment / CRLF
CRLF = CR LF ; carriage return and line feed
WSP = SP / HTAB ; space or horizontal tab
```

Fig. 2. Some rules of the ABNF grammar of ABNF

For example, the concrete syntax of numeric terminal notations such as %d1.3.10 and %x30-39 is defined in ABNF by num-val in Fig. 2, where the definitions of BIT, DIGIT, and HEXDIG are not shown but should be obvious from the names. In ACL2, the corresponding abstract syntax is formalized by num-val in Fig. 3, where: fty::deftagsum introduces a tagged sum type (disjoint union); num-val is the name of the type; :direct tags direct notations such as %d1.3.10 whose only component get is a list of natural numbers (type nat-list, whose recognizer is nat-listp) such as (1 3 10); and :range tags range notations such as %x30-39 whose components min and max are natural numbers (type nat, whose recognizer is natp) such as 48 and 57. This type definition introduces: a recognizer num-val-p for the type; constructors num-val-direct and num-val-range; destructors num-val-direct->get, num-val-range->min, and

---

[1] The meta circularity of the definition of the concrete syntax of ABNF in ABNF is broken by the human in the loop, who defines an abstract syntax of ABNF in ACL2.

num-val-range->max; and several theorems about these functions. Compared to the concrete syntax rule num-val in Fig. 2, the abstract syntax type num-val in Fig. 3 abstracts the binary, decimal, or hexadecimal notations to their natural number values.

As another example, the concrete syntax of rule definientia is defined in ABNF by alternation and mutually recursive companions in Fig. 2. In ACL2, the corresponding abstract syntax is formalized by alternation and mutually recursive companions in Fig. 3, where: fty::deftypes introduces mutually recursive types; fty::deflist introduces a type of lists over the element type that appears after :elt-type; fty::defprod introduces a product type similar to a fty::deftagsum summand; repeat-range is a type for repetition prefixes such as 1* or 3*6; rulename is a type for rule names; char-val is a type for string terminal notations such as %s"Ab"; and prose-val is a type for prose notations such as <host, see [RFC3986], Section 3.2.2>. These type definitions introduce recognizers, constructors, destructors, and theorems analogous to the ones for num-val above. Compared to the concrete syntax rules alternation and companions in Fig. 2, the abstract syntax types alternation and companions in Fig. 3 abstract away comments, white space, and line endings.

As a third example, the concrete syntax of grammars (i.e. lists of rules) is defined in ABNF by rulelist in Fig. 2. In ACL2, the corresponding abstract syntax is formalized by rulelist in Fig. 3, where the incremental component of rule is a boolean that says whether the rule is incremental (=/) or not (=). Compared to the concrete syntax rules rulelist and rule, the abstract syntax types rulelist and rule abstract away comments, white space, and line endings.

The syntactic structure of ABNF grammars is more complex than the syntactic structure of plain context-free grammars. ABNF rule definientia are expressions built out of various terminal notations (direct and range numeric notations, etc.) and operators (alternation, concatenation, repetition, etc.), while plain context-free rule definientia are sequences of symbols.

```
(fty::deftagsum num-val
  (:direct ((get nat-list)))
  (:range ((min nat) (max nat))))

(fty::defprod rule
  ((name rulename)
   (incremental bool)
   (definiens alternation)))

(fty::deflist rulelist
  :elt-type rule)
```

```
(fty::deftypes alt/conc/rep/elem
  (fty::deflist alternation :elt-type concatenation)
  (fty::deflist concatenation :elt-type repetition)
  (fty::defprod repetition
    ((range repeat-range) (element element)))
  (fty::deftagsum element
    (:rulename ((get rulename)))
    (:group ((get alternation)))
    (:option ((get alternation)))
    (:char-val ((get char-val)))
    (:num-val ((get num-val)))
    (:prose-val ((get prose-val)))))
```

Fig. 3. Some excerpts of the abstract syntax of ABNF formalized in ACL2

```
(fty::deftypes trees
  (fty::deftagsum tree
    (:leafterm ((get nat-list)))
    (:leafrule ((get rulename)))
    (:nonleaf ((rulename? maybe-rulename) (branches tree-list-list))))
  (fty::deflist tree-list :elt-type tree)
  (fty::deflist tree-list-list :elt-type tree-list))

(defun tree-match-num-val-p (tree num-val)
  (and (tree-case tree :leafterm)
       (let ((nats (tree-leafterm->get tree)))
         (num-val-case num-val
                       :direct (equal nats num-val.get)
                       :range (and (equal (len nats) 1)
                                   (<= num-val.min (car nats))
                                   (<= (car nats) num-val.max))))))

(mutual-recursion
  (defun tree-list-list-match-alternation-p (treess alt rules) ...)
  (defun tree-list-list-match-concatenation-p (treess conc rules) ...)
  (defun tree-list-match-repetition-p (trees rep rules) ...)
  (defun tree-list-match-element-p (trees elem rules) ...)
  (defun tree-match-element-p (tree elem rules)
    (element-case elem
      :rulename (tree-case tree
                           :leafterm nil
                           :leafrule (equal tree.get elem.get)
                           :nonleaf (and (equal tree.rulename? elem.get)
                                         (let ((alt (lookup-rulename elem.get rules)))
                                           (tree-list-list-match-alternation-p
                                            tree.branches alt rules))))
      :group ...
      :option ...
      :char-val ...
      :num-val (tree-match-num-val-p tree elem.get)
      :prose-val t)))

(defun parse-treep (tree string rulename rules)
  (and (treep tree)
       (tree-match-element-p tree (element-rulename rulename) rules)
       (equal (tree->string tree) string)))

(defun-sk languagep (nats rulenames rules)
  (exists (rulename tree) (and (nat-listp nats)
                               (in rulename rulenames)
                               (parse-treep tree nats rulename rules)))))
```

Fig. 4. Some excerpts of the semantics of ABNF formalized in ACL2

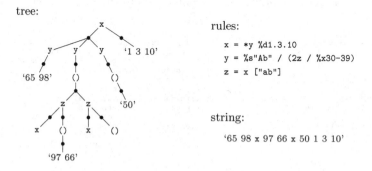

tree:

rules:
```
x = *y %d1.3.10
y = %s"Ab" / (2z / %x30-39)
z = x ["ab"]
```

string:

'65 98 x 97 66 x 50 1 3 10'

Fig. 5. An example of a tree for a string, given some rules

```
(defchoose parse-http (result) (string)
  (if (string-parsablep string *http-message* *http-grammar*)
      (and (parse-treep result string *http-message* *http-grammar*)
           (disambiguatep result))
      (equal result *error*)))
```

Fig. 6. A sketch of a declarative specification of an HTTP parser

3.2 Semantics

An ABNF grammar describes how a sequence of natural numbers (terminals) can be organized in tree structures according to the grammar's rules. Thus, the semantics of the abstract syntactic entities is formalized via matching relations with trees. The notion of language generated by a grammar is derived from that.

Since a single terminal notation like `%d1.3.10` or `%s"Ab"` denotes multiple natural numbers in sequence, it is convenient to use lists (i.e. strings) of natural numbers, instead of individual natural numbers, to label leaves of trees. A rule name (nonterminal) can label the root of a (sub)tree, with branches for one of the concatenations of the alternation that defines the rule name. Since a concatenation is a sequence of repetitions, and each repetition may denote multiple instances of its element, the branches are organized into a list of lists: the outer list matches the list of repetitions that form the concatenation, and each inner list matches the element instances of the corresponding repetition; this organization facilitates the formulation of the matching relations (see below). Rule names can also label leaves, to represent the tree structure of strings that include nonterminals. Round-bracketed groups and square-bracketed options are like anonymous rules: roots of (sub)trees that match groups and options are not labeled by rule names, but have lists of lists of branches for concatenations from the alternations inside the brackets, in the same way as named rules; additionally, a square-bracketed option is allowed to have an empty list of lists of branches, to represent the absence of the option.

Formally, (lists of (lists of)) trees are recursively defined by `tree` and mutually recursive companions in Fig. 4, where `maybe-rulename` is a type consisting of rule names and `nil`—the latter is used for roots not labeled by rule names. A function `tree->string` (whose definition is not shown here) collects the natural numbers and rule names at the leaves of a tree, from left to right, into a string (i.e. list).

Trees can be visualized as in Fig. 5. Leaves are labeled by lists of natural numbers or rule names. Roots of (sub)trees are labeled by rule names or, for groups and options, by () (which is another way to write `nil` in ACL2). Lines with joints represent lists of lists of branches.

A tree matches a direct numeric terminal notation iff it is a leaf labeled by the same list of natural numbers; a tree matches a range numeric terminal notation iff it is a leaf labeled by a list of one natural number in the range. This is formalized by `tree-match-num-val-p` in Fig. 4, where: `(tree-case tree:leafterm)` tests if `tree` is tagged by `:leafterm`; `(num-val-case num-val ...)` performs a case analysis on the tag of `num-val` (Fig. 3) that binds the variables with dots in their names to the corresponding components of the target variable `num-val` (e.g. `num-val.get` is bound to (`num-val-direct->get num-val`)); `len` returns the length of a list; and `car` returns the first value of a list.

Since an element (e.g. a numeric terminal notation) is matched by a tree, a repetition is matched by a list of trees: the length of the list must be within the repetition prefix's range, and each tree of the list must match the repetition's element. Since a concatenation is a list of repetitions, a concatenation is matched by a list of lists of trees: the length of the outer list must equal the length of the concatenation, and each inner list must match the corresponding repetition. Since an alternation denotes one of its concatenations at a time, an alternation is matched by a list of lists of trees, which must match one of the alternation's concatenations. A rule name is matched by either a leaf tree labeled by the rule name, or a non-leaf tree whose root is labeled by the rule name and whose branches match the alternation that defines the rule name. A group is matched by a non-leaf tree whose root is labeled by () and whose branches match the alternation inside the group; an option is matched by either a tree in the same way as a group, or by a non-leaf tree whose root is labeled by () and with an empty list of lists of trees as branches.

The assertions in the previous paragraph are formalized by `tree-list-list-match-alternation-p` and mutually recursive companions in Fig. 4, where: `mutual-recursion` introduces mutually recursive `defun`s; (`element-case elem ...`) and (`tree-case tree ...`) perform case analyses on the tags of `elem` (Fig. 3) and `tree` (Fig. 4), analogously to `num-val-case` as explained above; and `lookup-rulename` collects, from the rules of a grammar, all the alternatives that define a rule name. The termination of these mutually recursive functions is proved via a lexicographic measure consisting of the size of the trees followed by the size of the abstract syntactic entities.

A prose notation is matched by any tree, as far as the ABNF semantics alone is concerned. Predicates on trees, external to ABNF grammars, can be used to define the meaning of specific prose notations, and conjoined with the tree matching predicates to specify parsing requirements.[2] Some grammars use prose notations to refer to rules from other grammars, e.g. the HTTP grammar uses prose notations to refer to rules from the URI grammar (an example is in Sect. 2.1): the grammar composition operations briefly mentioned in Sect. 1 replace these prose notations with the referenced rules, resulting in a combined grammar without prose notations.

Given the rules of a grammar and a rule name, a parse tree for a string is a tree that matches the rule name and that has the string at the leaves, as formalized by `parse-treep` in Fig. 4. Given the rules of a grammar and a set of rule names, a string of the language generated by the rules starting from the rule names is a list of natural numbers at the leaves of some parse tree whose root is one of the rule names, as formalized by `languagep` in Fig. 4, where `in` tests set membership; since ABNF grammars do not have an explicit notion of

---

[2] Future work includes exploring mechanisms to "plug" such external predicates into the ABNF semantics.

start nonterminal, the start nonterminals of interest are specified by the second argument of `languagep`.

The `parse-treep` predicate can be used to write declarative specifications of correct parsing of ABNF-specified languages. For instance, a (non-executable) HTTP parser can be specified by something like `parse-http` in Fig. 6, where: `*http-grammar*` is a constant of type `rulelist` (Fig. 3) representing the rules of the ABNF grammar of HTTP; `*http-message*` is a constant of type `rulename` (Fig. 3) representing the top-level rule name `HTTP-message`; `string-parsablep` holds iff there exists a parse tree for the string; the predicate `disambiguatep` states disambiguating restrictions (since the grammar of HTTP is ambiguous); and `*error*` is a constant representing an error, distinct from trees. The function `parse-http` returns concrete syntax trees, because grammars do not specify abstract syntax; a practical HTTP parser can be specified as the composition of `parse-http` followed by a suitable HTTP syntax abstraction function (analogous to the ABNF syntax abstraction functions described in Sect. 3.3).

The semantics of ABNF grammars is more complex than the semantics of plain context-free grammars. ABNF parse trees have branches organized as lists of lists and have roots of non-leaf trees possibly labeled by (), while parse trees of plain context-free grammars have branches organized as lists and have roots of non-leaf trees always labeled by nonterminals. Accordingly, the ABNF tree matching relations are more complex than the tree matching relations of plain context-free grammars.

3.3   Concrete Syntax

The concrete syntax of ABNF is formalized in ACL2 using the rules of the ABNF grammar of ABNF, but "written in abstract syntax" because the concrete syntax is not available before it is formalized. This safely captures the meta circularity.

```
(def-rule-const *group*
  (/_ "(" (*_ *c-wsp*) *alternation* (*_ *c-wsp*) ")"))

(def-rule-const *num-val*
  (/_ "%" (!_ (/_ *bin-val*) (/_ *dec-val*) (/_ *hex-val*))))
```

Fig. 7. Some excerpts of the concrete syntax of ABNF formalized in ACL2

Since the FTY constructors of the abstract syntax are verbose, some specially crafted and named functions and macros are defined, and used to write abstract syntactic entities in a way that looks more like concrete syntax, easing not only their writing, but also their validation by inspection. For example, the rules `group` and `num-val` (Fig. 2) are written in abstract syntax as shown in Fig. 7.

After transcribing the 40 rules of the ABNF grammar of ABNF to this form, a constant `*abnf-grammar*` consisting of their list is defined. Since grammars, i.e. values of type `rulelist` (Fig. 3), are endowed with semantics (Sect. 3.2), this constant provides a formalization of the concrete syntax of ABNF in ACL2.

The link between the concrete and abstract syntax of ABNF is formalized by 51 executable ACL2 functions that map parse trees to their corresponding abstract syntactic entities: these are abstraction functions, which distill the abstract syntactic information from the concrete syntactic information. For example, a function `abstract-num-val` (whose definition is not shown here) maps a tree that matches the rule name `num-val` (Fig. 2) to a value of type `num-val` (Fig. 3). This function calls other abstraction functions on its subtrees, e.g. a function `abstract-*bit` (whose definition is not shown here) that maps a list of trees that matches `*BIT` to the big endian value of their bits. The top-level abstraction function `abstract-rulelist` (whose definition is not shown here) maps a tree that matches the rule name `rulelist` (Fig. 2) to the corresponding value of type `rulelist` (Fig. 3)—a grammar.

4   ABNF Grammar Parser

When specifying correct parsing of an ABNF-specified language as sketched in Fig. 6, a constant like `*http-grammar*` can be built by manually transcribing the grammar, as done for `*abnf-grammar*` (Sect. 3.3). A better alternative is to perform this transcription automatically, by running (i) the grammar parser described in the rest of this section, which produces a parse tree that matches `rulelist`, followed by (ii) `abstract-rulelist` (Sect. 3.3) on the resulting parse tree.

Since the grammar parser is verified as described below, and this automatic transcription process operates on the actual grammar text (e.g. copied and pasted from an Internet standard document), the resulting formal parsing specification is faithful to the grammar.

Running this process on the ABNF grammar of ABNF produces the same value as the manually built `*abnf-grammar*`. This provides a validation.

4.1   Implementation

The ABNF grammar of ABNF is ambiguous, as shown by the two different parse trees for the same string (of nonterminals, for brevity) in Fig. 8: the first `c-nl` can either end a `rule` (lower tree) or form, with the `WSP`, a `c-wsp` under `elements` (upper tree). The ambiguity only affects where certain comments, white space, and line endings go in the parse trees; it does not affect the abstract syntax, and thus the semantics, of ABNF. The parser resolves the ambiguity by always parsing as many consecutive `c-wsp`s as possible, as in the upper tree in Fig. 8.[3]

Aside from this ambiguity, the ABNF grammar of ABNF is mostly LL(1), with some LL(2) and LL(*) parts [1,21]. The parser is implemented as a recursive descent with backtracking. Backtracking is expected to be limited in reasonable grammars. Indeed, the parser runs very quickly on all the example grammars

---

[3] Future work includes exploring the formulation of an unambiguous ABNF grammar of ABNF that provably defines the same language as the current ambiguous one.

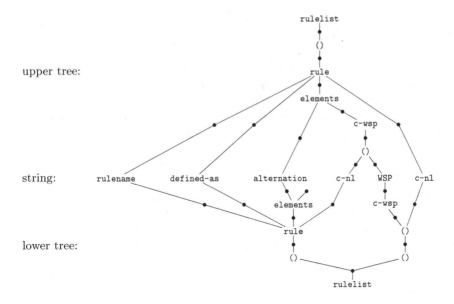

Fig. 8. An example showing the ambiguity of the ABNF grammar of ABNF

included in the development—fractions of a second, including file reading, which is adequate for the expected use of the parser outlined above.

The parser consists of 85 executable ACL2 functions. There is a parsing function for each rule, and parsing functions for certain groups, options, repetitions, and terminal notations. ACL2's Seq macro library for stream processing [25, seq] is used to define these functions in a more readable way. Each function takes a list of natural numbers to parse as input, and, consistently with Seq, returns (i) an indication of success (nil, i.e. no error) or failure (an error message, which is never nil), (ii) a (list of) parse tree(s) if successful, and (iii) the remaining natural numbers in the input.

For example, the parsing function for CRLF (Fig. 2) is parse-crlf in Fig. 9, where: first parse-cr parses a carriage return, yielding a CR parse tree that is assigned to tree-cr; then parse-lf parses a line feed, yielding an LF parse tree that is assigned to tree-lf; and finally return returns (i) nil (success), (ii) a CRLF parse tree with the two subtrees, and (iii) the remaining input after the carriage return and line feed. If parse-cr or parse-lf fails, parse-crlf fails. The threading of the input and the propagation of the failures is handled by the seq macro behind the scenes.

As another example, the parsing function for WSP (Fig. 2) is parse-wsp in Fig. 9, where: parse-sp attempts to parse a space, returning a WSP parse tree with a SP subtree if successful; otherwise parse-htab attempts to parse a horizontal tab, returning a WSP parse tree with a HTAB subtree if successful. If both parse-sp and parse-htab fail, parse-wsp fails. The backtracking is handled by the seq-backtrack macro behind the scenes.

As a third example, the parsing function for *BIT is parse-*bit in Fig. 9, which uses parse-bit to parse as many bits as possible, eventually returning the corresponding list of BIT parse trees; cons adds an element to the front of a list. The termination of parse-*bit is proved by the decrease of the length of the input. This function never fails: when no bits can be parsed, the empty list nil of parse trees is returned.

The parsing functions for alternation and mutually recursive companions (Fig. 2) are mutually recursive (their definitions are not shown here). Their termination is proved via a lexicographic measure consisting of the size of the input followed by a linear ordering of these functions—the length of the input alone is insufficient to prove termination, because some (e.g. parse-alternation) call others (e.g. parse-concatenation) on the same input.

The top-level parsing function is parse-grammar in Fig. 9, where b* binds the results of parse-rulelist to the three variables in the triple (mv ...). The function checks that there is no remaining input, returning just the parse tree if successful (or nil, i.e. no parse tree, if a failure occurs). There is also a wrapper function parse-grammar-from-file (whose definition is not shown here) that takes a file name as input and calls parse-grammar on the file's content.

```
(defun parse-crlf (input)
  (seq input
       (tree-cr := (parse-cr input))
       (tree-lf := (parse-lf input))
       (return (tree-nonleaf *crlf* (list (list tree-cr) (list tree-lf))))))

(defun parse-wsp (input)
  (seq-backtrack input
                 ((tree := (parse-sp input))
                  (return (tree-nonleaf *wsp* (list (list tree)))))
                 ((tree := (parse-htab input))
                  (return (tree-nonleaf *wsp* (list (list tree)))))))

(defun parse-*bit (input)
  (seq-backtrack input
                 ((tree := (parse-bit input))
                  (trees := (parse-*bit input))
                  (return (cons tree trees)))
                 ((return nil))))

(defun parse-grammar (input)
  (b* (((mv error? tree? rest) (parse-rulelist input)))
    (cond (error? nil) (rest nil) (t tree?))))
```

Fig. 9. Some excerpts of the ABNF grammar parser in ACL2

4.2   Verification

The correctness of the parser consists of:

– Soundness: the parser recognizes only ABNF grammars.
– Completeness: the parser recognizes all ABNF grammars (almost; see below).

```
(defthm parse-treep-of-parse-grammar
  (implies (and (nat-listp input)
                (parse-grammar input))
           (parse-treep (parse-grammar input) input *rulelist* *abnf-grammar*)))

(defthm input-decomposition-of-parse-crlf
  (implies (and (nat-listp input)
                (not (mv-nth 0 (parse-crlf input))))
           (equal (append (tree->string (mv-nth 1 (parse-crlf input)))
                          (mv-nth 2 (parse-crlf input)))
                  input)))

(defthm tree-match-of-parse-crlf
  (implies (and (nat-listp input)
                (not (mv-nth 0 (parse-crlf input))))
           (tree-match-element-p (mv-nth 1 (parse-crlf input))
                                 (element-rulename *crlf*)
                                 *abnf-grammar*)))
```

Fig. 10. Some excerpts of the ABNF grammar parser soundness proof in ACL2

```
(defthm parse-grammar-when-tree-match
  (implies (and (treep tree)
                (tree-match-element-p tree (element-rulename *rulelist*) *abnf-grammar*)
                (tree-terminatedp tree)
                (tree-rulelist-restriction-p tree))
           (equal (parse-grammar (tree->string tree)) tree)))

(defthm parse-wsp-when-tree-match
  (implies (and (treep tree)
                (nat-listp rest-input)
                (tree-match-element-p tree (element-rulename *wsp*) *abnf-grammar*)
                (tree-terminatedp tree))
           (equal (parse-wsp (append (tree->string tree) rest-input))
                  (mv nil tree rest-input))))

(defthm parse-*bit-when-tree-list-match
  (implies (and (tree-listp trees)
                (nat-listp rest-input)
                (tree-list-match-repetition-p trees (*_ *bit*) *abnf-grammar*)
                (tree-list-terminatedp trees)
                (mv-nth 0 (parse-bit rest-input)))
           (equal (parse-*bit (append (tree-list->string trees) rest-input))
                  (mv nil trees rest-input))))

(defthm fail-sp-when-match-htab
  (implies (and (tree-match-element-p tree (element-rulename *htab*) *abnf-grammar*)
                (tree-terminatedp tree))
           (mv-nth 0 (parse-sp (append (tree->string tree) rest-input)))))

(defthm constraints-from-parse-sp
  (implies (not (mv-nth 0 (parse-sp input)))
           (equal (car input) 32)))

(defthm constraints-from-tree-match-htab
  (implies (and (tree-match-element-p tree (element-rulename *htab*) *abnf-grammar*)
                (tree-terminatedp tree))
           (equal (car (tree->string tree)) 9)))

(defun-sk pred-alternation (input)
  (forall (tree rest-input)
    (implies (and (treep tree)
                  (nat-listp rest-input)
                  (tree-match-element-p tree (element-rulename *alternation*) *abnf-grammar*)
                  (tree-terminatedp tree)
                  ... ; 8 parsing failure hypotheses on rest-input
                  (equal input (append (tree->string tree) rest-input)))
             (equal (parse-alternation (append (tree->string tree) rest-input))
                    (mv nil tree rest-input)))))

(defthm parse-alternation-when-tree-match-lemma
  (pred-alternation input))
```

Fig. 11. Some excerpts of the ABNF grammar parser completeness proof in ACL2

More precisely, the parser not only recognizes ABNF grammars, but also returns the corresponding parse trees, as elaborated below.

The main soundness theorem is `parse-treep-of-parse-grammar` in Fig. 10, where `*rulelist*` represents the rule name `rulelist` (Fig. 2). Semi-formally, the theorem says:

> `input` is a list of natural numbers ∧
> `(parse-grammar input)` ≠ `nil` ⟹
> `(parse-grammar input)` is a parse tree
>   with `rulelist` at the root and `input` at the leaves

That is, if `parse-grammar` (Fig. 9) succeeds, it returns a parse tree that organizes the input into the tree structure of a grammar (i.e. a list of rules).

This main soundness theorem is proved via two theorems for each of the parsing functions that return triples:

- Input decomposition: if the function succeeds, the string at the leaves of the returned parse tree(s) consists of the natural numbers parsed from the input, and the function also returns the remaining natural numbers in the input.
- Tree matching: if the function succeeds, the returned parse tree/trees is/are consistent with the syntactic entity that the function is intended to parse.

For example, the input decomposition theorem of `parse-crlf` (Fig. 9) is `input-decomposition-of-parse-crlf` in Fig. 10, where `mv-nth` extracts the components (zero-indexed) of the triple returned by `parse-crlf`. The theorem says that if `parse-crlf` succeeds (i.e. its first result is `nil`, not an error), joining the string at the leaves of the returned tree with the returned remaining input yields the original input.

Each input decomposition theorem is proved by expanding the parsing function and using the input decomposition theorems of the called parsing functions as rewrite rules. For instance, in `input-decomposition-of-parse-crlf` (Fig. 10), expanding `parse-crlf` turns the `(append ...)` into one involving `parse-cr` and `parse-lf`, making their input decomposition theorems applicable.

As another example, the tree matching theorem of `parse-crlf` (Fig. 9) is `tree-match-of-parse-crlf` in Fig. 10. The theorem says that if `parse-crlf` succeeds (formulated in the same way as in the input decomposition theorem), the returned parse tree matches CRLF—which `parse-crlf` is intended to parse.

Each tree matching theorem is proved by expanding the parsing function and the tree matching predicate, and using the tree matching theorems of the called functions as rewrite rules. For instance, in the `tree-match-of-parse-crlf`, expanding `parse-crlf` and `tree-match-element-p` turns the conclusion into the assertion that the subtrees match CR and LF when `parse-cr` and `parse-lf` succeed, making their tree matching theorems applicable.

The input decomposition and tree matching theorems of the recursive parsing functions (e.g. `parse-*bit` in Fig. 9) are proved by induction on their recursive definitions.

The main soundness theorem, `parse-treep-of-parse-grammar` (Fig. 10), is proved from the input decomposition and tree matching theorems of parse-rulelist, and the fact that parse-grammar fails if there is remaining input.

Since the ABNF grammar of ABNF is ambiguous (Fig. 8) but the parser returns a single parse tree at a time, completeness is not provable. But it is provable relatively to trees consistent with how the parser resolves the ambiguity. A predicate tree-rulelist-restriction-p formalizes these restrictions on trees: each (*c-wsp c-nl) subtree, except the one (if any) that starts a rulelist, must not start with WSP.

The main completeness theorem is parse-grammar-when-tree-match in Fig. 11, where tree-terminatedp tests if a tree is terminated, i.e. if the string at its leaves has only natural numbers and no rule names. Semi-formally, the theorem says:

tree is a tree ∧
tree matches rulelist ∧
tree has no rule names at the leaves ∧
tree satisfies the disambiguating restrictions ⟹
(parse-grammar (tree->string tree)) = tree

That is, if a terminated tree matches a rulelist (i.e. it is a concrete syntactic representation of a grammar) and is consistent with how the parser resolves the ambiguity, parse-grammar succeeds on the string at the leaves of the tree and returns the tree.

This main completeness theorem is proved via an auxiliary completeness theorem for each of the parsing functions that return triples. The formulation of these auxiliary theorems is analogous to the main one, but with additional complexities: in the conclusions, the parsing functions are applied to the string at the leaves of the tree(s) joined with some remaining input; this makes these theorems usable as rewrite rules, and enables the addition of certain critical hypotheses to these theorems.

For example, the completeness theorem of parse-wsp (Fig. 9) is parse-wsp-when-tree-match in Fig. 11. As another example, the completeness theorem of parse-*bit (Fig. 9) is parse-*bit-when-tree-list-match in Fig. 11. The hypothesis that parse-bit fails on rest-input is critical: without it, parse-*bit might parse another bit from rest-input, and return a longer list of trees than trees.

Each auxiliary completeness theorem is proved by expanding the parsing function and the tree matching predicate, using the completeness theorems of the called functions as rewrite rules, and also using, as needed, certain disambiguation theorems.

The need and nature of these disambiguation theorems, in simple form, are illustrated by considering the proof of the completeness theorem of parse-wsp. The hypothesis that tree matches WSP expands to two cases:

1. The subtree matches the SP alternative of WSP. In this case, the completeness theorem of parse-sp applies, parse-sp succeeds returning the subtree, and parse-wsp succeeds returning tree.

2. The subtree matches the `HTAB` alternative of `WSP`. For the completeness theorem of `parse-htab` to apply, `parse-sp` must be shown to fail so that `parse-wsp` reduces to `parse-htab` and the proof proceeds as in the SP case.[4]

The theorem saying that `parse-sp` fails on the string at the leaves of a terminated tree matching `HTAB` is `fail-sp-when-match-htab` in Fig. 11. This theorem is proved via two theorems saying that `parse-sp` and `HTAB` induce incompatible constraints on the same value at the start of the input: the two theorems are `constraints-from-parse-sp` and `constraints-from-tree-match-htab` in Fig. 11. The incompatible constraints are that `parse-sp` requires the ASCII code 32, while `HTAB` requires the ASCII code 9.

There are 26 parsing constraint theorems similar to the one for `parse-sp`, and 49 tree matching constraint theorems similar to the one for `HTAB`. There are 87 disambiguation theorems similar to `fail-sp-when-match-htab` (Fig. 11): they say that certain parsing functions fail when trees match certain syntactic entities, effectively showing that the parser can disambiguate all the alternatives in the ABNF grammar of ABNF, including deciding when to stop parsing unbounded repetitions. The disambiguation theorems are used to prove not only some completeness theorems, but also other disambiguation theorems. Some disambiguation theorems critically include parsing failure hypotheses similarly to the completeness theorem of `parse-*bit` (Fig. 11). Many disambiguation theorems show incompatible constraints just on the first one or two natural numbers in the input, corresponding to LL(1) and LL(2) parts of the grammar. But for LL($*$) parts of the grammar, the disambiguation theorems show incompatible constraints on natural numbers that follow unbounded prefixes of the input; to "go past" these prefixes in the proofs of these disambiguation theorems, certain completeness theorems are used in turn.

Since the auxiliary completeness theorems call the parsing functions not on variables but on (`append ...`) terms, induction on the recursive parsing functions is not readily applicable [7, Chap. 15]. For the singly recursive functions like `parse-*bit`, induction on the list of trees is used. For the mutually recursive functions like `parse-alternation`, an analogous induction on the (lists of (lists of)) trees seems unwieldy due to the number (10) of mutually recursive parsing functions. Instead, the desired completeness assertions are packaged into predicates like `pred-alternation` in Fig. 11, where the tree and remaining input are universally quantified and a new variable `input` is equated to the argument of the parsing function. Given these predicates, theorems like `parse-alternation-when-tree-match-lemma` in Fig. 11 are proved by induction on the recursive parsing functions (now applicable to the variable `input`), from which the desired completeness theorems readily follow.

The main completeness theorem, `parse-grammar-when-tree-match` (Fig. 11), is proved from the auxiliary completeness theorem of `parse-rulelist` and the fact that the absence of remaining input fulfills the parsing failure hypotheses on the remaining input.

---

[4] Even though the roles of SP and HTAB are "symmetric" in the rule `WSP` in Fig. 2, the function `parse-wsp` in Fig. 9 "asymmetrically" tries to parse SP before HTAB.

All the theorems and proofs overviewed in this subsection are discussed in much greater detail in the documentation of the development [25, abnf]. Even the short overview above should convey that the completeness proof is considerably more laborious than the soundness proof, perhaps because the completeness proof must show that the parser can reconstruct any parse tree from its string at the leaves, while the soundness proof must show that the parser can just construct one appropriate parse tree when it succeeds.

5   Related Work

The author is not aware of other formalizations of the ABNF notation. There are formalizations of regular expressions [10], plain context-free grammars [4], and parsing expression grammars [16]. As explained at the end of Sects. 3.1 and 3.2, the syntax and semantics of ABNF are more complex than those of plain context-free grammars (and of regular expressions). The syntax of parsing expression grammars has some similarities with ABNF, but their semantics is operational, in terms of parsing steps, in contrast with ABNF's tree matching semantics. The referenced works formalize abstract syntax of the grammar notations, but not concrete syntax; in contrast, the work described in this paper formalizes both abstract and concrete syntax of ABNF, using the former to define the latter as faithfully to the meta circularity [9,18] as allowed by the theorem prover's define-before-use constraints, and validating the definition via the verified ABNF grammar parser as mentioned just before Sect. 4.1.

The author is not aware of other verified parsers of ABNF grammars. There are verified parsers of other languages [17,27]. Due to ABNF's role in Internet syntax specifications, a verified parser of ABNF grammars has a practical significance. There are verified generators of parsers, generators of verified parsers, verified parser interpreters, and verified parser validators [5,12,13,16,20,22]. Since they are based on different grammar notations from ABNF, using these tools for the verified parsing of ABNF grammars would require a trusted translation from the ABNF grammar of ABNF to the tools' grammar notations; in contrast, the verification of the parser described in this paper is based directly on the formalized ABNF notation. APG [26] is an ABNF parser generator, but it does not include or generate formal proofs.

Acknowledgements. This work was supported by DARPA under Contract No. FA8750-15-C-0007.

References

1. Aho, A.V., Lam, M.S., Sethi, R., Ullman, J.D.: Compilers: Principles, Techniques, and Tools, 2nd edn. Pearson, London (2007)
2. Avigad, J., Zach, R.: The epsilon calculus. In: Zalta, E.N. (ed.) The Stanford Encyclopedia of Philosophy, summer 2016 edn. Metaphysics Research Lab, Stanford University (2016). https://plato.stanford.edu/archives/sum2016/entries/epsilon-calculus/

3. Backus, J.W., et al.: Report on the algorithmic language ALGOL 60. Commun. ACM **3**(5), 299–314 (1960)
4. Barthwal, A.: A formalisation of the theory of context-free languages in higher-order logic. Ph.D. thesis. The Australian National University (2010)
5. Barthwal, A., Norrish, M.: Verified, executable parsing. In: Castagna, G. (ed.) ESOP 2009. LNCS, vol. 5502, pp. 160–174. Springer, Heidelberg (2009). https://doi.org/10.1007/978-3-642-00590-9_12
6. Berners-Lee, T., Fielding, R., Masinter, L.: Uniform Resource Identifier (URI): Generic syntax. Request for Comments (RFC) 3986, January 2005
7. Boyer, R.S., Moore, J.S.: A Computational Logic. Academic Press, Cambridge (1979)
8. Bray, T.: The JavaScript Object Notation (JSON) data interchange format. Request for Comments (RFC) 7159, March 2014
9. Crocker, D., Overell, P.: Augmented BNF for syntax specifications: ABNF. Request for Comments (RFC) 5234, January 2008
10. Doczkal, C., Kaiser, J.-O., Smolka, G.: A constructive theory of regular languages in Coq. In: Gonthier, G., Norrish, M. (eds.) CPP 2013. LNCS, vol. 8307, pp. 82–97. Springer, Cham (2013). https://doi.org/10.1007/978-3-319-03545-1_6
11. Fielding, R., Reschke, J.: Hypertext Transfer Protocol (HTTP/1.1): Message syntax and routing. Request for Comments (RFC) 7230, June 2014
12. Gross, J.S.: An extensible framework for synthesizing efficient, verified parsers. Master's thesis. Massachusetts Institute of Technology (2015)
13. Jourdan, J.-H., Pottier, F., Leroy, X.: Validating $LR(1)$ parsers. In: Seidl, H. (ed.) ESOP 2012. LNCS, vol. 7211, pp. 397–416. Springer, Heidelberg (2012). https://doi.org/10.1007/978-3-642-28869-2_20
14. Kaufmann, M., Moore, J.S.: The ACL2 theorem prover: Web page. http://www.cs.utexas.edu/users/moore/acl2
15. Kaufmann, M., Moore, J.S.: A precise description of the ACL2 logic. Technical report. Department of Computer Sciences, University of Texas at Austin (1998)
16. Koprowski, A., Binsztok, H.: TRX: a formally verified parser interpreter. Log. Methods Comput. Sci. **7**(2), 1–26 (2011)
17. Kumar, R., Myreen, M.O., Norrish, M., Owens, S.: CakeML: a verified implementation of ML. In: Proceedings of 41st ACM SIGPLAN Symposium on Principles of Programming Languages, POPL, pp. 179–191 (2014)
18. Kyzivat, P.: Case-sensitive string support in ABNF. Request for Comments (RFC) 7405, December 2014
19. Linhart, C., Klein, A., Heled, R., Orrin, S.: HTTP request smuggling. White paper, Watchfire (2005)
20. Nipkow, T.: Verified lexical analysis. In: Proceedings of 11th International Conference on Theorem Proving in Higher-Order Logics, TPHOL, pp. 1–15 (1998)
21. Parr, T., Fisher, K.: *LL(*)*: the foundation of the ANTLR parser generator. In: Proceedings of 32nd ACM SIGPLAN Conference on Programming Language Design and Implementation, PLDI, pp. 425–436 (2011)
22. Ridge, T.: Simple, efficient, sound and complete combinator parsing for all context-free grammars, using an Oracle. In: Combemale, B., Pearce, D.J., Barais, O., Vinju, J.J. (eds.) SLE 2014. LNCS, vol. 8706, pp. 261–281. Springer, Cham (2014). https://doi.org/10.1007/978-3-319-11245-9_15
23. Swords, S., Davis, J.: Fix your types. In: Proceedings of 13th International Workshop on the ACL2 Theorem Prover and Its Applications (2015)
24. The ACL2 Community: The ACL2 theorem prover and community books: Source code. http://github.com/acl2/acl2

25. The ACL2 Community: The ACL2 theorem prover and community books: User manual. http://www.cs.utexas.edu/~moore/acl2/manuals/current/manual
26. Thomas, L.D.: APG: ABNF Parser Generator. http://www.coasttocoastresearch.com
27. Wisnesky, R., Malecha, G., Morrisett, G.: Certified web services in Ynot. In: Proceedings of 5th International Workshop on Automated Specification and Verification of Web Systems, WWV, pp. 5–19 (2009)

Constructing Independently Verifiable Privacy-Compliant Type Systems for Message Passing Between Black-Box Components

Robin Adams[1(✉)] and Sibylle Schupp[2]

[1] Chalmers University of Technology, Gothenburg, Sweden
robinad@chalmers.se
[2] Technische Universität Hamburg, Hamburg, Germany
sibylle.schupp@tuhh.de

Abstract. *Privacy by design* (PbD) is the principle that privacy should be considered at every stage of the software engineering process. It is increasingly both viewed as best practice and required by law. It is therefore desirable to have formal methods that provide guarantees that certain privacy-relevant properties hold. We propose an approach that can be used to design a privacy-compliant architecture without needing to know the source code or internal structure of any individual component. We model an architecture as a set of *agents* or *components* that pass *messages* to each other. We present in this paper algorithms that take as input an architecture and a set of privacy constraints, and output an extension of the original architecture that satisfies the privacy constraints.

1 Introduction

Privacy by Design is the principle that privacy should be a consideration at every stage of the software design process [8]. It is increasingly seen as best practice for privacy protection, including by the International Conference of Data Protection and Privacy Commissioners [9] and the US Federal Trade Commission [14], and is a legal requirement in the EU since the General Data Protection Regulation (GDPR) came into force on 25 May 2018 [13].

It is therefore desirable to create methods that will provide a guarantee that software satisfies certain privacy-relevant properties. To this end, a substantial amount of research (both formal methods and other approaches) has been devoted to this problem, including static analysis of source code (e.g. [11,15]); real-time "taint tracking" of the data released by apps on a mobile device (e.g. [12,19]); refinement techniques that preserve privacy properties as we refine in stages from a high-level design to code (e.g. [1,10]); or the creation of new programming languages which include representations of privacy-relevant properties in types or annotations (e.g. [16,18]).

R. Piskac and P. Rümmer (Eds.): VSTTE 2018, LNCS 11294, pp. 196–214, 2018.
https://doi.org/10.1007/978-3-030-03592-1_11

We can thus design a privacy-safe application, or verify that a given application is privacy-safe, provided we can access and/or change its source code. However, in practice, many systems involve the interaction of different components, each controlled by a different person or organisation. The source code might not be available, or it might not be possible for us to change it. New versions of each component may come out regularly, so that a privacy analysis we did using an old component quickly becomes obsolete.

In this paper, we will show how we can design a type system for the *messages* that the components pass to each other, in such a way that we can formally prove that, if every message passed is typable under this typing system, then the privacy property must hold. We indicate how an existing unsafe component can be adapted into a component that uses this typing system by providing each component with an *interface* through which all messages must pass, without needing to read or modify the component's source code.

The structure of the paper is as follows. In Sect. 2, we give a relatively simple but realistic example of privacy constraints that we may wish to hold, and show the architecture that our algorithms generate. In Sect. 3, we provide the formal definition of architecture that we use. In Sect. 4, we define the algorithm for a simple constraint language and prove it correct. In Sect. 5, we do the same development again for a stronger language of constraints, of the form $\alpha \ni A \Rightarrow \beta \ni B$ ('if α possesses a term of type A then β must previously have possessed a term of type B'). Finally we survey some related work in Sect. 6, and conclude in Sect. 7.

2   Motivating Example

We now give an example of realistic privacy constraints that we might wish to introduce, and the architectures that are produced by our algorithms. The example is similar to an example considered by Barth et al. [4].

The US Children's Online Privacy Protection Act (COPPA) includes the clause:

> When a child sends protected information to the website, a *parent* must have previously received a privacy notice from the web site operator, [and] granted consent to the web site operator.

We propose to model a system as being composed of *agents* or *components* who pass *messages* to each other. The possible messages are provided by a *type system*, which consists of a set of *types* and a set of *constructors*. These two sets determine the set of *terms*, each of which has a type. We write $t : A$ to denote that the term t has type A.

A *message* is a triple (α, t, β), where α and β are agents and t is a term; this represents the agent α sending the piece of data t to β. If $t : A$, then we write this message as $\alpha \xrightarrow{t} \beta$ or $\alpha \xrightarrow{t:A} \beta$.

For the COPPA example, Fig. 1 suggests an architecture with three agents, Child, Website, and Parent. In the initial state, Child possesses a term info:

INFO, Website possesses policy: POLICY, and Child may send messages of type INFO to Website, etc. This represents a website which can send its privacy policy to the parent; the parent may send consent for the website to collect the child's protected info; and the child may send their protected info to the website. However, at the moment, there is nothing to prevent the protected info being sent to the website without either policy or consent having been sent.

Formally, an *architecture* is described by specifying the following (see Definition 2):

- for any agent α, which constructors an agent possesses in the initial state;
- for any two agents α, β, the set of types A such that α may pass a message of type A to β.

If A is a type, we shall sometimes say 'α can send A to β' to mean 'α may send messages of type A to β'.

We envision the designer beginning with a set Ag of agents and a type system $\mathcal{T}$ which describes the pieces of data they are interested in. They write down the set $\mathcal{C}$ of privacy constraints that they wish the finished system to have. For now, we consider constraints of these two forms (see Definitions 4 and 6):

- $\alpha \ni A \Rightarrow B$: If agent α has a piece of data of type A, then a piece of data of type B must have previously been created.
- $\alpha \ni A \Rightarrow \beta \ni B$: If agent α has a piece of data of type A, then agent β must previously have had a piece of data of type B.

The privacy constraints that we require for the architecture in Fig. 1 include

$$Website \ni INFO \Rightarrow Website \ni CONSENT$$
$$Website \ni CONSENT \Rightarrow Parent \ni POLICY$$

The first constraint specifies that agent Website possesses INFO only if it previously has received data of type CONSENT. The second constraint specifies that agent Website possesses CONSENT only if the Parent agent has received the POLICY before. (We will add a third constraint later, in Sect. 5.1.)

Fig. 1. An architecture that allows privacy breach

Given privacy constraints, we show how to extend $\mathcal{T}$ to a type system $\mathcal{T}_\mathbb{C}$. The type system $\mathcal{T}_\mathbb{C}$ includes a set of new types $C_\alpha(A)$. A term of type $C_\alpha(A)$ is called a *certified* term. As well as the plain INFO type, for example, the safe architecture contains the type $C_{Website}(INFO)$. A term of this type represents a piece of data from which *Website* can extract a term of type $INFO$, but no other agent can.[1] There are no restrictions on which agents may receive them or send certified terms.

The type system $\mathcal{T}_C$ also has types $P_\alpha(A)$, and constructors p_α that construct terms of type $P_\alpha(A)$. We may think of a term of type $P_\alpha(A)$ as a *proof* that α possesses a term of type A.

The architecture created by our Algorithm 2 is shown in Fig. 2. (For space reasons, we have listed only some of the constructors and messages, and omitted the subscripts on the types $C_\alpha(A)$ and $P_\alpha(A)$.) The algorithm creates new components *IWebsite*, the *input interface* to *Website*, and *OWebsite*, the *output interface* for *Website*; and similarly input and output interfaces for *Parent* and *Child*.

The constructor p_{POLICY} takes a term of type *POLICY* and constructs a term of type $P_{Parent}(POLICY)$—a proof that *Parent* has received a term of type *POLICY*. The constructor $m_{CONSENT}$ constructs a certified term of type $C_{Website}(CONSENT)$ out of a term of type *CONSENT*, plus the proof that the preconditions for *Website* to be allowed to read a term of type *CONSENT*, namely a term of type $P_{Parent}(POLICY)$. The constructor $\pi_{CONSENT}$ then extracts the term of type *CONSENT* from the certified term. Similar comments hold for m_{POLICY} and π_{POLICY}, and the other new constructors in Fig. 2.

It can be seen that, while *Child* may send *INFO* to *OChild* at any time, the only way for the data to travel any further is for a term of type $C_{Website}(INFO)$ to be created; this can only happen if a term of type $P_{Website}(CONSENT)$ has been created; this can only happen if a term of type *CONSENT* reaches *OWebsite*; and this can only happen if *Website* has a term of type *CONSENT*. Similar considerations hold for our other negative constraint.

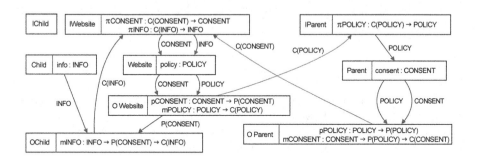

Fig. 2. A privacy-safe architecture

We can partition the agents in Fig. 2 into three sets: $\{Child, IChild, OChild\}$, $\{Website, IWebsite, OWebsite\}$, $\{Parent, IParent, OParent\}$. Each set thus consists of one of the agents from Fig. 1, plus its two new interfaces. Note that, if an agent from one set passes a message to an agent in another set,

---

[1] In practice, this would presumably be achieved by encryption, but we abstract from these implementation details here. See Sect. 2.1 for more discussion.

then that message has type $C_\alpha(A)$ or $P_\alpha(A)$ for some α, A. In the rest of this paper, we will prove two results (Theorems 1 and 2) that give general conditions such that, if an architecture can be partitioned in a way that satisfies these conditions, then a given set of privacy constraints are satisfied.

2.1   Note on Implementation

In practice, certification on the one hand, access on the other hand, could be implemented through encryption and decryption. But, other mechanisms possibly exist as well. The type systems we present in this paper abstract from these details. They specify which agents may and may not access which data, without specifying how this is to be done.

The terms of type $P_\alpha(A)$ should, in practice, ideally be an appropriate zero-knowledge proof which guarantees that α possesses a term of type A, without revealing the value of the term of type A. Again, in this paper we abstract from the details of how this would be implemented.

However, we expect it to be possible to implement these types in such a way that the designer could publish both the set of constraints $\mathbb{C}$ and the type system $\mathcal{T}_{\mathbb{C}}$, and an independent third party (the user, a regulatory authority, or anyone else) to verify both that our algorithm maps $\mathbb{C}$ to $\mathcal{T}_{\mathbb{C}}$, and that any given message is typable under $\mathcal{T}_{\mathbb{C}}$. This would greatly increase the trust that all parties can have that the global privacy policies $\mathbb{C}$ hold true.

We also note that, if there are large numbers of agents in our system, we will need a large number of types. In our motivating example, if we have many children and many parents, then we will need types $C_{CHILD_1}(CONSENT)$, $C_{CHILD_2}(CONSENT)$, etc. and a way to ensure that $\pi_{\alpha A}$ accepts terms of type $C_{\alpha'}(A)$ only if $\alpha = \alpha'$, requiring the use of dependent types. For now, this is left as work for the future.

3   Architectures

We now describe the language we use for specifying architectures. This system was inspired by work by le Métayer et al. [3] and Barth et al. [4].

An *architecture* consists of *agents* who pass *messages* to each other. Each message is a term that can be typed in a *type system*.

Definition 1 (Type System). *A type system is given by the following:*

- *A set of* atomic types. *The set of types is the defined inductively by:*
  - *Every atomic type is a type.*
  - *If A and B are types, then $A \rightarrow B$ is a type.*
- *A set of* constructors, *each with an associated type.*

The set of terms *of each type is then defined inductively by:*

- *Every constructor of type A is a term of type A.*

– If s is a term of type $A \to B$ and t is a term of type A, then st is a term of type B.

We write $t : A$ to denote that t is a term of type A.

In the example in Fig. 1, the atomic types are $INFO$, $CONSENT$ and $POLICY$. The constructors are $info$ which has type $INFO$, $policy$ which has type $POLICY$, and $consent$ which has type $CONSENT$. In the example in Fig. 2, the architecture has been extended with new atomic types such as $C_{Website}(INFO)$, and new constructors such as p_{POLICY}, which has type $POLICY \to P_{Parent}(POLICY)$.

Definition 2 (Architecture). *Given a type system T, an architecture $\mathcal{A}$ over T consists of:*

– *a set* Ag *of agents or components;*
– *for every agent α, a set H_α of constructors that α initially possesses or initially has;*
– *for every ordered pair of distinct agents (α, β), a set $M_{\alpha\beta}$ of atomic types that α may send in a message to β.*

We shall write $\alpha \overset{A}{\to} \beta$ to denote that $A \in M_{\alpha\beta}$.

(Note that only terms of atomic type can be passed between agents.)

In the example in Sect. 2, we have Ag $= \{Child, Website, Parent\}$. The agent $Child$ initially possesses the constructor $info$, and $Website$ initially possesses $policy$, and $Parent$ initially possesses $consent$. We have $M_{Child,Website} = \{INFO\}$; thus, $Child$ may send messages of type $INFO$ to $Website$. We also have $M_{Website,Parent} = \{POLICY\}$ and $M_{Parent,Website} = \{CONSENT\}$.

We will use lower-case Greek letters $\alpha, \beta, \ldots$ for agents, lower-case Roman letters $s, t, \ldots$ for terms, and capital Roman letters $A, B, \ldots$ for types. The letter c is reserved for constructors.

Let us say that an agent α can *compute* terms of type A iff it possesses a constructor of type $B_1 \to \cdots \to B_n \to A$ for some $B_1, \ldots, B_n$.

Definition 3. *Let $\mathcal{A}$ be an architecture.*

1. *An* event *or* message *is an expression of the form $\alpha \overset{t:A}{\to} \beta$, to be read as '$\alpha$ passes the term t of type A to β.'*
2. *A trace τ is a finite sequence of events.*
3. *A judgement is an expression of the form $\tau \vdash \alpha \ni t : A$, which we read as "After the trace τ, α has the term t of type A."*

We write τ_1, τ_2 for the concatenation of traces τ_1 and τ_2. We write $\tau_1 \sqsubseteq \tau'$ iff τ_1 is a prefix of τ', i.e. there exists τ_2 such that $\tau' = \tau_1, \tau_2$.

The *derivable* judgements are given by the rules of deduction in Fig. 3. We say that τ is a *valid* trace through $\mathcal{A}$ iff $\tau \vdash \alpha \ni t : A$ is derivable for some α, t, A. We say that an agent α *possesses* a term of type A after τ, and write

$$(init) \frac{}{\vdash \alpha \ni c : A} \ (c : A \in H_\alpha) \quad (message_1) \frac{\tau \vdash \alpha \ni t : A}{\tau, \alpha \overset{t:A}{\to} \beta \vdash \beta \ni t : A} \ (A \in M_{\alpha\beta})$$

$$(message_2) \frac{\tau \vdash \alpha \ni t : A \quad \tau \vdash \gamma \ni s : C}{\tau, \alpha \overset{t:A}{\to} \beta \vdash \gamma \ni s : C} \ (A \in M_{\alpha\beta})$$

$$(func) \frac{\tau \vdash \alpha \ni f : A \to B \quad \tau \vdash \alpha \ni t : A}{\tau \vdash \alpha \ni ft : B}$$

Fig. 3. Rules of deduction

$\tau \vdash \alpha \ni A$, iff there exists a term t such that $\tau \vdash \alpha \ni t : A$. We say that there *exists* a term of type A after τ, and write $\tau \vdash A$, iff $\tau \vdash \alpha \ni t : A$ for some α, t.

The rule (init) states that, if α initially possesses c, then α possesses c in the initial state. The rule (func) states that, if an agent possesses both a function f and term t of the appropriate types, it may compute the term ft. The rule (message_1) states that, after α has sent t to β, then β possesses t. The rule (message_2) states that, if γ possesses s before α sends a message to β, then γ still possesses s after the message is sent.

3.1 Metatheorems

We can establish the basic properties that our typing system satisfies.

Lemma 1.

1. **Weakening.** Suppose $\tau_1 \vdash \alpha \ni t : A$ and τ_1, τ_2 is a valid trace. Then $\tau_1, \tau_2 \vdash \alpha \ni t : A$.
2. If $\tau_1, \alpha \overset{t:A}{\to} \beta, \tau_2$ is a valid trace, then $A \in M_{\alpha\beta}$, and $\tau_1 \vdash \alpha \ni t : A$.
3. **Generation.** Suppose $\tau \vdash \beta \ni t : B$. Then there exist terms $t_1 : A_1, \ldots, t_m : A_m$ $(m \geq 0)$ and agents $\alpha_1, \ldots, \alpha_n$ $(n \geq 1)$ such that $t \equiv ft_1 \cdots t_m$, $\beta = \alpha_n$, and the following events occur in τ in order:

$$\alpha_1 \ni f : A_1 \to \cdots \to A_n \to B, \ \alpha_1 \overset{t:B}{\to} \alpha_2, \ \cdots, \ \alpha_{n-1} \overset{t:B}{\to} \alpha_n$$

   Further, we have $\tau \vdash \alpha_1 \ni t_1 : A_1, \ldots, \tau \vdash \alpha_1 \ni t_m : A_m$.
4. If $\tau \vdash \beta \ni t : B$, then either β can compute B, or there is an event $\alpha \overset{t:B}{\to} \beta$ in τ for some α.

Intuitively, Generation says that if agent β possesses a piece of data of type B, then it must have been computed by an agent α_1 that can compute terms of type B, and then passed to β in a sequence of messages.

The proofs of the first three properties are by straightforward induction on derivations. Part 4 follows easily from part 3.

4   The First Algorithm

In the rest of this paper, we will consider different sets of *constraints* that we may wish to place on our architectures. In each case, we shall show how, given an architecture $\mathcal{A}$ and a set of constraints $\mathbb{C}$, we can construct an architecture $\mathcal{B}$, which we call a *safe* architecture, that extends $\mathcal{A}$ and satisfies all the constraints.

For our first algorithm, we consider the following constraints:

Definition 4 (Constraint).

1. *A* negative constraint *has the form* $\alpha \ni A \Rightarrow B$, *where A and B are atomic types. We read it as: "If α receives a message of type A, then a term of type B must have previously been created." A trace τ complies with this constraint iff, for every $\tau_1 \sqsubseteq \tau$, if $\tau_1 \vdash \alpha \ni t : A$ for some t, then $\tau_1 \vdash \beta \ni s : B$ for some β, s.*
2. *A* positive constraint *has the form* $\mathsf{Pos}(\alpha, A)$, *where A is an atomic type. We read it as: "It must be possible for α to have a term of type A." A trace τ complies with this constraint iff $\tau \vdash \alpha \ni t : A$ for some term t.*

Note. To understand part 1 of this definition, note that, if it is possible to create a term $t : A$ without first creating a term $s : B$, then there is a trace τ such that $\tau \vdash \alpha \ni t : A$ for some α, and $\tau \nvdash \beta \ni s : B$ for all β. Thus, the condition "For every $\tau_1 \sqsubseteq \tau$, if $\tau_1 \vdash \alpha \ni t : A$ for some t, then $\tau_1 \vdash \beta \ni s : B$ for some β, s" captures the idea "If α receives a message of type A, then a term of type B must have previously been created."

Example. Consider an accountancy firm collecting personal data from the employees of a company in order to prepare a tax report. The principle of *data minimization* [13, Sect. 25] states that the accountancy firm should collect only the data that is necessary for this purpose. We can model this as follows: assume there are two types of tax return that can be prepared, TR_A and TR_B. Let *Employee* initially possess $a : A$ and $b : B$, where a is required to prepare TR_A and b is required to prepare TR_B. The company can send requests Q_A and Q_B to *Accountancy*, requesting a tax return of one of the two types. We could then write constraints *Accountancy* $\ni A \Rightarrow TR_A$ and *Accountancy* $\ni B \Rightarrow TR_B$ to express that the accountancy firm may only possess an employee's personal data if it is necessary for a tax return that it has been requested to prepare.

We now construct the type system that the safe architecture will use:

Definition 5 (Safe Type System). *Let $\mathcal{T}$ be a type system and Ag a set of agents. Let $\mathbb{C}$ be a finite set of negative constraints over $\mathcal{T}$ and Ag. The safe type system $\mathcal{T}_{\mathbb{C}}$ is defined as follows.*

- *The atomic types of $\mathcal{T}_{\mathbb{C}}$ are the atomic types of $\mathcal{T}$ together with, for every agent $\alpha \in \mathsf{Ag}$ and atomic type A in $\mathcal{T}$, a type $C_{\alpha}(A)$, the type of certified terms of type A that may only be read by α.*
- *Every constructor of $\mathcal{T}$ is a constructor of $\mathcal{T}_{\mathbb{C}}$.*

– *For every $\alpha \in \text{Ag}$ and type A of $\mathcal{T}$, let the constraints in $\mathbb{C}$ that begin with '$\alpha \ni A$' be*

$$\alpha \ni A \Rightarrow B_1, \ldots, \alpha \ni A \Rightarrow B_n \ .$$

Then the following are constructors of $\mathcal{T}_{\mathbb{C}}$:

$$m_{\alpha A}^{\beta_1 \cdots \beta_n} : A \rightarrow C_{\beta_1}(B_1) \rightarrow \cdots \rightarrow C_{\beta_n}(B_n) \rightarrow C_\alpha(A) \text{ for all } \beta_1, \ldots, \beta_n \in \text{Ag};$$
$$\pi_{\alpha A} : C_\alpha(A) \rightarrow A$$

The intention is that $m_{\alpha A}^{\beta_1 \cdots \beta_n}$ constructs a term of type $C_\alpha(A)$ out of a term of type A and n other terms which prove that the preconditions to $\alpha \ni A$ are all satisfied. The constructor $\pi_{\alpha A}$ then extracts the term of type A again.

Using the type system, we can state a set of conditions that guarantee that an architecture satisfies the negative constraints in $\mathbb{C}$.

Theorem 1. *Let $\mathcal{T}$ be a type system, Ag a set of agents, and $\mathbb{C}$ a set of negative constraints over $\mathcal{T}$ and Ag. Let $\mathcal{B}$ be an architecture over $\mathcal{T}_{\mathbb{C}}$ with set of agents Ag', where $\text{Ag} \subseteq \text{Ag}'$. Suppose there is a partition $\{\mathcal{P}_\alpha \subseteq \text{Ag}'\}_{\alpha \in \text{Ag}}$ of Ag' indexed by Ag such that:*

1. *$\alpha \in \mathcal{P}_\alpha$ for all $\alpha \in \text{Ag}$;*
2. *If $\beta \xrightarrow{A} \beta'$ and β, β' are in different sets of the partition, then A has the form $C_\gamma(B)$ for some γ, B;*
3. *If β possesses $\pi_{\alpha A}$ then $\beta \in \mathcal{P}_\alpha$;*
4. *For every constraint $\alpha \ni A \Rightarrow B$ in $\mathbb{C}$, if an agent $\beta \in \mathcal{P}_\alpha$ possesses a constructor with target A, then this constructor is $\pi_{\alpha A}$.*

Then every trace through $\mathcal{B}$ satisfies every negative constraint in $\mathbb{C}$.

The intuition behind the premises is this: the partition divides the system into parts. The part $\mathcal{P}_\alpha$ is the only part of the system that is allowed to look inside a term of type $C_\alpha(A)$ and extract the underlying term of type A. Only certified terms may be passed between the parts. Thus, the only way for an agent in $\mathcal{P}_\alpha$ to possess a term of type A is either for it to be computed within $\mathcal{P}_\alpha$, or for a term of type $C_\alpha(A)$ to be passed in from another part of the system.

Proof. Let τ be any trace through $\mathcal{B}$ and let $\alpha \ni A \Rightarrow B$ be one of the constraints in $\mathbb{C}$. We must show that, if $\tau \vdash \alpha \ni t : A$, then $\tau \vdash B$. We shall prove the more general result:

If $\tau \vdash \beta \ni t : A$ for some $\beta \in \mathcal{P}_\alpha$, then $\tau \vdash B$.

So suppose $\tau \vdash \beta \ni t : A$ for some $\beta \in \mathcal{P}_\alpha$. We may also assume without loss of generality that τ is the shortest trace for which this is true. By Generation and the minimality of τ, β possesses a constructor with target A. By our hypotheses, this is $\pi_{\alpha A}$, and $t = \pi_{\alpha A}(t')$ for some t'. Hence $\tau \vdash \beta \ni t' : C_\alpha(A)$ for some t'.

Now, looking at the construction of $\mathcal{T}_{\mathbb{C}}$, the only constructor with target $C_\alpha(A)$ is

$$m_{\alpha A}^{\beta_1 \cdots \beta_n} : A \to C_{\beta_1}(B_1) \to \cdots \to C_{\beta_n}(B_n) \to C_\alpha(A).$$

So applying Generation again, we must have $t \equiv m_{\alpha A}^{\beta_1 \cdots \beta_n} s t_1 \cdots t_n$ and there must be an agent γ which possesses $m_{\alpha A}^{\beta_1 \cdots \beta_n}$ with

$$\tau \vdash \gamma \ni s : A, \quad \tau \vdash \gamma \ni t_1 : B_1, \ldots, \tau \vdash \gamma \ni t_n : B_n .$$

Now, B is one of the types $B_1, \ldots, B_n$; let it be B_i. Then $\tau \vdash \gamma \ni C_{\beta_i}(B)$. By similar reasoning, there must be an agent δ that possesses one of the constructors $m_{\beta_i B}$, and $\tau \vdash \delta \ni B$. $\square$

We are now ready to construct the safe architecture.

Algorithm 1. *Given an architecture $\mathcal{A}$ and a finite set of constraints $\mathbb{C}$, construct the architecture $\mathtt{Safe}(\mathcal{A}, \mathbb{C})$ as follows:*

1. *The agents of $\mathtt{Safe}(\mathcal{A}, \mathbb{C})$ are the agents of $\mathcal{A}$ together with, for every agent α of $\mathcal{A}$, an agent I_α, which we call the interface to α.*
2. *The type system of $\mathtt{Safe}(\mathcal{A}, \mathbb{C})$ is $\mathcal{T}_{\mathbb{C}}$.*
3. *If an agent α possesses a constructor c in $\mathcal{A}$, then α possesses c in $\mathtt{Safe}(\mathcal{A}, \mathbb{C})$.*
4. *For every type A of $\mathcal{A}$, let the negative constraints that begin with $\alpha \ni A$ be*

$$\alpha \ni A \Rightarrow B_1, \ldots, \alpha \ni A \Rightarrow B_n .$$

   – *Every interface I_γ possesses $m_{\alpha A}^{\beta_1 \cdots \beta_n}$ for all $\beta_1, \ldots, \beta_n$.*
   – *I_α possesses $\pi_{\alpha A}$*
5. *For every atomic type A, the agents α and I_α may send A to each other.*
6. *Any two interfaces may send messages of type $C_\alpha(A)$ to each other for any α, A.*

Thus, in order to construct a certified term of type A readable by α, an interface must first obtain certified terms of all the types which the constraints require. The only way α can receive a term of type A is through its interface obtaining a term of type $C_\alpha(A)$. Interfaces may pass certified terms between each other at will. An agent and its interface may exchange uncertified terms at will.

Theorem 2. *Let $\mathcal{A}$ be an architecture and $\mathbb{C}$ a set of constraints. Suppose that:*

1. *For every negative constraint $\alpha \ni A \Rightarrow \beta \ni B$ in $\mathbb{C}$, we have that α cannot compute terms of type A.*
2. *For every positive constraint $\mathtt{Pos}(\alpha, A) \in \mathbb{C}$, there exists a trace through $\mathcal{A}$ that satisfies $\mathtt{Pos}(\alpha, A)$ and all the negative constraints in $\mathbb{C}$.*

Then the architecture $\mathtt{Safe}(\mathcal{A}, \mathbb{C})$ has the following properties:

1. *Every trace through $\mathtt{Safe}(\mathcal{A}, \mathbb{C})$ satisfies every negative constraint in $\mathbb{C}$.*

2. *For every positive constraint* $\text{Pos}(\alpha, A) \in \mathbb{C}$, *there exists a trace through* $\text{Safe}(\mathcal{A}, \mathbb{C})$ *that satisfies* $\text{Pos}(\alpha, A)$.

Proof. Part 1 follows from the previous theorem, taking $\mathcal{P}_\alpha = \{\alpha, I_\alpha\}$.

We now show that $\text{Safe}(\mathcal{A}, \mathbb{C})$ has the following property. Part 2 of the theorem follows immediately.

If $\tau \vdash \alpha \ni t : A$ in $\mathcal{A}$, A is an atomic type, and τ satisfies every negative constraint in $\mathbb{C}$, then there exists a valid trace τ' through $\text{Safe}(\mathcal{A}, \mathbb{C})$ such that $\tau' \vdash \alpha \ni t : A$ and $\tau' \vdash I_\alpha \ni t' : C_\alpha(A)$ for some t'.

The proof is by induction on τ, then on the derivation of $\tau \vdash \alpha \ni t : A$. We deal here with the case where the last rule in the derivation was $(message_1)$:

$$\frac{\tau \vdash \beta \ni t : A}{\tau, \beta \overset{t:A}{\to} \alpha \vdash \alpha \ni t : A.}$$

By the induction hypothesis, there exists τ' such that $\tau' \vdash_{\text{Safe}(\mathcal{A}, \mathbb{C})} \beta \ni t : A$. By the construction of $\text{Safe}(\mathcal{A}, \mathbb{C})$, we have $A \in C_{\beta I_\beta}$ and $A \in C_{I_\alpha \alpha}$. Hence $\tau, \beta \overset{t:A}{\to} I_\beta \vdash_{\text{Safe}(\mathcal{A}, \mathbb{C})} I_\beta \ni t : A$.

Now, let the negative constraints in $\mathbb{C}$ that begin with $\alpha \ni A$ be $\alpha \ni A \Rightarrow B_1, \ldots, \alpha \ni A \Rightarrow B_n$. By hypothesis, $\tau, \beta \overset{t:A}{\to} \alpha$ satisfies all these constraints. Therefore, $\tau \vdash_{\mathcal{A}} B_1, \ldots, \tau \vdash_{\mathcal{A}} B_n$.

Hence, by the induction hypothesis, there exists τ'' such that $\tau'' \vdash_{\text{Safe}(\mathcal{A}, \mathbb{C})} B_1, \ldots, \tau'' \vdash_{\text{Safe}(\mathcal{A}, \mathbb{C})} B_n$. Therefore,

$$\tau'' \vdash_{\text{Safe}(\mathcal{A}, \mathbb{C})} I_{\beta_1} \ni t_1 : C_{\beta_1}(B_1), \ldots, \tau'' \vdash_{\text{Safe}(\mathcal{A}, \mathbb{C})} I_{\beta_n} \ni t_n : C_{\beta_n}(B_n),$$

for some $t_1, \ldots, t_n$. By Weakening, we may assume $\tau' \sqsubseteq \tau''$.

After extending τ'' by passing $t_1, \ldots, t_n$ as messages to I_β, we have that I_β can construct a term of type $C_\alpha(A)$. After passing this term to I_α, we have that $I_\alpha(A)$ possesses a term of type $C_\alpha(A)$. From this, it can construct a term of type A which it may then pass to α, completing the required trace. $\qquad\square$

5   The Second Algorithm

Supposing it is important to us, not merely that a piece of data has been created, but that a particular agent has seen it. We can extend our system to handle this type of constraint as follows.

Definition 6. *In this section of the paper:*

- *a negative constraint is an expression of the form* $\alpha \ni A \Rightarrow \beta \ni B$. *A trace τ satisfies this constraint iff, for every $\tau' \sqsubseteq \tau$, if $\tau' \vdash \alpha \ni A$ then $\tau_1 \vdash \beta \ni B$.*
- *Positive constraints are as in Sect. 4.*

Note. If $(\alpha, A) \neq (\beta, B)$, then the constraint $\alpha \ni A \Rightarrow \beta \ni B$ is to be read as "if α possesses a term of type A, then β must previously have possessed a term of type B". (The condition $\alpha \ni A \Rightarrow \alpha \ni A$ is trivial.)

We show how to extend a given architecture $\mathcal{A}$ to an architecture that uses the new privacy-safe type system. Unfortunately, we have not found a way to do this that requires no modifications to the agents in $\mathcal{A}$. We present below (Algorithm 2) an algorithm that requires modifications which we expect would be minor in practice, and discuss in Sect. 5.2 ways in which this situation could be improved in future work.

Definition 7. *Given a type system $\mathcal{T}$, a set of agents Ag, and a set of negative constraints $\mathbb{C}$ over $\mathcal{T}$ and Ag, define the type system $\mathcal{T}_\mathbb{C}$ as follows.*

- *The types of $\mathcal{T}_\mathbb{C}$ are the types of $\mathcal{T}$ together with, for every agent α and atomic type A of $\mathcal{T}$, a type $C_\alpha(A)$ and a type $P_\alpha(A)$. (Intuition: a term $C_\alpha(A)$ is a certified term of type A that α is permitted to read. A term $P_\alpha(A)$ is proof that α has held a term of type A.)*
- *Every constructor of $\mathcal{T}$ is a constructor of $\mathcal{T}_\mathbb{C}$.*
- *For every agent α and type A, let the negative constraints in $\mathbb{C}$ that begin with $\alpha \ni A$ be*

$$\alpha \ni A \Rightarrow \beta_1 \ni B_1, \ldots, \alpha \ni A \Rightarrow \beta_n \ni B_n.$$

Then the following are constructors of $\mathcal{T}_\mathbb{C}$:

$$m_{\alpha A} : A \to P_{\beta_1}(B_1) \to \cdots \to P_{\beta_n}(B) \to C_\alpha(A)$$
$$\pi_{\alpha A} : C_\alpha(A) \to A$$
$$p_{\alpha A} : A \to P_\alpha(A)$$

Theorem 3. *Let $\mathcal{T}$ be a type system, Ag a set of agents, and $\mathbb{C}$ a set of negative constraints over $\mathcal{T}$ and Ag. Let $\mathcal{B}$ be an architecture over $\mathcal{T}_\mathbb{C}$ with set of agents Ag$'$, where Ag $\subseteq$ Ag$'$. Suppose that there is a partition $\{\mathcal{P}_\alpha\}_{\alpha \in \text{Ag}}$ of the agents of $\mathcal{B}$ such that:*

- $\alpha \in \mathcal{P}_\alpha$;
- *If $\beta \xrightarrow{A} \beta'$ and β and β' are in different sets in the partition, then A has either the form $C_\gamma(T)$ or $P_\gamma(T)$;*
- *If β initially possesses $\pi_{\alpha A}$ then $\beta \in \mathcal{P}_\alpha$;*
- *If β initially possesses $p_{\alpha A}$ then β cannot compute A.*
- *If β initially possesses $p_{\alpha A}$ and $\gamma \xrightarrow{A} \beta$ then $\gamma = \alpha$.*

Then every trace through $\mathcal{B}$ satisfies every constraint in $\mathbb{C}$.

Proof. Let τ be a trace through $\mathcal{B}$ and $\alpha \ni A \Rightarrow \beta \ni B$ be a constraint in $\mathbb{C}$. We must show that, if $\tau \vdash \alpha \ni A$, then $\tau \vdash \beta \ni B$. We shall prove the more general result:

If $\tau \vdash \gamma \ni A$ for any $\gamma \in \mathcal{P}_\alpha$, then $\tau \vdash \beta \ni B$.

So suppose $\tau \vdash \gamma \ni A$ for some $\gamma \in \mathcal{P}_\alpha$. We may assume without loss of generality that τ is the shortest such trace. By Generation and the minimality of τ, γ must possess a constructor with target A. By our hypotheses, this is $\pi_{\alpha A}$. Hence $\tau \vdash \gamma \ni t : C_\alpha(A)$ for some t. Now, let the constraints in $\mathbb{C}$ that begin with $\alpha \ni A$ be

$$\alpha \ni A \Rightarrow \beta_1 \ni B_1, \quad \cdots, \quad \alpha \ni A \Rightarrow \beta_n \ni B_n.$$

Applying Generation, we must have $t \equiv m_{\alpha A} s t_1 \cdots t_n$, and there must be an agent γ' that possesses $m_{\alpha A}$ such that

$$\tau \vdash \gamma' \ni s : A, \quad \tau \vdash \gamma' \ni t_1 : P_{\beta_1}(B_1), \ldots, \tau \vdash \gamma' \ni t_n : P_{\beta_n}(B_n).$$

Now, there is some i such that $\beta_i = \beta$ and $B_i = B$. We have $\tau \vdash \gamma' \ni t_i : P_\beta(B)$. Since a term of type $P_\beta(B)$ has been constructed, it must be that $\tau \vdash \beta \ni B$, as required.   □

We now show again how, given an architecture $\mathcal{A}$, we can construct an architecture that is privacy-safe.

Algorithm 2. *Given an architecture $\mathcal{A}$ and a finite set of constraints $\mathbb{C}$, construct the architecture* $\mathtt{Safe}(\mathcal{A}, \mathbb{C})$ *as follows:*

1. *The agents of* $\mathtt{Safe}(\mathcal{A}, \mathbb{C})$ *are the agents of $\mathcal{A}$ together with, for every agent α of $\mathcal{A}$:*
   - *an agent I_α, which we call the* input interface *to α;*
   - *an agent O_α, which we call the* output interface *to α*
2. *The type system of* $\mathtt{Safe}(\mathcal{A}, \mathbb{C})$ *is $\mathcal{T}_\mathbb{C}$.*
3. *If an agent α has a constructor c in $\mathcal{T}$, then it has the constructor c in $\mathcal{T}_\mathbb{C}$.*
4. *For any agent α and type A:*
   - *Every output interface O_γ possesses $m_{\alpha A}$*
   - *I_α possesses $\pi_{\alpha A} : C_{\alpha A} \to A$*
   - *O_α possesses $p_{\alpha A} : A \to P_{\alpha A}$*
5. *For any atomic type A of $\mathcal{T}$, I_α may send A to α, and α may send A to O_α.*
6. *Any two interfaces may send messages of type $C_\alpha(A)$ or $P_\alpha(A)$ to each other for any α, A.*

Theorem 4. *Let $\mathcal{A}$ be an architecture and $\mathbb{C}$ a set of constraints. Suppose that:*

1. *For every negative constraint $\alpha \ni A \Rightarrow B$ in $\mathbb{C}$, we have that α cannot compute terms of type A.*
2. *For every positive constraint $\mathtt{Pos}(\alpha, A) \in \mathbb{C}$, there exists a trace through $\mathcal{A}$ that satisfies $\mathtt{Pos}(\alpha, A)$ and all the negative constraints in $\mathbb{C}$.*

Then the architecture $\mathtt{Safe}(\mathcal{A}, \mathbb{C})$ *has the following properties:*

1. *Every trace through* $\mathtt{Safe}(\mathcal{A}, \mathbb{C})$ *satisfies every negative constraint in $\mathbb{C}$.*
2. *For every positive constraint $\mathtt{Pos}(\alpha, A) \in \mathbb{C}$, there exists a trace through* $\mathtt{Safe}(\mathcal{A}, \mathbb{C})$ *that satisfies $\mathtt{Pos}(\alpha, A)$.*

Proof. Part 1 follows from Theorem 3, taking $P_\alpha = \{\alpha, I_\alpha, O_\alpha\}$.

We shall now prove the following property, from which part 2 of the theorem follows.

If $\tau \vdash \alpha \ni t : A$ in $\mathcal{A}$ and τ satisfies every negative constraint in $\mathbb{C}$, then there exists a trace τ' through $\mathsf{Safe}(\mathcal{A}, \mathbb{C})$ such that $\tau' \vdash \alpha \ni t : A$.

The proof is by induction on τ, then on the derivation of $\tau \vdash \alpha \ni t : A$. We deal here with the case where the final step in the derivation is an instance of ($message_1$):

$$\frac{\tau \vdash \beta \ni t : A}{\tau, \beta \xrightarrow{t:A} \alpha \vdash \alpha \ni t : A}$$

By the induction hypothesis, there is a trace τ' such that $\tau' \vdash_{\mathsf{Safe}(\mathcal{A},\mathbb{C})} \alpha \ni A$. Let the negative constraints beginning with $\alpha \ni A$ be

$$\alpha \ni A \Rightarrow \beta_1 \ni B_1, \quad \ldots, \quad \alpha \ni A \Rightarrow \beta_n \ni B_n.$$

Then, by hypothesis,

$$\tau, \beta \xrightarrow{t:A} \alpha \vdash_{\mathcal{A}} \beta_1 \ni B_1, \quad \cdots, \quad \tau, \beta \xrightarrow{t:A} \alpha \vdash_{\mathcal{A}} \beta_n \ni B_n.$$

Using the fact that $(\alpha, A) \neq (\beta_i, B_i)$ for all i, the last step in each of these derivations must have been ($message_2$). Therefore,

$$\tau \vdash_{\mathcal{A}} \beta_1 \ni B_1, \quad \cdots, \quad \tau \vdash_{\mathcal{A}} \beta_n \ni B_n.$$

We may therefore apply the induction hypothesis to obtain traces $\tau_1, \ldots, \tau_n$ such that

$$\tau_1 \vdash_{\mathsf{Safe}(\mathcal{A},\mathbb{C})} \beta_1 \ni t_1 : B_1, \quad \cdots, \quad \tau_n \vdash_{\mathsf{Safe}(\mathcal{A},\mathbb{C})} \beta_n \ni t_n : B_n.$$

Now, let τ'' be the trace $\tau', \tau_1, \ldots, \tau_n$ followed by these events:

$$\beta \xrightarrow{t:A} O_\beta, \beta_1 \xrightarrow{t_1:B_1} O_{\beta_1}, \cdots, \beta_n \xrightarrow{t_n:B_n} O_{\beta_n},$$

$$O_{\beta_1} \xrightarrow{p_{\beta_1 B_1} t_1} O_\beta, \cdots, O_{\beta_n} \xrightarrow{p_{\beta_n, B_n} t_n} O_\beta,$$

$$O_\beta \xrightarrow{c_{\alpha A} t (p_{\beta_1 B_1} t_1) \cdots (p_{\beta_n B_n} t_n)} I_\alpha,$$

$$I_\alpha \xrightarrow{\pi_{\beta A} (c_{\alpha A} t (p_{\beta_1 B_1} t_1) \cdots (p_{\beta_n B_n} t_n))} \alpha$$

(Informally: the agent O_β collects the term of type A from β and all the necessary proofs, assembles the term of type $C_{\alpha A}$, and passes it to I_α, who decodes it with $\pi_{\alpha A}$ and passes the value of A to α.)

We thus have $\tau'' \vdash \alpha \ni A$ in $\mathsf{Safe}(\mathcal{A}, \mathbb{C})$, as required. $\square$

5.1 Example Revisited

We return to the example we presented in Sect. 2. We are now ready to formulate our third, positive constraint. We want to ensure it is possible for the website to receive the child's information once all legal requirements have been met. So the privacy constraints that we require for this architecture are:

Negative Constraint $Website \ni INFO \Rightarrow Website \ni CONSENT$
Negative Constraint $Website \ni CONSENT \Rightarrow Parent \ni POLICY$
Positive Constraint Pos ($Website, INFO$)

We can verify that the first constraint holds. The child can send the protected info to the interface $OChild$, but it cannot then be sent to another agent unless $OChild$ receives a term of type $P(CONSENT)$. And for a term of type $P(CONSENT)$ to be constructed, the parent must have sent consent to the website (via $OParent$ and $IWebsite$).

We can also verify that, in the architecture in Fig. 2, it is possible for the website to send the privacy policy to the parent, the parent to send consent to the website, and the child to send the protected info to the website. Formally, we describe a valid trace τ through the architecture that represents this sequence of events. The trace τ begins

$$Website \xrightarrow{policy:POLICY} OWebsite,$$

$$OWebsite \xrightarrow{mPOLICY(policy):C(POLICY)} IParent,$$

$$IParent \xrightarrow{\pi POLICY(mPOLICY(policy)):POLICY} Parent,$$

$$Parent \xrightarrow{consent:CONSENT} OParent,$$

$$Parent \xrightarrow{\pi POLICY(mPOLICY(policy)):POLICY} OParent$$

Let $p = \pi POLICY(mPOLICY(policy))$. The trace τ continues:

$$OParent \xrightarrow{mCONSENT(consent,p):C(CONSENT)} IWebsite,$$

$$IWebsite \xrightarrow{\pi CONSENT(mCONSENT(consent,p)):CONSENT} Website,$$

$$Website \xrightarrow{\pi CONSENT(mCONSENT(consent,p)):CONSENT} OWebsite,$$

Let $c = \pi CONSENT(mCONSENT(consent, p))$. The trace τ continues:

$$OWebsite \xrightarrow{pCONSENT(c):P(CONSENT)} OChild,$$

$$Child \xrightarrow{info:INFO} OChild,$$

$$OChild \xrightarrow{mINFO(info,pCONSENT(c)):C(INFO)} IWebsite,$$

$$IWebsite \xrightarrow{\pi INFO(mINFO(info,pCONSENT(c))):INFO} Website$$

This ends the trace τ which verifies that it is possible for $Website$ to receive a term of type $INFO$.

5.2   Note

In Fig. 2, we have had to modify the agents from Fig. 1. The agent $Parent$ needs to be able to output messages of type $POLICY$, and $Website$ needs to be able to output messages of type $CONSENT$. We believe these would be minor changes in practice. However, this is still unfortunate, because as discussed in the Introduction, we want our algorithms to apply in cases in which we are unable to change the source code of the agents in $\mathcal{A}$.

In practice, we could implement this by allowing $IParent$ to send $POLICY$ to $OParent$, and $IWebsite$ to send $POLICY$ to $OWebsite$, and adding the following local constraints to their behaviour:

- If $IParent$ sends $t : POLICY$ to $OParent$, then $IParent$ must previously have sent t to $Parent$.
- If $IWebsite$ sends $t : POLICY$ to $OWebsite$, then $IWebsite$ must previously have sent t to $Website$.

Obtaining a formal proof of correctness for this construction requires an architecture language in which this sort of local constraint can be expressed, and we leave this for future work.

6   Related Work

Le Métayer et al. [2,3,6,7] have described several languages for describing architectures and deciding privacy-related properties over them. Barth et al. [4] also give a formal definition of architectures, and show how to decide properties defined in temporal logic. Our work was heavily inspired by these systems; however, our aim was to give a method to design an architecture starting from a set of privacy properties, and not to decide whether a property holds of a given architecture.

Basin et al. [5] show how to describe privacy policies in metric first-order temporal logic (MFOTL), and how to build a component that monitors in real-time whether these policies are being violated. Nissenbaum et al. [4] also describe privacy policies using linear temporal logic (LTL), and this has inspired a lot of research into systems such as P-RBAC, which enforces low-level privacy-related conditions at run-time [17]. Most of this research has concentrated on verifying at run-time whether or not a given action is permitted by a given set of privacy policies. The work presented here concentrates instead on design-time, and ensures that a high-level privacy policy is followed, no matter what actions each individual component performs with the data it receives, as long as all messages follow the given type system.

Jeeves [20] is a constraint functional language motivated by separating business logic and confidentially concerns. We could implement our (architectural) constraints in Jeeves, but would no longer have static guarantees. Other work in formal methods for privacy includes static analysis of source code [11, 15] and refinement techniques for deriving low-level designs from high-level designs in a way that preserves privacy properties [1, 10]. These approaches complement ours well, addressing properties for individual components that cannot be expressed in our constraint language, while our algorithms provide formal guarantees of global properties of the system as a whole.

Other work in formal methods for privacy has tended to concentrate either on static analysis of source code [11, 15] or on refinement techniques for deriving low-level designs from high-level designs in a way that preserves privacy properties [1, 10]. These approaches should complement ours well, providing formal guarantees for individual components of properties that cannot be expressed in our constraint language, while our algorithms provide formal guarantees of global properties of the system as a whole.

7   Conclusion

We have given two algorithms which take an architecture, and a set of constraints on that architecture, and show how the architecture may be extended in such a way that we can produce a formal proof that the negative constraints hold on every trace through the architecture, and the positive constraints are satisfiable. Moreover, we do not need to read or modify the source code of the components from the original architecture in order to do this. We believe this is a promising approach to designing large, complex systems, with many different parts designed and maintained by different people, such that we can provide a formal proof of privacy-relevant properties.

For the future, we wish to expand the language that may be used for our constraints, for example by allowing the designer to express constraints using propositional, predicate or temporal logic. We hope then to express other properties that are desirable for privacy, such as the obligation to delete data. This will require in turn expanding our type systems T_C. We also plan to construct a prototype implementation of the interfaces described in this paper.

References

1. Alur, R., Černý, P., Zdancewic, S.: Preserving secrecy under refinement. In: Bugliesi, M., Preneel, B., Sassone, V., Wegener, I. (eds.) ICALP 2006. LNCS, vol. 4052, pp. 107–118. Springer, Heidelberg (2006). https://doi.org/10.1007/11787006_10
2. Antignac, T., Le Métayer, D.: Privacy architectures: reasoning about data minimisation and integrity. In: Mauw, S., Jensen, C.D. (eds.) STM 2014. LNCS, vol. 8743, pp. 17–32. Springer, Cham (2014). https://doi.org/10.1007/978-3-319-11851-2_2
3. Antignac, T., Le Métayer, D.: Privacy by design: from technologies to architectures. In: Preneel, B., Ikonomou, D. (eds.) APF 2014. LNCS, vol. 8450, pp. 1–17. Springer, Cham (2014). https://doi.org/10.1007/978-3-319-06749-0_1
4. Barth, A., Datta, A., Mitchell, J.C., Nissenbaum, H.: Privacy and contextual integrity: framework and applications. In: IEEE Symposium on Security and Privacy, pp. 184–198 (2006)
5. Basin, D., Klaedtke, F., Müller, S.: Monitoring security policies with metric first-order temporal logic. In: ACM SACMAT 2010 (2010)
6. Butin, D., Chicote, M., le Métayer, D.: Log design for accountability. In: IEEE Symposium on Security and Privacy Workshops, pp. 1–7 (2013)
7. Butin, D., Chicote, M., Le Métayer, D.: Strong accountability: beyond vague promises. Reloading Data Protection, pp. 343–369. Springer, Dordrecht (2014). https://doi.org/10.1007/978-94-007-7540-4_16
8. Cavoukian, A.: Privacy by design. IEEE Technol. Soc. Mag. **31**(4), 18–19 (2012)
9. Cavoukian, A., Stoddart, J., Dix, A., Nemec, I., Peep, V., Shroff, M.: Resolution on privacy by design. In: 32nd International Conference of Data Protection and Privacy Commissioners (2010)
10. Clarkson, M.R., Schneider, F.B.: Hyperproperties. J. Comput. Secur. **18**(6), 1157–1210 (2010)
11. Cortesi, A., Ferrara, P., Pistoia, M., Tripp, O.: Datacentric semantics for verification of privacy policy compliance by mobile applications. In: D'Souza, D., Lal, A., Larsen, K.G. (eds.) VMCAI 2015. LNCS, vol. 8931, pp. 61–79. Springer, Heidelberg (2015). https://doi.org/10.1007/978-3-662-46081-8_4
12. Enck, W., et al.: TaintDroid: an information-flow tracking system for realtime privacy monitoring on smartphones. ACM Trans. Comput. Syst. (TOCS) **32**(2), 5 (2014)
13. Regulation (EU) 2016/679 of the European parliament and of the council of 27 April 2016 on the protection of natural persons with regard to the processing of personal data and on the free movement of such data, and repealing directive 95/46/EC (general data protection regulation). Official journal of the European union L119, 1–88, May 2016. http://eur-lex.europa.eu/legal-content/EN/TXT/?uri=OJ:L:2016:119:TOC
14. Federal Trade Commission: Protecting consumer privacy in an era of rapid change. FTC report (2012)
15. Ferrara, P., Tripp, O., Pistoia, M.: MorphDroid: fine-grained privacy verification. In: Proceedings of the 31st Annual Computer Security Applications Conference, pp. 371–380. ACM (2015)
16. Myers, A.C., Zheng, L., Zdancewic, S., Chong, S., Nystrom, N.: Jif: Java information flow (2001)
17. Ni, Q., et al.: Privacy-aware role-based access control. ACM Trans. Inf. Syst. Secur. (TISSEC) **13**(3), 24 (2010)

18. Pottier, F., Simonet, V.: Information flow inference for ml. ACM Trans. Program. Lang. Syst. (TOPLAS) **25**(1), 117–158 (2003)

19. Schreckling, D., Köstler, J., Schaff, M.: Kynoid: real-time enforcement of fine-grained, user-defined, and data-centric security policies for Android. Inf. Secur. Tech. Rep. **17**(3), 71–80 (2013)

20. Yang, J., Yessenov, K., Solar-Lezama, A.: A language for automatically enforcing privacy policies. In: Proceedings of the 39th ACM SIGPLAN-SIGACT Symposium on Principle of Programming Languages, POPL 2012, Philadelphia, Pennsylvania, USA, 22–28 January 2012, pp. 85–96 (2012)

SideTrail: Verifying Time-Balancing
of Cryptosystems

Konstantinos Athanasiou[1], Byron Cook[2], Michael Emmi[3],
Colm MacCarthaigh[2], Daniel Schwartz-Narbonne[2(✉)], and Serdar Tasiran[2]

[1] Northeastern University, Boston, USA
konathan@ccs.neu.edu
[2] Amazon Web Services, Seattle, USA
{byron,colmmacc,dsn,tasirans}@amazon.com
[3] SRI International, Menlo Park, USA
michael.emmi@sri.com

Abstract. Timing-based side-channel attacks are a serious security risk
for modern cryptosystems. The time-balancing countermeasure used by
several TLS implementations (*e.g.* s2n, GnuTLS) ensures that execution timing is negligibly influenced by secrets, and hence no *attacker-
observable timing behavior* depends on secrets. These implementations
can be difficult to validate, since time-balancing countermeasures depend
on global properties across multiple executions. In this work we introduce the tool SIDETRAIL, which we use to prove the correctness of time-
balancing countermeasures in s2n, the open-source TLS implementation
used across a range of products from AWS, including S3. SIDETRAIL
is used in s2n's continuous integration process, and has detected three
side-channel issues that the s2n team confirmed and repaired before the
affected code was deployed to production systems.

1 Introduction

Timing-based side-channel attacks are a serious security risk for modern cryptosystems; the Lucky 13 attack is a recent example [1]. Current systems deploy
one of two prevailing countermeasures to prevent such attacks. One possible
mitigation against this threat is to apply the *constant-time* coding principle,
where secrets must not influence control-flow paths, memory access patterns,
or the cycle counts of instructions. This simplifies local reasoning about timing leaks: if secrets are not used in the prohibited manner, then the code does
not exhibit timing side-channels. However, constant-time coding often requires
replacing a program's natural control-flow with complicated bitwise operations,
and can require significant changes to standard data-structures and APIs, making it difficult to reason about functional correctness. The developers of OpenSSL
recently applied a 500+ LOC patch to perform constant-time cipher block chain-
ing (CBC) decoding; the complexity of which led to subsequent issues [2].

The second approach, dubbed *time-balancing*, ensures that execution time is
negligibly influenced by secrets. This relaxation from constant-time enables simpler and more readable countermeasures: developers must *balance* a program's

© Springer Nature Switzerland AG 2018
R. Piskac and P. Rümmer (Eds.): VSTTE 2018, LNCS 11294, pp. 215–228, 2018.
https://doi.org/10.1007/978-3-030-03592-1_12

executions to have similar timing footprints, allowing the use of standard operations that depend on secrets. The CBC code from s2n [3], for example, implements time-balancing in fewer than 20 additional lines, and s2n's time-balanced HMAC has been proven functionally correct [4]. However, since time-balancing countermeasures depend on global properties across multiple executions, programmers easily miss subtle timing leaks [5].

In this work, we introduce SIDETRAIL (and its implementation [6]), a deductive verifier for time-balancing countermeasures. SIDETRAIL uses an instruction-level precise timing model and encodes it via a *time counter*. It uses Boogie [7] to precisely reason about control flow and values, including the time counter. We automatically infer invariants over time-counter values with minimal user annotation, and use self-composition [8] to prove that the timing difference between every pair of executions with similar public inputs is below a given bound.

We have used SIDETRAIL to verify the correctness of the timing countermeasures for the data-packet processing stack in s2n. SIDETRAIL is used in s2n's Travis-based continuous integration system [9], has detected three issues that the s2n team has confirmed and repaired before the affected code was used in production systems, and has proved correctness of the repaired countermeasures.

1.1 Related Work

Prior work has proposed verification for constant-time [10–20] and power-balancing [21] side-channel countermeasures including the Everest project which has proven the functional correctness of a side-channel resistant TLS implementation in the constant-time model [22,23].

Different approaches have recently appeared in the context of *time-balancing* countermeasures [24,25]. Blazer [24] uses a *partitioning strategy* instead of self-composition and scales to examples of up to 100 basic blocks in size. Themis [25] uses *Quantitative Cartesian Hoare Logic* to capture timing differences between executions and scales to real-world Java applications. Themis requires functions to be time-balanced; it otherwise reports spurious violations. In contrast, SIDE-TRAIL takes a *path-based* approach, and can handle time-balancing countermeasures, such as those used in s2n's HMAC, which compose unbalanced functions to ensure that every execution path is time balanced. Both Blazer and Themis target Java programs while SIDETRAIL focuses on low-level C-code implementations. Unlike these two approaches, which approximate leakage using computational complexity and bytecode instruction counts respectively, SIDETRAIL supports fine grained cost models at the instruction level of LLVM's Intermediate Representation language.

The self-composition we describe in Sect. 3 builds on those of existing works [26–29], and our implementation follows ct-verif's [19], replacing its cross-product construction with self-composition; our novelty is in its application to time balancing. Contrary to approaches providing upper bounds of information leakage metrics [30], SIDETRAIL employs relational verification.

2   Time-Balancing

Time-balancing countermeasures provide the security assurance that program secrets have negligible influence on execution time, even in the presence of potentially malicious observers who can control the public inputs to the program. Formally, a program is δ-secure if for every possible public-input value, the timing difference between every pair of executions with different secrets is at most δ. In this work, we assume a standard adversarial model: a network man in the middle (MITM), who has the ability to observe and modify both the contents and the timing of any packet on the network, but who cannot execute arbitrary code on the targeted endpoints [31]. This model is powerful enough to capture a wide range of real TLS attacks, ranging from Bleichenbacher's attacks against PKCS #1 [32], to Brumley and Boneh's attack against RSA decryption [33], to the Lucky 13 family of attacks against the TLS HMAC [1].

```
1: procedure CBC-VULNERABLE              1: procedure CBC-TIMEBALANCED
2:     pad := packet[len − 1]            2:     pad := packet[len − 1]
3:     payload_len := len − pad          3:     payload_len := len − pad
4:     update(mac, packet, payload_len)  4:     update(mac, packet, payload_len)
                                         5:     update(dummyMAC, packet + payload_len, pad)
5:     digest(mac)                       6:     digest(mac)
```

Fig. 1. A vulnerable TLS CBC algorithm (a), and its time-balanced version (b).

Example 1. The Lucky 13 family of attacks [1] takes advantage of a weakness in the specification for SSL/TLS; CBC mode uses an HMAC to prevent adversaries from modifying incoming cipher-texts, but neglects to protect the padding [34]. A MITM attacker can trick a TLS implementation into decrypting a selected encrypted byte (*e.g.* from a password) into the padding length field. Figure 1a shows what happens in a naïve implementation: in line 4, len - pad bytes are hashed by the HMAC, whose timing strongly depends on the number of bytes hashed. Since len is known to the attacker, this creates a timing side-channel leaking the value of pad. A constant-time mitigation would be to rewrite the HMAC implementation so that its computation was independent of the value of pad. A simpler time-balanced countermeasure is shown in Fig. 1b: apply update on a dummy HMAC state dummyMAC (line 5), which ensures that no matter the value of pad, the HMAC will always process a total of len bytes, mitigating the timing side-channel.

Verifying Time-Balancing. Following previous approaches to verifying non-interference [26, 29], we reduce verification of δ-security, which is a 2-safety property, *i.e.* a property over pairs of executions, to the verification of a standard safety property, *i.e.* over individual executions. For technical simplicity, we consider a program P as a sequence of instructions $p_0; p_1; \ldots; p_n$ whose variables $V = Sec \uplus Pub$ are the disjoint union of secret and public variables, respectively;

a program state s maps the variables to values. A configuration c is a tuple (s, p) of program state s and the next instruction p to be executed. An execution is defined as a configurations sequence $c_1 c_2 \ldots c_m$.

Effective reasoning about δ-security requires (i) a timing model that accurately captures programs' timing behavior, and (ii) a verification technique able to relate the timing behavior of two distinct program executions. To capture timing, we introduce a leakage function $\ell(c)$, mapping configurations c to timing observations, *i.e.* the cost of executing the next program instruction using the values of variables in c. To keep track of the total cost of an execution we extend the set of variables with a *time counter* 1 as $V_L = V \uplus \{1\}$ and write the *time counter instrumented* program P_L as $l_1; p_1; l_2; p_2 \ldots; l_n; p_n$, in which each instruction l_i updates the time counter variable as $1 := 1 + \ell(s, p_i)$. Finally to relate the timing cost of two execution paths we compose P_L with its renaming $\hat{P}_L$ over variables $\hat{V}_L$, and form its self-composition $P_L; \hat{P}_L$ ranging over variables $V_L \cup \hat{V}_L$ [8,26]. Accordingly, δ-security can be specified as a safety property over the time-counter variables 1 and $\hat{1}$.

3   Implementation

SIDETRAIL uses the SMACK verification infrastructure [35], which leverages Clang [36] and LLVM [37] to generate and optimize LLVM bitcode before translation to the Boogie [7] intermediate verification language. Using LLVM intermediate representation (IR) allows SIDETRAIL to reason precisely about the effect of compiler optimizations, which can affect the timing of time-balancing countermeasures. Our initial experience verifying simple time-balanced examples showcased the importance of correctly accounting for compiler optimizations. In some cases, the compiler can notice that the extra code added for time-balancing

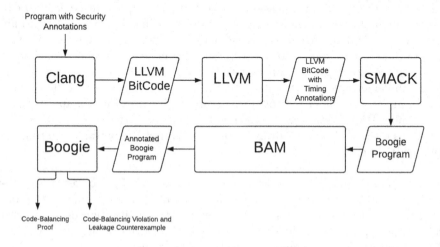

Fig. 2. SIDETRAIL architecture

```
#define DELTA 0        define i32 @plus(   procedure plus(       var l, _l: int;
                         i32, i32){           i0: int, i1: int)  procedure wrapper(
int plus(                %3 = add nsw i32    returns (r: int){      i0: int, i1: int,
  int a, int b){           %1, %0,           var i2: int;           _i0: int, _i1: int){
  public_in(a);          !TimeCost !19      bb0:                    assume i0 == _i0;
  assert_leakage(        ret i32 %3,          l  := l + 1;          call plus(i0, i1);
    DELTA);              !TimeCost !27        i2 := i0 + i1;        call _plus(_i0, _i1);
  return a + b;        }                      l  := l + 0;          assume l >= _l;
}                      !19 = !{i64 1}         r  := i2;             assert l - _l <= 0;
    ...                !27 = !{i64 0}         return;               return;
                                           }                     }
```

Fig. 3. Stages of SIDETRAIL translation, from left to right: (a) an annotated C-code add function; (b) the corresponding LLVM IR with timing annotations; (c) the translated Boogie code with time counter instrumentation; and (d) the Boogie code for the self-composition.

is side-effect free, and remove it, reintroducing the timing side-channel in the original algorithm.

In addition, using LLVM IR easily allows us to use an instruction-level-precise architectural timing model. We have extended SMACK to introduce the timing cost of LLVM instructions, and implement program transformations at the Boogie code-level, passing a time counter instrumented self-composition to the Boogie verifier [7]. If the program being verified is δ-secure, SIDETRAIL returns with a proof; if there is a violation of δ-security, SIDETRAIL provides a counter-example trace which includes the input values that triggered the exception, the trace leading to the exception, and the amount of leakage calculated for that trace. The SIDETRAIL flow is illustrated in Figs. 2 and 3.

Security Annotations: SIDETRAIL requires a small number of annotations at the source-code level to specify a δ-security proof. The programmer must annotate the appropriate entry-point arguments as public (unannotated arguments are treated as secrets) and specify the non-negative integer timing-difference bound (δ). The `public_in` and `assert_leakage` annotations of Fig. 3a serve these purposes.

Timing Model: SIDETRAIL uses LLVM's Cost Model Analysis for its instruction-level precise timing model. The analysis approximates the timing cost of each instruction when lowered to machine code by mapping it to a positive integer, and assumes that all memory accesses hit their respective caches; we discuss the soundness of this assumption in Sect. 4.3. Figure 3b shows how SIDETRAIL annotates the LLVM IR `add` (time cost: 1) and `ret` (time cost: 0) instructions with timing metadata, represented as metadata pointers `!19` and `!27` respectively. Figure 3c shows how the timing metadata are carried over to the Boogie code. A *time-modeling* transformation, implemented as a Boogie-code transformation, introduces the integer-type time counter variable `l` and updates it in lockstep with program instructions.

Loop Invariants: To capture how the values of the time counter variables are updated throughout a loop's execution, SIDETRAIL automatically inserts *loop-*

timing-invariants in the Boogie code, based on annotations provided by the user.

A loop's cost depends on two factors: the number of times it iterates, and the cost of each iteration. The number of iterations can be captured by annotating a simple continuation invariant—for example, loops of the form `for (i=0; i<n; ++i)` should be user-annotated with a continuation invariant (`i<=n`). In the common case where the execution time of the loop-body does not vary across iterations, SIDETRAIL can automatically infer the cost of each iteration. If the loop body contains nested control statements the user must provide annotations that describe how many times each branch of the control statement is visited, although we note that we encountered only a single loop with nested control in our experiments. In either case, SIDETRAIL automatically infers timing-invariants of the form (`l = l_prior + i*body_cost`), where `l_prior` is the value of `l` before entering the loop and `body_cost` is the timing cost of executing the loop body once, and inserts them in the Boogie code.

Self-composition: We implement the self-composition-based reduction of δ-security to assertion checking as an additional Boogie-code transformation, demonstrated in Fig. 3d. We duplicate the program to be verified, making a renamed copy of all functions (`plus` becomes `_plus`), and then transform these duplicated functions to use renamed copies of global variables including the time counter, and to perform nested procedure calls on the renamed procedures. Finally, a `wrapper` procedure enforces the equality of public inputs, makes two consecutive calls to the entry function of the program and its renamed copy, and adds an assertion to check δ-security.

Inter-procedural Analysis: SIDETRAIL supports inter-procedural analysis through function inlining, allowing the analysis of arbitrary entry points which may invoke individually unbalanced functions (s2n uses such functions in its path-balanced HMAC). As we discuss in Sect. 4, this approach is able to handle industrial codebases such as the s2n HMAC. SIDETRAIL also supports modular verification through timing stubs, described below.

Timing Stubs: SIDETRAIL allows the user to specify the expected leakage from a function by providing support for *timing stubs*. Users specify these stubs by adding `assume_leakage(expr)` statements to the body of a function, where `expr` is any expression computable within the function. When the *time-modeling* transformation encounters this call, it increases the time counter variable by `expr`. This allows stubs to represent complex timing behaviour which may depend on properties of both the input and current state of the function. It is the responsibility of the user to ensure that the stub correctly models the timing behaviour of the concrete implementation; we discuss how SIDETRAIL can be used to verify the correctness of stubs in Sect. 4.2.

4   Case Study of the s2n TLS Library

s2n is an open-source TLS library used by Amazon, including S3, and AWS services [38]. Its design goals are that it be: "small, fast, with simplicity as a priority" [39]. Its time-balanced CBC mode requires fewer than 20 additional lines of code, compared to the 500+ LOC patch to perform constant-time CBC decoding in OpenSSL. We have used SIDETRAIL to verify the correctness of the timing countermeasures for the whole data-packet processing stack (which includes CBC verification as a sub-component) in the current s2n release. In the process we have discovered three previously unknown issues that violate δ-security. We note s2n has a belt-and-suspenders security model with randomized delay on error and a secure default configuration [40], which would have prevented these issues from affecting data in production.

The proofs described below are automatically rerun as part of s2n's Travis based continuous integration system. This ensures that code changes are only accepted to the s2n repository after they have been validated using SIDETRAIL.

```
int s2n_hash_update(struct s2n_hash_state *state, const void *data, uint32_t size)
{
    assume_leakage(PER_BYTE_COST * size);
    state->currently_in_hash_block += size;
    int num_filled_blocks = state->currently_in_hash_block / BLOCK_SIZE;
    assume_leakage(num_filled_blocks * PER_BLOCK_COST);
    state->currently_in_hash_block = state->currently_in_hash_block % BLOCK_SIZE;
    return SUCCESS;
}
```

Fig. 4. Hash function timing stub.

4.1   Timing Stubs

s2n is written in a modular fashion, and does not implement its own cryptographic primitives – instead they are linked from the system `libcrypto`. We provide timing stubs for each cryptographic primitive used by s2n, following the approach described in Sect. 3. An example stub for `hash_update` is shown in 4. This stub has two components: a per-byte cost, representing the cost of `memcpy`ing the data, and a per-block cost, representing the cost of a hash compression round. The stubs were validated by using SIDETRAIL to verify that the stub had the same timing behaviour as a C implementation, as described in Experiment 3 (Sect. 4.2).

4.2   Experiments

Except as noted below, all experiments had approximatly 400 lines of initial source, 5 security annotations, 3 loop invariants, 100 lines of additional code (stubs + test harness), and expanded to an order of 1000 SMT clauses. All of the experiments listed below completed in less than 8 min on a 3.1 GHz Intel Core i7 with 16 GB of RAM running OSX 10.11, using Z3 4.6.0's integer arithmetic theory.[1] The code for all experiments is available online.[2]

For each experiment, we determined the precise amount of δ-leakage by varying δ to find the boundary where verification moved from unsuccessful to successful. Our experience in this process suggests that refuting values of δ that are too small is typically faster than verifying values of the correct size.

Properties Verified. We performed four related verification experiments using SIDETRAIL. Experiment 1 validated our ability to detect a previously reported timing issue in the CBC mode of s2n. Experiment 2 validated the correctness of the current implementation of this code. Experiment 3 validated the correctness of the timing stubs used in Experiment 2. Experiment 4 extends this proof to provide an end to end guarantee for data-packet processing.

[Experiment 1] One of the motivations for this work is a previously reported and repaired timing side-channel issue [41] in s2n's time-balanced CBC decoder. The issue is caused by an off-by-one error in the code that tracks how many bytes have been hashed and triggers for a particular edge-case in the padding size. SIDETRAIL reports an error trace that includes the concrete value of the padding size, as well as the expected leakage (equivalent to one hash compression round, approximately 1 μs).

[Experiment 2] In this experiment, we verify the correctness of the CBC mode time-balancing countermeasures for all protocol versions (SSL3, TLS[1.0–1.2]) and hash functions (MD5, SHA1, SHA-224, SHA-256, SHA-384, SHA-512) supported by s2n. In order to handle this wide range of modes and functions, both the test-harness and the hash-stubs were written in a generic fashion, allowing different modes to be tested by setting the appropriate compile-time constants. The experiment could then be rerun with varying parameters to cover all modes.

We experienced two types of scalability issues in this experiment. Firstly, s2n does not contain its own cryptographic primitives, leading us to use a modular verification approach using timing stubs as described in Sect. 4.1. Secondly, the CBC code makes branching decisions based on non-linear operators (`mod` and `div`), which the backend SMT solver had difficulty solving in a reasonable time. We worked around this issue by replacing the `div` operation with a handwritten variant that uses pre-calculated values for the block-sizes being tested. Our proofs for the various modes all showed a small δ-leakage, caused by the extra call to `hash_digest` necessary to affect time-balancing. Since this δ (approximately 0.03 μs) is significantly smaller than the time granularity visible to a network based attacker (estimated at 1 μs based on timing experiments done between

---

[1] Using integer arithmetic provides performance benefits at the cost of losing information about the underlying C types. In a few cases, we needed to annotate back this information, for example by adding `assume(x >= 0 && x < 256)` after an assignment to a `uint8_t x;`.

[2] https://github.com/danielsn/s2n/tree/sidetrail-vstte-artifact/tests/sidewinder.

co-located machines, which is in agreement with [31]), the code is successfully balanced.

[Experiment 3] The soundness of Experiment 2 depends on correct modeling of the timing behaviour of the timing stubs. In this experiment we verify that our SHA-1 timing stub accurately captures the timing cost of an open-source C implementation [42]. Our proof methodology is similar to the one used for δ-security, but in this case we form a composition of the timing stub (Fig. 4) with the C implementation and assert that their time counter variables are equal (i.e. $\delta = 0$). The SHA-1 C code contains a loop with a nested control statement, which requires us to indicate the times each branch is exercised via an additional invariant. After experimenting to find the correct values for `PER_BYTE_COST` and `PER_BLOCK_COST`, we verify that the δ between the stub and the C implementation is 0.

[Experiment 4] (450LOC Source, 150LOC stubs, 20LOC Annotations, 1860 SMT clauses) In this experiment we verify that data-packet processing is time-balanced, for all protocols (SSL3, TLS[1.0–1.2]) and modes (AEAD, CBC, Composite, and Stream) currently supported by s2n. This provides end-to-end confidence that from the time a data-packet is decrypted, until when the bytes are returned to the client, all paths are time-balanced.

The proof decomposes packet processing into three phases. Phase one, packet parsing, operates on public data, such as header fields, which are already known to a MITM attacker, and hence can be treated as public inputs. Phase two, decryption, is handled by stubs which havoc the decrypted data buffer, making the values non-deterministically different across the self-composed program executions. Phase three validates the decrypted data and returns it to the user. This phase uses the decrypted data from stage two, and hence is the stage which could potentially leak confidential information via a timing side-channel. We leverage the δ-security proof and the concrete value of δ reported from Experiment 2 to validate the timing stub for HMAC verification. All modes reported a $\delta < 0.05$ μs.

Previously Unknown Issues Discovered. Using SIDETRAIL, we reported three previously unknown issues in the s2n time-balancing countermeasures, which have been acknowledged and fixed by the s2n team, and validated the repaired code.

[Issue 1] s2n time-balancing code counts the number of bytes in the hash block, and uses this value as part of its time-balancing countermeasures. As an optimization, s2n took advantage of the fact that the standard HMAC specification [43] pads keys to be multiples of the hash-block in length, which means that hashing a padded key does not affect the number of bytes remaining in the hash block. Unfortunately, the SSLv3 specification follows this recommendation for MD5, but in SHA1 mode uses a padded key that is 4 blocks short of the hash

block size [44], causing the time-balancing code to incorrectly count the number of bytes.

[Issue 2] s2n's HMAC had two variables with similar names: `hash_block_size` and `block_size`. Due to a typo, the wrong variable was used in a modular operation which determines the need for time-balancing operations. Interestingly, this issue only exposes itself in SSLv3 mode; in all other modes, `block_size` and `hash_block_size` have the same value. This issue was accepted and repaired by the s2n team, who also renamed the variables to have more descriptive names.

[Issue 3] As discussed in Issue 1, s2n uses a count of the number of bytes hashed as part of its time-balancing countermeasures. In addition to the bytes directly added by calls to `hash_update()`, s2n must track the number of bytes added behind the scenes by the hash algorithm. In particular, before generating a hash digest, most hash algorithms append padding, which typically includes an integer specifying the total number of bytes that have been hashed. Most hash functions used in TLS (e.g. MD5, SHA1) use an 64-bit (i.e. 8-byte) integer for this purpose, and hence s2n's time-balancing code adds 8 to the number of bytes that have been hashed when determining the need for time-balancing operations. However, some hash algorithms, such as SHA-384 and SHA-512, append a 128 bit (16-byte) integer, which would cause s2n time-balancing code to miscount the number of bytes hashed when using these algorithms.

4.3 Discussion on the Timing Model

SIDETRAIL assumes an architectural timing model, which abstracts away microarchitectural features such as caching and branch prediction, similarly to other approaches [24,25]. This model captures the capabilities of a MITM network attacker against a TLS endpoint who can measure final execution time (with limited precision due to network jitter) but cannot affect or directly observe machine state. Consequently the attacker can only observe the cumulative number of cache hits/misses, and cannot influence them by altering the state of the cache. In the context of our s2n case study, the TLS code we verify preloads a data-packet whose maximum size is 16 KB into the cache, and then spends approximately 50 μs doing a linear scan across it (based on the speed of the hash functions used in TLS). Since the data-packet fits in the L1 cache (typically at least 32 KB), all memory accesses results in cache hits. Additionally, 50 μs are considerably less than the Linux quantum which is on the order of milliseconds, meaning that cache interference effects from context switches are minimal.

4.4 Verification Inspired Refactoring

Verifying an industrial code-base requires forming a clear understanding of the code being verified. As part of this effort, we discovered a number of refactorings that made the code more modular, clean, and easy to verify. These code changes were shared with the s2n team as GitHub PRs, and have been merged into the mainline code-base.

The proposed changes ranged from small optimizations such as removing an unnecessary loop, to refactoring of larger portions of the code-base. For example, as part of Experiment 2, we discovered that different HMAC modes had duplicated functionality; merging this functionality into a common function simplified both the code, and the proof effort. Conversely, in Experiment 4, the data-packet processing code interleaved functionality from several different modes, requiring a large number of local variables and making it difficult to write a test harness that covered all cases. We split the code into four simpler functions, with four simple test harnesses. The s2n team accepted the PR with the comment "this looks much better, thanks." The most interesting fix was to s2n's error handling which follows a disciplined methodology. As we analysed several error handling code paths, we realized that every case followed the same template, and could be simplified with a macro that made error-handling easier to annotate (since we only needed to add the annotation in one place). As an added benefit, this change removed 400 LOC from an approximately 6 KLOC code-base.

Formal verification both inspired and enabled these changes. Our refactoring touched large portions of the overall code-base, and made changes to security-critical functionality. Without automated formal proofs to give us confidence that our changes would not introduce new timing regressions, the amount of effort to manually validate the changes would have made these changes impractical.

5   Future Work

As future work we first aim to improve the accuracy of SIDETRAIL's timing model. Modeling the behaviour of micro-architectural components, such as the cache and the branch predictor, will extend the class of attackers that SIDETRAIL can reason about with on-machine active attackers. Additionally, replacing LLVM's instruction cost model with a model based on micro-benchmarks will increase the precision of SIDETRAIL, especially for operations such as `div` and `mod` which take a different number of cycles depending on the values of their input. We have demonstrated SIDETRAIL's capability to utilize and validate timing stubs. As a second direction of future work, we envision extending the tool's usability by inferring timing stubs in an automated fashion.

6   Conclusion

Ideal cryptographic practice is to design algorithms for an easy and straightforward implementation that is naturally constant-time. For legacy algorithms that were not designed with this restriction in mind, developers must use alternate approaches such as time-balancing. SIDETRAIL allows developers of industrial cryptographic code-bases such as s2n to verify the correctness of these mitigations, and to detect issues and regressions when they occur.

References

1. AlFardan, N.J., Paterson, K.G.: Lucky thirteen: breaking the TLS and DTLS record protocols. In: 2013 IEEE Symposium on Security and Privacy, SP 2013, Berkeley, CA, USA, 19–22 May 2013, pp. 526–540. IEEE Computer Society (2013)
2. Somorovsky, V.J.: Curious Padding oracle in OpenSSL (CVE-2016-2107) (2016). https://web-in-security.blogspot.co.uk/2016/05/curious-padding-oracle-in-openssl-cve.html. Accessed 15 Jan 2018
3. Amazon Web Services: s2n : an implementation of the TLS/SSL protocols (2018). https://github.com/awslabs/s2n
4. Dodds, J.: Part one: verifying s2n HMAC with SAW (2016). https://galois.com/blog/2016/09/verifying-s2n-hmac-with-saw/. Accessed 15 Jan 2018
5. Albrecht, M.R., Paterson, K.G.: Lucky microseconds: a timing attack on Amazon's *s2n* implementation of TLS. In: Fischlin, M., Coron, J.-S. (eds.) EUROCRYPT 2016. LNCS, vol. 9665, pp. 622–643. Springer, Heidelberg (2016). https://doi.org/10.1007/978-3-662-49890-3_24
6. Sidewinder: Time-balanced Verification Tests (2018). https://github.com/awslabs/s2n/tree/master/tests/sidewinder
7. Barnett, M., Chang, B.-Y.E., DeLine, R., Jacobs, B., Leino, K.R.M.: Boogie: a modular reusable verifier for object-oriented programs. In: de Boer, F.S., Bonsangue, M.M., Graf, S., de Roever, W.-P. (eds.) FMCO 2005. LNCS, vol. 4111, pp. 364–387. Springer, Heidelberg (2006). https://doi.org/10.1007/11804192_17
8. Barthe, G., D'Argenio, P.R., Rezk, T.: Secure information flow by self-composition. In: 2004 Proceedings of 17th IEEE Computer Security Foundations Workshop, pp. 100–114. IEEE (2004)
9. Amazon Web Services: s2n Travis CI integration page (2018). https://travis-ci.org/awslabs/s2n/
10. Agat, J.: Transforming out timing leaks. In: Wegman, M.N., Reps, T.W. (eds.) POPL 2000, Proceedings of the 27th ACM SIGPLAN-SIGACT Symposium on Principles of Programming Languages, Boston, Massachusetts, USA, 19–21 January 2000, pp. 40–53. ACM (2000)
11. Molnar, D., Piotrowski, M., Schultz, D., Wagner, D.: The program counter security model: automatic detection and removal of control-flow side channel attacks. In: Won, D.H., Kim, S. (eds.) ICISC 2005. LNCS, vol. 3935, pp. 156–168. Springer, Heidelberg (2006). https://doi.org/10.1007/11734727_14
12. Svenningsson, J., Sands, D.: Specification and verification of side channel declassification. In: Degano, P., Guttman, J.D. (eds.) FAST 2009. LNCS, vol. 5983, pp. 111–125. Springer, Heidelberg (2010). https://doi.org/10.1007/978-3-642-12459-4_9
13. Stefan, D., et al.: Eliminating cache-based timing attacks with instruction-based scheduling. In: Crampton, J., Jajodia, S., Mayes, K. (eds.) ESORICS 2013. LNCS, vol. 8134, pp. 718–735. Springer, Heidelberg (2013). https://doi.org/10.1007/978-3-642-40203-6_40
14. Almeida, J.B., Barbosa, M., Pinto, J.S., Vieira, B.: Formal verification of side-channel countermeasures using self-composition. Sci. Comput. Program. **78**(7), 796–812 (2013)
15. Barthe, G., Betarte, G., Campo, J.D., Luna, C.D., Pichardie, D.: System-level non-interference for constant-time cryptography. In: Ahn, G., Yung, M., Li, N. (eds.) Proceedings of the 2014 ACM SIGSAC Conference on Computer and Communications Security, Scottsdale, AZ, USA, 3–7 November 2014, pp. 1267–1279. ACM (2014)

16. Zhang, D., Wang, Y., Suh, G.E., Myers, A.C.: A hardware design language for timing-sensitive information-flow security. In: Özturk, Ö., Ebcioglu, K., Dwarkadas, S. (eds.) Proceedings of the Twentieth International Conference on Architectural Support for Programming Languages and Operating Systems, ASP-LOS 2015, Istanbul, Turkey, 14–18 March 2015, pp. 503–516. ACM (2015)

17. Doychev, G., Köpf, B., Mauborgne, L., Reineke, J.: Cacheaudit: a tool for the static analysis of cache side channels. ACM Trans. Inf. Syst. Secur. 18(1), 4:1–4:32 (2015)

18. Rodrigues, B., Pereira, F.M.Q., Aranha, D.F.: Sparse representation of implicit flows with applications to side-channel detection. In Zaks, A., Hermenegildo, M.V. (eds.) Proceedings of the 25th International Conference on Compiler Construction, CC 2016, Barcelona, Spain, 12–18 March 2016, pp. 110–120. ACM (2016)

19. Almeida, J.B., Barbosa, M., Barthe, G., Dupressoir, F., Emmi, M.: Verifying constant-time implementations. In: 25th USENIX Security Symposium, USENIX Security 16, Austin, TX, USA, 10–12 August 2016, pp. 53–70 (2016)

20. Blazy, S., Pichardie, D., Trieu, A.: Verifying constant-time implementations by abstract interpretation. In: Foley, S.N., Gollmann, D., Snekkenes, E. (eds.) ESORICS 2017. LNCS, vol. 10492, pp. 260–277. Springer, Cham (2017). https://doi.org/10.1007/978-3-319-66402-6_16

21. Fang, X., Luo, P., Fei, Y., Leeser, M.: Leakage evaluation on power balance countermeasure against side-channel attack on FPGAs. In: 2015 IEEE High Performance Extreme Computing Conference, HPEC 2015, Waltham, MA, USA, 15–17 September 2015, pp. 1–6. IEEE (2015)

22. Bond, B., et al.: Vale: verifying high-performance cryptographic assembly code. In: 26th USENIX Security Symposium, USENIX Security 2017, Vancouver, BC, Canada, 16–18 August 2017, pp. 917–934 (2017)

23. Bhargavan, K., et al.: Everest: towards a verified, drop-in replacement of HTTPS. In: Lerner, B.S., Bodík, R., Krishnamurthi, S. (eds.) 2nd Summit on Advances in Programming Languages, SNAPL 2017, Volume 71 of LIPIcs., Asilomar, CA, USA, 7–10 May 2017, pp. 1:1–1:12. Schloss Dagstuhl - Leibniz-Zentrum fuer Informatik (2017)

24. Antonopoulos, T., Gazzillo, P., Hicks, M., Koskinen, E., Terauchi, T., Wei, S.: Decomposition instead of self-composition for proving the absence of timing channels. In: Proceedings of the 38th ACM SIGPLAN Conference on Programming Language Design and Implementation, PLDI 2017, pp. 362–375. ACM, New York (2017)

25. Chen, J., Feng, Y., Dillig, I.: Precise detection of side-channel vulnerabilities using quantitative Cartesian hoare logic. In: Proceedings of the 2017 ACM SIGSAC Conference on Computer and Communications Security, CCS 2017, pp. 875–890. ACM, New York (2017)

26. Terauchi, T., Aiken, A.: Secure information flow as a safety problem. In: Hankin, C., Siveroni, I. (eds.) SAS 2005. LNCS, vol. 3672, pp. 352–367. Springer, Heidelberg (2005). https://doi.org/10.1007/11547662_24

27. Zaks, A., Pnueli, A.: CoVaC: compiler validation by program analysis of the cross-product. In: Cuellar, J., Maibaum, T., Sere, K. (eds.) FM 2008. LNCS, vol. 5014, pp. 35–51. Springer, Heidelberg (2008). https://doi.org/10.1007/978-3-540-68237-0_5

28. Barthe, G., Crespo, J.M., Kunz, C.: Relational verification using product programs. In: Butler, M., Schulte, W. (eds.) FM 2011. LNCS, vol. 6664, pp. 200–214. Springer, Heidelberg (2011). https://doi.org/10.1007/978-3-642-21437-0_17

29. Barthe, G., D'Argenio, P.R., Rezk, T.: Secure information flow by self-composition. Math. Struct. Comput. Sci. **21**(6), 1207–1252 (2011)
30. Pasareanu, C.S., Phan, Q.S., Malacaria, P.: Multi-run side-channel analysis using symbolic execution and max-SMT. In: 2016 IEEE 29th Conference on Computer Security Foundations Symposium (CSF), pp. 387–400. IEEE (2016)
31. Crosby, S.A., Wallach, D.S., Riedi, R.H.: Opportunities and limits of remote timing attacks. ACM Trans. Inf. Syst. Secur. **12**(3), 17:1–17:29 (2009)
32. Bleichenbacher, D.: Chosen ciphertext attacks against protocols based on the RSA encryption standard PKCS #1. In: Krawczyk, H. (ed.) CRYPTO 1998. LNCS, vol. 1462, pp. 1–12. Springer, Heidelberg (1998). https://doi.org/10.1007/BFb0055716
33. Brumley, D., Boneh, D.: Remote timing attacks are practical. In: Proceedings of the 12th Conference on USENIX Security Symposium, SSYM 2003, vol. 12, p. 1. USENIX Association, Berkeley (2003)
34. Rescorla, E., Dierks, T.: The Transport Layer Security (TLS) Protocol Version 1.2. RFC 5246, August 2008
35. Rakamarić, Z., Emmi, M.: SMACK: decoupling source language details from verifier implementations. In: Biere, A., Bloem, R. (eds.) CAV 2014. LNCS, vol. 8559, pp. 106–113. Springer, Cham (2014). https://doi.org/10.1007/978-3-319-08867-9_7
36. LLVM: clang: a C language family frontend for LLVM (2018). https://clang.llvm.org/
37. Lattner, C., Adve, V.: LLVM: a compilation framework for lifelong program analysis & transformation. In: Proceedings of the 2004 International Symposium on Code Generation and Optimization (CGO 2004), Palo Alto, California, March 2004
38. Schmidt, S.: s2n is now handling 100 percent of SSL traffic for Amazon S3 (2017). https://aws.amazon.com/blogs/security/s2n-is-now-handling-100-percent-of-of-ssl-traffic-for-amazon-s3/. Accessed 15 Jan 2018
39. Schmidt, S.: Introducing s2n, a new open source TLS implementation (2015). https://aws.amazon.com/blogs/security/introducing-s2n-a-new-open-source-tls-implementation/. Accessed 15 Jan 2018
40. MacCarthaigh, C.: s2n and Lucky 13 (2015). https://aws.amazon.com/blogs/security/s2n-and-lucky-13/. Accessed 15 Jan 2018
41. Almeida, J.B., Barbosa, M., Barthe, G., Dupressoir, F.: Verifiable side-channel security of cryptographic implementations: constant-time MEE-CBC. In: Peyrin, T. (ed.) FSE 2016. LNCS, vol. 9783, pp. 163–184. Springer, Heidelberg (2016). https://doi.org/10.1007/978-3-662-52993-5_9
42. Brad Conte: Basic implementations of standard cryptography algorithms, like AES and SHA-1 (2018). https://github.com/B-Con/crypto-algorithms. Commit: 02b66ec38b474445d10a5d1f0114bc0e8326707e
43. Krawczyk, H., Bellare, M., Canetti, R.: HMAC: Keyed-Hashing for Message Authentication. RFC 2104, RFC Editor, February 1997. http://www.rfc-editor.org/rfc/rfc2104.txt
44. Freier, A., Karlton, P., Kocher, P.: The Secure Sockets Layer (SSL) Protocol Version 3.0. RFC 6101, RFC Editor, August 2011. http://www.rfc-editor.org/rfc/rfc6101.txt

Towards Verification of Ethereum Smart Contracts: A Formalization of Core of Solidity

Jakub Zakrzewski[(✉)]

University of Warsaw, ul. S. Banacha 2a, 02-097 Warsaw, Poland
j.zakrzewski@mimuw.edu.pl

Abstract. Solidity is the most popular programming language for writing smart contracts on the Ethereum platform. Given that smart contracts often manage large amounts of valuable digital assets, considerable interest has arisen in formal verification of Solidity code. Designing verification tools requires good understanding of language semantics. Acquiring such an understanding in case of Solidity is difficult as the language lacks even an informal specification.

In this work, we evaluate the feasibility of formalization of Solidity and propose a formalization of a small subset of Solidity that contains its core data model and some unique features, such as function modifiers.

Keywords: Solidity · Ethereum · Smart contracts · Semantics

1 Introduction

Ethereum is a blockchain-based platform that provides a globally-consistent virtual general-purpose computer, called the Ethereum Virtual Machine. The programs to be executed on the EVM, called *smart contracts*, are provided in a stack-based machine language, which has a corresponding assembly language. But most smart contracts are written in higher-level languages. The most popular language of those is called Solidity. Given that Ethereum smart contracts often manage assets worth millions of US dollars, bugs in their design may lead to enormous harm. Since there is so little margin for error, considerable interest has arisen in formal verification of Solidity code.

To design accurate verification tools, one needs to know precisely what Solidity is. Superficially, Solidity seems to be a simple language that should be easy to understand for anyone familiar with mainstream programming languages of the C family, as it was designed with similarity to JavaScript in mind. However, after reading the freely available documentation while investigating the possibility of creating such a tool, we realized that we do not really understand the

J. Zakrzewski—This work was partially supported by the Polish NCN grant 2013/11/B/ST6/01381.

R. Piskac and P. Rümmer (Eds.): VSTTE 2018, LNCS 11294, pp. 229–247, 2018.
https://doi.org/10.1007/978-3-030-03592-1_13

language well. In the pursuit of providing high-level features, while maintaining the abstractions efficiently implementable for the Ethereum Virtual Machine, the creators of the language ended up with a language that has a very different type system and data model, and numerous unusual features. To improve our understanding of Solidity, we needed a precise specification.

Although much work has gone into formalizing and verifying the Ethereum Virtual Machine bytecode [1,7–9,12], there appears to be a paucity of studies on Solidity. A previous work on the topic by Bhargavan et al. [5] does not give explicit semantics. As such, we set out to create a new formalization. Since even an informal specification of the Solidity language does not exist, we had to design the semantics by studying the official documentation, doing experiments, and analysis of Solidity compiler sources. To enable establishing trust in the specification, we implemented it in an executable form in Coq, in a way such that it is possible to extract a working interpreter of the language. In the future, this will enable testing the semantics and comparing it with the real implementation.

Semantics for the complete Solidity language will be rather complex due to the multitude of features the language provides. In this paper:

- We give an overview of Solidity and highlight some surprising and, in our opinion, poorly documented features of the language, like modifiers and the data model (Sect. 2). We consider providing an accurate description of these language features to be a necessary step towards creating sound and complete verification tools for Solidity.
- We describe the dynamic semantics of several core Solidity constructs formally. Our semantics is given in an executable form in Coq, however here, it is described in conventional metanotation (Sect. 3). Our semantics omit many features we consider inessential to enabling deductive verification of contract state invariants. For example, we do not model transaction fees. Since providing insufficient funds for a transaction fee simply causes the whole transaction to abort without affecting the contract state.

2   Overview of Solidity

Solidity was originally designed as a JavaScript-like, but typed, programming language for the Ethereum platform. The language is structured into contract definitions, function and modifier definitions, statements, and expressions. A Solidity source unit is composed of contract definitions. Figure 1 presents the abstract syntax of the described fragment of Solidity.

2.1   Contracts and Messages

At source level, contracts appear similar to classes in object-oriented languages. They can contain declarations of *state variables* (analogous to class fields), definitions of functions (method), modifiers, constructors, and structs (record type), they support encapsulation (visibility attributes), and can even inherit from

e	::=	var	local variable access
		$\mid$ $var\{cname\}$	state variable access
		$\mid$ $funname$	internal function
		$\mid$ cst	bool or uint constants
		$\mid$ e_1 (e_2*)	function call
		$\mid$ $e_1[e_2]$	array access
		$\mid$ e . $fname$	member access
		$\mid$ op e	unary arithmetic or logic operation
		$\mid$ $e \ll op \gg e$	binary arithmetic or logic operation
		$\mid$ this	
		$\mid$ e_1 = e_2	assignment
		$\mid$ e^*	tuple
cst	::=	true $\mid$ false	Boolean constant
		$\mid$ n	integer constant
$StorageLocation$	::=	memory $\mid$ storage	
$LocalVarDef$	::=	$TyName$ $StorageLocation?$ var	local variable declaration
$TyName$	::=	uint	unsigned machine integer
		$\mid$ bool	boolean
		$\mid$ $sname$	struct
		$\mid$ $TyName[]$	dynamically sized array
		$\mid$ $TyName[n]$	fixed size array
		$\mid$ mapping($TyName$ => $TyName$)	mapping
$stmt$	::=	$stmt_1$; $stmt_2$	sequence
		$\mid$ if e then $stmt$ else $stmt$	conditional
		$\mid$ while (e) $stmt$	while loop
		$\mid$ throw;	
		$\mid$ return;	
		$\mid$ return e;	return statement
		$\mid$ _;	placeholder
		$\mid$ $LocalVarDef$;	local variable declaration
$StructFieldDef$	::=	$TyName$ id	
$StructDef$	::=	struct $sname$ { $StructFieldDef^*$ }	
$FunDef$	::=	function [$funname$]($LocalVarDef^*$)	
		[$mname$ (e^*)]*	
		[returns ([$TyName$ [var]]*)]	
		{ $stmt$ }	function definition
$ModifierDef$	::=	modifier $mname$(id^*) { $stmt$ }	modifier definition
$StateVarDef$	::=	$TyName$ $StorageLocation$ id	
$ContractDef$	::=	contract $cname$ is $cname^*$	
		{ $StateVarDef^*$ $FunDef^*$	
		$ModifierDef^*$ $StructDef^*$ }	contract definition

Fig. 1. Abstract syntax of our core Solidity.

multiple other contracts. All the defined entities reside in a single namespace. Functions can be statically overloaded. For resolving the visibility of inherited identifiers the creators of Solidity opted for the widely used C3 linearization algorithm [4].

To enable deployment on the Ethereum platform, the contract functions are compiled into EVM bytecode and a piece of code called *function selector* is added, which serves as an entry point into the contract code. The resulting EVM program is put in a *contract account* on the Ethereum network, which, in addition to storing code, also holds a certain amount of virtual currency. From that point on, other Ethereum accounts may trigger execution of contract functions or currency transfers by sending *messages* to the contract account. Whenever someone sends a message to the contract account, the contract code starts executing at the function selector. The selector decodes the message and jumps into an appropriate contract function (method). Solidity supports custom handling of messages that do not specify a concrete function to call, by the way of specifying *fallback functions*.

Functions return values using *return variables*. Their names can be either explicitly specified by the programmer, or it may be unique identifiers generated during the typechecking phase.

The declarations of local variables, in addition to type names and variable names can have a *storage location*. Local variables of simple scalar types, i.e. machine integers and Ethereum network addresses, do not need, or allow, this annotation. They always reside on the EVM stack. However, in addition to those simple types, we can declare *pointers* to compound types, such as structs and arrays. Objects of these types can reside in two locations: memory and storage. These are described in more detail in following subsections.

State Variables. State variables can store *storage objects*. Storage objects can be either scalars (machine integers, addresses, booleans), arrays of storage objects (either fixed-size or resizable), structs (records of storage objects) or mappings. Mappings are a sort of hash tables that are able to map certain hashable types to storage objects. However unlike typical hash tables, they do not store the keys alongside the values and do not implement any collision resolution mechanism. Instead, a key hashing scheme based on a collision resistant cryptographic hash function is used to derive an address where the value is stored [19] in the large 256-bit virtual address space of EVM storage. This lack of collision resolution complicates formal reasoning about operations on mappings, so we decided to treat this aspect as an implementation detail and abstract it away in our formalization, i.e. treat mappings as formal mappings, with no hashing involved.

The state variables reside in persistent *storage* of a given account, i.e. they are a part of the global state of the Ethereum network.

Note that the storage, as viewed from Solidity, does not behave like a traditional automatically managed heap of objects linked by pointers. Instead, storage objects are treated as values. As a result, assigning directly to a state variable causes deep copying, as demonstrated in Fig. 2. Notably though, this does not work for mappings, as they cannot be copied. Still, structs with a field of mapping type can be copied, though the problematic field in the destination object is simply left alone, preserving the old values.

That said, pointers to non-scalar storage objects can be taken and stored in local variables. An important thing to notice is that storage objects have automatic lifetimes, tied to reachability from a state variable. For example, calling the function `foo` of the following contract in Fig. 3 results in an error.

```
contract Z {
  int [] [] baz ;
  function foo () returns (int) {
    baz . length = 10;  // resize baz
    baz [0] . length = 10;   // resize baz [0]
    baz [1] . length = 1;    // resize baz [1]
    int [] storage bar = baz [0];   // bar is a storage pointer
    baz [0] = baz [1];  // deep copy
    return bar [9];   // error
  }
}
```

Fig. 2. Direct storage assignment example.

```
contract Z {
  int [] [] baz ;
  function foo () returns (int) {
    baz . length = 10;  // resize baz
    baz [0] . length = 10;
    int [] storage bar = baz [0];   // bar is a storage pointer
    baz . length = 0;   // bar becomes a dangling pointer !
    return bar [0];   // error
  }
}
```

Fig. 3. An example demonstrating storage data structure lifetime.

Modifiers. A unique feature of Solidity are the function modifiers, a functionality somewhat similar to Python decorators. They are often used to add precondition checks to contract functions. The modifiers assigned to a function are executed before entering the actual function body. The modifier hands over the control flow to the next modifier or the function body when so-called placeholder statement is encountered (_;).

```
address owner ;
modifier my_modifier (address a) {
  if (a != owner) { throw; }
  _; // enter the function body
}
function foo () my_modifier (msg . sender) returns (uint) {
  uint a; a += 1;
  return a;
}
```

The official Solidity documentation does not go into much detail on the semantics of modifiers. It only gives examples of the very simplest cases. For example, consider code in Fig. 4.

Multiple things are not obvious about the behavior of the function foo() and are not described by the documentation:

234   J. Zakrzewski

```
modifier my_modifier1 {
    _; _; _; // enter the function body three times
}
modifier my_modifier2 {
    uint a;
    if (a > 1) { _; }
    a += 1; _;
}
modifier my_modifier3(uint a) {
    if (a < 2) { _; }
}
function foo(uint a) my_modifier1 my_modifier2 my_modifier3
        (a) returns (uint) {
    a += 1; return a;
}
function bar() returns (uint) {
    return foo(0); // returns 2
}
```

Fig. 4. Example of confusing modifier code

- Are function's local variable values preserved when it is entered multiple times from modifiers? Our experiments indicate that they are;
- Are modifier's local variable values preserved when it is entered multiple times from other modifiers? In this case it seems that they are not;
- When are arguments passed to modifiers evaluated? They are evaluated anew each time the modifier is entered.

Struct Definitions. A struct definition in Solidity consists of a list of pairs of type names and field names. The definition can be used to instantiate both memory and storage objects, and the storage location of the object is propagated to fields. This means e.g. that pointers to storage objects cannot be stored in memory structs.

2.2 Type Names

The internal type system of the Solidity compiler is richer than the syntax suggests, as it tracks additional type attributes, like storage location for composite types. As a result, we have to differentiate type names from the actual types. The actual type of the declared entity depends on the context of the declaration and annotations provided by the programmer. This may be directly observed in error messages produced by the compiler. For example, a local variable declared as uint[] storage a has type uint[] storage pointer, while a storage variables declared as uint[] b has type uint[] storage ref.

2.3   Statements

We consider a limited set of simple control structures, such as if/then/else, while loops. Additional features such as for and do/while loops are left out, as their semantics are not particularly unusual.

One novel construct found in Solidity is the placeholder statement _;. It may appear only in function modifiers, where it denotes the point of entry into the next modifier or the function body.

The **return** statements interrupt the control flow and jump out of the function body. Providing an explicit value to the **return** statement causes it to have the side effect of assigning to the return variable. The control flow returns either to the caller or to a function modifier if one is used. The modifier may then reenter the function body. In that case all values of local variables, including return variables, are preserved.

2.4   Expressions

The annotation *cname* in state variable access and assignment statements of our abstract language denotes the contract (class) where the referenced variable is defined. It is not a part of Solidity's concrete syntax and is inferred by the type checker.

Function calls in Solidity can be of several types: internal, external, delegate, and calls to certain builtin functions. Internal function calls are simply jumps in the code of the current account. External calls cause a message to be sent over the Ethereum network, executing code on another account. Delegate calls exist to provide a functionality akin to shared libraries. That is, they allow code from another account to directly operate on the storage of calling account. The semantics of external and delegate calls are notorious source of bugs in contracts [2], notably the DAO [6] and Parity multi-sig contract [16] incidents. Since the code executed by outgoing external function calls may not be available, or not written in Solidity, we decided to specify the behavior of such calls only in terms of axioms that effectively state that arbitrary changes to the network state could be made. This is not very helpful for verification purposes, however a provision could be made for preservation of certain global invariants.

The semantics of **this** keyword in Solidity is quite unusual. In Solidity **this** is the address of the current account in the Ethereum network, which the contract can use to send an Ethereum message to itself. Directly accessing state variables using **this** is not possible, and though accessor functions are generated for public state variables, calling them incurs the cost of a message call. These phenomena are demonstrated by Fig. 5.

An especially unusual corner case is using **this** in constructors. The constructors execute *before* **this** account is actually able to receive and decode messages in the Ethereum network, which means that dispatching calls on **this** in a constructor, as in Fig. 6, causes a runtime error.

The order of evaluation of sub-expression in Solidity is explicitly left unspecified. Since this is tangential to the concepts we want to explore in this paper, we assume for simplicity a deterministic order.

```
contract Foo {
  uint private i;
  uint public j;
  function bar() returns (uint) {
    // return this.i;      // this would cause an error
    return this.j();       // externally calls an
      automatically generated getter
  }
}
```

Fig. 5. this cannot be used to access state variables directly.

```
contract Foo {
  constructor() { this.foo(); }   // this causes an error!
  function foo() { }
}
```

Fig. 6. this incorrectly used in a constructor.

Interestingly, the Solidity language has no constants of machine integer types. Instead, all numeric constants in the source are treated by the compiler as arbitrary precision rational numbers. At the typechecking stage, the constants are folded, and the results are converted to machine integers of type appropriate to the source context. However, since this step can be done entirely statically, we do not model this in our semantics.

2.5 Memory Objects in Solidity

As mentioned before, Solidity programs have access to auxiliary volatile memory. The view of memory as provided by Solidity is that of a mapping of pointers to memory objects. Memory objects can be either arrays or structs, which can contain scalars or pointers to other memory objects.

Note that there are no mappings in memory. Also, unlike in the case of storage, memory objects cannot be contained in other memory objects as values. Importantly, this means that a single struct declaration in Solidity can have two very different concrete representations.

```
struct S {
  int[8] a;
  mapping (int => int) m;
}
```

Fig. 7. An example struct declaration.

For example, when the struct definition in Fig. 7 is instantiated in memory, we get an object that contains a single field a that is a pointer to a memory array. An attempt to access m results in a type error. On the other hand, a state variable of type S, contains an object that has two fields, one of them being a storage array object (not a pointer), and the other a mapping.

Somewhat confusingly though, whenever a local variable of memory pointer type is defined, it is automatically initialized to point to a newly allocated memory object of given type and this initialization is recursive, i.e. all nested pointers in the object are initialized the same way. In fact, Solidity does not allow the programmer to explicitly allocate memory objects other than dynamically sized arrays, nor it provides any facility to free allocated objects or otherwise reclaim allocated memory. Thus, the code in Fig. 8, unlike the similar code in Fig. 2, does not result in an error being raised.

```
contract Z {
  function foo() returns (int) {
    int[][] memory baz = new int[][](10);
    baz[0] = new int[](10);
    baz[1] = new int[](1);
    int[] memory bar = baz[0];
    baz[0] = baz[1];
    return bar[9]; // OK
  }
}
```

Fig. 8. Memory allocation.

3   Formalization

Our formalization of Solidity focuses on dynamic semantics and it is written as an interpreter in Coq, in monadic functional big-step semantics style described by Owens et al. [15], however in this paper it is presented in a more conventional notation. Describing the semantics of the full Solidity language, including its type system, is too big to fit in a workshop paper. In order to make our presentation feasible, we focus here only on a subset of Solidity that captures the following features:

– contracts with storage,
– memory,
– inheritance,
– modifiers.

We omit other features, such as function overloading, visibility specifiers, rational constant types, integers of sizes less than 256 bits, packed byte array types, libraries, events, and most of Solidity's global built-in functions and variables. We assume all functions are callable both internally and externally. These features were left out, as they are either laborious to implement or not very interesting from the point of view of dynamic semantics. We have aimed for the formalization to be as abstract as possible, for example by not exposing the EVM data model, to make reasoning about programs simpler.

The Ethereum Network. The main effect of executing smart contract code is altering the state of the Ethereum network. From the point of view of our formalization, the Ethereum network σ is a partial mapping of addresses to accounts.

An account is a triple $\langle b, p, s \rangle$ of balance b (the amount of currency the account holds), the contract program p, and storage s. The contract program p can be thought of as a pair $\langle c, \textit{cdefs} \rangle$ of contract name and a list of definitions of the account contract, as well as all its parents in the inheritance hierarchy. To model the object-oriented nature of Solidity contracts, we abstract from the low-level EVM view of the account storage as a mapping of machine words to machine words, and instead we consider it to be analogous to a field table in Jinja [14]. Therefore, a storage s is a partial mapping from pairs $(\textit{var}, \textit{cname})$ to storage objects so, where var is the name of the variable and $cname$ is the identifier of the contract (class) where the variable was defined. Both those components are needed, since inheritance may lead to a single contract containing more than one variable of the same name. Storage objects can be thought of as trees containing values in their leaves and with mappings, arrays or structs as their nodes:

$so ::= $ Smapping (m), where $m \in v \to so$
   $|$ Sarray $(a, \textit{typ}, l)$, $a \in \mathbb{Z} \to$ option$(so), l \in \mathbb{Z}$
   $|$ Sstruct (s), $s \in$ ident $\to$ option(so)
   $|$ Sval (v)

This is similar to the model of C++ objects proposed by Ramananandro et al. [17]. Solidity mappings are total, initially mapping all keys to default objects of declared value type. Arrays contain, aside from partial mappings from indices to storage objects, length, and type information to allow bounds checking and initializing objects in new cells when resizing.

The contract execution is done as a part of a *transaction* which can be triggered by *messages* sent to the network. Two kinds of messages are currently of interest to us: creation messages, which are used to create new contract accounts in the network, and normal call messages. We do not attempt to formalize the Solidity ABI specification. Instead, for our purposes, creation messages are quadruples $\langle a_s, v, p, vs \rangle$ and normal messages are quintuples $\langle a_s, a_r, v, \textit{funname}, vs \rangle$, where a_s and a_r are the network addresses of the sender and recipient accounts, the *value* v that holds the amount of currency sent, p is contract code, *funname* is a name of a function to call, and vs is a list of values, which are the arguments to the constructor or the called function.

Memory. Memory m can be thought of as a mapping $loc \to mo$ from a set of locations to memory objects. Memory objects can be either arrays or structs that store values, including pointers to other memory objects:

$mo ::=$ Marray(a), $a \in \mathbb{Z} \to$ option(v)
   $|$ Mstruct(s), $s \in$ ident $\to$ option(v)

Since memory arrays are not resizable, unlike storage arrays, they do not need to carry type information. Storage references in memory are disallowed by the type system. We use m_{empty} to denote an empty memory.

Values. Values range over 256-bit machine integers, Booleans, storage references, memory pointers, and internal or external function pointers.

$$
\begin{aligned}
v \quad ::= \quad &\mathtt{Vbool}\ (b),\ b \in \{\mathrm{true}|\mathrm{false}\} & \text{booleans} \\
| \quad &\mathtt{Vint}\ (n),\ n \in \mathbb{Z}, 0 \le n < 2^{256} & \text{machine integers} \\
| \quad &\mathtt{Vaddr}\ (a),\ a \in \mathbb{Z}, 0 \le n < 2^{160} & \text{addresses} \\
| \quad &\mathtt{Vsref}\ (sref) & \text{storage references} \\
| \quad &\mathtt{Vmptr}\ (loc) & \text{memory pointers} \\
| \quad &\mathtt{Vifptr}\ (funname, cname) & \text{internal function pointers} \\
| \quad &\mathtt{Vefptr}\ (a, n, funname) & \text{external function pointers}
\end{aligned}
$$

$$
\begin{aligned}
sref ::= \quad &\mathtt{SRmapping\_val}(sref, v) \\
| \quad &\mathtt{SRarray\_cell}(sref, i),\ i \in Z \\
| \quad &\mathtt{SRsfield}(sref, funname) \\
| \quad &\mathtt{SRvar}(var, cname)
\end{aligned}
$$

Storage references are paths to (sub)objects in the storage of the current account. This accurately models the reachability and lifetimes of storage objects. Memory pointers, on the other hand, are simply locations. Internal function pointers contain a function name and the identifier of the contract where it is defined. External function pointers contain an address of an external account, value (i.e. the amount of currency to send along with the call), as well as a function name.

Lvalues. Lvalues are entities that designate an assignable location in one of the available storage locations. Lvalues may either point to locals, storage objects, cells in memory arrays, fields in memory structs, or tuples.

$$
\begin{aligned}
lv ::= \quad &\mathtt{LVlocal}\ (var) & \text{local variable} \\
| \quad &\mathtt{LVstorage}\ (sref) & \text{storage reference} \\
| \quad &\mathtt{LVmem\_arr\_cell}\ (loc, i),\ i \in \mathbb{Z} & \text{memory array cell} \\
| \quad &\mathtt{LVmem\_sfield}\ (loc, fname) & \text{memory struct field} \\
| \quad &\mathtt{LVtuple}\ (lv*) & \text{tuple}
\end{aligned}
$$

Most of these are self-explanatory. Tuple lvalues are a syntactic construct mostly used to retrieve multiple return values from a function. They are produced by tuple expressions appearing in an lvalue context. Tuple values do not exist, so they cannot be assigned to variables or passed as parameters.

3.1 Big Step Semantics

State. State μ is a tuple $\langle a, m, \sigma, l^f, l^m \rangle$ of the address a of the current account, memory m, network σ, function local store l^f, and modifier local store l^m. To accurately model the semantics of Solidity function modifiers, we introduce two stores for local variables: a function local store and a modifier local store. These stores are partial mappings from identifiers to values. A function store is used to hold local variables of the currently executing function, while a modifier store is used to hold local variables of currently executing modifier, if any. We use l_{empty} to denote an empty store.

Evaluation. The evaluation judgments are of the following forms:

$$\vdash msg, \sigma \Rightarrow \sigma' \qquad \text{transactions}$$
$$p, q, f \vdash stmt, \mu \Rightarrow out, \mu' \qquad \text{statements}$$
$$p \vdash e, \mu \Rightarrow out, \mu' \qquad \text{expressions}$$
$$p \vdash e, \mu \Leftarrow out, \mu' \qquad \text{expressions in lvalue position}$$

The entry point to our semantics is the transaction judgment. A transaction judgment relates a message msg and a network state σ to a new network state σ'. The judgments for statements, expressions, and lvalues relate corresponding syntactic elements to the outcomes of their execution in the given state μ. The symbol q denotes the *modifier stack*, while f is the function being executed. The modifier stack stores pairs $\langle fm, e* \rangle$ of function modifiers that are yet to be executed and lists of their unevaluated arguments (i.e. expressions). The top of the stack contains the modifier that is entered when the next placeholder statement is encountered. The return variables are used to store the return values of the currently executing function.

The rules for expressions and statements may produce one of the following outcomes:

$$out ::= \mathtt{OK}(v) \mid \mathtt{OK}(lv) \mid \mathtt{OK}(vs) \mid \mathtt{Return} \mid \mathtt{Fail}$$

The OK outcome means normal termination. A successful termination may yield a value v, lvalue lv, or a list of values vs. The OK notation is "overloaded" respectively. **Return** is used to interrupt control flow and jump out of the function body upon encountering a **return** statement. The **Fail** outcome is used to propagate exceptions, which cannot be caught and always cause the transaction to fail. In Solidity execution may fail for several reasons, like performing invalid storage accesses or transaction fees exceeding allowances, however we are currently not interested in tracing the causes of these failures.

Space constraints make it impossible to exhaustively list all the rules of our core language, so we give only a few examples of rules we consider interesting.

Account Creation. First things first, we give a rule describing contract account creation. Whenever someone wants to deploy a new contract on the Ethereum network, they have to send a creation message containing contract code. This results in a new account being created and the contract's constructor being run.

$$\frac{\begin{array}{c} msg = \langle a_s, v, p, vs \rangle \\ \sigma_1(a) = \mathtt{None} \qquad \sigma_2 = \sigma_1[a \to \langle v, p_{empty}, mkstorage(p) \rangle] \\ \mu = \langle a, m_{empty}, \sigma_2, mklocals(c, vs), l_{empty} \rangle \\ run\_constructors(p, \mu) = \mu' \qquad \mu' = \langle \dots, \sigma_3, \dots \rangle \qquad \sigma_4 = \sigma_3[a \to \langle \dots, p, \dots \rangle] \end{array}}{\vdash msg, \sigma_1 \Rightarrow \epsilon, \sigma_4}$$

Here, the account with address a_s (the sender) sends a creation message into the network, with the aim of deploying the contract p. The rule for handling creation messages generates a fresh network address a. Under this address, a new account with empty contract code, denoted by p_{empty}, is stored, resulting in a modified network σ'. The $mkstorage(p)$ function creates a new storage, with all storage variables in p set to default values. Similarly, $mklocals(c, vs)$ creates a new local variable store with the arguments of c mapped to vs and locals initialized to default values. Then, constructors of the contract and its superclasses are run according to reverse MRO (the C3 algorithm [4]), i.e. from the most basic to the most derived. Only when all these steps execute successfully, the contract code is actually stored[1] in the network σ_4. The result of the transaction is an empty list of values ϵ and the network σ_4. Note that executing constructors does not require special handling of internal virtual function calls. Our experiments show that functions called are always those of the most derived contract, even if its constructor has not yet finished executing.

Handling Normal Messages. Once we have a contract account on the network, we may execute its functions. This is done by sending messages with the appropriate value of the recipient field, as captured by the following rule:

$$
\frac{
\begin{array}{c}
msg = \langle a_s, a, v, fn, vs \rangle \qquad \sigma_1(a) = \langle b, p, s \rangle \qquad MRO(fn, p) = c \\
lookup(p, fn, c) = f \\
\mu_1 = \langle a, m_{empty}, \sigma_1[a \rightarrow \langle b + v, p, s \rangle], mklocals(f, vs), l_{empty} \rangle \\
p, modifiers(f, p), retvars(f) \vdash \_;, \mu_1 \Rightarrow \mathsf{OK}(\epsilon), \mu_2 \qquad \mu_2 = \langle \ldots, \sigma_2, l_2^f, \ldots \rangle \\
rvs = [l_2^f(retvar_1(f)), \ldots, l_2^f(retvar_n(f))]
\end{array}
}{
\vdash msg, \sigma_1 \Rightarrow rvs, \sigma_2
}
$$

where the function *retvars* simply extracts the return variables of a given function, while *modifiers* looks up modifier definitions and builds the modifier stack. Here, the sender a_s tries to trigger the execution of a function[2] called *fn*. This rule basically performs the role of the function selector. *MRO(funname, p)* returns the identifier of the contract where according to the method resolution order the function should be looked up. The *lookup* function retrieves the function definition. Then we set the modifier stack to contain all the called function's modifiers and reuse the rule for the placeholder statement to actually start executing the first function modifier, or otherwise enter the function body. After the execution of the function terminates, the values of its return variables $retvar_1(f), \ldots, retvar_n(f)$ are extracted and returned. Note that we are assuming any function can receive currency, but in Solidity only those declared as *payable* can do that.

Internal Function Calls. The internal call of a function given as a pointer is similar, however not messages are involved:

$$
\frac{
\begin{array}{c}
p \vdash e_1, \mu_1 \Rightarrow \mathsf{OK}(\mathtt{Vifptr}(fn, c)), \mu_2 \qquad p \vdash e_2*, \mu_2[\Rightarrow]\mathsf{OK}(vs), \mu_3 \\
lookup(p, fn, c) = f \qquad\qquad \mu_3 = \langle a, m_3, \sigma_3, l_3^f, l_3^m \rangle \\
\mu_4 = \langle a, m_3, \sigma_3, mklocals(f, vs*), l_{empty} \rangle \\
p, modifiers(f, p), f \vdash \_;, \mu_4 \Rightarrow \mathsf{OK}(\epsilon), \mu_5 \\
\mu_5 = \langle \ldots, l_4^f, \ldots \rangle \qquad rvs = [l_4^f(retvar_1(f)), \ldots, l_4^f(retvar_n(f))]
\end{array}
}{
p \vdash e_1(e_2*), \mu_1 \Rightarrow \mathsf{OK}(rvs), \mu_5
}
$$

---

[1] Readers acquainted with the internals of Solidity might notice that, unlike the real thing, we do store the constructor code in the network. However, after the account is created, the constructors become inaccessible anyway.

[2] For simplicity function overloading is not taken into account here. To make it work, Solidity ABI uses hashes of the function signature, instead of just names and this is a mechanism that we do implement in Coq.

where $[\Rightarrow]$ means extension of evaluation to lists of expressions.

External Function Calls. External calls are specified in terms of an *external_call* axiom:

$$\frac{p \vdash e_1, \mu_1 \Rightarrow \mathsf{OK}(\mathsf{Vefptr}(a, v, fn)), \mu_2 \quad p \vdash e_2*, \mu_2[\Rightarrow]\mathsf{OK}(vs), \mu_3}{\mu_3 = \langle a, m_3, \sigma_3, l_3^f, l_3^m \rangle}$$
$$\frac{external\_call(\sigma_3, a, v, fn) = v', \sigma_4 \quad \mu_4 = \langle a, m_3, \sigma_4, l_3^f, l_3^m \rangle}{p \vdash e_1(e_2*), \mu_1 \Rightarrow \mathsf{OK}(v'), \mu_4}$$

An external call may arbitrarily change the state of the network, including the invoking account. This is a important source of security issues [6], as well as a problem for verification, since we lose any knowledge about the state we had up to this point. However this is not a new problem, as it has long been known in the context of verification of object-oriented programs [3,10,11,13]. Several methodologies for reasoning about invariants across such calls have been proposed. Perhaps the simplest one is *visible-state semantics*, which would involve enforcing the invariants at all external call sites [11].

Modifiers and the Placeholder Statement. Next we give the semantics of the placeholder statement and function modifier execution. This rule may be triggered either as a part of the function call rules above, or when a placeholder statement is encountered inside a modifier. Once we are there, one of two possibilities may arise. The first one is that we have no more modifiers to execute, so we set the modifier local store to empty and enter the function body. This case is described by the following judgment:

$$\frac{\mu = \langle a, m, \sigma, l^f, l^m \rangle \quad \mu' = \langle a, m, \sigma, l^f, l_{empty} \rangle}{p, \epsilon, f \vdash body(f), \mu' \Rightarrow o, \mu'' \quad o \neq \mathbf{Fail}}{p, \epsilon, f \vdash \text{-;}, \mu \Rightarrow \mathsf{OK}(\epsilon), \mu''}$$

where the function *body* extracts the body of a given function. The second possibility is that we still have modifiers to execute:

$$\frac{\mu_1 = \langle a, m_1, \sigma_1, l_1^f, l_1^m \rangle \quad \mu_2 = \langle a, m_1, \sigma_1, l_1^f, l_{empty} \rangle}{p \vdash e*, \mu_2[\Rightarrow]\mathsf{OK}(vs), \mu_3 \quad \mu_3 = \langle a, m_3, \sigma_3, l_3^f, l_{empty} \rangle}{\mu_4 = \langle a, m_3, \sigma_3, l_3^f, mklocals(fm, vs) \rangle}{p, q', f \vdash body(fm), \mu_4 \Rightarrow o, \mu_5 \quad o \neq \mathbf{Fail}}{p, \langle fm, e* \rangle :: q, rv \vdash \text{-;}, \mu_1 \Rightarrow \mathsf{OK}(\epsilon), \mu_5}$$

where $\langle fm, e* \rangle :: q$ is a notation for list pattern matching. We evaluate the arguments, create a new modifier local store and fill it with default values of the next modifier's local variables, pop the next modifier off the modifier stack and enter its body.

Having a separate store for function and modifier locals allows us to ensure that if the actual function body is entered more than once, the values of function's local variables are preserved, in accordance with the observed behavior produced by the Solidity compiler.

Return Statement. The return statement is simple, but still interesting because of the return variable mechanism and its interaction with modifiers. The rule assigns values to the return variables and interrupts the control flow by using the `Return` outcome.

$$\frac{p \vdash e*, \mu[\Rightarrow] \texttt{OK}(vs), \mu' \qquad \mu' = \langle \ldots, l^f, \ldots \rangle}{\mu'' = \langle \ldots, l^f[retvar_1(f) \rightarrow vs_1, \ldots, retvar(f) \rightarrow vs_n], \ldots \rangle}{p, q, f \vdash \texttt{return } e*;, \mu \Rightarrow \texttt{Return}, \mu''}$$

Local Variables. Local variable scoping follows Solidity versions prior to 0.5.0, i.e. there is a single scope for the entire function body. The lvalue rule for local variable is very simple:

$$\frac{}{p \vdash var, \mu \Leftarrow \texttt{OK}(\texttt{LVlocal}(var)), \mu}$$

There are two rules for dereferencing locals, one for modifiers, and one for functions:

$$\frac{p \vdash e, \mu \Leftarrow \texttt{OK}(\texttt{LVlocal}(var)), \mu \qquad s = \langle a, m, \sigma, l^f, l^m \rangle \qquad l^m(var) = \texttt{Some}(v)}{p \vdash e, \mu \Rightarrow \texttt{OK}(v), \mu}$$

$$\frac{p \vdash e, \mu \Leftarrow \texttt{OK}(\texttt{LVlocal}(var)), \mu \qquad s = \langle a, m, \sigma, l^f, l^m \rangle}{l^m(var) = \texttt{None} \qquad l^f(var) = \texttt{Some}(v)}{p \vdash e, \mu \Rightarrow \texttt{OK}(v), \mu}$$

Local variables are first looked up in the modifier store and then, if this fails, in the function store. This could cause functions locals to be shadowed by modifier locals, but we ensure that this is not the case by setting the modifier store to empty when entering a function body. This trick allows us to forgo adding information about whether our current expression is evaluated within a function or modifier body. The possibility of accessing function locals from modifiers should be ruled out during the typechecking phase.

State Variables and Storage. Now we show the rules dealing with state variables and storage objects. The lvalue rules are straightforward:

$$\frac{}{p \vdash var\{cname\}, \mu \Leftarrow \texttt{OK}(\texttt{LVstorage}(\texttt{SRvar}(var, cname))), \mu}$$

$$\frac{p \vdash e, \mu \Rightarrow \texttt{OK}(\texttt{Vsptr}(sr)), \mu'}{p \vdash e.fname, \mu \Leftarrow \texttt{OK}(\texttt{LVstorage}(\texttt{SRstruct\_field}(sr, fname))), \mu'}$$

Analogous rules exist for element access of arrays or mappings.
The rules for dereferencing storage objects are as follows:

$$\frac{p \vdash e, \mu \Leftarrow \texttt{OK}(\texttt{LVstorage}(sr)), \mu \qquad \mu = \langle \ldots, s, \ldots \rangle \qquad s(sr) = \texttt{Some}(\texttt{Sval}(v))}{p \vdash e, \mu \Rightarrow \texttt{OK}(v), \mu}$$

$$\frac{p \vdash e, \mu \Leftarrow \texttt{OK}(\texttt{LVstorage}(sr)), \mu \quad \mu = \langle \ldots, s, \ldots \rangle \quad s(sr) \neq \texttt{Some}(\texttt{Sval}(\_))}{p \vdash e, \mu \Rightarrow \texttt{OK}(\texttt{Vsref}(sr)), \mu}$$

When the storage reference points to an $\texttt{Sval}$, the value it contains is returned. Otherwise a pointer is returned.

Assigning to a storage location in Solidity is quite complicated. Consider the rule for assigning from another storage location:

$$\frac{\begin{array}{cc} p \vdash e_1, \mu_1 \Leftarrow \texttt{OK}(\texttt{LVstorage}(sr_1)), \mu_2 & p \vdash e_2, \mu_2 \Rightarrow \texttt{OK}(\texttt{Vsref}\, sr_2), \mu_3 \\ \mu_3 = \langle a, m_3, \sigma_3, l_3^f, l_3^m \rangle & \sigma_3(a) = \langle b, p, s \rangle \\ s(sr_1) = \texttt{Some}(so_1) \quad s(sr_2) = \texttt{Some}(so_2) & copy\_over(so_1, so_2) = \texttt{Some}(so_3) \\ s' = s[sr_1 \rightarrow so_3] & \mu_4 = \langle a, m_3, \sigma_3[a \rightarrow \langle b, p, s', l_3^f, l_3^m \rangle] \rangle \end{array}}{p \vdash e_1 = e_2, \mu \Rightarrow \texttt{OK}(storage\_dereference(sr_1, s')), \mu_4}$$

As mentioned before, assigning a storage object to a storage location causes deep copying into that location. Intuitively, it should be sufficient to replace the storage object so_1 pointed to by sr_1 with so_2. Sadly, the inability to copy contents of mappings introduces an ugly corner case: when copying so_2 object over so_1, the contents of mappings reachable from so_1 are preserved. That behavior is modeled by the function $copy\_over$.

3.2 Current State of the Coq Development

As mentioned, we have written down our semantics in an executable form in Coq. This way, it can be combined with code that parses and typechecks Solidity to enable execution of basic contract code. Currently, a very rudimentary test environment has been implemented that enables running simple contract functions, such as the examples given in Sect. 2, except those involving external calls.

Solidity is quite a large language and a significant amount of work is still to be done claim any completeness or run real-world contracts. In particular, our typechecker is written in a mostly ad-hoc manner in Ocaml, still largely incomplete and limited to features necessary for execution, such as resolving state variable names and expression types. Other features of the type system, such as visibility and mutability specifiers are ignored. Solidity provides a number of syntactic sugar constructs, such as named arguments, that we left out. We still do not support the full range of available types and builtin functions. For example, support for small integer types, strings, and packed byte arrays is incomplete. Libraries (accounts containing reusable code), an another widely used feature yet to be formalized, are an significant omission, especially since their semantics can also be a source of serious problems [16]. Some features, like inline assembly, are incompatible with our high-level modeling and cannot be implemented.

Once we implement enough of the language, to establish trust in the specification, we plan to test the semantics against the Solidity compiler test suite. The way we plan to do this, is by implementing a mock Ethereum client with an RPC API that accepts Solidity code instead of EVM bytecode and modifying the Solidity test suite to work with it. The work on this infrastructure has been started, but it is not yet fully functional.

4 Related Work

Bhargavan et al. [5] provided a verification framework for a subset of Solidity by the way of shallow embedding in F*, a programming language aimed at program verification. However they have not provided explicit semantics, and we could not reproduce the data model of Solidity from the descriptions thereof.

Much work has been put into formally specifying the semantics of the Ethereum Virtual Machine. Hirai [9] defined EVM semantics in Lem, a language that can be compiled into specifications for several theorem provers, and then used it to prove safety properties of smart contracts. His formalization was extended with a program logic by Amani et al. [1]. Hildenbrandt et al. [8] defined complete executable EVM semantics in the K Framework, which passed the reference test suite for EVM implementations. Luu et al. have created Oyente [12], a static analysis tool for EVM bytecode. For that purpose, they have developed a simplified semantics of a fragment of EVM. Grishchenko et al. [7] present complete small-step semantics of EVM bytecode, formalized in F*.

Sergey et al. [18] describe SCILLA, an intermediate-level programming language for smart contracts that aims to provide clear operational semantics. They restrict the computation model to communicating automata and mandate external calls to occur at the end of a transaction. This makes the language more amenable to formal verification techniques.

5 Conclusions and Future Work

We have presented a formalization of what we consider to be the core of Solidity, in the form of big-step semantics. We have focused on high-level modeling of the data model and semantics of internal function calls with function modifiers. We have written down our semantics in an executable form in Coq.

Many features used in real contracts still remain to be formalized. In the near future we plan to specify semantics of a larger subset of Solidity. To establish trust in the specification, the executable semantics could then be tested against the official Solidity compiler test suite. Additionally, a coming release of Solidity (0.5.0) is planned to bring many changes to the language, like C99-like block scoping for local variables, and our semantics has to be adapted accordingly.

Verification of realistic contracts is still a somewhat distant goal. We do not consider raw operational semantics to be a practical tool for verification of contracts, for example due to axiomatization of external calls. Ultimately, our aim with this work is to provide a foundation for verification frameworks for smart contracts written in Solidity.

Acknowledgements. I would like to thank Aleksy Schubert for his helpful comments on the draft versions of this paper.

References

1. Amani, S., Bégel, M., Bortin, M., Staples, M.: Towards verifying ethereum smart contract bytecode in Isabelle/HOL. In: Proceedings of the 7th ACM SIGPLAN International Conference on Certified Programs and Proofs, CPP 2018, pp. 66–77. ACM, New York (2018). https://doi.org/10.1145/3167084
2. Atzei, N., Bartoletti, M., Cimoli, T.: A survey of attacks on ethereum smart contracts (SoK). In: Maffei, M., Ryan, M. (eds.) POST 2017. LNCS, vol. 10204, pp. 164–186. Springer, Heidelberg (2017). https://doi.org/10.1007/978-3-662-54455-6_8
3. Barnett, M., DeLine, R., Fahndrich, M., Leino, K.R.M., Schulte, W.: Verification of object-oriented programs with invariants. J. Object Technol. 3, 2004 (2003)
4. Barrett, K., Cassels, B., Haahr, P., Moon, D.A., Playford, K., Withington, P.T.: A monotonic superclass linearization for Dylan. In: Proceedings of the 11th ACM SIGPLAN Conference on Object-Oriented Programming, Systems, Languages, and Applications, OOPSLA 1996, pp. 69–82. ACM, New York (1996). https://doi.org/10.1145/236337.236343
5. Bhargavan, K., et al.: Formal verification of smart contracts: short paper. In: ACM Workshop on Programming Languages and Analysis for Security, Vienna, Austria, October 2016. https://doi.org/10.1145/2993600.2993611, https://hal.inria.fr/hal-01400469
6. Buterin, V.: CRITICAL UPDATE Re: DAO Vulnerability. https://blog.ethereum.org/2016/06/17/critical-update-re-dao-vulnerability/. Accessed 24 April 2018
7. Grishchenko, I., Maffei, M., Schneidewind, C.: A semantic framework for the security analysis of ethereum smart contracts. In: Bauer, L., Küsters, R. (eds.) POST 2018. LNCS, vol. 10804, pp. 243–269. Springer, Cham (2018). https://doi.org/10.1007/978-3-319-89722-6_10
8. Hildenbrandt, E., et al.: KEVM: a complete semantics of the ethereum virtual machine. Technical report (2017)
9. Hirai, Y.: Defining the ethereum virtual machine for interactive theorem provers. In: Brenner, M., et al. (eds.) FC 2017. LNCS, vol. 10323, pp. 520–535. Springer, Cham (2017). https://doi.org/10.1007/978-3-319-70278-0_33
10. Leino, K.R.M., Müller, P.: Object invariants in dynamic contexts. In: Odersky, M. (ed.) ECOOP 2004. LNCS, vol. 3086, pp. 491–515. Springer, Heidelberg (2004). https://doi.org/10.1007/978-3-540-24851-4_22
11. Leino, K.R.M., Stata, R.: Checking object invariants (1997)
12. Luu, L., Chu, D.H., Olickel, H., Saxena, P., Hobor, A.: Making smart contracts smarter. In: Proceedings of the 2016 ACM SIGSAC Conference on Computer and Communications Security, CCS 2016, pp. 254–269. ACM, New York(2016). https://doi.org/10.1145/2976749.2978309
13. Naumann, D.A., Barnett, M.: Towards imperative modules: reasoning about invariants and sharing of mutable state. Theor. Comput. Sci. 365(1), 143–168 (2006). https://doi.org/10.1016/j.tcs.2006.07.035. Formal Methods for Components and Objects
14. Nipkow, T.: Jinja: towards a comprehensive formal semantics for a Java-like language. In: Schwichtenberg, H., Spies, K. (eds.) Proof Technology and Computation, pp. 247–277. IOS Press, Amsterdam (2006)
15. Owens, S., Myreen, M.O., Kumar, R., Tan, Y.K.: Functional big-step semantics. In: Thiemann, P. (ed.) ESOP 2016. LNCS, vol. 9632, pp. 589–615. Springer, Heidelberg (2016). https://doi.org/10.1007/978-3-662-49498-1_23

16. A Postmortem on the Parity Multi-Sig Library Self-Destruct. https://paritytech. io/a-postmortem-on-the-parity-multi-sig-library-self-destruct/. Accessed 24 April 2018
17. Ramananandro, T., Dos Reis, G., Leroy, X.: Formal verification of object layout for C++ multiple inheritance. In: Proceedings of the 38th Annual ACM SIGPLAN-SIGACT Symposium on Principles of Programming Languages, POPL 2011, pp. 67–80. ACM, New York (2011). https://doi.org/10.1145/1926385.1926395
18. Sergey, I., Kumar, A., Hobor, A.: Scilla: a smart contract intermediate-level language. CoRR arXiv:abs/1801.00687 (2018)
19. Solidity documentation. https://solidity.readthedocs.io/en/develop/index.html. Accessed 22 April 2018

Relational Equivalence Proofs Between Imperative and MapReduce Algorithms

Bernhard Beckert, Timo Bingmann, Moritz Kiefer, Peter Sanders,
Mattias Ulbrich, and Alexander Weigl[✉]

Institute of Theoretical Informatics, Karlsruhe Institute of Technology,
Karlsruhe, Germany
weigl@kit.edu

Abstract. Distributed programming frameworks like *MapReduce*, *Spark* and *Thrill*, are widely used for the implementation of algorithms operating on large datasets. However, implementing in these frameworks is more demanding than coming up with sequential implementations. One way to achieve correctness of an optimized implementation is by deriving it from an existing imperative sequential algorithm description through a sequence of behavior-preserving transformations.

We present a novel approach for proving equivalence between imperative and deterministic *MapReduce* algorithms based on partitioning the equivalence proof into a sequence of equivalence proofs between intermediate programs with smaller differences. Our approach is based on the insight that proofs are best conducted using a combination of two kinds of steps: (1) uniform context-independent rewriting transformations; and (2) context-dependent flexible transformations that can be proved using relational reasoning with coupling invariants.

We demonstrate the feasibility of our approach by evaluating it on two prototypical algorithms commonly used as examples in *MapReduce* frameworks: k-means and PageRank. To carry out the proofs, we use a higher-order theorem prover with partial proof automation. The results show that our approach and its prototypical implementation enable equivalence proofs of non-trivial algorithms and could be automated to a large degree.

1 Introduction

Motivation. Frameworks for functional programming for distributed programs, such as *MapReduce* [10], Spark [25] and Thrill [4] address the challenges arising in the implementation of large-scale distributed algorithms by providing a limited set of operations whose execution is automatically parallelized and distributed among the nodes in a cluster. However, designing efficient algorithms in these frameworks is a challenge in itself. A good starting point for a distributed algorithm is an existing imperative algorithm which is then translated into a *MapReduce* framework. This initial program could be taken from a textbook on

© Springer Nature Switzerland AG 2018
R. Piskac and P. Rümmer (Eds.): VSTTE 2018, LNCS 11294, pp. 248–266, 2018.
https://doi.org/10.1007/978-3-030-03592-1_14

algorithms or could be a sequential implementation from an existing code base that is to be optimized. However, the translation into *MapReduce* can be non-trivial, and the original algorithmic structure is often lost during the translation since imperative constructs do not translate directly into the functional *MapReduce* primitives. Implementing efficient algorithms using *MapReduce* frameworks can thus require significant and elaborate alterations to a given imperative algorithm.

By proving the equivalence of the original imperative algorithm and its *MapReduce* version, one can verify that no bugs have been introduced during the translation. While such proofs do not directly provide correctness guarantees for the *MapReduce* algorithm, they transfer correctness results from the imperative version to the *MapReduce* implementation. The transferred correctness properties can be formal proofs whose reach then extends to the distributed implementation, but can also be informal arguments, e.g., if the algorithm is a well-known, simple textbook reference implementation or if it has been successfully applied previously.

In this paper, we use the term *"MapReduce"* in a broader sense than implied by the two functions "map" and "reduce". While some frameworks such as Hadoop's MapReduce [24] module are programmed strictly by specifying these two functions, the more popular and widely used distributed frameworks provide many additional primitives for performance reasons and to make them easier to program with. Theoretically, these additional primitives can be reduced to only map and reduce operations [6], but this overly complicates the program description and is generally not used in real-world applications.

Contribution of This Paper. We present an interactive verification approach with which a *MapReduce* implementation of an algorithm can be proved equivalent to an imperative implementation (to the best of our knowledge this is the first framework for the purpose of such equivalence proofs, see Sect. 6). Proofs are conducted as chains of individual, smaller behavior-preserving program transformations.

One novelty of the approach is that it brings together two approaches for equivalence reasoning: (1) proving equivalence by means of a series of uniform context-independent rewriting transformations; and (2) proving equivalence by means of relational deductive program verification using coupling invariants. We show how the approaches can be applied alternatingly. We identified a catalogue of 13 individual rules. Correctness of 10 of those rules was proven formally using the *Coq* theorem prover.

Our approach has a high potential for automation. The required interaction is designed to be as high-level as possible. The proof is guided by user-specified intermediate programs from which the individual transformations are derived. The rules are designed such that their side conditions can be proved automatically and we describe how pattern matching can be used to allow for a more flexible specification of intermediate steps.

We describe a workflow for integrating this approach with existing interactive theorem provers. We have successfully implemented the approach as a prototype within the interactive theorem prover *Coq* [22] and evaluated the feasibility of our approach by applying it to the k-means and PageRank algorithms. These two are prototypical algorithms commonly used as examples in *MapReduce* frameworks, because they exhibit the most common patterns found in large-scale distributed data processing applications. By showing that our approach can be applied to these two examples, we demonstrate that it can be extended to a much larger set of applications.

Interleaving Different Types of Proofs. We came to the important insight that the proof task requires the interplay of two kinds of sub-proofs:

(1) Uniform, context-independent and pattern-driven transformations that can locally change one program into another with a severely changed control flow. Rewriting techniques can be applied to perform such proof steps.
(2) Context-dependent but flexible equivalence proofs that preserve the control flow, but change the data representation. Relational deductive reasoning using coupling invariants allows us to conduct such proof steps.

In previous work [12,18], we have explored how equivalence proofs can be conducted effectively if the two programs to be compared exhibit a similar control flow. In this case, the relational reasoning approach (2) using coupling predicates that logically manifest the relation between the two program states at given synchronization points proved very successful, and often runs fully automatically. The reason for this is that if coupling predicates can be used, only the relationship between two current states needs to be captured in logic – functional properties (what the code actually computes) need not be formalized. The less similar the two compared programs are, the more difficult and less effective becomes this type of reasoning. However, differences in the control flows can often be bridged by aligning them through behavior-preserving rewriting rules of type (1) (like loop unrolling, loop peeling, function inlining) which are applied prior to the verification [17].

The presented approach now generalizes this idea by interleaving steps of both types. This permits us to apply relational reasoning even for the semantically larger gap between implementations of different programming paradigms. Both types of rules (context-independent rewriting and context-dependent relational reasoning) are necessary for such equivalence proofs: Rewriting rules can modify the control flow (and sometimes the data representation), but – being pattern-driven – are very inflexible in the input they can operate on. Relational reasoning on the other hand is not local; thus, it can be very flexible to show differently laid out programs are correct – as long the control flow is generally kept.

Overview of the Approach. The main challenge in proving the equivalence of an imperative and a *MapReduce* algorithm lies in the potentially large structural difference between two such algorithms. Existing relational verification approaches (like [12,13,19,23]) exploit the fact that the two program versions to

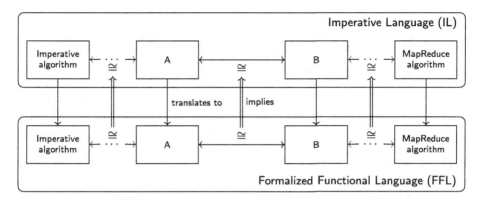

Fig. 1. Chain of equivalent programs is translated into formalized functional language

be compared are structurally similar, which allows the verification to focus on describing and proving the similarity of the implementations rather than describing what they actually compute. To deal with the complexity arising from the large structural differences, the equivalence of imperative and *MapReduce* algorithms is not shown in one step, but as a succession of equivalence proofs for structurally closer program versions.

To this end, we require that the translation of the algorithm is broken down (by the user) into a chain of intermediate programs. For each pair of neighboring programs in this chain, the difference is comparatively small and can usually be reduced to one isolated transformation.

The imperative algorithm, the intermediate programs, as well as the *MapReduce* implementation, are given in a high-level imperative programming language (IL). IL is based on a While language and supports integers, booleans, fixed-length arrays and sum and product types. It does not support recursion. Besides the imperative language constructs, IL supports *MapReduce* primitives. Given that we have stated previously that *MapReduce* programs tend to be of a more functional nature, it might seem odd at first to not use a functional language for specifying *MapReduce* algorithms. However, most existing *MapReduce* frameworks are not implemented as separate programming languages but as frameworks offered as APIs on top of imperative languages (Java for Hadoop, Scala for Spark, or C++ for Thrill). Thereby sequential parts of *MapReduce* algorithms can still be implemented using imperative language features.

Each program specified in the high-level imperative language is then automatically translated into the formalized functional language (FFL) described in Sect. 2. FFL is a deterministic language which might seem surprising given that for performance reasons *MapReduce* frameworks often do not guarantee determinism. However, the source of non-determinism in *MapReduce* algorithms are non-associative and non-commutative functions used with the "reduce" primitive. If all used reducer functions are associative and commutative, then the resulting algorithm is deterministic (some frameworks only require associativity).

Reducer associativity and commutativity are assumptions for the transformation into FFL which are not verified within our approach. Often, the justification is trivial, e. g., for addition on natural or rational numbers. For non-trivial cases, Chen et al. [8,9] present formal verification approaches.

The equivalence proofs are conducted on programs in FFL. An overview of this process can be seen in Fig. 1. For each pair of neighboring programs in the chain, a proof obligation is generated that requires proving their equivalence. These proof obligations are then discharged independently of each other (using the workflow described in Sect. 4). Since, by construction, the semantics of IL programs is the same as that of corresponding FFL programs, the equivalence of two IL programs follows from the equivalence of their translations to FFL. Figure 2 shows two example IL programs for calculating the element-wise sum of two arrays.

Function SumArrays(xs,ys)
begin
    sum ← replicate(n, 0);
    for i ← 0 **to** $n - 1$ **do**
      sum[i] ← xs[i] + ys[i];
    end
    return sum;
end

Function SumArraysZipped(xs,ys)
begin
    sum ← replicate(n, 0);
    zipped ← zip(xs,ys);
    for i ← 0 **to** $n - 1$ **do**
      sum[i] ← fst(zipped[i]) +
      snd(zipped[i]);
    end
    return sum;
end

Fig. 2. Two IL programs which calculate the element-wise sum of two arrays.

The implementation of our approach based on the *Coq* theorem prover has only limited proof automation and still requires a significant amount of interactive proofs. We are convinced, however, that our approach can be extended such that it becomes highly automatised and only few user interactions or none at all are required – besides providing the intermediate programs. Further challenges include the extension of our approach to features such as references and aliasing which are commonly found in imperative languages.

Structure of This Paper. In Sect. 2, we lay the formal groundwork for our approach by defining the programming language used for equivalence proofs and the notion of program equivalence used in this paper. Section 3 describes the two kinds of program transformations that we have identified and the techniques for proving equivalence using these transformations. The technical framework for equivalence proofs and the potential for automation are described in Sect. 4 and their its evaluation is in Sect. 5. In Sect. 6, we discuss work related to the ideas presented in this paper. Finally, we conclude in Sect. 7 and consider possible future work.

2   Formal Foundations and Program Equivalence

In this section, we briefly describe the language FFL, introduce a reduction big-step semantics for FFL and discuss the notion of equivalence for FFL programs.

The primary design goal of FFL is the capability to represent both imperative and *MapReduce* programs written in IL. To achieve this, we follow the work by Radoi et al. [21] and use a simply typed lambda calculus extended by the theories of sums, products, and arrays. Furthermore, the language also contains the programming primitives usually found in *MapReduce* frameworks. We also want to limit the number of primitives included in FFL while still retaining expressiveness. This simplifies proving general properties of FFL and proving the correctness of rewrite rules. We accomplish this by building upon the work of Chen et al. [7], who describe how to reduce the large number of primitives provided by *MapReduce* frameworks to a smaller core.

Two new primitives iter and fold were added to translate imperative loops directly. Compared to transforming imperative programs into a recursive form, this allows a translation closer to the original program formulation. The fold operator is used to translate bounded for-each iterator loops into FFL. The evaluation of the expression fold f v_0 xs starts with the initial loop state v_0 and iterates over each value of the array xs updating the loop state by applying f. General while loops are translated using the iter function. iter f v_0 is evaluated by repeatedly applying f to the loop state (which is initially v_0) until f returns unit to indicate termination. Program terms incorporating iter need not evaluate to a value since the construct allows formulating non-terminating programs.

The big-step operational reduction semantics [16] of FFL is defined as a binary relation $\Rightarrow_{bs}$. Note that, since FFL is based on lambda calculus, programs in FFL as well as values are FFL expressions. The semantics predicate is thus a partial, functional relation on FFL-terms.

Definition 1. *An FFL term t evaluates to an FFL term v if $t \Rightarrow_{bs} v$ holds. A term t is called* stuck *if there exists no v such that $t \Rightarrow_{bs} v$. Terms that evaluate to themselves are called* values.

A formal definition of the syntax and semantics of FFL can be found in [2]. The evaluation of a program t in an input state (i.e., for an argument tuple a) resulting in a output state v (a result tuple) can be formalized as the reduction evaluation of the application of the program to the arguments: $\langle t, a \rangle \Downarrow_{bs} v := \mathsf{app}(t, a) \Rightarrow_{bs} v$.

The semantics of FFL is deterministic. This may seem odd because most *MapReduce* frameworks take considerable leeway from fully deterministic execution in the name of performance. For example, some operations may be evaluated in a non-deterministic order depending on how fast data arrives over the network leading to non-determinism if these operations are not commutative and associative. However, non-determinism in *MapReduce* algorithms is usually not desired, and the problem of checking whether or not a *MapReduce* algorithm is deterministic is orthogonal to proving that it is equivalent to an imperative algorithm. We thus consider a deterministic language model to be suitable for our purposes and defer checking of determinism to other tools such as those developed by Chen et al. [8,9].

Since FFL includes the potential for run-time errors such as out-of-bound array accesses but does not include an explicit error term, the step-relation $\Rightarrow_{bs}$ is not total. The absence of an explicit error term also has the consequence that one cannot distinguish between non-termination and runtime errors according to the definition of program equivalence in Definition 2.

The introduction of the semantics relation allows us to define a notion of program equivalence for FFL terms.

Definition 2. *Two well-typed* FFL *terms* s *and* t *are called* equivalent *if they (a) are of the same type* τ *and (b) evaluate to the same values* v. *We write* $s \cong_\tau t$ *in this case. Using* $\vdash t : \tau$ *to denote that the closed* FFL *term* t *has type* τ, *this definition can be formalized as follows:*

$$
s \cong_\tau t \quad := \quad \begin{aligned} &\vdash s : \tau \wedge \vdash t : \tau \wedge \\ &\forall v. (s \Rightarrow_{bs} v) \Leftrightarrow (t \Rightarrow_{bs} v) \end{aligned} \tag{1}
$$

This definition of program equivalence also enforces *mutual termination* [11], i.e., the property that equivalent programs either both terminate or both diverge. In particular, two non-terminating terms of the same type are equivalent.

fold($\lambda sum. \lambda i.$
    write($sum, i, xs[i] + ys[i]$),
    replicate($n, 0$),
    range($0, n$))

snd(iter($\lambda(i, sum).$
    if $i < n$
    then inr $(i + 1,$
        write($sum, i, xs[i] + ys[i]$))
    else inl unit,
    $(0, $replicate$(n, 0))))$

(a)   (b)

Fig. 3. Translation of function SumArrays (see Fig. 2) into FFL using fold and iter (where inl and inr denote the left and right injection into a sumtype).

Example 1. Figure 3 shows two transformations of the function SumArrays (see Fig. 2) into FFL. In Fig. 3 (a), the loop is translated using fold, and in Fig. 3 (b) using the more general iter. In both cases, it can be observed that the local variables i and sum become λ-bound variables of the translation of the enclosing block, in this case the loop body.

The first translation has the initial state replicate($n, 0$), an array of length n with all values set to 0, and it iterates over the indices in the array ($[0; 1; \dots; n - 1]$), updating the array sum in each iteration using the *write* function of the McCarthy theory of arrays.

The translation in Fig. 3(b) starts from the initial loop state $(0, $replicate$(n, 0))$. In each iteration, an *if*-clause is used to check if the loop condition still evaluates to *true*. If that is the case, the index is incremented and *sum* is updated, otherwise the program exits the loop as indicated by inl unit and evaluates to the current loop state.

3   Program Transformations

With the reduction of imperative and *MapReduce* implementations to the common language FFL, we are able to prove equivalence between two programs by constructing a chain of single, isolated program transformations. We categorize the transformations by their dependence on the surrounding context. A *context-independent* transformation is an uniform transformation as it replaces only one isolated subterm in the program by an equivalent term. This replacement has no effects on other parts of the program and has only conditions on the replaced subterm. In contrast, *context-dependent* transformations do not replace individual terms but require many small changes throughout different parts of the programs.

For example, consider the IL programs in Fig. 2. In the left IL program, the loop iterates over two separate arrays xs and ys of the same length. In the right IL program, the loop iterates over a single array that represents the *zipped* version of xs and ys. Inspection of the FFL versions from Fig. 3 shows that a program transformation unifying both programs requires two changes to individual subterms: (a) the initial loop state, and (b) adaption of the read and write references.

We use two complementary techniques for proving the correctness of a transformation depending on whether it is context-independent or context-dependent: The equivalence of programs related by context-independent transformations is proven using rewrite rules (Sect. 3.1) while the equivalence of programs related by context-dependent transformation is shown using coupling predicates (Sect. 3.2).

$$\text{fold}(\lambda acc.\, \lambda x.\, f(acc, g(x)), \qquad \text{fold}(\lambda acc.\, \lambda y.\, f(acc, y),$$
$$i, \qquad\qquad\qquad \leftrightsquigarrow \qquad i,$$
$$xs) \qquad\qquad\qquad\qquad \text{map}(g, xs))$$

Side conditions: $acc \notin FV(f), x \notin FV(f), y \notin FV(f), x \notin FV(g), acc \notin FV(g)$

Fig. 4. Rewrite rule for separating a loop body into two functions f and g such that the evaluation of g is independent of all other iterations and can be computed in parallel. $FV(g)$ is the set of free, unbound variables in the term g.

3.1   Handling Context-Independent Transformations Using Rewrite Rules

Intermediate programs are mostly linked by uniform context-independent transformations on isolated subterms. Instead of performing and proving these local transformations manually, we can capture them into generalized rewrite rules. That equivalence is preserved when these generalized rewrite rules are applied, needs to be proven only once. By maintaining and using a collection of local transformations that have been proven correct, we can lower proof complexity and later increase the computer assistance and automation.

A rewrite rule describes a bidirectional program transformation that allows the replacement of a subterm within a program. It is composed of two patterns and a set of side conditions which are sufficient for the transformation to preserve program equivalence. A pattern is an FFL term containing metavariables.

To apply a rewrite rule on a program, we have to identify a subterm of the program that (a) matches the first pattern and (b) satisfies the side conditions. The transformed program is obtained by the instantiation of the other pattern with the matched metavariables. Since the sets of bound metavariables in the two patterns can be different, some metavariables may not be uniquely instantiated, leading to a degree of freedom in the translation. We will discuss the practical implications of this in Sect. 4.3.

While there is no hard limit on the complexity of the side conditions that can be part of rewrite rules, it is desirable to use side conditions that are simple and easy to check. This prevents the application of rewrite rules from producing auxiliary complex proofs due to complex side conditions. In our experiments we only encountered the following three different kinds of side conditions:

1. Two arrays xs and ys have the same length, i.e., $\mathsf{length}(xs) \cong_{\mathrm{int}} \mathsf{length}(ys)$.
2. t is not stuck.
3. $x \notin FV(t)$ where $FV(t)$ is the set of free variables in the term t.

Section 4.3 discusses how these side conditions could be discharged automatically.

To illustrate the kind of rewrite rules used in the equivalence proofs described in this paper, we present two of the most commonly used rewrite rules in detail. To demonstrate the feasibility of formal correctness proofs for rewrite rules, we have proven the correctness of most (10 out of 13 rules) of our rules in *Coq*. A full listing of all FFL rewrite rules can be found in the long version of this paper [2]. The first rule, shown in Fig. 4, decomposes the loop body of a `fold` expression into two separate functions f and g, where g is independent of other iterations. Thus, g can be computed in parallel using a `map` operation. This rewrite rule illustrates that rewrite rules used in proofs can often also function as guidelines for parallelizing and distributing imperative algorithms.

The second rule, shown in Fig. 5, is similar to the previous rule in that it tries to separate independent parts of the loop body so that they can be executed in parallel. However, in this case, the part that is extracted is only independent of other iterations that access different indices. The `group` operation can be used to group all accesses to the same index. Using `map` one can then calculate the new values for each index in xs in parallel and update ys with those new values.

$$\mathsf{fold}(\lambda acc.\,\lambda(i,x). \\ \quad \mathsf{write}(acc,i,f(i,x,acc[i])), \\ \quad ys, \\ \quad xs) \qquad \leadsto \qquad \begin{aligned} &\mathsf{fold}(\lambda acc.\,\lambda(i,v).\,\mathsf{write}(acc,i,v), \\ &ys, \\ &\mathsf{map}(\lambda(i,vs). \\ &\quad (i,\mathsf{fold}(\lambda x'.\,\lambda x.\,f(i,x,x'),ys[i],vs)), \\ &\quad \mathsf{group}(xs))) \end{aligned}$$

Side conditions: $acc \notin FV(f), x \notin FV(f), x' \notin FV(f), i \notin FV(f), vs \notin FV(f)$

Fig. 5. Rewrite rule for grouping loop iterations which access the same index of an array.

3.2 Handling Context-Dependent Transformations Using Coupling Predicates

While context-independent transformations are nicely handled using rewrite rules, context-dependent transformations can usually not be captured by patterns and simple side conditions. Coupling predicates provide a flexible and effective solution to proving the correctness of context-dependent transformations – at the cost of requiring more user interactions than rewrite rules. The use of coupling predicates is based on the observation that analyzing two loops in lockstep and proving that a relational property, i.e., the coupling predicate, holds after each iteration is sufficient to prove that it holds after the execution of both loops. Figure 6 shows the corresponding coupling invariant rule for `fold`. For the purpose of presentation, we ignore the distinction between syntactic terms and the values to which they evaluate. Besides this rule for `fold`, there is a similar rule for `iter`.

$$\begin{aligned} &\mathcal{C}(i_0,i_0') \\ \wedge\quad &(\forall i,i',j.\,\mathcal{C}(i,i') \implies \mathcal{C}(f(i,xs[j]),f'(i',xs'[j]))) \\ \implies\quad &\mathcal{C}(\mathsf{fold}(f,i_0,xs),\mathsf{fold}(f',i_0',xs')) \end{aligned}$$

Fig. 6. Coupling invariant rule for `fold` for a coupling predicate $\mathcal{C}$. Free variables are implicitly universally quantified.

One compelling example for using coupling predicates is given in the beginning of this section. The presented program transformation is provable equivalent with the coupling invariant rule from Fig. 2. If these arrays are part of the accumulator in a `fold` or `iter`, capturing this transformation by a rule patterns is not possible: While the transformation of the initial accumulator value can be captured using patterns, this is not sufficient since all references to the accumulator in the loop body also need to be updated. These references can be nested arbitrarily deep inside the loop body and there can be arbitrarily many references. This makes it impossible to capture them by a single pattern which can only bind a fixed number of variables and thereby only make a fixed number of transformations. To make matters worse, it is not even sufficient to just transform the loop itself since the loops are not equivalent: the right loop evaluates to two separate arrays while the other evaluates to an array of tuples. It is thus necessary to prove the equivalence of the enclosing terms under the assumption that the loop in one program evaluates to a tuple of two arrays pair(xs, ys) while the other loop evaluates to zip(xs, ys). This assumption can then be proven correct using the coupling predicate stating that this holds after each iteration.

Another commonly found transformation is the removal of unused elements from a tuple representing the loop accumulator. As it was the case for the previous transformation, the loops themselves are not equivalent and it is necessary to prove enclosing terms equivalent using the assumption that the values present in both loop accumulators are equivalent. As before, this assumption can be proven correct using a coupling predicate which states that this holds after each iteration.

4   Transformation Application Strategy

Splitting the translation into a chain of intermediate programs and translating these into FFL leaves us with the problem of proving neighboring programs equivalent. In order to reduce the amount of user interaction required to conduct these basic equivalence proofs, we define an iterative heuristic search strategy to identify the locations within the programs on which the program transformations described in Sect. 3 will be applied. Algorithm 1 depicts this search strategy as pseudocode. First, we use the structural difference operation (Diff, see Sect. 4.1) to identify subterms P' and Q' whose equivalence implies the equivalence of the full programs P and Q. Second, we start an iterative bottom-up process in which we try to prove the equivalence of the subterms P', Q' and their enclosing terms (ProveEquivalent), until we reached the top level programs P and Q. During the bottom-up process, the subterms P' and Q' may be found to be equivalent only in some cases but not in others. But that is fine as long as we are able to prove that the cases in which they are non-equivalent are not relevant in the context in which P' and Q' occur. Thus, we extract the premises under which P' and Q' are equivalent, and bubble them up to the equivalence proof for the parent terms (AddMissingPremises, Widen, see Sect. 4.2) If we arrive at the top-level terms and cannot prove those equivalent, the proof fails.

4.1   Using Congruence Rules to Simplify Proofs

While the difference between neighboring programs in the chain – which are more closely related – tends to be small, the size of these programs can still be large. This complicates interactive proofs for the user, and can also slow down automated proofs. To reduce the complexity, we prove the equivalence of subterms and then use congruence rules to derive the equivalence of the full programs. A concrete example of a congruence rule is shown in Fig. 7a.

```
input  : Two FFL terms P and Q
output : true if P and Q could be proven equivalent
Premises ← {};
(P',Q') ← Diff(P,Q);
repeat
    equivalent? ← ProveEquivalent(P',Q',Premises);
    if equivalent? then
    |   return true;
    else
    |   Premises ← AddMissingPremises(Premises);
    |   (P',Q') ← Widen(P',Q');
    end
until P' = P and Q' = Q;
return false;
```

Algorithm 1. Strategy for individual equivalence proofs between a pair of FFL programs.

We have found that a simple structural comparison (`Diff` in Algorithm 1) is well suited for finding smaller subterms whose equivalence implies the equivalence of the full programs. `Diff` computes the smallest two subterms such that replacing them by placeholders results in identical terms. An example of `Diff` can be seen in Fig. 7b.

(a)

$$\frac{xs \cong_{[\alpha]} ys \qquad i \cong_{\text{Int}} j}{\text{read}(xs,i) \cong_{\alpha} \text{read}(ys,i)}$$

(b)

$$\begin{aligned}
&\texttt{Diff}(\text{fold}(\lambda(x,y).\, x+y, 0, xs),\\
&\qquad\quad \text{fold}(\lambda(x,y).\, y+x, 0, xs))\\
&= (\lambda(x,y).\, x+y, \lambda(x,y).\, y+x)
\end{aligned}$$

Fig. 7. (a) Congruence rule for read (b) Example of applying `Diff`

4.2 Missing Premises and Widening

During the iterative bottom-up process in Algorithm 1, P' and Q' may turn out to be non-equivalent in some cases. The strategy then tries to extract required contextual conditions (premises) that are sufficient to ensure equivalence of P' and Q' (`AddMissingPremises`). In the next step, we try to prove the equivalence of enclosing terms (`Widen`), which contain P' and Q' as subterms. Additionally, in the widening-step, we take care of the generated premises. These have either to be shown to always hold in the context of $\texttt{Widen}(P', Q')$ or in the context of further widening.

These two steps – premise extraction and widening – are commonly required to prove the equivalence of loop bodies. The example in Fig. 8 illustrates this.

```
sum ← 0;                              sum ← 0;
for i ← 0 to n − 1 do                 for i ← 0 to n − 1 do
   │ sum ← sum + xs[i];                  │ zipped ← zip(xs,ys);
   │ xs ← F'(xs,ys);                     │ sum ← sum + fst(zipped[i]);
end                                      │ xs ← F(zipped);
                                      end
```

Fig. 8. Two potentially equivalent IL programs operating on two separate arrays (left) and the result of applying `zip` to these arrays (right). `xs`, `ys` are arrays of length n. `F` and `F'` return arrays of the length of their input.

Applying `Diff` instantiates P' and Q' with the two loop bodies, as they are the topmost non-equal subterms. A coupling invariant implying that the two loops are started in equivalent states is not sufficient to ensure equivalent loop states after execution since `zip` is only defined for arrays of the same length. Thus, the coupling invariant needs to include the premise that `xs` and `ys` are of equal length.

In some cases, additional premises sufficient for proving equivalence can be found by working backward from missing assumptions in failed proofs. In the example above, proving that the program states are equivalent at the end of each loop iteration assuming that they are equivalent at the beginning will fail due to the missing premise that `xs` and `ys` have the same length. We thus add this premise and try to prove the loop bodies equivalent using that premise. If that is successful, we widen the context to enclosing terms. In the outer context, we attempt to prove that the additional premises are satisfied and derive the equivalence of the full loops based on proved coupling invariant.

4.3   Potential for Automation of Proofs Using Rewrite Rules

Since equivalence proofs using rewrite rules are particularly common but also quite repetitive, this section is devoted to their potential for proof automation. A graphical overview of the individual steps can be found in Fig. 9.

1. We perform an approximate matching procedure to generate candidate programs which match the patterns in the rewrite rule.
2. We attempt to prove that these candidates are equivalent to the input programs or otherwise we reject them.
3. We prove that the side conditions hold for these candidates.

By the correctness of the rewrite rule, the candidates are equivalent.

4.3.1   Matching of Rewrite Rules

While automatic rewriting systems have been used in the related context of automatically translating imperative algorithms to *MapReduce* algorithms [21], the specific ways in which rewrite rules are used in our approach brings new challenges as well as simplifications.

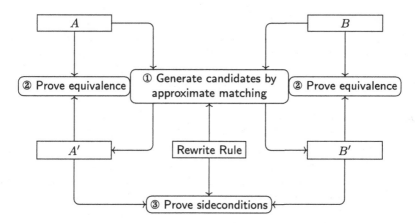

Fig. 9. Workflow for equivalence proofs using rewrite rules. The user has to provide the programs A, A', B, B' and also the rewrite rule. The equivalence proofs ③ are computer-aided in *Coq*.

The challenge lies in the fact that the intermediate programs often do not match the patterns found in rewrite rules directly. There are two typical solutions: normal forms and generalization of patterns. Both are not applicable here. First, there is no suitable normal form of FFL programs. Additionally, both programs are defined by the user, so we cannot assume a specific program structure. Second, the formulation of generalized rewrite rules for matching the large variety of user-defined programs is difficult to obtain and also their correctness proofs are harder to obtain.

The benefit of the programs A, A' (resp. B, B') being provided by the user is that this can reduce ambiguities. In particular, the schematic variables in the two patterns usually overlap to a large degree, but not fully. The matching of the program A against the corresponding pattern can lead to unassigned metavariables, which we need to instantiate with correct choices to prove the equivalence. Now, we have the benefit, that the target program A' is also defined by the user. So, we can obtain missing assignments by matching the other pattern against the other program.

To find the intermediate programs which match the patterns in rewrite rules, an approximate match procedure is used to find assignments for schematic variables in patterns. The approximate matching is an extension of the classical pattern matching with the background knowledge and heuristic of easy-to-prove differences. Applying these assignments to patterns yields candidates for the intermediate program. Once two candidates that match the patterns in a rewrite rule have been identified, it is necessary to prove that (a) the candidates are equivalent to the programs used as the input of the approximate matching procedure, and (b) the side conditions hold and the equivalence of the candidates follows thereby from the correctness of the rewrite rule.

While we have only implemented rudimentary partial automation of the equivalence proof construction, analyzing the *Coq* proofs produced in our experiments has shown that these proofs can be reduced to the correctness of a small number of simple transformations. Proving the correctness of these transformations automatically is feasible and could drastically reduce the need for user interaction.

During our evaluation, one of the most prevalent transformations is *call-by-name beta-reduction* or *lambda abstraction* depending on the direction of the transformation for proving the equivalence (② in Fig. 9). Call-by-name beta-reduction refers to the *beta-reduction* found in programming languages with lazy semantics, which contrary to *call-by-value beta-reduction*, does not evaluate the argument before applying substitution. Since we are working in a call-by-value setting, call-by-name beta-reduction does not always produce an equivalent program. However, the resulting program is equivalent if, for each case where the argument would have been evaluated in the original program, all occurrences in the new program will also be evaluated.

Most other transformations are special cases of constant-folding, e.g., reducing expressions such as $\mathsf{fst}(\mathsf{pair}(a,b))$ to a. Constant-folding does not produce an equivalent program in general if the terms that are being folded are inside the body of a lambda. A sufficient criterion for the resulting program to be equivalent is that the terms being folded are always evaluated.

4.3.2 Proving Side Conditions

In Sect. 3.1 we listed the three different kinds of side conditions used in our rewrite rules. The first of those, $x \notin FV(t)$, is purely syntactical and can easily be checked automatically. While proving that a term is not stuck can be difficult in general, in our experiments this could usually be reduced to the term being a value, which again is a syntactical condition. The third kind of side condition states that two arrays have the same length. This can usually be proven recursively by reduction to operations that produce arrays of a specific length, e.g.,

$$\forall n, a, b.\, \mathsf{length}(\mathsf{replicate}(n, a)) = \mathsf{length}(\mathsf{replicate}(n, b)) \ ,$$

or to length-preserving operations such as map. Note that it can be necessary to strengthen loop invariants to carry this fact through a loop, as explained in Sect. 4.2.

5 Evaluation and Case Study

To demonstrate the feasibility of our approach, we have created a toolchain. The user specifies a sequence of intermediate programs in a simple imperative language. These programs are then automatically translated into a formalization of the previously described functional programming language FFL in *Coq*. In addition to generating proof obligations, our toolchain reduces these obligations using the mentioned structural comparison `Diff`, and it applies congruence rules to reconstruct an equivalence proof of the full programs.

Using this toolchain, we have proven the equivalence of imperative and *MapReduces* implementations of the *PageRank* algorithm [5] and the *k-means* [20] algorithm in *Coq*. An extensive description of the *PageRank* example including all intermediate programs can be found in [3]. Figure 10 shows the imperative and the *MapReduce* implementation of *PageRank* that we have used in our experiments. The *MapReduce* implementation of *PageRank* shown here is deterministic when executed on rational numbers due to commutativity and associativity of addition. However, the algorithm is not deterministic when executed using floating point numbers since addition is not associative in this case. We have not attempted the verification of algorithms based on floating point numbers in this work.

While we have created the imperative implementations of the two algorithms ourselves, the *MapReduce* versions are very close to the implementations accompanying the Thrill [4] framework. This reinforces our claim that FFL is capable of representing *MapReduce* algorithms and is thereby suitable for this approach. In total, the formalization of FFL, the rewrite rules, and proofs of various properties, encompasses about 8000 lines of Coq code. The equivalence proofs of *PageRank* and *k-means* each require about 3700 lines of *Coq* proofs. That includes the automatically generated translation of the chain of equivalent programs (for *k-means* this chain consists of 9 programs while for *PageRank* it consists of 6 programs), which take up large parts of these proofs. The proofs rely on the rewrite rules which we have formalized in *Coq* as well as coupling predicates.

```
Function PageRank(links, numLinks, n)
begin
    ranks ←
        Replicate(numLinks, 1/numLinks );
    for i = 1 to n do
        ranks' ← Replicate(numLinks, 0);
        for p = 0 to numLinks − 1 do
            contrib ← ranks[p]/Length(links[p]) ;
            foreach q ← links[p] do
                ranks'[q] ←
                    ranks'[q] + contrib;
            end
        end
        for p = 0 to numLinks − 1 do
            ranks[p] ←
                Dampen(ranks'[p], numLinks);
        end
    end
    return ranks;
end
```

```
Function PageRank(links, numLinks, n)
begin
    ranks ←
        Replicate(numLinks, 1/numLinks );
    for i = 1 to n do
        outRanks ← Zip(links,ranks);
        contribs ←
            FlatMap(
                λ(ls,r).
                    Map(λl.(l, r/Length(ls) ), ls),
                outRanks);
        rankUpdates ←
            Reduce(+, 0, contribs);
        ranks' ← Replicate(numLinks, 0);
        foreach (l,r) ← rankUpdates do
            ranks'[l] ← r;
        end
        ranks ←
            Map(λr. Dampen(r, numLinks),
                ranks');
    end
    return ranks;
end
```

Fig. 10. Imperative (left) and *MapReduce* (right) versions of the *PageRank* algorithm (the function `Replicate(n, v)` creates an array of length `n` with all elements set to `v`; and `Dampen` is an arbitrary function).

6   Related Work

A common approach to relational verification and program equivalence is the use of product programs [1]. Product programs combine the states of two programs and interleave their behavior in a single program. *RVT* [13] proves the equivalence of C programs by combining them in a product program. By assuming that the program states are equal after each loop iteration, *RVT* avoids the need for user-specified or inferred loop invariants and coupling predicates.

Hawblitzel et al. [15] use a similar technique for handling recursive function calls. Felsing et al. [12] demonstrate that coupling predicates for proving the equivalence of two programs can often be inferred automatically. While the structure of imperative and *MapReduce* algorithms tends to be quite different, splitting the translation into intermediate steps yields programs which are often structurally similar. We have found that in this case, techniques such as coupling predicates arise naturally and are useful for selected parts of an equivalence proof.

Radoi et al. [21] describe an automatic translation of imperative algorithms to *MapReduce* algorithms based on rewrite rules. While the rewrite rules are very similar to the ones used in our approach, we complement rewrite rules by coupling predicates. Furthermore, we are able to prove equivalence for algorithms for which the automatic translation from Radoi et al. is not capable of producing efficient *MapReduce* algorithms. The objective of verification imposes different constraints than the automated translation – in particular, both programs are provided by the user, so there is less flexibility needed in the formulation of rewrite rules.

Chen et al. [7] and Radoi et al. [21] describe languages and sequential semantics for *MapReduce* algorithms. Chen et al. describe an executable sequential specification in the Haskell programming language focusing on capturing nondeterminism correctly. Radoi et al. use a language based on a lambda calculus as the common representation for the previously described translation from imperative to *MapReduce* algorithms. While this language closely resembles the language used in our approach, it lacks support for representing some imperative constructs such as arbitrary *while*-loops.

Grossman et al. [14] verify the equivalence of a restricted subset of Spark programs by reducing the problem of checking program equivalence to the validity of formulas in a decidable fragment of first-order logic. While this approach is fully automatic, it limits programs to Presburger arithmetic and requires that they are synchronized in some way.

To the best of our knowledge, we are the first to propose a framework for proving equivalence of *MapReduce* and imperative programs.

7   Conclusion

We have presented a new approach for proving the equivalence of imperative and *MapReduce* algorithms. This approach relies on splitting the transformation into a chain of intermediate programs. The individual equivalence proofs are then categorized in context-independent and context-dependent transformations. Equivalence proofs for context-independent transformations are handled using rewrite rules, while equivalence proofs for context-dependent transformations are based on coupling predicates. We have demonstrated the feasibility of end-to-end equivalence proofs using this approach by applying it two well-known non-trivial algorithms.

While we have hinted at the potential for automating this approach, implementing automation is left as future work. In particular, it would be interesting to explore whether existing tools for relational verification using coupling predicates can be used or if new tools are necessary. Further future work includes extending the approach presented here to support the full expressiveness provided by languages which are used to implement imperative and *MapReduce* algorithms.

References

1. Barthe, G., Crespo, J.M., Kunz, C.: Relational verification using product programs. In: Butler, M., Schulte, W. (eds.) FM 2011. LNCS, vol. 6664, pp. 200–214. Springer, Heidelberg (2011). https://doi.org/10.1007/978-3-642-21437-0_17
2. Beckert, B., Bingmann, T., Kiefer, M., Sanders, P., Ulbrich, M., Weigl, A.: Relational Equivalence Proofs Between Imperative and MapReduce Algorithms. ArXiv e-prints, January 2018. arXiv:1801.08766
3. Beckert, B., Bingmann, T., Kiefer, M., Sanders, P., Ulbrich, M., Weigl, A.: Proving equivalence between imperative and mapreduce implementations using program transformations. In: Third Workshop Models for Formal Analysis of Real Systems and Sixth International Workshop on Verification and Program Transformation. Electronic Proceedings in Theoretical Computer Science, vol. 268, pp. 185–199. Open Publishing Association (2018)
4. Bingmann, T., et al.: Thrill: high-performance algorithmic distributed batch data processing with C++. In: IEEE International Conference on Big Data, pp. 172–183. IEEE, December 2016. preprint arXiv:1608.05634
5. Brin, S., Page, L.: The anatomy of a large-scale hypertextual web search engine. Comput. Netw. ISDN Syst. **30**(1–7), 107–117 (1998). https://doi.org/10.1016/S0169-7552(98)00110-X
6. Chambers, C., et al.: FlumeJava: easy, efficient data-parallel pipelines. ACM SIGPLAN Notices **45**(6), 363–375 (2010)
7. Chen, Y.F., Hong, C.D., Lengál, O., Mu, S.C., Sinha, N., Wang, B.Y.: An Executable Sequential Specification for Spark Aggregation (2017). arXiv:1702.02439
8. Chen, Y.-F., Hong, C.-D., Sinha, N., Wang, B.-Y.: Commutativity of reducers. In: Baier, C., Tinelli, C. (eds.) TACAS 2015. LNCS, vol. 9035, pp. 131–146. Springer, Heidelberg (2015). https://doi.org/10.1007/978-3-662-46681-0_9
9. Chen, Y., Song, L., Wu, Z.: The Commutativity Problem of the MapReduce Framework: A Transducer-based Approach. CoRR abs/1605.01497 (2016). arXiv:1605.01497
10. Dean, J., Ghemawat, S.: MapReduce: simplified data processing on large clusters. Commun. ACM **51**(1), 107–113 (2008)
11. Elenbogen, D., Katz, S., Strichman, O.: Proving mutual termination. Form. Methods Syst. Des. **47**(2), 204–229 (2015). https://doi.org/10.1007/s10703-015-0234-3

12. Felsing, D., Grebing, S., Klebanov, V., Rümmer, P., Ulbrich, M.: Automating regression verification. In: Proceedings of the 29th ACM/IEEE International Conference on Automated Software Engineering, pp. 349–360. ASE 2014. ACM, New York, NY, USA (2014)
13. Godlin, B., Strichman, O.: Regression verification. In: Proceedings of the 46th Annual Design Automation Conference, pp. 466–471. DAC 2009. ACM, New York, NY, USA (2009)
14. Grossman, S., Cohen, S., Itzhaky, S., Rinetzky, N., Sagiv, M.: Verifying equivalence of spark programs. In: Majumdar, R., Kunčak, V. (eds.) CAV 2017. LNCS, vol. 10427, pp. 282–300. Springer, Cham (2017). https://doi.org/10.1007/978-3-319-63390-9_15
15. Hawblitzel, C., Kawaguchi, M., Lahiri, S., Rebêlo, H.: Mutual summaries: unifying program comparison techniques. In: Informal proceedings of BOOGIE 2011 workshop (2011). https://www.microsoft.com/en-us/research/publication/mutual-summaries-unifying-program-comparison-techniques/
16. Kahn, G.: Natural semantics. STACS **87**, 22–39 (1987)
17. Kiefer, M., Klebanov, V., Ulbrich, M.: Relational program reasoning using compiler IR - combining static verification and dynamic analysis. J. Autom. Reason. (2017)
18. Klebanov, V., Rümmer, P., Ulbrich, M.: Automating regression verification of pointer programs by predicate abstraction. J. Formal Methods Syst. Des. **52**, 229–259 (2017)
19. Lahiri, S.K., Hawblitzel, C., Kawaguchi, M., Rebêlo, H.: SYMDIFF: a language-agnostic semantic diff tool for imperative programs. In: Madhusudan, P., Seshia, S.A. (eds.) CAV 2012. LNCS, vol. 7358, pp. 712–717. Springer, Heidelberg (2012). https://doi.org/10.1007/978-3-642-31424-7_54
20. Lloyd, S.: Least squares quantization in PCM. IEEE Trans. Inf. Theor. **28**(2), 129–137 (1982). https://doi.org/10.1109/TIT.1982.1056489
21. Radoi, C., Fink, S.J., Rabbah, R., Sridharan, M.: Translating Imperative Code to MapReduce. SIGPLAN Not. **49**(10), 909–927 (2014)
22. The Coq development team: The Coq proof assistant reference manual. LogiCal Project, version 8.6 (2004). http://coq.inria.fr
23. Verdoolaege, S., Janssens, G., Bruynooghe, M.: Equivalence checking of static affine programs using widening to handle recurrences. ACM Trans. Program. Lang. Syst. **34**(3), 11:1–11:35 (2012). https://doi.org/10.1145/2362389.2362390
24. White, T.: Hadoop: The Definitive Guide. O'Reilly Media Inc., Sebastopol (2012)
25. Zaharia, M., Chowdhury, M., Franklin, M.J., Shenker, S., Stoica, I.: Spark: cluster computing with working sets. In: Proceedings of the 2nd USENIX Conference on Hot Topics in Cloud Computing, pp. 10–10. HotCloud 2010, USENIX Association, Berkeley, CA, USA (2010). http://dl.acm.org/citation.cfm?id=1863103.1863113

Practical Methods for Reasoning About Java 8's Functional Programming Features

David R. Cok$^{(\boxtimes)}$ and Serdar Tasiran

Amazon Web Services, Seattle, USA
{davidcok,tasirans}@amazon.com

Abstract. We describe new capabilities added to the Java Modeling Language and the OpenJML deductive program verification tool to support functional programming features introduced in Java 8. We also report on the application of the extensions to a secure streaming protocol library developed by Amazon Web Services and used as a foundation by services it provides. We found that the application under study used a small set of functional programming idioms; methods using these idioms could be verified by techniques that used only first-order logic and did not need all the features that might be required for full generality of functional programming.

1 Introduction

Java 8 introduced functional programming features to Java, permitting a functional programming (FP) style along with Java's imperative style. The features discussed in this work are function literals, functional interfaces, and implicit iteration in the Stream API. Verification of programs using these features requires new specification syntax in the Java Modeling Language (JML) and new proof techniques implemented in OpenJML. Nominally, reasoning about functions as first-class objects could require higher-order logic, instead of the first-order logic used in many current program verification tools. The authors faced this problem in applying the OpenJML deductive verification tool to an important Java security protocol library developed by Amazon Web Services (AWS).

We hypothesized that most use of Java 8 FP in practice follows a small set of functional programming patterns. We identified three such patterns, developed constructs in JML for specifying code that uses these FP patterns, and built support for verifying such specifications in OpenJML, while remaining within the existing first-order logic paradigm and the capabilities of SMT automated tools. OpenJML with support for these features was sufficient for us to successfully verify the AWS library, which consisted of some 5K lines of Java 8 code. We discuss the extensions to JML and OpenJML needed to perform deductive verification for these Java 8 FP patterns and our experience applying these to the AWS security protocol library. The enhanced version of OpenJML can be

© Springer Nature Switzerland AG 2018
R. Piskac and P. Rümmer (Eds.): VSTTE 2018, LNCS 11294, pp. 267–278, 2018.
https://doi.org/10.1007/978-3-030-03592-1_15

found at https://www.openjml.org; the GPLv2-licensed source code is available from the github repository at https://github.com/OpenJML/OpenJML.

2   Deductive Verification, the Java Modeling Language and the OpenJML Tool

Deductive verification (DV) is a technique in which software code and formal requirements are each translated into a logical form and then *automatically* and statically checked that the implementation conforms to the specification. Automation is critically important for the technique to become widespread and for efficiency in application. Thus we do not consider tools that translate into interactive proof environments. For the Java software under study, we used the Java Modeling Language (JML) to express specifications and OpenJML as the DV tool.

JML [4,19] is a language for specifying behavior of (non-concurrent) Java source code. Its syntax and semantics are similar to its host programming language, Java, with extensions appropriate to expressing assertions in a typed first-order logic appropriate to reasoning about software. JML is largely method-centric, with syntax to write pre-, frame- and post-conditions for each method, along with object invariants and other advanced features. JML is widely used in education about software specification and as a platform for research and experimentation in specification and reasoning about software.

An example of JML is given in Fig. 1. Syntacticly, JML specifications are written as structured Java comments (beginning with //@ or /*@). The method specification is expressed as a sequence of *clauses*: the *requires* clause is a pre-condition, *assignable* denotes a frame-condition, *ensures* a post-condition, and *signals* the post-condition on throwing an exception. Accompanying tools perform both static checking and runtime assertion checking using the JML specifications.

JML is similar in purpose and structure to other *Behavioral Interface Specification Languages* [11]; other examples are later languages such as ACSL for C programs [3], Spec# for C# [23], SPARK for Ada [15], and Dafny [14]; JML was designed using experience with the Larch tools [10] and with Eiffel [16]. The KeY tool [1] is also a program verification tool for Java, but addresses only the pre-generics (Java 4) subset of Java.

OpenJML [5–8,21] is a tool built on the OpenJDK [20] Java compiler; it translates both Java and JML into a logical form, eventually into SMT-LIB [2,22] and uses back-end SMT solvers to check whether method implementations and specifications are consistent.

Related Work. Our work builds on JML and on the OpenJML program verification tool. Like many other such tools, OpenJML translates the program and its specifications into a logical form and then uses an SMT solver (in our case, Z3 [9]) to check the logical verification conditions. Many other languages and associated program verification tools have supported functional programming for some time; examples are F*, Dafny, Leon, the Verifast tool for C programs,

C#, and Scala. Some proof systems, such as Coq and Isabelle, are partially inter-active, whereas OpenJML and most SMT-based tools aim for full automation, given program annotations. Kassios and Müller [13] showed first-order solutions to the general case of FP features; here we achieved practical program verifica-tion with simpler techniques. Unno et al. [18] describe how to infer the types we use for Specification Interfaces.

Our enhanced OpenJML reported here is unique in addressing the combina-tion of functional and imperative programming in Java, a widely used language, using techniques that build on existing verification technology. To some extent FP techniques could have been used within Java prior to Java 8, such as with object-oriented callbacks. However, such uses were not common. Now that FP is explicitly part of Java 8, programmers, such as the authors of the code used in our case study, are much more likely to use it extensively, making the speci-fication language and tool enhancements reported in this paper timely.

```
1 //@ requires i != Integer.MIN_VALUE;
2 //@ assignable \nothing;
3 //@ ensures \result >= 0 && (\result == i || \result == -i);
4 //@ signals (Exception e) false;
5 int abs(int i);
```

Fig. 1. Example JML specification of an absolute-value method

3   Verifying Java's FP Features

We observed that the uses of FP in the software under study consisted of three code patterns: (a) functional arguments that use general Java library interface types, (b) function literals as actual arguments, and (c) Stream objects and operations. These are discussed below, along with four techniques we developed that enable verification of these FP patterns.

Figure 2 shows examples of Java 8's FP features, modeled after code in the library, and discussed below.

3.1   Overly General Function Types

The first specification challenge is shown in Fig. 2(A). Here a function literal (a lambda expression) is the actual argument (line 7) in a call to a method whose body (line 5) applies the function to compute the method's effect. Program verification tools such as OpenJML work modularly. The implementation of each method is verified with respect to its specification, using only the specifications of called methods to model their effects. The method `modify` takes a `Function` argument. This argument type gives little information about `modify`'s argument, since `Function` and similar Java library function interfaces must necessarily have very general specifications. Thus, considering `modify` by itself, we can specify very little about its behavior, because we know very little about the argument

```
1  // Example A
2    // Function declaration with a FunctionalInterface parameter
3    int value;
4    void modify(Function<Integer,Integer> map)
5                              { value = map.apply(value); }
6    // Using the declaration above
7    { ... ;  modify( x->x+1 );   ... }
8
9  // Example B -- like Example A, but with a local variable
10   Function<Integer,Boolean> f = x->hasProperty(x);
11   if (f.apply(k)) ...
12
13 // Example C -- Stream API
14   boolean noNulls=true; void check(Object v) {noNulls = noNulls&&(v!=null);}
15   Stream<Object> s = ...; s.forEachOrdered(v -> check(v));
```

Fig. 2. Characteristic uses of FP features - function literals and Stream operations

map. The core issue in this first use pattern is that too much type information is lost when the formal argument has the general `Function` type. Local variable declarations (e.g., Fig. 2(B)) cause the same information loss.

In line 7, the argument of `modify` is a lambda expression (x -> x + 1). However, to reason about the effect of the lambda expression using existing OpenJML-style modular reasoning we need a specification of its effect. So the second, related syntactic challenge is that there is no place (in pre-Java-8 JML) to put a specification for lambda expressions. For this example, one could infer a specification, but in general the body of the lambda expression is an arbitrary block of code.

We devised and implemented three techniques to meet these two challenges.

Inlining `FunctionalInterface` Parameters. First we note that in this example the actual argument to `modify` is a function literal (line 7) (our second use pattern in the list at the beginning of this section). If the body of `modify` is available as source code, then the call to `modify` can be replaced by an inlined version of its body, with the actual arguments, in particular, the function literal, substituted and expanded. The call of `modify` then becomes simply `value = value + 1`, which is easily handled by existing verification techniques. Thus our first technique for handling type information loss is to inline the called method, avoiding the conversion to the general `Function` type. This technique works when the called method's body is available, is reasonably small, and any actual arguments of `FunctionalInterface` types are function literals. It can be used when the method does not have a specification. Inlining does not generate any new proof obligations and can avoid needing any specifications at all for the called method. Thus it is also a useful technique for small methods, such as getter and setter methods, independent of functional programming considerations. There are no new proof obligations because the body of the method is being used as its own specification, and so of course the specification and implementation are consistent.

JML Model Programs. Inlining a method body breaks modularity because it relies on knowing the body of called methods. If the called method is in a library, the body may not even be available. We devised a second technique that uses JML's *model programs*. A model program is an alternate specification syntax in which a method's behavior is specified using Java-like statements that abstract the effect of the method. We extended the model program syntax to allow more statements and in a more usable manner. The `modify` method is specified as

```
1  //@ public normal_behavior
2  //@   { value = map.apply(value); }
3  public void modify(Function<Integer,Integer> map);
```

In this example, the model program, which is the text within the braces, happens to duplicate the body of the method. In the more common case, it is a simplification or abstraction of the body. For instance, if we did not care about the final `value`, just that there were no other side-effects, we could write

```
1  //@ public normal_behavior
2  //@   { havoc value; } // changes value to an unspecified int
3  void modify(Function<Integer,Integer> map);
```

Here the `havoc` statement states that its argument, `value`, might change to some arbitrary value; since `value` is the only field listed, nothing else changes. So in this technique, a method is given a model program specification; where the method is called, the model program is inlined in place of the call, along with asserting or assuming any other specification clauses. This preserves modularity because we are only using the specification. Model programs work best when there is a succinct summary of the method being specified, as in this example.

Model programs are just another form of method specification. Thus there is a proof obligation that the model program, along with other specification clauses, matches the implementation. As model programs are more expressive, such proof obligations are typically more complicated than for specifications consisting of standard clauses. However, a model program is just a sequence of statements and can be translated just as the implementation is translated. So the translation of the model program uses the same infrastructure as translation of Java statements, albeit with some additional model-program-specific statements to be translated.

The extension to JML consisted of allowing model programs as simply another clause, written as a block of statements, with beginning and ending braces, along with relevant proof obligations. Previously model programs were a separate behavior type.

Specification with Model Interfaces. The above techniques apply in many cases and simplify the verification engine's work. But the core problem is that the type of function objects is usually too general. To solve that problem we insert a specification type that is more specific than the Java type (our third technique). For example, suppose it is required that all arguments of `modify` have a positive argument and produce a positive result, with no side effects. The specification for such a method can be encapsulated in an interface like this:

```
1  interface PositivePureFunction extends Function<Integer,Integer> {
2    //@ requires i > 0;
3    //@ assignable \nothing;
4    //@ ensures \result > 0;
5    Integer apply(Integer i);
6  }
```

So far these specifications are classic JML. In order to insert the new type as the type of a parameter (without changing non-comment Java source), we extended JML syntax as follows:

```
1  void modify(/*@{ PositivePureFunction }@*/  Function<Integer,Integer> map);
2
3  // also in a local declaration:
4  /*@{ PositivePureFunction }@*/  Function<Integer,Integer> f = ...
```

Here the type named within the new JML construct `/*@{...}@*/` (which is a Java comment) is the type to be used within specifications; the Java type is unchanged. Our extension enables such syntax in any declaration. Using such a specification type creates a *type checking* obligation that the specification type is indeed a subtype of the stated Java type. Also this new specification syntax has two new effects on proof obligations.

- First, the actual argument must be shown to meet the specification stated by the specification type of the formal argument. In the running example, the lambda expression `x -> x + 1` must be shown to obey the specifications for `apply` in `PositivePureFunction`.
- Second, when proving properties of the body of a method, the formal argument may be assumed to have the specification type and obey its specification, not just the more general Java type.

Note that the design of JML ensures that derived classes or interfaces are by definition behavioral subtypes because specifications are inherited. Thus the substitution principle automatically holds (if implementations conform to specifications). Though other syntax for specifying the behavior of Java functional objects could be designed, the syntax proposed here best fits with current JML syntax and with the style used by other BISLs.

3.2   Implicit Iteration

The third use pattern is the Stream API illustrated in Fig. 2(C). Here, a function with side effects is applied to a stream of values, with the iteration implicit. Operations on Java 8's Stream objects typically operate on each element of the stream. Imperative code would write such operations with explicit loops. Traditional specification paradigms, including JML and OpenJML, require loop invariants to state properties and reason about the effects of iteration. Stream operations pose two problems: (1) there are no explicit loops to which to attach loop invariants, and (2) existing JML syntax cannot express sufficiently strong specifications of Stream operations to enable successful verification. Our fourth technique is a means to address this combination of problems.

Specifying Stream Operations with Model Programs. Note though that Stream operations are typically very simple. For example, `forEachOrdered` in Fig. 2(C) is a Java library method that just applies the given function to each Stream element in turn. `forEachOrdered` can be specified using our enhanced JML model program syntax, where the model program contains an equivalent explicit loop with loop specifications and is inlined as part of verification. We have added such specifications to our Java system library specifications for `forEachOrdered` and other methods needed for this project. It is a task for future work to expand the system library specifications to be sufficient for general use. Here `count()` is a Java method giving the total number of elements in the stream; `\count` is a JML token denoting the number seen so far.

```
1  /*@  { loop_invariant i==\count && 0<=i && i<=this.count();
2           loop_modifies i;
3           for (int i = 0; i<this.count(); i++)
4                consumer.accept(this.values[i]);
5       } @*/
6  void forEachOrdered(Consumer<? super T> consumer);
```

This specification of `forEachOrdered` is provided by our enhanced OpenJML along with the Java library. However, it is independent of the context in which it is used and of `consumer`'s action; we need something more specific at the call site, as discussed next.

Reasoning About Implicit Iteration. In Fig. 2(C), `forEachOrdered` is used to accumulate the value `noNulls`, which states whether all stream elements so far are not null. Our partial specification of this example is shown next:

```
1  boolean noNulls = true;
2  //@ assignable noNulls;
3  //@ ensures noNulls == (\old(noNulls) && (v != null));
4  void check(Object v) { noNulls = noNulls && (v != null); }
5
6  s.forEachOrdered(v -> check(v));
7  //@ assert noNulls==(\forall int i; 0<=i&&i<s.count(); s.values[i]!=null);
```

Now we would like to establish the assertion on line 7, that `noNulls` is true if all stream elements are non-null. In addition to the library specifications, we need loop properties containing aspects of the user's code. In the solution we devised, we write

```
1  //@ loop_invariant noNulls==(\forall int j; 0<=j&&j<\count; s.values[j]!=null);
2  //@ loop_modifies noNulls;
3  //@ inlined_loop;
4  s.forEachOrdered(v -> check(v));
```

Note that the loop properties in lines 1–2 can only be stated in the calling program at the call site. The `inlined_loop` directive instructs the enhanced OpenJML (a) to inline the model program in `forEachOrdered`'s specification and the lambda expression `v -> check(v)` to produce the combined Java code (line 4 below) and (b) to combine the loop specifications in the model program and the user's loop properties to produce the effective specification in lines 1–3, enabling the proof of the assertion on line 5.

```
1 //@ loop_invariant i==\count && 0<=i && i<=s.count();
2 //@ loop_invariant noNulls==(\forall int j; 0<=j&&j<\count; s.values[j]!=null);
3 //@ loop_modifies noNulls, i;
4 for (int i = 0; i<s.count(); i++) check(s.values[i]);
5 //@ assert noNulls==(\forall int j; 0<=j&&j<s.count(); s.values[j]!=null);
```

So in the technique we devised, we have converted the implicit iteration verification problem into one that existing OpenJML can handle by combining a general library method specification with specific call site loop specifications.

4   Our Experience with a Case Study

4.1   Case Study Artifact

The subject of the case study is an implementation of a secure streaming communication protocol that underpins much of the communication between distributed components in Amazon and AWS (e.g., AWS's Kinesis service). The software was a useful target for the case study in this paper for several reasons. First, it was developed without deductive verification as a concern, and consequently it is an instance of legacy code implementing a design that was not affected by any constraints of a verification system. Second, it implements a secure communication protocol that is important to get right. Third, it is highly used and customers have expressed a desire for infrastructure software of this kind to be made publicly available along with demonstrations of its correctness. And fourth, the software uses Java 8 and thus is a test bed for verification technology that applies to both imperative and functional programming styles.

This code is not yet publicly available, as it is Amazon proprietary code. We are pursuing open-sourcing this code. It is particularly interesting that our open-sourcing efforts are driven by requests of some key particularly security-conscious AWS customers (e.g., military and financial). They are requesting that we open-source the code with our proofs, to help them understand and audit how we establish security on their behalf. This is why AWS previously open-sourced the TLS implementation s2n for example. Our proof activities are becoming a major asset for building customer trust.

4.2   Implementation

We used our enhanced OpenJML to verify this Java security protocol library developed by AWS. The library enables establishing secure network communication sessions and composing and decomposing the packet frames that constitute network messages. OpenJML was extended to be able to parse and type-check Java 8 syntax. Then, as described above, OpenJML was augmented

- to handle the logical interpretation of Java 8 features,
- to be able to inline the source code bodies of Java methods,
- to implement the syntax and semantics of enhanced JML model programs,
- to implement the syntax and semantics of specification types, and
- to implement the additions for verifying implicit iteration.

The properties checked for each method include all the behavioral properties needed to verify its use by calling methods. These include typical properties such as the absence of runtime errors, but also that, for example, output arrays contain the data that is expected given the inputs. At the top level of the library we used some example and test programs to verify that example end-to-end uses of the library performed as expected. We did not verify any features using multi-threaded execution, because that is not yet supported by JML (or Open-JML). All loops are checked for termination, but there is no automated check for termination of recursion. However a manual review shows only a single case of recursion in the library.

4.3 Observations

The source code under scrutiny consisted of about 5K lines of Java code across about 700 methods in 96 classes in 11 Java packages. The library was written well before this project and without any design for specification and verification. The specification task took about a person-month of effort and required about 5K lines of specification; verification requires about 16 h CPU time. After the informal observation that the techniques described in this paper handled all the FP uses in the library, we analyzed the FP patterns used:

(a) 20% of the methods contained at least one FP feature;
(b) a manual count identified 230 individual instances of FP features;
(c) 50% of FP uses consisted of function object literals, which in every case could be inlined for verification purposes;
(d) another 44% were instances of general functional formal parameters or return types; where needed these were specified by specification interface types; and
(e) the other 6% were uses of Stream operations.

Thus, the augmented OpenJML supports deductive program verification of all uses of FP-style code in this library. FP with unconstrained side-effects would be as difficult to verify as programs containing unconstrained callbacks; both would pose additional challenges to specification languages and verification technology. But the FP code under study was written in good FP style: methods were small, methods typically had no side-effects, objects were typically immutable, and exceptions were used only for error reporting and not for control-flow. In this context our set of solutions worked well. Though another programming style might emphasize a different mix of features, we expect that this basic set will be commonly used.

The work reported here focussed on verifying the FP features in the library. About 12% of the library's methods require as yet unimplemented non-FP features having to do with enums, maps, inner classes and concurrency. This remaining implementation and verification is currently in progress.

Note that when using a library (such as the Java system library) that has specifications, a client of the library simply uses the specifications. Those specifications do need to be shown to be self-consistent and the library implementation does need to be shown to conform to the specification, but that is not a task for the library client.

Although more general uses of FP features were not found in this in-the-wild software, it certainly is possible to write Java FP code that goes beyond the features that we found to be most prevalent. Consequently, we are in the process of implementing a general handling of methods that produce function objects as results and whose specifications depend on the specifications of function objects that are arguments to the method. In this we are following the work of Kassios and Müller mentioned above [13] and noting that of Kanig and Filliâtre [12].

A verification is only as strong as the properties that are verified. In this work, the specifications of lower-level methods are proved consistent with their own implementations but also are strong enough to verify routines that call those methods. At the top levels of the library, we chose a few example programs that exercise the library's end-to-end functionality and whose correctness depends on the correctness and strength of the specifications of the library components. Some aspects were left intentionally underspecified: for example, the human-readable content of error messages was not specified or verified, just the fact that errors were reported under the appropriate circumstances.

5   Conclusion

We identified a set of FP coding patterns that were used in an independently written Java library, implemented corresponding enhancements to JML and OpenJML, and successfully verified the FP code within a 5K-line networking library. We hypothesize that other FP-style Java software will also mostly use a constrained set of FP features, simplifying the task of implementing support in Java software analysis tools and enabling practical (industrial) program verification without full support of all language features. Our work was based on a real-world, moderate sized software library, but so far just on one; planned work on other software artifacts will determine to what extent our initial hypotheses will need to be extended and what additional proof techniques are in fact needed.

In the current state of the art, writing specifications sufficient for verifying behavioral properties can still require significant manual effort. It is certainly helpful in achieving correctness that the proof of consistency itself is automated using SMT solvers. Despite the manual effort, specifications (independent of the code) are essential to proving behavioral correctness; without specifications one can at best determine that a set of software does not result in runtime errors or violate any other implicit language issues. The usability issue of writing specifications is being partially addressed by separate, independent work on automated specification inference (e.g., [17]); however, there will always be the need to review specifications to ensure they match the informal expectations of a program. Specifications can also be verbose. That verbosity can also be addressed by specification inference and appropriate defaults. These usability issues were set aside in this project as future work that will be informed by our experience here.

Thus some of the topics for immediate work are these:

- completing the features needed to have a full verification of the target library
- further verification case studies to extend the results here and as further data to design improved usability
- generalizing the handling of function objects.

Tasks for future longer-term activities include the following:

- reducing the specification writing effort using specification inference
- implementing usability improvements to specification verbosity
- identifying specification idioms particularly useful for FP features
- extending the specifications of FP-centric features in the Java system library
- verifying the specifications for Java system library methods against actual implementations of the library.

References

1. Ahrendt, W., Beckert, B., Bubel, R., Hähnle, R., Schmitt, P.H., Ulbrich, M. (eds.): Deductive Software Verification - The KeY Book: From Theory to Practice, vol. 10001. Springer, Heidelberg (2016). https://doi.org/10.1007/978-3-319-49812-6
2. Barrett, C., Stump, A., Tinelli, C.: The SMT-LIB standard: version 2.0. In: Gupta, A., Kroening, D. (eds.) Proceedings of the 8th International Workshop on Satisfiability Modulo Theories, Edinburgh, England (2010)
3. Baudin, P., Filliâtre, J.C., Marché, C., Monate, B., Moy, Y., Prevosto, V.: ACSL: ANSI/ISO C Specification Language, version 1.10 (2013). http://frama-c.cea.fr/acsl.html
4. Burdy, L., et al.: An overview of JML tools and applications. In: Thomas, A., Wan F. (eds.) Eighth International Workshop on Formal Methods for Industrial Critical Systems (FMICS 2003). Electronic Notes in Theoretical Computer Science (ENTCS), vol. 80, pp. 73–89. Elsevier, June 2003
5. Cok, D.: Improved usability and performance of SMT solvers for debugging specifications. STTT **12**, 467–481 (2010)
6. Cok, D.R.: OpenJML: JML for Java 7 by extending OpenJDK. In: Bobaru, M., Havelund, K., Holzmann, G.J., Joshi, R. (eds.) NFM 2011. LNCS, vol. 6617, pp. 472–479. Springer, Heidelberg (2011). https://doi.org/10.1007/978-3-642-20398-5_35
7. Cok, D.R.: OpenJML: software verification for Java 7 using JML, OpenJDK, and Eclipse. In: Workshop on Formal Integrated Development Environment (F-IDE 2014). EPTCS, vol. 149, pp. 79–92, 06 April 2014, Grenoble, France (2014)
8. Cok, D.R., Kiniry, J.R.: ESC/Java2: uniting ESC/Java and JML. In: Barthe, G., Burdy, L., Huisman, M., Lanet, J.-L., Muntean, T. (eds.) CASSIS 2004. LNCS, vol. 3362, pp. 108–128. Springer, Heidelberg (2005). https://doi.org/10.1007/978-3-540-30569-9_6
9. de Moura, L., Bjørner, N.: Z3: an efficient SMT solver. In: Ramakrishnan, C.R., Rehof, J. (eds.) TACAS 2008. LNCS, vol. 4963, pp. 337–340. Springer, Heidelberg (2008). https://doi.org/10.1007/978-3-540-78800-3_24
10. Garland, S.J., Guttag, J.V.: A guide to LP, the larch prover. Technical report 82, Digital Equipment Corporation, Systems Research Center, 130 Lytton Avenue, Palo Alto, CA 94301, December 1991. Order from src-report@src.dec.com

11. Hatcliff, J., Leavens, G.T., Rustan, K., Leino, M., Müller, P., Parkinson, M.: Behavioral interface specification languages. Technical report CS-TR-09-01, University of Central Florida, School of EECS, Orlando, FL, March 2009

12. Kanig, J., Filliâtre, J.-C.: Who: a verifier for effectful higher-order programs. In: Proceedings of the 2009 ACM SIGPLAN Workshop on ML, ML 2009, pp. 39–48, New York. ACM (2009)

13. Kassios, I.T., Müller, P.: Modular specification and verification of delegation with SMT solvers. Technical report, ETH Zurich (2011)

14. Leino, K.R.M.: Dafny: an automatic program verifier for functional correctness. In: Clarke, E.M., Voronkov, A. (eds.) LPAR 2010. LNCS (LNAI), vol. 6355, pp. 348–370. Springer, Heidelberg (2010). https://doi.org/10.1007/978-3-642-17511-4_20

15. McCormick, J.W., Chapin, P.C.: Building High Integrity Applications with SPARK. Cambridge University Press (2015)

16. Meyer, B.: Object-Oriented Software Construction. Prentice Hall, New York (1988)

17. Singleton, J.L., Leavens, G.T., Rajan, H., Cok, D.R.: Poster: an algorithm and tool to infer practical postconditions. In: 2018 IEEE/ACM 40th IEEE International Conference on Software Engineering (ICSE). IEEE (2018)

18. Unno, H., Terauchi, T., Kobayashi, N.: Automating relatively complete verification of higher-order functional programs. SIGPLAN Not. 48(1), 75–86 (2013)

19. Many papers regarding JML can be found on the JML web site. http://www.jmlspecs.org

20. OpenJDK. http://www.openjdk.org

21. http://www.openjml.org

22. http://www.smtlib.org

23. The Spec# web site gives code, documentation and papers. http://research.microsoft.com/SpecSharp/

Verification of Binarized Neural Networks via Inter-neuron Factoring
(Short Paper)

Chih-Hong Cheng[(⊠)], Georg Nührenberg, Chung-Hao Huang,
and Harald Ruess

fortiss - Landesforschungsinstitut des Freistaats Bayern, Munich, Germany
{cheng,nuehrenberg,huang,ruess}@fortiss.org

Abstract. Binarized Neural Networks (BNN) have recently been proposed as an energy-efficient alternative to more traditional learning networks. Here we study the problem of formally verifying BNNs by reducing it to a corresponding hardware verification problem. The main step in this reduction is based on factoring computations among neurons within a hidden layer of the BNN in order to make the BNN verification problem more scalable in practice. The main contributions of this paper include results on the NP-hardness and hardness of PTAS approximability of this essential optimization and factoring step, and we design polynomial-time search heuristics for generating approximate factoring solutions. With these techniques we are able to scale the verification problem to moderately-sized BNNs for embedded devices with thousands of neurons and inputs.

1 Introduction

Neural networks are used for perception and scene understanding [12,16,20] and also for control and decision making [4,9,14,23] in autonomous systems. Implementations of artificial neural networks, however, are very power-intensive due to complex floating point arithmetics. Binarized Neural Networks (BNNs), which are based on bit-level arithmetic, have therefore recently been proposed [6,11] as an attractive alternative to more traditional neural networks for resource-constrained embedded applications (e.g. based on FPGAs [1]). BNNs also demonstrate satisfactory performance on a number of standard benchmark datasets in image recognition including MNIST, CIFAR-10 and SVHN [6].

Here we study the verification problem for BNNs. Given a trained BNN and a specification of its intended input-output behavior we develop verification procedures for establishing that the given BNN indeed meets its intended specification for all possible inputs. For solving the verification problem of BNNs, we build on well-known methods from the hardware verification domain (Sect. 4). However, even with efficient neuron-to-circuit encoding we were not able to verify BNNs with thousands of inputs and hidden nodes as encountered in some of our embedded systems case studies.

© Springer Nature Switzerland AG 2018
R. Piskac and P. Rümmer (Eds.): VSTTE 2018, LNCS 11294, pp. 279–290, 2018.
https://doi.org/10.1007/978-3-030-03592-1_16

Table 1. An example of computing the output of a BNN neuron, using bipolar domain (up) and using 0/1 boolean variables (down).

index j	0 (bias node)	1	2	3	4
$x_j^{(l-1)}$	+1 (constant)	+1	−1	+1	+1
$w_{ji}^{(l)}$	−1 (bias)	+1	−1	−1	+1
$x_j^{(l-1)} w_{ji}^{(l)}$	−1		+1	+1	−1	+1
$im_i^{(l)}$	+1				
$\mathsf{x}_i^{(l)}$	+1, as $im_i^{(l)} \geq 0$				
index j	0 (bias node)	1	2	3	4
$x_j^{(l-1)}$	1		1	0	1	1
$w_{ji}^{(l)}$	0 (bias)		1	0	0	1
$x_j^{(l-1)} \overline{\oplus} w_{ji}^{(l)}$	0		1	1	0	1
# of 1's in $x_j^{(l-1)} \overline{\oplus} w_{ji}^{(l)}$	3					
$\mathsf{x}_i^{(l)}$	1, as $(3 \geq \lceil \frac{5}{2} \rceil)$					

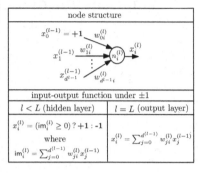

Fig. 1. Computation inside a neuron of a BNN, under bipolar domain ±1.

It turns out that one critical ingredient for efficient BNN verification is to factor computations among neurons in the same layer, which is possible due to the binary weights of inter-neuron connections in BNNs. Notice, however, that these factorings techniques are not directly applicable to floating-point based neural networks [5,7,10,15,19]. The key theorem regarding the hardness of finding optimal factoring as well as the hardness of inapproximability (Sect. 4.2) leads to the design of polynomial time search heuristics for generating factorings. These factorings substantially increase the scalability of formal verification via SAT solving (Sect. 5) to moderately-sized BNNs for embedded applications with thousands of neurons and inputs.

2   Related Work

There has been a flurry of recent results on formal verification of neural networks (e.g. [5,7,10,15,19]). These approaches usually target the formal verification of floating-point arithmetic neural networks (FPA-NNs). Huang et al. propose an (incomplete) search-based technique based on *satisfiability modulo theories* (SMT) solvers [8]. For FPA-NNs with ReLU activation functions, Katz et al. propose a modification of the Simplex algorithm which prefers fixing of binary variables [10]. This verification approach has been demonstrated on the verification of a collision avoidance system for UAVs. In our own previous work on neural network verification we establish maximum resilience bounds for FPA-NNs based on reductions to *mixed-integer linear programming* (MILP) problems [5]. The feasibility of this approach has been demonstrated, for example, by verifying a motion predictor in a highway overtaking scenario. The work of Ehlers [7] is based on sound abstractions, and approximates non-linear behavior in the activation functions. Scalability is the overarching challenge for these formal approaches to the verification of FPA-NNs. Case studies and experiments reported in the literature are usually restricted to the verification of FPA-NNs with a couple of hundred neurons.

Around the time (Oct 9th, 2017) we first release of our work regarding formal verification of BNNs, Narodytska et al have also worked on the same problem [17]. Their work focuses on efficient encoding within a single neuron, while we focus on computational savings among neurons within the same layer. One can view our result and their results being complementary.

3   Preliminaries

Let $\mathbb{B}$ be the set of *bipolar binaries* ± 1, where $+1$ is interpreted as "true" and -1 as "false". A *Binarized Neural Network* (BNN) [6,11] consists of a sequence of layers labeled from $l = 0, 1, \ldots, L$, where 0 is the index of the *input layer*, L is the *output layer*, and all other layers are so-called *hidden layers*. Superscripts $^{(l)}$ are used to index layer l-specific variables. Elements of both inputs and outputs vectors of a BNN are of bipolar domain $\mathbb{B}$.

Layers l are comprised of *nodes* $n_i^{(l)}$ (so-called neurons), for $i = 0, 1, \ldots, d^{(l)}$, where $d^{(l)}$ is the *dimension* of the layer l. By convention, $n_0^{(l)}$ is a *bias node* and has constant bipolar output $+1$. Nodes $n_j^{(l-1)}$ of layer $l - 1$ can be connected with nodes $n_i^{(l)}$ in layer l by a directed edge of *weight* $w_{ji}^{(l)} \in \mathbb{B}$. A layer is fully connected if every node (apart from the bias node) in the layer is connected to all neurons in the previous layer. Let $\boldsymbol{w}_i^{(l)}$ denote the array of all weights associated with neuron $n_i^{(l)}$. Notice that we consider all weights in a network to have fixed bipolar values.

Given an input to the network, computations are applied successively from neurons in layer 1 to L for generating outputs. Figure 1 illustrates the computations of a neuron in bipolar domain. Overall, the activation function is applied to the intermediately computed weighted sum. It outputs $+1$ if the weighted sum is greater or equal to 0; otherwise, output -1. For the output layer, the activation function is omitted. For $l = 1, \ldots, L$ let $x_i^{(l)}$ denote the output value of node $n_i^{(l)}$ and $\boldsymbol{x}^{(l)} \in \mathbb{B}^{|d^{(l)}|+1}$ denotes the array of all outputs from layer l, including the constant bias node; $\boldsymbol{x}^{(0)}$ refers to the input layer.

For a given BNN and a relation ϕ_{risk} specifying the undesired property between the bipolar input and output domains of the given BNN, the *BNN safety verification problem* asks if there exists an input $\boldsymbol{a}$ to the BNN such that the risk property $\phi_{risk}(\boldsymbol{a}, \boldsymbol{b})$ holds, where $\boldsymbol{b}$ is the output of the BNN for input $\boldsymbol{a}$.

It turns out that safety verification of BNN is no simpler than safety verification of floating point neural networks with ReLU activation function [10]. Nevertheless, compared to floating point neural networks, the simplicity of binarized weights allows an efficient translation into SAT problems, as can be seen in later sections.

Theorem 1. *The problem of BNN safety verification is NP-complete.*

Proof. Given a BNN and a relation ϕ_{risk} specifying the undesired property between the bipolar input and output domains of the given BNN, the *BNN safety verification problem* asks if there exists an input $\boldsymbol{a}$ to the BNN such that the risk property $\phi_{risk}(\boldsymbol{a}, \boldsymbol{b})$ holds, where $\boldsymbol{b}$ is the output of the BNN for input $\boldsymbol{a}$.

(NP) Given an input, compute the output and check if $\phi_{risk}(\boldsymbol{a}, \boldsymbol{b})$ holds can easily be done in time linear to the size of BNN and size of the property formula.

(NP-hardness) The NP-hardness proof is via a reduction from 3SAT to BNN safety verification. Consider variables $x_1, \ldots, x_m$, clauses $c_1, \ldots, c_d$ where for each clause c_j, it has three literals $l_{j_1}, l_{j_2}, l_{j_3}$. We build a single layer BNN with inputs to be $x_0 = +1$ (constant for bias), $x_1, \ldots, x_m, x_{m+1}$ (from CNF variables), connected to d neurons.

For neuron n_j^1, its weights and connection to previous layers is decided by clause c_j.

- If l_{j_1} is a positive literal x_i, then in BNN create a link from x_i to neuron n_j^1 with weight -1. If l_{j_1} is a negative literal x_i, then in BNN create a link from x_i to neuron n_j^1 with weight $+1$. Proceed analogously for l_{j_2} and l_{j_3}.
- Add an edge from x_{m+1} to n_j^1 with weight -1.
- Add an edge with weight -1 from x_0 to n_j^1 as bias term.

For example, consider the CNF having variables $x_1, \ldots, x_6$, then the translation of the clause $(x_3 \vee \neg x_5 \vee x_6)$ will create in BNN the weighted sum computation $(-x_3 + x_5 - x_6) - x_7 - 1$.

Assume that x_7 is constant $+1$, then if there exists any assignment to make the clause $(x_3 \vee \neg x_5 \vee x_6)$ true, then by interpreting the true assignment in CNF to be $+1$ in the BNN input and false assignment in CNF to be -1 in the BNN input, the weighted sum is at most -1, i.e., the output of the neuron is -1. Only when $x_3 =$ false, $x_5 =$ true and $x_6 =$ false (i.e., the assignment makes the clause false), then the weighed sum is $+1$, thereby setting output of the neuron to be $+1$.

Following the above exemplary observation, it is easy to derive that 3SAT formula is satisfiable *iff* in the generated BNN, there exists an input such that the risk property $\phi_{risk} := (x_{m+1} = +1 \rightarrow (\bigwedge_{i=1}^{n} x_i^{(1)} = -1))$ holds. It is done by interpreting the 3SAT variable assignment $x_i :=$ true in CNF to be assignment $+1$ for input x_i in the BNN, while interpreting $x_i :=$ false in 3SAT to be -1 for input x_i in the BNN. □

4 Verification of BNNs via Hardware Verification

The BNN verification problem is encoded by means of a *combinational miter* [3], which is a hardware circuit with only one Boolean output and the output should always be 0. The main step of this encoding is to replace the bipolar domain operation in the definition of BNNs with corresponding operations in the 0/1 Boolean domain.

We recall the encoding of the update function of an individual neuron of a BNN in bipolar domain (Eq. 1) by means of operations in the 0/1 Boolean domain [6,11]: (1) perform a bitwise XNOR ($\overline{\oplus}$) operation, (2) count the number of 1s, and (3) check if the sum is greater than or equal to the half of the number of inputs being connected. Table 1 illustrates the concept by providing the detailed computation for a neuron connected to five predecessor nodes. Therefore, the update function of a BNN neuron (in the fully connected layer) in the Boolean domain is as follows.

$$x_i^{(l)} = \mathsf{geq}_{\lceil \frac{|d^{(l-1)}|+1}{2} \rceil} (\mathsf{count1}(\boldsymbol{w}_i^{(l)} \overline{\oplus} \boldsymbol{x}^{(l-1)})), \tag{1}$$

where $\mathsf{count1}$ simply counts the number of 1s in an array of Boolean variables, and $\mathsf{geq}_{\lceil \frac{|d^{(l-1)}|+1}{2} \rceil}(x)$ is 1 if $x \geq \lceil \frac{|d^{(l-1)}|+1}{2} \rceil$, and 0 otherwise. Notice that the value $\lceil \frac{|d^{(l-1)}|+1}{2} \rceil$ is constant for a given BNN. Here we omit details, but specifications in the bipolar domain can also be easily re-encoded in the Boolean domain.

4.1   From BNN to Hardware Verification

We are now ready for stating the basic decision procedure for solving BNN verification problems. This procedure first constructs a combinational miter for a BNN verification problem, followed by an encoding of the combinational miter into a corresponding propositional SAT problem. Here we rely on standard transformation techniques as implemented in logic synthesis tools such as ABC [3] or Yosys [24] for constructing SAT problems from miters. The decision procedure takes as input a BNN network description, an input-output specification ϕ_{risk} and can be summarized by the following workflow:

1. Transform all neurons of the given BNN into neuron-modules. All neuron-modules have identical structure, but only differ based on the associated weights and biases of the corresponding neurons.
2. Create a BNN-module by wiring the neuron-modules realizing the topological structure of the given BNN.
3. Create a property-module for the property ϕ_{risk}. Connect the inputs of this module with all the inputs and all the outputs of the BNN-module. The output of this module is true if the property is satisfied and false otherwise.
4. The combination of the BNN-module and the property-module is the miter.
5. Transform the miter into a propositional SAT formula.
6. Solve the SAT formula. If it is unsatisfiable then the BNN is safe w.r.t. ϕ_{risk}; if it is satisfiable then the BNN exhibits the risky behavior being specified in ϕ_{risk}.

4.2   Counting Optimization

The goal of the counting optimization is to speed up SAT-solving times by reusing redundant counting units in the circuit and, thus, reducing redundancies

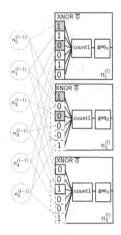

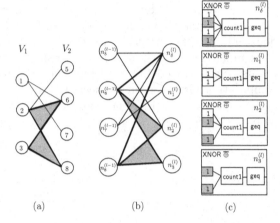

Fig. 2. One possible factoring to avoid redundant counting.

Fig. 3. From bipartite graph (a) to BNN where all weights are with value 1 (b), to optimal factoring (c).

in the SAT formula. This method involves the identification and factoring of redundant counting units, illustrated in Fig. 2, which highlights one possible factoring. The main idea is to exploit similarities among the weight vectors of neurons in the same layer, because the counting over a portion of the weight vector has the same result for all neurons that share it. The circuit size is reduced by using the factored counting unit in multiple neuron-modules. We define a factoring as follows:

Definition 1 (factoring and saving). *Consider the l-th layer of a BNN where $l > 0$. A factoring $f = (I, J)$ is a pair of two sets, where $I \subseteq \{1, \ldots, d^{(l)}\}$, $J \subseteq \{1, \ldots, d^{(l-1)}\}$, such that $|I| > 1$, and for all $i_1, i_2 \in I$, for all $j \in J$, we have $w_{ji_1}^{(l)} = w_{ji_2}^{(l)}$. Given a factoring $f = (I, J)$, define its saving $\mathsf{sav}(f)$ be $(|I| - 1) \cdot |J|$.*

Definition 2 (non-overlapping factorings). *Two factorings $f_1 = (I_1, J_1)$ and $f_2 = (I_2, J_2)$ are non-overlapping when the following condition folds: if $(i_1, j_1) \in f_1$ and $(i_2, j_2) \in f_2$, then either $i_1 \neq i_2$ or $j_1 \neq j_2$. In other words, weights associated with f_1 and f_2 do not overlap.*

Definition 3 (k-factoring optimization problem). *The k-factoring optimization problem searches for a set F of size k factorings $\{f_1, \ldots, f_k\}$, such that any two factorings are non-overlapping, and the total saving $\mathsf{sav}(f_1) + \cdots + \mathsf{sav}(f_k)$ is maximum.*

For the example in Fig. 2, there are two non-overlapping factorings $f_1 = (\{1, 2\}, \{0, 2\})$ and $f_2 = (\{2, 3\}, \{1, 3, 4, 5\})$. $\{f_1, f_2\}$ is also an optimal solution for the 2-factoring optimization problem, with the total saving being $(2 - 1) \cdot 2 + (2 - 1) \cdot 4 = 6$. Even finding one factoring f_1 which has the overall maximum saving $\mathsf{sav}(f_1)$, is computationally hard. This NP-hardness result is established by a reduction from the NP-complete problem of finding maximum edge biclique in bipartite graphs [18].

Theorem 2 (Hardness of factoring optimization). *The k-factoring optimization problem, even when $k = 1$, is NP-hard.*

Proof. The proof proceeds by a polynomial reduction from the problem of finding maximum edge biclique in bipartite graphs(MEB) [18][1]. Given a bipartite graph G, this reduction is defined as follows.

1. For $v_{1\alpha}$, the α-th element of V_1, create a neuron $n_{\alpha}^{(l)}$.
2. Create an additional neuron $n_{\delta}^{(l)}$
3. For $v_{2\beta}$, the β-th element of V_2, create a neuron $n_{\beta}^{(l-1)}$.
   - Create weight $w_{\beta\delta}^{(l)} = 1$.
   - If $(v_{1\alpha}, v_{2\beta}) \in E$, then create $w_{\beta\alpha}^{(l)} = 1$.

This construction can clearly be performed in polynomial time. Figure 3 illustrates the construction process. It is not difficult to observe that G has a maximum edge size κ biclique $\{A; B\}$ iff the neural network at layer l has a factoring (I, J) whose saving equals $(|I| - 1) \cdot |J| = \kappa$. The gray area in Fig. 3-a shows the structure of maximum edge biclique $\{\{2, 3\}; \{6, 8\}\}$. For Fig. 3-c, the saving is $(|\{n_{\delta}^{(l)}, n_2^{(l)}, n_3^{(l)}\}| - 1) \cdot 2 = 4$, which is the same as the edge size of the biclique. $\square$

Furthermore, even having an approximation algorithm for the k-factoring optimization problem is hard - there is no polynomial time approximation scheme (PTAS), unless NP-complete problems can be solved in randomized subexponential time. The proof follows an intuition that building a PTAS for 1-factoring can be used to build a PTAS for finding maximum complete bipartite subgraph which also has known inapproximability results [2].

Theorem 3. *Let $\epsilon > 0$ be an arbitrarily small constant. If there is a PTAS for the k-factoring optimization problem, even when $k = 1$, then there is a (probabilistic) algorithm that decides whether a given SAT instance of size n is satisfiable in time $2^{n^{\epsilon}}$.*

Proof. We will prove the Theorem by showing that a PTAS for the k-factoring optimization problem can be used to manufacture a PTAS for MEB. Then the result follows from the inapproximability of MEB assuming the exponential time hypothesis [2].

---

[1] Let $G = (V_1, V_2, E)$ be a bipartite graph with vertex set $V_1 \uplus V_2$ and edge set E connecting vertices in V_1 to vertices in V_2. A pair of two disjoint subsets $A \subset V_1$ and $B \subset V_2$ is called a *biclique* if $(a, b) \in E$ for all $a \in A$ and $b \in B$. Thus, the edges $\{(a, b)\}$ form a complete bipartite subgraph of G. A biclique $\{A; B\}$ clearly has $|A| \cdot |B|$ edges.

Assume that $\mathcal{A}$ is a ρ-approximation algorithm [2] for the k-factoring optimization problem. We formulate the following algorithm $\mathcal{B}$:
Input: MEB instance M (a bipartite graph $G = (V, E)$)
Output: a biclique in G

1. perform reduction of proof of Theorem 2 to obtain k-factoring instance $F :=$ reduce(M)
2. factoring $(I, J) := \mathcal{A}(F)$
3. return $(I \setminus \{n_\delta^{(l)}\}, J)$

Remark: step 3 is a small abuse of notation. It should return the original vertices corresponding to these neurons.

Now we prove that $\mathcal{B}$ is a ρ-approximation algorithm for MEB: Note that by our reduction two corresponding MEB and k-factoring instances M and F have the same optimal value, i.e., $\text{OPT}(M) = \text{OPT}(F)$.

In step 3 the algorithm returns $(I \setminus \{n_\delta^{(l)}\}, J)$. This is valid since we can assume w.l.o.g. that I returned by $\mathcal{A}$ contains $n_\delta^{(l)}$. This neuron is connected to all neurons from the previous layer by construction, so it can be added to any factoring. The following relation holds for the number of edges in the biclique returned by $\mathcal{B}$:

$$\|I \setminus \{n_\delta^{(l)}\}\| \cdot \|J\| = (\|I\| - 1) \cdot \|J\| \tag{2a}$$
$$\geq \rho \cdot \text{OPT}(F) \tag{2b}$$
$$= \rho \cdot \text{OPT}(M) \tag{2c}$$

The inequality in step (2b) holds by the assumption that $\mathcal{A}$ is a ρ-approximation algorithm for k-factoring and (2c) follows from the construction of our reduction. Equations (2) and the result of [2] imply Theorem 2.   □

As finding an optimal factoring is computationally hard, we present a *polynomial time heuristic algorithm* (Algorithm 1) that finds factoring possibilities among neurons in layer l. The **main** function searches for an unused pair of neuron i and input j (line 3 and 5), considers a certain set of factorings determined by the subroutine **getFactoring** (line 6) where weight $w_{ji}^{(l)}$ is guaranteed to be used (as input parameter i, j), picks the factoring with greatest **sav()** (line 7) and then adds the factoring greedily and updates the set **used** (line 8).

The subroutine **getFactoring()** (lines 10–14) computes a factoring (I, J) guaranteeing that weight $w_{ji}^{(l)}$ is used. It starts by creating a set $\mathbb{I}$, where each element $I_{j'} \in \mathbb{I}$ is a set containing the indices of neurons whose j'-th weight matches the j'-th weight in neuron i (the condition $(w_{j'i'}^{(l)} = w_{j'i}^{(l)})$ in line 11). In the example in Fig. 4a, the computation generates Fig. 4b where $I_3 = \{1, 2, 3\}$ as $w_{31}^{(l)} = w_{32}^{(l)} = w_{33}^{(l)} = 0$. The intersection performed on line 12 guarantees that the set $I_{j'}$ is always a subset of I_j – as weight w_{ji} should be included, I_j already defines the maximum set of neurons where factoring can happen. E.g., I_3 changes from $\{1, 2, 3\}$ to $\{1, 2\}$ in Fig. 4c.

Algorithm 1. Finding factoring possibilities for BNN.

Data: BNN network description (cf Sect. 3)
Result: Set F of factorings, where any two factorings of F are non-overlapping.
1 **function** main():
2   let used := $\emptyset$ and $F := \emptyset$;
3   **foreach** neuron $n_i^{(l)}$ **do**
4   let f_i^{opt} := empty factoring;
5   **foreach** weight $w_{ji}^{(l)}$ where $(i,j) \notin$ used **do**
6       $f_{ij} =$ getFactoring$(i, j,$ used$)$;
7   **if** sav$(f_{ij}) >$ sav(f_i^{opt}) **then** $f_i^{opt} := f_{ij}$;
8   used := used $\cup \{(i,j) \mid (i,j) \in f_i^{opt}\}$; $F := F \cup \{f_i^{opt}\}$;
9   **return** F;

10 **function** getFactoring(i, j, used):
11   **build** $\mathbb{I} := \{I_0, ..., I_{d^{(l-1)}}\}$ where $I_{j'} :=$
    $\{i' \in \{0, ..., d^{(l)}\} \mid w_{j'i'}^{(l)} = w_{j'i}^{(l)} \wedge (i', j') \notin$ used$\}$;
12   **foreach** $I_m \in \mathbb{I}$ **do** $I_m := I_m \cap I_j$;
13   **build** $\mathbb{J} := \{J_0, \ldots, J_{j'}, \ldots, J_{d^{(l-1)}}\}$ where $J_{j'} :=$
    $\{j'' \in \{0, ..., d^{(l-1)}\} \mid I_{j'} \subseteq I_{j''}\}$;
14   **return** $(I, J) := (I_{j^*}, J_{j^*})$ where $I_{j^*} \in \mathbb{I}, J_{j^*} \in \mathbb{J}$, and
    $(|I_{j^*}| - 1) \cdot |J_{j^*}| = \max_{j' \in \{0,...,d^{(l-1)}\}} (|I'_j| - 1) \cdot |J'_j|$;

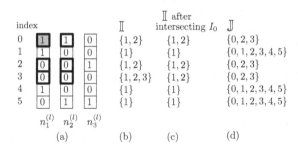

index				$\mathbb{I}$	$\mathbb{I}$ after intersecting I_0	$\mathbb{J}$
0	1	1	0	$\{1,2\}$	$\{1,2\}$	$\{0,2,3\}$
1	1	0	0	$\{1\}$	$\{1\}$	$\{0,1,2,3,4,5\}$
2	0	0	1	$\{1,2\}$	$\{1,2\}$	$\{0,2,3\}$
3	0	0	0	$\{1,2,3\}$	$\{1,2\}$	$\{0,2,3\}$
4	1	0	0	$\{1\}$	$\{1\}$	$\{0,1,2,3,4,5\}$
5	0	1	1	$\{1\}$	$\{1\}$	$\{0,1,2,3,4,5\}$
	$n_1^{(l)}$	$n_2^{(l)}$	$n_3^{(l)}$			
		(a)		(b)	(c)	(d)

Fig. 4. Executing getFactoring$(1, 0, \emptyset)$, meaning that we consider a factoring which includes the top-left corner of (a). The returned factoring is highlighted in thick lines.

The algorithm then builds a set $\mathbb{J}$ of all the candidates for J. Each element $J_{j'}$ contains all the inputs j'' that would benefit from $I_{j'}$ being the final result I. Based on the observation mentioned above, $J_{j'}$ can be built through superset computation between elements of $\mathbb{I}$ (line 13, Fig. 4d). After we build $\mathbb{I}$ and $\mathbb{J}$, finally line 14 finds a pair of (I_{j^*}, J_{j^*}) where $I_{j^*} \in \mathbb{I}, J_{j^*} \in \mathbb{J}$ with the maximum saving $(|I_j^*| - 1) \cdot |J_j^*|$. The maximum saving as produced in Fig. 4 equals $(|\{1,2\}| - 1) \cdot |\{0,2,3\}| = 3$.

There are only polynomial operations in this algorithm such as nested for loops, superset checking and intersection which makes the heuristic algorithm polynomial. When one encounters a huge number of neurons and long weight vectors, we further partition neurons and weights into smaller regions as input to Algorithm 1. By doing so, we find factoring possibilities for each weight segment of a neuron and the algorithm can be executed in parallel.

5   Evaluation and Outlook

We have created a verification tool, which first reads a BNN description based on the Intel Nervana Neon framework[2], generates a combinational miter in Verilog and calls Yosys [24] and ABC [3] for generating a CNF formula. No further optimization commands (e.g., refactor) are executed inside ABC to create smaller CNFs. Finally, Cryptominisat5 [21] is used for solving SAT queries. The experiments are conducted in a Ubuntu 16.04 Google Cloud VM equipped with 18 cores and 250 GB RAM, with Cryptominisat5 running with 16 threads. We use two different datasets, namely the MNIST dataset for digit recognition [13] and the German traffic sign dataset [22]. We binarize the gray scale data to ±1 before actual training. For the traffic sign dataset, every pixel is quantized to 3 Boolean variables.

Table 2 summarizes the result of verification in terms of SAT solving time, with a timeout set to 90 min. The properties that we use here are characteristics of a BNN given by numerical constraints over outputs, such as "simultaneously classify an image as a priority road sign and as a stop sign with high confidence" (which clearly demonstrates a risk behavior). It turns out that factoring techniques are essential to enable better scalability, as it halves the verification times in most cases and enables us to solve some instances where the plain approach ran out of memory or timed out. However, we also observe that solvers like Cryptominisat5 might get trapped in some very hard-to-prove properties. Regarding the instance in Table 2 where the result is unknown, we suspect that

Table 2. Verification results for each instance and comparing the execution times of the plain hardware verification approach and the optimized version using counting optimizations.

ID	# inputs	# neurons hidden layer	Properties being investigated	SAT/UNSAT	SAT solving time (normal)	SAT solving time (factored)
MNIST 1	784	3×100	$out_1 \geq 18 \wedge out_2 \geq 18$ ($\geq 18\%$)	SAT	2m 16.336 s	0m 53.545 s
MNIST 1	784	3×100	$out_1 \geq 30 \wedge out_2 \geq 30$ ($\geq 30\%$)	SAT	2m 20.318 s	0m 56.538 s
MNIST 1	784	3×100	$out_1 \geq 60 \wedge out_2 \geq 60$ ($\geq 60\%$)	SAT	timeout	10m 50.157 s
MNIST 1	784	3×100	$out_1 \geq 90 \wedge out_2 \geq 90$ ($\geq 90\%$)	UNSAT	2m 4.746 s	1m 0.419 s
Traffic 2	2352	3×500	$out_1 \geq 90 \wedge out_2 \geq 90$ ($\geq 18\%$)	SAT	10m 27.960 s	4m 9.363 s
Traffic 2	2352	3×500	$out_1 \geq 150 \wedge out_2 \geq 150$ ($\geq 30\%$)	SAT	10m 46.648 s	4m 51.507 s
Traffic 2	2352	3×500	$out_1 \geq 200 \wedge out_2 \geq 200$ ($\geq 40\%$)	SAT	10m 48.422 s	4m 19.296 s
Traffic 2	2352	3×500	$out_1 \geq 300 \wedge out_2 \geq 300$ ($\geq 60\%$)	unknown	timeout	timeout
Traffic 2	2352	3×500	$out_1 \geq 475 \wedge out_2 \geq 475$ ($\geq 95\%$)	UNSAT	31m 24.842 s	41m 9.407 s
Traffic 3	2352	3×1000	$out_1 \geq 120 \wedge out_2 \geq 120$ ($\geq 12\%$)	SAT	out-of-memory	9m 40.77 s
Traffic 3	2352	3×1000	$out_1 \geq 180 \wedge out_2 \geq 180$ ($\geq 18\%$)	SAT	out-of-memory	9m 43.70 s
Traffic 3	2352	3×1000	$out_1 \geq 300 \wedge out_2 \geq 300$ ($\geq 30\%$)	SAT	out-of-memory	9m 28.40 s
Traffic 3	2352	3×1000	$out_1 \geq 400 \wedge out_2 \geq 400$ ($\geq 40\%$)	SAT	out-of-memory	9m 34.95 s

[2] https://github.com/NervanaSystems/neon/tree/master/examples/binary.

the simultaneous confidence value of 60% for the two classes out_1 and out_2, is close to the value where the property flips from satisfiable to unsatisfiable. This makes SAT solving on such cases extremely difficult for solvers as the instances are close to the "border" between SAT and UNSAT instances.

In the future, we plan to directly synthesize propositional clauses without the support of third party tools such as Yosys in order to avoid extraneous transformations and repetitive work in the synthesis workflow. Similar optimizations of the current verification tool chain should result in substantial performance improvements.

Acknowledgments. We thank Dr. Ljubo Mercep from Mentor Graphics for indicating to us some recent results on quantized neural networks, Dr. Alan Mishchenko from UC Berkeley for his kind suggestions and support regarding ABC, and Hugo A. Andrade from Xilinx for exchanging the view of BNN.

References

1. Umuroglu, Y., et al.: FINN: a framework for fast, scalable binarized neural network arXiv preprint arXiv:1612.07119 (2017)
2. Ambühl, C., Mastrolilli, M., Svensson, O.: Inapproximability results for maximum edge biclique, minimum linear arrangement, and sparsest cut. SIAM J. Comput. **40**(2), 567–596 (2011)
3. Brayton, R., Mishchenko, A.: ABC: an academic industrial-strength verification tool. In: Touili, T., Cook, B., Jackson, P. (eds.) CAV 2010. LNCS, vol. 6174, pp. 24–40. Springer, Heidelberg (2010). https://doi.org/10.1007/978-3-642-14295-6_5
4. Chen, C., Seff, A., Kornhauser, A., Xiao, J.: Deepdriving: learning affordance for direct perception in autonomous driving. In: ICCV, pp. 2722–2730 (2015)
5. Cheng, C.-H., Nührenberg, G., Ruess, H.: Maximum resilience of artificial neural networks. In: D'Souza, D., Narayan Kumar, K. (eds.) ATVA 2017. LNCS, vol. 10482, pp. 251–268. Springer, Cham (2017). https://doi.org/10.1007/978-3-319-68167-2_18
6. Courbariaux, M., Hubara, I., Soudry, D., El-Yaniv, R., Bengio, Y.: Binarized neural networks: training deep neural networks with weights and activations constrained to +1 or -1. arXiv preprint arXiv:1602.02830 (2016)
7. Ehlers, R.: Formal verification of piece-wise linear feed-forward neural networks. In: D'Souza, D., Narayan Kumar, K. (eds.) ATVA 2017. LNCS, vol. 10482, pp. 269–286. Springer, Cham (2017). https://doi.org/10.1007/978-3-319-68167-2_19
8. Huang, X., Kwiatkowska, M., Wang, S., Wu, M.: Safety verification of deep neural networks. In: Majumdar, R., Kunčak, V. (eds.) CAV 2017. LNCS, vol. 10426, pp. 3–29. Springer, Cham (2017). https://doi.org/10.1007/978-3-319-63387-9_1
9. Huval, B., et al. An empirical evaluation of deep learning on highway driving. arXiv preprint arXiv:1504.01716 (2015)
10. Katz, G., Barrett, C., Dill, D.L., Julian, K., Kochenderfer, M.J.: Reluplex: an efficient SMT solver for verifying deep neural networks. In: Majumdar, R., Kunčak, V. (eds.) CAV 2017. LNCS, vol. 10426, pp. 97–117. Springer, Cham (2017). https://doi.org/10.1007/978-3-319-63387-9_5
11. Kim, M., Smaragdis, P.: Bitwise neural networks. arXiv preprint arXiv:1601.06071 (2016)

12. Krizhevsky, A., Sutskever, I., Hinton, G.E.: Imagenet classification with deep convolutional neural networks. In: NIPS, pp. 1097–1105 (2012)
13. LeCun, Y.: The MNIST database of handwritten digits (1998). http://yann.lecun.com/exdb/mnist/
14. Lenz, D., Diehl, F., Le, M.T., Knoll, A.: Deep neural networks for Markovian interactive scene prediction in highway scenarios. In: Intelligent Vehicles Symposium IV. IEEE (2017)
15. Lomuscio, A., Maganti, L.: An approach to reachability analysis for feed-forward relu neural networks. arXiv preprint arXiv:1706.07351 (2017)
16. Long, J., Shelhamer, E., Darrell, T.: Fully convolutional networks for semantic segmentation. In: CPVR, pp. 3431–3440. IEEE (2015)
17. Narodytska, N., Kasiviswanathan, S.P., Ryzhyk, L., Sagiv, M., Walsh, T.: Verifying properties of binarized deep neural networks. arXiv preprint arXiv:1709.06662 (2014)
18. Peeters, R.: The maximum edge biclique problem is NP-complete. Discret. Appl. Math. **131**(3), 651–654 (2003)
19. Pulina, L., Tacchella, A.: An abstraction-refinement approach to verification of artificial neural networks. In: Touili, T., Cook, B., Jackson, P. (eds.) CAV 2010. LNCS, vol. 6174, pp. 243–257. Springer, Heidelberg (2010). https://doi.org/10.1007/978-3-642-14295-6_24
20. Sermanet, P., Eigen, D., Zhang, X. , Mathieu, M., Fergus, R., LeCun, Y.: Overfeat: integrated recognition, localization and detection using convolutional networks. arXiv preprint arXiv:1312.6229 (2013)
21. Soos, M.: The Cryptominisat 5 set of solvers at sat competition 2016. In: Sat Competition 2016, p. 28 (2016)
22. Stallkamp, J., Schlipsing, M., Salmen, J., Igel, C.: The German traffic sign recognition benchmark: a multi-class classification competition. In: IEEE International Joint Conference on Neural Networks, pp. 1453–1460 (2011)
23. Sun, L., Peng, C., Zhan, W., Tomizuka, M.: A fast integrated planning and control framework for autonomous driving via imitation learning (2017). arXiv preprint arXiv:1707.02515
24. Wolf, C., Glaser, J., Kepler, J.: Yosys-a free verilog synthesis suite. In: Proceedings of the 21st Austrian Workshop on Microelectronics (Austrochip) (2013)

The Map Equality Domain

Daniel Dietsch, Matthias Heizmann, Jochen Hoenicke, Alexander Nutz$^{(\boxtimes)}$,
and Andreas Podelski

University of Freiburg, Freiburg im Breisgau, Germany
{dietsch,heizmann,hoenicke,nutz,podelski}@cs.uni-freiburg.de

Abstract. We present a method that allows us to infer expressive invariants for programs that manipulate arrays and, more generally, data that are modeled using maps (including the program memory which is modeled as a map over integer locations). The invariants can express, for example, that memory cells have changed their contents only at locations that have not been previously allocated by another procedure. The motivation for the new method stems from the fact that, although state-of-the-art SMT solvers are starting to be able to check the validity of more and more complex invariants, there is not much work yet on their automatic inference. We present our method as a static analysis over an abstract domain that we introduce, the *map equality domain*. The main challenge in the design of the method lies in scalability; given the expressiveness of the invariants, it is *a priori* not clear that a corresponding static analysis can be made scalable. Preliminary experiments with a prototypical implementation of the method allow us to cautiously conclude that may indeed be the case.

1 Introduction

At least since McCarthy's theory of arrays [20], it has been standard to use logical properties over arrays or maps in program analysis and verification.[1] The need for expressive properties over maps becomes urgent when we model dynamically allocated memory (the heap of a program) as maps, which has become the standard, e.g., in the setting where the Boogie verification language is used [19] . Many of the state-of-the-art SMT solvers used for program verification support the theory of maps; see, e.g., [1,3,6,7,11,13].

These SMT solvers can check the validity of increasingly complex invariants, which is useful in the setting of verification where invariants are provided, typically in the annotation of the program. The automatic inference of such invariants is, however, an altogether different task, and it is fair to say that work in this direction has just started (see Sect. 3 on related work).

Following the framework of abstract interpretation [8,9], we phrase our method as a static analysis that is constructed from an abstract domain. Specifically, we introduce the map equality domain, an abstract domain for three categories of logical properties over maps: equalities between arbitrary expressions

---

[1] We use the mathematical term of *maps* in order to keep the distinction with the idiom of arrays in practical programming languages such as C and Java.

© Springer Nature Switzerland AG 2018
R. Piskac and P. Rümmer (Eds.): VSTTE 2018, LNCS 11294, pp. 291–308, 2018.
https://doi.org/10.1007/978-3-030-03592-1_17

involving (an arbitrary number of) maps (this includes the pointwise equality between two maps), disequalities between arbitrary expressions involving maps, and a third category called *weak equivalences* which is original to this work (for the relationship to existing concepts see Sect. 3).

The formulation of logical properties with weak equivalences accommodates the situation where it is more convenient to specify the positions where two maps may differ ("equal up to ...") rather than specifying the set of positions where they don't. For example, in a program, the present value of an array may arise from the initial value of the array from a series of updates after the execution of a loop over the array indices. Thus, for example, weak equivalences allow us to express a logical property saying that memory cells have changed their contents only at locations that have not been previously allocated by another procedure. It is generally quite common that we need to put different maps into relation (say, the map that models the contents of memory cells and the map that tracks which memory cells have been allocated). Thus, we will use weak equivalences to express that two maps are equal up to a set of positions, where the set of positions itself is defined by the value of each position under a third map.

The three categories in the abstract domain are mutually intertwined in the sense that the presence of one immediately entails the need of the two other ones. Thus, the derivation of a weak equivalence may necessitate the prior derivation of an equality and the prior derivation of a disequality, and so on. For example to derive the disequality $i \neq j$ one may need to derive the equality $a = b$ and the disequality $a[i] \neq b[j]$; to derive the equality between the maps a and b one may need to derive the weak equivalence $a \stackrel{q=i}{=\!=\!=} b$ (meaning "a and b may only differ at indices q where $q = i$ holds") and the equality $a[i] = b[i]$; and to derive the equality $a[i] = b[i]$ one may need to derive the weak equivalence $a \stackrel{c[q]=1}{=\!=\!=} b$ and the equality $c[i] \neq 1$.

Contribution. The contribution of this paper is to introduce the new method, a static analysis based on an abstract domain with the new notion of weak equivalences. We argue that this analysis infers highly expressive invariants and is sufficiently scalable to be useful in practice.

The expressivity of the derived invariants is witnessed by the fact that they suffice to prove a rather complex framing condition of a procedure that writes to an unbounded number of newly allocated non-contiguous memory cells, as our example in Sect. 2 shows. We are not aware of any other method that derives a safe inductive invariant for this example (and certainly not one for which scalability has been demonstrated).

Given the expressiveness of the invariants, it is not clear that a corresponding static analysis can be made scalable. Preliminary experiments with a prototypical implementation of the method allow us to cautiously conclude that this is the case. Our experiments on a set of benchmarks from SV-COMP [2] show that the method can derive invariants in an acceptable time frame on a large number of programs.

Road Map. We will continue with the example, which gives an intuition for our notion of weak equivalence and its expressive power. After that we will describe the map equality domain formally and give proofs that its abstract operators overapproximate their concrete counterparts. Last, we present an evaluation of the scalability of our domain.

2 Example

Figure 1 shows an example program, in the syntax of Boogie [19], an intermediate language which is used for the verification of programs in practical programming languages such as C and Java. The correctness is specified through the assert statement in line 10. It amounts to a framing condition: *a memory cell that is marked valid before a procedure call is never overwritten during execution of the call.* We do not know of an existing method that can derive this invariant. We will next explain how our method based on the map equality domain can derive the required invariant.

The Program. The program uses three global variables, the maps (over the integers) `content`, `next`, and `valid`. They represent, respectively, the contents of the memory, a linked list (where each entry in `next` is interpreted as a pointer to the next element of the list), and the account of which memory locations are already in use (here `valid[i]` = 1 means that the memory at location i has already been allocated). The procedure `main` has three parts. First, it picks an allocated memory location `p` and stores the memory content at `p` into the variable `value`. Next, it calls the procedure `initList` (which may possibly change the value of the global variables). The assertion in line 10 expresses that the procedure call does not change the `content`-map at position `p`. The procedure `initList` initializes a list of nondeterministic length. It makes sure that the memory cells have not been allocated before and are marked as allocated afterwards. It returns a variable that stores the head position of the list. The task of lines 19 to 21 is to pick a formerly unallocated memory location and mark it as allocated. In the remainder of the loop, the new memory location is prepended to the list and `content` is set to −1 at the newly allocated location.

Correctness of the Program. To prove correctness we need to show that `content[p]` remains unchanged during execution of the procedure call in line 9. Thus we have to show that the value that i has in line 24, is never the same as `p`. However `p` is not visible in `initList`, so it cannot be the essence of why `initList` has the desired property. The deeper reason why `initList` never writes to `p` is that the program tracks which positions have already been written to in the `valid`-map and never writes to the same position twice. Thus a safe inductive invariant for `initList` could state the fact that content remains unchanged for all positions q that are marked as already taken (`valid[q]` = 1) at procedure entry.

```
 1   var valid , next , content : [int] int;
 2
 3   procedure main ();
 4   modifies valid , next , content;
 5   implementation main () {
 6     var p, newListHead , value : int;
 7     assume valid [p] == 1;
 8     value := content [p];
 9     call newListHead := initList ();
10     assert content [p] == value;
11   }
12
13   procedure initList () returns (res : int);
14   modifies valid , next , content;
15   implementation initList () returns (res : int) {
16     var i , head : int;
17     head := 0;
18     while (∗) {
19       havoc i;
20       assume valid [i] == 0;
21       valid [i] := 1;
22       next [i] := head;
23       head := i;
24       content [i] := −1;
25     }
26     res := head;
27   }
```

Fig. 1. Example program in Boogie syntax with assert statement (line 10). Our method derives the required invariant ("the procedure `initList` never writes the map `content` at any position that has the value 1 under the map `valid`").

Weak Equivalences. So we need to relate the maps, `content` and `old(content)` in way that allows us to express that they only differ at positions q where `old(valid)[q] = 0`. (The Boogie-keyword `old` refers to the state of each global variable at procedure entry.) Fortunately, (extended) weak equivalences are a perfect match for this kind of property.

We write a weak equivalence between a and b with exceptions $\Phi(q)$ like this:

$$a \xrightarrow{\Phi(q)} b$$

The intuitive meaning of the above weak equivalence is:

a and b are equal on all index positions except for the positions q where $\Phi(q)$ evaluates to *true*; no statement is made about these positions.

Weak equivalences can be expressed as formulas in the theory of maps with one universal quantifier. The following weak equivalence is an inductive invariant for the procedure `initList`:

$$\text{content} \xrightarrow{\;\text{old(valid)}[q]=0\;} \text{old(content)}$$

This constraint precisely captures the property of `initList` we described already. Before the procedure call the following holds.

$$\text{valid}[p] = 1 \wedge \text{content}[p] = \text{value}$$

In order to show the assertion correct, the procedure invariant must guarantee that `content` at position p remains unchanged through the procedure execution, i.e., $\text{content}[p] = \text{old(content)}[p]$. The above weak equivalence allows us to draw this conclusion if the following formula is unsatisfiable.

$$\text{valid}[p] = 1 \wedge \text{valid} = \text{old(valid)} \wedge \text{old(valid)}[q] = 0 \wedge q = p$$

The first three conjuncts represent our base knowledge when combining the information from directly before the procedure call and directly before procedure exit. The last conjunct is used to test if, given the base knowledge, p is a valid choice for q, where q represents all the positions where the weak equivalence edge does *not* make an equality statement $\text{content}[q] = \text{old(content)}[q]$. Because the formula is unsatisfiable, we can conclude that p is not one of these exceptions. Thus $\text{content}[p] = \text{old(content)}[p] = \text{value}$ holds in line 10, after the procedure call and our analysis derives the desired property.

3   Related Work

Our work is related to the line work that uses abstract interpretation to infer low-level information about a program's dynamically allocated memory. Chang and Leino [4] propose an abstract domain with equalities, congruence and a weaker notion of weak equivalence than ours. Their domain does not accomodate the propagation of disequalites, which is crucial in the context of our work.

The notion of weak equivalence was also used in the context of decision procedures. Both Stump et al. [21] and Christ and Hoenicke [5] presented decision procedures for the quantifier-free theory of arrays using weak (also called partial) equivalences. The weak equivalences used in all those works are a special case of ours where the formula describing the exceptions to equivalence is limited to set of index terms, i.e., the quantified variable q cannot appear inside an array access.

Gulwani and Tiwari [16] introduce an abstract domain that tracks equalities and disequalities (they actually track equalities and may-equalities). In contrast to our domain their domain allows quantifier alternation and a much higher nesting depth of quantifiers, while we only allow (implicit) universal quantification where the depth is bounded to the maximum dimension of the maps that occur in the program. Thus our domain can be expected to scale to significantly more complex programs. Gange et al. [14] apply congruence with uninterpreted functions to enhance an existing abstract interpretation by inferring additional equality information. In contrast to our work they don't consider disequalities nor do they have a special treatment for maps (in particular updates to maps).

Cousot, Cousot and Logozzo propose a functor domain for extending existing abstract domains to array analyses [10]. Although instantiations of their functor also reasons about maps their approach is mostly orthogonal to ours. Their focus lies in reasoning about the contents of the maps in some parameter domain, while our domain has its strength in relating different maps as a whole by weak (or strong) equivalences.

To summarize, in the above line of work, precursors of our abstract domain have been defined. None of them is able (has been shown to be able) to derive the expressive invariants that our analysis is able to derive.

Another way of inferring invariants about maps is by Craig interpolation. Brillout et al. [3] present a way derive quantified Craig interpolants in the theory of arrays. Hoenicke and Schindler [18] present a way to derive quantifier-free predicates in the theory of maps (enhanced by a special predicate) through Craig interpolation.

4   Preliminaries

In this section we fix our notation for map expressions and programs. Our analysis will derive constraints over *map expressions* given by the following grammar.

$$Exp ::= x \mid lit \mid e[e']$$

x represents a variable from some variable set V, lit represents a literal, and $e[e']$ represents a select-expression. To highlight that an expression e depends on some variables in the set X, we write $e \in Exp(X)$. For expressions that are used as maps (indices) we also use the letters a, b (i, j).

Note that the *store* function, which is also in the theory of arrays' signature, does not occur in Exp. We write store-expressions as $e\langle e' \triangleleft e'' \rangle$. While the programs we consider may contain store-expressions, we do not include them in Exp because they can be expressed by weak equivalences and thus do not occur in the values of the abstract domains we will present.

We assume a nonempty set $Sort$ as our base sort. From $Sort$ we construct map sorts of any dimensionality, so our expression can have any sort in

$$Sorts \overset{def}{=} \bigcup_{n \in \mathbb{N}_0} (Sort^n \to Sort).$$

The function $sort \colon Exp \to Sorts$ assigns a sort to each expression. If e, e' are two expressions with $sort(e) = Sort^n \to Sort$ for $n > 0$ and $sort(e') = Sort$, then the select expression $e[e']$ has the sort $Sort^{n-1} \to Sort$.

The interpretation function $[\![\cdot]\!] \colon Exp \to \bigcup_{n \in \mathbb{N}_0} (Sort^n \to Sort)$ assigns each expression a value from the corresponding sort. The interpretation of a literal is always the same, for variables it depends on some additional valuation function.

The interpretation of a select-expression $e[e']$ is the evaluation of the map e at position e', i.e., $[\![e[e']]\!] = [\![e]\!]([\![e']\!])$.

We fix a set of *program variables* Var. A *program state* s is a mapping from the program variables to their respective sort, formally:

$$States \stackrel{def}{=} \{s \mid s\colon Var \to Sorts\}$$

Our formulas are generated by the following grammar.

$$Formulas ::= \top \mid \bot \mid e = e' \mid e = e'\langle e'' \triangleleft e'''\rangle \mid \neg\varphi \mid \varphi \wedge \varphi' \mid \varphi \vee \varphi' \mid \exists x.\, \varphi \mid \forall x.\, \varphi$$

$e = e'$ is a proper formula only if the expressions $e, e' \in Exp$, have the same sort. In addition to (dis-)equalities between expressions in Exp we allow equalities between expressions and store-expressions. If the input program has nested stores, they are flattened by introducing auxilliary variables. For $e\langle e' \triangleleft e''\rangle$ to be a proper expression, e has to have some map-sort $Sort^n \to Sort$ for $n > 0$, e' must have sort $Sort$, and e'' must have the sort $Sort^{n-1} \to Sort$. $e\langle e' \triangleleft e''\rangle$ has the same sort as e. The interpretation of the store-expression $e\langle e' \triangleleft e''\rangle$ is a copy of the map e, where the element at index e' has been replaced by value e'', formally:

$$[\![e\langle e' \triangleleft e''\rangle]\!] \stackrel{def}{=} v \mapsto \begin{cases} [\![e'']\!] & \text{if } v = [\![e']\!] \\ [\![e]\!](v) & \text{otherwise} \end{cases}$$

An *interpretation* of a formula is a pair $(\mathcal{A}, s)$. The structure $\mathcal{A}$ must give the above-described symbols their according meaning. Valuation s maps variables to values in their sorts. We write $(\mathcal{A}, s) \models \varphi$ if an interpretation fulfills a formula.

A formula over the program variables $\varphi \in Formulas(Var)$ denotes the set of program states that fulfills the formula, formally:

$$[\![\varphi]\!] = \{s \in States \mid \text{there exists a structure } \mathcal{A} \text{ s.t. } (\mathcal{A}, s) \models \varphi\}$$

A *program* is given through a *transition formula*, which is a formula over the primed and unprimed program variables: $T \in Formulas(Var \cup Var')$, where $Var' = \{v' \mid v \in Var\}$. The concrete *post -operator* relates a set of states, given through a formula over the program variables $S \in Formulas(Var)$, to a new set of states as follows. We first conjoin the respective formulas. Second we project away all unprimed program variables, through existential quantification. Third we substitute all primed program variables by their unprimed versions (denoted by $\cdot[Var' \hookleftarrow Var]$). Formally:

$$post([\![S]\!], T) \stackrel{def}{=} [\![\exists x_1 \ldots x_n.\, S \wedge T[Var' \hookleftarrow Var]]\!] \quad \text{where} \quad Var = \{x_1, \ldots, x_n\}$$

The basic ingredients of an *abstract domain*, as introduced in [8], are a set of elements D, also called the *abstract values*, and a *concretisation function* $\gamma\colon D \to 2^{States}$, which gives the elements a meaning by assigning each abstract value a set of program states. An abstract domain also requires a *partial order* operator $\sqsubseteq$, a *join* operator $\sqcup$, and a *meet* operator $\sqcap$. Last, we need an *abstract post operator* $post^\#\colon D \times Formulas(Var \cup Var') \to D$. An abstract domain induces a static analysis that will compute an inductive invariant for each given program by repeatedly applying $post^\#$ to the program until a fixpoint is reached. In our setting, convergence of this operation has to be ensured by the above operators (we do not use a widening operator). Two abstract domains D, D' can be combined to the Cartesian product domain $D \times D'$. The operators of the subdomain can be used to obtain operators for the product in a straightforward manner. The precision of the Cartesian product can be increased by giving a reduction operator $\rho\colon D \times D' \to D \times D'$. ρ may propagate constraints between the values of the subdomains D and D' in order to obtain a smaller abstract value while not changing its concretisation, the following has to hold: $\rho((A, A')) \sqsubseteq (A, A')$ and $\gamma(\rho((A, A'))) = \gamma(A) \cap \gamma(A')$.

Intuitively, we call operators *sound* with respect to the concretisation function γ if we can guarantee that a program analysis built from them will over-approximate the program's behaviour, we speak of a *precision loss* insofar the overapproximation is not tight. Let $A, B \in D$ be any two elements from the abstract domain D, then we call the operators $\sqsubseteq, \sqcup, \sqcap$ *sound with respect to* γ if 1. γ is monotonous with respect to $\sqsubseteq$, i.e., $A \sqsubseteq B \implies \gamma(A) \subseteq \gamma(B)$, 2. $\sqcup$ overapproximates the union of state sets, i.e., $\gamma(A \sqcup B) \supseteq \gamma(A) \cup \gamma(B)$, 3. $\sqcap$ overapproximates the intersection of state sets, i.e., $\gamma(A \sqcap B) \supseteq \gamma(A) \cap \gamma(B)$. We call an abstract post operator $post^\#$ sound if it overapproximates the concrete post operator $post$, i.e., for any abstract value A and any transition relation T the following holds: $post(\gamma(A), T) \subseteq \gamma(post^\#(A, T))$.

Typically, abstract value represents conjunctive constraints. The disjunctive completion allows for disjunctive abstract values by maintaining sets of abstract values. The generalisations of the operators for this case are straightforward.

5   The Map Equality Domain

We introduce the map equality domain by introducing its building blocks, the domain of equalities and disequalities, and the weak equivalence domain, and then combining them in a reduced product. Afterwards we define the abstract post operator for the map equality domain.

5.1   The Domain of Equalities and Disequalities

The domain of equalities and disequalities (short: *ED*) tracks equalities and disequalities over program expressions and keeps them closed under function congruence. Handling equalities with uninterpreted functions is standard knowledge, however some aspects still require special attention. First, the full-precision join operator for a domain involving congruence closure is not computable [17]. Therefore, each element of *ED* maintains a finite set of tracked expressions to which propagations are limited. Furthermore, complete propagation of disequalities is expensive, so we limit ourselves to those that can be done by a simple propagation rule.

An abstract value in ED consists of three parts: a finite set of expressions, $exp \subset_{fin} Exp$, and two relations $\sim$ and $\not\sim$ over these expressions $\sim, \not\sim \subseteq exp \times exp$. We define the *reduction operator for* domain of equalities and disequalities, ρ_{ED}, as the exhaustive application of the rules in Fig. 2. The operator ρ_{ED} applies a closure such that $\sim$ is a congruence relation with respect to $\not\sim$ and with respect to the select-function $\cdot[\cdot]$, but only insofar expressions in exp are concerned.

Formally, we define the *domain of equalities and disequalities* as follows.

$$ED \overset{def}{=} \{\rho_{ED}((\sim, \not\sim, exp)) \mid \sim, \not\sim \subseteq exp^2, exp \subset_{fin} Exp\} \cup \{\bot_{ED}\}$$

To describe an abstract value in the domain of equalities and disequalities, we sometimes use informal notation like $(a \sim b \wedge i \not\sim j)$ to denote the value $\rho_{ED}((\{(a,b)\}, \{(i,j)\}, \{a,b,i,j\})) \in ED$.

Semantically, the relation $\sim$ represents equality while the relation $\not\sim$ represents disequality, as is reflected by the *concretisation function* γ:

$$\gamma((\sim, \not\sim, exp)) \overset{def}{=} [\![\bigwedge_{(e,e') \in \sim} e = e' \wedge \bigwedge_{(e,e') \in \not\sim} e \neq e']\!] \qquad \gamma(\bot_{ED}) \overset{def}{=} \emptyset$$

We will sometimes abuse notation and use $\gamma(A)$ to denote the corresponding formula instead of the formula's denotation.

Operators for ED. As a first step, all of our operators align the expression sets of their operands.

$$(\sim_A, \not\sim_A, exp_A) \circ (\sim_B, \not\sim_B, exp_B) \overset{def}{=} \rho_{ED}((\sim_A, \not\sim_A, exp_A \cup exp_B))$$
$$\circ \, \rho_{ED}((\sim_B, \not\sim_B, exp_A \cup exp_B)) \text{ where } \circ \in \{\sqsubseteq, \sqcup, \sqcap\}$$

After this alignment, we can define inclusion, meet, and join using standard set operators $\supseteq, \cap, \cup$ respectively. Furthermore, $\bot_{ED}$ is smaller than all elements, it is neutral with respect to the join operator, and an annihilator with respect to the meet operator.

Intuitively an abstract value A is smaller (i.e. stronger) than abstract value B, if it has the same or more equality and disequality constraints. The join operator keeps exactly those constraints that are present in both operands, whereas the meet operator keeps those that are present in at least one of the operands. A detailed definition and soundness proof can be found in the appendix.

Precision of ED. Our propagation rules in ρ_{ED} are complete in the sense that whenever an abstract value $A \in ED$ has an empty concretisation, it is reduced to $\bot_{ED}$ as they incorporate the standard decision procedure for the theory of equality with uninterpreted functions [12].

On the other hand the join operator does not compute the *least* upper bound of its operand in ED and thus incurs a precision loss. An example is the join $A \sqcup B$ where $A = a[i] \sim 0 \wedge i \sim b[j]$ and $B = a[k] \sim 0 \wedge k \sim b[j]$. Here, the value $C = a[b[j]] \sim 0$ is an upper bound and is smaller than $A \sqcup B$, which does

$$\frac{}{e \sim e} \; (refl) \qquad \frac{e \circ e' \quad \circ \in \{\sim, \nsim\}}{e' \circ e} \; (symm) \qquad \frac{e \sim e' \quad e' \sim e''}{e \sim e''} \; (trans)$$

$$\frac{e \nsim e'' \quad e \sim e'}{e' \nsim e''} \; (\nsim\text{-}cong) \qquad \frac{e \sim e' \quad e \nsim e'}{\bot_{ED}} \; (contr) \qquad \frac{}{lit \nsim lit'} \; (lit)$$

$$\frac{a \sim b \quad i \sim j \quad \{a[i], b[j]\} \subseteq exp}{a[i] \sim b[j]} \; (fw\text{-}cong) \qquad \frac{a \sim b \quad a[i] \nsim b[j]}{i \nsim j} \; (bw\text{-}cong)$$

Fig. 2. The propagation rules that the reduction operator ρ_{ED} applies. The rules ensure that $\sim$ is an equivalence relation, that $\sim$ and $\nsim$ are compatible, and that two syntactically different literals are unequal. The rule *fw-cong* (*bw-cong*) introduces equalities (disequalities) according to the congruence axiom of the select-function

not contain any constraints. Furthermore, the reduction operator ρ_{ED} does not derive all disequalities that follow from a constraint. The rule *bw-cong* derives some disequalities. However for performance reasons no complete rule is given. For example the implication $a[i][j] \neq a[j][i] \implies i \neq j$ is valid but it is is not covered by one of our rules.

Disjunctive Completion Operators for ED. As a preparation for the next subsection, we extend the lattice operators for *ED* to disjunctions of elements of *ED*. The concretisation γ is given as the disjunction of the element's concretisations. Let $\Phi, \Phi' \subseteq ED$ be subsets of *ED*, then we define the usual operators as follows.

$$\Phi \sqsubseteq \Phi' \text{ if for each } \varphi' \in \Phi' \text{ there exists } \varphi \in \Phi \text{ such that } \varphi \sqsubseteq \varphi'$$

$$\Phi \sqcup \Phi' \overset{def}{=} \Phi \cup \Phi' \qquad \Phi \sqcap \Phi' \overset{def}{=} \{\varphi \sqcap \varphi' \mid \varphi \in \Phi, \varphi' \in \Phi'\}$$

It is easy to see that the operators $\sqcap$ and $\sqcup$ for the disjunctive completion are sound and precise with respect to γ. However, the partial order operator is only sound, as we have no efficient precise way of checking if an element of *ED* implies a disjunction of elements of *ED*.

5.2   The Weak Equivalence Domain

The elements of the weak equivalence domain (short: *WE*) are *weak equivalence graphs*. Like an element of *ED*, a weak equivalence graph keeps a finite set of expressions, $exp \subset_{fin} Exp$. The expressions in exp form the nodes of a weak equivalence graph.

Let $a, b \in exp$ be two maps. An edge $a \overset{\Phi(q)}{=\!=\!=} b$ in a weak equivalence graph is labeled with an element Φ of the disjunctive completion of *ED*. Φ constrains elements from $exp \cup Q$ where $Q = \{q_1, q_2 \ldots\}$ is a set of special variables disjoint from *Exp*. Intuitively, $\Phi(\boldsymbol{q})$ expresses all *exceptions to equivalence* of a and b. Note that $\boldsymbol{q}$ represents indices for multidimensional maps; the i-th component of $\boldsymbol{q}$, is used to access the maps a and b at dimension i. At every index $\boldsymbol{q}$ such that $\Phi(\boldsymbol{q})$ holds, $a \xlongequal{\Phi(\boldsymbol{q})} b$ does not constrain a or b. At every index $\boldsymbol{q}$ such that $\Phi(\boldsymbol{q})$ does not hold, $a \xlongequal{\Phi(\boldsymbol{q})} b$ implies that $a[\boldsymbol{q}] \sim b[\boldsymbol{q}]$ must hold.

Weak equivalence graphs. A weak equivalence graph has the following form.

$$(\overset{\Phi}{\sim}, exp) = \{a \xlongequal{\Phi(\boldsymbol{q})} b) \mid a, b \in exp, sort(a) = sort(b), \Phi \subseteq ED,$$
$$\varphi \in \Phi \text{ have expression set } exp\}$$

The weak equivalence domain contains all *weak equivalence graphs*, formally:

$$WE \overset{def}{=} \{(\overset{\Phi}{\sim}, exp) \mid (\overset{\Phi}{\sim}, exp) \text{ is a weak equivalence graph}\}$$

We give the concretisation functions for a weak equivalence edge and for a weak equivalence graph as follows.

$$\gamma(a \xlongequal{\Phi(\boldsymbol{q})} b) \overset{def}{=} [\![\forall \boldsymbol{q}. (\bigvee_{\varphi(\boldsymbol{q}) \in \Phi(\boldsymbol{q})} \gamma(\varphi(\boldsymbol{q}))) \vee a[\boldsymbol{q}] = b[\boldsymbol{q}]]\!]$$

$$\gamma((\overset{\Phi}{\sim}, exp)) \overset{def}{=} [\![\bigwedge_{w \in \overset{\Phi}{\sim}} \gamma(w)]\!]$$

We maintain certain well-formedness conditions on weak equivalence graphs. Instead of keeping two parallel weak equivalence edges $a \overset{\Phi}{=\!=} b$ and $a \overset{\Phi'}{=\!=} b$, we insert a single edge whose label expresses the conjunction of the two labels, $a \xlongequal{\Phi \sqcap \Phi'} b$ and we drop the other two edges.

Also, weak equivalence edges are propagated in a graph, in order to fulfill a variant of the triangle inequality. Intuitively, when maps a and b are equal except for some exceptions described by Φ, and b and c are equal except for some exceptions described by Φ', then a and c must be equal except for at indices that fulfill Φ or Φ'. We exhaustively apply the following propagation rule.

$$\frac{a \overset{\Phi}{=\!=} b \quad b \overset{\Phi'}{=\!=} c}{a \xlongequal{\Phi \cup \Phi'} c} \ (\Delta)$$

We give the standard operators for abstract interpretation for WE as follows.

$(\overset{\Phi}{\sim}, exp) \sqsubseteq (\overset{\Phi'}{\sim}, exp)$ if for all a, b in exp with $a \overset{\Phi'}{=\!=} b \ \in \overset{\Phi'}{\sim}, a \overset{\Phi}{=\!=} b \in \overset{\Phi}{\sim}: \Phi \sqsubseteq \Phi'$

$(\overset{\Phi}{\sim}, exp) \circ (\overset{\Phi'}{\sim}, exp) \overset{def}{=} (\{a \xlongequal{\Phi \circ \Phi'} b \mid a \overset{\Phi}{=\!=} b \in \overset{\Phi}{\sim}, a \overset{\Phi'}{=\!=} b \in \overset{\Phi'}{\sim}\}$ for $\circ \in \{\sqcup, \sqcap\}$

Proposition 1. *The operators* $\sqsubseteq, \sqcup, \sqcap$ *on weak equivalence graphs are sound with respect to* γ.

Proof. Weak equivalence graphs directly inherit their soundness from the operators for the disjunctive completion of *ED*, which they are built from. $\qquad \square$

$$\frac{a \xlongequal{\Phi(q)} b \quad \psi \quad \Phi(\boldsymbol{q}) \sqcap \psi \sqsubseteq \bot}{a \sim b} \; (ext) \qquad\qquad \frac{a \sim b}{a \xlongequal{\bot} b} \; (strongtoweak)$$

$$\frac{a \xlongequal{\Phi(q_1,\boldsymbol{q}^+)} b \quad i \sim j \quad \{a[i], b[j]\} \subseteq exp}{a[i] \xlongequal{\Phi(i,\boldsymbol{q})} b[j]} \; (roweq) \qquad \frac{a[i] \xlongequal{\Phi(\boldsymbol{q})} b[j] \quad i \sim j}{a \xlongequal{\{q_1 \not\sim i\} \cup \Phi(\boldsymbol{q}^+)} b} \; (roweq^{-1})$$

Fig. 3. Propagation rules for the map equality domain. The reduction operator ρ is defined as the exhaustive application of these rules. The $+$-operator shifts the variable indices in a vector of q_i-variables, i.e., $(q_1, q_2, \ldots)^+ = (q_2, q_3, \ldots)$.

Store-expressions vs. Weak Equivalences. An equality between an expression and a store-expression can be expressed through an equality and a weak equivalences according to the equivalence below. We will later exploit this to convert the transition formula T to an abstract value $T^{\#}$.

$$a = b\langle i \lhd v \rangle \equiv (a[i] = v \wedge \forall q.\, q = i \vee a[q] = b[q])$$

5.3 The Map Equality Domain

The map equality domain is the reduced product of the domain of equalities and disequalities with the domain of weak equivalences, formally:

$$MED \overset{def}{=} \{\rho((\sim, \not\sim, \overset{\Phi}{\sim}, exp)) \mid (\sim, \not\sim, exp) \in ED, (\overset{\Phi}{\sim}, exp) \in WE\}$$

The reduction operator ρ is given through the propagation rules in Fig. 3.

The rule *ext* allows us to convert a weak equivalence to an equality, provided we can show that the label of the weak equivalence edge is inconsistent in conjunction with all other constraints we have derived. In order to check if the label of a weak equivalence edge $\Phi(\boldsymbol{q})$ is inconsistent with some other constraints we have derived, we have to compute the meet of the label with the whole abstract value, possibly including weak equivalences.

In general we don't store weak equivalence edges whose labels do not depend on any variable from the set Q. If such a label is inconsistent, we store an equality instead, according to the *ext*-rule. If it is consistent, we overapproximate it to the tautological constraint. We have to reflect equalities between maps not only in the *ED*-part of an abstract value, but also in the weak equivalence graph according to the *strongtoweak*-rule.

The rule *roweq* states that we can propagate a weak equivalence constraint between two maps a, b with label $\Phi(q_1, \boldsymbol{q})$ to the submaps of a and b at position i, when we replace the variable q_1 in Φ by i and decrement the subscript of each variable in the vector $\boldsymbol{q}$. Intuitively we project Φ to the statements it makes about a and b at position i. The rule *roweq*$^{-1}$ states that any weak equivalence constraint between maps a and b we have derived for some index position i can be propagated to the encompassing maps of higher dimension when we shift the

q_j-indices by one and state that we put no constraint on any position other than i by adding a disjunct $q_1 \not\sim i$.

Applying ρ does not alter the concretisation of an abstract value: We consider the concretisation formulas of each constraint in the rules and observe that the implication formula corresponding to each rule is valid.

Operations and Properties. The operators $\sqsubseteq, \sqcup, \sqcap$ for the map equality domain are defined as is standard for a reduced product, i.e., let $A = (A_{ED}, A_{WE})$, $B = (B_{ED}, B_{WE})$ be two elements of the map equality domain, then

$$A \sqsubseteq B \text{ if } A_{ED} \sqsubseteq B_{ED} \text{ and } A_{WE} \sqsubseteq B_{WE}$$

$$A \circ B \stackrel{def}{=} \rho(A_{ED} \circ B_{ED}, A_{WE} \circ B_{WE}) \qquad \text{where } \circ \in \{\sqcap, \sqcup\}$$

Proposition 2. *The operators $\sqsubseteq, \sqcup, \sqcap$ for the map equality domain are sound with respect to γ.*

Proof. The soundness of the reduced product follows directly from the soundness of the factor domains and the reduction operator.

To give a feeling for the reduction rules of ρ and the precision of the map equality domain we give to examples.

Example 1. The *roweq*-rules allow us to handle multidimensional stores transparently. Say we have an equality between a map and a two-dimensional store expression $b = a\langle i_1 \triangleleft a[i_1]\langle i_2 \triangleleft x \rangle\rangle$. We expect to obtain the weak equivalence edge $a \xrightarrow{q_1 = i_1 \wedge q_2 = i_2} b$. We convert the nested store to two weak equivalences:

$$b \xrightarrow{q_1 = i_1} a \wedge b[i_1] \xrightarrow{q_1 = i_2} a[i_1] \wedge b[i_1][i_2] = x$$

From $roweq^{-1}$ we get $b \xrightarrow{q_1 \neq i_1, q_2 = i_2} a$, which strengthens the leftmost conjunct to our expected result as we can see through the following equivalence.

$$(q_1 \sim i_1) \sqcap (q_1 \not\sim i_1 \wedge q_2 \sim i_2) \equiv (q_1 \sim i_2 \wedge q_2 \sim i_2)$$

Example 2. A source of imprecision of the ρ-operator is that it does not consider on *how many* positions two weakly equivalent maps might differ, for instance the abstract value written below is not reduced to $\bot$ even though its concretisation is empty.

$$a \xrightarrow{q = i} b \wedge a[k] \not\sim b[k] \wedge a[j] \not\sim b[j] \wedge k \not\sim j$$

5.4   Abstract Post Operator

We define the abstract post operator for the map equality domain analogously to the concrete post operator in Sect. 4. We replace the transition formula T by an abstract value $T^\# \in MED$, we replace projection through existential quantification by a special abstract projection operator $\pi^\#$, and we replace conjunction by the meet operator. We define the *abstract post operator* $post^\# : MED \times Formulas(Var \cup Var') \to MED$ for the map equality domain as follows.

$$post^\#(A, T) \overset{def}{=} \pi^\#_{Var}(A \sqcap T^\#)[Var' \hookleftarrow Var]$$

Next, we will define $\pi^\#$ and $T^\#$ and prove soundness of $post^\#$.

Abstract Transition Formula $T^\#$. We assume without restriction that T is purely conjunctive (use disjunctive completion otherwise). We can write T as follows.

$$T = \bigwedge_{(e,e') \in \sim} e = e' \land \bigwedge_{(e,e') \in \not\sim} e \neq e' \land \bigwedge_{(e,i,e') \in weq} \forall q.\, q = i \lor e[q] = e'[q]$$

We construct a weak equivalence graph $\overset{\Phi}{\sim}$, and an expression set exp using the above-define sets $\sim$, $\not\sim$, weq.

$$\overset{\Phi}{\sim} \overset{def}{=} \{e \xrightarrow{q_1 = i} e' \mid (e, i, e') \in weq\} \qquad exp \overset{def}{=} \{e \mid e \text{ occurs in } \sim, \not\sim \text{ or } weq\}$$

From these ingredients we construct $T^\#$: $T^\# \overset{def}{=} \rho(\sim, \not\sim, \overset{\Phi}{\sim}, exp)$

Proposition 3. *$T^\#$ precisely captures the meaning of T, i.e., $\gamma(T^\#) \equiv T$.*

Proof. The formula $\gamma(T^\#)$ is syntactically equal to the rewritten form of T.

Abstract Projection Operator $\pi^\#$. The operator $\pi^\#$ must fulfill two prerequesites. First, the resulting abstract value may not contain any of the projected-away variables. Second, the projected value must overapproximate the original value, i.e., $\gamma(\pi^\#_V(A)) \supseteq \gamma(A)$. We start with the naive projection operator π^{nv} and later refine it to the more precise operator $\pi^\#$. We will define how to project away one variable, the generalization to a set of variables is straightforward.

Projecting away a variable affects all expressions that depend on the variable. We define dependent expressions and dependent pairs for variable x in expression set exp as the least fixpoint of the following constraints:

$$x \in dep_{exp}(x)$$
$$e \in dep_{exp}(x) \land e[e'] \in exp \implies e[e'] \in dep_{exp}(x)$$
$$e' \in dep_{exp}(x) \land e[e'] \in exp \implies e[e'] \in dep_{exp}(x)$$

We lift the notion of dependent expressions to expression pairs as follows.

$$dep^{pairs}_{exp}(x) \overset{def}{=} (dep_{exp}(x) \times exp) \cup (exp \times dep_{exp}(x))$$

We define a naive projection operator π^{nv} as follows.

$$\pi^{nv}_x((\sim, \not\sim, \overset{\Phi}{\sim}, exp)) \overset{def}{=} (\sim \setminus dep^{pairs}_{exp}(x), \not\sim \setminus dep^{pairs}_{exp}(x), \pi^{nv}_x(\overset{\Phi}{\sim}), exp \setminus dep_{exp}(x))$$

$$\pi^{nv}_x(\overset{\Phi}{\sim}) \overset{def}{=} \{a \xrightarrow{\{\pi^{nv}_x(\varphi_1),...,\pi^{nv}_x(\varphi_n)\}} b \mid a, b \notin dep_{exp}(x), a \xrightarrow{\{\varphi_1,...,\varphi_n\}} b \in \overset{\Phi}{\sim}\}$$

Intuitively, π^{nv} simply drops all constraints that contain the projected variable x or an expression that depends on x.

While π^{nv} is a proper projection according to our criteria, we would incur a drastic precision loss if we used it without further customization.

Example 3. Let $A = (i \sim j \wedge a[i] \sim k)$ with $exp = \{i, j, k, a[j]\}$ be a value in *MED* and assume we want to project i. Then, because $a[i]$ depends on i we have to project it, too, and we would end up with the empty abstract value. But if $a[j]$ were in exp we could retain the constraint $a[j] \sim k$.   □

This loss in precision is a consequence of our strategy to restrict all propagations to expressions in exp. In order to avoid this problem as much as possible we allow $\pi^{\#}$ to enhance exp before removing any constraints.

Let $A \in MED$ be an abstract value and let x be a variable we want to project from A. The projection operator $\pi^{\#}$ proceeds in two steps. In the first step it alternates applications of the rules from 4 and the reduction operator ρ until no more new expressions can be introduced. Afterwards it applies the naive projection operator π^{nv}.

One danger of using $\pi^{\#}$ is that it may introduce unboundedly many expressions during repeated applications of $post^{\#}$. In our experience this case is very rare in practice. We avoid nontermination by setting a limit to the nesting depth of the expressions that are added, which effectively limits the number of added expressions during a run of the analysis to a finite amount.

$$\frac{a \sim b \quad i \sim j \quad a[i] \in dep(x, exp)}{b[j] \in exp} \ (\pi^{\#}\text{-}fw\text{-}cong)$$

$$\frac{a \xrightarrow{\Phi(q_1, q^+)} b \quad i \sim j \quad a[i] \in dep(x, exp) \quad \Phi(i, q^+) \sqsubseteq \bot}{b[j] \in exp} \ (\pi^{\#}\text{-}roweq)$$

$$\frac{a \xrightarrow{\Phi(q_1, q^+)} b \quad i \sim j \quad a[i] \in dep(x, exp) \quad \Phi(i, q^+) \text{ depends on } q}{b[j] \in exp} \ (\pi^{\#}\text{-}roweq')$$

Fig. 4. Inference rules describing how $\pi^{\#}$ may add expressions to exp. The rules correspond to rules from ρ and are tailored such that ρ can infer a constraint for each newly introduced expression. The upper two rules allow ρ to add an equality constraint, the third rule allows ρ to add a weak equivalence.

Proposition 4. *The abstract projection $\pi^{\#}$ overapproximates projection through existential quantification, i.e., $[\![\exists x.\,\gamma(A)]\!] \subseteq \gamma(\pi_x^{\#}(A))$.*

Proof. Pick $A \in MED$. Step 1 in our algorithm does not change the concretisation of A because neither enhancing exp nor applying ρ does so. Clearly $\pi_x^{nv}(A)$ is weaker than A, i.e., $\gamma(A) \subseteq \gamma(\pi_x^{nv}(A))$. Because $\exists$ is monotonous we can conclude $\exists x.\,\gamma(A) \subseteq \exists x.\,\gamma(\pi_x^{nv}(A))$. Because $\pi_x^{nv}(A)$ does not depend on x, we also know $\exists x.\,\gamma(\pi_x^{nv}(A)) \equiv \gamma(\pi_x^{nv}(A))$ holds.   □

Soundness of the map equality domain. We show that the map equality domain is sound and that a fixpoint computation in it terminates.

Theorem 1 (Soundness of $post^\#$). *The abstract post operator $post^\#$ is sound, i.e., for any abstract value $A \in MED$ and any transition $T \in Formulas(Var, Var')$ the following holds.*

$$post(\gamma(A), T) \subseteq \gamma(post^\#(A, T))$$

Proof. The proof goal follows directly from the fact that $T^\#$ overapproximates T, that the meet operator $\sqcap$ is sound (i.e. overapproximates $\wedge$), and that the projection operator overapproximates projection through existential quantification. □

Theorem 2 (Termination of fixpoint computation). *$post^\#$ converges on any program, i.e., for every transition relation T, there is a number of iterations $n \in \mathbb{N}$ such that $post^{\#^n}(\top, T)$ is a fixpoint.*

Proof. The proof goal holds because $T^\#$ has a finite number of expressions, $\pi^\#$ may only introduce a finite number of expressions, and there are only finitely many elements of MED for a fixed set of expressions exp. □

Table 1. The results of running our implementation on the benchmarks from the *memsafety* category of the SV-COMP benchmarks. The rows correspond to subfolders in the benchmark set. The columns show on how many benchmarks a fixpoint was found after a given amount of time up to five minutes as well as the total amount of files in each folder.

Folder	#files	<30 s	<120 s	<300 s
array-examples	4	4	4	4
array-memsafety	65	46	54	58
forester-heap	25	0	0	0
heap-manipulation	7	1	1	1
ldv-memsafety	105	82	82	82
ldv-memsafety-bitfields	10	10	10	10
list-ext-properties	19	8	10	10
list-properties	6	0	0	0
locks	13	13	13	13
memsafety	287	170	192	197
memsafety-ext	18	0	0	0
memsafety-ext2	10	0	0	0
ntdrivers-simplified	10	3	9	10

6   Evaluation

We have implemented our method within the abstract interpretation plugin [15] of the ULTIMATE framework[2]. For elements of ED we use a union-find data structure and the standard congruence closure algorithm [12]. The full reduction operator (in particular triggering the expensive rules Δ and ext) is applied only before operations that may suffer from a precision loss, namely join and projection. We have implemented basic caching to represent the order relation $\sqsubseteq$.

As our benchmark set we chose the programs from the *memsafety* category of SV-COMP 2018[3]. This category is focused on memory operations, which ULTIMATE translates into operations on maps.

We ran ULTIMATE in version 0.1.23-a5595af with a memory limit of 6 GB and a timelimit of 300 s on a machine with an 3.4 GHz Intel i7-2600 CPU. Table 1 shows the results of our experiments. While the method finished in under thirty seconds on the majority of benchmark tasks there is still a large set of benchmarks where the analysis needs more time. Still the experiments allow us to cautiously conclude that our method can be made scalable. Nevertheless a lot of work, in particular in exploring a wide range of possible optimizations, lies ahead of us until we obtain a practical tool.

References

1. Barrett, C., et al.: CVC4. In: Gopalakrishnan, G., Qadeer, S. (eds.) CAV 2011. LNCS, vol. 6806, pp. 171–177. Springer, Heidelberg (2011). https://doi.org/10.1007/978-3-642-22110-1_14

2. Beyer, D.: Software verification with validation of results. In: Legay, A., Margaria, T. (eds.) TACAS 2017. LNCS, vol. 10206, pp. 331–349. Springer, Heidelberg (2017). https://doi.org/10.1007/978-3-662-54580-5_20

3. Brillout, A., Kroening, D., Rümmer, P., Wahl, T.: Program verification via Craig interpolation for presburger arithmetic with arrays. In: VERIFY@IJCAR of EPiC Series in Computing, vol. 3, pp. 31–46. EasyChair (2010)

4. Chang, B.-Y.E., Leino, K.R.M.: Abstract interpretation with alien expressions and heap structures. In: Cousot, R. (ed.) VMCAI 2005. LNCS, vol. 3385, pp. 147–163. Springer, Heidelberg (2005). https://doi.org/10.1007/978-3-540-30579-8_11

5. Christ, J., Hoenicke, J.: Weakly equivalent arrays. In: Lutz, C., Ranise, S. (eds.) FroCoS 2015. LNCS (LNAI), vol. 9322, pp. 119–134. Springer, Cham (2015). https://doi.org/10.1007/978-3-319-24246-0_8

6. Christ, J., Hoenicke, J., Nutz, A.: SMTInterpol: an interpolating SMT solver. In: Donaldson, A., Parker, D. (eds.) SPIN 2012. LNCS, vol. 7385, pp. 248–254. Springer, Heidelberg (2012). https://doi.org/10.1007/978-3-642-31759-0_19

7. Cimatti, A., Griggio, A., Schaafsma, B.J., Sebastiani, R.: The MathSAT5 SMT solver. In: Piterman, N., Smolka, S.A. (eds.) TACAS 2013. LNCS, vol. 7795, pp. 93–107. Springer, Heidelberg (2013). https://doi.org/10.1007/978-3-642-36742-7_7

---

[2] https://github.com/ultimate-pa/ultimate.

[3] https://sv-comp.sosy-lab.org/2018.

8. Cousot, P., Cousot, R.: Abstract interpretation: a unified lattice model for static analysis of programs by construction or approximation of fixpoints. In: POPL, pp. 238–252. ACM (1977)

9. Cousot, P., Cousot, R.: Systematic design of program analysis frameworks, pp. 269–282, ACM Press, New York (1979)

10. Cousot, P., Cousot, R., Logozzo, F.: A parametric segmentation functor for fully automatic and scalable array content analysis. In: POPL, pp. 105–118. ACM (2011)

11. de Moura, L., Bjørner, N.: Z3: an efficient SMT solver. In: Ramakrishnan, C.R., Rehof, J. (eds.) TACAS 2008. LNCS, vol. 4963, pp. 337–340. Springer, Heidelberg (2008). https://doi.org/10.1007/978-3-540-78800-3_24

12. Downey, P.J., Sethi, R., Tarjan, R.E.: Variations on the common subexpression problem. J. ACM **27**(4), 758–771 (1980)

13. Dutertre, B.: Yices 2.2. In: Biere, A., Bloem, R. (eds.) CAV 2014. LNCS, vol. 8559, pp. 737–744. Springer, Cham (2014). https://doi.org/10.1007/978-3-319-08867-9_49

14. Gange, G., Navas, J.A., Schachte, P., Søndergaard, H., Stuckey, P.J.: An abstract domain of uninterpreted functions. In: Jobstmann, B., Leino, K.R.M. (eds.) VMCAI 2016. LNCS, vol. 9583, pp. 85–103. Springer, Heidelberg (2016). https://doi.org/10.1007/978-3-662-49122-5_4

15. Greitschus, M., Dietsch, D., Podelski, A.: Loop invariants from counterexamples. In: Ranzato, F. (ed.) SAS 2017. LNCS, vol. 10422, pp. 128–147. Springer, Cham (2017). https://doi.org/10.1007/978-3-319-66706-5_7

16. Gulwani, S., Tiwari, A.: An abstract domain for analyzing heap-manipulating low-level software. In: Damm, W., Hermanns, H. (eds.) CAV 2007. LNCS, vol. 4590, pp. 379–392. Springer, Heidelberg (2007). https://doi.org/10.1007/978-3-540-73368-3_42

17. Gulwani, S., Tiwari, A., Necula, G.C.: Join algorithms for the theory of uninterpreted functions. In: Lodaya, K., Mahajan, M. (eds.) FSTTCS 2004. LNCS, vol. 3328, pp. 311–323. Springer, Heidelberg (2004). https://doi.org/10.1007/978-3-540-30538-5_26

18. Hoenicke, J., Schindler, T.: Efficient interpolation in the theory of arrays. In: SMT Workshop (2017). http://smt-workshop.cs.uiowa.edu/2017/papers/SMT2017_paper_4.pdf

19. Leino, R.: This is Boogie 2. Microsoft Research, June 2008

20. McCarthy, J.: Towards a mathematical science of computation. In: IFIP Congress, pp. 21–28 (1962)

21. Stump, A., Barrett, C.W., Dill, D.L., Levitt. J.R.: A decision procedure for an extensional theory of arrays. In: LICS, pp. 29–37. IEEE Computer Society (2001)

Loop Detection by Logically Constrained Term Rewriting

Naoki Nishida[1]🆔 and Sarah Winkler[2](✉)🆔

[1] Department of Computing and Software Systems, Graduate School of Informatics, Nagoya University, Nagoya, Japan
`nishida@i.nagoya-u.ac.jp`
[2] Department of Computer Science, University of Innsbruck, Innsbruck, Austria
`sarah.winkler@uibk.ac.at`

Abstract. Logically constrained rewrite systems constitute a very general rewriting formalism that can capture simplification processes in various domains as well as computation in imperative programs. In both of these contexts, nontermination is a critical source of errors. We present new criteria to find loops in logically constrained rewrite systems which are implemented in the tool Ctrl. We illustrate the usefulness of these criteria in three example applications: to find loops in LLVM peephole optimizations, to detect looping executions of C programs, and to establish nontermination of integer transition systems.

Keywords: Constrained rewriting · Nontermination · Loops

1 Introduction

Rewriting in presence of side constraints captures simplification processes in various areas, such as expression rewriting in compilers, theorem provers, or SMT solvers [11,14,15,17]. But also computations in an imperative program can be seen as rewrite sequences according to a constrained rewrite system describing the control flow graph [7]. In both cases the imposed side constraints can typically be expressed as formulas over a decidable logic. *Logically constrained term rewrite systems* (LCTRSs) [12] formalize a very general rewriting mechanism that can express both of these settings, as well as earlier formalisms of constrained rewriting (cf. [12]). Side constraints of LCTRSs can employ an arbitrary first-order logic which contains propositional logic and equality, though their application for practical analysis tasks requires decidability of the logic under consideration. But thanks to the impressive progress of SMT solving in the last two decades, we can use theories including, for instance, integer as well as bitvector arithmetic and arrays. This renders LCTRSs a powerful analysis tool in a wide range of areas, including program verification [7].

This work is partially supported by JSPS KAKENHI Grant Number JP18K11160 and FWF (Austrian Science Fund) project T789.

R. Piskac and P. Rümmer (Eds.): VSTTE 2018, LNCS 11294, pp. 309–321, 2018.
https://doi.org/10.1007/978-3-030-03592-1_18

Termination is a key property of simplification and computation processes, and loops are the most common violation thereof. We consider an example from the field of compiler optimizations.

Example 1. The Instcombine pass in the LLVM compilation suite performs *peephole optimizations* to simplify expressions in the intermediate representation. The current optimization set contains over 1000 simplification rules to e.g. replace multiplications by shifts or perform bitwidth changes. About 500 of them have recently been translated into the domain-specific language Alive [14,15]. The following simplification is an example rule in this format.

```
Name: MulDivRem 9
Pre: C < 0 && isPowerOf2(abs(C))
%Op0 = sub %Y, %X
%r = mul %Op0, C
  =>
%sub = sub %X, %Y
%r = mul %sub, abs(C)
```

It consists of a precondition labelled `Pre`, a left-hand side (the expression before the arrow `=>`), and the right-hand side (the expression after the arrow). Both expressions are defined by a sequence of variable assignments. The last variable on each side—in this case `%r`—identifies the pattern to be replaced. This simplification can also be represented by the following LCTRS rule, using a side constraint over bitvector arithmetic:

$$\mathsf{mul}(\mathsf{sub}(y, x), c) \rightarrow \mathsf{mul}(\mathsf{sub}(x, y), \mathsf{abs}(c)) \; [c <_s \#\mathsf{x0} \wedge \mathsf{isPowerOf2}(\mathsf{abs}(c))] \quad (1)$$

The Instcombine optimization suite is community-maintained, and unintended interference of rules may occur. For instance, for 16-bit integers where #x8000 is the smallest representable integer value, Rule (1) in combination with constant folding admits the following loop since abs(#x8000) evaluates to #x8000:

$$\mathsf{mul}(\mathsf{sub}(x, x), \#\mathsf{x8000}) \rightarrow \mathsf{mul}(\mathsf{sub}(x, x), \mathsf{abs}(\#\mathsf{x8000})) \rightarrow \mathsf{mul}(\mathsf{sub}(x, x), \#\mathsf{x8000})$$

In this paper we present new criteria to recognize loops in LCTRSs. We implemented them in the Constrained Rewrite tooL Ctrl [13], which can now for instance detect the loop shown in Example 1. In order to illustrate the usefulness of our criteria, we discuss applications in three example domains: (1) finding loops in the Instcombine optimization suite, (2) detecting loops in C programs, and (3) establishing nontermination of integer transition systems.

The remainder of this paper is structured as follows. In Sect. 2 we recall preliminaries about logically constrained rewrite systems. We present our nontermination criteria in Sect. 3. Afterwards, we outline our implementation within the tool Ctrl in Sect. 4, and report on detecting loops in some example application areas in Sect. 5. In Sect. 6 we conclude.

2   Preliminaries

We assume familiarity with term rewrite systems [1], but briefly recapitulate the notion of logically constrained rewriting [7,12] that our approach is based on.

We consider an infinite set of variables $\mathcal{V}$ and a sorted signature $\mathcal{F} = \mathcal{F}_{\text{terms}} \cup \mathcal{F}_{\text{theory}}$ such that $\mathcal{T}(\mathcal{F}, \mathcal{V})$ denotes the set of terms over this signature. Symbols in $\mathcal{F}_{\text{terms}}$ are called *term symbols*, while $\mathcal{F}_{\text{theory}}$ contains *theory symbols*. A term in $\mathcal{T}(\mathcal{F}_{\text{theory}}, \mathcal{V})$ is called a theory term. For a non-variable term $t = f(t_1, \ldots, t_n)$, we write $\text{root}(t)$ to obtain the top-most symbol f. A position p is an integer sequence used to identify subterms of a given term. The *subterm* of t at position p is defined as $t|_\epsilon = t$, and if $t = f(t_1, \ldots, t_n)$ then $t|_{ip} = t_i|_p$. The result of replacing the subterm of a term t at position p by s is denoted $t[s]_p$. A *context* C is a term with a single occurrence of a designated constant $\square$, and we write $C[t]$ to denote the term obtained by replacing $\square$ in C by t. A *substitution* σ is a mapping from variables to terms. We write $\mathcal{D}om(\sigma)$ and $\mathcal{R}an(\sigma)$ for its domain and range, while $t\sigma$ denotes the application of σ to a term t.

Terms over logical symbols are associated with a fixed semantics. To this end, we assume a mapping $\mathcal{I}$ that assigns to every sort ι occurring in $\mathcal{F}_{\text{theory}}$ a carrier set $\mathcal{I}(\iota)$, and an interpretation $\mathcal{J}$ that assigns to every symbol $f \in \mathcal{F}_{\text{theory}}$ a function $f_{\mathcal{J}}$. For every sort ι occurring in $\mathcal{F}_{\text{theory}}$ we assume a set $\mathcal{V}al_\iota \subseteq \mathcal{F}_{\text{theory}}$ of *value* symbols, such that all $c \in \mathcal{V}al_\iota$ are constants of sort ι and $\mathcal{J}$ constitutes a bijective mapping between $\mathcal{V}al_\iota$ and $\mathcal{I}(\iota)$. Hence there exists a constant symbol for every value in the carrier set. We write $\mathcal{V}al$ for $\bigcup_\iota \mathcal{V}al_\iota$. The interpretation $\mathcal{J}$ naturally extends to theory terms without variables by setting $[f(t_1, \ldots, t_n)]_{\mathcal{J}} = f_{\mathcal{I}}([t_1]_{\mathcal{J}}, \ldots, [t_n]_{\mathcal{J}})$. Theory symbols and term symbols are supposed to overlap only on values, i.e., $\mathcal{F}_{\text{terms}} \cap \mathcal{F}_{\text{theory}} \subseteq \mathcal{V}al$ holds. We assume a sort bool such that $\mathcal{I}(\text{bool}) = \mathbb{B} = \{\top, \bot\}$ with values $\mathcal{V}al_{\text{bool}} = \{\text{true}, \text{false}\}$ such that $\text{true}_{\mathcal{J}} = \top$, and $\text{false}_{\mathcal{J}} = \bot$. Moreover we consider a theory symbol $\approx$ for equality. Theory terms of sort bool are called *constraints*. A substitution σ which satisfies $\sigma(x) \in \mathcal{V}al$ for all $x \in \mathcal{D}om(\sigma)$ is also called an *assignment*. A constraint φ is *valid* if $[\varphi\gamma]_{\mathcal{J}} = \top$ for all assignments γ, and *satisfiable* if $[\varphi\gamma]_{\mathcal{J}} = \top$ for some assignment γ.

Logically Constrained Rewriting. We consider constrained rewriting as developed in [7,12]. A *constrained rewrite rule* is a triple $\ell \to r \; [\varphi]$ where $\ell, r \in \mathcal{T}(\mathcal{F}, \mathcal{V})$, $\ell \notin \mathcal{V}$, φ is a constraint, and $\text{root}(\ell) \in \mathcal{F}_{\text{terms}} \setminus \mathcal{F}_{\text{theory}}$. If $\varphi = \text{true}$ then the constraint is omitted, and the rule denoted as $\ell \to r$. A set of constrained rewrite rules is called a *logically constrained term rewrite system* (LCTRS for short).

In order to define rewriting using constrained rewrite rules, a substitution σ is said to *respect* a constraint φ if $\varphi\sigma$ is valid and $\sigma(x) \in \mathcal{V}al$ for all $x \in \mathcal{V}ar(\varphi)$. A *calculation step* $s \to_{\text{calc}} t$ satisfies $s = C[f(s_1, \ldots, s_n)]$ for some $f \in \mathcal{F}_{\text{theory}} \setminus \mathcal{V}al$, $t = C[u]$, $s_i \in \mathcal{V}al$ for all $1 \leqslant i \leqslant n$, and $u \in \mathcal{V}al$ is the value symbol of $[f(s_1, \ldots, s_n)]_{\mathcal{J}}$. In this case $f(x_1, \ldots, x_n) \to y \; [y \approx f(x_1, \ldots, x_n)]$ is a *calculation rule*, where y is a variable different from $x_1, \ldots, x_n$. A *rule step* $s \to_{\ell \to r \; [\varphi]} t$ satisfies $s = C[\ell\sigma]$, $t = C[r\sigma]$, and σ respects φ. For an LCTRS

$\mathcal{R}$, we also write $\rightarrow_{\mathsf{rule},\,\mathcal{R}}$ to refer to the relation $\{\rightarrow_\alpha\}_{\alpha\in\mathcal{R}}$, and denote $\rightarrow_{\mathsf{calc}} \cup$ $\rightarrow_{\mathsf{rule},\,\mathcal{R}}$ by $\rightarrow_\mathcal{R}$. The subscript $\mathcal{R}$ is dropped if clear from the context.

Example 2. Consider the sorts int and bool, and let $\mathcal{F}_{\mathsf{theory}}$ consist of symbols $\cdot$, $+$, $-$, $\leqslant$, and $\geqslant$ as well as values n for all $n \in \mathbb{Z}$, with the usual interpretations on $\mathbb{Z}$. Let $\mathcal{F}_{\mathsf{terms}} = \mathcal{V}al \cup \{\mathsf{fact}\}$. The LCTRS $\mathcal{R}$ consisting of the rules

$$\mathsf{fact}(x) \rightarrow 1 \quad [x \leqslant 0] \qquad \mathsf{fact}(x) \rightarrow \mathsf{fact}(x-1)\cdot x \quad [x-1 \geqslant 0]$$

admits the following rewrite steps:

$$
\begin{aligned}
\mathsf{fact}(2) &\rightarrow_{\mathsf{rule}} \mathsf{fact}(2-1)\cdot 2 && (\text{as } 2-1 \geqslant 0 \text{ is valid})\\
&\rightarrow_{\mathsf{calc}} \mathsf{fact}(1)\cdot 2 \quad\quad \rightarrow_{\mathsf{rule}} (\mathsf{fact}(1-1)\cdot 1)\cdot 2 && (\text{as } 1-1 \geqslant 0 \text{ is valid})\\
&\rightarrow_{\mathsf{calc}} (\mathsf{fact}(0)\cdot 1)\cdot 2 \rightarrow_{\mathsf{rule}} (1\cdot 1)\cdot 2 && (\text{as } 0 \leqslant 0 \text{ is valid})\\
&\rightarrow^+_{\mathsf{calc}} 2
\end{aligned}
$$

An LCTRS $\mathcal{R}$ is *terminating* if $\rightarrow_\mathcal{R}$ is well-founded. A *loop* is a rewrite sequence of the form $t \rightarrow^+_\mathcal{R} C[t\sigma]$. Due to the sequence $t \rightarrow^+_\mathcal{R} C[t\sigma] \rightarrow^+_\mathcal{R} C^2[t\sigma^2] \rightarrow^+_\mathcal{R} \cdots$ existence of a loop implies nontermination. For example, a rewrite rule $\mathsf{f}(x,y) \rightarrow \mathsf{h}(\mathsf{f}(-x,\mathsf{g}(y)))$ $[x \geqslant 0]$ gives rise to the loop where $t = \mathsf{f}(0,y)$, $C = \mathsf{h}(\square)$, and $\sigma = \{y \mapsto \mathsf{g}(y)\}$:

$$\mathsf{f}(0,y) \rightarrow_{\mathsf{rule}} \mathsf{h}(\mathsf{f}(-0,\mathsf{g}(y))) \rightarrow_{\mathsf{calc}} \mathsf{h}(\mathsf{f}(0,\mathsf{g}(y))) \rightarrow_{\mathsf{rule}} \mathsf{h}(\mathsf{h}(\mathsf{f}(-0,\mathsf{g}(\mathsf{g}(y))))) \rightarrow_{\mathsf{calc}} \cdots$$

Rewriting Constrained Terms. The notion of rewriting for *unconstrained* terms considered so far is used to model the actual simplification and computation processes in practice. But for the sake of analysis it is convenient to also define a notion of rewriting on *constrained* terms, for instance to capture the composition of rewrite rules.

To that end, a *constrained term* is a pair $s\ [\varphi]$ of a term s and a constraint φ. Two constrained terms $s\ [\varphi]$ and $t\ [\psi]$ are *equivalent*, denoted by $s\ [\varphi] \sim t\ [\psi]$, if for every substitution γ respecting φ there is some substitution δ that respects ψ such that $s\gamma = t\delta$, and vice versa. For example, $\mathsf{fact}(x)\cdot x\ [x = 1 \wedge x < y] \sim \mathsf{fact}(1)\cdot y\ [y > 0 \wedge y < 2]$ holds, but these terms are not equivalent to $\mathsf{fact}(x)\cdot y\ [x = y]$ or $\mathsf{fact}(1)\ [\mathsf{true}]$. Next we define rewriting on constrained terms.

Definition 1

- A *calculation step* $s\ [\varphi] \rightarrow_{\mathsf{calc}} t\ [\varphi \wedge x \approx f(s_1,\ldots,s_n)]$ needs to satisfy $s = C[f(s_1,\ldots,s_n)]$ for some $f \in \mathcal{F}_{\mathsf{theory}} \setminus \mathcal{F}_{\mathsf{terms}}$ and $t = C[x]$ such that $s_1,\ldots,s_n \in \mathcal{V}ar(\varphi) \cup \mathcal{V}al$ and x is a fresh variable.
- A constrained rewrite rule $\alpha\colon \ell \rightarrow r\ [\psi]$ admits a *rule step* $s\ [\varphi] \rightarrow_\alpha t\ [\varphi]$ if φ is satisfiable, $s = C[\ell\sigma]$, $t = C[r\sigma]$, $\sigma(x) \in \mathcal{V}al \cup \mathcal{V}ar(\varphi)$ for all $x \in \mathcal{V}ar(\psi)$, and $\varphi \Rightarrow \psi\sigma$ is valid.

Given an LCTRS $\mathcal{R}$, we again write $\rightarrow_{\mathsf{rule},\,\mathcal{R}}$ for $\{\rightarrow_\alpha\}_{\alpha\in\mathcal{R}}$. The main rewrite relation $\rightarrow_\mathcal{R}$ on constrained terms is defined as $\sim \cdot (\rightarrow_{\mathsf{calc}} \cup \rightarrow_{\mathsf{rule},\,\mathcal{R}}) \cdot \sim$.

For example, the LCTRS from Example 2 and the constraint $\varphi = x \geqslant 1 \land y \geqslant 0$ admit the rule step $\mathsf{fact}(x + y) \; [\varphi] \to_{\mathsf{rule}} \mathsf{fact}(x + y - 1) \cdot (x + y) \; [\varphi]$, while $\mathsf{fact}(x + y) \; [\varphi] \to_{\mathsf{calc}} \mathsf{fact}(z) \; [\varphi \land z \approx x + y]$ is a possible calculation step.

We next define narrowing on constrained terms (cf. the notion of *chains* [4]).

Definition 2. A constrained rewrite rule $\alpha \colon \ell \to r \; [\psi]$ admits a narrowing step $s \; [\varphi] \rightsquigarrow_{\alpha,p}^{\mu} t \; [\varphi']$ if $s = s[s']_p$, the terms s' and ℓ are unifiable with mgu μ, the resulting term is $t = (s[r]_p)\mu$, $\varphi' = (\varphi \land \psi)\mu$, and φ' is satisfiable.

We also write $s \; [\varphi] \; {}_{\alpha}^{\mu}{\rightsquigarrow} \; t \; [\varphi']$ if $\alpha \colon \ell \to r \; [\psi]$ admits a step $t \; [\varphi'] \rightsquigarrow_{r \to \ell}^{\mu} {}_{[\psi]} \; s \; [\varphi]$. The following lemma shows the crucial correspondence between narrowing and rewriting, which ensures correctness of our loop detection shown in Sect. 4.

Lemma 1 (Lifting Lemma). *Suppose* $\alpha \colon \ell \to r \; [\psi]$ *admits a narrowing step* $s \; [\varphi] \rightsquigarrow_{\alpha,p}^{\mu} t \; [\varphi']$, *where* $\varphi' = (\varphi \land \psi)\mu$. *Then* $s\mu \; [\varphi'] \to_{\alpha,p} t \; [\varphi']$.

Proof. We have $s\mu|_p = \ell\mu$ and can perform a rewrite step because $\varphi' = (\varphi \land \psi)\mu$ is satisfiable, and $\varphi' \Rightarrow \psi\mu$ is valid. The result is indeed $s\mu[r\mu] = (s[r]_p)\mu = t$. $\square$

3   Loop Criteria

Our aim is to detect loops in LCTRSs. More precisely, given an LCTRS $\mathcal{R}$ we want to find rewrite sequences $t \to_{\mathcal{R}}^+ C[t\sigma]$ on *unconstrained* terms. A natural approach to this end from standard rewriting is *unfolding* [19]: one tries to compose (instances of) rewrite rules such that the final term of the resulting rewrite sequence contains (an instance of) the initial term. For our setting, this requires to rewrite *constrained* terms. But a rewrite sequence $t \; [\varphi] \to_{\mathcal{R}}^+ C[t\sigma] \; [\psi]$ on constrained terms where the final term contains the initial term need not imply a loop: this depends on whether the constraints can remain satisfied after repeated execution of the respective rewrite steps. In this section we consider a rewrite sequence $t \; [\psi] \to_{\mathcal{R}}^+ C[t\sigma] \; [\psi]$ and look for sufficient criteria such that these steps give rise to a loop. If there exists a ψ as above then we abbreviate this by $t \to_{\psi,\mathcal{R}}^+ C[t\sigma]$ and call it a *loop candidate*.

The following criterion was presented in [18, Theorem 2].

Lemma 2. *Let* $\mathcal{R}$ *be an LCTRS, and* ψ *a constraint. Suppose* $t \to_{\psi,\mathcal{R}}^+ C[t\sigma]$ *for a term* t, *context* C, *and substitution* σ *such that* $\sigma(x) \in \mathcal{T}(\mathcal{F}_{\text{theory}}, \mathcal{V})$ *for all* $x \in \mathcal{V}\mathrm{ar}(\psi)$, ψ *is satisfiable, and* $\psi \Longrightarrow \psi\sigma$ *valid. Then* $\mathcal{R}$ *is nonterminating.*

As a nontermination criterion, Lemma 2 has the disadvantage that it cannot detect loops which occur only for *specific* input values, such as the loop from Example 1. We next propose two criteria which remedy this shortcoming.

Lemma 3. *Let* $\mathcal{R}$ *be an LCTRS, and* ψ *a constraint. Suppose that* $t \to_{\psi,\mathcal{R}}^+ C[t\sigma]$ *for some term* t, *context* C, *and substitution* σ *such that* $\sigma(x) \in \mathcal{T}(\mathcal{F}_{\text{theory}}, \mathcal{V})$ *for all* $x \in \mathcal{V}\mathrm{ar}(\psi)$, *and* $\psi \land \bigwedge_{y \in \mathcal{D}\mathrm{om}(\sigma)} y \approx y\sigma$ *is a constraint satisfied by some assignment* α. *Then* $\mathcal{R}$ *is nonterminating because of the loop* $t\alpha \to_{\mathcal{R}}^+ C[t\sigma\alpha]$.

Proof. If $\psi \wedge \bigwedge_{y \in \mathcal{D}om(\sigma)} y \approx y\sigma$ is satisfied by an assignment α then $\psi\alpha$ is valid, and $[y\alpha]_{\mathcal{J}} = [y\sigma\alpha]_{\mathcal{J}}$ for all $y \in \mathcal{D}om(\sigma)$. Thus $t\sigma\alpha \rightarrow_{\mathsf{calc}}^{*} t\alpha$ such that there is a loop $t\alpha \rightarrow_{\mathcal{R}}^{+} C[t\sigma\alpha] \rightarrow_{\mathsf{calc}}^{*} C[t\alpha] \rightarrow_{\mathcal{R}}^{+} \cdots$. $\qquad\square$

Example 3. Returning to Example 1, the two rewrite steps

$$\mathsf{mul}(\mathsf{sub}(y, x), c) \; [\varphi] \rightarrow_{\mathsf{rule}} \mathsf{mul}(\mathsf{sub}(x, y), \mathsf{abs}(c)) \; [\varphi] \rightarrow_{\mathsf{calc}} \mathsf{mul}(\mathsf{sub}(x, y), c') \; [\psi]$$

constitute a loop candidate, where $\varphi = c <_s \#\mathsf{x0000} \wedge \mathsf{isPowerOf2}(\mathsf{abs}(c))$ and $\psi = \varphi \wedge c' = \mathsf{abs}(c)$. We thus have $t \; [\psi] \rightarrow_{\mathcal{R}}^{+} C[t\sigma] \; [\psi]$ for $t = \mathsf{mul}(\mathsf{sub}(y, x), c)$, $C = \square$, and $\sigma = \{y \mapsto x, c \mapsto c'\}$, such that $\sigma(z)$ is a logical term for all z in ψ. The formula $\psi \wedge x = y \wedge c = c'$ is satisfiable by any assignment such that $\alpha(x) = \alpha(y)$ and $\alpha(c) = \alpha(c') = \#\mathsf{x8000}$, which exhibits the loop in Example 1:

$$\mathsf{mul}(\mathsf{sub}(x, x), \#\mathsf{x8000}) \rightarrow \mathsf{mul}(\mathsf{sub}(x, x), \mathsf{abs}(\#\mathsf{x8000})) \rightarrow \mathsf{mul}(\mathsf{sub}(x, x), \#\mathsf{x8000})$$

The criterion of Lemma 3 is rather restrictive in that it demands the starting term to occur again as a subterm after some (calculation) steps. The next criterion adds some flexibility in this respect.

Lemma 4. *Let $\mathcal{R}$ be an LCTRS, and ψ a constraint. Suppose that $t \rightarrow_{\psi,\mathcal{R}}^{+} C[t\sigma]$ for some term t, context C, and substitution σ such that $\sigma(x) \in \mathcal{T}(\mathcal{F}_{\text{theory}}, \mathcal{V})$ for all $x \in \mathcal{V}ar(\psi)$. Suppose $\mathcal{D}om(\sigma) = \{y_1, \ldots, y_n\}$, and let $\rho = \{y_1 \mapsto z_1, \ldots, y_n \mapsto z_n\}$ be a renaming to fresh variables $z_1, \ldots, z_n$.*

If $\forall y_1 \ldots y_n.(\psi \implies \psi\sigma) \wedge \psi\rho$ is satisfiable by α then $\mathcal{R}$ is nonterminating because of the loop $t\rho\alpha \rightarrow_{\mathcal{R}}^{+} C[t\sigma\rho\alpha]$.

Proof. We write $\overline{y}$ for $y_1 \ldots y_n$ and assume that $\chi = \forall\overline{y}.(\psi \implies \psi\sigma) \wedge \psi\rho$ is satisfied by some assignment α, so $\mathcal{R}an(\alpha) \subseteq \mathcal{V}al$. We can assume $\mathcal{D}om(\alpha) \cap \{\overline{y}\} = \varnothing$ since there are no free occurrences of y_i in χ. There must be some assignment β such that $\alpha = \beta \uplus \alpha|_{\{z_i\}}$, and we abbreviate $\gamma = \rho\alpha|_{\{z_i\}}$. By assumption $\psi\rho\alpha$ holds, which coincides with $\psi\beta\gamma$ because $\mathcal{R}an(\beta) \subseteq \mathcal{V}al$ and $\mathcal{D}om(\beta) \cap \{\overline{y}\} = \varnothing$. Moreover $\forall\overline{y}.(\psi \implies \psi\sigma)\beta\alpha|_{\{z_i\}}$ holds, and we have

$$
\begin{aligned}
(\forall\overline{y}.(\psi \implies \psi\sigma)\beta\alpha|_{\{z_i\}}) &= (\forall\overline{y}.(\psi\beta \implies \psi\sigma\beta))\alpha|_{\{z_i\}} && \text{as } \mathcal{D}om(\beta) \cap \{\overline{y}\} = \varnothing \\
&= (\forall\overline{y}.(\psi\beta \implies \psi\sigma\beta)) && \text{because } \overline{z} \text{ are fresh} \\
&= (\forall\overline{y}.(\psi\beta \implies \psi\beta\sigma)) && \text{as } \mathcal{D}om(\beta) \cap \{\overline{y}\} = \varnothing
\end{aligned}
$$

Thus $\psi\beta\gamma'$ implies $\psi\beta\sigma\gamma'$ for all substitutions γ' with $\mathcal{D}om(\gamma') = \{\overline{y}\}$. Since $\mathcal{D}om(\sigma^k\gamma) = \{\overline{y}\}$ the constraint $\psi\beta\sigma^k\gamma = \psi\sigma^k\beta\gamma = \psi\sigma^k\rho\alpha$ holds for all $k \geqslant 0$. Hence we have the loop

$$t\rho\alpha \rightarrow_{\mathcal{R}}^{+} C[t\sigma\rho\alpha] \rightarrow_{\mathcal{R}}^{+} C^2[t\sigma^2\rho\alpha] \rightarrow_{\mathcal{R}}^{+} \cdots \qquad\square$$

Example 4. Consider the following LCTRS $\mathcal{R}_0$ with constraints over the integers:

$$\mathsf{f}(x, y) \rightarrow \mathsf{f}(x + 1 - y, y) - 1 \; [y \neq 1 \wedge x \geqslant 0]$$

The rule constitutes a loop candidate: We have $t \to^+_{\psi, \mathcal{R}} C[t\sigma]$ for $t = f(x, y)$, $C = \Box - 1$, and $\sigma = \{x \mapsto x + 1 - y\}$ with $\mathcal{D}om(\sigma) = \{x\}$. The formula

$$\forall x \ (y \neq 1 \wedge x \geq 0 \implies (y \neq 1 \wedge (x + 1 - y) \geq 0)) \wedge y \neq 1 \wedge z \geq 0$$

is satisfied e.g. by the assignment $\alpha(y) = \alpha(z) = 0$. Thus we can detect the loop

$$f(0, 0) \to_{\mathcal{R}} f(0 + 1 - 0, 0) \to^+_{\mathsf{calc}} f(1, 0) \to_{\mathcal{R}} f(1 + 1 - 0, 0) \to^+_{\mathsf{calc}} f(2, 0) \to \cdots$$

Note that this loop is not captured by the criteria in Lemmas 2 and 3.

It is clear that Lemma 4 subsumes Lemma 2— satisfiability of ψ and validity of $\psi \implies \psi\sigma$ in Lemma 2 implies satisfiability of $\forall y_1 \ldots y_n.(\psi \implies \psi\sigma) \wedge \psi\rho$ in Lemma 4. The LCTRS $\mathcal{R}_0$ from Example 4 indicates the existence of an example for which Lemma 4 can detect a loop but Lemmas 2 or 3 do not. The following example shows the remaining relationship between Lemmas 2, 3, and 4.

Example 5. A loop of the LCTRS $\mathcal{R}_1 = \{ f(x) \to f(x) \ [x \geq 0] \}$ can be detected by Lemmas 2, 3, and 4. A loop of the LCTRS $\mathcal{R}_2 = \{ f(x) \to f(x+1) \ [x \geq 0] \}$ can be detected by Lemmas 2 and 4 but not by Lemma 3. A loop of the LCTRS $\mathcal{R}_3 = \{ f(x, y) \to f(x + y, y) \ [x \geq 0] \}$ can be detected by Lemmas 3 and 4 but not by Lemma 2. A loop of the LCTRS $\mathcal{R}_4 = \{ f(x, y) \to f(y + 1, x - 1) \ [x \geq 0 \wedge y \geq 0] \}$ can be detected by Lemma 3 but not by Lemmas 2 or 4.

The relationship between the different criteria is summarized in Fig. 1.

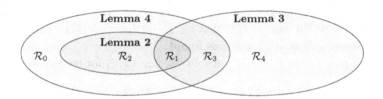

Fig. 1. Relationship between the criteria implied by Lemmas 2, 3, and 4.

4   Implementation

We extended the tool Ctrl [13] by nontermination techniques that exploit the criteria presented in Sect. 3. Optionally a starting term can be given, i.e., two modes are supported:

(a) Given an LCTRS $\mathcal{R}$, find a loop $t \to^+_{\mathcal{R}} C[t\sigma]$.
(b) Given an LCTRS $\mathcal{R}$ and a starting term u, find a loop reachable from u, i.e., a sequence $u \to^*_{\mathcal{R}} t \to^+_{\mathcal{R}} C[t\sigma]$.

To that end our implementation searches loop candidates $t \rightarrow^+_{\varphi,\mathcal{R}} C[t\sigma]$ which satisfy the criteria in Lemmas 2–4. An input file in the ctrs format specifies the logical theory to be used, the signature, the rewrite rules, and a query to fix the problem statement for Ctrl, i.e., the requested analysis or transformation task. To support nontermination analysis, we provide loops as a query in input files:

QUERY loops t

where the optional argument t is a term from which a loop should be reachable. Ctrl offers theory specifications for integers and arrays, and we added bitvectors for this work. Alternatively, a user-defined theory specification can be used.

We next describe how our implementation detects loops. Following the idea of unfolding [19], we construct *sequence tuples* $(s \rightarrow t\ [\psi], S)$ where $s \rightarrow t\ [\psi]$ is a constrained rewrite rule, $S = [(\alpha_1, p_1), \dots, (\alpha_k, p_k)]$, α_i is a rule of the form $\ell_i \rightarrow r_i\ [\varphi_i]$ and p_i are positions for all $0 \leqslant i \leqslant k$ such that there is the rewrite sequence $s\ [\psi] \rightarrow_{\alpha_1,p_1} \cdots \rightarrow_{\alpha_k,p_k} t\ [\psi]$.. In either of the modes (a) and (b), we proceed in five steps as follows.

(1) Using the dependency pair (DP) framework present in Ctrl [12], the problem is split into strongly connected components of the dependency graph. This results in a set of DP problems of the form $(\mathcal{P}, \mathcal{R})$, where $\mathcal{P}$ is a set of dependency pairs and $\mathcal{R}$ the given LCTRS. (Basically this amounts to splitting the problem into rules $\mathcal{P}$ that are applied at the root of a term and rules $\mathcal{R}$ that can be applied below. Then potential cycles in the call graph are identified, and only upon these the analysis continues; see [12] for details.)

The following steps are then performed for each of these DP problems:

(2) The set of initial sequence tuples T_0 is determined. In case of (a), we take the set of all single-step sequences $(\ell \rightarrow r\ [\varphi], [(\ell \rightarrow r\ [\varphi], \epsilon)])$ such that $\ell \rightarrow r\ [\varphi] \in \mathcal{P}$. In case of (b), this set is restricted to those tuples where a rewrite sequence $u \rightarrow_{\varphi,\mathcal{R}} v[\ell]$ was found.

(3) Given tuples T_i, we define T^f_{i+1} for forward and T^b_{i+1} for backward unfolding:

$$T^f_{i+1} = \{(s\tau \rightarrow u\ [\chi],\ S_f) \mid (s \rightarrow t\ [\psi], S) \in T_i,\ \beta \in \mathcal{Q} \text{ and } t\ [\varphi] \rightsquigarrow^\tau_{\beta,q} u\ [\chi]\}$$

$$T^b_{i+1} = \{(u\tau \rightarrow t\ [\chi],\ S_b) \mid (s \rightarrow t\ [\psi], S) \in T_i,\ \beta \in \mathcal{Q} \text{ and } u\ [\varphi]\ {}_{\beta,q}{}^\tau\!\!\leftsquigarrow s\ [\chi]\}$$

Here $\mathcal{Q}$ abbreviates $\mathcal{P} \cup \mathcal{R}$, $S_f = S \mathbin{+\!\!+} [(\beta, q)]$ and $S_b = [(\beta, q)] \mathbin{+\!\!+} S$, where $\mathbin{+\!\!+}$ denotes list concatenation.

(4) Let $T = \bigcup_{i \leqslant n} T_i$ for some n. By the construction of T_i and Lemma 1, we have $s\ [\psi] \rightarrow^+_{\mathcal{R} \cup \mathcal{P}} t\ [\psi]$ for all $(s \rightarrow t\ [\psi], S) \in T$. If $t = C[s']$ for some C and s' such that s and s' are unifiable with mgu μ and $\psi\mu$ is satisfiable, then $s\mu\ [\psi\mu] \rightarrow^+_{\mathcal{R} \cup \mathcal{P}} C[s\mu]\ [\psi\mu]$ is a loop candidate.

(5) We finally use Lemmas 2, 3, and 4 to check whether there are input values for which the loop candidates correspond to actual loops.

Since it is known that forward and backward unfolding are incomparable in general [19], both methods are supported. The tool as well as input files corresponding to the examples used in this paper can be found on-line[1].

---

[1] http://cl-informatik.uibk.ac.at/users/swinkler/lctrs_loops.

5 Applications

We now illustrate the loop support of Ctrl in three different application domains.

LLVM Instcombine Simplifications

We transformed the around 500 simplifications in the Alive language mentioned in Example 1 into LCTRSs using bitvector theory as background logic. These simplifications are split into domains. We tested Ctrl on the simplification sets for addition and subtraction, multiplication and division, shifts, bitwise logical operations, and select operations, as well as on their union. Table 1 summarizes our results. The columns refer to the different domains, and loops refers to the set of rules involved in all loops found in the work [16] discussed below. The rows indicate how many loops of length at most 3 were found by Ctrl using forward (fw) and backward (bw) unfolding, respectively, and how much time was required. In general forward unfolding seems to be more useful than backward unfolding.

Table 1. Instcombine loops found via forward (fw) and backward (bw) unfolding.

	# rules	add-sub	mul-div	shift	and-or	select	loops	all
		66	118	75	180	85	43	518
fw	3-loops	4	8	4	22	2	40	51
	Time (s)	16	80	9	3601	24	25	>32k
bw	3-loops	4	8	4	10	2	27	TO
	Time (s)	29	727	9	8400	21	24	TO

A dedicated tool `alive-loops` to detect loops in the Instcombine optimizations was presented in [16]. We briefly compare our criteria to their approach: First of all, we found the same loops with Ctrl that were exhibited by `alive-loops`, modulo combination and nesting of loops. But the loop check applied in `alive-loops` is different: It amounts to the search for a loop candidate $t \rightarrow^+_{\psi,\mathcal{R}} C[t\sigma]$ such that $\psi \implies \psi\sigma$ is satisfiable. While this is obviously a necessary condition it is in general not sufficient:

Example 6. As an (artificial) example, consider the constrained rewrite rule $\mathsf{and}(\#\mathsf{x0}, x) \rightarrow \mathsf{and}(\#\mathsf{x0}, x \gg_u \#\mathsf{x1})\ [x > \#\mathsf{x0}]$. It gives rise to a loop candidate $t \rightarrow^+_{\psi,\mathcal{R}} t\sigma$ where $\psi = x > \#\mathsf{x0}$, $t = \mathsf{and}(\#\mathsf{x0}, x)$, and $\sigma = \{x \mapsto x \gg_u \#\mathsf{x1}\}$. The constraint $\psi \implies \psi\sigma$ is satisfiable. But logically shifting x to the right will eventually result in a bit vector $\#\mathsf{x0000}$, hence no such loop exists. Indeed `alive-loops` finds a spurious loop in this example, but Ctrl does not.

By the correctness proofs of Lemmas 3 and 4, such false positives can be excluded for Ctrl. Moreover `alive-loops` is limited in that it restricts to loop candidates which are not size-increasing.

We remark that not all loops found by Ctrl or `alive-loops` can actually occur in the LLVM Instcombine pass since the rule set is applied with a particular strategy, such that certain optimizations can "shadow" other ones. Thus it needs to be checked by hand whether the detected potential loops can actually occur.

Loops in Integer Transition Systems

Integer term rewriting has been introduced as a rewriting formalism which natively supports integer operations, to be applied to rewrite-based program analysis [6]. The integer transition system `Velroyen08-alternKonv.jar-obl-8` from the Termination Problem Database 9.0[2] corresponds to the following LCTRS:

$$f1\_0\_main(x,y) \rightarrow f81\_0(x',y') \quad [\, x > 0 \land y > -1 \land y = x' \,] \tag{1}$$
$$f81\_0(x,y) \rightarrow f81\_0(x',y') \quad [\, x < 0 \land x > -3 \land x + 2 = x' \,] \tag{2}$$
$$f81\_0(x,y) \rightarrow f81\_0(x',y') \quad [\, x > 0 \land x < 3 \land x - 2 = x' \,] \tag{3}$$
$$f81\_0(x,y) \rightarrow f81\_0(x',y') \quad [\, x < -2 \land x < -1 \land x < 0 \land -x - 2 = x' \,] \tag{4}$$
$$f81\_0(x,y) \rightarrow f81\_0(x',y') \quad [\, x > 2 \land -x + 2 = x' \,] \tag{5}$$
$$init(x,y) \rightarrow f1\_0\_main(x',y') \tag{6}$$

where the starting term is of the form $init(x, y)$. It admits the following rewrite steps which contain a loop:

$$init(1,1) \xrightarrow{(6)} f1\_0\_main(1,1) \xrightarrow{(1)} f81\_0(1,-1) \xrightarrow{(3)} f81\_0(-1,0) \xrightarrow{(2)} f81\_0(1,-1)$$

(where the arrows are decorated with the applied rule). Ctrl can easily show nontermination within less than 2 seconds by exploiting Lemma 3. This is also the case for the similar system `alternKonv_rec`, while in the Termination Competition 2017[3] both of these problems remained unsolved.

Loops in C Programs

Consider the following C program implementing binary search [10]:

```c
int bsearch(int a[], int k, unsigned int lo, unsigned int hi) {
  unsigned int mid;
  while (lo < hi) {
    mid = (lo + hi)/2;
    if (a[mid] < k)
      lo = mid + 1;
    else if (a[mid] > k)
      hi = mid - 1;
    else
      return mid;
  }
  return -1;
}
```

---

[2] http://termination-portal.org/wiki/TPDB.
[3] http://www.termination-portal.org/wiki/Termination_Competition_2017.

It admits a loop for inputs `lo=1` and `hi=UINT_MAX` if `a[0]` < `k`. Abstracting from the array accesses, this program can be represented by the following LCTRS:

$\mathsf{bsearch}(k_1, lo_1, hi_1) \to u_2(k_1, lo_1, hi_1, rnd_1)$

$u_2(k_1, lo_1, hi_1, mid_2) \to u_3(k_1, lo_1, hi_1, (lo_1 + hi_1) /_u \#x02) \quad [\, lo_1 <_u hi_1 \,]$

$u_3(k_1, lo_1, hi_1, mid_2) \to u_5(k_1, (mid_2 + \#x01), hi_1, mid_2) \quad [\, mid_2 <_u k_1 \,]$

$u_3(k_1, lo_1, hi_1, mid_2) \to u_6(k_1, lo_1, (mid_2 - \#x01), mid_2) \quad [\, mid_2 \geqslant k_1 \wedge mid_2 > k_1 \,]$

$u_6(k_1, lo_1, hi_1, mid_2) \to u_9(k_1, lo_1, hi_1, mid_2)$

$u_3(k_1, lo_1, hi_1, mid_2) \to \mathsf{return}(mid_2) \quad [\, mid_2 \geqslant k_1 \wedge mid_2 \leqslant k_1 \,]$

$u_5(k_1, lo_1, hi_1, mid_2) \to u_9(k_1, lo_1, hi_1, mid_2)$

$u_9(k_1, lo_1, hi_1, mid_2) \to u_{10}(k_1, lo_1, hi_1, mid_2)$

$u_{10}(k_1, lo_1, hi_1, mid_2) \to u_2(k_1, lo_1, hi_1, mid_2)$

$u_2(k_1, lo_1, hi_1, mid_2) \to \mathsf{return}(\#xff) \quad [\, lo_1 \geqslant_u hi_1 \,]$

Ctrl can prove existence of a loop that is reachable from a term of the form $\mathsf{bsearch}(x, y, l, h)$ below one second, using Lemma 3.

6   Conclusion

We presented new criteria to recognize loops in LCTRSs, and implemented these in the constrained rewrite tool Ctrl. In order to demonstrate applicability of such nontermination support, we investigated three example domains.

For the case of LLVM Instcombine optimizations, we confirmed all loops found by the tool `alive-loops` [16], and argued that in contrast to this previous work our criteria do not give rise to false positives. We moreover showed how Ctrl can be used to detect loops in a C program and in integer transition systems.

Extensive work on nontermination detection has been done in the past for both domains, c.f. [2,5,10] and [3,9], for example. A thorough evaluation of our criteria by means of comparison with tools such as [2,3,9] is left for future work. Rather than claiming our implementation superior to other tools, we consider the work presented in this paper a proof of concept that nontermination criteria for LCTRSs are applicable to a wide range of domains. In contrast to tools designed for integer transition systems, C programs, or LLVM Instcombine optimizations, we can treat all these applications *uniformly* with our criteria: Due to the generality of LCTRSs, the same implementation can be applied to a variety of background theories such as integer or bitvector arithmetic or arrays.

In future work we want to investigate further application domains such as simplifications performed in the preprocessing phase of SMT solvers [8,17]. Moreover, it would be interesting to find criteria for nonlooping nontermination of LCTRSs.

Acknowledgements. The authors thank the anonymous referees for their helpful comments.

References

1. Baader, F., Nipkow, T.: Term Rewriting and All That. Cambridge University Press, Cambridge (1998)
2. Borralleras, C., Brockschmidt, M., Larraz, D., Oliveras, A., Rodríguez-Carbonell, E., Rubio, A.: Proving termination through conditional termination. In: Legay, A., Margaria, T. (eds.) TACAS 2017. Heidelberg, vol. 10205, pp. 99–117. Springer, Cham (2017). https://doi.org/10.1007/978-3-662-54577-5_6
3. Brockschmidt, M., Cook, B., Ishtiaq, S., Khlaaf, H., Piterman, N.: T2: Temporal property verification. In: Chechik, M., Raskin, J.-F. (eds.) TACAS 2016. LNCS, vol. 9636, pp. 387–393. Springer, Heidelberg (2016). https://doi.org/10.1007/978-3-662-49674-9_22
4. Falke, S., Kapur, D.: A term rewriting approach to the automated termination analysis of imperative programs. In: Schmidt, R.A. (ed.) CADE 2009. LNCS (LNAI), vol. 5663, pp. 277–293. Springer, Heidelberg (2009). https://doi.org/10.1007/978-3-642-02959-2_22
5. Falke, S., Kapur, D., Sinz, C.: Termination analysis of C programs using compiler intermediate languages. In: Proceedings of the 22nd RTA, Leibniz International Proceedings in Informatics, vol. 10, pp. 41–50 (2011). https://doi.org/10.4230/LIPIcs.RTA.2011.41
6. Fuhs, C., Giesl, J., Plücker, M., Schneider-Kamp, P., Falke, S.: Proving termination of integer term rewriting. In: Treinen, R. (ed.) RTA 2009. LNCS, vol. 5595, pp. 32–47. Springer, Heidelberg (2009). https://doi.org/10.1007/978-3-642-02348-4_3
7. Fuhs, C., Kop, C., Nishida, N.: Verifying procedural programs via constrained rewriting induction. ACM TOCL 18(2), 14:1–14:50 (2017). https://doi.org/10.1145/3060143
8. Ganesh, V., Berezin, S., Dill, D.: A decision procedure for fixed-width bit-vectors. Technical report, Stanford University (2005)
9. Giesl, J., et al.: Analyzing program termination and complexity automatically with AProVE. JAR 58(1), 3–31 (2017). https://doi.org/10.1007/s10817-016-9388-y
10. Gupta, A., Henzinger, T., Majumdar, R., Rybalchenko, A., Xu, R.G.: Proving non-termination. SIGPLAN Not. 43(1), 147–158 (2008). https://doi.org/10.1145/1328897.1328459
11. Hoder, K., Khasidashvili, Z., Korovin, K., Voronkov, A.: Preprocessing techniques for first-order clausification. In: Proceedings of the 12th FMCAD, pp. 44–51 (2012)
12. Kop, C., Nishida, N.: Term rewriting with logical constraints. In: Fontaine, P., Ringeissen, C., Schmidt, R.A. (eds.) FroCoS 2013. LNCS (LNAI), vol. 8152, pp. 343–358. Springer, Heidelberg (2013). https://doi.org/10.1007/978-3-642-40885-4_24
13. Kop, C., Nishida, N.: Constrained term rewriting tooL. In: Davis, M., Fehnker, A., McIver, A., Voronkov, A. (eds.) LPAR 2015. LNCS, vol. 9450, pp. 549–557. Springer, Heidelberg (2015). https://doi.org/10.1007/978-3-662-48899-7_38
14. Lopes, N., Menendez, D., Nagarakatte, S., Regehr, J.: Provably correct peephole optimizations with Alive. In: Proceedings of the 36th PLDI, pp. 22–32 (2015). https://doi.org/10.1145/2737924.2737965
15. Lopes, N., Menendez, D., Nagarakatte, S., Regehr, J.: Practical verification of peephole optimizations with Alive. Commun. ACM 61(2), 84–91 (2018). https://doi.org/10.1145/3166064
16. Menendez, D., Nagarakatte, S.: Termination-checking for LLVM peephole optimizations. In: Proceedings of the 38th International Conference on Software Engineering, pp. 191–202 (2016). https://doi.org/10.1145/2884781.2884809

17. Nadel, A.: Bit-vector rewriting with automatic rule generation. In: Biere, A., Bloem, R. (eds.) CAV 2014. LNCS, vol. 8559, pp. 663–679. Springer, Cham (2014). https://doi.org/10.1007/978-3-319-08867-9_44
18. Nishida, N., Sakai, M., Hattori, T.: On disproving termination of constrained term rewriting systems. In: Proceedings of the 11th WST (2010)
19. Payet, É.: Loop detection in term rewriting using the eliminating unfoldings. Theor. Comput. Sci. **403**(2–3), 307–327 (2008). https://doi.org/10.1016/j.tcs.2008.05.013

Store Buffer Reduction in the Presence of Mixed-Size Accesses and Misalignment

Jonas Oberhauser[✉]

Saarland University, Saarbrücken, Germany
`jonas@wjpserver.cs.uni-saarland.de`

Abstract. Naïve programmers believe that a multi-threaded execution of their program is some simple interleaving of steps of individual threads. To increase performance, modern Intel and AMD processors make use of store buffers, which cause unexpected behaviors that can not be explained by the simple interleaving model.

Programs that in the simple interleaving model obey one of various programming disciplines do not suffer from these unexpected behaviors in the presence of store buffers. These disciplines require that the program does not make use of several concrete features of modern processors, such as mixed-size/misaligned memory accesses and inter-processor interrupts. A common assumption is that this requirement is posed only to make the formal description and soundness proof of these disciplines tractable, but that the disciplines can be extended to programs that make use of these features with a lot of elbow grease and straightforward refinements of the programming discipline.

In this paper we discuss several of such features where that assumption is correct and two such features where it is not, namely mixed-size/misaligned accesses and inter-processor interrupts. We base our discussion on two programming disciplines from the literature. We present solutions and discuss some context, including a claim in the C11 standard that contradicts our findings.

Our work is based directly on the roughly 500 page PhD thesis of the author, which includes a formal treatment of the extensions and a detailed soundness proof.

1 Introduction

Memory speed has not been able to keep up with the growth of processor speed for decades. To avoid a serious performance bottleneck, processor designers decouple memory and processing by several optimizations, such as introducing special buffers and executing instructions out of order. The effect of these methods is visible at the program level, where in multi-threaded executions they cause behaviors that can not be explained by any simple interleaved executions, such as accesses to a lock protected data structure being executed outside the critical section.

As a result, programmers designing safety-critical systems have three choices: (1) understand in depth the specific architecture and optimizations used by the

© Springer Nature Switzerland AG 2018
R. Piskac and P. Rümmer (Eds.): VSTTE 2018, LNCS 11294, pp. 322–344, 2018.
https://doi.org/10.1007/978-3-030-03592-1_19

```
0  x = 1;                      y = 1;
1  if (y == 0)                 if (x == 0)
2    // critical section         // critical section
```

Listing 1: A mutual exclusion protocol. In simple interleavings, at most one of the threads (possibly neither) can enter the critical section. In the presence of store buffers, both threads can enter the critical section.

target platform, and show that the code works on that specific platform, (2) use a tool that analyzes the program and proves that the code is correct on the target platform, or (3) use a reduction theorem which proves that if the program obeys some programming discipline in the idealized interleaving model, the platform will execute the code as if the platform implemented the idealized interleaving model.

We believe that in most cases, the third option is the best one, especially when the system in question is developed in a high-level language, where compiler optimizations can interact with hardware optimizations in unexpected ways. To make this work, high-level languages in practice come themselves with a programming discipline, which is then used to make sure that the compiled code for each platform obeys a software discipline for that platform. Reduction theorems are then used to prove the correctness of the compiler, rather than just of individual programs.

One of the less aggressive hardware optimizations, used among others by x86-64 processors, are so called store buffers, which work like thread-local FIFO to-do lists: when a thread executes a store to a memory location, the store is not actually performed but rather added to its local store buffer as a 'to-do item', and the program can continue execution without needing to wait for the store to be performed. When executing a load, the processor forwards from the most recent local store buffer item that stores to the same location, or from memory if no such item exists. This preserves the expected semantics in single-threaded executions.

The canonical example for how store buffers cause unexpected behaviors is shown in Listing 1. As in all examples we assume all variables are initialized to zero. The shown code provides mutual exclusion in all simple interleaved executions: the first thread to make a step will change x resp. y to 1 and thus prevent the other thread from entering the critical section. In the presence of store buffers, the first step of each thread does not change memory, only the local store buffer. By the time the threads read y resp. x to evaluate the condition of the if-statements, assignments to x resp. y can still be in the store buffers of the other thread; thus both threads can potentially read zero and enter the critical section.

To avoid this behavior, programmers can add so called memory barriers, which drain the store buffer. Interlocked read-modify-write operations (RMW) are memory barriers, as well as the stand-alone barrier for which we will used the keyword `fence`. By adding a `fence` between lines 0 and 1 in both threads, the mutual exclusion is restored: the first thread to execute the memory barrier must have executed its assignment to x resp. y, which is therefore 1 and prevents the other thread from entering the critical section.

The goal is then to find a software discipline that is easy for a compiler to implement, and which uses memory barriers sparingly as they negate the performance benefits of store buffers. Several programming disciplines and variations thereof have been developed ([Obe15, CS10, CCK14, Owe10] and others), but all require that the program does not make use of several concrete features of modern processors, such as:

1. memory accesses which completely ignore the store buffer and therefore have the potential to break even single-threaded code
2. mixed-size accesses or misaligned accesses, which create memory accesses that overlap but do not have the same memory footprint
3. inter-processor interrupts, which create a second channel through which communication is possible
4. transport-triggered memory, which performs complex operations as a side-effect of a store, and can possibly affect multiple memory locations
5. untrusted code that may violate the discipline, e.g., in the form of code calling into a library, or user programs
6. code modification, e.g., for operating systems that can swap code pages, or for just-in-time compilation

The reason that the usage of these features is precluded is that they considerably blow up the formal models of computation and the soundness proof of the disciplines. The simplification comes with the hope that the software disciplines can survive in the presence of these features with only minor changes. In his recent PhD thesis [Obe17], the author carried out that work for one particularly efficient and practical discipline from the literature, the dirty-bit method of Cohen and Schirmer [CS10]. That hope is justified for most features listed above, with the following two exceptions:

1. for mixed-size/misaligned accesses, where the discipline requires a new, and not-so-obvious rule
2. for inter-processor interrupts (IPIs), certain guarantees that can be provided by hardware *must* be discarded in the idealized model, i.e., the semantics of IPIs in the idealized model is weaker than that in those hardware implementations.

In this paper we discuss two particular software disciplines from the literature, the well-known triangular-race-freedom (TRF) of Owens [Owe10], and the more efficient dirty-bit method (more precisely, its ownership-free restatement by Oberhauser [Obe15]). We show how they fail in minor and easily-repaired ways for most of these features and in major ways for mixed-size memory and IPIs by providing counterexamples. We also show how the dirty-bit method can be extended to deal with these features.

2   Data Races and Shared Accesses

Informally, a data race occurs if multiple threads concurrently access the same memory location, and at least one of the accesses modifies that memory location. Two terms in this description are ambiguous:

'concurrently'. There are several ways to make this precise; for us, two memory operations are concurrent if they are executed by different threads and right after each other.

'modifies'. An atomic compare-and-swap (CAS) operation

$$t = \text{cas}\, x\, c \to v$$

returns the current value of a memory location x, and if that value compares equal to compare value c, changes the value of x to a new value v. If the values of c and v are equal, or the values of c and x are unequal, does the CAS modify memory? We consider the answers to these questions to be yes and no, respectively.

We require that all memory operations involved in a data race are tagged as shared in some way in the program code. In listings we will use curly braces around a variable in a memory operation if the access caused by that memory operation is involved in a data race on that variable. For example, a correctly annotated version of the code from Listing 1 is given in Listing 2.

```
0  {x} = 1;              {y} = 1;
1  if ({y} == 0)         if ({x} == 0)
2     // critical section    // critical section
```

Listing 2: A correctly annotated version of the mutual exclusion protocol from Listing 1.

In a sense, this is our high-level language software discipline. Note how it does not mention specifics about hardware optimizations or memory barriers. This is very similar to programming disciplines of real languages, such as Java or C11/C++11, where memory operations that have data races need to be tagged in some way—such as use of the `volatile` keyword in Java—but one has to be careful, as the definitions of 'concurrently' and 'modifies' can be subtly different from those given here, as discussed in detail in Sect. 8.

3   Low-Level Programming Disciplines

Triangular race freedom (TRF) was one of the first non-trivial programming disciplines for store buffer reduction. It defines as a triangular race a race between a read and a write, where the thread executing the read may have a write (to a different address) in its store buffer. The part of the different address makes little difference in practice and in the examples discussed here, so we drop that portion. Note that the read in question must be shared, which allows us to simplify the discipline to the following rule.

TRF. Between each write and a later shared read on the same thread, the thread must execute a memory barrier.

Note there does not need to be a unique memory barrier between each pair of writes and shared reads on the same thread; multiple writes can be separated from multiple shared reads by a single memory barrier.

The dirty-bit[1] discipline (DB) is a more efficient version of the previous discipline. Rather than all writes, only shared writes make a memory barrier necessary:

DB. Between each *shared* write and a later shared read on the same thread, the thread must execute a memory barrier.

Observe that both TRF and DB require that in the code in Listing 2, a memory barrier must be placed between lines 0 and 1.

4   Formal Model and Relation to the Real World

Computation in multi-core systems above the hardware level is inherently non-deterministic. Even more so in the presence of store buffers, inter-processor interrupts, and asynchronous components such as devices or memory management units (MMUs). Not only is the order of steps non-deterministic between these units, but also within each step there may be non-deterministic choices: for example, an MMU step may non-deterministically choose to translate one of several virtual addresses.

We model this non-determinism by using labels (or actions) in deterministic labeled transition systems (LTS): the non-determinism is encoded in the actions. These actions thus both distinguish between the threads (and asynchronous components, which are modeled as threads), and provide any non-deterministic choices. For example, the label of an MMU transition would identify the exact virtual address to be translated, thus replacing a single non-deterministic choice by several deterministic transitions. States record the state of each unit, of the shared memory, and of the store buffer of each processor, which is a finite but unbounded sequence of outstanding stores. Processor actions can add new elements to the tail of their store buffer, and store buffer actions pop the head of the store buffer and commit it to memory.

Not all states have an outgoing transition for each possible action. For example, store buffer actions are only enabled when the store buffer is non-empty, and MMU actions that translate a virtual address can be disabled when the page table does not allow translation of that virtual address at the moment.

---

[1] We call the discipline the dirty-bit discipline because in the original paper, Cohen and Schirmer use a dirty bit for each thread that records whether a shared write has been executed by a thread since its last memory barrier; to check whether a program obeys the discipline, one checks that the dirty bit is zero when executing a shared read (which is not itself a memory barrier).

We distinguish between two machines: the store buffer machine, which is implemented by the real hardware, and the idealized machine without store buffers, which is seen by the programmer. Each machine is modeled as its own LTS. In a simplified setting, these LTS's differ in only one central point[2]: an action which would place a store into the store buffer in the store buffer machine will in the idealized machine execute the store immediately.

To sidestep irrelevant details and to make our results reusable, e.g., for custom ISAs or other TSO architectures such as RISCV zTSO, we leave most of the transition systems uninterpreted. To show that we have not abstracted away any relevant details, we have instantiated[3] our generalized transition systems with the formal model of MIPS86 of Schmaltz [Sch13], which takes the base ISA of MIPS and adds to it several features of x86, as described in the formal model of x86 of Degenbaev [Deg12]. This instantiation also shows that our formalizations of the extensions described in this paper match the formal model of x86 of Degenbaev.

In 2016 in the classroom our group presented a gate-level design of a pipelined MIPS86 multi-processor and a simulation proof between the deterministic gate-level design and the non-deterministic ISA [LOP16]. Except for store buffers and inter-processor interrupts, this design has also been implemented and tested[4] on FPGA in Verilog/HDL by Zahran [Zah16].

Our model can also be instantiated with simplified processor models that do not include any of the features presented in this paper, such as the abstract operational model of x86-TSO presented in [OSS09]. However, this match is not 1:1 as the model presented there spreads interlocked operations across multiple transitions, whereas we use a single transition for each interlocked operation, which is allowed at most to (1) fetch an instruction, (2) read any number of values from the memory system, (3) write back to memory and the processor registers (where each of these steps may depend on the values returned by previous steps). We are not aware of any interlocked operations of x86 that can not be modeled with a single such transition, but if the need should arise, one could extend the model to allow for an arbitrary number of nested reads and writes. As a final note, all additional restrictions placed by our software discipline (beyond those of [Obe15]) are always satisfied on simplified processor models; thus the programmer only has to 'pay' for those extensions to the programming model she uses.

---

[2] For technical reasons, store buffer actions are allowed in the idealized machine, but are simply no-ops.

[3] The instantiation with MIPS86 can be found in the PhD thesis of the author [Obe17] and takes up 36 pages (not counting arithmetic and logical operations, for which we could literally reuse the definitions of Schmaltz). For comparison, the formal specification of MIPS86 takes up 52 pages, the condensed formal model of x86 by Degenbaev takes up 200 pages, and the informal instruction manual of x86 [Int10] takes up over 2000 pages.

[4] During testing, a few bugs were still found and fixed in this design; mostly indexing and spelling errors that we overlooked when checking the pencil and paper proofs. Mechanizing these proofs and thus fully eliminating all such bugs is future work.

5 Theorem and Correctness Proof

We define as a computation an infinite sequence of transitions. We say two computations are equivalent if they agree for all n and each thread i on (1) what the n-th action of thread i is, and (2) what values are returned from the memory system during that transition.

Our theorem then states that if every computation of the idealized machine obeys the software discipline, then for each store buffer machine computation we can find an equivalent idealized computation.

The theorem is proven by a reordering of the sequence of actions of the store buffer machine execution, where actions are only reordered if they do not race. Clearly one would like to use the conditions of the software discipline to show that the actions in question can not race, but this is not immediately possible because we require that the software discipline be obeyed only in the idealized machine. As a result, the proof of this theorem is rather long and difficult. The original mechanized proof by Cohen and Schirmer for the baseline machine, published in text form only in Chen's PhD thesis [Che16], takes up roughly 70 pages. A simpler pencil-and-paper proof (described by the author in [Obe15]) still takes up 15 pages as a detailed proof sketch, and when written down in full detail takes up 30 pages (this version of the proof is unpublished). We briefly discuss the structure of this simpler proof. We focus only on high-level ideas, and omit several details and strategies that are necessary to make the proofs go through; for these, we refer the reader to [Obe17].

The proof has three central steps. In the first step, we define a synchronization relation between actions in a computation: an earlier action t and a later action k are synchronized iff any of the following hold:

1. t executes a shared store and k executes a shared read which reads from the store executed in action t,
2. they belong to the same thread,
3. t executes a shared read-modify-write operation such as a compare-and-swap operation (CAS) which reads from an address modified by k, and which could thus be prevented from modifying memory if executed after k,
4. t is synchronized with some action l which is itself synchronized with k.

We then show that in all idealized machine computations, if an action t executes a store and a later action k reads from or overwrites one of the addresses modified by that store, then t and k must be synchronized or shared. Another way to view this is that the same races are found by considering adjacent memory accesses (as we have defined in Sect. 2) and by looking at synchronization relations.

To prove this theorem, we try to reorder the two actions next to each other. In a nutshell, this either fails because we hit upon a data race that prevents us from reordering two transitions, in which case the racing accesses must be shared and we can construct the chain of shared accesses we are looking for; or the reordering succeeds, and now have a data race between the two transitions in question, which must thus be shared.

In the second step, we show a weakened form of the main theorem where we only prove for store buffer machine computations of a certain form that there is an equivalent idealized machine computation. In particular, only for those where no thread executes a shared action while another thread has a shared store in its store buffer.

The key insight here is that any store s which is in the store buffer of any thread i can only be read or overwritten by other threads if there is a chain involving a shared write r (for release) of thread i and a later shared read a (for acquire) of some other thread; but because store buffers are first-in first-out, that releasing store r can not leave the store buffer before the original store s. The shared read a can by assumption only be executed when shared store r, and by extension store s, have left the buffer, and thus idealized machine (where the store was executed immediately) and store buffer machine (where the store was executed when it left the buffer) agree about the state of memory; thus the shared read a will see the same values in both machines.

In the third step, we show that all store buffer computations can be reordered into an equivalent store buffer computation of that form. The key idea is to recursively unroll the sequence of actions in the order of shared accesses, while keeping the order of actions of each thread intact. In the recursive step from t to $t+1$, we have by recursion created a computation equivalent to the original one where the computation consisting of the first t actions has the desired form. If the next action does not enter a store into a store buffer, nothing has to be reordered and we are done. Otherwise, we choose the first action k made by the thread that makes the next shared access, and reorder that action to position t. We then show that the resulting computation is still equivalent to the original computation.

To show equivalence, we need to show in particular that all transitions after t observe the same values in memory. This is the most difficult part of the proof. The central issue is the fact that actions between t and k which do not execute a shared access in the store buffer machine can still execute a shared access in the idealized machine, namely if they put a shared store into the store buffer (which in the idealized machine is executed immediately). These stores may race with transition k in the idealized machine. Let for the sake of argument s be such a store which modifies some value read by action k. Imagine now that action k executes a compare-and-swap operation (CAS) which only writes back to memory if that value satisfies some condition, which happens to become false when s changes memory. Note that in the store buffer machine, s is not executed and k changes memory. Consider now an action l—executed after the action that executes s, but before action k—which reads from the memory region modified by k. In the original store buffer machine computation l would not see any values written by k because it is executed before k; but after the reordering action k is now executed before l, which could thus potentially see the value written by action k, in which case the computations would not be equivalent.

Without mixed-size accesses, this situation is only possible if store s and actions k and l all access the same address. In this case, one can show that store

$$\{x\} = 1; \,\, // \,\, T \,\| \, \{y\} = 1; \,\, // \,\, T$$
$$t = y; \quad // \,\, U \,\| \, u = \{x\}; \,\, // \,\, T$$

Listing 3: A mixture of trusted (T) code and untrusted (U) code. The trusted code obeys the programming discipline and correctly annotates all races as shared. The untrusted code does not.

s and action l must be executed by the same thread, and that in the store buffer machine, action l will forward the value from store s and ignore values written by action k. With this key observation, it is a pure technicality to complete the proof.

Obviously, the last part of this proof falls apart in the presence of mixed-size accesses, and we need a new, more complicated argument. We will get into more detail in Sect. 8. Apart from this, the structure of the proof stays the same.

6   Untrusted Code

Operating systems need to be correct no matter the code of user processes. When operating system and untrusted user processes can concurrently access the same memory, this raises several questions: how to deal with races between user processes and the OS? How can we model the transition between the OS, which obeys the software discipline, and user processes, which may ignore the software discipline out of ignorance or malice? Can malicious user code somehow break the idealized programming model of an OS that otherwise obeys the discipline, leading to unsound verification results?

Clearly, races between the untrusted code and the trusted code can break the correctness of trusted code. Consider, for example, Listing 3, where the load from y is part of untrusted code. Disciplines TRF and DB do not require us to insert a memory barrier between the store to x and the load from y in Thread 1. Thus if Thread 1 is executed before Thread 2, but its store is still buffered when Thread 2 reads from x, both threads can read a zero—a result impossible in simple interleavings.

Obviously the problem here is that the untrusted code can race with the trusted code without using the necessary memory barriers. The simplest way to resolve the problem in this example is to add a new rule, which is to drain the store buffer when entering untrusted code. To completely hide store buffers during execution of trusted code, we strengthen this and add the following rule:

Switch. While a write may be in the store buffer, a thread may not switch between trusted and untrusted code.

In our formal model, the transition relation of the idealized machine is now defined by a case split: if a thread is currently executing trusted code, actions of that thread use the simplified semantics where stores that would be placed into the store buffer in the store buffer machine are instead executed immediately. If a thread is currently executing untrusted code, actions of that thread behave exactly like they would in the store buffer machine, i.e., they put stores into the store buffer.

We allow races between threads running trusted code, and threads running untrusted code as well as with their store buffers, in which case the memory access of the trusted code must be annotated as shared[5]. As long as the memory accesses of untrusted code are restricted by some means, e.g., memory protection in case the untrusted code is a user thread, this works well.

As a final remark, we believe that the memory barrier upon switching from untrusted to trusted code is not strictly necessary. We believe that without it, one would obtain a slightly weaker programming model, where the store buffer of the untrusted code is visible and still active during the execution of trusted code, until one reaches either (1) a memory barrier or (2) a shared write. In this model, stores of the trusted code would still be executed immediately, and local stores would bypass the untrusted code's store buffer completely. Note that on x86-64, both jumps to the interrupt service routine (e.g., after a system call) and returns to user code are memory barriers, so it may be that in most cases there is nothing to be gained by relaxing this restriction.

7   Transport-Triggered Memory

Some memory-mapped registers in x86 do not behave like normal memory. Stores to these registers have atomic side-effects on other registers. Among others these are the end-of-interrupt (EOI) port in the local advanced programmable interrupt controller (APIC), and the I/O register select port (ioregsel) of the I/O APIC. The EOI port is coupled with the in-service register (ISR), which in a bit-array records all interrupt levels that are currently being serviced by an interrupt handler; any store to the EOI register atomically clears the bit corresponding to the highest priority active interrupt in the ISR. The value written to the EOI is dropped and the value of the EOI remains unchanged by the store. We call such memory regions, which do not behave like regular memory, transport-triggered registers (TTRs)[6].

In our formal model, this side effect is applied as part of the transition that executes a store to a TTR (possibly the store buffer step committing that store to memory), thus ensuring atomicity. For example, after a transition that executes store to the EOI, the bit corresponding to the highest priority active interrupt in the ISR is cleared; but the ISR is unchanged while that store is being buffered in the store buffer.

We also need to widen our definition of races: a store to a TTR is considered racing with loads and stores to one of the registers that may be modified as a side effect of the store.

---

[5] In contrast, in [Obe17], operations of untrusted code are considered shared by default, so technically all accesses are shared, but the rule DB must only be satisfied by trusted code. The results are the same.

[6] After transport-triggered architectures [Cor97], which forego normal instructions in favor of transport-triggered registers.

```
EOI = 1;
done = (ISR == 0);
```

Listing 4: A hypothetical program finishing an interrupt, and then checking whether all interrupts have been resolved.

$$o: \texttt{cas } \{\texttt{x}\} \; 0 \rightarrow t; \; \left\| \begin{array}{l} s: \; \{\texttt{x}\} = u; \\ l: \; v = \texttt{x}; \end{array} \right.$$

Listing 5: A simple program with two racing accesses to variable x.

To see how TTRs can interfere with store buffer reduction, consider the program[7] in Listing 4.

In a simple interleaved execution of a single thread, the instructions are carried out in order, and the value of ISR is changed as an atomic side-effect of the store to EOI.

In the presence of store buffers, the store to EOI might still be in the store buffer when the thread executes the load from ISR. Since the store has not been executed yet, the value of ISR has not yet been updated either; the thread will read a stale value and incorrectly conclude that there are still unresolved interrupts when the last interrupt has just been resolved.

Obviously, there are no races in the code in Listing 4, as there is only a single thread. Thus none of the accesses have to be shared and no memory barriers are needed based on the rules of the programming discipline we have so far. Even more restrictive disciplines such as data-race freedom (DRF) [Owe10], which requires a complete absence of races except on lock variables, is insufficient, since there are no races. We add a simple rule[8]:

TTR: Insert a memory barrier between a store to a TTR and a read from any register that could be modified as a side-effect of that store.

Compilers of high-level languages such as C are usually not aware of which memory regions are TTRs, but rely on the programmer to point out these regions, e.g., by use of the `volatile` qualifier in C.

8   Mixed-Size/Misaligned Accesses

In a simple processor where each memory access changes a single, indivisible memory location, multiple memory accesses that race must have the same memory footprint. Therefore in the code in Listing 5, all three possible execution orders for CAS operation o racing with store s, and a later load l, have the same final state:

---

[7] In real x86, the ISR is too large to allow this simple test for zero; this does not matter for the sake of argument given here.

[8] The PhD thesis uses a stronger rule, where all accesses to transport-triggered memory regions are considered shared. This rule is only used in a single lemma, which is also implied by the rule below.

$$o:\ \texttt{cas}\ \{\texttt{x[0:3]}\}\ 0 \to t_0, \ldots, t_3;\ \Big\|\ \begin{array}{l} s:\ \{\texttt{x[0:1]}\}\ =\ u_0,\ u_1; \\ l:\ v\ =\ \texttt{x[0:3]}\,; \end{array}$$

Listing 6: Accesses to the four bytes of variable x. CAS o modifies all four bytes x[0:3], writing the value t_i into byte i. Store s only modifies the first two bytes x[0:1]. Load l can therefore also see the combination u_0, u_1, t_2, t_3 of bytes written by o and s.

$o \to s \to l$: Load l sees the value written by s, which overwrites o and leaves the final memory state as

$$\texttt{x} = u \ \wedge \ v = u$$

Since l and o are not adjacent, they are not concurrent, and do not race.

$s \to o \to l$: The comparison of o fails, and o does not modify memory. Thus load l sees the value written by s, and the final state is

$$\texttt{x} = u \ \wedge \ v = u$$

Since l and o do not modify memory, they do not race.

$s \to l \to o$: The comparison of o fails, and o does not modify memory. Load l sees the value written by s, and the final state is

$$\texttt{x} = u \ \wedge \ v = u$$

Since l and o do not modify memory, they do not race.

We observe that the annotation of l as local is correct. When executing the program in the presence of store buffers, store s can be in the store buffer when load l and store o are executed, which gives rise to an additional interesting possibility:

$l \to o \to s$: In this case, l will forward from the value of s, which overwrites the value of o

$$\texttt{x} = u \ \wedge \ v = u$$

This execution happens to be indistinguishable from the interleaved executions above, since the store s completely hides the successful execution of CAS operation o.

In the presence of mixed-size or misaligned accesses, however, memory accesses can overlap without having the same footprint. The CAS operation o in the adapted program in Listing 6 can not be hidden by the smaller store s.

In the interesting store buffer execution $l \to o \to s$, load l does not see any bytes written by o, but the final state of x includes such bytes

$$\texttt{x[0:3]}\ =\ u_0,\ u_1,\ t_2,\ t_3 \ \wedge \ v\ =\ u_0,\ u_1,\ 0,\ 0.$$

$$o\text{:}\texttt{cas} \ \{\texttt{x[1:2]}\} \ 0 \to t_1, t_2;\ \Big\|\ \begin{array}{l} s\text{:} \ \{\texttt{x[0:1]}\} \ = \ u_0, u_1; \\ l\text{:} \ v \ = \ \texttt{x[2:3]}; \end{array}$$

Listing 7: The problem can be replicated using same-size accesses with different alignment.

```
struct lockref {
    union {
        aligned_u64 lock_count;
        struct {
            spinlock_t lock;
            unsigned int count;
        };
    };
};
```

Listing 8: A lockref. One thread may use a double-word CAS access to update the lock and the reference count while another thread may concurrently access lock and count individually.

In the interleaving model, the only state in which bytes written by o are in the final value of x is $o \to s \to l$, where o is executed before s, but in this execution l also sees the bytes written by o

$$v \ = \ u_0, u_1, t_2, t_3.$$

Again we observe that there is no race between l and o in the idealized model, and there is still no need to annotate l as a shared read. Thus the program as written above obeys DB and also the stricter TRF, but has new behaviors in the presence of store buffers; the disciplines are unsound.

Almost the same program can also be written using misalignment instead of mixed-size accesses, as the code in Listing 7 shows.

One simple way to forbid this is to require that accesses involved in a data race must have the same size and alignment. This would forbid the program in Listing 6 since operations o and s have different size. However, some efficient algorithms actually would like to use concurrent mixed-size memory accesses. A good example is the code of a Linux lockref [loc] shown in Listing 8, which implements a lock protected reference counter. A thread can go through the lock by locking, operating on the counter, and then unlocking. Alternatively, a thread can use a single double-word CAS operation that accesses both lock and reference count, checks that the lock is free, and changes the reference count only if the lock is free, without ever taking the lock. Obviously the code involves mixed-size races between CAS and LOCK operations, but also concurrent accesses between a local read to count (in code that acquired the lock) and double-word CAS to lock_count which is not modifying.

Our solution is to forbid executions of the shape given in Listing 9, which we call delayed RMW races, and which satisfy all of the following conditions:

```
cas {x,y} c → t;  ║ {x} = u;
                  ║ .../* no memory barrier,
                  ║       no stores to y */
                  ║ v = y;
```

Listing 9: A delayed RMW race. A CAS modifies variables x and y just before a store to x by a second thread might prevent the CAS from succeeding. A later load reads from y (which is not an alias for x), with no memory barriers or stores to y preventing us from witnessing the store to x after the load from y in the presence of store buffers.

1. A read-modify-write operation (RMW) is executed right before a store of a second thread, and the RMW reads variables that will be modified by the store
2. by executing only actions of the second thread, one eventually executes a read that sees some part of the write of the RMW, i.e., their memory footprints overlap and there are no writes between the store and the read that completely overwrite the overlapping region
3. the store can be in the store buffer when the read is executed.

NoDelayedRMW. There are no delayed RMW races.

Note that TRF is a strengthening of DB since all writes, not just shared writes, require a memory barrier. There is a dual strengthening where instead all reads, not just shared reads, require a memory barrier. We call this rule FRT.

FRT. Between each shared write and a later read on the same thread, the thread must execute a memory barrier.

This rule implies freedom from delayed RMW-races: the store is shared, and can thus not be in the store buffer when the read is executed. Unlike TRF or DB, it would thus be sound in the presence of mixed-size/misaligned accesses.

Unlike the other extensions described in this document, this extension and the rule **NoDelayedRMW** add considerable proof effort. The proof outlined in Sect. 5 fails in the proof of step three, where our simplifying observation—that all memory accesses involved in the races must be using the same address—is no longer valid. Let like in that outline k execute the CAS operation that we wish to reorder to position t, s be a store racing with k, and l execute a load accessing some addresses modified by k.

We want to apply the rule **NoDelayedRMW** to show that any modifications made by k are invisible to l due to forwarding. Ideally, store s and actions k and l would be part of a delayed RMW race; but this is not necessarily the case because not all actions between s and l belong to the same thread. We now create an auxiliary computation in with a delayed RMW race by sorting all actions between t and l by thread, with the lowest thread being the thread executing action l. For sorting we use bubble sort [Knu98], which has the advantages of being stable and only swapping adjacent actions, which together with the fact that those actions are by choice of k not shared makes it easy to show that the actions between t and l still observe the same values from memory. In the auxiliary (sorted) computation, all actions from position t until action l are now made by the same thread.

In the auxiliary computation, we now move action k right before the first store s' before action l that races with it (the case where no such store exists is handled more easily and omitted here). Now we show with rule **NoDelayedRMW** that there are no delayed RMW races, and thus the overlapping region between k and l must be completely overwritten by some other writes between actions k and l. These other stores obviously already exist in the original computation. Since all actions between k and l in the auxiliary (sorted) computation are made by the same thread as l and bubble sort is stable, these stores are also already between position t and action l in the original schedule.

Thus when we move action k to position t in the original schedule, modifications by action k are not observed by action l because all loads from the overlapping region are resolved via forwarding from these other writes.

Another important comparison to make here is with the C11/C++11 memory model and its definition of a data race. Rather than looking at memory accesses of adjacent accesses in a computation, C11 uses a synchronization relation like the one defined in Sect. 5 to define races. Recall that we proved that there is no difference between these two methods of identifying races. Boehm and Adve [BA08] proved a similar theorem for a formal memory model of C11. Indeed, their proof is used as a justification [c11b] for the following excerpt of the C11 draft [c11a] in Sect. 5.1.2.4.

"[...] data races, as defined here, and with suitable restrictions on the use of atomics, correspond to data races in a simple interleaved (sequentially consistent) execution."

Surprisingly, this claim is wrong. The reason for this is that each of these three documents defines 'concurrently' and 'modifies' (cf. Sect. 2) differently.

1. In our definition, a CAS with a failed test is not 'modifying'. For 'concurrently' we either use adjacent memory accesses or those not synchronized by our synchronization relation.
2. In C11 (both in the standard draft and in the formalization of Batty [BOS+11]), a CAS with a failed test is also not considered to be 'modifying' memory and 'concurrently' is defined by the C11 synchronization relation, *but that synchronization relation is missing the third part of our definition* (which synchronizes an RMW with a later store that 'disables' it).
3. Boehm and Avde define 'concurrently' using the C11 synchronization relation, but define a CAS to always be 'modifying' (even if the test fails).

In other words, we have here three subtly distinct classifications of races, two of which can be stated either in terms of adjacent accesses or of unsynchronized accesses. Sadly, the classification used by the C11 standard is not among them. Recall in particular the example from Listing 5, where in the simple interleaved model there is no race between o and s; but in the C11 definition of a synchronization relation, CAS operation o is not synchronized with l in the execution $o \rightarrow s \rightarrow l$ and thus there is a race which is not correctly annotated.

As a final note, observe that including RMWs that do not modify memory in the definition of a data race is a strengthening of our suggested solution, since it implies that the read in a delayed RMW race would need to be shared—and both DB and TRF would require a memory barrier between the shared write and the shared read, precluding the write from possibly being in the store buffer when the read is executed.

9 Inter-processor Interrupts

There are generally two possible types of semantics for inter-processor interrupts (IPIs), which are easily explained by analogy. The first type is the 'fire alarm' semantics. When you receive the interrupt, you drop everything you are doing right now and head for the interrupt service routine. The second type is the 'tax return' semantics. When you receive the interrupt, you let it rest on your desk for a long (and possibly unbounded) time, but eventually you have to sit down and spend the time resolving the interrupt.

In our formal models, when an APIC action delivers a 'fire alarm' IPI, it modifies a processor register of the receiving processor which is read during each action of that processor. Thus the receiving processor reacts to the IPI on its next action. When an APIC delivers a 'tax return' IPI, it changes instead a memory-mapped register which is read by the processor only during special actions that snoop for pending interrupts, thus allowing the processor to ignore the interrupt by executing actions that do not snoop for interrupts.

While the first type of semantics seems preferable and has been suggested in some work (e.g., in the formal semantics of MIPS86 by Schmaltz [Sch13]), this semantics is not stable under store buffer reduction, and hardware that implements 'fire alarm' IPIs must for store buffer reduction be abstracted by a model that only supports tax return interrupts, unless the store buffers are drained as a side-effect of the APIC action that delivers the IPI. This is not done by any real processor that we are aware of, and so formal models of IPIs in a simple interleaving model should always use 'tax return' semantics for IPIs.

We begin by detailing the way interrupts are sent. A thread has access to two 'magic' variables that allows it to send interrupts, the interrupt controller's target

$$\texttt{APIC.target}$$

which contains the id of a thread to be interrupted, and the interrupt controller's status flag

$$\texttt{APIC.pending}$$

which distinguishes whether the interrupt has been received by the target (value is 0) or not (value is 1).

```
APIC.target = Thread2;   s: x = 1;
APIC.pending = 1;
while (APIC.pending);
l: t = x;
```

Listing 10: Thread 1 interrupts Thread 2 by setting the target to Thread 2, the status flag to 1, and then polling the status flag until it becomes zero.

To send an interrupt a thread sets the target and changes the status flag to 1, then polls the status flag until it becomes zero. An example is shown in Listing 10, where load l can only be executed after the IPI was received by Thread 2. We observe that the semantics of this program depends on the semantics of interrupts. With fire alarm interrupt semantics, store s can only be executed before the interrupt is received, since after receiving the interrupt Thread 2 must immediately go to the interrupt service routine (not shown here). This allows for the following orders of load l, store s, and delivery of the IPI (step ipi):

$s \to ipi \to l$: The load sees the store, the final configuration is

$$x = t = 1$$

$ipi \to l$: The store is never executed, the final configuration is

$$x = t = 0$$

Observe that in none of these execution orders there is a race between s and l, since they are never concurrent. Thus the lack of shared annotations in the code in Listing 10 is in accordance with our programming discipline.

With tax return interrupt semantics, the store s can be executed after the interrupt is received, since the interrupt only has to be taken eventually, not immediately. This allows two additional executions:

$ipi \to s \to l$: The load sees the store, the final configuration is

$$x = t = 1$$

$ipi \to l \to s$: The load does not see the store, which still changes the value of x

$$x = 1 \land t = 0$$

Not only is there now a race between s and l, which therefore need to be annotated, but also there is a new possible final configuration. To make sure that the thread which received the IPI has really been interrupted, one needs therefore a slightly more complicated protocol: the interrupt service routine of the interrupted thread has to acknowledge the interrupt through a shared variable.

We also look at what happens in the presence of store buffers, which can be either drained when receiving an IPI or not drained. The presence of store buffers does not change the possible final states of the individual executions, only

Table 1: A matrix of all possible combinations of executions and IPI semantics. 'FA' stands for fire-alarm, 'TR' for tax-return, 'No SB' for the absence of store buffers, 'Drain' for the presence of store buffers which are drained when receiving the IPI, 'No Drain' for the presence of store buffers which are not drained when receiving the IPI. Entries with a lightning symbol (⚡) indicate that the execution is not possible using this combination of IPI semantics, entries with a checkmark (✓) that the execution is possible

Execution	FA/No SB	FA/Drain	FA/No Drain	TR/No SB	TR/Drain	TR/No Drain
$s \to ipi \to l$	✓	✓	✓	✓	✓	✓
$ipi \to l$	✓	✓	✓	✓	✓	✓
$ipi \to s \to l$	⚡	⚡	✓	✓	✓	✓
$ipi \to l \to s$	⚡	⚡	✓	✓	✓	✓

```
IC.target = Thread2;                   s: fence; {x} = 1;
fence; IC.pending = 1;                 f: fence;
do fence; while (IC.pending);
l: fence; t = {x}; fence;
```

Listing 11: A fully fenced and annotated program.

which executions are allowed. We list all possible executions with all combinations of interrupt semantics in Table 1. We observe that the only semantics which matches the fire-alarm semantics in the idealized machine is an implementation that provides fire-alarm semantics and drains the store buffers of threads that receive an IPI. We try to adjust the discipline to solve this problem by requiring that after and before each memory access, the programmer must introduce a memory barrier (note that this is an extremely strict discipline, which is even stronger than DRF of [Owe10]). We use the keyword **fence** to indicate a memory barrier and obtain the program in Listing 11. We observe that Thread 2 can be interrupted after putting store s into the store buffer, but before executing fence f. Therefore the fully fenced program has exactly the same possible executions and final states as the program without fences. We conclude that no simple programming discipline can maintain a fire alarm semantics for IPIs if the implementation does not drain the store buffers of threads that receive an interrupt. To the best of our understanding of the Intel and AMD manuals, x86-64 processors do not do this. They only drain the store buffer when the thread reaches the interrupt service routine (which is a subtle difference, but enough to make the executions above valid).

This leaves us with two alternatives: (1) never use fire alarm semantics for IPIs in simple interleaving models, even if the underlying processor implements them or (2) use a more complicated programming discipline which entails an IPI protocol, stating that the interrupting thread must ignore the status flag of its interrupt controller and instead wait for an acknowledgment from the interrupt service routine of the interrupted thread. But that is exactly the programming

$$x = 1; \quad \| \quad y = 1;$$
$$t := x; \quad \| \quad y := 2;$$

Listing 12: Two threads without races that use bypassing accesses (indicated by :=) to create inconsistent executions. Thread 1 may read 0 and the final value of y may be 1.

model one obtains if one does not use fire alarm semantics, so for the purpose of programming the system, the two options are likely indistinguishable. Since option (1) is simpler, that is the option we recommend.

10   Bypassing the Store Buffer

Modern processors have autonomous units which modify processor-local variables but may completely bypass the store buffer. One such unit is the memory management unit (MMU), which modifies a variable called the translation look-aside buffer (TLB) but otherwise behaves like a separate thread that bypasses the store buffer; thus a store to a page table entry is only seen by the MMU after it leaves the store buffer.

A reduction theorem can deal with such units in at least two ways: either by treating them as separate threads, but hiding in some way the races on the local variables, or by treating them as the same thread but allowing accesses of the thread to bypass the store buffers.

For example, if the MMU is treated as a separate thread, each of its accesses to the TLB will race with accesses to the TLB by the processor. Without special treatment of TLBs, almost every processor step now involves a shared read to the TLB, which in both TRF and DB would be impossible to deal with. Thus one would need a specific argument about the TLB, such as monotonicity [CCK14], to apply a store buffer reduction theorem without introducing these shared reads. If on the other hand we allow steps of the processor to explicitly bypass the store buffer, we can simply model MMU steps as steps of the processor which happen to bypass the store buffer.

The second solution is not perfect in general, since it implies that racing steps of the MMU become shared steps of the processor thread, with which the disciplines can not deal (since we do not know when they occur and hence can not insert the necessary memory barriers). As long as the MMU does not race—e.g., because it does not set accessed and dirty bits and one never modifies page tables while an MMU could be walking them; or at least not while the processor is executing trusted code (e.g., in kernel mode)—this is completely fine, and so our method of dealing with MMUs works at least in some useful cases, but not in all.

Obviously, bypassing the store buffer can already break single-threaded (or non-racing) code, as the examples in Listing 12 show. We require five new rules[9]

---

[9] In the presence of transport-triggered registers, all rules below concerning shared writes also apply to writes to such registers.

to restrict the usage of these bypassing accesses in a sound way, but none of them are particularly exciting or surprising. The first two simply deal with the problems shown in Listing 12. Rule AtomicWrite prevents torn writes. Rule AtomicRMW prevents the RMW from becoming non-atomic due to other writes of other threads being executed between the read and the write of the RMW. Rule MessagePassing prevents us from, e.g., releasing a lock (with a bypassing shared write) before modifications of the lock-protected data (which are still in the buffer) become visible to other threads.

WriteWriteOrder. Do not execute a bypassing write to a variable that is modified by a write that could be in the store buffer.

WriteReadOrder. Do not execute a bypassing read to a variable that is modified by a write that could be in the store buffer.

AtomicWrite. If a write is shared, it must be either bypassing or buffered, but not a mix.

AtomicRMW. If an RMW is shared, its write must be bypassing.

MessagePassing. A shared write must be buffered if a write could be in the write buffer.

Note that when bypassing accesses are used for autonomous units, such as the MMU, these rules have subtle implications. For example, if a thread modifies a page table entry, it must use a memory barrier before it allows the MMU to access that page table entry. If this is not possible, for example because the MMU is always running, one needs an additional theorem to deal with this, e.g., by showing that it suffices to have a memory barrier and then a TLB invalidation before the page table entry is used for the first time (we have not shown this).

As a final remark, observe that the existence of bypassing memory accesses in the theorem is actually a weakening of the store buffer programming model. It shows that the proof does not hinge on some of the order between local operations that is provided by store buffers, and reminds us of the multi-copy atomic release-acquire model (used, e.g., by ARMv8 [FGP+16] and planned for RISCV), where only the order with so-called release stores and acquire loads is maintained. It is plausible that a programming discipline similar to DB can be found for such memory models, which only requires that all shared writes be marked release, and all shared reads be marked acquire. We leave this as future work.

11 Modifying Code

When teaching about programming, many experts strongly advise against writing self-modifying code. Sadly in the real world, modification of code can not be avoided in at least four places: (1) the bootloader loading code of the operating system before executing it, (2) the operating system loading code pages of a user process, e.g., after a page fault on fetch, (3) a just-in-time compiler, which generates instructions on-the-fly and later executes them, and (4) programmable controllers in the processor, such as the APIC.

To verify software such as operating systems that touches these places, one needs a realistic formal model that includes the effects of code modification. Multiple options exist. From the programmer's viewpoint, the simplest model is for instructions to be fetched and executed atomically. We allow this in our formalization by splitting each transition into up to three phases: (1) a fetch phase, which depends only on local registers, (2) a read phase, which in addition depends on the values fetched from memory in phase 1, and (3) a write back phase, which in addition depends on the values read from memory in phase 2. This means we can fetch and execute an RMW in a single transition. Note that even if the processor does not itself provide mixed-size accesses for reads and writes, such transitions are in effect mixed-size accesses, since each transition can read from up to two distinct addresses. This gives rise to exactly the same challenges already discussed in Sect. 8.

In hardware, single cycle fetch-and-execute turns out to be difficult to implement due to pipelining: an instruction can enter the pipeline right before the pipeline discovers a store to the instruction address, or before such a store is committed to memory, possibly by another processor. To provide the simple formal model above in hardware, the processor needs to discover such stores and roll back the fetched, stale instruction. In particular, x86 processors do implement such mechanisms and provide single cycle fetch-and-execute, if the same *virtual* address is used for the instruction and the stores modifying the instructions.

Custom processors which do not implement such fancy mechanisms must either rely on a stronger software discipline—such as not executing code recently written by stores, and avoiding concurrent code modification where possible [LOP16]—or implement a weaker ISA, where the possibility for stale instructions is accounted for in some way—such as allowing pre-fetch of instructions into an instruction buffer, which may become stale and is flushed by instructions that drain the pipeline [Obe17]. Details are beyond the scope of this document.

12   Conclusion

We have focused here on a high-level view of how several features of modern processors affect triangular-race freedom [Owe10] and the dirty-bit discipline of Cohen and Schirmer [CS10], and have provided solutions for the cases where the disciplines are insufficient. This work is based directly on the roughly 500 page PhD thesis of the author [Obe17], which presents a formal treatment of the problems, a monolithic solution, and its soundness proof. The extensions presented here differ from those proven correct in that work in two ways: we present a slightly more efficient way to deal with transport-triggered registers and we discard the assumption that partial hits drain the store buffer. To date, the proofs only exist as fully-detailed pencil and paper proofs. Erring is human, and especially a proof of this size would benefit from a machine-checkable version.

There are still features of modern processors that we have not dealt with, or dealt with insufficiently. The first feature we are aware of are non-temporal memory accesses, which have weaker ordering constraints. The second feature are MMUs which set accessed and dirty bits, and which thus race with other MMUs walking the same page tables. Also, modern processors use other, more aggressive optimizations, for which efficient programming disciplines have not yet been verified. All of these are left as future work.

There has been more work on dealing with store buffers, mostly on automated tools that insert fences into insufficiently annotated programs, e.g., [BDM13, AKNP14]. Since this is a computationally hard problem we do not expect this to be a general efficient solution. To the best of our knowledge these tools currently only apply to idealized processors, but we suspect that they can be extended easily to mixed-size accesses.

The only other results that go beyond simple idealized processors are extensions of the dirty-bit discipline by (1) Kovalev, Cohen, and Chen [CCK14], who deal with MMUs as separate threads by a monotonicity argument, and (2) by Chen [Che16] who introduces a mixed-size environment, but falsely assumes that the processor will detect and prevent delayed RMW races.

References

[AKNP14] Alglave, J., Kroening, D., Nimal, V., Poetzl, D.: Don't sit on the fence. In: Biere, A., Bloem, R. (eds.) CAV 2014. LNCS, vol. 8559, pp. 508–524. Springer, Cham (2014). https://doi.org/10.1007/978-3-319-08867-9_33

[BA08] Boehm, H.-J., Adve, S.V.: Foundations of the C++ concurrency memory model. In: ACM SIGPLAN Notices, vol. 43, pp. 68–78. ACM (2008)

[BDM13] Bouajjani, A., Derevenetc, E., Meyer, R.: Checking and enforcing robustness against TSO. In: Felleisen, M., Gardner, P. (eds.) ESOP 2013. LNCS, vol. 7792, pp. 533–553. Springer, Heidelberg (2013). https://doi.org/10.1007/978-3-642-37036-6_29

[BOS+11] Batty, M., Owens, S., Sarkar, S., Sewell, P., Weber, T.: Mathematizing C++ concurrency. SIGPLAN Not. 46(1), 55–66 (2011)

[c11a] C11 draft n1570. https://port70.net/~nsz/c/c11/n1570.html. Accessed 14 Apr 2018

[c11b] Comments on the C++ memory model following a partial formalization attempt. http://www.open-std.org/jtc1/sc22/wg21/docs/papers/2009/n2955.html. Accessed 14 Apr 2018

[CCK14] Chen, G., Cohen, E., Kovalev, M.: Store buffer reduction with MMUs. In: Giannakopoulou, D., Kroening, D. (eds.) VSTTE 2014. LNCS, vol. 8471, pp. 117–132. Springer, Cham (2014). https://doi.org/10.1007/978-3-319-12154-3_8

[Che16] Chen, G.: Store buffer reduction theorem and application. Ph.D. thesis, Saarland University (2016)

[Cor97] Corporaal, H.: Microprocessor architectures: from VLIW to TTA (1997)

[CS10] Cohen, E., Schirmer, B.: From total store order to sequential consistency: a practical reduction theorem. In: Kaufmann, M., Paulson, L.C. (eds.) ITP 2010. LNCS, vol. 6172, pp. 403–418. Springer, Heidelberg (2010). https://doi.org/10.1007/978-3-642-14052-5_28

[Deg12] Degenbaev, U.: Formal specification of the x86 instruction set architecture. Ph.D. thesis, Saarland University (2012)

[FGP+16] Flur, S., et al.: Modelling the ARMv8 architecture, operationally: concurrency and ISA. SIGPLAN Not. **51**(1), 608–621 (2016)

[Int10] Intel, Santa Clara, CA, USA. Intel®64 and IA-32 Architectures Software Developer's Manual: Volumes 1–3b, June 2010

[Knu98] Knuth, D.E.: The Art of Computer Programming, Volume 3: Sorting and Searching, 2nd edn. Addison Wesley Longman Publishing Co. Inc., Redwood City (1998)

[loc] Introducing lockrefs. https://lwn.net/Articles/565734/. Accessed 14 Apr 2018

[LOP16] Lutsyk, P., Oberhauser, J., Paul, W.: Multicore system architecture. Lecture notes (2016)

[Obe15] Oberhauser, J.: A simpler reduction theorem for x86-TSO. In: Gurfinkel, A., Seshia, S.A. (eds.) VSTTE 2015. LNCS, vol. 9593, pp. 142–164. Springer, Cham (2016). https://doi.org/10.1007/978-3-319-29613-5_9

[Obe17] Oberhauser, J.: Justifying the strong memory semantics of concurrent high-level programming languages for system programming. Ph.D. thesis, Saarland University (2017). https://dx.doi.org/10.22028/D291-27208

[OSS09] Owens, S., Sarkar, S., Sewell, P.: A better x86 memory model: x86-TSO. In: Berghofer, S., Nipkow, T., Urban, C., Wenzel, M. (eds.) TPHOLs 2009. LNCS, vol. 5674, pp. 391–407. Springer, Heidelberg (2009). https://doi.org/10.1007/978-3-642-03359-9_27

[Owe10] Owens, S.: Reasoning about the implementation of concurrency abstractions on x86-TSO. In: D'Hondt, T. (ed.) ECOOP 2010. LNCS, vol. 6183, pp. 478–503. Springer, Heidelberg (2010). https://doi.org/10.1007/978-3-642-14107-2_23

[Sch13] Schmaltz, S.: MIPS-86-a multi-core MIPS ISA specification. Technical report, Saarland University, Saarbrücken (2013)

[Zah16] Zahran, S.: Implementing and debugging a pipelined MIPS machine with interrupts and multi-level address translation. Master's thesis, Saarland University (2016)

Author Index

Printed in the United States
by Baker & Taylor Publisher Services